Third Edition

Family Therapy

A Systemic Integration

Dorothy Stroh Becvar
St. Louis Family Institute, Inc.

Raphael J. Becvar
Northeast Louisiana University

Allyn and Bacon
Boston • London • Toronto • Sydney • Tokyo • Singapore

Editor-in-Chief, Social Sciences: Susan Badger
Senior Editor: Mylan Jaixen
Senior Editorial Assistant: Sue Hutchinson
Production Administrator: Rob Lawson
Production Coordinator: Susan Freese
Editorial-Production Service: Kailyard Associates
Composition Buyer: Linda Cox
Manufacturing Buyer: Megan Cochran
Cover Administrator: Linda Knowles
Cover Designer: Marshall Henrichs

Library of Congress Cataloging-in-Publication Data

Becvar, Dorothy Stroh.
    Family therapy: a systemic integration/Dorothy Stroh Becvar,
Raphael J. Becvar.—3rd ed.
        p.   cm.
    Includes bibliographical references and index.
    ISBN 0–205–17275–X (alk. paper)
    1. Family psychotherapy.   I. Becvar, Raphael J., 1931– .
II. Title.
RC488.5.B388   1996
616.89'156—dc20   95–20640
                                                           CIP

Printed in the United States of America

10   9   8   7   6   5   4   97   96   95   94

Acknowledgements:
Excerpts from A. M. Horne and M. M. Ohlsen, *Family Counseling and Therapy,* Copyright ©
1984. Reproduced by permission of the publisher, F. E. Peacock Publishers Inc., Itasca,
Illinois. Excerpts from *Two Cybernetic Frontiers* by Stewart Brand, copyright © 1974 by
Stewart Brand. Reprinted by permission of Random House. Selected excerpts from pp. xii,
202–203, 206–208, and 474–475 from *Steps to an Ecology of Mind* by Gregory Bateson.
Copyright © 1972 by Harper & Row, Publishers, Inc. Reprinted by permission of the
publishers. Figures 16.1 and 16.2 reprinted from *American Journal of Psychiatry, 137*(5), p. 537,
May 1980. Copyright © 1980, the American Psychiatric Association. Reprinted by
permission of the authors and publisher. Selected excerpts throughout from *The Saturated
Self* by Kenneth J. Gergen. Copyright © 1991 by Basic Books, Inc. Reprinted by permission
of Basic Books, a division of Harper Collins Publishers, Inc.

For John

Contents

Foreword to the Third Edition

Longevity is one of the major marks of a fine textbook. *Family Therapy: A Systemic Integration* by Dorothy and Raphael Becvar is now into its third edition, and, in my judgment, is destined to go into several more updates as the field of family therapy changes. It has already established its claim as a premier introduction and guide to the field. The values of the book as a travel guide and the authority and skill of the Becvars as teachers have already been described in the Forewords to the first and second editions. I would suggest that the reader peruse carefully the thoughts expressed by Bradford Keeney and Bruce Lackie. They reflect nicely part of the reasons that *Family Therapy: A Systematic Integration* has marked out its place in the growing world of family therapy texts.

Rather than to repeat some of what has been written in the earlier Forewords, my intent is to build on the well-established foundation of those Forewords. That seems appropriate and consistent with what the Becvars have done in this revision of the book; they have built on the solid base they constructed earlier. Keeping track with trends, conflicts, and controversy leading into the 1990s, they have added a chapter on "Postmodernism and Social Constructionism," have discussed the feminist critique of family therapy—much of which is focused on system theory and its rejection of unilateral control, and have given a brief description of the family therapy-family medicine rapprochement, which continues to develop as an important specialty. Embodied in the postmodernism and social constructionism developments is a new appreciation of the role of language in social interaction. Were this book written for different purposes other than to serve as an introductory textbook, it would be interesting to see a discussion of similarities between the recent emphasis on language and social constructionism and the work of Harry Stack Sullivan and others who were educated or taught at the University of Chicago several decades ago. From somewhere in Sullivan's writings I recall the ideas (freely recalled) that "reality is that which is consensually validated." From another Chicagoan came the idea that "that which is defined as real is real in its consequences." Sullivan's attention to the linguistic theory and research of Sapir certainly seems to have anticipated some of the social constructivism of current days.

Let the Becvars speak for themselves:

> *It is through language that we both assimilate and influence our world as it is expressed in cultural norms and values. It is in language that we perceive, make meaning, and thus create our reality. And it is by means of language that client and therapist share stories in an ongoing, reciprocal conversation, the outcome of which is a narrative authored by all participants (p. 120).*

For those who are concerned with flexibility and with avoiding fitting treatment to the clients rather than crowding families, couples, and individuals into a single Procrustean bed, the Becvars offer such guidance as the following:

> *. . . while we may talk at the level of process about how to work with families, at the level of content our specifics will need to vary from context to context (p. 91).*

> *. . . there is no prescribed form that therapy must take, nor should there be. The basic limitation for acceptable therapist behavior is not exceeding the limits of ethical behavior (p. 91).*

The emphasis on social constructivism is not new in the Becvars' writing; they have made more explicit what was present previously in a more muted form. We are the beneficiaries of their decision to spell out the implications of their thinking.

This is a book that reflects intellectual integrity, compassion, ethical concern, and, rarest of all in a field too often dominated by an emphasis on action and technique, thoughtfulness and wisdom.

William C. Nichols, EdD
The Family Workshop, Atlanta

Foreword to the Second Edition

Given the numerous writers who seek to contain the full range of the family therapy field, the Becvars are among the most prominent. This second edition of their widely used text both defines the expanding horizon of family therapy and brings higher resolution to the more familiar aspects of the landscape. They are unusually available to the reader as guides. Throughout their text, they display empathy for the inherent uncertainty of the learner. They are a continuing, benign presence, inviting a dialogue with the reader. If one were to think of the family therapy field as a series of rooms in a museum, with well-displayed tapestries of both prominent and lesser known artists still emerging out of invisibility, the Becvars would serve as seasoned museum guides, their voices nonintrusive yet informative.

Their authority is apparent, and if authority is the capacity to see the invisible, the reader shares in and gains from their capacities, leaving at the end of the book well informed, enlightened. They evoke curiosity in the reader about the range of schools and make sense of the taffeta pattern of family therapy history. The reader is thus inclined to pay as much attention to the narration as the object of inquiry.

If travel is the best education, then traveling with the Becvars is time well spent. What lies ahead in the following pages invites attention; their capacity to contain and convey the complex pattern that is family therapy invites admiration.

Bruce Lackie, Ph.D.
Hahnemann University

Foreword to the First Edition

I am delighted to introduce you to Dorothy and Raphael Becvar's book, *Family Therapy: A Systemic Integration*. At last, a clearly written, accurate, and engaging presentation of the territories of family therapy is available. The Becvar's book is a superb travel guide that introduces the reader to the history, language, action, and major orientations of family therapy.

For the beginner it provides an overview and immediate access to the field. For the more seasoned practitioner it is a handy reference guide and reminder of how rich and diverse family therapy has become. Whether as an introductory text, desk reference, or an entertaining read, many will discover this book to be an indispensable part of their family therapy library.

As you will soon see, *Family Therapy: A Systemic Integration* is more than a travel guide that maps what can be observed in the field. It is an invitation to examine one's own participation in observing family therapy. This shift in perspective toward a view of "how one is viewing" brings the reader into the very core of systemic thinking—what the Becvars accurately call "cybernetics of cybernetics." The implication of this systemic shift is that the reader is challenged to take full responsibility for what he or she sees, knows, decides, and does with the ideas evoked by this text.

Seldom does a preface make a statement about the personhood and interactional style of the book's authors. Since this book seriously underscores the importance of intertwining the observed and the observer as well as the family and the therapist, I will take liberty to propose a beginning connection between the text and the people who wrote it.

Dorothy and Raphael Becvar are masterful teachers, serious scholars, dedicated clinicians, and most importantly, warm and caring human beings. Their commitment to systemic thinking and ethical conduct is part of their personal and professional lives. As simply as I know how to say it, this is a book you can trust. In what follows, the authors, their ideas, and their readers will find ways of connecting.

Bradford Keeney
Lubbock, Texas

Preface

As we noted in the preface to the second edition of this book, the significance of a particular historical period in the lives of individuals/families, in professions, or in the larger society certainly cannot be determined by its length. Although only two years have passed, we once again find ourselves, our profession, and society in very different places. Since the last writing we became fully acquainted with the commuter marriage lifestyle, departing on Sunday evenings for full-time faculty positions in Virginia (Dorothy) and Louisiana (Ray) and meeting in the airport on our Thursday evening returns to St. Louis, where we continued our work as teacher/trainers and therapists on a part-time basis. While Ray continues to commute, Dorothy is once again in full-time private practice in St. Louis. Our daughter, Lynne, works as a therapist in a residential treatment center for abused and neglected teenagers.

Although recognized in many significant ways as a separate and legitimate mental health profession, family therapy continues to be the focus of considerable debate. Internally, the discussion revolves around such issues as marginalization, gender and context sensitivity, and the impact of postmodernism and social constructionism. Externally, the primary concern has been with issues related to health care reform and survival in the world of managed care.

Looming large on the national horizon are the changes and challenges associated first with the election of Bill Clinton, and two years later, with a shift in Congress from Democratic to Republican majorities. Internationally, the communist system has been abolished in Russia and the IRA has declared a truce in Northern Ireland. Meanwhile, developments in technology continue to shrink our world and make thinking in terms of a global community more of a universal reality. The larger context also includes an awareness that we are but a few short years away from the beginning of a new century, a time considered by most to be extremely significant. However, even with all of these changes there is much that remains the same, much that provides us with the stability that enables such changes to occur.

Similarly, this book may best be described in terms of morphogenesis/morphostasis, or change in the context of stability/stability in the context of change. That is, the basic theoretical foundation remains consistent with the previous two editions, with changes throughout representing expansions rather than revisions. In Part One, we follow the discussion of two different world views with an updated look at the historical perspective. While adding a chapter on postmodernism and social constructionism after the discussion of the paradigmatic shift of systems theory, we see this movement within the field as more a change in emphasis rather than as a whole new way of thinking which falls outside the cybernetic paradigm. The ramifications of this change in emphasis are included in an expanded discussion of therapeutic intervention and strategies. The family process chapter also takes this change in emphasis into consideration. In Part Two we continue to describe the seminal approaches to and modalities of family therapy which we see as fundamental to an understanding of the family therapy field. And we once again have chosen to leave to the reader the option of comparing, contrasting, and integrating the various ways of conceptualizing the family therapy process. The chapter on evolving therapeutic models is, by definition, an updated consideration of current developments in the field. Finally, Part Three continues to include a chapter on assessment and research and one on pathologies of epistemology. The major change in this section is an expanded discussion of qualitative research methodologies. Once again, our aim has been to provide a more complete overview of the family therapy world in a manner consistent with our systemic perspective/bias.

It is our belief that the field of family therapy has done more to create a consciousness about mental health and its practice than any other profession. It certainly has also provided a far greater awareness of the systemic paradigm than might otherwise have been the case. This perspective, with its different kinds of questions that point to different sorts of solutions, is to us the most valuable aspect of family therapy. For by it we are directed to knowledge of our connectedness, and with it we may therefore one day succeed in transcending a view of difference as divisive.

As with the first two editions, this book will probably be different from most other textbooks you have encountered, and the most obvious differences will emerge from the use of a systems perspective. Perhaps the first thing you will notice will be a focus on *process* as we attempt to engage you, the reader, in an ongoing interaction or dialogue. As systems theorists and family therapists, we see, and thus construct, the world in relational, reciprocal terms. We view the writing of a book as involving those who read it. This is quite similar to our belief that without students, our roles as teachers would be meaningless. In both cases, we are as much concerned about the process as we are about the content.

However, in making this comparison we have immediately encountered the dilemma that challenged us to write a book on family therapy in the first place. After all, there were dozens of books on the subject, but few of them dealt with the difficulty involved in (1) writing about one language while (2) using the words of another language when (3) these two languages have fundamental assumptions that are logically inconsistent with one another.

So what does that have to do with our comparison between writing/readers and teaching/students? In a word, everything, for when we write, we are involved in sending messages without the possibility of responding to immediate feedback from the receiver of those messages. On the other hand, when we teach, we are influenced by the reactions of our students just as they are influenced to react by the ideas we share with them. To compound the difficulty, the language we must use as we attempt to transmit information in written form is linear (i.e., *A* causes *B*), while the language of systems theory is based on the notion of circularity (i.e., *A* and *B* mutually influence one another). Hence our dilemma.

Therefore, in this book we continue to attempt to keep you, the reader, in mind, to anticipate your reactions and to provide answers to the kinds of questions we think you might have based on those that typically arise in our discussions with co-learners in this field. We coin words and phrases to convey concepts. We also stray from the normal format when this appears to be the best way to illustrate a point. And we do our best to write in a nonlinear fashion as we strive for consistency within our theoretical perspective. When it becomes appropriate to make use of such distinctly linear words as *why, goal,* and *purpose,* we indicate that we must step outside the *framework* of systems theory in order to do so.

We have touched on three key concepts that merit further development before we proceed: *process, assumptions,* and *frameworks.* So let's backtrack a little. (In systems thinking that's not at all unusual; you can begin and end where you choose, retrace your steps, or punctuate a series of events however you see fit.)

First of all, we mentioned our concern with process. As we will discuss more completely in Chapter 3, systems theory focuses on the *what, when,* and *how* of patterns of interactions rather than on either the *why* or the specific *content* of those interactions. In other words, if we wanted to analyze our relationship as teachers and students, we would look at *what* role each of us plays, *when* various behaviors occur, and *how* we are with you, as you are with us as we are with you. We would not ask why each of us behaves as we do nor would it be particularly useful to know the details (i.e., the *content*) of our discussions with each other. Rather, the systemic hypothesis is that over time, we tend to establish fairly stable habits of how we are with each other, or patterns of interaction, regardless of the topics of our conversations. Therefore, if we wanted to understand our relationship, it is on this process that we would focus our attention.

Thus, in the writing of all three editions of this book, an important part of our task concerned the kind of relationship we as authors could establish with you as readers. Indeed, an essential aspect was the ongoing awareness and implementation of objectives at the level of process. At the same time, the rest of our challenge involved that sharing of information (i.e., the writing of a textbook), which certainly necessitated that we be concerned with the content. But the requirements for the latter aspect of our task emerge from a frame of reference other than that of systems theory.

It probably makes the most sense to talk about the other two concepts—assumptions and frameworks—together. Indeed, in our usage of these terms, each helps to explain the other. And together they take us into an area of crucial importance, that of epistemology.

In philosophy, epistemology refers to the study of how we know what we know, or how we can make valid knowledge claims based on a particular theoretical framework. Among other areas, this study focuses on the assumptions that underlie a particular framework and on whether the knowledge claims made by the theory are logically consistent with its own assumptions. For example, one of the fundamental assumptions of psychodynamic theory is the existence of an unconscious. However, the claim to know that we have an unconscious is illogical, or self-referentially inconsistent, because by definition the unconscious is unknowable.

Epistemology also may be used as a synonym for one's personal framework or interpretive system. In this case, the term refers to the belief system according to which each of us operates in every aspect of life. Although we rarely are aware of it, we each have internalized a set of theories that enables us to give order and predictability to our lives. They are the means by which each of us constructs our personal reality. These theories were learned in our families of origin, in school, and from other experiences that have been particularly meaningful to us. Each of our personal theories rests on some basic assumptions about how we believe the world is or will be. Inevitably, because we both create these theories and operate out of them, the kind of paradox described in our example of psychodynamic theory and the unconscious will occur. Sometimes this is problematic, and sometimes it is not. Certainly the concept of an unconscious has been extremely valuable in the progress of psychology, and we would be the last to suggest doing away with it. On the other hand, we do feel it is extremely important to be conscious of the frameworks we use, the assumptions on which they are based, and the possibility of logical inconsistency, or what Bateson (1972) calls "pathologies of epistemology."

Therefore, as students of family therapy and thus, by our definition of systems theory, we believe that each of us is challenged to examine his or her personal framework and personal set of assumptions about reality. When what we are doing is not working, we may recognize that it is we who create our reality and that perhaps our creation needs some revamping. In the same way, as family therapists we may challenge the interpretive systems of our clients, helping them to expand their beliefs about reality in such a way that new behaviors become appropriate and thus possible. In other words, for students, therapists, and clients, creating new, more useful constructions of reality is a shared goal. Thus, being aware of our assumptions, of inconsistencies between our assumptions and our actions, and of the possibility that other choices are available to us may be the means of finding solutions for many problems.

At this point, we have reached a good stopping/starting place, for in its most basic sense, epistemology is what this book is all about. That is, how do we describe the theoretical framework of systemic family therapy? How is this framework different from that on which traditional intrapsychic theories have been built? What are the basic assumptions of these two types of frameworks? On which fundamental assumptions do certain family therapists agree and on which do they differ? How do we understand the process of change from a systems perspective? How does the problem of paradox and theoretical inconsistency relate both to clients and therapists? Enough, you say! But this is only the beginning! For these are the sorts of questions that we will attempt to answer in the following chapters.

We are aware from our work with other students that you will probably experience frustration and confusion in the first sections of this book. In fact, we suspect you may already have some of these feelings. At times you will probably feel as though you have arrived in a foreign country where everyone is speaking another language you can't understand. We certainly felt that way upon first entering into the world of systems thinking. The best advice we can give you is to hang in there and allow yourself to be muddled for a time. Indeed, this is not unlike the experience we help to create for our clients in the process of change, and it may be very valuable for you to know how it feels.

It also may be important to know that there have been many travelers in this land before you, and many of them have found the trip to be extremely worthwhile. Certainly we look forward to accompanying you as your interpreters and guides, and we attempt to facilitate the journey by pointing out important guideposts to understanding along the way. Although you may feel that you are getting lost, you never will be out of our sight, and we hope you will find this excursion to be both interesting and enjoyable.

Plan for the Text

We present a brief glimpse of the book's organization, or our travel plan, before we continue our journey. In Chapter 1 we will learn about the world views consistent with both individual psychology and systemic family therapy. In Chapter 2 we will visit some of family therapy's historical sites and review some early research in the field as well as some of the models used by theorists, practitioners, and students of family therapy. We will also briefly consider some current influences in the field. In Chapter 3 we will experience the shift involved in internalizing systems thinking; here we will encounter the language of cybernetics, with all its ramifications for theorizing and conducting therapy. In Chapter 4 we provide a chapter on the background and influence of postmodernism and social constructionism on the theory and practice of family therapy. In Chapter 5 we will take a brief excursion into the theory of change consistent with a systems perspective, including in this consideration the use of narrative approaches and the role of stories and storytelling. We will also consider some important ethical issues. After that the going gets a little easier. In Chapter 6 we will consider family processes and their assessment relative both to accepted standards of normalcy and to cultural variation.

In Part Two, Chapters 7 through 12, we will visit particular schools of family therapy and meet some of the prominent spokespersons for each. We will highlight concepts and strategies which characterize, as well as the systemic consistency of, the following schools: psychodynamic, experiential, structural, communications, strategic, and behavioral. Chapter 13 will review a variety of approaches that have emerged most recently in the family therapy field. And Chapter 14 will include brief stops for observation of family therapy done at a variety of systems levels: individual, couple, group, intergenerational, and network.

Chapters 15 and 16, comprising Part Three, conclude our journey. Research issues are presented as well as dilemmas facing family therapists who operate out of a systemic perspective. Also included are some final thoughts.

Acknowledgments

The initial process of creating this tour guide for you was assisted by the reviewers whose suggestions and comments provided valuable feedback along the way. We continue to express our gratitude to Dick Dustin, Margaret Hoopes, Bradford Keeney, and Allan Wilcoxin. Preparation of the second edition was greatly facilitated by users of the text who responded to a survey conducted by Allyn and Bacon. Although we do not know your names, we wish to thank you for your assistance.

We would also like to thank the editors, staff, and freelancers at Allyn and Bacon who worked with us, first to produce this book and then to revise it: Susan Badger, Laura Pearson, Beth Brooks, Susan Freese, Dana Hayes, Mylan Jaixen, Annette Joseph, Susan Lundgren, Karen Mason, Susan Mesner, Grace Sheldrick, Sue Hutchinson, Rob Lawson, Jane Jacobi, and Laurie Lach. A special thanks to typesetter Yoram Mizrahi.

$P \quad a \quad r \quad t$ 1

The Systemic Framework

The first part of our journey into the world of systems theory and family therapy will provide you with some of the basics. Our goal is that you be well equipped to venture on, not only into the rest of this book but also into the vast array of references and resources in the family therapy field. However, certain parameters need acknowledgment if this experience is to be as meaningful for you as we would wish.

Our bias throughout this book is obviously based on our espousal of a systemic/cybernetic perspective. From this perspective, we assume bias is inevitable and the best one can do is recognize that bias. However, although we espouse a systemic/cybernetic perspective, we do not feel it is the *right* way, the *only* way, or the *best* way to think. *It is a way to think.* Similarly, we do not assume that doing family therapy necessarily requires operating upon the assumptions underlying a systemic/cybernetic perspective. Rather, it is our belief (bias) that one of the major contributions of the family therapy movement was its introduction of a systemic/cybernetic perspective into the theory and practice of the behavioral sciences.

Given these biases, we feel it essential to delineate the nature of the systemic/cybernetic perspective as well as its ramifications for the concepts of stability and change, health and dysfunction, and for the whole notion of ethics. Consistent with our basic assumptions, we begin by presenting a context, or historical framework, within which to understand the current flowering of family therapy. With each of the topics addressed in this and the other two sections of the book, we will make every effort to remain consistent with our framework. While it may therefore appear that we are trying to convince you of the "truth" of a systemic/cybernetic perspective, we would ask you to remember that such a position would be inconsistent with our basic assumptions and that our challenge is to describe and not to persuade.

In equipping you for this and future journeys, we hope to assist you in becoming better students and consumers of the field. We are keenly aware of the popularity of family therapy, of the number of programs being offered, of the variety of possible approaches, and of the complexity of the literature. Indeed, becoming a family therapist is not a simple process. It requires excellence in training, clinical experience, and supervision. But above all, we believe it requires a solid theoretical grounding so that you may understand and assess what is appropriate both for you and your clients. Whether you decide to accept or reject a systemic/cybernetic perspective, you will need knowledge of this theory and its fundamental assumptions as well as the related areas of history, strategy creation, ethics, and family process, all of which are presented in Part One.

Chapter 1

Two Different World Views

Welcome to the world of systems theory and family therapy! We suspect that if you read the Preface you are already having second thoughts about undertaking this journey. (If you have not read the Preface, we suggest that you go back and do so now.) Hesitation and second thoughts are perfectly normal at this point, and we would be surprised if you were feeling otherwise. Approach the systems world just as cautiously as you would when visiting any foreign area.

This chapter describes the frameworks that underlie two different world views: individual psychology and systemic family therapy. The former framework or world view is familiar to you because it is so much a part of our culture. The latter world view is not only different but is also *countercultural*. That is, its assumptions are inconsistent with those basic to American society. Hence the discomfort students of family therapy usually experience when first they encounter systems theory. In time the language will become familiar and you probably will become comfortable with the concepts. You may even find your own viewpoint has changed so that you will decide to take up residence in systems territory yourself. But that possibility is going to seem remote for quite some time.

The Framework of Individual Psychology

Most of us have been socialized into a world whose philosophical assumptions (basic epistemology) are firmly rooted in a Western, Lockean, scientific tradition. By *socialized* we mean the processes, both implicit and explicit, by which we learn appropriate behavior and ways of thinking consistent with a particular social group. For most of us, informal socialization occurs in our families and formal socialization occurs in school. In both places we are taught the rules that enable us to become productive members of society. Thus, if you, and especially if your parents as well, were educated in Western society, you were totally immersed in a perspective derived from the thinking of John Locke, and those who followed him, about the appropriate rules for theory construction and methodology in the physical sciences. That is, you have been immersed in what is currently referred to as the world of modernism (Gergen, 1991).

You probably have been taught, for example, that linear cause/effect thinking is appropriate and that any problem is solvable if we can find an answer to the question Why? From this perspective, event *A* causes event *B* ($A \rightarrow B$) in a linear (unidirectional) fashion. We therefore hold *A* responsible for *B* or blame *A* for causing *B*. Why did *B* happen? Because *A* did such and such. Or another way of expressing the same idea is to say that *A* bumped into *B* and then *C* happened ($A \rightarrow B \rightarrow C$).

Also, you probably have been taught, consistent with the Lockean tradition, to understand the world as consisting of subjects and objects, or *A*s operating on *B*s. From this point of view, reality is considered to be external to us, to exist outside our minds. Thus, meaning comes from external experience and we are recipients: we recognize order rather than create it. Further, if we can reduce sequences of reality, which are out there, into their smallest possible components (reductionism), then we can uncover the laws according to which the world operates. We understand the world to be deterministic and to operate according to lawlike principles, the discovery of which will reveal some absolute truths about reality. We as individuals are seen as reacting to our reality rather than creating it.

According to this tradition, the appropriate scientific methodology is empirical and quantitative; knowledge must be pursued by means of observation and experimentation. The results of such experimentation must be measurable and objective. And not only is the subject separate from the object of his observations, but reality and the theories about reality are seen as either/or, black or white, right or wrong explanations.

When these beliefs were translated from the physical sciences into the behavioral sciences, they were interpreted into theories that described human behavior as determined either by internal events or external environmental sequences to which we may react. Behavioral scientists embraced the notion of mind/body dualism inherent in the belief that mind and reality exist independently of one another. Thus, I as an *A* (subject/mind) can view *B* (object/reality) from a distance without imposing my values or beliefs on *B*. This premise has led us to believe that both objective measurement and a value-free science are possible and to distrust the subjective dimension as being nonscientific.

The particular assumptions outlined above have served researchers, especially those in the so-called hard sciences, extremely well for generations and no doubt will continue to do so for many more. It is not surprising, therefore, that this scientific tradition has been and continues to be well respected in Western societies. It is also not surprising that psychologists, in their early efforts to gain credibility within the scientific community, adopted this tradition wholeheartedly. We in the behavioral, the so-called soft, sciences have accepted the importance of objectivity and the value of measurable, quantifiable data. We were taught and hence believe that our focus should be on root causes. We therefore have directed our attention toward history, or previous events that led to current problems, so we can understand human behavior and find solutions to such problems. If our goal is to reduce behavior to the lowest common denominator, then we must focus either on the individual and the individual's specific behaviors or on the internal events of the human mind.

Such premises are consistent with many of our basic American values. Not only do we have a great respect for science in this country, but part of the tradition that we as Americans hold most dear is a belief in individualism. Indeed, the individual rather than the community is at the heart of all our social and political speculation (Becvar, 1983). Thus, with its emphasis on the individual as well as its consistency with the Lockean scientific tradition, psychodynamic theory fit and was well received and warmly embraced in the United States. Have you ever noticed, for example, how often the following psychodynamic terms occur in our everyday conversations: *Freudian slip; rationalization; unconscious behavior; defense mechanism?*

Throughout the first half of the twentieth century, theories based either on Freudian notions or on reactions to them proliferated. As a result we have a variety of individual psychologies, intrapsychic theories, learning theories, and therapies that combine elements of these psychologies and theories, all of which, though they may look different on the surface, have basically the same world view. Although some of these theories and therapies are clearly more humanistic than scientific or mechanistic, they all focus on the individual and share similar fundamental beliefs. An examination of individual psychologies such as psychoanalysis (Freud), analytical psychology (Jung), individual psychology (Adler), Rogerian therapy (Rogers), behaviorism (Skinner), rational emotive therapy (R.E.T.)(Ellis), reality therapy (Glasser), and transactional analysis (T.A.)(Berne), for example, reveals that each is based on a foundation that includes most of the following assumptions about reality and its appropriate description:

Asks Why?

Linear cause/effect

Subject/object dualism

Either/or dichotomies

Value-free science

Deterministic/reactive

Laws and lawlike external reality

Historical focus

Individualistic

Reductionistic

Absolutistic

To illustrate this world view, let us think of these intrapsychic/learning theories as slices of an individual psychology pie (see Figure 1.1). Let us think of the foundation, or crust in which the pie is baked, as being made up of the ingredients contained in the above list of basic assumptions (see Figure 1.2).

As anyone who appreciates good cooking knows, the pie and its crust need to fit, or complement, each other or the pie will not be very tasty. Similarly, theories and the assumptions on which they are based must have a good fit if they are to have a logical consistency. Just as we need to know the ingredients of a crust to know if it is appropriate to its filling, part of understanding a theory involves knowing the assumptions that flavor and give meaning to theories built on these assumptions. Thus, if we put assumptions and theories together, we come up with a pie as illustrated in Figure 1.3.

As you, the students of family therapy, attempt to journey into the systems world and understand the concepts according to which its natives are socialized, the dilemma you face is not unlike that encountered by the cook who only knows how to bake a pumpkin pie and must now learn how to bake a cheese pie. Even though both pies have creamy fillings, they are made in different ways and, most importantly, their crusts contain entirely different ingredients.

FIGURE 1-1   **Filling for an Individual Psychology Pie**

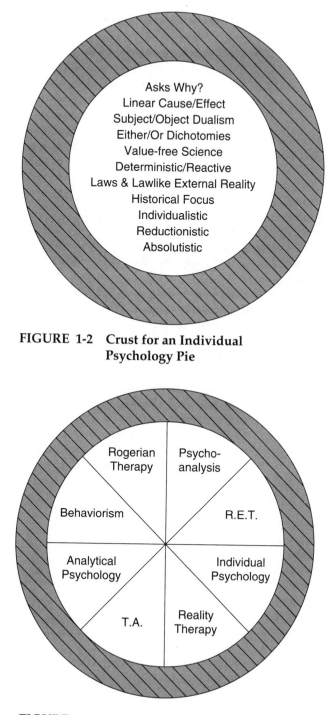

**FIGURE 1-2   Crust for an Individual
                 Psychology Pie**

FIGURE 1-3   Individual Psychology Pie

The Framework of Systemic Family Therapy

While the individual psychology pie is built on particular assumptions underlying intrapsychic and learning theories, the family therapy pie is built on a different set of assumptions, which underlie systems theory. In the former case, these assumptions are consistent with such basic American values as individual responsibility and autonomy. In the latter case, however, the underlying assumptions are contradictory to our traditional ways of thinking in this society. Hence, our use of the term *countercultural* to characterize systems theory.

Systems theory directs our attention away from the individual and individual problems in isolation and toward relationships and relationship issues between individuals. In contrast to the Lockean tradition, systems theory is consistent with the tradition labeled as Kantian. Accordingly, the observer replaces the observed as the focus of attention. Thus, subjectivity is seen as inevitable as the observer perceives, acts on, and creates her own reality. In addition, the interdependence of observer and observed is an important aspect of a wholistic perspective that takes into account the context of their interaction. Such interaction is seen as a noncausal, dialectical process of mutual influence in which both are equally involved. Finally, understanding requires assessing patterns of interaction with an emphasis on what is happening rather than why it is happening.

Just as the individual psychology pie contains slices representing various theories and therapies, so there are several different slices, or schools, of family therapy. Some of these schools look deceptively like slices cut from the individual psychology pie. (We might illustrate the filling for the family therapy pie as in Figure 1.4.)

It is important to emphasize, however, that the part of the family therapy pie that gives it a unique flavor and makes it difficult to learn how to bake is the crust. Systemic family therapy is based on a different foundation of assumptions about reality and its appropriate description, which include the following:

Asks What?

Reciprocal causality

Wholistic

Dialectical

Subjective/perceptual

Freedom of choice/proactive

Patterns

Here-and-now focus

Relational

Contextual

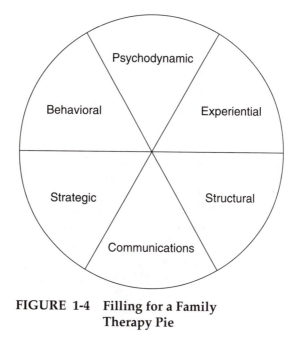

FIGURE 1-4   Filling for a Family
Therapy Pie

Systems theory, or the crust for the family therapy pie, is illustrated in Figure 1.5. And putting the pie and crust together gives us the final product, comparable to the individual psychology pie (see Figure 1.6 and compare with Figure 1.3).

What follows is an introduction to the important concepts that form the foundation of systems theory. A much fuller discussion is contained in Chapter 3. Nevertheless, you might anticipate the recurrence of that muddled feeling as we turn the corner into more unfamiliar territory.

Basic Concepts of Systems Theory

In the world of systems theory, linear causality does not exist. Instead we find an emphasis on reciprocity, recursion, and shared responsibility. *A* and *B* exist in the context of a relationship in which each influences the other and both are equally cause and effect of each other's behavior: (A⤫B) or "I am with you as you are with me as I am with you."

Over time, *A* and *B* establish patterns characteristic of their particular relationship. If we wish to understand the events of their relationship, we do not ask *why* something happened. Rather we ask *what is going on* in an effort to describe these patterns. Our perspective is wholistic, and our focus is on the processes, or context, that give meaning to events instead of only on the individuals or the events in isolation. Our focus is also present-centered: We examine here-and-now interactions rather than look to history for antecedent causes.

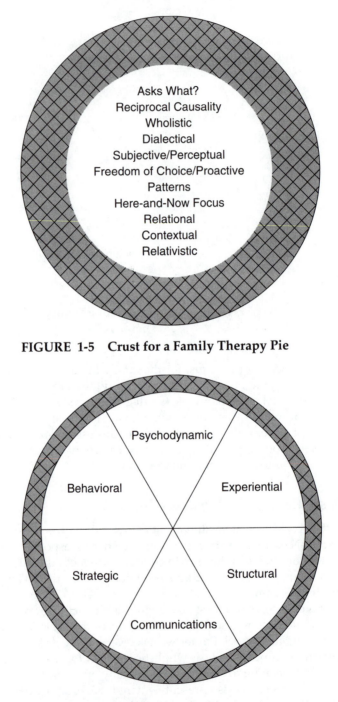

FIGURE 1-5   Crust for a Family Therapy Pie

FIGURE 1-6   Family Therapy Pie

Thus, in this world we are all concurrently subjects and objects; we are all involved in each other's destiny. Reality is not external to us but is constructed by us as we bring our own personal perceptions to bear on it and give meaning and order to it. We are proactive. We act on the world and have choices relative to the creation of our own destiny. We recognize that mind and body are inseparable, that subjectivity is inevitable, and that a value-free science is therefore not possible.

We attempt to transcend either/or dichotomies by acknowledging the necessity for, or complementarity of, both sides of the coin, if the coin is to exist at all. Thus, we do not reject one side of the coin in favor of the other: we attempt to consider the utility of each side of the coin relative to a given context. For example, to understand the concept of light we must have darkness. Only as they are contrasted can we observe difference and thereby understand the meaning of each. Just because we may prefer the light, we cannot do away with darkness. Further, there are times when darkness may be equally useful. Certainly it is easier for many of us to create an atmosphere of romance with darkness and candlelight than it would be in broad daylight. Therefore, the utility of each is decided situationally.

The characteristic of the systems world just described is *theoretical relativity.* According to this concept, we realize that just as we cannot reject one side of a coin or issue without destroying it entirely, embracing one theory does not require or imply the rejection of an opposite theory. Rather, we recognize that each theory gives meaning to the other and each has utility relative to a given context. Thus, entry into the systems world does not require rejection of the individual psychology world. Just as light and darkness are contrasted to each other and enable us to observe difference, so the individual psychology world and the systems theory world are intricately connected as each gives meaning to the other.

By making use of systems theory, with the notions of transcendence of dichotomies and utility relative to context, as explained above, we recognize that sometimes a pumpkin pie is the appropriate dessert and at other times the better choice is a cheese pie. The final selection must be made relative to the rest of the meal, or the larger context. Therefore, the table on which the pies are placed and whose rules will be employed in passing judgment are those of theoretical relativity. Figure 1.7 illustrates this idea. Both pies are placed on the menu, but one will be selected because it complements the meal rather than because it is good and the other is bad.

Similarly, entry into the systemic family therapy world does not require that you leave the individual psychology world behind forever. Rather, we find that systems theory provides us with a passport to travel freely back and forth between both worlds. Systems theory may therefore be said to be a theory of theories, or metatheory. It is descriptive only and suggests that we suspend judgments about what is good and bad, right and wrong. Rather, we are urged to consider goodness and badness relative to context. The important issue is utility, or appropriateness, neither of which can be decided out of context.

Another way to describe systems theory is as a "skeleton of science" (Boulding, 1968), whose bones may be fleshed out by whatever discipline one chooses.

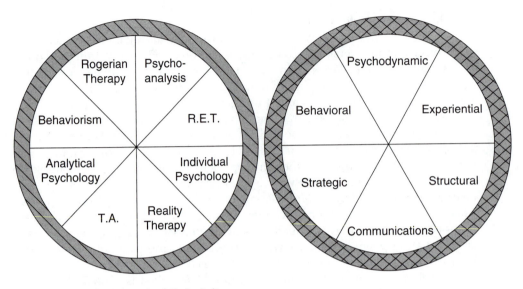

FIGURE 1-7   Theoretical Relativity

Thus, it is just as appropriate to talk about pies as it is to talk about theories when using this perspective.

What systems theory is not, however, is a pragmatic theory. Even though it can be used to describe the relationship between pies, between theories, and between human behaviors and can tell us where to focus our attention if we wish to understand events or make changes, it cannot tell us what to do to make those changes. Once again, it is not a pragmatic theory. Many of the seminal thinkers in family therapy adopted systems theory because of its utility in describing human interaction and then fleshed out its bones with concepts drawn from a variety of sources, including individual psychology, anthropology, biology, cybernetics, and communications theory. This in part accounts for the evolution of the various schools of thought within the field of family therapy. It may also account in part for the differences of these schools in terms of their consistency with the systemic/cybernetic perspective.

Family Therapy or Relationship Therapy?

It is important to note that the term *family therapy* is probably a misnomer. When family therapy is built on the assumptions of systems theory, a more appropriate label would probably be *relationship therapy*. As mentioned previously, systems theory enables us to describe relationships and patterns of interaction. Therefore, the choice to work with families to solve everyday human problems is one of expediency rather than of necessity. Since the family is the primary group from which each of us derives meaning and is the context in which most of us live. it is the family to which we as therapists have directed most of our attention. However, it is just as appropriate to work at the individual level, the couple level, the extended family level, the neighborhood level, or the societal level, and indeed many family therapists do that. But more about that in Part Two.

Summary

This concludes the introductory portion of our trip. We have briefly discussed the world view underlying individual psychology, noting its basic assumptions and the fit of this perspective in Western societies. We also have outlined the bare essentials of a systems perspective and have addressed its countercultural aspects. It is important to emphasize the fact that systems theory, as a metaperspective, is inclusive of individual psychology and does not require the student of family therapy to make either/or choices between these two world views. Finally, we have indicated our belief that family therapy based on systems theory might more appropriately be called relationship therapy.

Chapter 2

The Historical Perspective

The seeds of the family therapy movement can be said to have been planted in the late 1930s and early 1940s. Having found fertile soil, the movement put down roots in the 1950s, began to bud in the 1960s, and finally blossomed in the 1970s. However, now that we have made such an assertion, it is important to remember that much that preceded this era can also be said to have influenced the timing and shape of the emergence of family therapy as a viable clinical modality. Thus, making a division at the 1940s is somewhat arbitrary and is done in light of our personal perceptions and interpretations of particular historical events.

In the same vein, it is interesting to note the varied and sometimes conflicting accounts of the development of family therapy written by those who were there (e.g., Ackerman, 1967; Guerin, 1976; Keith & Whitaker, 1982). Such variations make sense in at least two ways. First, human beings are unique in terms of their ability to be both actors and observers of their own actions. As we discuss more fully in the next chapter, the observer's perceptions always color what is being observed. Nowhere is this more the case, and possibly a dilemma, than when the subjects are also the objects of their own observations. Indeed, one goal of therapy is to enable clients to gain some distance from life experiences in which they are involved and thus, as we say, to gain some perspective on them.

Secondly, history writing, particularly by people who helped create the history, is a process by which the historians (in this case family therapists) distance themselves from their actions and record them from the perspective of observers. The process of distancing, reflecting on, and describing is necessarily different from the process of experiencing. The same events will vary in degree of importance relative to the framework of each observer. Further, just as Maturana (Simon, 1985) indicates that each member of the same family (from the perspective of an outsider) lives in a slightly different family (from the perspective of the insider), so each historian gives different meaning to, and writes a slightly different account of, the same experience.

No single description of the family or one historical account of family therapy is any more right or accurate than any other. From a systems perspective we live in a multiperspectival, multiconstructed universe in which each viewer creates his or her own reality and for whom that reality is his or her own truth. We will be returning to this important point many times and we discuss it in great detail in Chapter 3.

It is important to remember that we are second-generation family therapists. We have integrated various accounts filtered through the frameworks of both first- and second-generation family therapists and then through our own cognitive lenses. We hope, however, that this particular historical perspective will provide a full sense of the development and ramifications of the movement. In addition to giving our account of the main events, key people, and various climates in which family therapy sprouted and grew, we feel that a thorough understanding also requires a delineation and examination of the historical context that both nurtured and was influenced by this developmental process. Therefore, we have provided you with a historical table (see Table 2.1 at the end of this chapter), in which we have recorded highlights in the development of family therapy and some background world events we feel capture a sense of the environment in which family therapy flowered. Our discussion focuses on both.

We have divided our historical survey into periods corresponding to decades beginning with the 1940s and continuing through the 1990s. Having guided you up to the present, we then take you back before the so-called beginning. That is, we briefly look at the period before the forties and at the contributions of various theorists or therapists who helped to prepare the soil in which the seeds of family therapy were sown. Perhaps you may feel we are putting the cart before the horse, and in a sense we are. But given our perspective, it makes sense to use this format in order to emphasize the circularity we see in all processes and the difficulty we see in designating beginnings.

Planting the Seeds: The 1940s

Cybernetics

The seeds of the family therapy movement were sown by a disparate group of researchers and theorists from a variety of disciplines who were early explorers in the realm of cybernetics. Included in this group were mathematicians Norbert Wiener, John Von Neumann, and Walter Pitts; physician Julian Bigelow; physiologists Warren McCulloch and Lorente de No; psychologist Kurt Lewin; anthropologists Gregory Bateson and Margaret Mead; economist Oskar Morgenstern; as well as others from the fields of anatomy, engineering, neurophysiology, psychology, and sociology (Wiener, 1948).

In what has since been recognized as a major departure in the way we study and come to know our world, the science of cybernetics early on concerned itself with organization, pattern, and process rather than with matter, material, and content. In the words of Ashby (1956), another pioneer, cybernetics "treats, not things but *ways of behaving*. It does not ask 'what does it do?'... It is thus essentially functional and behavioristic" (p. 1).

The field of cybernetics dates from approximately 1942, and Norbert Wiener is usually given credit for naming the science. Wiener, writing in 1948, defines the term and also traces its roots:

> *The word cybernetics is taken from the Greek kybernetes, meaning steersman. From the same Greek word, through the Latin corruption gubernator, came the term governor, which has been used for a long time to designate a certain type of control mechanism and was the title of a brilliant study written by the Scottish physicist James Clark Maxwell eighty years ago. The basic concept which both Maxwell and the investigators of cybernetics mean to describe by the choice of this term is that of a feedback mechanism, which is especially well represented by the steering engine of a ship. (p. 14)*

By means of a focus not only on feedback mechanisms but also on information processing and patterns of communication, cyberneticians began in the early 1940s to study and compare inanimate machines with living organisms in an effort to understand and control complex systems. Much of the early work in this area, as well as its interdisciplinary nature, was both assisted by and emerged out of the events of World War II (Heims, 1975).

Development of Interdisciplinary Approaches

By tradition, research had always tended to take place within the fairly rigidly maintained boundaries of particular disciplines housed in separate university departments. During the war, however, many efforts were undertaken by teams of researchers whose areas of expertise cut across various disciplines in both the physical and social sciences. Thus, for example, Norbert Wiener was a member of an interdisciplinary team at the Massachusetts Institute of Technology. His assignment was to section D–2 of the National Defense Research Committee, and his focus was on antiaircraft fire. At the same time, John Von Neumann was a consultant in mathematics to the Manhattan Project in Los Alamos, New Mexico—where the first nuclear weapons were constructed (Heims, 1977).

While their goal was the improvement of the technology of war, many concepts forthcoming from these research efforts have had an impact that continues to be felt. In a 1943 article entitled "Behavior, Purpose and Teleology," Rosenblueth, Wiener, and Bigelow state: "In classifying behavior the term 'teleology' was used as synonymous with 'purpose controlled by feedback'....It may be pointed out, however, that purposefulness, as defined here, is quite independent of causality, initial or final" (p. 22). With ideas such as these, an alternate perspective on knowledge and reality came into being.

In addition to belonging to multidisciplinary teams, Wiener and Von Neumann communicated with one another during this period. Indeed, as early as 1943 they had begun to share their thoughts about the relative advantages of studying organisms and machines together. By the time the war ended in 1945, they had organized a small study group and were beginning to plan ways to implement some of their ideas.

Gregory Bateson

Meanwhile, anthropologist Gregory Bateson had been formally introduced to the world of hypnosis and the ideas of Milton Erickson at two conferences held in New York City, the first on December 7, 1941, and the second on May 14–15, 1942. According to Bateson (Bateson & Mead, 1976), psychologist Lawrence Kubie played an important role in this drama. Through both the earlier conference and joint writings, he helped "respectabilize" hypnotist Erickson. Indeed, the title of the latter conference, "Cerebral Inhibition," was, as Bateson noted (Bateson & Mead, 1976), nothing more than "a respectable word for hypnosis" (p. 32). The upshot of these conferences for Bateson

> *was a solution to the problem of purpose. From Aristotle on, the final cause has always been the mystery. This came out then. We didn't realize then (at least I didn't realize it, though McCulloch might have) that the whole of logic would have to be reconstructed for Recursiveness. (p. 33)*

At the 1942 conference, Bateson also became acquainted with the as-yet-unpublished contents of the Rosenblueth, Wiener, and Bigelow paper mentioned previously. Although an article by Ross Ashby would achieve a prior publication date of 1940, Bateson was not aware of it at the time and thus considered the 1943 article to be the first great paper on cybernetics (Bateson & Mead, 1976).

During the war, Bateson, an Englishman, worked for the U.S. Office of Strategic Services in India, China, and Ceylon. At the same time he continued to ponder and be intrigued by the concepts to which he recently had been introduced. He was particularly interested in creating new and better ways of interpreting the data he had collected during his studies of the Balinese and Iatmul cultures before the war. His overriding goal was to find a more appropriate framework for the behavioral sciences than those currently in use (Heims, 1977). With this in mind, Bateson corresponded with physiologist Warren McCulloch, who shared similar interests. By the end of the war they were among those who were pushing the Josiah Macy, Jr., Foundation to sponsor another conference (Bateson & Mead, 1976).

By March 1946 the scientists who had been employed in the defense effort were looking for new projects and for ways to explore new ideas that had emerged in relation to their war research. In the United States the prestige of science was high, there was great faith in the potential of science to solve most problems, and money was available to support civilian research. Thus, it was without much difficulty that the Macy Foundation was persuaded to sponsor a multidisciplinary conference on "Teleological Mechanisms" (Heims, 1977).

At this point it seems appropriate to note that Gregory Bateson is considered to be one of the most important figures in the development of systemic family therapy, especially in the delineation of the philosophical framework underlying this movement. His translation of the concepts of engineering and mathematics into the language of the behavioral sciences was crucial. However, Bateson himself was neither an engineer, a mathematician, nor a family therapist. Rather, he has been variously labeled *anthropologist* and/or *ethnologist,* and his ultimate contributions were in the realm of epistemology. At the 1946 Macy Conference, Bateson's talk focused on his search for an adequate framework for the social sciences and the limitations of learning theory for describing stability mechanisms in various cultures. At future conferences and in subsequent communications, he continued his conversations with other cyberneticians, particularly Wiener and Von Neumann. Thus, Bateson played a vital role in the process of bridging the worlds of the physical and behavioral sciences.

During the 1946–47 academic year, Bateson was a visiting professor at the New School for Social Research in New York City. In 1947–48 he was a visiting professor at Harvard University. Failing to receive a permanent appointment at Harvard, he then went to join Juergen Ruesch as a research associate in the department of psychiatry at the University of California Medical School. He worked full-time at the Langley Porter Institute for the next two years and, according to Bateson (1977), "In those two years, my beginnings as well as the premises of *Steps to an Ecology of Mind* (1972) were established" (p. 332). Bateson (1977) noted, however, that

> *the credit for discovering the importance of Principia in engineering and in human natural history goes, surely, to Norbert Wiener and Warren McCulloch. I learned this discovery from them and brought this powerful insight with me to the Langley Porter Institute. Juergen Ruesch and I were indeed "standing on the shoulders of giants." (p. 334)*

What were the contributions to which Bateson refers? By *Principia* Bateson meant *Principia Mathematica,* written by Alfred North Whitehead and Bertrand Russell and published in 1910. The major contribution of this work was its delineation of the theory of logical types, with mathematical proofs for the inevitability of self-reference and paradox in all formal systems, due to a discontinuity between a class and the members of that class. We will return shortly to these extremely important, if somewhat complicated, concepts.

Applying these notions within the context of a cybernetic perspective, Wiener had already begun by the 1940s to see such psychological constructs as Freud's id and unconscious and Jung's archetypes as informational processes. The importance for Bateson of such insights cannot be underestimated. For him cybernetics resolved the ancient problem posed by dualistic thinking about mind and body. Rather than being considered transcendent, mind could now be described as immanent in systems. Thus, in the company of Juergen Ruesch and equipped with both his communication expertise and knowledge gained from Wiener and other members of the Macy group, Bateson set about translating the practice of psychiatry into a theory of human communication (Heims, 1977).

Putting Down Roots: The 1950s

Bateson (Continued)

The 1946 Macy Conference was the first in a series of ten small conferences held during the next seven years, the final one taking place in April 1953. Continuing to attract theorists from a variety of disciplines, "each conference included about twenty-five participants, of which approximately twenty were regular conferees and five were guests. The title of the conferences, 'Circular Causal and Feedback Mechanisms in Biological and Social Systems' was later changed to 'Cybernetics'" (Heims, 1975, p. 368). However, the term *cybernetics* was not as widely adopted in this country as it was in Europe, where Wiener had taken the label as well as the concepts (Bateson & Mead, 1976). Rather, in the United States it was *systems theory*, following Ludwig von Bertalanffy's use of "general system theory" in articles published during the 1950s, with which the family therapy movement became identified. As we repeatedly observe, many strands of thought eventually converged as various researchers and practitioners arrived at a similar theoretical position from different initial starting points. Bateson (1972) acknowledged the importance of this phenomenon:

> *Now I want to talk about the other significant historical event which has happened in my lifetime, approximately in 1946–47. This was the growing together of a number of ideas which had developed in different places during World War II. We may call the aggregate of these ideas cybernetics, or communication theory, or systems theory. The ideas were generated in many places: in Vienna by Bertalanffy, in Harvard by Wiener, in Princeton by Von Neumann, in Bell Telephone labs by Shannon, in Cambridge by Craik, and so on. All these separate developments in different intellectual centers dealt with different communication problems, especially with the problem of what sort of a thing is an organized system. (pp. 474–475)*

As Bateson indicated, his ideas had already begun to crystallize by the time he went to California to work with Juergen Ruesch. After two years there he changed his status at the Langley Porter Institute from full- to part-time and initiated what would become a lengthy association with the Veteran's Administration Hospital in Palo Alto. In 1951 Ruesch and Bateson published *Communication: The Social Matrix of Psychiatry,* in which they delineated the "role of feedback and information theory in communication" (Foley, 1974, p. 5).

In 1952 Bateson received a grant from the Rockefeller Foundation to direct a research project on the role of the paradoxes of abstraction in communication. This study was aimed at an examination of the levels of communication in terms of the theory of logical types. Jay Haley and John Weakland became part of Bateson's research team in early 1953, joined later that year by William Fry. Haley was a communication specialist, Weakland a chemical engineer turned cultural anthropologist, and Fry a psychiatrist interested in studying humor. This disparate group undertook research on a variety of aspects of animal and human behavior. In all cases, however, the focus was on the levels of communication and, more importantly, on conflicts between these levels. In the process they studied the language of schizophrenics, popular movies, and humor, as well as guide-dog training and otters at play (Nichols, 1984).

In 1954 the Macy Foundation awarded Bateson a two-year grant to direct a research project on schizophrenic communication. The original team of researchers was soon joined by Don D. Jackson. Jackson, a psychiatrist, became clinical consultant to the group and supervised the therapy with schizophrenic patients. At this point the goal of the research project shifted to outlining a theory of communication that would explain both schizophrenia in general and schizophrenia in the context of the family in particular. However, this idea was not entirely new; the Bateson group had hypothesized about the appropriateness of family versus individual therapy in some instances as early as 1949. In addition, Bateson had subsequently questioned the traditional concept of psychosis as an illness. Thus, he had considered the possibility of defining a schizophrenic episode as a "spontaneous initiation ceremony" (Heims, 1977, p. 153).

The Double-Bind Hypothesis

Although the group did not begin to see families until 1956 or 1957 (Simon, 1982), by 1954 Bateson had developed his now-famous double-bind hypothesis. In 1956 the landmark paper "Toward a Theory of Schizophrenia" was published. An interesting historical note recounted by Haley (Simon, 1982) reveals that "we wrote the double-bind paper in June 1956; it was published in September 1956—the fastest journal publication ever done, I think" (p. 22). Why such immediate attention? To answer this question we must consider the theory in some detail. It will also help clarify previously unexplained concepts.

According to the theory's authors (Bateson, 1972), the necessary ingredients for a double-bind situation include:

1. *Two or more persons, one of whom is designated the "victim."*
2. *Repeated experience.*
3. *A primary negative injunction.*
4. *A secondary injunction conflicting with the first at a more abstract level, and like the first enforced by punishments or signals which threaten survival.*
5. *A tertiary negative injunction prohibiting the victim from escaping the field.*
6. *Finally, the complete set of ingredients is no longer necessary when the victim has learned to perceive his universe in double-bind patterns. Almost any part of a double-*

*bind sequence may then be sufficient to precipitate panic or rage. The pattern of con-
flicting injunctions may even be taken over by hallucinatory voices. (pp. 206–208)*

In assessing the effects of the double bind, it is hypothesized that "there will
be a breakdown in any individual's ability to discriminate between Logical Types
whenever a double-bind situation occurs" (Bateson, 1972, p. 208). The further requirements for such a situation are:

1. *When the individual is involved in an intense relationship; that is, a relationship in
   which he feels it is vitally important that he discriminate accurately what sort of message is being communicated so that he may respond appropriately.*
2. *And, the individual is caught in a situation in which the other person in the relationship is expressing two orders of messages and one of these denies the other.*
3. *And, the individual is unable to comment on the messages being expressed to correct
   his discrimination of what order of message to respond to, i.e., he cannot make a metacommunicative statement. (p. 208)*

According to this theory, the victim of such a double-bind situation will, following a psychotic breakdown, show symptoms that can be characterized in the
following manner:

1. *The individual will not share with normal people a sensitivity to signals that accom-
   pany messages to indicate what a person means.*
2. *The individual's metacommunicative system—the communications about communication—will have broken down, and he or she will not know what kind of message a
   message is. (p. 210)*

The authors summarized the double-bind theory by stating:

*Our approach is based on that part of communications theory which Russell has
called the Theory of Logical Types. The central thesis of this theory is that there is
a discontinuity between a class and its members. The class cannot be a member of
itself nor can one of the members be the class, since the term used for the class is
of a different level of abstraction—a different Logical Type—from terms used for
members. Although in formal logic there is an attempt to maintain this discontinuity between a class and its members, we argue that in the psychology of real
communications this continuity is continually and inevitably breached, and that
a priori we must expect a pathology to occur in the communication between mother and child. We will have symptoms whose formal characteristics would lead the
pathology to be classified as schizophrenia. (pp. 202–203)*

Although elements of this theory still assume a linear epistemology, its basic
message was revolutionary. What the Bateson group did was to focus on schizo-

phrenia as an interpersonal, relational phenomenon rather than to view it as an intrapsychic disorder of the individual that secondarily influences interpersonal relationships. However, appreciating the significance of this paper requires that we again turn our attention to the historical context: at the time of its publication, psychodynamic theories dominated therapy, and insight was understood as the only means of change (Simon, 1982).

As we indicated in Chapter 1, it was little wonder that such psychodynamic theories were dominant. Their basic tenets were consistent with fundamental American beliefs in both rugged individualism and the power of science. Indeed, individualism is the most frequently cited characteristic of our society (Becvar, 1983), and "what Freud did was to legitimize and, eventually, institutionalize an emphasis on the individual and the self" (Reeves, 1982, p. 119). In addition, science is revered in the United States "with a veneration approaching worship" (Truxall & Merrill, 1947, p. 47), and faith in the limitless possibilities of science forms part of the characteristically American belief in man's ability to reform and/or master the environment (Smelser & Halpern, 1978). Certainly Freudian theory was consistent with this thrust. Thus, when we say that systems theory and family therapy are countercultural, these are some of the aspects to which we refer. No longer is our attention directed at the internal workings of the mind, which can be controlled through examination and understanding. Rather, we are now charged with considering the external dimensions of relationships.

Nathan Ackerman

The Bateson group was not totally alone in proposing such a radical shift in thinking as was represented by the double-bind theory. Several other so-called voices in the wilderness had also begun to question the traditional focus on individuals in terms of its effectiveness in dealing with mental illness. In the clinical world, the primary bridge between the intrapsychic and systemic approaches to therapy was provided by Nathan Ackerman, M. D., a psychoanalytically trained child psychiatrist. His article, "The Family as a Social and Emotional Unit," which appeared in 1937, gets credit for being the earliest publication in the field, and Ackerman is considered by some (Foley, 1974), including himself, to be the grandfather of family therapy. Indeed, "Ackerman saw his work and the work of his colleagues in the Child Guidance Movement as the 'real' beginning of the family movement" (Guerin, 1976, p. 4). Thus, while much of the other early work with families was an outgrowth of research in the area of schizophrenia, Ackerman believed that undue emphasis on that fact obscured what he considered to be family therapy's true origins "in the study of nonpsychotic disorders in children as related to the family environment" (Ackerman, 1967).

Let us briefly consider, then, the events that led Ackerman to play such an important role in the family therapy drama. Following completion of his medical training, he was part of a research project looking at mental health problems among unemployed miners in western Pennsylvania. This experience was significant in terms of revealing the impact of environmental factors on mental well-being as well as their ramifications for the well-being of the entire family. Subsequently, Ackerman began his professional career as a staff member at the children's division of the Menninger Clinic in Topeka, Kansas. In 1937 he was promoted to chief psychiatrist of the Child Guidance Clinic, where by the 1940s he had begun to experiment with having both mother and child seen by the same therapist rather than splitting their treatment in the usual manner. In addition, consistent with his interest in the effects of chronic economic hardship on family life (from his experience with the miners), he began in the 1940s and 1950s to send members of his staff on home visits in order to study families (Guerin, 1976).

In 1955 Ackerman organized and led the first session on family diagnosis and treatment at the American Orthopsychiatry Association meeting in New York City (Nichols, 1984). In 1957 he was secretary to a panel on the family at the annual meeting of the American Psychiatric Association in Chicago. He also began in the 1950s to produce numerous articles about his work with families, and in 1958 he published *The Psychodynamics of Everyday Life*, "the first full-length study combining theory and practice, in which he emphasized the importance of role relations within the family" (Foley, 1974, p. 6).

Ackerman was responsible for establishing the Family Mental Health Clinic of Jewish Family Services in New York City in 1957, and in 1960 he opened the Family Institute, also in New York City. In 1962 he and Don Jackson began publishing what is today one of the most influential journals in the field, *Family Process,* with Jay Haley as the first editor. During this period Ackerman was a professor of psychology at the College of Physicians and Surgeons at Columbia University, and from 1964 to 1967 also served as a consultant to the family studies section at the Albert Einstein College of Medicine. Nathan Ackerman died in 1971, and soon thereafter the Family Institute was renamed the Ackerman Family Institute in his honor.

Throughout its early years, the family therapy movement was divided along ideological lines between those who leaned more toward an intrapsychic approach and those who espoused a more systemic orientation. Ackerman was the most outstanding proponent of the former position. He combined both psychodynamics and the notion of an individual's social role to understand the ongoing interaction between heredity and environment and the maintenance of homeostasis within and between the person, the family, and ultimately, society. However, "he emphasized the intrapsychic effects of families on individuals more than the behavioral sequences, communication, and interaction that systems-oriented family therapists stressed" (Nichols, 1984, p. 56).

Further, even though Ackerman's contributions should not be underestimated, they lie more in the realm of a shift in focus from individuals to interpersonal interactions and of clinical artistry than in the area of theory construction. Thus, although the Ackerman Family Institute continues to be a thriving center for family therapy, no school of thought in family therapy is distinctly traceable to the man himself.

With Ackerman's death, tension between ideological camps lessened and family therapists in general tended to move more toward a systems perspective. However, there were others in the first generation who also had intrapsychic training, and their work with families continues to be flavored by this initial orientation. These people include such early entrants into the field as Murray Bowen and Carl Whitaker.

Murray Bowen

Murray Bowen became a staff member at the Menninger Clinic in Topeka, Kansas, in 1946. Having switched from neurosurgery to psychiatry, he was by then a fully trained psychoanalyst. He was among those influenced by John Rosen's work with schizophrenic patients and their families when Rosen, a psychiatrist from Bucks County, Pennsylvania, visited the clinic in 1948. However, by 1950 Bowen had begun to focus on mother/child symbiosis on the assumption that "schizophrenia was the result of an unresolved tie with the mother" (Hoffman, 1981, p. 29). In 1951 he instituted a treatment plan at Menninger in which mothers and their schizophrenic children resided together for several months in cottages on the clinic grounds. Continuing in this direction, Bowen left Kansas in 1954 and went to the National Institute of Mental Health (NIMH), where he instituted and directed the classic study in which whole families of schizophrenic patients were hospitalized for observation and research.

In 1957 Bowen was part of a panel on family research at the meeting of the American Orthopsychiatry Association. This significant event marked the first public acknowledgment, at the national level, of studies that previously were unrecognized and somewhat underground. The panel, organized by John Spiegel, also included Theodore Lidz of Yale University and David Mendel of Houston, Texas. Bowen, along with Lidz and Don Jackson, was also part of the family research panel for which Nathan Ackerman served as secretary at the APA meeting in Chicago that same year.

At the time of these meetings, Bowen, who had left NIMH in 1956, was a faculty member in the department of psychiatry at Georgetown University Medical School. Although he had intended to take the family research project with him, these plans did not materialize as the department chairman who had hired him died shortly after Bowen switched his affiliation to Georgetown. However, the change in plans did not seem to deter him because "during his years at Georgetown, Bowen developed his comprehensive theory of family therapy, inspired an entire generation of students, and became an internationally renowned leader of the family therapy movement" (Nichols, 1984, pp. 346–347).

Indeed, Bowenian family therapy has made many important contributions to the field in terms of such concepts as triangulation, intergenerational transmission, differentiation of self, and undifferentiated family ego mass. We study Bowen's theory in some detail in Chapter 7, "Psychodynamic Approaches," and at that point we also look more closely at Bowen's background and evolution as a family therapist.

Carl Whitaker

Another clinical pioneer of family therapy is Carl Whitaker. Although a psychiatrist by profession, his training was anything but orthodox, and the impact of early experiences in the field was instrumental in the evolution of his self-professed atheoretical stance and unique style. Whitaker and his therapy are the subject of detailed examination in Chapter 8, "Experiential Approaches."

Like the early cyberneticians, Whitaker's career was much affected by World War II. Personnel shortages in both his initial hospital placements and at the University of Louisville resulted in training that emphasized play therapy and a behavioral rather than an intrapsychic focus and led to his teaching psychotherapy to medical students while still a resident himself. Further, as a staff psychiatrist at the Oak Ridge Hospital in Oak Ridge, Tennessee, from 1944 to 1946, the pressures associated with living and working in the shadow of the U.S. Army's atomic plant just before the development of the bomb also made their mark. Due to lack of experience, psychological stress, and inordinately heavy client loads and schedules, Whitaker and John Warkentin, who had a doctorate in psychophysiology, started working together as a cotherapy team. Eventually they involved the spouses and children of patients as part of their treatment approach.

In 1946 Whitaker (as chairman) and Warkentin went to Emory University in Atlanta, Georgia, to establish the Medical School's first department of psychiatry. They were joined in 1948 by Thomas Malone, Ph.D., whose training was in psychoanalytic psychology. During his tenure at Emory, Whitaker continued his experiments with family therapy and focused increasingly on the treatment of schizophrenia. As a part of this emphasis, in 1948 he initiated a series of ten four-day weekend conferences on schizophrenia. In addition to the group from Emory, these conferences included at various times John Rosen, Edward Taylor, Michael Hayward, and Albert Scheflen, from the Philadelphia area, as well as anthropologist George Devereau. At the final conference in 1955 at Sea Island, Georgia, "the first major meeting of the family therapy movement" (Nichols, 1984, p. 62), Gregory Bateson and Don Jackson were also in attendance. The format included a demonstration by each participant of his approach to therapy. Both individual clients and client families from Atlanta were involved in this process. Following observation of therapy, issues that emerged during the demonstrations were debated and discussed (Broderick & Schrader, 1981).

In 1955 Whitaker left Emory to go into private practice in Atlanta, and ten years later he left private practice to become a professor of psychiatry at the University of Wisconsin Medical School in Madison. By the time of his arrival in Madison in 1965, Whitaker thought of himself as a family therapist and was evolving what he later defined as his "psychotherapy of the absurd" (Whitaker, 1975). Although initially less well known than some of his peers, he is regarded today as one of the greats, and "even among the company of strong-willed and colorful founders of family therapy, Carl Whitaker stands out as the most dynamic and ir-reverent" (Nichols, 1984, p. 61).

Theodore Lidz

The research and treatment of schizophrenia were also the focus of two other orig-inal players in the family therapy drama—Theodore Lidz and Lyman Wynne. However, both are more like Bowen than Whitaker in terms of their initial psycho-dynamic orientation and both are usually identified more with specific conceptual contributions than with comprehensive models of their own devising. Further, Wynne is the only pioneer who continues his research with schizophrenics up to the present (Nichols & Schwartz, 1995).

After receiving his M.D. from Columbia University in 1936, Lidz went to Lon-don to study neurology at the National Hospital. He returned to the United States in 1938 to begin a residency in psychiatry at Johns Hopkins University, completed in 1941. During his final year as a resident, Lidz initiated his studies of schizo-phrenics with an examination of the characteristics of their families, concluding (Lidz & Lidz, 1949) that the influence of fathers could be at least as important as that of mothers.

Lidz was a faculty member at Johns Hopkins from 1942 to 1946. From 1942 to 1951 he also trained at the Baltimore Institute of Psychoanalysis, although from 1946 to 1951 he was no longer affiliated with Johns Hopkins but was serv-ing as a lieutenant colonel in the U.S. Army. During this period he also under-took a longitudinal study of sixteen middle- and upper-middle-class families of schizophrenics.

As in his earlier study, Lidz consistently found patterns of severe dysfunction and pathology in these families, and ultimately he challenged some major beliefs in the field. He rejected the Freudian notion that fixation in the oral stage followed by stress-induced regression in young adulthood causes schizophrenia. Based on his research he also refuted the belief that schizophrenia is caused by maternal re-jection, as proposed by Frieda Fromm-Reichman and John Rosen. In addition, Lidz widened his focus to include both the entire maturation period rather than just in-fancy and the role of fathers rather than just that of mothers (Nichols, 1984).

Following completion of both his military service and his training in psycho-analysis, Lidz moved from Baltimore to New Haven, Connecticut, where he be-came a professor of psychiatry at Yale University. There he continued to study the relationship between schizophrenia and the family. *Marital schism* and *marital skew* are two concepts that grew out of this research.

Spouses who are unable to achieve role reciprocity or complementarity of pur-pose are characteristic of marital schism. Each may attempt to coerce the other into meeting his or her expectations, may distrust the other's motivations, and may un-dermine the position of the other, particularly in the area of parenting. By contrast, the presence of one strong and one weak spouse is characteristic of marital skew. In this case, the strong one allows the weak one to dominate so that conflict is masked and the discrepancy between what is felt as opposed to what is admitted is not openly acknowledged (Simon, Stierlin, & Wynne, 1985).

Lidz thus embraced a relational focus and a wholistic perspective that included more than the symptom-bearing patient. Indeed, the significance of his work is in his early emphasis on the interaction of family communication patterns and role relationships with individual developmental processes, characterizing the context within which schizophrenia emerges. He therefore moved from a belief in individual pathology to an emphasis on family dysfunction as the matrix out of which pathology may arise. This concept was one of the fundamental building blocks of family therapy.

Lyman Wynne

Like Lidz, Lyman Wynne also concluded from his studies of schizophrenia that the significance of the family could not be underestimated, that role relationships are crucially important, and that understanding pathology requires a consideration of communication patterns. It is to Wynne that credit is due for the concepts of *pseudo-mutuality, pseudohostility,* and the *rubber fence,* all instrumental in helping people working with families to view and understand them at the level of process rather than of content.

Wynne graduated from Harvard Medical School in 1948. He then continued his studies at Harvard in the graduate department of social relations, where he received his Ph.D. in 1952. During these four years he was introduced to the association between family problems and ulcerative colitis, and in 1947 he began to see whole families as part of the treatment process (Broderick & Schrader, 1981). Wynne joined NIMH in 1952, quickly moving from staff psychiatrist to clinical investigator. When Murray Bowen came to NIMH in 1954, the two men began to share their thoughts and struggles on issues related to mental illness and family treatment. In 1956 Wynne became chief of the family research section, when Bowen left for Georgetown University.

Wynne began research on the families of schizophrenics in 1954. At the 1956 and 1957 meetings of the American Psychiatric Association, he and Bowen began dialogues with Ackerman, Jackson, and Lidz. By 1958, Wynne had introduced the concept of pseudomutuality, "a predominant absorption in fitting together at the expense of the differentiation of identities of the persons in the relation" (Wynne, Ryckoff, Day, & Hirsch, 1958, p. 207). That is, affirmation of individual identity is seen as a threat to the family as a whole, whereas in well-functioning families there is a more appropriate balance between separateness and togetherness. In addition, there is a lack of humor and spontaneity, roles are rigidly assigned and maintained, and family members insist on the desirability and appropriateness of this rigid role structure.

Families characterized by a pseudomutual pattern are totally focused on the whole. Such family-centeredness is maintained by a flexible but nonstable boundary Wynne referred to as a "rubber fence." The rules comprising this type of boundary are in continual flux as the family opens to admit what it considers acceptable and closes in an unpredictable manner to exclude what is not acceptable. Communication, individual perceptions, and identity formation are all problematic in this context of confusion and enmeshment. Consistent with systemic theory, the schizophrenic is seen as a symptom of family dysfunction rather than as an example of individual pathology or as the victim of inappropriate, schizophrenogenic parenting. Togetherness in such families is valued above all else, and significant relationships outside the family are not tolerated. Thus, it may take the acting-out characteristic of schizophrenic behavior to achieve recognition of individual difference. Having succeeded in attaining this recognition, however, the now separate individual is labeled as a schizophrenic and, accordingly, is ejected from the family: "And like mud oozing back over the place where a rock has been removed from a swamp, the family's pseudomutuality is thereupon restored" (Nichols, 1984, p. 34).

On the other hand, pseudohostility refers to a superficial alienation of family members that masks both members' needs for intimacy and affection and chronic conflict and alienation at a deeper level. But like its counterpart, pseudomutuality, pseudohostility reflects a distortion of communication and perceptual impairment as rational thinking about relationships is obstructed. In both cases the focus is on descriptions of family alignments and splits that define the emotional system of which the schizophrenic is a part.

Although these concepts constitute some of Wynne's most significant contributions to the field, during his twenty years at NIMH he and his colleagues authored numerous articles detailing the results of their research and therapy with schizophrenics and revising and updating their earlier theorizing. This emphasis on keeping theory consonant with practice has continued since his move to the University of Rochester in 1972 to become a professor in the department of psychiatry. An active researcher and practitioner, Wynne continues to add to our knowledge of communication deviance in the families of schizophrenics. Wynne is also one of those who have spoken to the issue of the marginalization of family therapy (Shields, Wynne, McDaniel, & Gawinski, 1994a, 1994b) and who urges greater collaboration with other health care professions.

Ivan Boszormenyi-Nagy

As you probably have noticed throughout this review, several contributors mentioned peripherally were from the Philadelphia area. In fact, in 1957 Ivan Boszormenyi-Nagy founded the Family Therapy Department at the Eastern Pennsylvania Psychiatric Institute (E.P.P.I.), a large, state-owned research and training facility. With its emphasis on research and training in schizophrenia and the family, E.P.P.I. became one of the earliest family therapy centers. It has included among its staff at various times such key figures as Ray Birdwhistell, James Framo, John Rosen, David Rubenstein, Geraldine Spark, Ross Speck, Albert Scheflen, and Gerald Zuk. One of the earliest published volumes in the field was the 1965 book entitled *Intensive Family Therapy*, edited by Boszormenyi-Nagy and Framo.

Boszormenyi-Nagy, a Hungarian psychiatrist with psychoanalytic training, emigrated to the United States in 1948. In the mid-1950s he teamed up with Spark, whose background was in psychiatric social work and psychoanalysis and whose previous experience was in a child guidance clinic. Over the years they worked out a theory of families that focused on the impact of intergenerational processes in families. In 1973 they published *Invisible Loyalties: Reciprocity in Intergenerational Family Therapy.*

The approach to treatment created by Boszormenyi-Nagy, discussed more fully in Chapter 7, is known as intergenerational-contextual. One of his most significant contributions was the introduction of an ethical dimension to therapy (Nichols, 1984). It is his belief that trust and loyalty are the crucial dimensions in relationships and that families must have what he refers to as "balanced ledgers" in this area. Thus, the goal of therapy is the "ethical redefinition of the relational context" (Boszormenyi-Nagy, 1966) such that trustworthiness is a mutually merited phenomenon and concern for future generations provides the impetus for health.

John Elderkin Bell

In contrast to the well-known figures previously described, a rarely mentioned and often excluded person among the founders of family therapy is John Elderkin Bell. Although he is associated with family group therapy, his early work with families is often overlooked because he did not begin publishing until the 1960s. "Further, unlike the other parents of family therapy, he had few offspring. He did not establish an important clinical center, develop a training program, or train well-known students" (Nichols, 1984, p. 41).

However, Bell was one of the first to see families conjointly, although his initial decision to do so was based on a serendipitous experience while on a visit to England. At the time, Bell, a professor of psychology at Clark University in Worcester, Massachusetts, was visiting the home of the medical director of London's Tavistock Clinic, Dr. John Sutherland. Sutherland was describing for Bell the work of a psychiatrist on his staff, Dr. John Bowlby. He had just mentioned that Bowlby had begun having the whole family come in with the patient when the conversation was interrupted, never to be completed.

On his way home, Bell began thinking about the idea of seeing the whole family, and once back in the United States was presented with a case that seemed a likely prospect for such an approach. By the second session, Bell was convinced that it was the family that had the problem rather than the thirteen-year-old son, who had initially been identified as the patient. Only years later did he learn that Bowlby had not been seeing whole families but had been treating all the members of the family on an individual basis, occasionally calling them together for a group conference.

Having stumbled onto family treatment, however, and finding it a viable option, Bell created an approach based on the theory of group dynamics and group psychotherapy. In 1961 he published *Family Group Therapy,* which has become one of the classics in the field. This therapeutic modality will be one subject of discussion in Chapter 14.

Christian F. Midelfort

Even less well known than Bell is Christian F. Midelfort. Like Bell, his relative anonymity seems to be a function of his isolation from a particular school or training center in the early days of the family therapy movement rather than of the value of his work or the timing of his entry into the field. Indeed, Midelfort's introduction to family therapy came through observing his father's techniques in the latter's medical practice. Midelfort's own experiments with this approach were some of the earliest and most innovative in this area.

Midelfort was a psychoanalyst who received his training at the Payne-Whitney and Henry Phipps psychiatric clinics. He then went into practice at the Lutheran Hospital in La Crosse, Wisconsin. In 1952 he delivered a paper on the use of family therapy techniques at the meeting of the American Psychiatric Association (APA). In 1957 he published *The Family in Psychotherapy,* one of the first books on the subject. In it he describes some practices used in his setting:

> *At this hospital relatives of psychiatric patients stayed as nurses' aides and companions in consistent attendance to supervise occupational, recreational, and insulin therapies, to minimize suicidal risk, fear, aggression, and insecurity and to take part in therapeutic interviews with patient and psychiatrist. . . . Family treatment is also extended to the out-patient department for all types of mental illness. (pp. v–vi)*

However, despite his innovations and orientation, Midelfort was outside the mainstream, and thus his potential as an early contributor to family therapy was never fully realized.

Overview of the 1950s

We find that even though many voices were beginning to speak the language of family therapy, some were heard more than others. When we survey the events of the 1950s, both within and without the movement, relevant to the development of family therapy, we can discern several other themes. In terms of the social, economic, and political context, these themes include the aftermath of the war, the infancy of the nuclear age, the McCarthy era, and by the end of the decade, the beginning of a countercultural movement. Accordingly, increased prosperity was balanced by the increased stress of reunited families, war-delayed marriages, and the baby boom. Peace at the international level was balanced by domestic suspicion and threats to internal freedoms. Pride in technology and the power of science was balanced by insecurity related to an awareness of the realities of nuclear power and the potential for annihilation. And optimism and complacency were balanced by hippies and the beginnings of the civil rights and ecology movements.

Moving from the level of the system to that of some of its members, we find that within both the physical and the behavioral sciences change was a major theme: "This change was facilitated by the many viable options open to scientists in that period of high prestige and economic support of science, the same period (the McCarthy era) during which other freedoms were at a low ebb" (Heims, 1977, p. 142). Thus, we may say that the ability of family therapy to put down roots that would support healthy growth and development was logical to context. As we look into the movement itself, we also find several key themes that support this view.

Perhaps most obvious is the enormous influence of research on schizophrenia. Although the world of therapy was dominated by psychiatry, psychodynamic explanations, and individual interventions, family treatment could be legitimized as part of a scientific endeavor to understand schizophrenia. Indeed, observation of a family for purposes of research justified what would otherwise have been considered a breach of appropriate therapist behavior. Contact with a patient's family was frowned on if not prohibited in then-standard treatment approaches (Goldenberg & Goldenberg, 1985). In an era of high scientific prestige, schizophrenia loomed as a mystery not amenable to solution by current therapeutic modalities. Thus, researchers were able to obtain grant money for the support of studies in this area, a factor whose importance must never be underestimated.

The second theme immediately apparent is the number of pioneers who stumbled onto, sailed into, and otherwise discovered the world of family therapy. Although we have highlighted a significant number of individuals whom we feel were most influential, we might have added many others had our emphasis been different. Something seems to have facilitated the simultaneous but separate occurrence of similar events. Jung (Rychlak, 1981) would have called it "synchronicity"; Sheldrake (Briggs & Peat, 1984) would call it "seeding." We would say that the context was able to support and help maintain the development of family therapy, and vice versa, and thus it was a logical occurrence.

The third and final major theme was the movement from isolation to community, cooperation, and shared creation. The fifties saw the coming together and intermingling, at various times and in various places, of many participants. Family therapy was therefore nurtured by the encouragement and support of fellow travelers in this as-yet-uncharted land. Having traced the history of this process, we find that by the end of the 1950s there was a pattern of connection. While the process may not have been neat and orderly, the root system was now well in place. Indeed, it was time for the movement to sprout and grow.

The Plant Begins to Bud: The 1960s

Paradigm Shift

In *The Structure of Scientific Revolutions,* Thomas Kuhn (1970) describes the process by which a scientific community shifts from being dominated by one particular paradigm to accepting another. By *paradigm* Kuhn refers to the set of presuppositions about what the world is like, about the problems worthy of investigation, and about the methods appropriate for the investigation of these problems. During periods of so-called normal science, the major focus is on puzzle solving done according to the assumptions and rules characterizing the currently accepted theoretical and methodological belief system or paradigm. Thus, solutions to problems are sought from within a given frame or perspective as normal science attempts "to force nature into the preformed and relatively inflexible box that the paradigm supplies" (Kuhn, 1970, p. 24).

If, in time, serious problems arise or events occur that are not explainable according to the rules of the prevailing paradigm, an anomaly is said to exist and the search for new explanations begins. This is the point of crisis, and it is followed by a period of so-called extraordinary science, in which the old rules are loosened and a process of reconstruction of basic beliefs is undertaken:

> *Confronted with anomaly or crisis, scientists take a different attitude toward existing paradigms, and the nature of their research changes accordingly. The proliferation of competing articulations, the willingness to try anything, the expression of explicit discontent, the recourse to philosophy and to debate over fundamentals, all these are symptoms of transition from normal to extraordinary research. (Kuhn, 1970, pp. 90–91)*

When the old belief system is ultimately replaced by a new one, the experience is similar to that of a gestalt switch. That is, the old world is seen from an entirely different perspective and old events take on new meaning. According to Kuhn, "the resulting transition to a new paradigm is scientific revolution" (Kuhn, 1970, p. 90). Obviously, such revolutions do not occur easily or without great resistance, nor should they:

> *By ensuring that the paradigm will not be too easily surrendered, resistance guarantees that scientists will not be lightly distracted and that the anomalies that lead to paradigm change will penetrate existing knowledge to the core. The very fact that a significant scientific novelty so often emerges simultaneously from several laboratories is an index both to the strongly traditional nature of normal science and to the completeness with which that traditional pursuit prepares the way for its own change. (p. 65)*

Acceptance of a new paradigm requires that it "seem better than its competitors, but it need not, and in fact never does, explain all the facts with which it can be confronted" (Kuhn, 1970, pp. 17–18). Once accepted, the process comes full circle as scientists return to their normal-science, puzzle-solving activities of "extending the knowledge of those facts that the paradigm displays as particularly revealing, by increasing the extent of the match between those facts and the paradigm's predictions, and by further articulation of the paradigm itself" (p. 24).

Certainly the acceptance of a cybernetic epistemology, which had occurred during the 1940s, is illustrative of the process of scientific revolution described by

Kuhn. Indeed, the gestalt-switch shift from a linear to a recursive world view that took place within the larger scientific community was, as Bateson noted, one of the great events of his lifetime. Although by the late 1950s family therapy was not yet widespread within the behavioral sciences, the movement was clearly consistent with the cybernetic revolution. For researchers and clinicians who had adopted or were moving toward a systemic framework, the time had now come to return to such normal-science, puzzle-solving activities as expanding their knowledge, delineating concepts, and enlarging the repertoire of techniques logical to the basic assumptions of the new perspective. Thus the 1960s saw the expansion of family therapy in several directions: there was increasing recognition of this modality at professional meetings, a continuation of previously begun research, initiation of new research projects, and increasing publication of books and articles on the subject.

MRI

One case in point involved those working in California. In 1962 the Bateson Project at the Veteran's Administration Hospital in Palo Alto, California, ended, and subsequently the Mental Research Institute (MRI) widened its horizons in terms of both personnel and treatment focus. The MRI was opened on March 19, 1959, by Don Jackson, who had invited Jules Riskin and Virginia Satir to join him in this enterprise. According to Satir (1982), "it was originally conceived of as an institute dedicated to researching the relationship of family members to each other, and how those relationships evolved into the health and illness of its members" (p. 19). Although initially focused on schizophrenia, MRI now also began working with families around such issues as delinquency, school-related problems, psychosomatic disorders, and marital conflict. Further, the staff was increased to include Richard Fisch, Jay Haley, Paul Watzlawick, and John Weakland. Much of the credit for enhancing public awareness of family therapy, as well as for developing two of its major approaches, goes to the members of this group.

Although he would live only until 1968, Don Jackson "perhaps published more material on family therapy than any other theorist" (Foley, 1974, p. 70). Two books that he coauthored, now considered classics, are *Pragmatics of Human Communication* (Watzlawick, Beavin, & Jackson, 1967) and *Mirages of Marriage* (Lederer & Jackson, 1968). As previously mentioned, in 1962 Jackson and Nathan Ackerman also established the first and one of the most prestigious journals in the field, *Family Process*. In terms of his orientation, Jackson was a communications theorist, and some of his most important contributions include his basic rules of communication as well as the notion of homeostasis, or balance, in families. This will be explained in Chapter 10.

In addition to Jackson, Virginia Satir became, and continued until her death in 1988 to be, one of the most popular spokespersons for the family therapy movement. Not only did she start making presentations at professional meetings early in her career, but following publication in 1964 of *Conjoint Family Therapy*, she also earned her place as "one of the major forces in the field of family therapy" (Foley,

1974, p. 92). Like Jackson, Satir was concerned with communication, but she added to this emphasis the dimensions of emotional growth and self-esteem and was thus considered to be the humanist in the group. Satir (1982) labeled her approach a "process model." She too will be a focus of further discussion in Chapter 10.

Jay Haley has been an equally important influence on the field of family therapy as the first editor, in 1962, of *Family Process*, the author of numerous books and articles, and the person most closely associated with the strategic school of family therapy (see Chapter 11). As a coauthor of the double-bind theory, Haley's attention was initially focused on levels of communication, but this ultimately took him into the study of relationships with an emphasis on the power tactics he felt were an inevitable part of all human interaction. In 1963 Haley published *Strategies of Psychotherapy*, his first delineation of this approach.

By the end of the decade, even though Jackson had died, Satir had moved to Esalen, and Haley had gone to Philadelphia, MRI had begun the Brief Therapy Project, which continues to be its hallmark. It also had established itself as a major center of family research in the United States. In the process of its normal-science activities, it spawned both the strategic and the communications approaches to family therapy.

Salvador Minuchin

The 1960s saw the emergence of another spokesperson whose work would evolve into one of the major schools of family therapy. Salvador Minuchin is the architect of the structural approach to family therapy (Chapter 9 will deal with this approach). Minuchin is a native of Argentina, where he received his medical training and planned to pursue a speciality in pediatrics. However, after the state of Israel was established in 1948, Minuchin volunteered as an army doctor during the war with the Arab nations. Following the war, he came to the United States, where he pursued further training in child psychiatry at the Jewish Board of Guardians in New York City. He also studied psychoanalysis at the William Alanson White Institute during this period. Minuchin then returned to Israel to work with children who had survived the Holocaust as well as with Jews who had immigrated there from Arab countries. Minuchin's interest in working with whole families can be traced to this point in his career.

After his second stay in Israel, Minuchin came back to the United States, and in 1960 began working at the Wiltwyck School for Boys in New York. Here he was involved with male juvenile delinquents, many of whom were either blacks or Puerto Ricans from New York City. It was also here that Minuchin began focusing on low-income and ghetto families and had to develop techniques appropriate to this population. Ultimately, he published *Families of the Slums* (1967), with Montalvo, Guerney, Rosman, and Schumer, a book that was an outgrowth of his work at Wiltwyck.

In 1965 Minuchin became director of the Philadelphia Child Guidance Clinic, which had begun as a small facility in the heart of the black ghetto. Under Minuchin's leadership, it became one of the largest centers of its kind ever to be established. A modern medical complex now affiliated with the University of Pennsylvania's Children's Hospital, the Philadelphia Child Guidance Clinic is one of the few in the country in which ghetto families outnumber all other clients (Goldenberg & Goldenberg, 1985).

When Minuchin came to Philadelphia he brought Montalvo and Rosman with him, and in 1967 they were joined by Jay Haley. Other family therapists associated with this group include Harry Aponte, Stephen Greenstein, and Marianne Walters. The Philadelphia Child Guidance Clinic has become outstanding not only for the treatment it offers but also as a center for family therapy training in general and structural approach training in particular.

Other Developments

Meanwhile during the 1960s, the Family Institute in New York City was growing and expanding under the directorship of Nathan Ackerman, who in 1966 published *Treating the Troubled Family;* Lidz was at Yale; Wynne was at NIMH; Bowen was at Georgetown; Whitaker moved to the University of Wisconsin; Bell published *Family Group Therapy* (1961); Boszormenyi-Nagy and Framo published *Intensive Family Therapy* (1965); and in 1967 Mara Selvini Palazzoli established the Institute for Family Studies in Milan. Further, in 1968 Ludwig von Bertalanffy published *General System Theory,* perhaps the clearest and certainly the most comprehensive articulation of the cybernetic revolution, or paradigm shift previously noted, emerging in this case out of the biological sciences.

Although considered to be less mechanistic than cybernetics, general systems theory is equally concerned with feedback mechanisms and recursion and, in fact, there is little that separates the two theories from each other. It was Bertalanffy, a biologist, who after first presenting general systems theory in 1945, ultimately "showed how it might be applied specifically in the field of psychiatry" (Foley, 1974, p. 40). Consistent with Kuhn's notion that during periods of extraordinary science similar ideas arise in different laboratories, both cybernetics and systems theory were born in the 1940s, the former in engineering, the latter in biology. However, as mentioned in Chapter 1, in the United States systems theory rather than cybernetics was the catch phrase that caught on, and the detailed explanations in Bertalanffy's book were a key to this turn of events. Between the occurrences both in and outside the movement, the time for family therapy to bloom clearly had arrived.

Blossom Time: The 1970s

The 1970s witnessed the development of the newly created approaches to family therapy into full-blown schools and, in some cases, elaborate theoretical models. Indeed, publications by the founders reached their peak in this decade. Students began flocking to the various centers for training by the masters. The boundaries of the major approaches were more clearly demarcated. The following is a summary of highlights of this decade relative to the models created by key originators of family therapy. It is important to be aware, however, that this review does not represent a complete survey of everyone working in the field. Rather, the aim is to preview the work of representative figures of the major approaches that had evolved by the 1970s. These approaches will be examined in some detail in later chapters.

Psychodynamic Approaches

Although Murray Bowen, as well as some of his followers, has characterized his model as Bowenian, or family systems theory, his intrapsychic origins are clearly discernible, hence his inclusion under the heading of psychodynamic approaches. Not only was he representative of this approach, but he was also one of the field's major theoreticians. Indeed, one of Bowen's overriding concerns was that family therapy be guided by a coherent and comprehensive theory, and his framework provided an attempt to achieve this goal. Following his death in 1990, it was noted (Wylie, 1991) that "Bowen's preoccupation with discovering a new science of human behavior—an overarching *natural systems* theory—set him apart from other pathbreakers of the field" (p. 26). Bowen's theory evolved over four decades of research and clinical work during which he authored approximately fifty articles. In 1978 he also published *Family Therapy in Clinical Practice*, detailing his theoretical position as well as techniques consistent with his model.

Basically, Bowen was concerned with the individual's differentiation of self from family of origin as well as with the internal separation of intellectual and emotional functioning. Bowenian therapy involves the supervision of an individual or couple with a view to avoiding triangles and emotional entanglement and to encouraging cognitive processes on the part of the client(s). Bowen's theory is comprised of eight interlocking concepts and related strategies. The model is clearly delineated and has attracted numerous students over the years. Since 1965, Georgetown University has sponsored an annual forum on family therapy that has grown from its initial forty participants to over a thousand attendees each year. Thus, Bowen became a leading trainer in the practice of family therapy. His students and followers include Elizabeth Carter, Thomas Fogarty, Philip Guerin, Michael Kerr, and Monica McGoldrick.

Also in the psychodynamic category is Ivan Boszormenyi-Nagy, who focuses on the intergenerational context of families. He believes that symptom formation is a process involving unresolved issues from previous generations that are being lived out in the present. The goal of therapy is to help family members become aware of these invisible loyalties and achieve a better balance in their obligations so that healthy individual and family functioning may be achieved. Members of both the parent and grandparent generations are invited to attend therapy, and more mature relationships are encouraged.

Certainly Nathan Ackerman must be included in the category of psychodynamic approaches. However, his death in 1971 cut short any further direct contributions to the field. Nevertheless, his influence lives on in the clinical artistry of both Salvador Minuchin and Israel Zwerling.

Experiential Approaches

Turning to the realm of experiential therapy, in 1977 David Keith and Carl Whitaker provided a chapter for Peggy Papp's *Family Therapy: Full Length Case Studies* entitled "The Divorce Labyrinth." Napier and Whitaker published *The Family Crucible* in 1978. In both instances family therapy is described in terms of detailed case studies and personal accounts of and reactions to the process. In direct contrast to Bowen, the members of this school, and particularly Whitaker, are staunchly atheoretical in their approach. In a 1976 article entitled "The Hindrance of Theory in Clinical Work," Whitaker states that rather than theory he prefers to use

> *the accumulated and organized residue of experience, plus the freedom to allow the relationship to happen, to be who you are with the minimum of anticipatory set and maximum responsiveness to authenticity and to our own growth impulses.* (p. 163)

As a function of this position, Whitaker's approach is necessarily difficult to pin down, and therefore the members of his school consist mainly of those who have worked with him as cotherapists, for example, Napier and Keith.

Walter Kempler (1972) is also firmly committed to the experiential approach:

> *Upon these two commandments hang all the laws upon which experiential psychotherapy within families stands: attention to the current interaction as the pivotal point for all awareness and interventions; involvement of the total therapist-person bringing overtly and richly his full personal impact on the families with whom he works (not merely a bag of tricks called therapeutic skills).* (p. 336)

Kempler is a Gestaltist, and his philosophy and orientation are derived from this theoretical position—that people do not see isolated events but rather they see in terms of *Gestalten,* or meaningful wholes, which contain qualities not present in their individual parts (Capra, 1983). Although this modality is often associated with Fritz Perls and an individual focus, Kempler inaugurated in 1961 the "idea of Gestalt therapy as a clinically viable basis for the treatment of families" (Kempler, 1982, p. 144) by opening the Kempler Institute for the Development of the Family in Los Angeles.

During the late 1960s and 1970s Kempler traveled throughout the United States and northern Europe advocating his model, and in 1973 he published *Principles of Gestalt Family Therapy.* Like Whitaker, Kempler proposes a general approach rather than a specific model. The goal of therapy is "the awakening and restoration of the family to its rightful place as the primary promoter of personal potentials for all its members, parents and children alike.... The therapist is a temporary catalyst who uses whatever talents are available to revitalize the family" (Kempler, 1982, p. 147).

Structural Approaches

In direct contrast to the experientalists, proponents of the structural approach have created a clearly delineated model of therapy that is relatively easy to learn and practice. Salvador Minuchin outlined this approach in his 1974 book, *Families and Family Therapy.* The model focuses on the organization of the whole family, or on the rules, boundaries, coalitions, and so on that characterize its structure. This school of thought has been extremely appealing to hundreds of trainees, and "by the late 1970s, structural family therapy had become perhaps the most influential and widely practiced of all systems of family therapy" (Nichols, 1984, p. 471). Minuchin himself has had particular success with his approach in the research and treatment of such chronic disorders as asthma and anorexia nervosa. In 1978 he, Rosman, and Baker documented this work in their book entitled *Psychosomatic Families: Anorexia Nervosa in Context.* Basically they see these disorders as symptoms rooted in a particular family context, and it is the structure that must be changed if the problem is to be resolved.

Strategic Approaches

From 1967 to 1976 Jay Haley worked with Minuchin at the Philadelphia Child Guidance Clinic, and certainly each had a significant impact on the work of the other. However, Haley is best known as the leading spokesperson for the strategic approach to family therapy. Haley's model was strongly influenced both by his initial focus on communication and by his studies of hypnotist Milton Erickson. In 1973 Haley published *Uncommon Therapy,* in which he places Erickson's approach in a family development framework and describes the latter's hypnotic techniques. Indeed, the strategic approach is often equated with the use of paradox, and Haley's descriptions of Erickson's therapy provided some of the clearest examples of paradoxical interventions. Haley continued to develop his model during his years in Philadelphia, and he acknowledges help in this enterprise from Minuchin, Montalvo, and Cloé Madanes. In 1976 he published *Problem-Solving Therapy.* In the introduction Haley notes that "although the book focuses on problems, the approach here differs from other symptom-oriented therapies in that it emphasizes the social context of human problems" (p. 1). In 1976 Haley and Madanes moved to Washington, D.C., where they established the Family Therapy Institute and where they continue today to run one of the most popular training programs in the country although operating in slightly different ways.

The other major proponents of the strategic approach were the original Milan Associates, including Mara Selvini Palazzoli, Luigi Boscolo, Gianfranco Cecchin, and Guiliana Prata. They incorporated the theory and techniques of Haley and other strategic therapists into a unique team approach. In 1977 they made their first visit to the United States, and in 1978 they published *Paradox and Counterparadox,* which outlined their approach and described its use with a number of clients at the Institute for Family Studies in Milan. In the foreword to this book, Helm Stierlin notes the requirements of their model:

1. *The therapists establish a positive relationship with all family members. To do so, they accept and "connote positively" anything the family offers, avoiding even the faintest hint which might be construed as a moralizing stance or accusation, or which might otherwise induce anxiety, shame or guilt.*
2. *The therapists aim at a radical reshuffling of the relational forces operating in these families: they shake the family out of its destructive clinch, as it were, and try to give all members a new chance to pursue their own individuation and separation. (p. ix)*

Disagreements among the original team members about the nature of therapy and appropriate ways to proceed led to a parting of the ways in the early 1980s.

Communication Approaches

Although the members of the Mental Research Institute are also strategic in their approach, their fundamental theorizing and problem-solving techniques focus on the important distinctions between the levels of communication and on the function of language in the creation of reality. Thus Watzlawick, Weakland, and Fisch will be discussed in detail under the heading of communication approaches. For the moment, it is important to note that they were responsible for one of the most significant books in the field, *Change: Principles of Problem Formation and Problem Resolution* (1974). They described the process of first- and second-order change, basing their assumptions and explanations on Russell's theory of logical types.

In 1977 Watzlawick and Weakland edited *The Interactional View: Studies at the Mental Research Institute, Palo Alto, 1965–74.* Watzlawick also published *How Real is Real?* in 1976 and *The Language of Change* in 1978. In addition, MRI is well known for its brief family therapy project initiated in 1967 and continuing to this day. According to the brief therapy format, treatment is limited to a maximum of ten sessions, and the goal is the solution of the presenting problem in the most expedient fashion.

Although we found placing Virginia Satir something of a challenge, including her with the communication theorists is probably most appropriate. Given her emphasis on process, however, her model might also be discussed with the experiential approaches. Satir's *Conjoint Family Therapy* (1964) and *Peoplemaking* (1972) are certainly two of the most readable books in the field. Satir also coauthored *Helping Families to Change* with Stachowiak and Taschman in 1975 and *Changing with Families* with Bandler and Grinder in 1976. Satir's influence was most profound in terms of her direct work with families and students in both private therapy and public workshops conducted around the world. Writing in 1974, Foley noted that Satir

> brings a dimension of feeling to communicational theory that helps to counterbalance its obvious intellectual base. Satir exudes warmth and caring in her therapy. In the past few years she has moved off into the wider areas of the encounter and human potential growth movements. Of all the therapists studied, she is the one most involved in the emotional or the feeling level of people. (p. 93)

In a tribute to Satir, who died in 1988, Fred Duhl (*Remembering Virginia,* 1989) wrote: "She was brilliant, theoretically and technically creative, and she taught more people to be real and human than any other non-religious person in our time" (p. 32).

Behavioral Approaches

In the category of behavioral approaches are practitioners who have applied learning theory principles to the practice of family therapy. Developed in the mid- to late sixties, this approach is represented by Robert Weiss and his Oregon Marital Studies Program; Richard Stuart; Gerald Patterson and John Reid of the Oregon Social Learning Center; Neil Jacobson; Gayola Margolin; Robert Lieberman; Arthur Horne; and in the area of sex therapy, William Masters, Virginia Johnson, and Helen Singer Kaplan. According to Horne (1982), this modality

> *attempts to provide an environment in which effective learning may occur: behavioral alternatives are expanded, and new options are presented, so that families and couples may remedy deficits and develop new skills for dealing with the problems of living in close human relationships. This learning occurs in a systematic teaching-modeling program which emphasizes learning procedures derived from psychology and related behavioral sciences. (p. 360)*

Like its individually oriented counterpart, important aspects of behavioral family therapy are research and evaluation. Thus, even though it is the most recent entrant into the field, it has been the most carefully studied of all the approaches. The influence of this model has been directly felt through the work of its advocates in the areas of behavioral marital therapy, behavioral parent training, and conjoint sex therapy. An indirect impact can be found in the application of such principles as conditioning, reinforcement, shaping, and extinction by proponents of other approaches, most notably Minuchin and Haley.

Gregory Bateson

Finally, the 1970s marked the appearance of two major works by Gregory Bateson: an article entitled "The Cybernetics of 'Self': A Theory of Alcoholism" (1971) and the book *Steps to an Ecology of Mind* (1972). In the foreword to his book, Bateson noted that it contained "everything that I have written, with the exception of items too long to be included, such as books and analyses of data; and items too trivial or ephemeral, such as book reviews and controversial notes" (p. xii). It is fitting to point out that Bateson, the nonclinician, would find a wide audience, including those involved not only with the family movement but also with the Vietnam War protests, student unrest, and an evergrowing concern for ecology. Not surprisingly, Bateson's work won great acceptance in these areas:

The younger generation of the widespread, popular countercultural movement slowly discovered Bateson, the man who found aspiration for holistic understanding to be compatible with science; who asserted that clear thinking, theoretical formulations, and detailed observations are means rather than hindrances to holistic understanding; who disassociated himself from conventional cultural assumptions.

Bateson's approach was also congenial to the later ecology movement; for whether he talked of a New Guinea culture, or of the family interactions of a schizophrenic, or of cybernetics, his emphasis had always been on ecological pattern. (Heims, 1977, p. 155)

Bateson's theme was the "pattern which connects," which, appropriately enough, brings us to the 1980s.

Connecting and Integrating: The 1980s

At a workshop attended by the authors in 1985, Salvador Minuchin noted that the 1980s were to be the period of integration: the period when family therapists would need to know and be able to use something of each of the approaches if they were to become effective clinicians. That, indeed, is the theme of this book, which was originally published in 1988. But not only does expertise require knowledge in all the dimensions of family therapy, it also requires an awareness of the movements' various precursors who in some ways were ahead of their time and yet in other ways are timeless. Thus, in an appropriately recursive move, we preface a review of the present and future by looking again at some of our roots.

Other Voices

As noted at the beginning of this chapter, making a cut at the 1940s and choosing to highlight particular theorists and events was somewhat arbitrary. Now that we have nearly completed our summary of what we feel was the crucial sequence of events in the early years of the family therapy movement, we would like to mention some other people, too important to ignore, whose work influenced the context out of which family therapy emerged.

Freud
Although Sigmund Freud chose to focus on individual and intrapsychic, rather than family, dynamics, he was aware of the interactional context within which symptoms evolved. Freud (1856–1939) was the father of personality theory, and his influence on the development of modern psychology was enormous. For Freud, an unresolved or poorly resolved Oedipal conflict was at the root of all neurosis. The dynamics of this conflict, which originates in infancy, include a desire to kill the

same-sexed parent and marry the parent of the opposite sex. In addition, "certain unconscious thoughts which frame wishes for external objects cannot be enacted overtly because of their hostile and/or sexual nature. Parents and other family members are the first objects of these culturally unacceptable wishes" (Rychlak, 1981, p. 108). Further, successful progression through the psychosexual stages by the developing child requires appropriate responses by parents. Freud was aware of the role of family relationships in the development of schizophrenia and other illnesses, and his strict prohibition against seeing anyone other than the patient in therapy was based on a knowledge of this role. Indeed, "Freudians excluded the real family in order to uncover the unconscious introjected family" (Nichols, 1984, p. 68).

However, in at least one classic case, Freud broke his own rule and arrived at a cure for "Little Hans" by supervising treatment of the boy by his father. Freud may thus have been the first to practice family therapy in the sense of working with more than one family member. He was aware of family influences, even though his focus was always on the individual and on the resolution of intrapsychic conflicts. Therefore, he was clearly a forerunner of the family therapy movement both in terms of his contextual awareness and his provision of a coherent framework against which to rebel.

Jung

One theorist who chose to rebel and move away from a strict Freudian position was Carl Gustav Jung. In contrast to Freud, who died just as the cybernetic era was being born, Jung (1875–1961) saw the emergence of both psychoanalysis and family therapy. Although he is more clearly associated with the former rather than the latter movement, his "basic concepts clearly transcended the mechanistic models of classical psychology and brought his science much closer to the conceptual framework of modern physics than any other psychological school" (Capra, 1983, pp. 186–187). That is, Jung was concerned with wholeness and the totality of the psyche relative to its wider environment. His was a dialectical framework characterized by fluctuations between opposite poles and movement toward integration or synthesis of both. These positions put him close to modern physics, and they are quite similar to those of systems thinkers and family therapists. About psychotherapy, Jung (1928) noted that "by no device can the treatment be anything but the product of mutual influence, in which the whole being of the doctor as well as that of his patient plays its part" (p. 71). Thus, Jung's thinking was in many ways consistent with the assumptions underlying the practice of family therapy, although one is hard pressed to find any mention of his thought in the family therapy literature.

Adler

Another Freudian dissenter, whose ideas have more often been acknowledged as having influenced the family therapy movement, is Alfred Adler (1870–1937). Although Adler called his theory "individual psychology," this label was chosen in acknowledgment that the word "individual" derives from the Latin word *individ-*

uum, meaning indivisible. Indeed, he wished to describe a wholistic perspective and a recognition that to be understood, behavior must be considered in context. Accordingly, Adlerian psychology "seeks explanations to all problems by considering the interrelationship of the parts and the whole" (Nicholl, 1989, p. 3).

Adler's thought evolved into a practical, applied psychology for living, whose notions he sought to give away to those responsible for the development of children—teachers and parents. As early as 1922, he was instrumental in the creation of both child guidance clinics for teachers and family counseling clinics in which the whole family was involved. Initially, his child guidance clinics were aimed at helping teachers learn skills for dealing with children in order to help overcome negative family influences. His later family counseling centers sought to empower families. Thus, teachers, schools, and parents were the focus of Adler's efforts to foster positive child development processes and to help children deal with feelings of inferiority.

While Freud developed his theory out of curiosity, Adler developed his theory out of a concern with social interest, perhaps the most fundamental aspect of his theory (Lowe, 1982). Social interest involves an inherent desire for people to become members of and make contributions to the community without promise or expectation of reward or status. It carries with it the feeling of belonging and requires cooperation, participation, and contribution. It recognizes the equality of all people. It requires that one solve personal problems in harmony with the welfare of all. Thus, "whatever increases one's feelings of belonging, or gives equal social status and significance increases his/her social interest" (Lowe, 1982, p. 311).

In addition to social interest, another important construct in Adlerian theory is that of faulty lifestyle, which describes the struggle to overcome inferiority and create goals for personal success. These two constructs are related inasmuch as the achievement of one's personal goals may be contradictory to attainment of goals consistent with social interest. However, Adler's perspective is an optimistic one. That which others might label disease, Adler called failure to solve life's problems. He saw people as discouraged, and rightly so, when their goals were inappropriate and the methods used to attain those goals seemed to move them further away from what they desired. Because he believed in discouragement, the complementary concept of encouragement is an important part of Adlerian therapy.

Although Adler is an important historical voice in the field, his approach is not generally included in what is considered to be mainstream in the field of family therapy. His theory is alive and well, however, as disseminated in the United States by Rudolph Dreikurs. Dreikurs developed the concept of democratic parenting methods based on Adlerian thought, which he described as distinct from a laissez-faire approach. Dreikurs believed that all behavior is goal-directed and that the purposes of children's behavior may include striving for attention, striving for power, striving for revenge, and/or striving to assume or display a disability. Consistent with the concept of social interest, children need to be aware that their behavior affects others. In order to help the child learn this idea, parents and teachers are urged to use natural and logical consequences and encouragement rather than punishment.

While often neglected in discussions of family therapy, Adlerian theory continues to be influential. Important works on parenting based on Adlerian theory are offered by Dinkmeyer and McKay (1973, 1976), and applications for couples therapy are exemplified by Kern, Hawes, and Christensen (1989) and for family counseling by Dinkmeyer and Dinkmeyer (1991). Perhaps the foremost proponent of the Adlerian perspective in North America and Europe today is Oscar Christensen, who coedited a seminal text of Adlerian approaches to family counseling (Christensen & Schramski, 1983).

Sullivan
Another theorist whose work and interest paralleled and certainly influenced many of the early thinkers in the family therapy field was Harry Stack Sullivan (1892–1949). Sullivan had been influenced by both sociologists and anthropologists, and his personality theory is an interpersonal framework that challenges the "illusion of personal individual personality" (Ruitenbeek, 1964, p. 122). In Sullivan's view, personality is inseparable from interpersonal relationships and, indeed, it consists chiefly of interpersonal behavior. Thus, people are the product of interpersonal situations, and the idea of personality is a purely hypothetical entity. Consistent with this model, in the 1920s Sullivan created a treatment program for schizophrenics that focused on altering the patient's social environment. He also suggested that a therapist was not just an observer but a participant in an interpersonal situation. Rather than thinking of therapy in terms of the so-called medical cure, he saw the process as being akin to education.

Fromm-Reichman
Frieda Fromm-Reichman, a follower of Sullivan, extended his work more directly to a focus on the family. She introduced the term *schizophrenogenic mother* and articulated the Sullivanian view of schizophrenia: "The schizophrenic is painfully distrustful and resentful of other people, due to the severe early warp and rejection he encountered in important people of his infancy and childhood, as a rule, mainly in a schizophrenogenic mother" (Fromm-Reichman, 1948, p. 265). Fromm-Reichman argued that schizophrenia evolves in the context of the mother-child relationship and, following Sullivan, she believed that there is no developmental period when the individual exists outside the realm of interpersonal relatedness. She further modified psychoanalytic techniques in order to take advantage of the vestiges of normal interpersonal development residing within each schizophrenic, pioneering so-called clear directness and active therapeutic moves. Schultz (1984) suggests that "Fromm-Reichman's enduring legacy for family therapy lies perhaps in the boldness with which she undertook these changes in technique, revealing a willingness to sacrifice psychoanalytic convention to the needs of her patients" (p. 11).

Allport
The work of Gordon Allport (1897–1967) reflects a conscious awareness of the theoretical options available to him and to all social scientists of his era. He was knowledgeable of general systems theory as well as of the current personality the-

ories, and he acknowledged the tension between psychological and sociocultural science that had emerged during his lifetime:

> *Western theorists, for the most part, hold the integumented view of the personality system. I myself do so. Others, rebelling against the setting of self over against the world, have produced theories of personality written in terms of social interaction, role relations, situationism or some variety of field theory. Still other writers, such as Talcott Parsons and F. H. Allport, have admitted the validity of both the integumented personality system and systems of social interaction, and have spent much effort in harmonizing the two types of systems thus conceived. (Allport, 1964, pp. 158–159)*

While aligning with the view of personality that sees it as residing within the skin and not purporting to resolve the issue presented above, Allport (1964) nevertheless suggests that

> *our work is incomplete unless we admit that each person possesses a range of abilities, attitudes, and motives, which will be evoked by the different environments and situations which he encounters.... The personality theorist should be so well trained in social science that he can view the behavior of an individual as fitting any system of interaction; that is, he should be able to cast this behavior properly in the culture where it occurs, in its situational context and in terms of role theory and field theory. (p. 159)*

Lewin

The field theory to which Allport refers was the label Kurt Lewin used to describe his theoretical framework. When Lewin (1890–1947) came to the United States from Germany in 1933, he brought with him principles evolved from a movement that included many disciplines and that basically took exception to the idea that natural events were simple forces acting between unalterable particles. Rather, proponents of field theory believed that in addition to being influenced by internal characteristics, the behavior of particles also reflected the state of the field and the presence or absence of other particles. According to Lewin, behavior is a function of life space, which is a function of the person and the environment. His formulation challenged the individualistic, mechanistic, linear cause/effect perspective, and it is not surprising that he was present at some of the early Macy conferences on cybernetics. Even though his work did not focus specifically on the family, his ideas as applied to groups influenced many professionals, who began to use his theory as a basis for seeing the whole family as the client.

Dewey and Bentley

John Dewey, generally regarded as an educational philosopher and associated with the progressive education movement, was also a psychologist and served as president of the American Psychological Association. Arthur Bentley was a philosopher, an economist, and a journalist who had been one of Dewey's students. Dewey (1859–1952) seems to have had an awareness of himself and his profession in social context in a way that others of his day did not. Indeed, he challenged many basic assumptions then important to the evolving field of psychology, for instance, the move away from philosophy to establish the legitimacy of psychology as a science and the tendency to remain in the laboratory rather than making experiments relevant to the real problems of the social context. He noted the relationship between psychological theory and political ideology: "A theory about human behavior, Dewey asserted, could not be independent of the ideological foundations of a society and the psychologist's place in that social order" (Sarason, 1981, p. 137). In their 1949 book entitled *Knowing and the Known*, which grew out of an eleven-year correspondence (Plas, 1986), Dewey and Bentley discussed the relationship between the observer and the observed, or the transactional reality created by the interaction of the knower and the known. According to their conception, dimensions of this reality were closely tied to the language used in naming what was observed. Dewey and Bentley noted further that there is more than one "correct" description of any event and that within transactional inquiry a description need not make reference to a notion of causality. Thus, their transactional reality was

> *neither subjective nor objective. In transactional science, a person's subjective world is a matter for existential or spiritual consideration; an objective reality is impossible to know. The transactional reality that is available for study is born of the engagement between the knower and that which is to be known.* (Plas, 1986, p. 23)

As will become clearer in our discussions in Chapter 3, such notions are clearly consistent with the cybernetic paradigm.

Barker
Roger Barker (1968; Barker & Wright, 1955; Barker & Associates, 1978) can be viewed as an ecological psychologist who thinks systemically. For Barker, the *behavior setting* is the fundamental unit of analysis, and he has challenged the concept that personality belongs solely to the individual. As a systemic ecologist he focuses on relationships and wholes. The concept of behavior setting is akin to that which systems thinkers refer to as context. The relationship between the person and other persons, things, and ideas all interact to comprise the behavior setting. In this view there is no cause that can be isolated and thus there is no blame. Further, the whole is understood as larger than the sum of the parts, whether one is speaking of nations or of families (Plas, 1986).

Still More
A few other people should also be mentioned. Karen Horney (1885–1952) was a psychoanalyst who focused attention on the importance of social and cultural factors in the development of mental illness. Psychologist William James (1842–1910) was "a fervent critic of the atomistic and mechanistic tendencies in psychology, and an enthusiastic advocate of the interaction and interdependence of mind and

body" (Capra, 1983, p. 171). Kurt Goldstein's (1878–1965) organismic approach has the air of helping people address themselves and their environment, and "he recognizes the importance of the objective world both as a source of disturbance with which the individual must cope and as a source of supplies by means of which the organism fulfills its destiny" (Hall & Lindzey, 1978, pp. 250–251). Finally, there were those individuals associated with what in the field of psychology is referred to as transactional functionalism. This group included, among others, Adelbert Ames, Hadley Cantril, Albert Hastorf, and William Ittelson. Like Dewey and Bentley, they asserted that reality can never be known in any absolute sense. Rather, it was their belief that where, when, and how we perceive things influence how each of us defines reality.

The Limits of History

Although these people we selected were chosen for different reasons, all are similar to the extent that their theories dealt in some way with social context rather than merely with individuals. Thus, they all illustrate both the pervasiveness of wholistic thinking that emerged during the first half of the twentieth century as well as the extensive overlapping of ideas in the intrapsychic and systemic views from their beginnings.

Nevertheless, none of these voices was systemic in the purest sense of the term; none had made the paradigmatic shift to a cybernetic epistemology. But in order to be able to agree or disagree with this judgment, it is necessary to have an awareness of the basic tenets of a systems framework. Further, from this perspective, there is a limit to what history can tell us. Maturana (1978) has noted: "History is necessary to explain how a given system or phenomenon came to be, but it does not participate in the explanation or the operation of the system or phenomenon in the present" (p. 39). For a look at what is happening in the present, we move now to a consideration of the 1990s.

Controversy, Conflict, and Beyond: The 1990s

The final decade of the twentieth century continues to be a period of challenge and innovation as the field both maintains an intensive self-critique and implements efforts to forge new partnerships. In their review of the decade of the 1980s, Piercy and Sprenkle (1990) note the dramatic increase in family therapy literature dealing with theory, research, and practice and the evolution of traditional models of therapy, as well as the creation of new models, to accommodate both individual and societal influences. They state further that "lively debates have also characterized the decade" (p. 1116). Two of the primary debates, which have important ramifications for current practice, center around the discussion of social constructionism and the feminist critique of family therapy. The former has become an issue of such prominence that we have written a new chapter (see Chapter 4) in order to deal adequately with this topic. Another development of great significance is the relatively new collaborative relationship between family therapy and family medicine.

The Feminist Critique

Even as the field was coming of age, the late 1970s and early 1980s saw the emergence of the feminist critique of family therapy. That is, just when many family therapists were beginning to feel confident and perhaps complacent about what they had wrought (Nichols & Schwartz, 1991), others were protesting the lack of attention that had been paid to gender-related issues in both theory and therapy. Beginning with a groundbreaking article by Rachel Hare-Mustin in 1978, family therapists began to be criticized for (1) failing to consider the larger context when describing family dysfunction; (2) adhering to the notion that all parties to a problem have contributed equally and thus share equal responsibility for that problem; (3) continuing to view mothers as the source of pathology in families; and (4) assuming a neutral stance vis-à-vis families. Further, much of the feminist critique has been focused specifically on systems theory.

The use of systems theory has been seen as problematic to the extent that it encourages the use of mechanistic metaphors to describe family dysfunction and blinds its adherents to a consideration of the social, political, and economic conditions that contribute to such dysfunction. In addition, since systems theory rejects the idea of unilateral control, its proponents have been severely chastised for failing to acknowledge the realities of the power relationships that characterize our patriarchal society. Family therapists thus have been criticized for their participation, inadvertent or otherwise, in maintaining a sexist status quo. Similarly, circular causality has been seen as particularly repugnant when applied to problems such as battering, rape, and incest. The argument is that, rather than looking for cause or placing blame, the family therapist "subtly removes responsibility for his behavior from the man while implying that the woman is coresponsible, and in some ways plays into the interactional pattern which results in violence and abuse" (Avis, 1988, p. 17).

Having made the covert overt relative to previous applications of family systems theory, advocates of a feminist perspective have suggested the inclusion of discussions of gender-related issues in therapy, self-disclosure regarding the therapist's biases, and an emphasis on the strengths of women, their individual needs, and the ways in which women may be empowered (Avis, 1988). Indeed, according to Goldner (1985a) the feminist critique challenges family therapists to accept "gender as an irreducible category of clinical observation and theorizing" (p. 22). Wheeler (1985) notes further that feminism requires an on-going examination by family therapists regarding their honesty, responsibility, and integrity and a consideration of whether their practice "is the most ethical, effective, and humane treatment for women" (p. 55). To this discussion Nichols (1985) adds the following reflections:

I think that sexual politics is so personal and consequential a subject that thera-
pists are especially prone to lose their objectivity and to become directive where sex
role inequity is concerned. . . . We should, I believe, always keep in mind that our
clients may choose to balance their relationship in ways differently than we think
they should. Finally, I think that all of us, men and women, should beware that
intervening to rescue women is an invidious form of sexual bias, according to
which women are helpless victims and need someone to take over for them. (p. 77)

We would also suggest that it is important to make a distinction between theory and theorist. For example, while family therapists may indeed have ignored
the larger context and may have operated in a sexist manner, consistent with the
society in which they were socialized, they were not directed to do so by systems
theory:

To be true to its own aspirations, GST [General Systems Theory] can and must
emphasize that families, like all human systems, are inseparably embedded in the
historical, social, cultural, economic and political context in which they exist. So,
too, are theory building and ways of knowing. (Germain, 1991, p. 123)

In order to avoid gender bias, therefore, it behooves theorists, therapists, and researchers to become conscious of their personal values and beliefs and to recognize
the degree to which the observer influences that which he or she observes. To do
otherwise is not only to participate in maintaining the problem of sexism but also
to be inconsistent with a systems perspective. Applications of the theory, however,
have often been confused with the theory itself.

After many years of tension and conflict, Virginia Goldner noted at a conference presentation in 1991 that within the previous two years family therapists and
feminists had begun a more collegial dialogue. While agreeing with the radical
constructivists that families may not be real in the crude sense of a living organism,
feminists remind us that people and societies live and act as if families were real.
Further, while there is a deemphasis on political liberties and social options, we
must recognize that political categories determine quality of life and that it is too
easy to ignore the social consequences of our therapeutic conversations. Thus,
while not as heated, the debate continues, and much of it revolves around developments in family therapy theory, particularly as an outgrowth of the perspective
provided by social constructionism.

For example, in what she termed a "postmodern analysis of therapy," Hare-
Mustin (1994) examines the impact of society's dominant discourses which inevitably influence the interaction between client and therapist. She notes that "our society privileges a discourse of heterosexual relations, obscures a discourse of
female desire, and promotes a discourse of female victimization" (p. 24) and suggests that to the extent that therapists are not self-reflexively aware of their use of
language, they participate in maintaining prevailing ideologies. For despite attempts to view clients as equal participants, there is at best an implicit hierarchy as

ultimately therapists are perceived as having the greater expertise and it is they whom the clients pay.

Simon (1993) has addressed the issue of hierarchy and suggests that it be recast in "temporal and developmental terms" (p. 154), rather than in terms of power. While acknowledging that hierarchical phenomena are "crucial to the therapeutic process itself" (p. 151), he suggests that therapists must move away from a judgmental, pathologizing, and controlling stance and instead provide a context which allows the client to confront aspects of his or her sociocultural environment in which an inadequacy of fit is being experienced. Goldner (1993), however, sees this suggestion as a "rhetorical sleight of hand" (p. 157) and states that "power is a problem for family therapy because power is a problem" (p. 157). Her solution is to "cultivate an attitude of critical inquiry about the larger social context" which considers not only the therapeutic conversation but the issues which have been excluded from the conversation. Similar to Hare-Mustin, she advocates a stance which includes self-reflexiveness and an awareness that our personal truths do not represent *the* truth.

Family Therapy and Family Medicine

Family medicine emerged as a separate specialty in 1969, in reaction to the increasing specialization and reductionism within the medical field. However, it was many years before family practitioners and family therapists began first to acknowledge each other and then to establish formal working relationships. In 1983 William Doherty, Ph.D., and Macaran Baird, M.D., published *Family Therapy and Family Medicine: Toward the Primary Care of Families,* the first book to focus on the interface of family medicine and family therapy. This was followed by the creation of a journal entitled *Family Systems Medicine.* Numerous books and articles have since been published and not long ago it was noted that "as the national health care crisis deepens, family therapy and family medicine are developing a partnership with good prospects for combining physical and mental health care in a new model for clinical practice" (*Family Therapy and Family Medicine,* 1990, p. 9).

In the spring of 1990, the American Association for Marriage and Family Therapy (AAMFT) and the Society of Teachers of Family Medicine (STFM) established a joint task force "to identify existing collaborative practices; to promote collaborative practices in a variety of settings; and, to promote the education and training of family therapists and family physicians to work collaboratively" (Tilley, 1990, p. 1). For despite differences in training, professional socialization, theoretical orientation, styles of practice, and reimbursement methods, the two disciplines share a common approach to health based on a systemic, or wholistic, perspective. Thus, there is a shared belief in the importance of context, including the biological system, the psychological system, the family system, and the social system (Henao, 1985), for understanding how problems emerge, how they are maintained, and how they may be solved. Teamwork between family physicians and family therapists may therefore become an important means of dealing with the complexities of both physical and emotional problems.

Further, separating mind and body is no longer considered to be a valid activity, and healing includes the facilitation of health as well as the treatment of disease (Becvar, Becvar, Newell, & Andresen, 1991). Implementation of a systemic approach to both illness and wellness permits family physicians "to set limits on individual involvement and risk-taking by transferring part of the care of the family to other individuals and organizations" (Doherty & Baird, 1983, p. 279). The physician is thus seen as one part of a community network from which helping resources may be derived and to which the patient may be connected, so that no one bears the burden of sole responsibility for problem solving.

Within the medical field, George Engel (1977; 1992) has long been a primary proponent of a biopsychosocial model. And family therapists have been admonished to overcome their ambivalence about the notion of illness and to "conceptualize and differentiate the varieties of illness/distress from one another in order to clarify, strengthen, and broaden the scope of family therapy, theory, and clinical practice" (Wynne, Shields, & Sirkin, 1992, p. 16). Indeed, the field of family therapy is paying increasing attention to collaboration with physicians (Seaburn, Gawinski, Harp, McDaniel, Waxman, & Shields, 1993) and in recent years has seen the emergence of a variety of practice models (Cohen & Milberg, 1992; Leff & Walizer, 1992; McDaniel, Hepworth, & Doherty, 1992; Miller, 1992; Stein, 1992).

Summary

This chapter provided an overview of many of the voices and events that shaped the emergence of systems theory and family therapy. The sociohistorical context of the movement was stressed and the chart of noteworthy occurrences integrated the development of systems theory with the larger context. World War II, for example, was shown to have a significant influence in terms of the creation of interdisciplinary research teams and the opening of doors into the realm of cybernetics.

The immediate postwar period saw separate researchers and clinicians reaching similar conclusions about the treatment of whole families. This was followed by an era in which researchers and clinicians began to come together and share their findings. The word spread and received national attention via the publication of journal articles and books. Finally, distinct schools of, or approaches to, family therapy evolved as the field matured.

Having come of age, family therapy found itself, in the 1980s, in an era in which achieving expertise required knowledge and training in all of the approaches. Also required was an appreciation of those outside the field who nevertheless contributed to its development. Thus, a summary of other voices heard in the era before the emergence of family therapy was provided. Finally, we concluded with a look at two forces whose impact will continue to be felt as we proceed through the decade of the 1990s: the feminist critique and the partnership between family therapy and family medicine.

TABLE 2.1

	Background World Events	Development of Family Therapy
1937	F.D.R. signs U.S. Neutrality Act Wall Street stock market decline signals serious recession Karen Horney: *The Neurotic Personality of Our Time* Alfred Adler dies (b. 1870)	Ackerman at Menninger Clinic Ackerman: "The Family as a Social & Emotional Unit"
1938	F.D.R. appeals to Hitler & Mussolini to settle European difficulties amicably Franz Boas: *General Anthropology*	Lidz at Johns Hopkins
1939	Freud dies (b. 1856) World War II (1939–1945) U.S. economy recovers	
1940	F.D.R. reelected to 3rd term as president of U.S. Carl Jung: *The Interpretation of Personality* Bertrand Russell appointed to lectureship at Harvard Penicillin developed as a practical antibiotic	
1941	Pearl Harbor bombed by Japan U.S. enters the war Manhattan Project on atomic research begins	Conference on hypnosis, Psychoanalytic Institute, NY
1942	Gandhi's demand for India's independence defeated Mass murder of Jews in Nazi gas chambers begins Erich Fromm: *The Fear of Freedom*	May 15–17 Conference on Cerebral Inhibition, NY Ashby paper
1943	Italy surrenders to U.S. & declares war on Germany Polio epidemic in U.S. Rationing of meat, cheese, fats, & all canned foods Nobel Prize for physics: Otto Stern (U.S.), for work with molecular beam theory, proton movement	Von Neumann & Wiener communicate re: shared ideas Rosenblueth et al.: "Behavior, Purpose & Teleology"
1944	D-Day (June 6) F.D.R. reelected to 4th term as president of U.S. Cost of living in U.S. rises almost 30%	Whitaker at Oak Ridge, TN
1945	F.D.R. dies; Truman becomes president of U.S. VE day ends war in Europe (May 8) U.S. drops bombs on Hiroshima (August 6) and Nagasaki (August 9) Japan surrenders; war ends (August 14)	Bateson & McCulloch push for Macy conference Bertalanffy presents general systems theory Wiener & Von Neumann organize study group

	Background World Events	Development of Family Therapy
1946	Atomic Energy Commission created Dr. Benjamin Spock: *Baby and Child Care* Electronic brain built by University of Pennsylvania	Bateson at New School for Social Research Macy conference Bowen at Menninger Clinic Whitaker at Emory
1947	India independent, partitioned into India & Pakistan Alfred North Whitehead dies (b. 1861) Bell Laboratories scientists invent the transistor Michael Polanyi: *Science, Faith and Society* Kurt Lewin dies (b. 1890)	Bateson at Harvard
1948	Gandhi is assassinated (b. 1869) Truman is reelected president of U.S. State of Israel established Alfred Kinsey: *Sexual Behavior in the Human Male*	Bateson at Langley Porter Rosen visits Menninger Clinic Whitaker begins conferences on schizophrenia
1949	Communist People's Republic proclaimed in China Apartheid program established in South Africa George Orwell: *Nineteen Eighty-Four* Psychologist Edward L. Thorndike dies (b. 1874) Harry Stack Sullivan dies (b. 1892)	
1950	Sen. Joseph McCarthy advises president that State Department is riddled with communists Truman instructs U.S. Atomic Energy Commission to develop hydrogen bomb N. Korean forces invade S. Korea, capture Seoul Miltown comes into wide use in U.S. as a tranquilizer	Bateson begins work at V.A. in Palo Alto, CA Bowen focuses on mother/child symbiosis
1951	22nd Amendment to U.S. Constitution passes limiting presidential terms Julius & Ethel Rosenberg sentenced to death for espionage against the U.S. Color TV first introduced J. Andre-Thomas devises a heart-lung machine	Ruesch & Bateson: *Communication: The Social Matrix of Psychiatry* Bowen: Residential treatment of mothers & children Lidz at Yale
1952	King George VI of England dies; succeeded by his daughter, Queen Elizabeth II Eisenhower resigns as Supreme Commander in Europe; elected president of U.S.	Palo Alto research project on paradoxes Wynne at NIMH

Continued

TABLE 2.1   *(Continued)*

	Background World Events	Development of Family Therapy
1952 *Cont'd*	Nobel Peace Prize: Albert Schweitzer Contraceptive pill of phospheridin produced John Dewey dies (b. 1859) Karen Horney dies (b. 1885)	Midelfort presents paper on family therapy at APA
1953	Stalin dies; succeeded by Malenkov; Beria dismissed & executed; Khrushchev promoted to First Secretary of Russian Communist Party Dag Hammarskjold elected Secretary- General of U.N. U.S. creates Secretary of Health, Education and Welfare cabinet post Korean armistice signed B.F. Skinner: Science and Human Behavior	Final Macy conference on cybernetics
1954	U.S. Supreme Court rules that segregation by color in public schools violates 14th Amendment Televised McCarthy hearings; formal censure of McCarthy & condemnation by U.S. Senate Aldous Huxley: *The Doors of Perception* Concern in Europe & U.S. about fallout and disposal of radioactive wastes Antipolio serum administered by Jonas Salk	Palo Alto research: Schizophrenic communication Bowen at NIMH
1955	Blacks in Montgomery, AL, boycott segregated city bus lines Ultra-high frequency waves produced at MIT Albert Einstein dies (b. 1879) U.S. & U.S.S.R. announce plan to launch earth satellites in International Geophysical Year 1957–1958	American Orthopsychiatry Association meeting, NY Conference on schizophrenia, Sea Island, GA Whitaker in private practice, Atlanta, GA Satir begins teaching family dynamics in Chicago
1956	Soviet troops march into Hungary Eisenhower reelected president of U.S. Martin Luther King emerges as leader of campaign for desegregation John F. Kennedy: *Profiles in Courage* Bell Telephone Company developing "visual telephone"	Bateson group: "Toward a Theory of Schizophrenia" Bowen at Georgetown Wynne takes over family research section at NIMH
1957	U.S.S.R. launches Sputnik I & II International Atomic Energy Agency established Ayn Rand: *Atlas Shrugged* John Von Neumann dies (b. 1903) Desegregation crisis in Little Rock, AR	Panel on family research: American Orthopsychiatry Meeting, NY Family panel at APA meeting, Chicago Midelfort: *The Family in Psychotherapy*

	Background World Events	Development of Family Therapy
1957 Cont'd	"Beat" and "beatnik" emerge as popular labels	Boszormenyi-Nagy opens Family Therapy Department at Eastern Pennsylvania Psychiatric Institute Satir visits family research project at NIMH
1958	European Common Market comes into being John B. Watson dies (b. 1878) Alaska becomes 49th state Pope Pius XII dies; Cardinal Roncalli elected Pope John XXIII Stereophonic recordings come into use	Ackerman: *The Psychodynamics of Family Life* Wynne introduces pseudomutuality Satir begins private practice in California
1959	Fidel Castro becomes Premier of Cuba Charles DeGaulle proclaimed President of Fifth French Republic Pierre Teilhard de Chardin: *The Phenomenon of Man* Hawaii becomes 50th state	Jackson opens MRI in Palo Alto, with Satir & Riskin
1960	J.F.K. elected president of U.S. Harper Lee: *To Kill a Mockingbird* First weather satellite launched by U.S. to transmit TV images of cloud cover around the world Former Gestapo chief Adolph Eichmann arrested U.S. scientists develop laser device	Ackerman opens Family Institute, NY Minuchin begins Wiltwyck Project, NY
1961	Cuban exiled rebels attempt an unsuccessful invasion of Cuba at Bay of Pigs Berlin Wall constructed Gordon Allport: *Pattern and Growth in Personality* Carl Jung dies (b. 1875) Yuri Gagarin (U.S.S.R.) orbits earth in 6-ton satellite Alan Shepard makes first U.S. space flight	Bell: *Family Group Therapy* Kempler Institute for the Development of the Family opens in Los Angeles
1962	Cuban missile crisis Second Vatican Council opens in Rome Eleanor Roosevelt dies (b. 1884) Thalidomide causes birth defects Nobel Prize for Medicine & Physiology: F.H.C. Crick, M.H.F. Wilkins, & J.D. Watson for determining molecular structure of DNA	Bateson project ends Haley goes to MRI *Family Process* begins publication

Continued

TABLE 2.1   *(Continued)*

	Background World Events	Development of Family Therapy
1963	J.F.K. assassinated; L.B.J. becomes president of U.S. Pope John XXIII dies; succeeded by Cardinal Montini, Pope Paul VI Dr. Michael DeBakey first uses artificial heart to take over circulation during surgery 200,000 Freedom Marchers demonstrate in Washington, DC	Haley: *Strategies of Psychotherapy*
1964	Prime Minister Nehru of India dies (b. 1890) L.B.J. elected president of U.S. Eric Berne: *Games People Play* Norbert Wiener dies (b. 1894) A U.S. destroyer is allegedly attacked off N. Vietnam; U.S. aircraft attack N. Vietnam bases in reprisal; escalation of war, heavy fighting	Philadelphia Family Institute founded
1965	Winston Churchill dies (b. 1874) Ralph Nader: *Unsafe at Any Speed* Legislative momentum gains for antipollution laws on a national scale in U.S. Senate Power blackout in northeastern U.S. affects 30 million Kurt Goldstein dies (b. 1878)	Whitaker at University of Wisconsin Boszormenyi-Nagy & Framo: *Intensive Family Therapy* Minuchin director of Philadelphia Child Guidance Clinic
1966	Indira Gandhi becomes Prime Minister of India International Days of Protest against U.S. policy in Vietnam Floods ravage northern Italy; thousands of art treasures ruined at Venice & Florence	Ackerman: *Treating the Troubled Family*
1967	Six-Day War between Israel and Arab nations Dr. Christiaan Barnard performs first human heart transplant operation in Cape Town, S. Africa Desmond Morris: *The Naked Ape* Svetlana Alliluyeva, Stalin's daughter, arrives in U.S. Gordon Allport dies (b. 1897)	Satir: *Conjoint Family Therapy* Watzlawick, Beavin, & Jackson: *Pragmatics of Human Communication* Brief family therapy project begins at MRI Haley at Philadelphia Minuchin et al.: *Families of the Slums* Selvini Palazzoli founds Institute for Family Studies, Milan, Italy
1968	Martin Luther King, Jr., is assassinated Sen. Robert F. Kennedy is assassinated Richard Nixon elected president of U.S. Worldwide confusion in university life created by student unrest Pope Paul VI: encyclical "Humanae Vitae" against all artificial means of birth control	Satir at Esalen Jackson dies Bertalanffy: *General System Theory*

	Background World Events	**Development of Family Therapy**
1969	Golda Meir becomes Israel's 4th prime minister Gallup poll shows that 70% of those questioned feel that the influence of religion is declining in U.S. Apollo II lands on moon J. Weber of U. of Maryland observes gravitational waves first postulated by Einstein in 1916 U.S. government takes steps to ban use of DDT	
1970	Student protests against Vietnam War lead to killing of 4 students at Kent State U., OH Bertrand Russell dies (b. 1872) First complete synthesis of a gene announced by scientists at University of Wisconsin	
1971	Federal & state aid to parochial schools ruled unconstitutional by U.S. Supreme Court 26th Amendment allowing 18-year-olds to vote ratified Nixon orders 90-day wage & price freeze to curb inflation Erich Segal: *Love Story* Church of England & Roman Catholic Church end 400-year dispute: agree on "essential meaning of the Eucharist"	Ackerman dies Bateson: "The Cybernetics of 'Self'"
1972	U.S. returns Okinawa to Japan Nixon visits China and Russia "Watergate Affair" begins Nixon reelected president of U.S.	Bateson: *Steps to an Ecology of Mind* Wynne at University of Rochester Satir: *Peoplemaking*
1973	Vice President Spiro Agnew resigns over income tax evasion; Gerald Ford named to replace him U.S. Supreme Court rules that states may not prohibit abortion during first 6 months of pregnancy Pablo Picasso dies (b. 1881) American Skylab I (unmanned), II, & III (manned) space missions completed successfully Energy crisis created by gasoline shortages	Boszormenyi-Nagy & Spark: *Invisible Loyalties* Haley: *Uncommon Therapy* Kempler: *Principles of Gestalt Family Therapy* Speck & Attneave: *Family Networks*
1974	Worldwide inflation Nixon resigns and Ford becomes 39th president of U.S. Limited amnesty granted to Vietnam War draft evaders and military deserters	Watzlawick, Weakland, & Fisch: *Change* Minuchin: *Families and Family Therapy*

Continued

TABLE 2.1   *(Continued)*

	Background World Events	Development of Family Therapy
1974 Cont'd	Aleksandr Solzhenitsyn: *The Gulag Archipelago* U.S. Secretary of State Kissinger facilitates cease-fire on Golan Heights between Syria and Israel Four U.S. Episcopal bishops defy church law and ordain 11 women as priests	
1975	Ella Grasso elected governor of Connecticut U.S. ends two decades of military involvement in Vietnam Egypt reopens Suez Canal 8 years after closing New York City's Council of Churches rejects membership for Unification Church of Rev. Sun Myung Moon U.S. Apollo & Soviet Soyuz 19 spacecrafts link up 40 miles above earth American Revolution Bicentennial celebration begins in Boston	Satir, Stachowiak, & Taschman: *Helping Families to Change*
1976	Mao Tse-Tung dies (b. 1893) U.S. & U.S.S.R. sign treaty limiting size of underground nuclear explosions for peaceful purposes; provides for first on-site inspection of compliance Jimmy Carter elected president of U.S. Dixie Lee Ray elected governor of Washington Alex Haley: *Roots* U.S. Air Force Academy admits 155 women, ending all-male tradition at U.S. military academies	Haley: *Problem-Solving Therapy* Bandler, Grinder, & Satir: *Changing with Families* Watzlawick: *How Real Is Real?* Haley to Washington, DC
1977	President Carter grants pardon to almost all American draft evaders of Vietnam War era U.S. Department of Energy established Scholastic Aptitude Test of college-bound students shows steady decline since 1963 U.S. confirms testing of neutron bomb, which kills with massive radiation, leaving most buildings intact	Watzlawick & Weakland: *The Interactional View* Papp: *Family Therapy: Full Length Case Studies*
1978	Hubert Humphrey dies (b. 1911) U.S. Senate ratifies new Panama Canal treaties U.S. & People's Republic of China announce establishment of full diplomatic relations	Napier & Whitaker: *The Family Crucible* Minuchin et al.: *Psychosomatic Families*

	Background World Events	**Development of Family Therapy**
1978 *Cont'd*	Israeli Premier Begin & Egyptian President Sadat agree on framework for Mideast peace at Camp David Pope Paul VI dies; John Paul I dies; John Paul II, Karol Wojtyla, first non-Italian in 456 years, first Pole, elected Pope First test-tube baby born in England Nuclear accident at Three Mile Island	Bowen: *Family Therapy in Clinical Practice* Selvini Palazzoli et al.: *Paradox and Counterparadox* Watzlawick: *The Language of Change* Hare-Mustin: "A Feminist Approach to Family Therapy"
1979	Elaine Pagels: *Gnostic Gospels* Margaret Thatcher becomes West's first female prime minister Voyager II on mission to Jupiter Sandinistas come to power in Nicaragua; El Salvador civil war begins Israeli-Egyptian Peace Treaty signed in Washington	Bateson: *Mind and Nature* Haley: *Leaving Home* Rueveni: *Networking Families in Crisis*
1980	Reagan elected U.S. President Mt. St. Helens erupts Iraq-Iran war begins Polish Trade Union Solidarity founded West boycotts 20th Olympic Games held in Moscow William Golding: *Rites of Passage* Vaccine for hepatitis B developed	Gregory Bateson dies (b. 1904) First International Congress on Ericksonian Hypnotherapy Selvini Palazolli/Prata and Boscolo/Cecchin form separate teams
1981	Artificial skin for burn victims developed Egyptian President Sadat killed President Reagan and Pope John Paul II wounded First flight of space shuttle Columbia First woman appointed to U.S. Supreme Court	Kempler: *Experiential Psychotherapy with Families* Madanes: *Strategic Family Therapy* Hoffman: *The Foundations of Family Therapy* Von Foerster: *Observing Systems*
1982	Falklands War Soviet President Brezhnev dies U.S. backs Nicaraguan Contras against the Sandinistas First transplant of an artificial heart (USA) First woman Supreme Court Judge in Canada	Gilligan: *In a Different Voice* Walsh: *Normal Family Processes* Fisch, Weakland, & Segal: *Tactics of Change*
1983	Reagan's "Star Wars" speech U.S. intervenes militarily in Grenada First U.S. woman, Sally K. Ride, in space Anti-apartheid protests increase in U.S. and Europe *Pioneer 10,* the first space probe, leaves the solar system	Keeney: *Aesthetics of Change* Doherty & Baird: *Family Therapy and Family Medicine*

Continued

TABLE 2.1   *(Continued)*

Background World Events	Development of Family Therapy
1984 Multinational peacekeeping force withdraws from Lebanon 21st Olympic Games held in Los Angeles without the U.S.S.R. Indira Gandhi killed President Reagan reelected First female candidate for V.P. Joseph Heller: *God Knows* Madeleine Kunin elected governor of Vermont	Madanes: *Behind the One-Way Mirror* Watzlawick: *The Invented Reality*
1985 Gorbachev becomes Soviet leader South Africa declares state of emergency Palestinian terrorist attacks on Rome and Vienna airports Warsaw pact renewed for 30 years Canada rejects "Star Wars" invitation Reagan-Gorbachev summit in Geneva	Gergen: "Social Constructivist Movement in Psychology" de Shazer: *Keys to Solution in Brief Therapy* Goldner: "Feminism and Family Therapy"
1986 U.S. space shuttle Challenger explodes Philippines President Marcos forced into exile; Mrs. Aquino succeeds U.S. planes bomb Libya Nuclear accident at Chernobyl U.S. Iran-Contra scandal exposed DNA finger-printing developed at Leicester University	Selvini Palazzoli: "Towards a General Model of Psychotic Family Games"
1987 Syrians intervene in Beirut Chad defeats Libya Western navies begin escorting Gulf ships India intervenes in Sri Lanka "Black Monday" on world stock markets Mrs. Thatcher wins third general election in Britain	Boszormenyi-Nagy: *Foundations of Contextual Therapy* Bateson & Bateson: *Angels Fear* Tom Andersen: "The Reflecting Team"
1988 Soviet withdrawal from Afghanistan begins 22nd Olympic Games in Seoul Galaxy 4C41.17, most distant yet, discovered Mitterand reelected President of France Salman Rushdie: *The Satanic Verses* George Bush elected U.S. President	Virginia Satir dies (b. 1916) de Shazer: *Clues* Walters, Carter, Papp, & Silverstein: *The Invisible Web*
1989 Berlin Wall dismantled Tiananmen Square massacre in China San Francisco earthquake Ayatollah Khomeini dies Exxon-Valdez oil spill	O'Hanlon & Weiner-Davis: *In Search of Solutions*

	Background World Events	Development of Family Therapy
1990	First authorized use of gene therapy to control illness Ann Richards elected governor of Texas John Updike: *Rabbit at Rest*	Murray Bowen dies (b. 1913) White & Epston: *Narrative Means to Therapeutic Ends* Madanes: *Sex, Love, and Violence*
1991	"Desert Storm" War in Mideast Soviet Union dissolves Isaac Bashevis Singer dies (b. 1904) Thurgood Marshall resigns from U.S. Supreme Court	Feminist boycott as presenters at AAMFT annual conference Gergen: *The Saturated Self* Harold Goolishian dies (b. 1924)
1992	Clinton elected U.S. president Earth Summit Somalia intervention Moore: *Care of the Soul*	McDaniel, Hepworth, & Doherty: *Medical Family Therapy*
1993	Health care controversies Ethnic cleansing in Bosnia Angelou: *Wouldn't Take Nothing for My Journey Now*	Boscolo & Bertrando: *The Times of Time* Hoffman: *Exchanging Voices* Israel Zwerling dies (b. 1917)
1994	Republicans win majority in Congress Accords between Israel and Jordan and Israel and Palestine Murray & Hernstein: *The Bell Curve* United Nations International Year of the Family Cease-fire in Ireland	de Shazer: *Words Were Originally Magic* Schwartz: *Internal Family Systems Therapy* William H. Masters retires, Masters & Johnson Institute closes

Chapter *3*

The Paradigmatic Shift of Systems Theory

The next part of the journey requires a change in our mode of transportation. The ride will feel different, and we must now orient ourselves to a different set of circumstances. In Chapter 2 we enjoyed a peaceful cruise through the valley of history. The waters were never choppy, the weather was balmy, and the sights along the shore were often familiar and only rarely unsettling. However, as your pilots on this flight to look more closely at the systems world, we feel several reminders are in order. We will be flying at high altitudes, so the atmospheric conditions may be unfamiliar. The cabin is equipped to compensate for this but the pressure may change from time to time and you may experience discomfort in your ears. Turbulence may also cause some bouncing. However, we want to assure you that this plane is outfitted for your safety and we will make the ride as comfortable as possible. Now, please fasten your seatbelts—we are ready for takeoff.

A Cybernetic Epistemology

As our plane leaves terra firma and climbs up through the clouds we may look out of the window and find that familiar landmarks become more difficult to recognize. The world looks different from this perspective; we get a sense of the whole and how the parts relate to each other. Rather than seeing cars, highways, houses, yards, rivers, and river banks as isolated units, we see cars-on-highways, yards-with-houses, and banks-divided-by-rivers. All of these units of interconnectedness are now seen as parts of larger wholes, such as cities or towns. Such a view of the relationships and interdependence of the elements and inhabitants of the world below is not unlike the perspective offered by systems theory at the level of simple cybernetics.

To avoid confusion it is important to repeat how we use the terms *general systems theory* and *cybernetics*. As Beer (1974) has indicated: "For some, cybernetics and General Systems Theory are co-extensive, while those could be found who regard each as a branch of the other" (p. 2). However, this debate seems to be primarily concerned with applications of the perspective rather than with disagreement over basic concepts and theoretical positions. Indeed, both are built on the same fundamental assumptions described in Chapter 1. These assumptions include the following: asks What?, reciprocal causality, wholistic, dialectical, subjective/perceptual, freedom of choice/proactive, patterns, here-and-now focus, relational, contextual, and relativistic. We thus use the terms synonymously and make no distinction between *systems theory* and *cybernetics*. However, we do make a distinction between *simple cybernetics* and *cybernetics of cybernetics*.

Returning to our analogy of the view from the plane, at the level of simple cybernetics, we place ourselves outside the system as observers of what is going on inside the system. We use the metaphor of the black box to describe a system whose operation we attempt to understand by observing what goes into and what comes out of it. We do not see ourselves as either part of the system or concerned with why it does what it does. Our focus is on describing what is happening. We therefore ask such questions as, Who are the members of the system? What are the characteristic patterns of interaction in this system? What rules and roles form the boundaries of the system and distinguish it as separate from other systems? We attempt to define the degree of openness or closedness of these boundaries; that is, how freely is information able to be transmitted into or out of the system? We look at the balance between stability and change. Although we acknowledge history as providing an important part of the context of a system, our focus is on the present, on the here-and-now rather than on the past. We are also concerned with the tendency of the system to move either toward or away from order. And all of our questions are asked from a framework that understands reality as operating according to the principles of recursiveness and feedback/self-correction, the two basic elements of a cybernetic system (Keeney, 1983).

Recursion

Dealing first with the issue of recursive organization, when we are viewing the world from a cybernetic/systemic perspective, we do not ask the question Why? We are not interested in cause. Consistent with the assumption of recursiveness, or reciprocal causality, we see people and events in the context of mutual interaction and mutual influence. Rather than examining individuals and elements in isolation, we look to their relationship and how each interacts with and influences the other. We see the behavior of *A* as a logical complement to the behavior of *B*, just as *B*'s behavior is a logical complement to the behavior of *A*. Thus a sadist requires a masochist, just as a masochist requires a sadist, if each is to be able to perform a particular behavioral role. Similarly, while dominance may look more powerful than submission, one cannot dominate another unless that other agrees to submit;

one cannot be submissive without the cooperation of another to dominate. Looking from the airplane window to the world below, yards have meaning as such only when they have a house perched on them; the river defines its banks; and highways would be meaningless without the cars that require them, and vice versa.

Thus, from a systems perspective, meaning is derived from the relation between individuals and elements as each defines the other. Causality becomes a reciprocal concept to be found only in the interface between individuals and between systems as they mutually influence each other. Responsibility or power exists only as a bilateral process, with each individual and element participating in the creation of a particular behavioral reality. As Bateson states (1970): "Any complex person or agency that influences a complex interactive system thereby becomes a part of that system, and no part can ever control the whole" (p. 362). Each of us, therefore, shares in the destiny of the other and with Bronowski (1978) we understand ourselves as members of a constantly conjoined universe.

Given this recursive perspective, we see every system influencing and being influenced by every other system and every individual influencing and being influenced by every other individual. We understand ourselves as being members of a world community, and we see patterns of connection at every level of the system. Indeed, one beauty of systems theory is its ability to increase our awareness of this range of levels, and one frustration of systems theory is this same awareness. Recognition of the whole requires an acknowledgement of the degree to which we are but a small part of the whole. Further, "the ecological systems in which man participates are likely to be so complex that he may never have sufficient comprehension of their content and structure to permit him to predict the outcome of many of his own acts" (Rappaport, 1974, p. 59). Considered as a totality, comprehension of the whole is impossible and would require what Bronowski (1978) has called a "God's-eye view."

Traditionally, however, we have thought in linear cause/effect terms. That is, we have isolated events and looked at them out of context. From a systems perspective we need to be aware that an isolated cause/effect event is but a partial arc of a larger pattern of circularity. And we are therefore brought to the awareness that "a unilineal focus on part of a system will disrupt and fractionate the balanced diversity of an ecosystem" (Keeney, 1983, p. 126).

Feedback

Turning to the second important criterion of cybernetic systems, let us consider feedback, or the aspect of recursion involving self-correction. Feedback refers to the process whereby information about past behaviors is fed back into the system in a circular manner. Indeed, feedback is behavior and is thus all-pervasive, for "we know nothing of our own behavior but the feedback effects of our own inputs" (Powers, 1973, p. 351).

At the level of simple cybernetics, we may talk about both positive and negative feedback. However, it is important to remember that these concepts do not connote value judgments. Rather they refer to the impact of the behavior upon the system and the response of the system to that behavior. Thus, positive feedback acknowledges that a change has occurred and has been accepted by the system, and negative feedback indicates that the status quo is being maintained. What is more, both feedback processes may refer to something that is good and/or something that is bad. The goodness or badness of a feedback process can only be evaluated relative to context.

Because the concepts of negative and positive feedback are difficult to understand in light of our usual use of these terms to indicate particular value judgments, perhaps an analogy from the medical profession will help illustrate their application from a systems perspective. In the process of attempting to diagnose certain diseases, the doctor may request that some tests be performed. If the results of these tests come back labeled *negative*, that means no change in body function has occurred. The status quo is being maintained. This is a *good* outcome. If the same tests were to come back indicating the presence of certain disease processes, they would be labeled *positive*. In this case the outcome is a *bad* one. On the other hand, consider the case of a young woman who would like to have a baby. Suspecting that she is pregnant, she goes to the doctor, who performs certain tests. If the tests come back labeled *positive*, indicating that she is pregnant, they provide information that certain changes have occurred in her body and that she is going to have a baby. In this case the outcome would be considered a *good* one. Were the tests to have come back labeled *negative*, indicating that she was not pregnant, that no changes had occurred in her body, the outcome would be a *bad* one. However, the same positive results of a pregnancy test done for a woman who does not want a baby would be labeled as a *bad* outcome, and so on.

Thus, *good* and *bad* are relative terms in systems theory and can only be decided within a particular context that defines them one way or the other. In addition, it is important to remember that neither positive nor negative feedback causes anything. Rather, they are descriptors of processes in a given system at a particular time. Understanding the feedback process requires looking both at the behavior and the response of the system to that behavior. For example, consider the heating system in your home. You set the thermostat at 70° and turn on the furnace. The furnace continues to run until the temperature in your home reaches 70°. At that point the furnace shuts off. As long as the thermostat indicates that a 70° temperature is being maintained, the furnace remains off. The thermostat indicating 70° and the continuation of the furnace in its off position are an illustration of negative feedback processes. The status quo is being maintained. However, should the temperature in the house fall below the desired 70° level, the furnace will kick back on and will continue to run until the temperature comes back up to 70°. The combination of an indication that the temperature has fallen below a desired level and the response of the furnace to turn back on are illustrative of a positive feedback process; that is, change has occurred and knowledge of that change has been incorporated into the system, which responds to it accordingly.

As noted, feedback processes are self-corrective mechanisms; they indicate variations and fluctuations which serve to increase the probability of the survival of the system. However, both change and stability are necessary aspects of the process of any system's survival. Positive feedback is said to be an error-activated process inasmuch as it describes a process whereby information about a deviation from a previously established norm is fed back into the system and is responded to in a manner such that the difference is accepted. Thus, system maintenance behavior occurs in response to change. Indeed, the occurrence of a new behavior in a system suggests that change may be necessary in order for the system to remain stable in a functional way. On the other hand, negative feedback processes indicate that fluctuations or disturbances are being opposed and a particular level of stability is being maintained. Information about this stability is being fed back into the system and responded to accordingly.

For example, as members of a family grow and develop, maintenance of stability in a functional manner may require that the system allow for change at various points in the family's life cycle. Initiation of such changes can come from both parents and children. Indeed, one reality of a growing, evolving family is the need for a gradual shift in the balance between dependence and independence in the relationship between parents and children. When children are very young, the balance is on the dependent end of the continuum. As they get older, their need for independence increases. Ideally, parents will anticipate this need and allow for increased independence on the part of children and thus preclude the necessity for rebelliousness. As parents acknowledge a growing maturity on the part of their children by giving them more privileges and responsibility, and as privileges are handled appropriately and responsibility is accepted, positive feedback processes are operative. On the other hand, perhaps a parent continues to behave with a fifteen-year-old child as though that child were still ten. At this point, the fifteen-year-old may choose to violate some family rules, to stay out late, to become rebellious. No matter how the parent responds to and acknowledges this new behavior on the part of the fifteen-year-old—either by accepting the need for change or resisting the need for change—positive feedback processes are operating. Once a pattern of acceptance and cooperation or resistance and rebelliousness is incorporated into the system, negative feedback processes are operating. In either case, whether in a functional or dysfunctional manner, the stability of the system is maintained in the context of both negative and positive feedback processes.

Morphostasis/Morphogenesis

A system's ability to remain stable in the context of change and to change in the context of stability are defined by the concepts known as *morphostasis* and *morphogenesis*. Morphostasis describes a system's tendency toward stability, a state of dynamic equilibrium. Morphogenesis refers to the system-enhancing behavior that allows for growth, creativity, innovation, and change, all of which are characteristic of functional systems. In well-functioning systems both morphogenesis and morphostasis are necessary. They cannot be separated; they represent two sides of the same coin. That is, "cybernetics proposes that change cannot be found without a roof of stability over its head. Similarly, stability will always be rooted to underlying processes of change" (Keeney, 1983, p. 70).

While either extreme of the morphogenesis/morphostasis continuum would probably be dysfunctional, in healthy systems an appropriate balance will be maintained between the two. The rules of the system will allow for a change in the rules of the system when such changes are in order.

To illustrate, think back to the growing family as it moves through the life cycle. As each new stage is anticipated and appropriate changes are incorporated into the system, the family's level of functioning is maintained. By contrast, in the case of the fifteen-year-old whose family did not allow for needed changes, an overemphasis on morphostasis at the expense of morphogenesis threatens the system's well-being. In the same way, if too frequent or too much change were permitted, the previously established degree of functioning of the family or system would also be threatened. In both cases, however, it is at the level of the rules that either change occurs or stability is maintained.

Rules and Boundaries

The rules according to which a system operates are comprised of the characteristic relationship patterns within the system. These rules express the values of the system as well as the roles appropriate to behavior within the system. A system's rules are what distinguish it from other systems, and therefore rules may be said to form the boundaries of a system. However, such rules, or boundaries, are not visible but must be inferred from the repeated patterns of behavior of a system. A system exists only in the eye of a beholder. In other words, a system exists only as I, the observer, choose to define it as such, only as I infer rules and patterns of relationship within a system that define it as such and form its boundary. The rules of a system are implicit for the most part, existing outside the conscious awareness of the members of the system.

To understand this notion of rules and boundaries, we invite you to reflect for a moment on the family in which you grew up. In your family there were certain things that you just did, that you knew were expected. Other things were not permitted. No one specifically told you these things. You found out about what was or was not permitted mainly when you crossed over the line of acceptable behavior. Perhaps, in your family, dinner was always served at 6:00 and children were to be seen but not heard. Perhaps there were certain expectations about religious attendance or school performance. Perhaps there were certain jobs for the males in the family and others for the females. This set of behavioral norms for your particular family is what we would call rules from a systems perspective. They were unique for your family, helped to define it, and enabled others to identify it as the Smith family or the Jones family. They formed the boundary around your particular system.

The concept of boundary also implies the notion of a hierarchy of systems. Any system, or *holon* (Anderson & Carter, 1990), exists as part of a larger system, or suprasystem, and has smaller subsystems for which it is the suprasystem. The concept of boundary connotes the separateness of a system from a larger system and yet a belongingness to that suprasystem. Thus, a family is a system and is also a part of the system of all families. Similarly, subsystems of sibling and parental relationships exist within the larger system of the family. A system's boundary, its rules, acts as a gatekeeper for the flow of information into and out of the system. Thus, maintenance of a system's identity involves a process in which the boundary functions as a buffer for information from outside the system, screening it for compatibility with the family's value system. For example, as a child, you might have heard one of your parents say, "That is not the way we do things in this family," or "I don't care what Susie is allowed to do, in this family we...." The message was that input from outside the system was not consistent with your family's values and therefore was not going to be accepted by the system.

The boundary of a system also describes the exit for information from the system. Such information is different from the inputs of other systems and is not purely what happened within the system. Rather, incoming information is transformed by the system and is then emitted as new information to other systems. For example, when children begin attending school, the family gets bombarded with all kinds of new information. Johnny comes home from school feeling smart because he has learned to use some new words. However, his parents consider such words to be profanity. After being informed that swearing is not acceptable behavior, Johnny will return to school not only with the new vocabulary words but with a message about when and when not to use such words, which he will think about and may or may not share with his friends the next time the subject arises.

Openness and Closedness

The extent to which a system screens out or permits the input of new information into the system refers to the openness or closedness of that system. All living systems are open to some extent, so openness and closedness refer to a matter of degree. An appropriate balance between the two is desirable for healthy functioning. The particular end of the continuum that is more appropriate in a given circumstance can only be determined relative to context. When a system and its identity are threatened by a context very different from its own, closedness would be the more viable option if that identity is to be maintained. For example, perhaps a particular religious group finds itself a minority within the larger cultural system. In order for the members of that religious group to maintain their uniqueness, information and input that might lead to change within the system need to be screened out, and thus the boundary must be more closed than open to new information. It is therefore not surprising that parents often insist children marry someone of the same religion so that a particular religious identity may be maintained. On the other hand, immigrants to a new country are often very open to the ways of the new society and allow in a great deal of information as part of their efforts to be assimilated by that society and to accommodate its rules and values. In this case, openness is the more appropriate end of the continuum.

Entropy/Negentropy

If a balance between openness and closedness is appropriate, then conversely, being either too open or too closed will probably be dysfunctional. At either extreme, the system may be said to be in a state of entropy, or is tending toward maximum disorder and disintegration. By allowing in either too much information or not enough information, the identity and thus the survival of the system are threatened. On the other hand, when the appropriate balance between openness and closedness is maintained, we may say that the system is in a state of negentropy, or negative entropy; it is tending toward maximum order. The system is allowing in information and permitting change as appropriate, while screening out information and avoiding changes that would threaten the survival of the system.

The way energy is used within the system also helps locate its particular position on the entropy/negentropy continuum. Some energy needs to be used to organize and maintain the system and some needs to be directed toward task functions. Too much energy devoted to one at the expense of the other can be problematic. For example, family tasks may be pursued diligently but in a conflictual or haphazard manner and nothing ever seems to get done. A sense of coherence or order seems to be lacking. In this case, a relative absence of organization, or inattention to maintenance aspects of the system, may be undermining the ability of the family members to successfully complete their tasks. The movement of the system at this point is toward entropy.

Equifinality/Equipotentiality

Whatever the particular balance between morphogenesis and morphostasis, openness and closedness, or entropy and negentropy, all systems can be described according to the concept of equifinality. That is, the system, as it is, is its own best explanation of itself, for regardless of where one begins, the end will be the same. Literally meaning equal ending, *equifinality* is "the tendency towards a characteristic final state from different initial states and in different ways based upon dynamic interaction in an open system attaining a steady state" (Bertalanffy, 1968, p. 46).

People in relationships tend to develop habitual ways of behaving and communicating with one another. We refer to these habits and characteristic processes as redundant patterns of interaction; systems are comprised of patterns and these patterns tend to repeat. Thus, no matter what the topic, the way the members of a given relationship argue, solve problems, discuss issues, and so forth will generally be the same. These redundant patterns of interaction are the characteristic end state referred to by the term "equifinality."

By contrast, the notion of *equipotentiality* reminds us that different end states may be arrived at from the same initial conditions. In either case "the implication is that it is not possible to make deterministic predictions about developmental processes" (Simon, Stierlin, & Wynne, 1985, p. 115). The concept of equifinality/equipotentiality, therefore, directs our attention to the level of process and to a focus on *what* is going on. At the same time, it precludes our need for history or for asking *why* something is. Our concern is with the here-and-now, with the particular organization and ongoing interaction in a system rather than with the origins of these characteristic patterns and processes.

This shift in emphasis from the why to the what, from the past to the here-and-now, is one of the major differences between the individual psychology and systems theory perspectives. As we will describe more fully in our discussion of change in Chapter 5, achieving insight is not the route to problem solution from a systems perspective. Rather, the goal is first to understand the context within which a problem fits, the patterns maintaining that problem, and then to change the context. While an historical framework may provide understanding about the context of such a problem, we do not seek to place blame or locate cause. Instead, we are concerned with attempted solutions and current communication about the problem, all of which have become part of the problem rather than of its solution. Given the concept of equifinality, we may be fairly certain that the system has become stuck, that the processes currently in use are no longer effective, and that what is needed is new information, new ways of communicating, and thus behaving, relative to the problem.

Communication and Information Processing

Communication and information processing are at the heart of the matter when thinking systemically. Whether we are talking about behavior, boundaries, change, closedness, energy, entropy, equifinality, feedback, input, openness, output, perception, relationship, stability, structure, or wholeness, we are making reference to communication and information processing. Three basic principles form the foundation of this concept:

Principle 1: One cannot not behave.

Principle 2: One cannot not communicate.

Principle 3: The meaning of a given behavior is not the *true* meaning of the behavior; it is, however, the personal truth for the person who has given it a particular meaning.

According to Principle 1, we can never do nothing. Even so-called doing nothing is doing something. Just for fun, try for a moment not to do anything, not to behave. If someone were watching you, what would that person have seen? Or how would you have described not doing anything to someone else? Probably your description would be something like, "I sat very still, didn't move my hands, and didn't talk." These are behaviors and thus deny the message of doing nothing and affirm the principle that one cannot not behave.

Principle 2 follows from Principle 1 inasmuch as "all behavior in the context of others has message value" (Becvar & Becvar, 1982, p. 13). Even your behavior as described above, sitting silently and not moving, conveys a message to an observer. How often, however, have you heard or used the phrase, "We just don't communicate"? What that means is that communication at the verbal level may be less than satisfactory, but at least at the nonverbal level, communication is taking place, and meaning is given to behavior even if the behavior is silence.

Principle 3 refers to the fact that a particular message or behavior may be interpreted in many different ways and no one interpretation is necessarily more correct than any other. Reality is subjective rather than objective, and how I create reality will be a function of the set of assumptions and frame of reference I bring to bear upon an event or experience. However, this is just my perception, which may or may not match your perception, and for each of us that perception is equally true and equally valid.

In addition to these three general principles, we may talk about communication occurring in three different modes: the verbal or digital mode, the nonverbal mode, and the context. The combination of the nonverbal mode and the context is called the analog. The verbal or digital mode refers to the spoken word, or the report aspect of the message. However, this is only one part of the message and is the least powerful in defining how the message is received. According to Watzlawick, Beavin, and Jackson (1967), "Whenever relationship is the central issue of communication, we find that digital (verbal) language is almost meaningless" (p. 63). For example, if a mother and daughter are talking and the mother turns to her daughter and says, "This room is sure a mess," whether the daughter is to hear these words as a comment on a particular situation or a command to clean up will depend on where they are and how the words are spoken. That is, the explicit content of a message must be qualified by the nonverbal and context modes in order to be able to decide the meaning of a message, and thus it is the analog that is more powerful.

The nonverbal mode is the command aspect of the message. It refers to voice tone, inflection, gestures, facial expression, and so forth, and tells how a message is to be received. It is therefore the relationship-defining mode of communication in that it defines the intent of the sender of the message. For example, the words "I love you" said, on the one hand, in a gruff tone with clenched fists, and on the other hand, gently while delivering a bouquet of flowers, make statements about two different kinds of relationships. The context even further modifies the meaning of a message.

Where we are, who we are with, and when, comprise the elements of context. The context defines how we are to relate to one another. Thus, you as student and I as teacher will behave one way in a classroom and another way if we go to a movie together. Indeed, a change in context usually means a change in the rules of the relationship. How we perceive each other, and thus behave with each other, are influenced by the circumstances.

Inasmuch as the meaning of the verbal message is influenced by the nonverbal mode and the context modifies the nonverbal, it is possible to understand how it is that the analog is the more powerful aspect of communication. Returning to the example of the mother and daughter, we can now see that the message "This room is sure a mess" said in amazement while visiting a friend is simply a statement shared between equals. By contrast, the same words said harshly in the daughter's room indicate that mother is in charge and that daughter had better get to work.

Congruent and Incongruent Communication

We therefore have two levels of communication: the content, referring to the digital portion, and the process, referring to the analog. When these two levels match, the members of a relationship have a pretty good idea about where they stand with each other; they are sending and receiving straight, or congruent, messages. When the two levels do not match, however, problems may arise. Since more attention is paid to the analog, or process level, responses to a mixed message are generally made to that portion of the communication. To illustrate, the recipient of the message "I love you" sent in a gruff tone with clenched fists is not likely to respond with "I love you, too." Rather, she will probably retort with something like "Why are you mad at me?" or "What's wrong with you?" From this you can conclude that their interchange will probably not be very productive.

Avoiding Communication Traps

There are two ways to avoid jumping into such a communication trap. First, whenever you receive an incongruent message, the safer alternative is to respond to the words, to the content of the message, rather than to the analog, or the process. Such a response tosses the responsibility ball back into the other's court. By simply replying "I love you, too" or "I'm glad you feel that way" and ignoring the analogical message, it is up to the other person to say what is on his mind. By choosing to respond in such a manner, you are not participating in allowing the other to insert a negative comment into the relationship via an incongruent message.

The second way to avoid this kind of trap is by metacommunication, or talking about the way you are communicating. Thus, in response to the kind of double message noted above you might say something like "I get the impression that your words are saying one thing while your voice, tone, and body seem to be saying something else. Could you clarify this for me?" The trick with metacommunication, however, is that there needs to be a rule that says metacommunication is acceptable in your relationship. Otherwise, such a response may be greeted by anger or defensiveness for which you are at least in part responsible.

Another communication trap involves mind reading. As you may recall from our discussion of equifinality, as a relationship evolves, rules are established and characteristic patterns of behavior develop. The members become sensitive to each other's analog and to unspoken definitions of their mutual interaction. However, each member of a relationship still perceives things in a unique way, and mind reading simply is not possible. No matter how well they feel they know the other, meaning will be ascribed relative to a personal frame of reference. Thus, everyone will receive messages differently, and the only way to be sure of the meaning of an unclear or double message is to make the implicit explicit. That takes us back to the two solutions described previously.

It is probably clearer to you now why we said that communication and information processing are the heart of the matter from a systems perspective. Indeed, information flow—within, into, and out of—is the basic process of social systems. How we communicate, how information is shared and handled, provides a key to understanding more completely the notions of relationship and wholeness.

Relationship and Wholeness

As noted, two individuals relating together are not independent; they mutually influence one another. We have also mentioned that relationships are characterized by redundant patterns of interaction. What we have not mentioned previously is the fundamental rule in systems theory that the whole is greater than the sum of its parts, or $1 + 1 = 3$. The three elements in this equation are the two individuals plus their interaction. As you now know, it is this interaction that provides the context of a relationship. Thus, even though in therapy we may work with a single individual we do not consider that person in isolation. Rather, our perspective is relational and our focus is on the context, or the whole, without which behavior cannot be fully understood.

Not only does $1 + 1 = 3$, but as the size of a family or system increases additively, the complexity of the system increases geometrically. Indeed, the addition of a new member to a two-person dyad multiplies the number of relationships from one to three and the number of units from three to seven. To complicate things even further, with three people we now have the possibility of a triangle. Thus, we have three people, three relationships, and one triangle, for a total of seven units. In a family of five, we have five persons, ten relationships, and twenty-seven triangles, bringing the total number of units to forty-two. The whole is indeed greater than the sum of its parts!

Triangles

The notion of triangles is an important one in family therapy, particularly in the theory of Murray Bowen. According to Bowen (1976), the triangle may be "the smallest stable relationship system" (p. 76). Thus a dyad, or two-person relationship system, may be relatively stable when things are going well. However, when a problem arises a triangle will inevitably emerge as a third person is drawn into the situation by one or the other members of the relationship. For example, Mary and Tom Smith have an argument at breakfast about money. Tom leaves for work, Mary calls her best friend to complain about what a skinflint her husband is, and the best friend agrees with Mary. We now have a two-against-one situation in which Mary gets support for her opinion from a third party, and a triangle is born. Given the kind of dilemma that now looms, we advocate a basic rule: only two to a relationship, only two to an argument. That is, Mary and Tom have a much better chance of working things out if the issues are not confused by a third party. Similarly, children will eventually reach a truce if parents do not attempt to referee their battles or arrange a cease-fire.

Relationship Style

Another important notion is that of relationship style. Rather than assessing individuals and assigning to them labels such as *dominant, submissive, aggressive, passive, cruel,* or *kind,* we assess relationships and label them according to their characteristic patterns of interaction. Derived mostly from the process level, or analogic behavior, the focus once again is on the whole, on the context within which a behavior exists and is maintained. Three relationship styles have been identified: *complementary, symmetrical,* and *parallel.*

Complementary relationships are characterized by a high frequency of opposite kinds of behavior. For example, aggressiveness on the part of one is maintained by passivity on the part of the other, and vice versa. Or the pattern is one of dominance and submission, or cruelty and kindness. Conversely, in symmetrical relationships the exchange involves a high frequency of similar kinds of behavior. In this case, the more she screams, the more he screams back, and so forth. Or he responds to her withdrawal with more withdrawal. The third relationship style is a combination of the other two styles and has been labeled parallel. In parallel relationships, both complementary and symmetrical exchanges occur, and when functioning in the complementary style, the members alternate in the one-up and one-down positions. Role flexibility exists within the relationship, and both members are able to accept responsibility as appropriate.

Although, as with most aspects of systems theory, the goodness or badness of a particular relationship style can be judged only in context, parallel relationships seem to be of a higher logical order than the other two styles (Harper, Scoresby, & Boyce, 1977). There is greater variation in behaviors, rather than being locked into one type of exchange. The issue of a power struggle seems to be bypassed in parallel relationships, and there also seems to be an implicit awareness of the bilateral nature and mutual responsibility inherent in the concept of relationship.

Finally, it is important to note that, given wholeness and interdependence as characteristic aspects of systems, a change in one part will have an impact on the whole. A system has a particular coherence or structure based on the interrelatedness of members, and a change in any one reverberates throughout the whole, not unlike the ripple effect you observe after tossing a stone into a pond. Therefore, it is possible to work with one member of a family to facilitate a change in the larger context. However, just as waters in the pond soon return to their previous state of calm, a family often struggles to regain its previous level of stability when faced with change in one member. Indeed, it was this phenomenon that led some founders of family therapy to consider working with the whole family after failing to treat individual patients successfully. Particularly in the case of long-standing problems, the family has organized itself around the problem, which is thus logical to its context. Treating the problem in isolation, as individual pathology, fails to acknowledge the systemic idea that a problem is a symptom of system dysfunction and that a lasting solution requires a change in the larger context. Again, it is necessary to think wholistically. Indeed, "dualisms between health and pathology are mended when one views symptoms as well as signs of health as simply relationship metaphors—communication or indicators of the ecology of relationship systems" (Keeney & Sprenkle, 1982, p. 9).

Goals and Purposes

The one topic remaining in our overview of simple cybernetics is goal or purpose. This is a bit tricky. According to Dell (1982), "the concept of purpose is and has been very problematic for accounts of human behavior in both psychology and philosophy. All attributions of purpose are made by an observer who is *interpreting* the behavior in question" (p. 26). Systems theory provides no exception to this dilemma, since we can only invent the purpose of a system and state it according to our own perceptions as an outsider looking in.

On the one hand, we may say that all cybernetic systems behave as though they are goal directed (Pask, 1969). On the other hand, it is not consistent with a systems perspective to speak of goal or purpose because this concept implies such intrapsychic notions as motivation or intention and is causal or linear in nature. If the best definition of the system is itself, the only logical claim we can make is that the system exists in order to exist, or to do what it does. That, however, is tautological, or circular reasoning, and begs the question of goal or purpose. In fact, while we may infer a goal, this requires someone outside the system to do so, an activity that is legitimate only at the level of simple cybernetics: "In essence, of course, the purpose *for* or the purpose *of* the system is invented by the observer himself and it is stated in an observer's metalanguage for talking about the system" (Pask, 1969, p. 23).

A common question students often ask, and one probably running through your head now, is "Why talk about goal or purpose if it is not systemic to do so?" The answer is that we are part of a culture and it is out of our culturally-based frameworks that we typically ask questions. In U.S. society that framework is not systemic; it is neopositivistic, or Newtonian, and linearity, causality, and purposefulness are basic assumptions. Thus, we almost instinctively ask Why?, attempt to assign motive, and assume all behavior is goal directed. The notion of system provides no exception to this rule.

While it is often useful for family therapists to operate at the level of simple cybernetics, as observers of the black box we think of as a system, or family, we must also be aware of the system level that includes us and defines us as a part of the context. Indeed, according to Keeney (1983), "the inadequacy of applying simple cybernetics to human phenomena was that it failed to prescribe higher-order punctuations that connect the therapist or observer to the client or observed" (p. 158). Accordingly, it is time to move into a discussion of cybernetics of cybernetics.

This will probably be the most difficult part of our flight, attaining the highest altitude. The best way to deal with this part of the trip is to simply fly through it, getting an overview, while saving your attempts to sort things out until we land.

Cybernetics of Cybernetics

Cybernetics of cybernetics moves us up a level of system so that we are no longer merely observers of black boxes. As you may recall, we said that at the level of simple cybernetics we use the metaphor of the black box to describe the system that we attempt to understand as outside observers analyzing inputs to and outputs from that system. This view, illustrated in Figure 3.1, is problematic in that it puts the observer in another black box and fails to take into account the interactions of the two systems as they both exist within a larger context.

At the level of cybernetics of cybernetics, on the other hand, we no longer view systems only in the context of the inputs and outputs of, or relationships with, other systems. Rather, we are moved to that larger context that includes the black box plus the observer, and is illustrated in Figure 3.2.

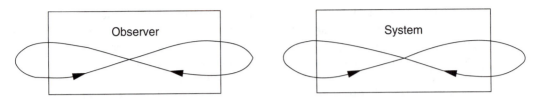

FIGURE 3-1   Simple Cybernetics

At this higher level of abstraction, the observer becomes part of, or a participant in, that which is observed. Everything that is going on is entirely self-referential: "whatever you see reflects your properties" (Varela & Johnson, 1976, p. 30). There is no reference to an outside environment; the boundary is unbroken and the system is closed. A closer approximation of wholeness is attempted. At this level we speak only of negative feedback.

We also define the autonomy, or organizational closure, of systems. At the level of cybernetics of cybernetics, the focus shifts from a behavioral analysis based on inputs and outputs with an emphasis on the environment to a recursive analysis that emphasizes the internal structure of the system and the mutual connectedness of the observer and the observed (Varela, 1979).

Wholeness and Self-Reference

Now, having presented this introduction, let's back up a bit. You may recall that we said that systems exist in the eye of the beholder, only as we choose to define them as such. We make distinctions based on our own frames of reference, and we punctuate reality according to these epistemological premises. Indeed, "we should never forget that the cybernetic system we discern is a consequence of the distinctions we happen to draw" (Keeney, 1983, p. 142). In the same manner, we can punctuate systems at the level of either simple cybernetics or cybernetics of cybernetics as either open to the inputs of other systems or closed, hence autonomous. In other words, we create our own reality, which "is a domain specified by the operations of the observer" (Maturana, 1978, p. 55). However, all the assertions in this paragraph are self-referential in that we are making them based on our own epistemological premises. Thus, they are paradoxical in the sense that we cannot know them

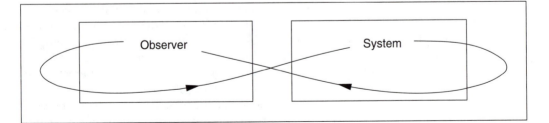

FIGURE 3-2   Cybernetics of Cybernetics

as true in any absolute way, and their truth exists only as we choose to punctuate reality at the level of cybernetics of cybernetics.

This kind of paradox is inevitable in any system of thinking inasmuch as such a system necessarily includes the thinker. It is the "human dilemma," as defined by Rollo May (1967), that we can define ourselves as both subject and object but cannot get outside ourselves to observe the process of defining ourselves. According to Varela and Johnson (1976),

> *the fact that wholes have this closed organization implies that in order to describe them we have to deal with self-referential descriptions. You wind up with functions that are functions of themselves, or interactions that intersect with themselves, properties that compute themselves, and so on. (p. 27)*

It is self-reference, this mutualness or simultaneity of interactions, that gives whole systems their sense of organizational closure, or autonomy. Indeed, understanding the autonomy of a system precludes reference to an outside and can be described only through references to itself (Keeney, 1983). Autonomy thus refers to the highest order of recursion or feedback processes of a system, and the range of deviation or level of stability maintained is that of the organization of the whole. At this level, systems have identity as particular unities—for example, as cells, organisms, individuals, families, animal populations, economic systems, and so forth.

Openness and Closedness

This notion of organizational closure requires a second look at the concept of a system's openness or closedness. Remember that at the level of simple cybernetics, openness and closedness are defined relative to the input/output ratio between a system and its environment. At this level, we are the observers of a black box that we understand as a control system interacting in a given context. On the other hand, at the level of cybernetics of cybernetics, the system plus the observer are understood to be mutually interacting within a larger system whose boundary is closed, and thus no reference is made to an external environment. From this perspective the identity of the system "is specified by a network of dynamic processes whose effects do not leave that network" (Maturana & Varela, 1987, p. 89). However, neither possibility denies the other. Rather, it is a matter of emphasis. Each view is both legitimate and flawed, and each is a function of the level at which we choose to punctuate our experience, the systemic reality we wish to create.

Autonomous systems are interactive and changes may occur at this level. However, such changes involve structure, or the way in which the organization of the whole is maintained. Therefore, interactions of systems at the level of autonomy must be referred to as perturbations rather than as inputs. As used systemically, structure refers to the relations between the parts, as well as the identity of the parts, that constitute the whole. Organization refers to the relations that define a system as a unity as well as determine its properties, with no reference to the identity of the parts. Indeed, the parts may be anything as long as they meet the requirements of the particular relations that define a system as a particular unity. "Therefore, two systems have the same organization if the relations that define them as unities are the same, regardless of how these relations are obtained, and accordingly, two systems that have the same organizations may have different structures" (Maturana, 1974, p. 467).

Thus, for example, as long as we have individuals operating according to some kind of generational hierarchy in support of the mutual welfare of all and the individual development of each, we may define that unity as a family. Such a definition holds for this particular organization regardless of whether the structure is defined by relations between a mother and father who are married and their children, or between an unmarried woman, her child, and the child's paternal grandmother. Similarly, if the members of the traditional family in the former example should experience divorce, they are still a family despite the fact that one parent no longer lives in the same household. In each case, "the identity of a system is determined by its organization and remains unchanged as long as this remains unchanged, regardless of whether the system is static or dynamic and regardless of whether the structure of the system changes or not" (Maturana, 1974, pp. 467–468).

Autopoiesis

It is *the way the parts relate,* rather than the nature of the parts, that generates a unity with particular properties by means of which we define that unity. This process of self-generation has been labeled autopoiesis. According to Maturana and Varela (1987), "the most striking feature of an autopoietic system is that it pulls itself up by its own bootstraps and becomes distinct from its environment through its own dynamics, in such a way that both things are inseparable" (pp. 46–47). In other words, a boundary is necessary in order to be able to distinguish a family from the larger context. At the same time, the dynamics of interaction and particular relationships between members, which specify the unity we call "family," are necessary in order to be able to distinguish a boundary. The boundary does not cause the family nor does the family cause the boundary. Rather, each requires the other and both are part of the unitary process of autopoiesis.

The product of an autopoietic system is always itself. That is, the system does what it does in order to do what it does, "with no separation between producer and product. The being and doing of an autopoietic unity are inseparable, and this is their specific mode of organization" (Maturana & Varela, 1987, p. 49). Therefore, at the level of cybernetics of cybernetics, we can only talk about negative feedback. Negative feedback, you recall, refers to system maintenance behavior. Therefore, to describe positive feedback is to look at deviation or change in isolation rather than in the context of the larger autonomous system. In that larger context the system operates to maintain itself, according to the rules of autopoiesis. Cybernetic descriptions are therefore always made in terms of negative feedback (Bateson, 1972). A positive feedback punctuation, or a description of deviation amplification, is "a partial arc or sequence of a more encompassing negative feedback process" (Keeney, 1983, p. 72).

Similarly, to look at families from the black box perspective and to operate accordingly is not truly consistent with a systems perspective. On the one hand, the therapist working at the pragmatic level often needs to think in terms of black boxes. It makes sense to talk about positive and negative feedback as long as they are recognized as complementary concepts. In this sense, positive feedback is understood "as an approximation for higher orders of negative feedback" (Keeney, 1983, p. 72). On the other hand, the therapist who fails to acknowledge personal membership in the context within which a family exists and problems are defined, and therefore simply treats families, does not operate differently from the therapist who chooses to see problems residing within the mind of individuals and therefore treats patients. Systemic therapists recognize their inability to extricate themselves from the context within which problems emerge and solutions are attempted. They are aware that what may look like instability at one level is part of stability at a higher order of recursion. They are thus also aware of the larger ecological balance that may be disturbed by virtue of their interventions. However, they know the limits of what is possible from such intervention efforts.

Structural Determinism

At the level of autonomy, we say that systems are structurally determined:

> They can be perturbed by independent events, but the changes that they undergo as a result of these perturbations, as well as the relations of autopoiesis that these changes generate, occur, by their constitution, as internal states of the system regardless of the nature of the perturbation. (Maturana, 1974, pp. 460–461)

Thus, the system itself determines the range of structural variations acceptable without loss of identity. The system is limited, by virtue of its structure, to what it can and cannot do. For example, a rubber ball rolls as it does as a function of the relations between its parts: its weight, mass, constitutive elements, and so on, in the context of roundness. While the interaction of the ball and a foot creates a context for movement, or change, the kind of movement—in this case, rolling—is a function of the structure of the rubber ball and not of the kick. Thus, while it may look similar, if we were to kick a bubble, it would pop. If we were to kick a cannon ball, we would hurt our feet. In all three instances the particular organization of elements defines each unity as a sphere, but what each does or can do is determined by its specific structure. The environment, therefore, does not determine what a system does. At best, the environment, as a perturbing agent, may provide the context or historical instance for the occurrence of what the system's structure determines it can do.

This shift in perspective significantly influences our thinking about growth and change relative to the interaction between organisms and the environment. According to the notion of negative explanation (Bateson, 1972), what is possible is a function of the structure of the organism and the constraints placed upon it by the environment. The organism can do or become whatever its structure allows as long as that choice is not forbidden by the environment. Thus, "we can think of the continually changing environment continually opening up further possible habitats for species to evolve *into* through their internal pressures, their 'curiosity,' and their vast richness of possibilities" (Hayward, 1984, p. 134).

Structural Coupling and Nonpurposeful Drift

In addition, given the notion of structural determinism, what a system does is always correct. It is correct because it does only what its structure determines it can do. Only from the perspective of an observer can we define the action of a system as an error. However, systems do exist within a medium that includes other systems and observers. The degree to which these systems are able to mutually coexist is defined by the concept of structural coupling. According to this concept, organisms survive by fitting with one another and with other aspects of their context, and will die if that fit is insufficient:

> *What you do with the closure of a system is actually what we do all the time, i.e., we interact with a system by poking at it, throwing things at it, and shouting at it and doing things like that, in various degrees of sophistication. That is a perturbation on the stability of the system, which it will compensate or will not compensate (and hence disintegrate). If it does compensate then we sense in it a stability for that interaction. (Varela & Johnson, 1976, p. 28)*

Therefore, change is a process of structural transformation in the context of organizational invariance.

The context within which systems exist is not deterministic. As we have said, there is no cause and effect. Rather, the life of a system is a process of a nonpurposeful drift within a medium. Even though there may be continual perturbation/compensation interactions, both internally and externally, and thus constant change, such interactions are not determined and will continue until the time of disintegration, which can occur at any time. Learning

> *appears as the continuous ontogenic structural coupling of an organism to its medium through a process which follows a direction determined by the selection exerted on its changes of structure by the implementation of the behavior that it generates through the structure already selected in it by its previous plastic interactions. (Maturana, 1978, p. 45)*

In other words, systems interact with each other in a given context. How they interact in that context is a recursive process of mutual influence/feedback/adaptation within a range determined by the structure of their respective systems. This structure exists as a function of such mutual influence/feedback/adaptation interactions in previous instances of structural coupling. Therefore, change occurs in response to a change in a context for whose creation both systems are responsible. As therapists or anyone else, we do not change systems or treat families. Rather, we change our behavior, examine the impact of this new behavior in terms of reactions to it, and then react to reactions in an ongoing modification process. If the interaction thus described is characterized by a change in the system, we may say that feedback has been established and a change in context has occurred. The strategy is to create a context in which the desired outcome—a change in behavior—is a logical response.

Epistemology of Participation

The notion of structural coupling has enormous ramifications for how we think about reality. For example, we are no longer able to consider progress as a move forward toward greater accuracy and/or truth as we attempt to understand the universe in which we live. The most we can say is that we "create new and different ways to coordinate our actions with one another" (Efran & Lukens, 1985, p. 25). We cannot act as observers who delineate more accurate representations of reality. We must return again to the notions that the observer and the observed are inextricably bound up with each other and that objectivity, as we normally understand it, is impossible. We refer to this as an epistemology of participation. Accordingly, humanity is seen in continuity with the natural world:

> Knowledge comes into being in autonomous units through an interwoven mesh of frozen histories, like a castle of cards—structured, yet boot-strapping its content and solidarity from within. Conversely it sees nature as human history, where every factual statement has a hermeneutics from which it derives and which contains its possibilities. The successor to objectivism is not subjectivism, by way of negation, but rather the full appreciation of participation, which is a move beyond either of them. (Varela, 1979, p. 276)

"Full appreciation of participation" requires a focus on how the observer and the observed are bound up with one another. Specifically, whether we are attempting to question, describe, or attribute meaning, these are all interactive processes involving perturbation and compensation within a context. For example, according to Maturana (1974),

> a problem is a question. A question is a perturbation that the questioned system must compensate for by generating a conduct that satisfies certain criteria specified in the same domain as the perturbation. Therefore, to solve a problem is to answer a question in the same domain in which it is asked. (p. 469)

Such processes, therefore, have no explanatory power relative to an understanding of the whole from the perspective of a so-called objective outsider. Rather, understanding is possible only from the perspective of the subject who is doing the questioning, describing, or explaining.

Reality as a Multiverse

Indeed, as living systems we operate in consensual domains generated through structural coupling in the context of a common language system. First-order consensual domains are those we study. Second-order consensual domains are those of which we are a part. What we do as observers is operate as though we were external to a situation and observe it (first-order) and ourselves (second-order) observing. However, in the process of observing we are inevitably interacting and therefore are creating the reality of the consensual domain we are attempting to observe:

> *Since a description always implies an interaction, and since the describing systems describe their components via their interaction through their components, there is a constitutive homomorphism between descriptions, and behavior in general, and the operations of the systems they describe. Therefore, we literally create the world in which we live by living it. (Maturana, 1978, p. 61)*

Each of us lives in and creates reality in a slightly different manner based on our own unique combinations of heredity, experiences, presuppositions, and thus perceptions. Each of us therefore lives in and creates a slightly different reality. Recalling the third rule of communication, for each of us this reality is both true and equally valid. According to Maturana (Simon, 1985), the significance of this view, as we move from simple cybernetics to cybernetics of cybernetics, is as follows:

> *Systems theory first enabled us to recognize that all the different views presented by the different members of a family had some validity. But systems theory implied that these were different views of the same system. What I am saying is different. I am not saying that the different descriptions that the members of a family make are different views of the same system. I am saying that there is no one way which the system is; that there is no absolute, objective family. I am saying that for each member there is a different family, and that each of these is absolutely valid. (p. 36)*

From this perspective, we can no longer talk about a universe. Instead we must concede that we live in a multiverse of many equally valid observer-dependent realities. From this perspective there is no objectivity, and without objectivity we cannot talk about subjectivity. (You may want to refer at this point to Chapter 1 and our discussion of darkness being defined by light.) What we may refer to is "objectivity in parentheses" (Simon, 1985), or an acknowledgment of the interrelatedness of observer and observed.

In addition, perception now becomes a process of construction; we invent the environment in which we live as we perceive/construct it. We create our reality, our world, by assimilating and accommodating input via our conceptual structures or personal world view. Thus, it becomes exceedingly important to understand the presuppositions and assumptions according to which we perceive/

construct reality. We are directed toward a consideration of mental processes. As therapists we are confronted with the task of helping our clients create, via their perceptions, a reality within which they may operate more effectively and thereby may construct a reality more supportive of their effectiveness. Before moving into directions for therapy derived from this framework, however, let us first circle back (even as our plane is now circling in preparation for landing) and summarize its key aspects.

Summary

From the perspective of first-order cybernetics, while we think in terms of recursion and feedback, morphostasis and morphogenesis, rules and boundaries, openness and closedness, entropy and negentropy, equifinality and equipotentiality, communication and information processing, relationship and wholeness, our stance is still one of seeing reality as "out there," able to be observed without being influenced. Thus therapists "discover" and "treat" problems and direct change from outside the system. By contrast, from the perspective of cybernetics of cybernetics we must consider:

1. The observer plus the black box.
2. The observer as part of the observed.
3. Reality as self-referential.
4. No reference to an outside environment.
5. Closed systems with unbroken boundaries.
6. Negative feedback.
7. Autonomy, or organizational closure.
8. An emphasis on internal structure.
9. Interactions as recursive perturbation/compensation processes.
10. Autopoiesis, or self-generation.
11. Structural determinism.
12. Structural coupling.
13. Nonpurposeful drift.
14. New coordinations rather than progress.
15. An epistemology of participation.
16. Consensual domains.
17. Reality as a multiverse of individual perceptions/constructions.
18. A focus on mental processes.

Accordingly, therapists are aware that what they work with are perceptions and constructions, both their own and those of their clients. They acknowledge that ours is a storied reality which never can be known in either a complete or an absolute sense. They are aware that their observations influence what is seen and that there are many other equally valid ways to view the same phenomena.

In Part Two, which considers the basic approaches to family therapy, the discussion of each model concludes with a section on systemic consistency. We will thus be returning to these concepts. They will form the basis of analysis of systemic consistency relative to the levels of both first-order or simple cybernetics and cybernetics of cybernetics.

Although there is much about the world of cybernetics of cybernetics that may be distressing at worst and elusive at best, comfort can be found in its sense of inclusiveness. We are not required to make either/or choices. Rather, we think in terms of both/and: for example, both light and dark, both linearity and recursiveness, both simple cybernetics and cybernetics of cybernetics. Each is understood as an integral part of a complementarity comprising a larger whole.

While we may lose the security provided by the notions of a lawful universe and the possibility of an accessible absolute truth, freedom can be gained from a proactive perspective that understands men and women as cocreators of reality. Thus we also gain a measure of control by virtue of our sense of shared responsibility for the world we live in and the larger world community of which we are a part.

In terms of therapy, some rather sobering implications, as well as some freeing aspects, can also be derived from this world view. On the one hand, we are led to an awareness that while we may talk at the level of process about how to work with families, at the level of content our specifics will need to vary from context to context. Attempting to provide a family therapy cookbook is to commit an epistemological error based on a linear epistemology. The rule regarding change from a systems perspective is differentness. A change in behavior requires a behavior that is not logical in that context. Thus, there is no prescribed form that therapy must take, nor should there be. The basic limitation for acceptable therapist behavior is not exceeding the bounds of ethical practice.

On the other hand, since therapists can neither treat, join, nor understand a family except as they experience it through interactions with various members of that family, therapists are freed to work together with family members, to codrift, and to help define a new, more functional family. However, before moving to a consideration of the theory of change consistent with a systemic perspective, as well as a consideration of ethical behavior, which are the focuses of Chapter 5, we move to a discussion of postmodernism and social constructionism.

That concludes our flight. Although we realize that it probably was not the most comfortable experience you have ever had, we suspect that this portion of our journey will not soon be forgotten.

Chapter 4

Postmodernism and Social Constructionism

This part of the journey will give you a sense of the terrain you are likely to encounter when our tour is complete, for it provides a brief background for and explanation of current events in the family therapy field. The constructionist debate referred to at the end of Chapter 2 describes an ongoing tension between those who theorize and practice in a manner consistent with the level of first-order cybernetics, on the one hand, and those who operate in a manner consistent with the level of second-order cybernetics, on the other hand. It also refers to conflict between advocates of a modernist stance and those who support the assumptions upon which postmodernism is based. This is a dispute which "has been characterized as the principal intellectual issue of our time" (Lowe, 1991, p. 41).

As indicated in Chapter 3, from the perspective of first-order cybernetics, therapists/theorists describe what is going on inside the system from a position outside the system. They assess and accordingly attempt to change behavior relative to the normative standards and criteria accepted within the larger societal context. At the level of second-order cybernetics, the observer is understood to be part of that which is observed, and thus may only describe observing systems. From the former perspective, one may define problems as existing "out there" in a real, knowable reality. From the latter perspective, reality is understood to be constructed as a function of the belief systems that one brings to bear on a particular situation and according to which one operates. At the level of second-order cybernetics, there is a concern with not only the problem but also the context in which it is embedded in terms of the meaning of each as described by both the client and the therapist. Rather than discovering behavior we create it, or believing is seeing, and how we language something becomes crucial.

The use of such terms as individual responsibility, homeostasis, resistance, pathology, and objectivity has been called into question by proponents of the "new epistemology" (Piercy & Sprenkle, 1990). Similarly, research in the logical-positivist, empirical tradition, based on a belief in the possibility of objectivity and with a focus on reductionism, has also become suspect, with a more qualitative approach being advocated in its stead (Atkinson, Heath, & Chenail, 1991). Indeed, with social constructionism and the postmodern era has come greater acceptance of a higher-order awareness, or of an epistemology that has a conscious awareness of itself. Such awareness has led to an examination of the totalizing discourses that organize our society, revealing that these discourses tend to have a deficit focus and, in normative social science and mental health practice, to be pathology-based. Attention is also given to an awareness of knowledge as framework-relative, challenging the hierarchy of the expert with his/her privileged information, hence power. All people thus regain the right to develop their personal expertise relative to their own lives. At the same time, the concept of relatedness consistent with that of the systemic/cybernetic perspective is understood to be of primary importance. All of these changes in assumptions are understood to comprise a far more ethical perspective which acknowledges the equal engagement of client and therapist as co-creators of a shared reality.

With this shift in emphasis regarding ethics, constructionism has spawned a variety of new approaches, or what we refer to as evolving therapeutic models, which will be discussed more fully in Chapter 13. While we disagree, for some this shift necessarily represents a perspective outside that of cybernetics of cybernetics. But in either case, "for constructivists, the *entire therapeutic venture* is fundamentally an exercise in ethics, it involves the inventing, shaping, and reformulating of codes for living together" (Efran, Lukens, & Lukens, 1988, p. 27). Therapy is thus understood as a dialogue whose goal is the creation of a context in which accommodation of the needs and desires of all the participants is facilitated. Such therapy is said to be consistent with a postmodern stance. In order to fully understand the significance of constructionism and postmodernism, we feel it is important to put the current events in historical perspective. Following this discussion we then examine not only the implications of constructionism for the role of language and the role of the individual but also some of the debates which characterize the constructionist context.

Postmodernism in Historical Perspective

Gergen (1991) has categorized the late eighteenth and nineteenth centuries as the period which saw the flowering of romanticism, a perspective which "lays central stress on unseen, even sacred forces that dwell deep within the person, forces that give life and relationships their significance" (p. 19). Accordingly, the world of reason and observation was replaced by "the world of the *deep interior,* lying beneath the veneer of conscious reason" (p. 20). The language of passion, purpose, depth, and personal significance was used to speak of heroism, genius, inspiration, and love. Moral values and a sense of ultimate purpose to life characterized a world view which continues today to influence our descriptions of people and their behavior.

Toward the end of the nineteenth century and the beginning of the twentieth century, the romanticist perspective was upstaged by that of modernism. This was a more practical view in which truth was to be sought through "systematic observation and rigorous reasoning" (Gergen, 1991, p. 29). Continuous progress toward a greater goal achieved by scientific means characterized the *"grand narrative"* of society, and the search for the essential, irreducible essence permeated endeavors of all kinds. It was also during this period that the machine metaphor was invoked and human behavior was understood to be determined by environmental conditions. Further, the independent, autonomous individual was valued as the ideal of maturity.

There are still those, of course, who long for the "good old days" of romanticism although there is also much to be said for the newer world of modernism. According to Gergen (1991, p. 47):

> *Many lament the loss of the romanticist languages of the person. However, it is possible to appreciate the allure of the modernist replacement. In many ways modernism is both more optimistic and more democratic. The romantic individual was forever a mystery—the vital essence quixotic and out of reach. The modernist self, by contrast, is knowable, present in the here and now, just slightly below the surface of his actions. He is not likely to be transported by sudden inspiration, be smitten by some great passion, or give way to a rush of suicidal urges. Rather, he is reliable and trustworthy. His word today is good tomorrow and the next. The modernist self is not likely to have his reason clouded by intense emotional dramas; his reasons guide his actions and his voice is clear and honest. And we must not await the arrival of some naturally gifted, inspired, or insightful man to lead our nation or our institutions. Everyone is created equal, and it is up to us as parents and good citizens to mold the young. With proper molding, and the help of science, we create the future of our dreams.*

In the modern era we thus have learned to rely on the power of science and the knowledge of objective experts who supposedly possess the truth about a reality which is out there, and which can be represented accurately and understood via reliable research data. Further, we trusted that we were progressing toward a greater good through the creation of ever more significant technological advances. Consistent with this tradition, the role of therapist and social scientist has been that of the social engineer.

In the most recent era, referred to as that of postmodernism, the belief in the possibility of objective knowledge and absolute truth is being undermined on many fronts. In its stead we find the notion that ours is a reality that is inevitably subjective and that we do indeed dwell in a multiverse which is constructed through the act of observation. Facts are being replaced by perspectives and with this shift comes a challenge to the power and privilege previously attributed to the possessors of "knowledge." Hence the issues of hierarchy and power which characterize much of the debate regarding ethical therapist behavior. That is, if we are to be consistent with the fundamental assumptions of the postmodern world view, clients must be understood as possessing equally valid perspectives and we must become aware that there is no "transcendent criterion of the correct" (Gergen, 1991, p. 111). And hence also the discomfort of those grounded in the modernist paradigm which assumes "that knowledge can be founded upon, or grounded in absolute truth ... is 'about' something external to the knower, and can present itself objectively to the knower" (Lowe, 1991, p. 43). Perhaps the most significant aspect of this shift from a belief in facts to an awareness of perspectives is the degree to which our attention is now focused on discourse and the role of language.

Deconstruction and the Role of Language

Indeed, in the postmodern era the role of language has moved to center stage. That is, "Discourse has become a central concept, not only in postmodern thought, but in the general sphere of contemporary social and cultural theory" (Lowe, 1991, p. 44). In philosophy it was Wittgenstein (1963) who proposed that it is social practice rather than a referential base by means of which language acquires meaning and Foucault (1978, 1979) who explored the power of discourse, or culturally embedded bodies of language, to expand or oppress (Gergen, 1994). Rorty (1979) is also cited as having had a major influence through his "invitation to philosophers to abandon attempts at transcendent truth and to participate pragmatically in the broader dialogues of society" (Gergen, 1994, p. 413). Similar explorations in the fields of sociology, semiotics, literary deconstruction theory, communication theory, and psychology have characterized a large segment of intellectual inquiry for the past twenty years. The outcome of such inquiry is a warning against reifying the language of a community as true for anyone other than the members of that community and a focus on the limitations of local languages in terms of what they exclude.

For the postmodernist, language is understood as the means by which individuals come to know their world and in their knowing simultaneously to construct it. In the process, the idea of minds and objects as separate phenomena is *deconstructed*, or is shown to be self-referentially inconsistent. That is, a statement about the nature of things is demonstrated to depend upon assumptions which are denied by the statement in question (e.g., the "fact" of an unconscious). Considerable impetus to the deconstructionist movement has been provided by French theorist Derrida, who opposes "the presumption that words reflect the workings of the mind as it converts the surrounding chaos into logical order" (Gergen, 1991, p. 107). Rather, we are urged to consider that if we can only know reality via our perceptions, then that which we perceive is a function of our mental processes, or mind, and thus the two are inseparable. Therefore, rather than thinking of mind as something bounded by the skin of the individual, we accept the concept of a nonlocal mind which is universal and empowering of all creatures and things. Further, we experience and express our knowing through a system of language which has a separate existence. Accordingly, "Social constructionist inquiry is principally concerned with explicating the processes by which people come to describe, explain, or otherwise account for the world (including themselves) in which they live" (Gergen, 1985, p. 266).

Each of us is born into and assimilates preexisting forms of language in a culturally created linguistic system. In the process of socialization we learn to speak in accepted ways and simultaneously to adopt the shared values and ideology of our language system. Thus our words express the conventions, the symbols, the metaphors of our particular group and we cannot speak in a language separate from that of our community:

> *The terms in which the world is understood are social artifacts, products of historically situated interchanges among people. From the constructionist position the process of understanding is not automatically driven by the forces of nature, but is the result of an active, cooperative enterprise of persons in relationship. In this light, inquiry is invited into the historical and cultural bases of various forms of world construction. (Gergen, 1985, p. 267)*

Accordingly, for the postmodernist, the goal is to deconstruct "facts" by delineating the assumptions, values, and ideologies upon which they rest and to consider ourselves and our constructions about life and living with skepticism and even perhaps humor. As this posture is translated into therapy, a "healthy irreverence for all teachers and teachings" is advocated (Keeney, 1990, p. 5) along with respect for the uniqueness of the client. For example,

> *In our small world of therapy, it is the irreverent therapist's job to undermine those aspects of the clients' reality that are restricting them from making the changes they desire. The irreverent therapist is skeptical toward polarities, thereby affording himself freedom from both the passive position of, "I must not go and introduce an idea about how people change," and the strategic position of, "I've got to come up with a tactic." With irreverence the therapist introduces an idea but does not necessarily believe that people should follow it. (Cecchin, Lane, & Ray, 1992, p. 10)*

The postmodernist must also recognize that the self is not an isolated, autonomous being but rather is constructed in relationship: "In the postmodern world, selves may become the manifestations of relationships, thus placing relationships in the central position occupied by the individual self for the last several hundred years of Western history" (Gergen, 1991, p. 147). What is more, if we cannot know truth or reality in any objective sense, but can only evaluate from within a perspective, then the traditional Logical-Positivist scientific enterprise becomes suspect. No longer are we able to think of the outcomes of empirical research as representing the "real world," but rather we must consider the subjectivity of the researcher and the likelihood that we may produce only partial images that are more or less useful (Longino, 1990; Newmark & Beels, 1994). This latter issue is a primary focus of Chapter 15. For the present, however, let us return to the issue of the individual self.

The Role of the Individual

According to Gergen (1991, p. 251), in the postmodern era, "the individual is viewed as a participant in multiple relationships, with 'the problem' only a problem because of the way it is constructed in certain of these relations." That is, both the "self" and the "problems" which an individual may be experiencing take shape and have meaning only in the context of specific relationships and are expressed through the language of the consensual domain within which these relationships occur. Decontextualized individuals and problems are an impossibility (Minuchin, 1984), although the same society of which we are all a part often suggests otherwise (Watts, 1972), thereby creating a double-bind situation.

Within psychology, this view of the self-in-relationship, as well as the undermining of traditional science, has been protested strongly by Smith (1994), who sees Gergen's position as representing "fin de siécle hopelessness" (p. 405). In response, Gergen (1994) articulates his belief that rather than eradicating the self, the postmodernist stance brings with it the potential to enrich the self through accounts that acknowledge the "reality of relatedness" (p. 415). Within family therapy the possible loss of the individual through a relational focus has long been a concern and most recently has been addressed by Nichols (1987), Schwartz (1994), and Nichols and Schwartz (1995). For example, Nichols (1987, p. x.) writes:

> *The difference is that human beings interact on the basis of conscious and unconscious expectations of each other. However impossible it may be to understand people without considering their relationships, it is equally impossible to understand those relationships if we only think of external behavior without considering interior realities. At the heart of human experience is a central self, an "I," who feels, thinks, and acts—as well as interacts.*

In a manner consistent with postmodernist thinking, however, we must acknowledge with Watts (1972) the argument that "our most private thoughts and emotions are not actually our own. For we think in terms of languages and images which we did not invent, but which were given to us by society" (p. 64). We would also note that given the importance of each individual's perception from a social constructionist perspective, the self, though differently defined, gains in significance. Or, as Steinglass (1991) has indicated relative to family therapy, "Constructivist models, with their emphasis on differing individual perspectives of reality, have led to models of therapy that have underscored the importance of conversation, of co-construction of problems and proposed solutions, of respect for individual differences" (p. 268). Nevertheless, we anticipate that this debate will continue along with those regarding not only first-order versus second-order therapies but also the fit of postmodern thinking and cybernetics.

The Debates

With the shift by many theorists to an emphasis on constructionism and the creation of approaches more consistent with postmodernist thinking have come arguments about hierarchy, power, and the role of the therapist as well as about whether the espousal of either a first-order or a second-order approach requires the rejection of the other. A second debate revolves about whether postmodern thinking fits within the cybernetic paradigm or instead represents an anomaly outside this paradigm, and thus a new epistemology. Although a resolution of these issues may not be forthcoming in the near future, we believe it is important for you to hear some of the voices of those most overtly engaged in these debates. And we would caution you to be aware that from the systemic/cybernetic perspective, the proponents on either side of both issues make valid points and that neither side is necessarily right or wrong. Rather, all are offering their perspectives on some very complex issues. Further, it is possible that such conflicting perspectives may each be "true" for the speaker/writer based on the framework out of which she or he is operating.

First-Order versus Second-Order Therapy

Making reference to Varela's (Maturana & Varela, 1980) distinction between the first-order, allopoietic, control model and the second-order, autopoietic, autonomy model of living systems, Hoffman (1985) notes the prevalence of family therapy approaches consistent with the former model, approaches which are the subject of Chapters 7 through 12 and Chapter 14 in this book. Hoffman predicts a shift in the future to approaches consistent with the latter model, and thus having the following characteristics:

1. *An "observing system" stance and inclusion of the therapist's own context.*
2. *A collaborative rather than a hierarchical structure.*
3. *Goals that emphasize setting a context for change, not specifying a change.*
4. *Ways to guard against too much instrumentality.*
5. *A "circular" assessment of the problem.*
6. *A non-pejorative, non-judgmental view. (p. 395)*

According to Hoffman, second-order approaches that are more constructivist in nature, such as those of Boscolo and Cecchin, two of the members of the original Milan team, would enable the therapist to unhook from the position of power and control. However, Golann (1988a) responds that:

> *Despite the good intentions of such leading theorists as Boscolo, Cecchin, and Hoffman, constructivism and the observing-system stance have not yet led to a substantially less intrusive or hierarchical family therapy practice.... Although there may be some positive consequences from the introduction of constructivism into family practice and theory, one major negative consequence is the potential*

use of theory to rationalize or obscure the introduction of a disingenuous or mis-
guided form of therapist powerlessness into practice. Power obscured eventually
emerges—a therapeutic wolf clad as a second-order sheep. (p. 56)

While in response acknowledging the inevitability of influence, Hoffman (1988) advocates a stance which removes control as a central issue in therapy and removes the therapist as an "expert system." She believes that rather than providing strategies, interpretations, or suggestions for behavioral change, the therapist's job is to create a context for epistemological change. She also notes that in talking about second-order therapy she is not talking about second-order cybernetics: "By 'second-order' I am talking about changes in the premises that govern pieces of behavior, rather than change in the behaviors themselves. I don't think this kind of change can ever be directly imposed" (p. 66). Golann's (1988b) reply reiterates his concern about "the potential misuse of constructivism to rationalize or to obscure instances of disingenuous or naive therapist 'powerlessness'" (p. 68). We note that "although certainly valid, the fear that it may be inappropriately utilized is applicable to all theories and not specific to constructivism" (Becvar & Becvar, 1993, p. 54).

Similarly, Atkinson and Heath (1990a) write that "any existing family therapy model can be applied in a way that is or is not consistent with the implications of second-order cybernetics" (p. 154). These authors believe it to be appropriate for therapists to continue to draw upon the more pragmatic, first-order models as long as they do not become too attached to clients' acceptance of their suggestions and interventions. Thus "willful determination" to change must be addressed by therapists even as therapists must address this issue with their clients.

Simon (1992) criticizes the debate over first-order and second-order therapies, which he considers to have been overemphasized in the literature. He proposes a both-and, dialectical perspective whereby one may have "a second-order mind while doing first-order therapy." His conclusion is that:

Language is productive of social organization. As a result, if the family therapy
field evolves over the next several years in the direction of increasing polarization
between the first- and second-order perspectives on the therapeutic enterprise, it
will be because family therapists have chosen to speak the language of either-or
rather than the language of both-and. (p. 386)

To speak in terms of either-or, as you now know, is inconsistent with the systemic/cybernetic perspective. Further, while we as systemic "purists" find operating with a second-order mind to be a more respectful and appropriate choice, we are cognizant not only of the fact that the pragmatics of the first-order therapies can inform our practice in a useful way, but also that we, most of our clients, and many other professionals dwell in a first-order world. If we are to work meaningfully within this world, at the very least we must understand it, and at best we can retain that which has served us well in the past. Similarly, we believe a constructionist perspective is consistent with the world view of cybernetics of cybernetics, although this too has become the subject of much debate.

Postmodernism and Cybernetics

Indeed, the debate about first-order therapy versus second-order therapy also includes a discussion of the appropriateness of the cybernetic perspective as well as its fit with postmodernism and social constructionism. As articulated by Anderson and Goolishian (1990) in their response to Atkinson and Heath (1990a), "We believe, as we think Bateson later did, that the language of cybernetics is not appropriate or sufficient to deal with the issues of human systems and therapists' work with them" (159). It is the conclusion of Anderson and Goolishian that the polarizing issues around the use of power, intervention, and change are implicit in a cybernetic epistemology, which rests on an assumption of mechanical control. They prefer a "'post-cybernetic' interest in human meaning, narrative, and story" (p.161) to make up for what they perceive as the inability of cybernetics to understand humans in their cultural and relational contexts or to describe them relative to their ability to make meaning and act accordingly:

> For us, psychotherapy is in a conversational domain, and the art of psychotherapy is a conversational art. The theoretical base that informs and develops the vocabulary of understanding for therapy should reflect this position. Our thesis is that a clinically responsible and effective position can evolve from a science of narrative and semantics. (p. 161)

Atkinson and Heath (1990b) disagree, noting that a cybernetic epistemology requires awareness of the limits to certainty given the inevitability of self-reference, acknowledges the interaction of ideas and the appropriateness of dialogue, and challenges the use of conscious control.

Hoffman, having stated (1990) that she, along with Anderson and Goolishian, believes that the systemic cybernetic paradigm has run its course, indicates (1992) "a preference for a mutually influenced process between consultant and inquirer" (p. 127) and opts for an "ethic of participation" (p. 22).

Our bias is that the idea of control is inconsistent with the perspective of cybernetics of cybernetics within which influence is understood to be mutual and responsibility is seen as a shared or bilateral process. Indeed, to us the ethic of participation and the epistemology of participation define very similar stances. Further, given the assumption of subjectivity, with reality being understood as perceptually constructed or created, we see the postmodernist, social constructionist stance as logically consistent with the systemic/cybernetic paradigm. Also consistent are both the focus on context and the importance of communication. Indeed, an understanding of context requires an exploration of individual perceptions and meanings, as well as a consideration of the ecology of ideas and the larger social system within which relationships are embedded. Our focus is relational; we understand that all behavior has communication value and that communication and information processing are basic systemic processes. We believe that to the extent that family therapy approaches fail to be consistent with such assumptions, they are lacking in systemic consistency. Moreover, while the emphasis may shift, we see cybernetics of cybernetics as a world view consistent with that of postmodernism and social constructionism. Such a world view, however, is not without its challenges, especially as we attempt to translate it into clinical practice.

The Challenge of Second-Order Therapy

It has been said that in the postmodern era, therapy practices must be discourse-sensitive, both to ongoing conversation and to culturally established forms of speaking (Lowe, 1991). Therapists thus focus in a self-critical manner upon the use of language and its impact. The goal is a more humane and a more socially and politically sensitive understanding of families and of therapy as one becomes aware of those discourses which are and are not "privileged." Despite such aspirations, however, there remain several challenges to those who would espouse such a stance.

Constructionism as a clinical theory has been challenged (Held & Pols, 1987; Held, 1990) as being self-referentially inconsistent. That is, if the only thing we can describe is an approximation of reality, we cannot make claims about how things "really" are, either for clients or for therapists. More recently, Amundson (1994) has written that "there is an emerging danger that postmodernist narrative clinical practice is being sent up the modernist river" (p. 83), and therapists are advised to beware of assuming certainty with the creation of our new stories about therapy. Similarly, Lowe (1991) warns against the creation of a family therapy scenario in which

> therapists would be cast as Experts on postmodernism, and Master deconstructionists, editors, conversationalists and story-tellers. All kinds and levels of human experience would be reduced to abstract conceptions of 'conversation' and 'discourse' which would become 'natural' foundational terms for a new form of universal knowledge. (p. 51)

However, these seem to us to be problems of application, for if one assumes constructivism as an ontological position rather than using it as a clinical theory to describe what is going on in an absolute sense, one recognizes that any theory is at best a story whose ultimate truth can never be known.

Another challenge, according to Gergen (1991, p. 251), with which the therapist may be faced is that of facilitating:

> renegotiation of the meaning system within which "the problem" exists. The therapist actively enters dialogue with those who maintain the problem definition, not as a clairvoyant, but as a coparticipant in the construction of new realities. The

emphasis may be placed on new narratives, and metaphors for understanding one's life and improving skills for negotiating meaning.

Indeed, Tom Andersen (1993), one of the first to operate out of a constructionist perspective and a strong adherent of the collaborative, conversational approach, acknowledges, "What I myself found important, but extremely difficult, to do was to try to listen to what clients say instead of making up meanings about what they say. Just listen to what they say" (p. 321). Thus, the focus returns to the level of process.

That is, at the level of process, we must observe *what* is going on and *how* we are behaving. In terms of our therapy practice, we must consistently ask ourselves whether or not we believe that we offer truth to our clients and we must guard against the seduction of certainty. We must consider whether or not we are behaving in a manner that is consistent with what it is we say we believe and avoid portraying ourselves as experts. We must also avoid pathologizing language and must be sensitive to the impact of discourse at many levels. We must be aware of the larger social context and its influence on both our clients and ourselves. We must consider what we are communicating, both by what we say and by what we don't say, what we do and what we don't do. We must be respectful of our clients, of their stories, and of the meanings which their stories have for them. Finally, we must recognize the limits of what we can know. For the reality created by social constructionism and postmodernism is that there is no reality that we can know for sure. Or, in the words of Watzlawick (1984, p. 326):

["What reality is constructed by constructivism itself?"] is a fundamentally wrong question. But we also see that this mistake had to be committed in order to reveal itself as a mistake. Constructivism does not create or explain any reality "out there"; it shows the subjective, rather, it shows that the subject-object split, that source of myriads of "realities," does not exist, that the apparent separation of the world into pairs of opposites is constructed by the subject, and that paradox opens the way into autonomy.

Summary

In this chapter we have considered some of the most recent developments and debates impacting upon and characteristic of the family therapy field as well as of the Western intellectual tradition. Some of society's most basic values and assumptions have been called into question with the emergence of postmodernism and social constructionism. Accordingly, science and the scientific endeavor focused on discovering and disseminating truth is being critiqued from a perspective which underscores the role of mind in all meaning-making. Of central importance is language, which is understood to be a socially constructed system and which, through dominant and privileged discourses, empowers some and oppresses others. As the impact of this perspective has been experienced among family therapists, debates have ensued regarding the appropriateness of therapy at a first-order, pragmatic level versus a second-order, aesthetic level, versus a combination of the two. Also debated is the fit of postmodernism and social constructionism with the systemic/cybernetic paradigm. We conclude with a consideration of the challenges presented by postmodernism and social constructionism as the assumptions of this stance are translated into clinical practice. Accordingly therapists are cautioned to be wary of an expert posture, to operate out of a more respectful, ethical stance, and to acknowledge the limits of what can be known. In the following chapter we will look more closely at the theory of change consistent with the systemic/cybernetic paradigm. We will also consider the ramifications of postmodernism and social constructionism vis-à-vis specific techniques and interventions. And finally, we will consider ethical behavior and codes of ethics from both first-order and second-order perspectives.

Chapter *5*

Therapeutic Intervention and Strategies

Like the theory of systems/cybernetics, the theory of change consistent with this perspective is based on the same basic assumptions. Thus, although some of the things you will read may be different and therefore challenging, we doubt that you will experience this difference with as much discomfort as you may have felt in Chapter 3. We might compare the next part of our journey with a road trip from one state to another within the same country. Despite the fact that you might never have been to this state before, you will find some of the same stores, restaurants, and so on, which are part of national chains, and thus you will quickly begin to feel right at home. So this time we invite you to relax and enjoy the ride.

A Theory of Change

The theory of change we are about to describe was delineated in the 1974 book by Paul Watzlawick, John Weakland, and Richard Fisch entitled *Change* and subtitled *Principles of Problem Formation and Problem Resolution*. It is important for you to be aware that, according to these authors, understanding how to solve problems also requires understanding how problems are created and maintained. It is their belief that, ultimately, the attempted solution becomes the problem and that it is this so-called solution that must be changed if the problem is to be solved.

First, change can either be first-order or second-order in nature. *First-order change* is a difference that occurs within the system, according to the rules of that system. *Second-order change*, on the other hand, involves a change in the rules of the system and thus in the system itself. The classic illustration of the difference between these two types of change is provided by the nine-dot problem, as illustrated in Figure 5.1. The only instruction for this problem is that you connect the nine dots

FIGURE 5-1   Nine-Dot Problem

with four straight lines without lifting your pencil from the paper. Before looking ahead to the solution, we would like you to try this exercise. Were you successful? If you were not, you were certainly not alone. Now let's see if we can explain the dimensions of the problem.

First attempts at solution usually bog down in the assumption (implicit rule) that the nine dots form a square. However, all attempts to find a solution by following this rule and staying within the square are examples of first-order change solutions, and in this instance they are doomed to failure. By contrast, as soon as one changes the rule to allow for the possibility of drawing lines extending beyond the square, solution is possible and second-order change has occurred, as illustrated in Figure 5.2.

Change from the perspective of systems theory requires a change in context. Such a change in the rules of the game, as illustrated above by the move from an assumption of square to an assumption of not-square, is what we mean by a *change in context*. By changing the rules we change our perception, or the way we view the problem, and new behavioral alternatives become possible in the process. By seeing the nine dots differently, we can allow our pencil to go outside the perceived square and solve the problem.

Second-order change has been compared to the leap of imagination experienced in moments of creativity. It requires a response that is illogical to context, paradoxical, or crazy when considered within the framework of the existing rules. While not all change needs to be of the second-order variety in order to be effective, there are many instances in which it offers the only hope of solution:

> *A system which may run through all its possible internal changes (no matter how many there are) without effecting a systemic change, i.e., second-order change, is said to be caught in a Game Without End. It cannot generate from within itself the conditions for its own change; it cannot produce the rules for the change of its own rules. (Watzlawick, Weakland, & Fisch, 1974, p. 22)*

First-order change is what we think of as the logical solutions to problems. For example, it is logical to turn up the heat inside when it gets colder outside (less heat plus more heat equals comfort). Similarly, it is logical to turn on a light when it gets dark (less light plus more light equals visibility). In both situations the problem is solved by doing the opposite of what has occurred. However, while these examples demonstrate the effectiveness of logical, first-order change, in many other instances change at this level does not produce the desired effect because the opposite equals more of the same.

To illustrate the notion that the opposite is more of the same, let's think of a couple, Susie and Harry, who are having a heated argument. At first they just disagree. Pretty soon the disagreement escalates into a shouting match, with Susie yelling at Harry and Harry yelling at Susie. But yelling back at someone who is yelling at you probably will not solve the problem at hand. So, Susie decides to switch tactics and ignore Harry. However, ignoring the other person, who is still doing the yelling, is an opposite behavior and probably will not solve the problem either. In fact, it may make the problem worse, for ignoring is just a quieter way of yelling and is an attempt at unilateral control of a bilateral relationship. Susie and Harry are stuck in the mud and the more they spin their wheels, the deeper they go. In this case, the attempted solutions have become problematic and second-order change is necessary if they are going to break out of their impasse, or get out of the mud.

The focus now shifts to the attempted solutions and to the consideration that a change in context is needed—an illogical response to the hostile context that defines Harry and Susie as yeller-yeller or yeller-ignorer. Such an illogical response, by definition, would allow new behaviors to occur inasmuch as it is part of a new frame that redefines the context. If Harry responds to Susie's yelling or ignoring by standing on his head, the rules of the game are immediately changed and the pattern within which the yelling is maintained is broken. Standing on his head is logical in a context of silliness, and thus the context of hostility is redefined. Indeed, as soon as Harry behaves in such an apparently crazy manner, Susie will probably not be able to continue to yell or ignore for very long. She will probably begin to respond to Harry in a different manner, possibly by laughing, just as he responded differently to her.

The keys to understanding problem formation and resolution, therefore, are the awareness of the reciprocal nature of behavior, the importance of the context that defines behavior and in which particular behaviors have meaning, and thus (once again), the significance of process. It does not matter *what* Susie and Harry were arguing about—the *content* of their argument is unimportant. Given the notion of equifinality, we can be pretty certain that regardless of the topic, whenever they get into the kind of "game without end" we described, the pattern repeats and the problem is not solved. Indeed, what matters at this point is *how* they are fighting—the *process*. Thus, what they need is a change in the rules so that solution is possible, for changing the context equals changing the rules.

Perhaps another illustration will help you to understand better the change process we are describing here. This time we shall refer to an example provided by the creative genius of Albert Einstein. Einstein, with his so-called beginner's mind, redefined problems that had been puzzling physicists for decades and in so doing created the theory of relativity. Typical of what was obviously a much

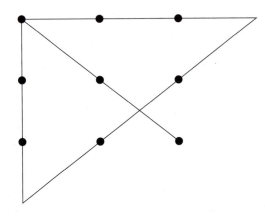

FIGURE 5-2   Nine-Dot Problem Solution

more complicated process was his handling of the question as to how the speed of light could always be 186,000 miles per second regardless of the observer's state of motion:

> *In an ingenious mental turnaround, Einstein turned this puzzle into a postulate! Instead of worrying for the moment about how it can happen, he simply accepted the experimentally irrefutable fact that it does happen. This evident (to us) recognition of the obvious was the first step in a logical process, which, once set in motion was to explain not only the puzzle of the constant speed of light, but a great deal more. (Zukav, 1980, p. 135)*

While none of us may possess the genius of an Einstein, we do have the potential to be equally creative in our response to problems that require second-order solutions. Probably all of us have experienced the success of this kind of action at one time or another without having been aware of the principles underlying our behavioral strategy. Indeed, Watzlawick, Weakland, and Fisch created their theory of change after studying, in an effort to explain, the success of such creative therapists as Milton Erickson and Virginia Satir. The result was the delineation of the process according to which problems are created and maintained and thus may be solved. Whether problems appear unsolvable because we deny their existence, because we attempt solutions at the wrong level, or because no solution is possible, how we perceive and define the problem (the context) is the focus of change.

Reframing

The change in perception that characterizes the Gestalt switch from, for example, seeing a square to seeing a not-square has been defined as a *reframe* (Watzlawick, Weakland, & Fisch, 1974). Indeed, the technique of reframing underlies the use of paradox so often equated with family therapy. However, while reframing may be a relatively new label, the process to which it refers certainly is not.

A reframe takes a situation and lifts it out of its old context (set of rules) and places it in a new context (set of rules) that defines it equally as well. However, this new context offers an alternative understanding, or new meaning, to which new and different responses are logical and thus possible. For example, a brother and sister are constantly fighting. The parents are worried about sibling rivalry and its possible deleterious effects. They have attempted to stop the fighting by separating the pair, by lecturing them both separately and together, and by various punishments, but the fighting continues and the parents' concerns increase. All of the parents' attempted solutions are of the first-order variety and they are not working. They are a function of the fact that the parents are defining the fighting as a problem. On the other hand, the therapist may define the fighting to the parents as normal sibling behavior and ask them to allow it to occur. If the children perceive a decrease of concern, and hence attention, on the part of their parents when they fight, some of the fun may go out of the fighting and it is likely to decrease. Similarly, to the children, the therapist may reframe the fighting as loving behavior: "Did you know that every time your sister hits you she is really trying to let you know how much she loves you?" or "We all know that at your ages it is not 'cool' for brothers and sisters to hug each other, so instead they hit. But this is really their way of saying how much they like each other." All of these are examples of reframes.

The key to successful reframing, however, is to provide a new frame for the situation that is acceptable to the clients. Thus, the therapist needs to have a good sense of the world view according to which the clients are currently operating. The therapist must then present the reframe in terms that make sense to the client and are believable by the clients. Defining the children's fighting as normal will only be effective if it fits the circumstances of the situation and is couched in language consistent with the parents' frames of reference. Similarly, the children would need to be able to accept a definition of their behavior as loving. If they do, however, new actions consistent with the new meaning may replace the old behaviors, and it will be very difficult for them to operate according to their previous perceptions.

The process involved here is the creation of reality as we perceive/define it. This means that we categorize objects and events into classes of action with particular meanings. Once we assign an object or event to such a class, it is extremely difficult to see it belonging to another class, and thus as having a different meaning. Reframing, on the other hand, changes the class of the object or event:

> *What makes reframing such an effective tool of change is that once we do perceive the alternative class membership(s) we cannot so easily go back to the trap and the anguish of the former view of "reality." Once somebody has explained to us the solution of the nine-dot problem, it is almost impossible to revert to our previous helplessness and especially our original hopelessness about the possibility of a solution. (Watzlawick, Weakland, & Fisch, 1974, p. 99)*

Paradoxical Interventions

Like reframing, a *paradoxical intervention* is also an example of second-order change. Indeed, it operates exactly like the reframe inasmuch as it redefines the context, thus changing the meaning of a situation and opening up new behavioral alternatives. The classic example of a paradoxical intervention is prescribing the symptom. That is, rather than telling a depressed person to cheer up (a logical first-order response), we tell that person he or she obviously needs to be depressed and should certainly not try to change (a "crazy" second-order response). In the former instance, the command to cheer up is consistent with a context whose implicit rule is that feeling bad is not O.K. The dilemma, however, is that feelings are not something we can control. Rather, feelings occur spontaneously, and to tell someone to do consciously what can only be done spontaneously is to put the person in a "be spontaneous" paradox—a double bind. In addition to feeling bad, that person probably will also feel guilty about feeling bad—a double whammy. Our well-intentioned, commonsense effort to help has not only helped to maintain the problem, but it may also have helped to make it worse. On the other hand, the therapeutic paradox of giving the depressed person permission to feel depressed redefines the context as one in which the implicit rule is that feeling bad is O. K. Once one is freed up to feel what one is feeling, and thus stop fighting what is happening, spontaneous remission of the problem is more likely to occur. If the depression lifts, then we may say that second-order change has taken place.

A more familiar illustration concerns the dilemma of insomnia. Perhaps you have had trouble sleeping. Usually when this happens, the more you try to fall asleep the wider awake you become. Just as in the above example, you have put yourself in a "be spontaneous" paradox. If you can't sleep, we recommend that you try to stay awake. This reframe of the situation will allow you to do other things. And even though you may know exactly what is happening, in the course of doing other things you will probably get sleepy and the problem will solve itself. If such is the case, once again second-order change has occurred.

Problem Formation/Resolution

As we think about the business of problem formation/resolution, we are often reminded of a well-known dictum: "If men define situations as real, they are real in their consequences" (Thomas & Thomas, 1928, p. 572). Similarly, according to Maturana (Efran & Lukens, 1985), problems occur in the process of naming a situation a problem. Until a problem is perceived as such and is so labeled, there is no such thing as a problem. Thus, like a system, a problem exists only in the eye of the beholder. Further,

> *the form of a problem—the domain in which it exists—determines the form of its "cure." The phrasing of a question establishes the kinds of answers that can be formulated. When "reframing" proves effective, it may be because the domain in*

which the problem occurs has shifted, and new answers become available and acceptable. (Efran & Lukens, 1985, p. 28)

Or, in the words of Alan Watts (1972), p. 55): "Problems that remain persistently insoluble should always be suspected as questions asked in the wrong way." Maturana (Efran & Lukens, 1985) also points out that a problem only exists for the person who is speaking about it. Thus, while a parent may label a child as a problem, the person with the problem is the parent and not the child. What is more, to speak of family problems is epistemologically problematic. A family cannot talk and therefore cannot label something as a problem. Rather, each member of a family may define a particular issue as problematic. In this case, while action may occur simultaneously, each person has a problem and will interact around the issue in unique ways. System change is therefore a function of changes in individuals as they change their perceptions and thus their interactions around particular issues.

Stochastic Processes

From a systems perspective, change is said to occur in a *stochastic,* or partially random, manner. While the context may change, thereby defining new behaviors as logical responses, one cannot predict the exact nature of these responses. Given that systems are structurally determined, and that all behavioral responses are understood as instances of negative feedback or system-maintaining responses at the level of autonomy, there is a limit to the number of behaviors possible. However, one cannot know in advance which particular behavior will be selected relative to a particular change in context. In the words of Paul Dell (1980):

> *The "pattern which connects" is not accessible to conscious design; it may only be impacted upon in stochastic fashion. That is, one can only intervene at the level of objects and thereby bring about a change in the pattern, but the exact nature of the change can be neither predicted nor designed. In short, patterns can be changed by disrupting them, but they cannot be sculpted to a planned design. (p. 329)*

Perturber versus Change Agent

Finally, just as we cannot speak to a family, we cannot join it nor do we treat it or change it. Rather, by virtue of our presence we help define a new context and thus a new family within which the members behave differently. When a client system chooses to enter into a therapeutic relationship with us, we may consider that we "have been invited to co-drift with members of families" (Efran & Lukens, 1985, p. 74) rather than thinking of ourselves as change agents. Our goal is to perturb the system in such a way that it compensates in more functional behaviors for the system. In other words, we must provide new information, which the system may choose to incorporate into a self-corrective process that at the same time facilitates self-maintenance. We do this, according to Keeney (1983), by creating meaningful noise in a context of both stability and change.

Meaningful Noise

We would like to introduce this section with the following statement made by Varela (1981):

> *A key idea of this period is the extension of the Shannonian theory to characterize self-organization, in the now well-known principle of order-from-noise, where noise is capable of increasing the redundancy. . . . This increase can be understood by noting the many ways in which the components of the system will "select" those perturbations from ambient noise which contribute to increase in order of the system. (p. xii)*

To begin the process of teasing apart the meaning of Varela's message, we note that the system must have something new to draw upon, a source of the random, in order to behave in new ways or to create alternative structures. When clients come into therapy, it is safe to assume that they are stuck, that they have run through all the solutions available to them given their current frames of reference. What they need is new information that will allow them to see things differently and thus behave differently. The new information the therapist provides is the so-called noise referred to in the quote from Varela. However, this noise must be meaningful. That is, it must be couched in the clients' language and must fit their world view.

Language and World Views

As we said when describing reframes, the clients must be able to accept what we are saying. They must also assume that there is meaning to be found, for the "search for meaning will then generate new structure and pattern" (Keeney, 1983, p. 170). The creation and presentation of meaningful noise requires that the therapist understand the clients' world view and be able to speak in the clients' language. This means having an awareness of the metaphors according to which clients operate. For example, if we are working with a computer programmer, what we say will be more easily understood and more readily accepted if we are able to phrase it in the language of writing programs, systems runaway, and other computer terms. Thus, how we say something (the process) is once again more important than what we say (the content).

Stability and Change

The new information, or meaningful noise, must also be presented in such a way that it acknowledges both stability and change. That is, when clients come into therapy they are simultaneously requesting that the therapist change them and that the therapist allow them to remain the same. We like to think of this as a push me—pull you situation which may be defined as follows: even though none of us particularly likes having problems, at least we are familiar with the problems we have. There is a certain security in problems in terms of the predictability of our behavior relative to them. On the other hand, change equals the unknown, and the unknown is frightening in terms of its lack of both predictability and familiarity. At the same time that we, or our clients, may be requesting change, there is usually a second, although not conscious, message of "Don't change me." The therapist's task, therefore, becomes one of responding in such a manner that both requests are acknowledged.

The process involved is that of the change of change defined in the previous section as second-order change. The system needs to change how it changes in order to remain stable. The therapist helps to provide a context in which this can happen, presenting information in such a way that the client can find meaning in it and thereby create and perceive a new reality. In addition, the requirements of the system for both stability and change must be affirmed in the process.

To illustrate, we often delineate a set of alternative behaviors clients might try, which we feel might be useful ways to deal with problematic situations. After a rather lengthy description and acknowledgment by the clients that these probably would be effective solutions, we then request that the clients not try to implement them just yet. We provide a rationale that suggests that although we know they don't like the problem, it did not develop overnight. We state that change is difficult, that it needs to be undertaken slowly, and that probably they are not ready for it just yet. We therefore ask that, at least for the time being, they remain exactly as they are and keep their problem for a little while longer.

This approach provides a response to the double request for stability and change while also offering new information. We have met the criteria for the presentation of meaningful noise. You might also recognize this strategy as a paradoxical intervention inasmuch as we have asked the clients to have the problem they have asked us to fix.

We have also kept in mind the logic of problem formation and resolution from a systemic/cybernetic perspective. That is, all symptoms are understood as logical to context—there is a way in which the problem makes sense and is being maintained. The efforts at change are part of the stability of the system, and the system needs to maintain its stability as it changes how it changes. Only the system can do this. A system corrects itself and therapy merely provides a context in which this self-corrective process is facilitated. Thus, even though clients may come in looking for answers and solutions, and while we may phrase our suggestions in such terms, we are aware that the most we can provide is new information. This involves a constant recursive process of responding, learning, feedback, and adaptation on the part of the therapist as well as the clients.

Information and Perturbation

As the therapist perturbs and the client responds, the therapist is also being provided with information that allows for self-correction in terms of their joint interaction. Indeed, therapists do not make "mistakes," nor can client behaviors be considered "mistakes." Information may be accepted or not, but what doesn't happen provides as much information as what does happen. Every piece of rejected information enables the therapist to narrow the range of possible acceptable alternatives. Therefore, every so-called mistake becomes a therapeutic opportunity in which the therapist/client system evolves a relationship within which a context is defined such that the problem behavior/maintaining responses are no longer logical.

If clients decide to ignore our instruction and try out some new behaviors, we have information that they are ready to change. We also learn which of our suggestions they chose to implement, which they chose not to implement, and how well what they tried worked. Even though we were *wrong* in their eyes about their not being ready to change, we were *right* to the extent that they thought our suggestions were good enough to try. If what they tried worked, so much the better. If what they tried didn't work, we were right in that they were probably not ready to change just yet. In this last instance, however, while we may say that to our clients, we also need to be aware that how we are interacting must be changed if change is going to occur. This is the same information we have if the clients decide to follow our instructions and keep the problem. That is, we have feedback that indicates meaningful noise was not perceived; we will need to alter our strategy if we are going to help define a context that facilitates self-correction. This is the same process the clients will mirror as they perceive meaningful noise and alter their structure relative to their changed perceptions.

Key concepts in our discussion to this point include the following:

1. Second-order change equals a change in context, or in the rules of the system.
2. A change in context is facilitated through a change in perception, or the way a problem is viewed.
3. It is the context which defines behavior and in which particular behaviors have meaning.
4. Reframing takes a situation and lifts it out of its old context and places it in a new context which defines it equally as well but offers new meaning and thus provides new behavioral alternatives.
5. Problems and solutions evolve in the context of relationships, which are reciprocal in nature.
6. Systems change themselves as a function of individuals as they change their perceptions.
7. The role of therapy is to provide a context within which change may be facilitated.
8. The role of the therapist is to be a perturber by providing meaningful noise.
9. Meaningful noise refers to a source of the random that is acceptable to the client and acknowledges both stability and change.
10. In order to provide meaningful noise, the therapist must understand the client's world view, be sensitive to the client's metaphors, and be able to speak the client's language.

These concepts define a process which has been translated into practice in many different ways, as exemplified by the approaches described in Part Two of this book. However, as you will become aware, most of the earlier approaches (Chapters 7 through 12 and Chapter 14) are more consistent with the perspective of simple cybernetics and thus may be seen as falling into the category of first-order therapy. Although the development of approaches consistent with cybernetics of cybernetics, or second-order therapy (Chapter 13), is still in its early stages, we believe the above process also describes clinical work characteristic of postmodernist, social constructionist clinical practice.

The Theory of Change, Meaningful Noise, and the Postmodernist/Social Constructionist Perspective

As described in Chapter 4, social constructionists emphasize the role of language in the context of social interaction. It is through language that we both assimilate and influence our world as it is expressed in cultural norms and values. It is in language that we perceive, make meaning, and thus create our reality. And it is by means of language that client and therapist share stories in an ongoing, reciprocal conversation, the outcome of which is a narrative authored by all participants. Therapy is thus a collaborative process in which everyone is an expert and no one has the "Truth." The therapeutic dialogue has a here-and-now focus in which understanding is always evolving and continues to emerge in the context of conversational questioning. Respect and sensitivity are of primary importance as therapists look for unique outcomes (White & Epston, 1990) and/or are solution-focused (deShazer, 1985, 1988). Accordingly, change in the client's context is facilitated as "the therapist challenges the coherence of the reflexive circle between beliefs and actions (constructions) and when the therapist takes a different point of view" (Fruggeri, 1992, p. 51). Thus the meaning system which underlies behavior is changed through a focus on language.

Translated into the theory of change described and summarized above, we would say that second-order change is facilitated as therapist and client co-create a new context in which old, problem-saturated stories are deconstructed and new, solution-focused stories are authored by client and therapist through mutual interaction and feedback. This occurs in the process of respectful dialogue in which situations may be perceived differently and thus are reframed. That is, "I find it most useful here to think in terms of shifting the discourse in which the client is currently engaged to another discourse in which the problem does not exist" (Lax, 1992, p. 74). Rather than attempting to change the system, the therapist offers perturbations by means of questions and comments. Ideally, therapy is thus a conversation experienced by the client as meaningful and productive of new possibilities for the future, or new behavioral alternatives.

While we have defined the process of change and the creation of meaningful noise and have also provided a brief description of this process as it relates to postmodernist, social constructionist, narrative clinical practice, perhaps you are wondering where else to go for the content of therapy. The answer to this question is surprisingly simple: almost anywhere. We may feel free to draw on many of the techniques delineated by the vast array of intrapsychic theories and therapies as well as on those outlined by the various schools of family therapy. The difference is that the former must be translated into a systemic framework, while, to greater or lesser degrees, in the latter case this has already been done. Given the metaperspective provided by systems theory, we have a framework, or skeleton, whose bones may be fleshed out in whatever way we choose. Given the fact that both/and rather than either/or thinking is consistent with this perspective, we do not need to eliminate linear thinking and strategies consistent with a linear perspective from our behavioral repertoire. An important proviso, however, is the necessity for an awareness of the recursive/feedback process within which our behaviors are imbedded and relative to which our reality is perceived/created. Another important proviso concerns an awareness of the ethical issues relative to a systemic/cybernetic framework.

Ethical Issues

For several reasons, we have chosen to include our discussion of ethics at this point in our journey. First of all, ethical issues arise in the context of therapy and the facilitation of change, and they exist regardless of one's particular approach or style. Secondly, when operating out of a systemic/cybernetic epistemology, a whole new set of ethical issues emerges. And third, as noted previously, a defining characteristic of therapy consistent with the assumptions of postmodernism and social constructionism is its emphasis on ethics. Awareness of these issues, therefore, is central both to a complete understanding and to increasing the potential for operating in a logically consistent manner. We therefore feel that the topic is too important to be relegated to the back of the book, where it may be perceived as an afterthought, or worse, overlooked.

In August 1991 The American Association for Marriage and Family Therapy (AAMFT) published its revised AAMFT Code of Ethics. Like much of the practice of therapy, this code deals primarily with pragmatic issues at the level of simple cybernetics. Indeed, it is not markedly different from the standards of ethical conduct of other professional groups, each of which has its own code of ethics. A commonality exists across these codes inasmuch as they are built on similar assumptions and are concerned with similar issues related to the nature of therapy. Because of our belief in its importance, however, we present the AAMFT code to you in its entirety.

AAMFT Code of Ethics

The Board of Directors of the American Association for Marriage and Family Therapy (AAMFT) hereby promulgates, pursuant to Article 2, Section 2.013 of the Association's Bylaws, the Revised AAMFT Code of Ethics, effective August 1, 1991.

The AAMFT Code of Ethics is binding on Members of AAMFT in all membership categories, AAMFT Approved Supervisors, and applicants for membership and the Approved Supervisor designation (hereafter, AAMFT Member).

If an AAMFT Member resigns in anticipation of, or during the course of an ethics investigation, the Ethics Committee will complete its investigation. Any publication of action taken by the Association will include the fact that the Member attempted to resign during the investigation.

Marriage and family therapists are strongly encouraged to report alleged unethical behavior of colleagues to appropriate professional associations and state regulatory bodies.

1. RESPONSIBILITY TO CLIENTS

Marriage and family therapists advance the welfare of families and individuals. They respect the rights of those persons seeking their assistance, and make reasonable efforts to ensure that their services are used appropriately.

1.1   Marriage and family therapists do not discriminate against or refuse professional service to anyone on the basis of race, gender, religion, national origin, or sexual orientation.

1.2   Marriage and family therapists are aware of their influential position with respect to clients, and they avoid exploiting the trust and dependency of such persons. Therapists, therefore, make every effort to avoid dual relationships with clients that could impair professional judgment or increase the risk of exploitation. When a dual relationship cannot be avoided, therapists take appropriate professional precautions to ensure judgment is not impaired and no exploitation occurs. Examples of such dual relationships include, but are not limited to, business or close personal relationships with clients. Sexual intimacy with clients is prohibited. Sexual intimacy with former clients for two years following the termination of therapy is prohibited.

1.3   Marriage and family therapists do not use their professional relationships with clients to further their own interests.

1.4   Marriage and family therapists respect the right of clients to make decisions and help them to understand the consequences of these decisions. Therapists clearly advise a client that a decision on marital status is the responsibility of the client.

1.5   Marriage and family therapists continue therapeutic relationships only so long as it is reasonably clear that clients are benefiting from the relationship.

1.6   Marriage and family therapists assist persons in obtaining other therapeutic services if the therapist is unable or unwilling, for appropriate reasons, to provide professional help.

1.7   Marriage and family therapists do not abandon or neglect clients in treatment without making reasonable arrangements for the continuation of such treatment.

1.8   Marriage and family therapists obtain written informed consent from clients before videotaping, audiorecording, or permitting third party observation.

2. CONFIDENTIALITY

Marriage and family therapists have unique confidentiality concerns because the client in a therapeutic relationship may be more than one person. Therapists respect and guard confidences of each individual client.

2.1   Marriage and family therapists may not disclose client confidences except: (a) as mandated by law; (b) to prevent a clear and immediate danger to a person or persons; (c) where the therapist is a defendant in a civil, criminal, or disciplinary action arising from the therapy (in which case client confidences may be disclosed only in the course of that action); or (d) if there is a waiver previously obtained in writing, and then such information may be revealed only in accordance with the terms of the waiver. In circumstances where more than one person in a family receives therapy, each such family member who is legally competent to execute a waiver must agree to the waiver required by subparagraph (d). Without such a waiver from each family member legally competent to execute a waiver, a therapist cannot disclose information received from any family member.

2.2   Marriage and family therapists use client and/or clinical materials in teaching, writing, and public presentations only if a written waiver has been obtained in accordance with Subprinciple 2.1(d), or when appropriate steps have been taken to protect client identity and confidentiality.

2.3   Marriage and family therapists store or dispose of client records in ways that maintain confidentiality.

3. PROFESSIONAL COMPETENCE AND INTEGRITY

Marriage and family therapists maintain high standards of professional competence and integrity.

3.1   Marriage and family therapists are in violation of this Code and subject to termination of membership or other appropriate action if they: (a) are convicted of any felony; (b) are convicted of a misdemeanor related to their qualifications or functions; (c) engage in conduct which could lead to conviction of a felony, or a misdemeanor related to their qualifications or functions; (d) are expelled from or disciplined by other professional organizations; (e) have their licenses or certificates suspended or revoked or are otherwise disciplined by regulatory bodies; (f) are no longer competent to practice marriage and family therapy because they are impaired due to physical or mental causes or the abuse of alcohol or other substances; or (g) fail to cooperate with the Association at any point from the inception of an ethical complaint through the completion of all proceedings regarding that complaint.

3.2   Marriage and family therapists seek appropriate professional assistance for their personal problems or conflicts that may impair work performance or clinical judgment.

3.3   Marriage and family therapists, as teachers, supervisors, and researchers, are dedicated to high standards of scholarship and present accurate information.

3.4   Marriage and family therapists remain abreast of new developments in family therapy knowledge and practice through educational activities.

3.5   Marriage and family therapists do not engage in sexual or other harassment or exploitation of clients, students, trainees, supervisees, employees, colleagues, research subjects, or actual or potential witnesses or complainants in investigations and ethical proceedings.

3.6   Marriage and family therapists do not diagnose, treat, or advise on problems outside the recognized boundaries of their competence.

3.7   Marriage and family therapists make efforts to prevent the distortion or misuse of their clinical and research findings.

3.8   Marriage and family therapists, because of their ability to influence and alter the lives of others, exercise special care when making public their professional recommendations and opinions through testimony or other public statements.

4. RESPONSIBILITY TO STUDENTS, EMPLOYEES, AND SUPERVISEES

Marriage and family therapists do not exploit the trust and dependency of students, employees, and supervisees.

4.1   Marriage and family therapists are aware of their influential position with respect to students, employees, and supervisees, and they avoid exploiting the trust and dependency of such persons. Therapists, therefore, make every effort to avoid dual relationships that could impair professional judgment or increase the risk of exploitation. When a dual relationship cannot be avoided, therapists take appropriate professional precautions to ensure judgment is not impaired and no exploitation occurs. Examples of such dual relationships include, but are not limited to, business or close personal relationships with students, employees, or supervisees. Provision of therapy to students, employees, or supervisees is prohibited. Sexual intimacy with students or supervisees is prohibited.

4.2   Marriage and family therapists do not permit students, employees, or supervisees to perform or to hold themselves out as competent to perform professional services beyond their training, level of experience, and competence.

4.3   Marriage and family therapists do not disclose supervisee confidences except: (a) as mandated by law; (b) to prevent a clear and immediate danger to a person or persons; (c) where the therapist is a defendant in a civil, criminal, or disciplinary action arising from the supervision (in which case supervisee confidences may be disclosed only in the course of that action); (d) in educational or training settings where there are multiple supervisors, and then only to other professional colleagues who share responsibility for the training of the supervisee; or (e) if there is a waiver previously obtained in writing, and then such information may be revealed only in accordance with the terms of the waiver.

5. RESPONSIBILITY TO RESEARCH PARTICIPANTS

Investigators respect the dignity and protect the welfare of participants in research and are aware of federal and state laws and regulations and professional standards governing the conduct of research.

5.1   Investigators are responsible for making careful examinations of ethical acceptability in planning studies. To the extent that services to research participants may be compromised by participation in research, investigators seek the ethical advice of qualified professionals not directly involved in the investigation and observe safeguards to protect the rights of research participants.

5.2   Investigators requesting participants' involvement in research inform them of all aspects of the research that might reasonably be expected to influence willingness to participate. Investigators are especially sensitive to the possibility of diminished consent when participants are also receiving clinical services, have impairments which limit understanding and/or communication, or when participants are children.

5.3   Investigators respect participants' freedom to decline participation in or to withdraw from a research study at any time. This obligation requires special thought and consideration when investigators or other members of the research team are in positions of authority or influence over participants. Marriage and family therapists, therefore, make every effort to avoid dual relationships with research participants that could impair professional judgment or increase the risk of exploitation.

5.4   Information obtained about a research participant during the course of an investigation is confidential unless there is a waiver previously obtained in writing. When the possibility exists that others, including family members, may obtain access to such information, this possibility, together with the plan for protecting confidentiality, is explained as part of the procedure for obtaining informed consent.

6. RESPONSIBILITY TO THE PROFESSION

Marriage and family therapists respect the rights and responsibilities of professional colleagues and participate in activities which advance the goals of the profession.

6.1   Marriage and family therapists remain accountable to the standards of the profession when acting as members or employees of organizations.

6.2   Marriage and family therapists assign publication credit to those who have contributed to a publication in proportion to their contributions and in accordance with customary professional publication practices.

6.3   Marriage and family therapists who are the authors of books or other materials that are published or distributed cite persons to whom credit for original ideas is due.

6.4   Marriage and family therapists who are the authors of books or other materials published or distributed by an organization take reasonable precautions to ensure that the organization promotes and advertises the materials accurately and factually.

6.5   Marriage and family therapists participate in activities that contribute to a better community and society, including devoting a portion of their professional activity to services for which there is little or no financial return.

6.6   Marriage and family therapists are concerned with developing laws and regulations pertaining to marriage and family therapy that serve the public interest, and with altering such laws and regulations that are not in the public interest.

6.7   Marriage and family therapists encourage public participation in the design and delivery of professional services and in the regulation of practitioners.

7. FINANCIAL ARRANGEMENTS

Marriage and family therapists make financial arrangements with clients, third party payors, and supervisees that are reasonably understandable and conform to accepted professional practices.

7.1   Marriage and family therapists do not offer or accept payment for referrals.

7.2   Marriage and family therapists do not charge excessive fees for services.

7.3   Marriage and family therapists disclose their fees to clients and supervisees at the beginning of services.

7.4   Marriage and family therapists represent facts truthfully to clients, third party payors, and supervisees regarding services rendered.

8. ADVERTISING

Marriage and family therapists engage in appropriate informational activities, including those that enable laypersons to choose professional services on an informed basis.

General Advertising

8.1   Marriage and family therapists accurately represent their competence, education, training, and experience relevant to their practice of marriage and family therapy.

8.2   Marriage and family therapists assure that advertisements and publications in any media (such as directories, announcements, business cards, newspapers, radio, television, and facsimiles) convey information that is necessary for the public to make an appropriate selection of professional services. Information could include: (a) office information, such as name, address, telephone number, credit card acceptability, fees, languages spoken, and office hours; (b) appropriate degrees, state licensure and/or certification, and AAMFT Clinical Member status; and (c) description of practice. (For requirements for advertising under the AAMFT name, logo, and/or the abbreviated initials AAMFT, see Subprinciple 8.15, below).

8.3   Marriage and family therapists do not use a name which could mislead the public concerning the identity, responsibility, source, and status of those practicing under that name and do not hold themselves out as being partners or associates of a firm if they are not.

8.4   Marriage and family therapists do not use any professional identification (such as a business card, office sign, letterhead, or telephone or association directory listing) if it includes a statement or claim that is false, fraudulent, misleading, or deceptive. A statement is false, fraudulent, misleading, or deceptive if it (a) contains a material misrepresentation of fact; (b) fails to state any material fact necessary to make the statement, in light of all circumstances, not misleading; or (c) is intended to or is likely to create an unjustified expectation.

8.5   Marriage and family therapists correct, wherever possible, false, misleading, or inaccurate information and representations made by others concerning the therapist's qualifications, services, or products.

8.6   Marriage and family therapists make certain that the qualifications of persons in their employ are represented in a manner that is not false, misleading, or deceptive.

8.7   Marriage and family therapists may represent themselves as specializing within a limited area of marriage and family therapy, but only if they have the education and supervised experience in settings which meet recognized professional standards to practice in that specialty area.

Advertising Using AAMFT Designations

8.8   The AAMFT designations of Clinical Member, Approved Supervisor, and Fellow may be used in public information or advertising materials only by persons holding such designations. Persons holding such designations may, for example, advertise in the following manner:

- *Jane Doe, Ph.D., a Clinical Member of the American Association for Marriage and Family Therapy.*

Alternately, the advertisement could read:

> *Jane Doe, Ph.D., AAMFT Clinical Member.*

- *John Doe, Ph.D., an Approved Supervisor of the American Association for Marriage and Family Therapy.*

Alternately, the advertisement could read:

> *John Doe, Ph.D., AAMFT Approved Supervisor.*

- *Jane Doe, Ph.D., a Fellow of the American Association for Marriage and Family Therapy.*

Alternately, the advertisement could read:

> *Jane Doe, Ph.D., AAMFT Fellow.*

More than one designation may be used if held by the AAMFT Member.

8.9 Marriage and family therapists who hold the AAMFT Approved Supervisor or the Fellow designation may not represent the designation as an advanced clinical status.

8.10 Student, Associate, and Affiliate Members may not use their AAMFT membership status in public information or advertising materials. Such listings on professional resumes are not considered advertisements.

8.11 Persons applying for AAMFT membership may not list their application status on any resume or advertisement.

8.12 In conjunction with their AAMFT membership, marriage and family therapists claim as evidence of educational qualifications only those degrees (a) from regionally accredited institutions or (b) from institutions recognized by states which license or certify marriage and family therapists, but only if such state regulation is recognized by AAMFT.

8.13 Marriage and family therapists may not use the initials AAMFT following their name in the manner of an academic degree.

8.14 Marriage and family therapists may not use the AAMFT name, logo, and/or the abbreviated initials AAMFT or make any other such representation which would imply that they speak for or represent the Association. The Association is the sole owner of its name, logo, and the abbreviated initials AAMFT. Its committees and divisions, operating as such, may use the name, logo, and/or the abbreviated initials AAMFT in accordance with AAMFT policies.

8.15 Authorized advertisements of Clinical Members under the AAMFT name, logo, and/or the abbreviated initials AAMFT may include the following: the Clinical Member's name, degree, license, or certificate held when required by state law, name of business, address, and telephone number. If a business is listed, it must follow, not precede the Clinical Member's name. Such listings may not include AAMFT offices held by the Clinical Member, nor any specializations, since such a listing under the AAMFT name, logo, and/or the abbreviated initials, AAMFT, would imply that this specialization has been credentialed by AAMFT.

8.16 Marriage and family therapists use their membership in AAMFT only in connection with their clinical and professional activities.

8.17 Only AAMFT divisions and programs accredited by the AAMFT Commission on Accreditation for Marriage and Family Therapy Education, not businesses nor organizations, may use any AAMFT-related designation or affiliation in public information or advertising materials, and then only in accordance with AAMFT policies.

8.18 Programs accredited by the AAMFT Commission on Accreditation for Marriage and Family Therapy Education may not use the AAMFT name, logo, and/or the abbreviated initials AAMFT. Instead, they may have printed on their stationery and other appropriate materials a statement such as:

The (name of program) of the (name of institution) is accredited by the AAMFT Commission on Accreditation for Marriage and Family Therapy Education.

8.19 Programs not accredited by the AAMFT Commission on Accreditation for Marriage and Family Therapy Education may not use the AAMFT name, logo, and/or the abbreviated initials AAMFT. They may not state in printed program materials, program advertisements, and student advisement that their courses and training opportunities are accepted by AAMFT to meet AAMFT membership requirements.

Violations of this Code should be brought in writing to the attention of the AAMFT Ethics Committee, 1133 15th Street, NW, Suite 300, Washington, DC 20005, (telephone 202/452–0109).

Effective August 1, 1991.

Ethics and Cybernetics of Cybernetics

The AAMFT guidelines seek to safeguard our clients and uphold the highest standards of professional behavior. As professionals, we feel it is essential that all practitioners be familiar with and follow such codes to the best of their ability. However, as family therapists, we feel we must also deal with another set of ethical issues. We would suggest that at the level of cybernetics of cybernetics, the nature of the concerns and the types of questions we must ask change somewhat. Some of these issues may challenge the practices implied by the *AAMFT Code of Ethics*. The following is an attempt to address some of these concerns and questions.

The ethical issues that emerge with the application of a cybernetic framework are, like the theory, more inclusive than those with which we traditionally deal. Indeed, they arise out of the same ecological awareness that allows us to punctuate relationship, recursion, and a "constantly conjoined universe" (Bronowski, 1978). However, they are only ethical issues as we choose to define them as such as perceivers and creators of a systemic/cybernetic reality.

In the section on problem formation, we said that until a problem is perceived and so labeled there is no such thing as a problem. We have also said, in Chapter 3, that given the notion of structural determinism, what a system does is always correct. Thus, we must confront the dilemma of labeling the behavior of a family or one of its members as "mad" or "bad," for, in essence, we are thereby giving that system a problem it did not previously have by virtue of not having perceived it as such.

To illustrate, let us consider abusive behavior (which we in no way condone). For a long period in history, both child and wife abuse were not only accepted but were publicly sanctioned. In other words, in the early days of this country, family violence had community support. Thus, "good" parents often beat their children in order to "get the devil" or the "sin-nature" out of them, and a "good" husband routinely beat his wife to keep her in subjection (Morgan, 1956). The fact that abuse exists today is therefore not really evidence of so-called family breakdown as we are often invited to believe. It is not really new and different. What is different is how we perceive this behavior and the fact that we now define it as bad.

However, in the process of defining this behavior as a problem, we may have given families in which abusive behavior was a part of their heritage an even greater problem than we intended. Now their forebears are also seen as "bad," even though at the time their behavior may well have been a logical response given the particular cultural context that defined it as acceptable. We have also told the members of such families that the negative consequences of this problem will, in all likelihood, remain with them all their lives—and they probably will, inasmuch as these persons will create their own reality, at least in part, based on this perception. This is one of those instances in which we as "experts" have claimed knowledge that we can't have in an absolute sense.

The fact is, we do define problems and we probably will continue to do so for all time. As members of a society that, of necessity, evolves appropriate rules of conduct, we will always be part of a context that defines acceptable and unacceptable behaviors. The ethical imperative, however, is to avoid pathologizing, avoid the implication that we have access to the Truth, and avoid narrowing the range of health to the point where there is little we do that is not illness. Let us consider, for example, the issue of happiness in our society.

According to Schofield (1964), the liberalization of the definition of mental illness has reached the stage where unhappiness, or a failure to be free of anxiety, falls into the category of mental illness. In our attempts as therapists to help, we seem to have given the impression, inadvertently or not, that cures for the so-called pathologies of unhappiness or the failure to be free of anxiety are known and that treatments are available:

> *What has changed is man's relative freedom to think about his condition, to be anxious about his anxiety, and to live in a cultural epoch which entertains the thesis that personal frustration of any sort is abnormal, that avoidance of anxiety should be a primary personal goal and that society can provide both the knowledge and the experts for the successful prevention of unhappiness. (Schofield, 1964, p. 44)*

Thus, in the process of selling ourselves and our skills, we must be careful that our claims do not create more problems than they solve. To reiterate what to us is an important theme: in our efforts to help, "let us first do no harm" (Becvar, Becvar, & Bender, 1982, p. 385).

A similar issue is raised when we go about treating symptoms without an awareness of the ecology of which they are a part and which will be disturbed if a supposed cure is effected. For many years family therapists have spoken of problems as symptoms of system dysfunction rather than as manifestations of individual illness. Certainly this makes sense at the level of simple cybernetics and certainly such a conceptualization is indicative of a major shift relative to the way we traditionally have understood pathology. However, at the level of cybernetics of cybernetics, we can see the logic of all behaviors and thus are precluded from defining dysfunction. Rather, all actions are understood as part of higher order negative-feedback/system-maintaining behaviors. Given the interrelatedness of all phenomena posited by this framework, as well as the undisputed fact that ours is an incredibly vast universe, we can never know the full consequences of our therapeutic interventions. It therefore behooves us to consider carefully the possible ripples before we toss our pebble into the pond. By the time we are able to assess the full impact of our behavior, it may be too late to change it. When we realize that the water we have stirred up will overturn the small child's boat, our pebble is already at the bottom of the pond. Accordingly, "therapists who seriously face this dilemma will strive toward careful planning of their interventions, always with an eye toward higher order effects" (Keeney, 1983, p. 122).

Another issue concerns the dread disease known as manipulation, which according to some theories is to be avoided at all costs. However, it follows that if one cannot not influence or be influenced, one cannot not manipulate or be manipulated. Any behavior in the presence of another communicates something about the nature of that relationship, thereby influencing it. Any therapist's behavior in the presence of a client exerts at least as much, and probably more, influence on that relationship. Inasmuch as influence and thus manipulation (both of which refer to modifying or determining the behavior of another) are inevitable, we must consider the issue somewhat differently: "The problem, therefore, is not how influence and manipulation can be avoided, but how they can best be comprehended and used in the interest of the patient" (Watzlawick, Weakland, & Fisch, 1974, p. xvi).

Therefore, manipulation occurs, but its goodness or badness can be decided only relative to context. From the perspective of higher order cybernetics, manipulation is bad in a context that doesn't consider a "symptom as part of the organizational logic of its ecology" (Keeney, 1983, p. 8). It is also bad when techniques that are part of "packaged cookbook cures" are implemented without their being "adequately coupled to the ecology of which they are a part" (Keeney & Sprenkle, 1982, p. 16). Thus, in a very real sense, those family therapists who have defined themselves as atheoretical and who have been willing only to describe the experiential process that characterizes their work are, at least in terms of this aspect, most consistent with a cybernetic perspective. Even though they have tended to be the most difficult to imitate because they do not provide us with a specific set of tried and true therapeutic interventions, they have been excellent models in terms of their attempts to respond to each encounter with a client in ways logical to that particular context. And in the newer, evolving therapeutic models described in Chapter 13, you will find examples of conscious attempts to avoid behavior which may be construed as disrespectful and unethical.

As we approach our clients from a particular theoretical perspective, we must consider the possibility that our definition of health may be too idealized to be attainable by most couples and families. We must also ask whether or not our model is functional for a particular family in a given cultural context and whether our theory of effective family process is desirable for this family. We must consider carefully the nature of an intervention relative to the assumed good it can provide and whether it is potentially constructive or destructive. The sincerest purposes of professionals whose belief in a theoretical model approaches a religious fervor will not necessarily produce positive outcomes. Despite our enthusiasm for a particular model, which seems to have successfully supported therapy in the past either for ourselves or for others, we must be aware of the limitations of all theories and not endow them with a certainty they may not deserve. To do otherwise is to allow our theoretical constructs, by virtue of our enthusiasm for the good implicit in their labels, to become sources of pathology. Indeed, the postmodernists would say that we need to "check our theories at the door." That is, we need to suspend our stories and allow the client's story, as it evolves in the context of the therapeutic interaction, to be our primary focus.

The postmodernists would also say that we must include a consideration of the larger social context. We must be aware of and sensitive to the prevailing discourses about, for example, gender relationships. We must consider how our language may continue to be experienced as oppressive by virtue both of what we say and what we do not say.

Finally, we come to the issue of economics in general and of third-party payments in particular. In order to be therapists, we need to have problems to solve. In order to make our living as therapists, we need to have clients who will pay us a fee for helping to solve their problems. Theoretically, if we were to do our jobs effectively, we would work ourselves right out of business by virtue of the fact that there would be no more problems to solve. The chances of our doing this, however, are downright minuscule. The fact is, we are error-activated systems and we live in a problem-defining society. Indeed, "ours is a negative, problem oriented perspective" (Becvar, 1983, p. 18), and our traditional orientation is to "pathology rather than normalcy, to treatment and rehabilitation rather than to prevention and promotion" (Dempsey, 1981, p. 132). The ethical imperative, therefore, is not that we stop defining problems but that we not define problems in order to keep ourselves in business. Similarly, we need to remind ourselves that our responses to situations defined as problems have as much potential to maintain those problems as to solve them.

The issue of third-party payments is sticky on a couple of levels. In the first place, as our society is currently structured, those mental health professionals who may receive reimbursement for their services from their clients' insurance companies are limited, in most states, to psychiatrists and psychologists. Such reimbursements require an individual diagnosis according to the categories delineated in the fourth edition of the Diagnostic and Statistical Manual (DSM-IV) (American Psychiatric Association, 1994). While we don't have any simple answers, we would nevertheless like to pose the following questions for your consideration:

- Is it ethical for family therapists to assign a diagnostic label to an individual, thereby defining him or her as dysfunctional, while operating out of a perspective that, even at the level of simple cybernetics, sees family rather than individual dysfunction?
- At the level of cybernetics of cybernetics, what are the consequences of the above action for our clients? What are the consequences for the larger society of our creating and maintaining a belief in pathology defined as individual rather than contextual?
- What is our ethical responsibility when we realize that we participate in a pathologizing discourse while at the same time recognizing that diagnostic categories and illness labels are our creation and do not exist outside of our constructions?

Certainly, you may argue, family therapists deserve to be paid for their services as much as psychiatrists and psychologists, and the reality is that many of our clients could not afford to pay our fees without recourse to their insurance companies. We would agree. However, we would also argue that we need to ask ourselves about our methods for receiving payment and question whose best interests are being served by our present behavior relative to this process. We must consider the larger ecology of our behavior and recognize that if we wish to define a context as different and create a different (i.e., systemic) reality, we must behave in ways that are different and not more of the same. Although idealistic, we would agree with Heinz von Foerster (1981) that "at any moment we are free to act toward the future we desire" (p. 199).

The bottom line is that if we are to be consistent with a systemic epistemology, our actions must reflect the premises of this belief system not only in our work with clients but in all aspects of our personal and professional lives. Ethical behavior requires consistency at the levels of both simple cybernetics and cybernetics of cybernetics. However, this poses yet another dilemma, not necessarily ethical in nature, and thus we will save a fuller discussion for Chapter 16, "Pathologies of Epistemology, Cybernetics of Cybernetics, and Family Therapy." For now, we have reached the end of yet another leg of our journey. We invite you to ponder these concepts and issues before we resume our travels together in a slightly different direction.

Summary

Our discussion began with a delineation of the differences between first-order and second-order change, or change within a system as compared with change of the system itself. The notion that the opposite is more of the same and that change often requires behavior of a different logical order was described. Reframing and paradoxical interventions were offered as illustrations of such second-order change strategies.

According to the theory of change consistent with a systemic/cybernetic epistemology, problems must be perceived as such in order for them to exist. System change requires changes in individuals. Even though therapists participate in and facilitate a change in context, they can neither predict the exact nature of the change nor speak to or change families. Rather, therapists may perturb the organization of the system, which may or may not respond, in a partially random manner within the limits of its structure, in such a way that we may say change has occurred.

In the process of facilitating change, the therapist's task is to provide new information, or meaningful noise, using metaphors that fit the frameworks of the clients. This information must also be presented in a manner that acknowledges the requirements of the system for both stability and change. Therapy proceeds through a recursive cycle of perturbation/feedback/perturbation, during which both the presence and the absence of new behaviors are considered as information. We noted that this description of the change process may also be used to describe the therapeutic stance of the postmodernist/social constructionist. We also noted that techniques may be selected from a wide variety of sources and should be tailored to the specific needs of each client. They must also meet the standards of ethical conduct.

In the area of ethics, the AAMFT Code of Ethics was provided. This was followed by a discussion of the kinds of ethical issues faced by both those who espouse a systemic/cybernetic epistemology and those who place themselves only in the postmodernist, social constructionist camp. Specifically, we considered the issues of creating problems for our clients—defining dysfunctions, liberalizing our definitions of illness, the ecology of therapist behavior, the claim to expertise, manipulation, cookbook therapies, and labeling and pathologizing. We concluded with the observation that consistency with this perspective may well require alteration of traditional beliefs and behaviors, especially in the area of ethics.

Chapter *6*

Family Process

The family as a focus of methodologically consistent study is a relatively recent phenomenon, and multidisciplinary approaches to the topic are still in their infant stages. It is important to note that as recently as 1963 the following assessment was made:

> *One of the paradoxes of contemporary sociology is that the family has been studied as much, perhaps, as any institution in our society, and yet the theoretical organization and development of the voluminous materials that have been gathered are even more conspicuously absent than in other fields of sociological inquiry. (Frankel, 1963, p. 3)*

In the field of history it has been noted that "studies of the family have come into vogue only within the past decade, specifically since the publication of Aries' *Centuries of Childhood* (1963)" (Hareven, 1971, p. 211).

Efforts at understanding family functioning have traditionally employed a deficit model focused on structure rather than on process (Billingsley, 1968; Marotz-Baden, Adams, Bueche, Munro, & Munro, 1979). Thus, the topics of concern for researchers have generally been problems and pathology, while the major independent variables consisted of structural dimensions such as father-absence or family type, for example, divorced or single-parent. In fact, the use of a deficit model is consistent with a national concern with family problems nearly as old as our country (Abbot, 1981). Forecasts of the impending breakdown of the family are hardly a new phenomenon (Becvar, 1983). Currently, this pattern of doomsday thinking is most apparent in discussions revolving around concerns that the prevalence of deviations from the traditional two-parent family will inevitably produce negative consequences for children (Coontz, 1992).

Recent changes in both the study of the family and in approaches to this study are of crucial importance to family therapy and, indeed, some have occurred in conjunction with the growth of this field. Scholars have begun to recognize the limitations of a negativistic, structural approach to the study of families (Bronfenbrenner, 1979; Pedersen, 1976). They are aware, for example, that single-parent families are capable of being cohesive, warm, supportive, and favorable to the development of children (Herzog & Sudia, 1972). Researchers have attempted to describe healthy families and to take note not only of the process dimensions within healthy families (Lewis, Beavers, Gossett, & Phillips, 1976) but also of the variety of family forms that may be supportive of normal growth and development for both adults and children. As the importance of contextual considerations has been acknowledged and a focus on the ecology of human development established (Bronfenbrenner, 1979), real attention has been given to the fact that both individual and family health are indeed complex issues and that "characteristically, psychological events . . . are multiply determined, ambiguous in their human meaning, polymorphous, contextually environed, or embedded in complex and vaguely bounded ways, evanescent and labile in the extreme" (Koch, 1981, p. 218).

In the following section we will consider the topic of family health and dysfunction by summarizing a variety of process dimensions characteristic of well-functioning families, regardless of their particular structure. Then we will discuss several theories of development that provide maps for understanding the territory we think of as family. Finally, we will take note of cultural and structural dimensions that may characterize various groups of families within our society. This chapter will be somewhat like a visit to a museum or an art gallery. Accordingly, you will have an opportunity to get a sense of the complexity of the family as well as to see a variety of pictures that depict families and family life.

Health and Dysfunction

Consistent with the systemic/cybernetic perspective underlying family therapy, our discussion of health and dysfunction will focus on process rather than on content. We will be concerned with the patterns that characterize families defined as functional, and thus implicitly, those defined as dysfunctional. However, our first task is to attempt to define these terms. In so doing we must recognize that any definition that implies goodness or badness is inconsistent with systems theory at the level of cybernetics of cybernetics. As you recall, it is only at the pragmatic level of simple cybernetics that we as observers may look at a system and decide its health or pathology. Given the notion of structural determinism (Maturana, 1978), we recognize that a system responds to various perturbations in a manner determined by or consistent with its structure. Thus, all systems do what they do, and what they do is not pathological unless we so define it. With that thought in mind, we feel that any definition of health or dysfunction must include the members of the family we are observing. We would therefore concur with Walsh (1982) who states that "the guiding question is that of how families, with variant forms and requisites, organize their resources and function to accomplish their objectives" (p. 9). Accordingly, we are more concerned with *how* families do best what it is *they* want to do than we are with *what* they are doing. Consistent with this position, we would define health as *the family's success in functioning to achieve its own goals.* We would emphasize the fact that we are not defining how a family should be structured or what its goals should be. At the same time, we must recognize that all of us live in a society characterized by a range of norms, established by law and tradition, deemed acceptable by that society. These norms must be taken into consideration when working with families. We believe, however, that this issue must be dealt with situationally and is more appropriately evaluated relative to context.

In our own practice of family therapy, as we have noted elsewhere (Becvar & Becvar, 1982), we have found several process dimensions to be characteristic of healthy families. While no one family is ever likely to possess all these dimensions, the more successful families seem to have a combination that includes at least a majority of the following:

1. *A legitimate source of authority, established and supported over time.*
2. *A stable rule system established and consistently acted upon.*
3. *Stable and consistent shares of nurturing behavior.*
4. *Effective and stable childrearing and marriage-maintenance practices.*
5. *A set of goals toward which the family and each individual works.*
6. *Sufficient flexibility and adaptability to accommodate normal developmental challenges as well as unexpected crises. (Becvar & Becvar, 1982, p. 74)*

Similarly, Lewis et al. (1976) found optimal family functioning was characterized by a variety of processes interacting with one another. In their study of healthy families, these authors also concluded "that health at the level of the family was not a single thread, and that competence must be considered as a tapestry, reflecting differences in degree along many dimensions" (p. 206).

These dimensions include (1) a caring, affiliative attitude versus an oppositional approach to human encounters; (2) respect for the subjective world views, differences, and values held by self and others, or the ability to agree to disagree, versus authoritarianism; (3) belief in complex motivations and the ability to be flexible and to change both form and structure in active resonation with a complex environment, versus rigidity in approach to the world at large; (4) high levels of initiative, versus passivity, as manifested in high degrees of community involvement; (5) flexible structures characterized by a strong parental/marital coalition, with clear individual and generational boundaries, an absence of internal or external coalitions, and high levels of reciprocity, cooperation, and negotiation; (6) high levels of personal autonomy, which is expressed by clarity of communication, acknowledgment of what each other feels and thinks, and strong encouragement of individual responsibility for feelings, thoughts, and actions; (7) a congruent mythology, with family members perceiving themselves in a manner consistent with how others perceive them; (8) openness in the expression of affect, a prevailing mood of warmth, affection, and caring, a well-developed capacity for empathy, and a lack of lingering conflict or resentment; and (9) high degrees of spontaneity and humor.

Building on the above information and adding the findings of several other researchers and clinicians, Kaslow (1982) reports that healthy families reflect a systems orientation, with a sense of mutuality, a clear and definite structure, openness to growth and change, and shared roles and responsibilities. In such families, boundaries are distinct and appropriate, and the need for both individual and relational privacy is respected. Communication in well-functioning families is effective, and power issues are handled hierarchically yet with strong, egalitarian parental leadership gradually giving way to greater freedom for children relative to their development. Autonomy and initiative are encouraged in a context that nurtures and supports even as it facilitates emancipation and independence. A wide variety of emotions are expressed in the healthy family, and individual members are permitted to be angry with one another as well as to be able to play well together. There is a pervasive feeling of optimism and humor, and negotiation is favored over compromise or conciliation. Finally, well-functioning families have a transcendental value system that embodies a sense of relatedness and continuity in terms of both time and space. While it is perhaps debatable as to whether this final dimension must necessarily refer to a religious value system, Kaslow notes she has

> yet to find a family that rates a 1 or 2 score on the Beavers-Timberlawn Scale (indicating high functioning) that does not speak with certainty of a belief in the harmony of the universe, some sense of a Supreme Being or Force in nature, and a humanistic and ethical system of values. (Kaslow, 1982, p. 22)

The observance of shared rituals and traditions is another important aspect of healthy families (Becvar, 1985; Otto, 1979; Sawin, 1979). Indeed, rituals tend to enhance group identity and allow members to accept growth, change, and loss while maintaining their basic continuity. The ritual acknowledges not only tangible but also intangible realities inasmuch as it involves both content and process. Thus, it may help to strengthen the whole family or relationships within it, encourage and/or acknowledge role performance, and influence the structure—rules and boundaries—characterizing the family:

> The word "ritual" implies action.... Ritual transforms the state of powerlessness ("life just happens to me") to one of effectiveness. Its prescribed form and predictability are part of its power to give shape to joy, form to grief and order to the assertion of might—and in so doing contain and relieve our anxieties. (LaFarge, 1982, p. 64)

Moreover, recent research regarding the role of rituals in alcoholic families has shown that "extreme ritual disruption was significantly related to greater intergenerational recurrence of alcoholism, whereas ritual protection was associated with less transmission" (Wolin & Bennett, 1984, p. 403). The authors of this study feel rituals relate to the core quality of the family and its ability to conserve its basic identity even during periods of disruption. They believe that to keep rituals relevant, flexibility of the family through the life cycle is extremely important. Traditions may be just as effective in symbolizing transition as they are in reinforcing the status quo. Perhaps you remember the opening lines of a well-known play in which the following question is asked: "How do we keep our balance?" The answer: "Tradition." And Tevye goes on to conclude that "without our traditions, our life would be as shaky as a fiddler on the roof."

Healthy families also tend to have a natural network of relationships outside the family. On the other hand, when a family sees itself, or is perceived by others, as being different, the natural network may drop off. Not only can social isolation be detrimental to family functioning, it also has been found to be a characteristic of families in which abuse occurs. What abusing families lack is a lifeline, so that during particularly stressful times they have no network of resources, either emotional or material, to which they can turn for help (Cochran & Brassard, 1979).

An area of such great importance to healthy family functioning that it requires further elaboration is that of communication. Well-functioning families speak clearly and congruently so that both verbal and nonverbal levels match. Messages are acknowledged and attention is direct. Discussions are neither chaotic nor are they characterized by the taking of rigid and inflexible positions on issues. Individuals are able to assert themselves yet they tend to agree more than they disagree. The environment is one of friendliness, good will, and optimism with evidence of a good sense of humor. Mind reading and intrusiveness rarely occur and arguments are followed quickly by friendly interactions. Individual differences are encouraged and respected, and cooperation and collaboration are the norm when working together on a task. The uniqueness of each individual is encouraged and successes are acknowledged appropriately (Becvar, 1974; Riskin, 1982; Satir, 1982). Indeed, by practicing effective communication healthy processes are modeled and thus encouraged.

Closely related to the issue of effective communication is our position that a happy family is one in which happy things happen. If we think systemically, we see all behavior as communication or information, and we see information flow as the basic process of social systems such as the family. The more energy devoted to positive processes the less energy available for negative processes, and vice versa. Further, positive processes tend to revitalize while negative processes tend to wear down the system. Thus, it is not surprising to find that healthy families enjoy each other, are able to play, and have fun together. While happiness certainly involves more than the ability to play, it is an ingredient all too often overlooked (Becvar & Becvar, 1994).

For example, consider the young man and woman who, after a delightful courtship, marry and quickly settle down into the routines of an old married couple. Some years down the road, they find themselves complaining that the magic has gone out of their relationship. It is little wonder, since even the magician has to learn and practice his tricks if he is to remain skillful. Similarly, romance requires a loving attitude, and keeping fun in families requires a lighthearted stance and the ability to be a little bit creative in directing energy toward maintaining the romantic and fun aspects of relationships.

Thus, in healthy families the members celebrate each other. They enjoy uniqueness and togetherness as individuals and as a family. They fight, but always they belong, and the surety of this knowledge provides them with the courage to be imperfect. Beavers's summary (1982) supports this: At the healthy end of the continuum, families are characterized by the ability to negotiate, an absence of intimidation, and respect for individual choice as well as openness and clarity in communication. At the other end of the continuum are the dysfunctional families, with fuzzy or inflexible generational boundaries, confused communication, and lack of shared focus of attention. Beavers concludes that

> *healthy families have a capacity for and seek intimacy. Less fortunate families in the midrange of functioning competence seek control, and family members endlessly attempt to obtain a power edge and to intimidate others successfully. Severely dysfunctional families flounder in unsuccessful efforts at achieving coherence and reaching out to others. (Beavers, 1982, p. 66)*

We feel it is important to reiterate that the labels "healthy," "midrange," and "dysfunctional" are attributions that we make consistent with our personal values and those of the society in which we live and (more importantly) practice family therapy. With Dell (1983) we believe in the necessity of emphasizing that objective knowledge is not accessible to us and that therefore "our conventional understanding of pathology (i.e., that it is an objective, scientific phenomenon) is utterly indefensible" (p. 29). As family therapists who operate at the level of simple cybernetics but who also have an awareness of cybernetics of cybernetics, we must take responsibility for labeling a family as dysfunctional and acting to change it because we *believe* it is somehow sick or bad rather than because it *is* sick or bad:

> *Clinical epistemology de-constructs pathology and leaves us to dwell in a world of our values. It confronts us with a set of questions. Will we take responsibility for our perceptions and reactions? Will we back our projections? Will we face life without the aid and comfort of "pathology"? (Dell, 1983, p. 64)*

Keep in mind this same issue, with its related questions, as we turn to a consideration of theories of individual and family development.

Developmental Frameworks

Various theories of individual development and models of the family life cycle, especially when employed in combination, are extremely useful tools for family therapists. They assist in the processes of understanding and assessing functioning, as well as of creating therapeutic strategies and interventions, by offering a set of guidelines for considering individual and family growth and development. A few of the frameworks for individual development we have found particularly useful include the psychosocial model of Erik Erikson (1963), the cognitive development model of Jean Piaget (1955), the moral development models of Lawrence Kohlberg (1981) and Carol Gilligan (1982), and the adult development models of Marjorie

Fiske Lowenthal and David Chiriboga (1973) and Bernice Neugarten (1976). For resources in the area of family development through the life cycle, we look to Reuben Hill and Roy Rodgers (1964), Evelyn Duvall (1962), Barnhill and Longo (1978), and Elizabeth Carter and Monica McGoldrick (1980, 1988).

The individual models are appropriately linear in nature, depicting development through the stages of life from an individual psychology perspective. However, the stage models of family development, which also tend to be linear, may present a dilemma to the systems therapist who attempts to apply them in clinical practice. Some of the characteristics of this dilemma are that (1) they describe isolated moments, or arbitrary punctuations, in what, from the systems perspective, is an ongoing and interactive process; (2) they tend to describe a traditional model reflective of only a small portion of U.S. families today; (3) they tend to focus on the developmental milestones of one individual, usually the first child, and are weak in their ability to capture the complexity or reflect the many levels of family interaction; (4) even though the general characteristics of each stage may be outlined, specific issues and tasks, as well as style of progress through the life cycle, may vary a great deal from family to family; and (5) like many theories that attempt to define living phenomena, periodic revisions are necessary in order for them to reflect the developmental processes of individuals and families relative to changes in the larger society.

The issues of specific style and cultural relevance (as well as that of sex bias), may also be pertinent to models of individual development. Further, if one views each nuclear family's progress through its life cycle as part of a larger spiral that includes the extended family, one does get a sense of circularity. However, our particular concern here is to provide a framework that captures the essence of the recursive context defined by a systems perspective. We therefore propose to use what we call the *dynamic process model* of family development. But before delineating that model, we will need to outline at least one model of individual development and one family life-cycle model.

The theory of individual development we have selected is Erik Erikson's (1963). Erikson built on Freud's model of psychosexual development, adding to it a consideration of the impact of society on the individual and extending the stages to include adult as well as child development. It is probably a familiar model and thus we will provide only a brief overview of its contents. According to Erikson, each individual progresses through a series of eight stages during the course of his or her life cycle. In each of these stages the individual is challenged by a particular developmental issue, or crisis, which offers the potential for either "progress" or "regression, integration, and retardation" (p. 271). The degree of task resolution achieved at each stage affects all those that follow, with lack of resolution impeding all later development. The first four stages of Erikson's model define the relevant issues of infancy and early childhood, and the last four stages describe adolescence through adulthood. Table 6.1 presents this model in outline form.

Frameworks of individual development like that of Erikson's help us anticipate and understand the predictable challenges we and our clients may expect to face during our lives. They help us to grasp the nature of the individual's internal

TABLE 6.1 Erik Erikson's Eight Ages of Man

Stage	Developmental Task
I. Oral-sensory	Basic trust vs. mistrust
II. Muscular-anal	Autonomy vs. shame and doubt
III. Locomotor-genital	Initiative vs. guilt
IV. Latency	Industry vs. inferiority
V. Puberty and adolescence	Identity vs. role confusion
VI. Young adulthood	Intimacy vs. isolation
VII. Adulthood	Generativity vs. stagnation
VIII. Maturity	Ego integrity vs. despair

struggle at a given point in time. However, each provides us with only one piece of the puzzle of human development and is most effective when coupled with theories offering insight into such other aspects as cognitive and moral development. But even taken together, these models provide us with nothing more than a map or guide and are not to be adhered to as "this is the way it should be," or "if they are not doing this by such and such an age, there must be something wrong." Indeed, in the postmodernist era, therapists are warned against using developmental theories because of the inherent danger of perceiving them as universal standards of behavior (Gergen, 1982; Hoffman, 1992). We would reiterate this proviso and note that it applies as well to theories describing the family life cycle.

Stage-critical family life-cycle schema provide us with models of the family context in which individual tasks are or are not mastered and which have their own developmental issues relative to particular stages in the life of the family. The developmental conceptual framework

> *brings together from rural sociologists the idea of stages of the life cycle, from child psychologists and human development researchers concepts of developmental needs and tasks, from the sociology of the professions the idea of a family as a set of mutually contingent careers, and from the structure function and interaction theorists such concepts as age and sex roles, plurality patterns, functional prerequisites, and other concepts which view the family as a system of interacting actors.* (Hill & Rodgers, 1964, p. 171)

Table 6.2 combines and updates information drawn from Barnhill and Longo (1978), Becvar and Becvar (1982), Carter and McGoldrick (1980), and Duvall (1962).

Even though this model captures something of the complexity of family issues, it is still one-dimensional. Thus, we would recommend combining the individual and family models. As we have noted:

> *By using the two conceptualizations just outlined in combination, we are able to understand the individual in terms of the process of growth and development, to*

TABLE 6.2 Stages of the Family Life Cycle

Stage	Emotional Issues	Stage-Critical Tasks
1. Unattached adult	Accepting parent-offspring separation	a. Differentiation from family of origin b. Development of peer relations c. Initiation of career
2. Newly married	Commitment to the marriage	a. Formation of marital system b. Making room for spouse with family and friends c. Adjusting career demands
3. Childbearing	Accepting new members into the system	a. Adjusting marriage to make room for child b. Taking on parenting roles c. Making room for grandparents
4. Preschool-age child	Accepting the new personality	a. Adjusting family to the needs of specific child(ren) b. Coping with energy drain and lack of privacy c. Taking time out to be a couple
5. School-age	Allowing child to establish relationships outside the family	a. Extending family/society interactions b. Encouraging the child's educational progress c. Dealing with increased activities and time demands
6. Teenage child	Increasing flexibility of family boundaries to allow independence	a. Shifting the balance in the parent-child relationship b. Refocusing on mid-life career and marital issues c. Dealing with increasing concerns for older generation
7. Launching center	Accepting exits from and entries into the family	a. Releasing adult children into work, college, marriage b. Maintaining supportive home base c. Accepting occasional returns of adult children
8. Middle-aged adult	Letting go of children and facing each other	a. Rebuilding the marriage b. Welcoming children's spouses, grandchildren into family c. Dealing with aging of one's own parents
9. Retirement	Accepting retirement and old age	a. Maintaining individual and couple functioning b. Supporting middle generation c. Coping with death of parents, spouse d. Closing or adapting family home

*see him or her in the context of his or her family at any given point in its develop-
mental process, and to anticipate the normal issues with which families in general
must contend as they grow and evolve. (Becvar & Becvar, 1982, p. 37)*

An additional concern is that the family life-cycle model basically follows the
progress of a couple through a traditional pattern of marriage, childbearing, and
childrearing. Certainly this was appropriate when such models were first created.
However, given the enormous variations in family lifestyle over the past three decades and the likelihood that families will continue to evolve and change in the future, a model that can accommodate and describe such modifications is necessary.
This brings us to the dynamic process model of the family life cycle.

The dynamic process model of the family life cycle allows us to capture and
depict more accurately the particular characteristics of each family's life cycle.
Rather than solely defining each stage relative to the absence or presence of children and/or the particular developmental milestones characteristic of individuals
living more traditional patterns of family life, this model is applicable to the wide
variety of couples and families whom the therapist is often called upon to help.
The dynamic process model integrates both individual and family models and can
reflect the interaction between the generations and the broader family context in
which the client system exists. However, illustration of the model also requires outlining a model that depicts the stages of the marital relationship.

For a model that depicts the stages of a marriage, we have taken relevant pieces of the family life-cycle model as well as information derived from clinical practice. Somewhat arbitrarily, we have defined four stages of the marital relationship,
as outlined in Table 6.3.

TABLE 6.3   Stages of a Marriage

Stage	Emotional Issues	Stage-Critical Tasks
1. Honeymoon period (0–2 years)	Commitment to the marriage	a. Differentiation from family of origin b. Making room for spouse with family and friends c. Adjusting career demands
2. Early marriage period (2–10 years)	Maturing of relationship	a. Keeping romance in the marriage b. Balancing separateness and togetherness c. Renewing marriage commitment
3. Middle marriage period (10–25 years)	Post-career planning	a. Adjusting to mid-life changes b. Renegotiating relationship c. Renewing marriage commitment
4. Long-term marriage (25+ years)	Review and farewells	a. Maintaining couple functioning b. Closing or adapting family home c. Coping with death of spouse

The dynamic process model of the family life cycle integrates individual and marital development theories. Diagrams of these theories are presented in Figure 6.1. To illustrate the use of the model, let us consider a traditional family of four. Mary and John Smith are in their mid-twenties and this is the first marriage for each of them. The year is 1980. Married five years, they have two children, a three-year-old daughter and an infant son. If we wish to examine their nuclear family in detail we may use the dynamic process model to depict their family as illustrated in Figure 6.2.

Thus we have two adults, both in stage VI (young adulthood) according to Erikson, each of whom is subject to the individual issues described by that theory. As a couple, they are in the second stage of their marriage and must deal with the issues relevant to the early marriage period. The family is also characterized by concerns relevant to both the childbearing and the preschool-age child stages of the family life cycle. The parents' relationships with their children are further impacted by issues for their older child from the muscular-anal phase of development and for their younger child from the oral-sensory phase.

By adding Mary and John's parents and siblings, we are also able to reflect characteristics and concerns at several other levels of the family hierarchy. Thus, we get a perspective on the interaction between the generations and the broader family context of this nuclear family. For example, Mary was the fourth of four children. Her parents, Jane and Bill Jones, have been married forty years and thus are in the long-term marriage phase of their relationship. They are also in the retirement stage of the family life cycle. Bill is sixty-five and Jane is sixty, and therefore both are in transition from adulthood to maturity in terms of individual development. John, however, was an only child, and his parents are considerably younger

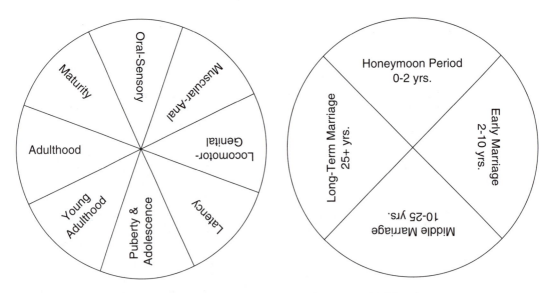

FIGURE 6-1   Erik Erikson's Eight Ages of Man and Stages of a Marriage

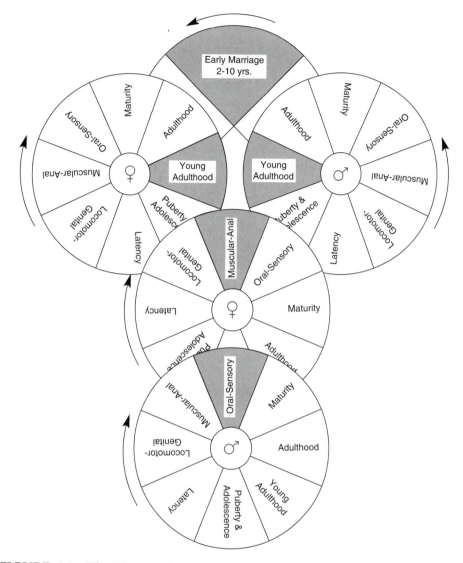

FIGURE 6-2   The Mary and John Smith Family, 1980

than Mary's. Helen and Jack Smith are both fifty and have been married for twenty-five years. They are moving into the long-term marriage phase of their relationship, are dealing with issues of adulthood, and are in the middle-age stage of the family life cycle. Thus, the two sets of parents have different sets of concerns and challenges, and their interactions with Mary and John will be influenced accordingly. The Smiths's extended family is illustrated in Figure 6.3.

Knowledge of the issues and concerns at several generational levels helps a therapist define the point in the family life cycle at which a particular system may

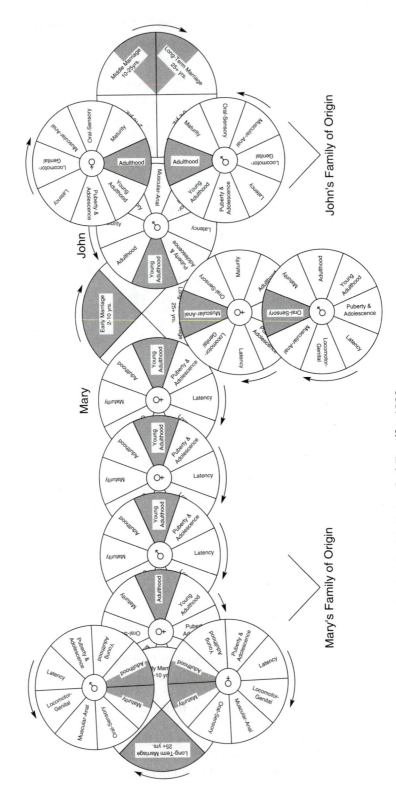

FIGURE 6-3 The Mary and John Smith Extended Family, 1980

be stuck or is having problems and thus identify specific challenges the family may need to face. The dynamic process model, which is capable of integrating a number of theories and illustrating various contexts of family life, may be used to describe the unique characteristics and individual differences in each client family. It allows for a three-dimensional perspective and assumes continued growth, change, and development as indicated by the arrows. Consistent with a cybernetic epistemology, the focus is on family process at various levels rather than on content.

Family Form

By substituting for the stages of a marriage model an alternate diagram that illustrates the stages and developmental challenges of family contexts punctuated by divorce, single parenthood, remarriage, or stepparenting, or by various cultural differences, a broad range of family styles and types may be more clearly described. Given the reality of our so-called melting pot society as well as the current context of change, awareness of different family forms is essential to full understanding of family process. We therefore will briefly consider structural variations and then cultural variations in families.

Structural Variations

As the rates of divorce, single parenting, stepparenting, and remarriage continue to increase (or even remain stable), therapists will continue to be called upon to help clients deal with the additional challenges associated with these crises of reorganization in family living. Thus, a developmental perspective that enables us to understand and anticipate the structural and emotional requirements necessitated by a divorce or remarriage is essential. A single-model perspective of the family no longer provides sufficient information but rather must be enhanced by models that include the tasks faced by different types of families. For example, according to Garfield (1982), those experiencing divorce and the challenge of single parenthood must deal with the following:

1. Self-acceptance by the marital partners and resolution of losses.
2. Acceptance of new roles and responsibilities.
3. Renegotiation of relationships with family and friends.
4. Transformation of relationships with ex-spouses.

On the other hand, according to Visher and Visher (1982), the necessary tasks for achievement of stepfamily integration include:

1. Mourning losses involved.
2. Development of new traditions.
3. Formation of new interpersonal relationships.
4. Maintenance of relationship(s) with child(ren)'s biological parents.
5. Satisfactory movement between households.

A consideration of both sets of tasks reveals that in each case, an overriding issue is the formation of a new identity, which necessarily includes a sense of each system's own legitimacy as a family unit. Part of the difficulty of this issue arises from the radical break with the past that occurs when the single-parent or stepparent family emerges fully grown, like a phoenix rising from the ashes of previous marriages. Parents and children are thrust into a situation they probably have little or no prior experience with, and all must work together to create a context that will appropriately meet both individual and family needs in the midst of loss, disruption, and change.

To illustrate, let us return to John and Mary Smith, who have decided to get a divorce after fifteen years of marriage. They are now in their late thirties and have to begin dealing with individual issues associated with adulthood. Their children are in the puberty and adolescence phases of their development. The family life-cycle issues are those of the teenage child. All of these issues must be faced in a context punctuated by divorce and single parenthood and thus characterized by the appropriate challenges outlined above. Their situation is further impacted by the serious illness of Mary's mother, who is now a widow, as well as the decision of John's parents to retire and move to a warmer climate, leaving the family without much extended family support. Once again, we can illustrate the family using the dynamic process model, as in Figure 6.4.

Part of the challenge associated not only with divorced and single-parent families but also with stepparent or blended families involves the issue of parenting. In the former, the key to providing a healthy context is the health of the custodial parent (Tessman, 1978). That is, children are better able to accept the stress and adapt to the changes associated with life in a single-parent family when the parent with whom they reside handles these stresses and changes in a responsible manner. That does not mean the custodial parent cannot show his or her grief. It does mean, however, that he or she is able to get on with the business of living despite the pain; does not rely on the children for emotional support or place them in inappropriate parental roles; does not demean the noncustodial parent in front of the children; does not try to be both mother and father; and is the best father or mother he or she knows how to be (Becvar, 1986).

In blended families, the biological parent has the challenge of doing the main job of parenting, and the stepparent assumes the role of marriage partner and support system to his or her spouse and friend to his or her spouse's children. If, on the other hand, the biological, custodial parent has not been able to take charge and assume an appropriate parental role and thus decides to remarry in order to secure a disciplinarian for the children, problems are likely to arise. Children need to see their parents as effective adults, and it does not help them to build a relationship with a stepparent if that person is seen as the heavy. Assuming the role of friend precludes the possibility of one day being told by an angry stepchild, "You can't tell me to do that; you're not my mother/father!" Indeed, no matter where the noncustodial parent resides and regardless of his or her degree of involvement, the child knows of that parent's existence and usually does not want it denied, either explicitly or implicitly.

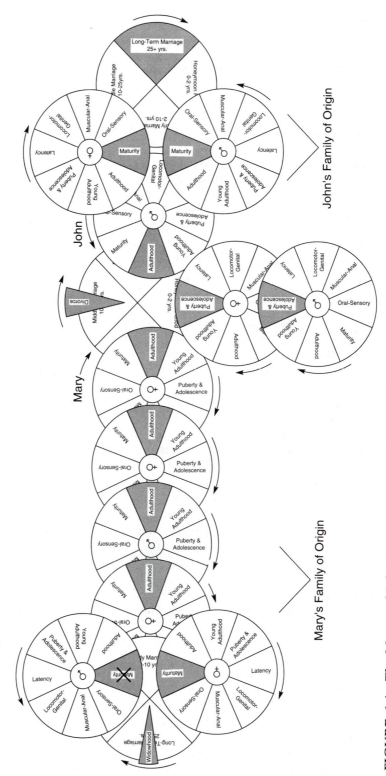

FIGURE 6-4 The Mary and John Smith Extended Family, 1990

In the case of blended families, the myths of "instant readjustment" and the "recreated nuclear family" (Jacobsen, 1979) also require attention. Thus, if either John or Mary Smith decides to remarry, they need to be aware that remarriage is not an easy transition. Rather, remarriage brings along with the issues of the honeymoon period noted in the stages of a marriage model several additional complications. These include (1) family members with different loyalties and different amounts of previously shared history; (2) the lack of an adjustment period without children; and (3) increased sexual tensions rising out of the newly formed husband-wife relationship as well as the lack of incest taboos between stepparents and stepchildren (Kleinman, Rosenberg, & Whiteside, 1979). Indeed, the "Brady Bunch" notwithstanding, all members will not automatically become a single family unit similar to the one experienced in previous families, and the new family can never hope to be just like the old one.

Cultural Variations

Structural variations are only one aspect of the present discussion. The other equally important aspect is that of cultural variations. We would therefore like to pose the following questions: As you read through the descriptions of the Smith family and considered the illustrations of their system at two different points in time, did you question their ethnicity or the cultural group of which they are members? We would guess you assumed this to be a middle-class white family. This assumption makes sense given the usual models of family life presented in the literature on the family—it is certainly consistent with the model presented above. On the other hand, we can use generalizations about ethnic groups only to increase our level of awareness and to alert us to the possibility of normal differences in behavior that might otherwise be described as signs of pathology. We can never assume that ethnic-group stereotypes accurately describe the family actually sitting with us in the therapy room.

For example, let us briefly consider the African American family. In March 1965 the Office of Policy Planning and Research of the United States Department of Labor released a study entitled *The Negro Family: The Case for National Action,* written by Daniel Patrick Moynihan. Subsequently known as the Moynihan Report, this study defined the Negro family as a "tangle of pathology," which was seen as the major source of the enormous difficulties faced by blacks in America. Having thus labeled it as a deviant family form, programs were enacted to overcome the so-called cultural deprivation of African Americans and to "strengthen" the black family.

However, based on knowledge gained in the intervening years since the publication of the Moynihan Report, it would be possible to redefine the black family as a cultural variant (Allen, 1978) having a distinctive African heritage (Ladner, 1973; Lewis, 1975; Mathis, 1978; Nobles, 1978) and characterized by an extensive kin network that provides both economic and emotional support to its members. That is, the African American extended family network may spread across geographical areas and usually includes more than one household (Martin & Martin, 1978). It very often includes non-kin, or "fictive kin" members (Billingsley, 1968).

Support among extended family members is manifested in a variety of ways including doubling up of households (Hill, 1980) and informal adoption (Martin & Martin, 1978). Economic aid is also a major support mechanism within the kin network (McAdoo, 1980).

Like the research on African American families, studies of Mexican American or Chicano families also reveal discrepancies between older and newer perspectives. However, according to Staples and Mirandé (1980), there are at least four characteristics on which proponents of both views would agree. These include (1) dominance by sex—male over female; (2) dominance by age—older over younger; (3) support systems characterized by mutual assistance among family members; and (4) familism, or the priority of family needs over the needs of individuals. But Hamner and Turner (1985) have noted several significant aspects of the research on Chicano families, including:

> *(1) the lack of empirical data to support the stereotyped traditional view of the Chicano family as rigid, patriarchal, and damaging to children; (2) the lack of control in research for socioeconomic status and level of education variables, thereby often confusing cultural values with social conditions; and (3) the tendency to generalize that Chicano families are homogeneous in their family interaction and child-rearing patterns and to ignore the evidence of diversity among these families, taking into account structural family variables. (pp. 149–150)*

The bottom line is that as members of a society to which people with a myriad of ethnic origins have immigrated, many of whom continue to live according to their traditional heritage, it behooves us to be aware of the broadest range of cultural variation and of the inevitability of variation within ethnic groups. We must therefore thoroughly familiarize ourselves with the characteristics of our client populations. When we are able to recognize and understand difference not as deviance but as simply another way of life, we respond accordingly and are thus potentially more helpful. We take our clients where they are, we help them to achieve their goals, and we facilitate health in the way most useful for them.

Indeed, according to McGoldrick (1982), cultural identity influences the definition of family, family life-cycle phases, emphasis placed on various traditions and celebrations, occupational choice, characteristic problems, and logical solutions as well as attitudes toward the process of therapy. Further, this author believes that awareness of cultural variation changes one's view of therapy. Conflicts in this area, either within families or between families and the larger society, may be the underlying context of symptomatic behavior. This may be the appropriate focus for problem resolution, and thus therapists must raise their consciousness "beyond the level of family to a perspective on the cultural relativity of all values systems" (McGoldrick, 1982, p. 23).

We would suggest that a similar consciousness raising is also appropriate relative to such other factors as socioeconomic status, religious orientation, handicapping conditions, career choices, and cross-cultural relationship issues. Further, such nontraditional variations as communal families, families with cohabiting parents, and families with homosexual parents have their own requirements and special challenges with which the therapist needs to be familiar in order to be effective. Regardless of the particular dimensions in questions, the issue of family process must be considered first and foremost, and then always in the context of structural and cultural relativity. Time and space do not permit elaboration here of all the varieties of families with whom we might work, but we would strongly recommend further study in this area.

Speaking of time and space, it looks as if our museum tour has ended and we need to move on. The entire first phase of our journey is now complete. In Part One we outlined a basic framework for understanding families and family therapy. By contrast, in Part Two we will be making several brief visits to the schools where the pragmatics of family therapy are the focus of the curriculum. We will become better acquainted with the founders of these schools and we will discuss some of the strategies advocated by each. We will also consider the issue of theoretical consistency relative to a cybernetic framework. We would therefore suggest that if you are still feeling a bit muddled about some aspects of the journey, this would be a good time to review and reflect before venturing on. We know from our own experience that each reading brings with it new insights, and slowly the pieces of the puzzle fit together and the muddle decreases. So going backward may indeed be a step forward as we recursively travel on.

Summary

In contrast to traditional, structural, or content-focused approaches to understanding family functioning, this chapter considered health and dysfunction at the level of process. We described a number of characteristics that define so-called healthy families and pointed out that at the level of cybernetics of cybernetics all behaviors or characteristics fit, and thus the punctuation of health or dysfunction is logically inconsistent. At the pragmatic, cultural level, however, the following dimensions were found to exist in some combination in well-functioning families:

1. A hierarchical structure with a strong parental/marital coalition and appropriate generational boundaries.
2. A caring and nurturing atmosphere supportive of both individual differences and family growth and development.
3. Flexibility and adaptability within a context of predictability and stability.
4. Initiative, reciprocity, cooperation, and negotiation.
5. Effective communication.
6. A congruent mythology.
7. Openness in the expression of all feelings.
8. A systemic orientation.
9. Optimism and a sense of humor.
10. A transcendental value system and shared goals and beliefs.
11. Rituals, traditions, and celebrations.
12. A viable network of support.

We then considered the integration of several developmental frameworks into a dynamic process model. Such a model may be used to assess and understand families in terms of their unique characteristics and contexts. Further, it accommodates a focus on process as well as both structural and cultural variations in families.

We concluded the chapter with a discussion of family forms defined by such structural variations as divorce or remarriage or by differences in cultural heritage, as illustrated by African American or Mexican American families. On the one hand, an awareness of the ramifications of differences is important for effective therapist behavior. On the other hand, it is important that knowledge of such differences not be generalized to all families within a particular structural or cultural group.

Part 2

Models of Family Therapy

Now we move to more familiar territory. In all likelihood you have already had exposure to theories of personality and individual counseling/therapy. According to the framework we have given you in Part One of this book, these theories are based on assumptions which are different from but complementary to those upon which the systemic/cybernetic paradigm is based. Most of the individual personality theories evolved in a context in which the individual was the unit of analysis and the focus of treatment, and a rich variety of stories has emerged in this tradition.

Within the systemic/cybernetic paradigm we have made a distinction between simple cybernetics and cybernetics of cybernetics. Just as the individual theories proliferated, many models of family therapy have emerged. We would place most of these models in the category of simple cybernetics because they are nonsystemic in the purest sense of cybernetics of cybernetics. That is, these theories often punctuate family organization and processes in linear and nonrecursive ways. While this can be considered a fault, it can also be viewed as increasing the probability that the explanation provided by the model will be meaningful to families and individuals who have been socialized into and have internalized a linear, nonrecursive, nonsystemic paradigm. Indeed, the systemic/cybernetic paradigm probably would not constitute meaningful noise to people socialized in a Western culture. (This may also explain the difficulty you as a student of cybernetics of cybernetics may have in your efforts to shift to a systems perspective.)

In Part One we also explicated the postmodern, social constructionist world view which evolved from, among other things, a discontent with the mechanistic, instrumental feel of simple cybernetics. In so doing we also created both a distinction and a bridge between simple cybernetics and a cybernetics of cybernetics/postmodern/social constructionist perspective.

In Part Two we explicate several pragmatic, simple-cybernetics models of family therapy which are comparable to the personality and counseling theories consistent with individual psychology. As we present each model we also call your attention to the degree to which it is systemic from the perspective of cybernetics of cybernetics. For this latter consideration we shall refer back to the concepts summarized at the end of Chapter 3. Specifically, in Chapters 7, 8, 9, 10, 11, and 12 we describe selected psychodynamic, experiential, structural, communications, strategic, and behavioral approaches. In Chapter 14 we present models that are logical extensions of systems theory or represent particular modalities for therapeutic work. There you will find discussions of individual family therapy, couples therapy, group family therapy, couples group therapy, multiple family therapy, family networking, and systems consultation. In Chapter 13 we present a cluster of evolving models of family therapy, or second-generation approaches, many of which have been created in response to the constructionist influence.

To us the models presented in Chapters 7 through 12 and those presented in Chapter 14 illustrate the distinction between modernism/simple cybernetics and postmodernism/cybernetics of cybernetics. As noted in Chapter 4, modernism emerged early in the twentieth century and continues to pervade much of our thinking today. A defining characteristic of modernist thinking is structuralism:

> *A broad movement influencing many disciplines, structuralism was a late-modernist attempt to identify the universal codes and structures underlying and governing all human languages, customs and behaviors, whatever the particular cultural context. Structuralism, derived in part from the work of French anthropologist Claude Levi-Strauss, strongly influenced American literary criticism in the 1970s as well as linguists and psychology. . . . With its quest for universal truths, structuralism was perhaps the high watermark of 20th century modernism. (Doherty, 1991, pp. 39–40)*

The goal of structuralism is to discover, map, and know the objective truth of the world of human behavior, consistent with traditional, empirical science. The modernist/structuralist influence in family therapy may be seen, in general, in the search for characteristics of healthy and unhealthy families, and more specifically, as exemplified by structural family therapy, according to which families are assumed to have universal patterns of organization. Armed with expert knowledge, the therapist takes charge of and sets the goals for therapy. The therapist is the coach, choreographer, and director, and the goals for therapy are dictated by the therapist's theory. The therapist treats the *real* problem, the underlying structural flaw that is built into the system and which necessarily gives rise to symptoms:

> *The modernist/structuralist idea is, in fact, built into the word "symptom" itself . . . and points to the idea that symptoms are the result of some underlying problem, a psychic or structural problem, such as incongruent hierarchies, covert parental conflicts, low self-esteem, deviant communication, "dirty games," etc. (de Shazer, 1991, pp. 30–31)*

Theories consistent with the modernist/structuralist perspective thus define the kind of individuals, marriages, and families needed/valued by society, and mental health professionals, among others, become social engineers who have the knowledge and the technology available to produce such needed/valued individuals, marriages, and families. "Science based metaphors" (Lowe, 1991, p. 45) and the world (and people) as machines are dominant themes in this tradition. An additional contribution is the "myth of naturalism," which suggests that, for example, childrearing cannot be left to the untrained. In this tradition, language represents reality or what Gergen (1994) calls "representationalism,... the assumption that there is (or can be) a determinant (fixed or intrinsic) relationship between words and world" (p. 412).

The modernist/structuralist world view is that of normative social science and the mental health practice sequence of observation (from a position outside the person or system), diagnosis, treatment planning, and treatment. The therapist is the expert since she/he bases her/his work on the "knowledge" derived from science. This position as expert gives the therapist "privileged access to what is 'really' going on below or beyond the family's articulation of their predicament, the latter being consigned to the status of symptoms or raw material to be diagnosed, or transformed" (Lowe, 1991, p. 46) by the therapist as the agent of change. The therapy process is thus consistent with the tradition of logical positivism and empiricism:

1. *Make unprejudiced observations, and discover facts*
2. *Form a theory or hypothesis to explain the facts*
3. *Make a prediction from this theory*
4. *Test the prediction by making another unprejudiced observation. (Hayward, 1984, p. 65)*

By contrast, the postmodernists are suspicious of the search for ultimate truths and the concomitant delineation of universal theories. Postmodernists focus on the historical and value contexts within which theories evolve and outside of which no valid knowledge claims may be made. Indeed, cultural historian Foucault "even proposed that explanatory theories about the world and humankind, far from representing objective truths, are essentially instruments of social power and are inherently imperialistic" (Doherty, 1991, p. 40).

By way of review, we note the following perspectives consistent with postmodernism:

• Language is viewed as mediating or even constituting reality rather than reflecting or representing reality.
• The possibility of direct access to experience or direct expression of experience is questioned.
• Totalizing discourses are critiqued with an eye to what they omit, obscure, and express relative to power relations.
• Therapy as science is replaced by the idea of therapy as conversation, as a collaborative process.
• Therapists are aware that they must include themselves in their theorizing.
• The content of the family's predicament as storied or narrated by the family provides the focus of the therapeutic conversation.

Family therapists in the postmodern tradition can be characterized as participant-observers in the sense of second-order cybernetics. They are constructionists who view therapy as a collaborative process between the therapist and the client. The therapist participates with the client in deconstructing the universal truth story the client brings to therapy and collaborates with the client in constructing a new story that solves problems the presenting story did not. In a sense, the therapist might be viewed as more *client centered* than *theory centered* (i.e., the focus is more on the client than on some preconception of what is "really" going on in the individual, between the couple, and/or among family members). The therapist does not attempt to impose some normative way (according to the theory of the therapist) about how individuals, couples, and families should be. Nor is the "real" problem dictated by a theory. Rather, therapy is more likely to resemble a conversation or a recursive dance between therapist and client.

As students and practitioners of family therapy, you will be expected to know the formal models presented in this section because they are a part of the received view of the field as well as of some of its controversies. However, they are but a beginning in your growth as therapists. We would concur with Raymond Corsini (1984): "I believe that if one is to go into the fields of counseling and psychotherapy then the best theory and methodology to use has to be one's own!" (p. 11). Indeed, your repertoire of models and techniques, or your disparagement of same, will grow through your many experiences in therapy, reading, playing, and just plain living.

As a delineation of the received view of the field of family therapy, this portion of the book might be called What Every Family Therapist Should Know to Be Considered a Family Therapist. Thus, you will be exposed to psychodynamic, experiential, structural, communications, strategic, and behavioral approaches as well as to more recently emerging therapeutic approaches. You will also be exposed to those theorists and clinicians who are generally subsumed under these categories. There may be rich differences between the people subsumed within a category as well as many similarities between people in different categories, but we leave this to you to discover for yourself. In forming the categories and in fitting certain people within the categories, we have influenced you enough. We hope you will create your own categories for understanding the field. At the same time, if you are to communicate meaningfully with others in the field, you need to know the received view.

As interpreters of these general models of family therapy we are secondary sources. What you learn here of the models may be useful to you, but we encourage you to experience the descriptions of the models in original sources. Thus, we conclude each chapter with a list of seminal books and articles for further reading.

Chapter 7

Psychodynamic Approaches

In psychodynamic approaches to family therapy we find a mixture of systemic thinking and psychodynamic, or analytic, psychology. Such approaches are often referred to as transgenerational therapies, or extended family therapies, which of course makes reference to their analytic roots. Murray Bowen noted that

> *the growing multitudes of mental health professionals who use all the different theories and therapies still follow two of the basic concepts of psychoanalysis. One is that emotional illness is developed in relationship with others. The second is that the therapeutic relationship is the universal "treatment" for emotional illness. (Bowen, 1976, p. 44)*

Bowen's observation seems valid in that the assumption that emotional disorders are amenable to treatment in the context of another person implies that the etiology of emotional illness includes the interpersonal dimension and that the illness is maintained in the context of others. Indeed, Freudian theory can be viewed as a description of the dynamics of family relationships explained in the rich, metaphoric language of the psychoanalytic model. There is a paradox involved, however, with speaking of psychoanalytic family therapy—psychoanalysis focuses on individuals and the concern is the intrapsychic domain; family therapy focuses on relationships and the concern is the domain of social systems. As Nichols (1984) asks, "How, then, can there be a psychoanalytic family therapy?" (p. 179).

The answer to this question is object relations theory, or

> *the psychoanalytic study of the origin and nature of interpersonal relationships, and of the intrapsychic structures which grew out of past relationships and remain to influence present interpersonal relations. The emphasis is on those mental structures that preserve early interpersonal experiences in the form of self- and object-images. (Nichols, 1984, p. 183)*

The difference is that from the perspective of psychoanalysis, greater emphasis is on the internal world of fantasized objects, while in the case of family therapy greater emphasis is on the external world and the objects about whom such fantasies are created.

While there is no unified object relations theory, many theorists have developed their own idiosyncratic object relations perspective that roughly fits the root theory of Freud. These theorists draw upon the concepts and constructs invented by Freud while also inventing new concepts and constructs to flesh out object relations theory. In addition, a great number of the pioneers of the family therapy movement—Ackerman, Alger, Boszormenyi-Nagy, Bowen, Jackson, Lidz, Minuchin, Whitaker, and Zwerling, for example—were trained in psychoanalytic theory, and not surprisingly, many have retained at least a flavor of this early training in the development of their own models. In fact, a more recent entrant into the field is specifically labeled *object relations family therapy.*

An assumption of psychodynamic/psychoanalytic family therapy is that resolving problems in relationships in the clients' current family or in their lives necessitates intrapsychic exploration and resolution of those unconscious object relationships internalized from early parent-child relationships. It is further assumed that these early influences affect and explain the nature of present interpersonal difficulties. Thus, psychodynamic family therapy is often a therapy with individuals and is focused on helping clients deal with issues they bring with them from their families of origin. It is concerned with helping individuals grow and become more mature, focusing on the personality rather than on the family per se. Interpretations in therapy often involve use of a variety of constructs from Freudian psychology.

There are many models we could have selected in order to illustrate the psychodynamic approach to family therapy. The two seminal models we have chosen are those developed by Murray Bowen and Ivan Boszormenyi-Nagy. As with most of the models discussed in this book, we view their creators as first-generation theorists in the evolution of the field known as family therapy. Both Bowen and Nagy (pronounced Naahge) retain the strong intergenerational focus of psychoanalytic theory and yet diverge from it through the creation of concepts and constructs that also involve interpersonal, relational phenomena. We have also included a brief overview of object relations family therapy, which is an explicit attempt to integrate the individual and the systemic perspectives. Like the majority of the theories we will review in Part Two, these models are theories at the level of simple cybernetics in that each offers a cluster of concepts and constructs that may be useful explanations, as well as a set of pragmatic guidelines for conducting therapy.

Murray Bowen

When Murray Bowen died in October 1990, the field lost not only one of its greatest masters but also one of its severest critics. According to Bowen, most family therapists had missed his point by focusing on technique rather than on theory (Wylie, 1991). Indeed, for Bowen the idea of theory in family therapy was all-important. One of his basic beliefs was that with theory as a guide to therapeutic action, the personal issues of the therapist are less likely to influence the therapy, particularly if the therapy builds on techniques and processes without a unifying framework. He described the problem family as an emotional field having the potential to involve the therapist in its emotionality. He saw both theory, and the therapeutic practice consistent with that theory, as crucial in helping the therapist remain emotionally detached. In fact, as we shall see when we get into the specifics, such emotional detachment in the form of separation of the feeling process from the intellect is an important aspect of the functional family as well as a basic goal of therapy. According to Bowen (1976), the lack of a clearly articulated theory has led to an "'unstructured state of chaos' in family therapy" (p. 51). Thus, unlike many other models of family therapy about which you will learn in the following chapters, the Bowenian approach is very rich and is perhaps the only true theory in the field. It gives us a method of organizing and categorizing events, helps us predict future events, explains past events, gives a sense of understanding about what causes events, and gives us the potential for control of events. This potential for the control of events is basic to the idea of Bowenian family therapy.

Basic Concepts/Theoretical Constructs

Bowen defined family therapy relative to the conceptual model employed in the process and not according to who is being seen in therapy. Therefore, as the therapist thinks in terms of the family system as an entity in its own right rather than in terms of the dynamics of individual members, he is doing family therapy regardless of who is in the room.

To Bowen, the family is an emotional system composed of the nuclear family—all those living in a household—as well as the extended family, whether living or dead and regardless of where they reside. All of these living or deceased, absent or present members "live" in the *nuclear family emotional system* in the here-and-now, in the processes that mark the family's unique configuration. That is, the family as an emotional system is a universal and transgenerational phenomenon. Indeed, the nuclear family emotional system is a key concept in Bowen's theory. Thus, while the nuclear family may be the unit with which the therapist works, the emotional systems of previous generations of the family are alive and well and very much a part of the family and the therapeutic process.

Another key concept in this theory is that of *differentiation of self.* For Bowen there are two aspects to the differentiation process: (1) the differentiation of *self from others;* and (2) the differentiation of *feeling processes from intellectual processes.* A related construct is that of the *undifferentiated family ego mass,* or *fusion.* This construct describes a family's emotional oneness. (In later work Bowen demonstrated a preference for the use of the latter term [Nichols, 1984].) The theory distinguishes between people who are fused and those who are differentiated. The preferred characteristic is *differentiation,* or individuals who can transcend not only their own emotions but also those of the family system. Such people can extricate themselves from emotional entanglements. People who have differentiated are also flexible, adaptable, and more self-sufficient. The problem with being undifferentiated according to Bowen is that such individuals tend to be more rigid and more emotionally dependent on others for their well-being. In effect, differentiated persons are ones who feel their own feelings and, while not unaware of the feelings of others around them, are able to maintain a degree of objectivity and emotional distance. Thus, differentiated persons have a conscious (intellectual) awareness of the emotional dynamics around them and can transcend this level of interaction.

Bowen also distinguished between the *solid-self* and the *pseudo-self.* Again, this distinction is closely tied to a valuing of the transcendence of the intellectual over the emotional. That is, the person with the solid-self operates on the basis of clearly defined beliefs, opinions, convictions, and life principles developed through the process of intellectual reasoning and the consideration of alternatives. Conversely, the notion of a pseudo-self is consistent with the idea of emotional fusion in that it is characteristic of the person who makes choices on the basis of emotional pressures rather than on the basis of reasoned principles. For such people decisions and choices made at different points in time may be inconsistent, but there is a lack of awareness of this inconsistency. Bowen (1976) described the pseudo-self as a pretend self, which to the person may feel real.

The concepts of differentiation of self and fusion are also important in Bowen's intergenerational hypothesis. People who leave their families of origin with a pseudo-self or who are fused to their families of origin tend to marry others to whom they can also become fused. Two undifferentiated people thus tend to find one another. The result is an emotional cutoff from the family of origin and the subsequent fusion of spouses. In addition, the unproductive family processes of the previous generation get passed on to the next generation through such a marriage.

In a marriage in which spouses are fused, each pseudo-self attempts to rely on the pseudo-self of the other for the stability and emotional distance, or differentiation, that each lacks. In effect, one has two undifferentiated people who are pretending to be differentiated while they are simultaneously looking to the other for cues as to how to respond emotionally and what choices to make. This is a relatively unstable field, with husband looking to the wife who is looking to the husband, who is looking to the wife, and so on.

The instability in this marital fusion can lead to (1) reactive emotional distances between spouses as each fails to get stability from the other; (2) physical or emotional dysfunction in one of the spouses; (3) overt marital conflict; or (4) projection of the problem onto one or more of the children. However, the extent of the lack of differentiation is related to the severity of the problems, the degree of emotional cutoff from families of origin, and the level of stress in the family (Nichols, 1984).

The idea of projection of the problem onto one or more of the children brings us to another important concept in Bowen's theory—the *triangle,* or *triangulation.* To Bowen, the dyad, or two-person system, is stable as long as it is calm. If the stress or anxiety this system encounters is transitory or not chronic, the dyad can remain relatively stable. Further, the degree of anxiety or stress needed to destabilize the system is somewhat relative to the degree of undifferentiation in the spouses. On the other hand, chronic stress can destabilize almost any but the most differentiated dyads, and even these will be challenged under some circumstances.

When situational or chronic anxiety is increased beyond the level of tolerance of the dyad, a vulnerable other person may become triangulated. That is, a third party is sought by one of the members of the dyad as an ally to support his or her position in a conflict with the other member of the dyad. In cases where the anxiety is too great for this threesome, others may become involved, forming a series of interlocking triangles. Although such triangles are usually created in an effort to achieve resolution, they actually tend to prevent resolution and the instability remains, with more family members participating in an escalating and increasingly unstable emotional field. Thus, we find ourselves back at the starting place, and the transmission of the emotional fusion of the family of origin continues.

It is through the *family projection process* that the parents transmit their lack of differentiation to their children. Emotional fusion between spouses produces anxiety, which is evidenced in marital conflict and tension. The projection process involving a child is manifested in attempts by the parents to seek stability and assurance from the child, who needs stability and assurance from the parents. The more typical pattern of triangulation is one in which the child resonates the mother's instability and lack of confidence in herself as mother, which the mother interprets as a problem in the child. Mother therefore increases her attention to and overprotectiveness of the child, who thus becomes more impaired. The father's role, as the third leg of the triangle, is to seek to calm the mother and play a supportive role in dealing with the child. The couple coalesces and stabilizes around the child's problems, and the triangle is now a stable field (Singleton, 1982).

This sequence builds on the mother-child dyad, but it must be noted that the degree of the projection process is in direct proportion to the degree of undifferentiation in both spouses. The mother-child dyad is punctuated to describe the sequence, yet the process of projection and the development of the triangle requires co-collaborators—both spouses.

We have mentioned Bowen's notion of *emotional cutoff*. This concept refers to the way people handle their attachments to their parents or their families of origin at the point of separation. In the fused family triangulation is a common pattern, and being in a triangle implies some level of undifferentiation. That is, the greater the triangulation, the lower the level of differentiation, the more intense the involvement with the family of origin, and thus the more challenging the separation process. Indeed, leaving the family of origin does not necessarily mean that one has differentiated.

Bowen referred to the lack of differentiation at the point of departure from the family of origin as *unresolved emotional attachments*. Unresolved emotional attachments may be handled via either denial or isolation of self and the development of a pseudo-self, which are forms of emotional cutoff. The undifferentiated individual may therefore choose to live close to the parents, move far away from the parents, emotionally isolate from the parents, or may evidence a combination of emotional isolation and physical distancing. Of course, such attempts at emotional cutoff will not be successful. Bowen suggested the more intense the attempts at cutoff with the past, the more likely it is that the individual will possess an exaggerated version of the parent's family in the family of procreation formed with a spouse. Further, children of such parents are more likely to attempt emotional cutoff in their families. There is, of course, a great deal of variation in the degree of intensity relative to the way in which the subsequent emotional cutoff is manifested, but it will occur (Bowen, 1978).

In the above discussion of the transmission of the emotional process across two generations, you have already been introduced to another important concept in Bowenian theory, that of *multigenerational transmission.* However, it is important to note that the level of undifferentiation, or fusion, transmitted across generations is not constant. Rather, each subsequent generation tends to move toward a lower level of differentiation (Singleton, 1982). Bowen (1976) indicated that "there is no way to chi square a feeling and make it qualify as a scientific fact" (p. 45). Yet for purposes of understanding, if we were to give a family a differentiation score of ten, we would predict that the next generations would, according to this theory, have scores of nine, eight, seven, and so on down the line. That is, there is an increasing lack of differentiation and an increase in emotional fusion with each subsequent generation. Thus, emotional problems, which are at base interpersonal problems, are the result of a multigenerational sequence in which all members are actors and reactors (Nichols, 1984). The multigenerational transmission process will continue until unresolved emotional attachments and cutoffs are dealt with successfully.

Another important concept in Bowenian theory is that of *sibling position,* according to which Bowen incorporated the ten basic sibling profiles developed by Toman (1976). The hypothesis of this concept is that children develop certain fixed personality characteristics on the basis of their sibling position in the family. These would include such roles as the oldest brother of brothers, the middle child, twin, and so forth. Bowen noted that the concept of sibling position enables the therapist to predict the part a child will play in the family emotional process as well as which family patterns will be carried over into the next generation.

The concept of *process of society* is also a key notion in Bowen's model. With this concept, Bowen extended the principles of the emotional dynamics of the family to hypothesize that the same processes of dysfunction observed in the family can be seen in the larger society. To reiterate a point, humankind can handle acute, situational stress very well, but not chronic stress. Under conditions of chronic stress, both the family and society will lose contact with their intellectually determined principles and will resort to an emotional basis for decisions that offer short-term relief. The dilemma is that legislation that has an emotional basis for decisions tends to be a mere Band-Aid on a more basic problem. Thus, even though it may well provide short-term relief, such legislation maintains the overall chronic nature of the problems. Good intentions at any social level, without the appropriate distance that allows for a measure of objectivity to see the whole pattern of the family or the society, tend not only to be unhelpful but also to foster helplessness (Bowen, 1976).

Theory of Health/Normalcy

In a way, Bowen's theory does away with the concept of normalcy as we usually think of it. Normalcy is typically contrasted with its identity member, abnormalcy, which is generally tied to the presence of symptoms or behavior outside the so-called normal range. By contrast, Bowen talked about optimal functioning based on an individual's level of differentiation and intellectual functioning. He saw normality, neurosis, and schizophrenia as residing on a continuous scale from the highest level of functioning or differentiation to the lowest. This assessment of level of functioning is, of course, mediated by the degree of stress present at a given point in time. Even the most highly differentiated person will, under conditions of chronic stress, exhibit what from another viewpoint might be called symptoms, or abnormalcy. Thus, a well-differentiated person can be stressed into dysfunction. On the other hand, highly differentiated persons will tend to recover more quickly because they have a larger repertoire of coping mechanisms. Bowen valued the more highly differentiated person and society, which can respond on the basis of reasoned principles rather than succumbing to short-term, emotionally-based decisions. At the same time, he acknowledged that this is but a theoretical ideal, and thus probably not fully attainable.

Similarly, the ideal marriage according to Bowenian theory is one in which the partners have attained a high degree of differentiation and are capable of emotional intimacy without loss of autonomy. The spouses as parents have an investment in raising their children to be their own persons without pressuring them to develop into images of their parents' projections. In this ideal family, each member is self-reliant and succeeds or fails on the basis of his or her own efforts. This is not an uncaring family, but its members do not project responsibility for their emotions onto other family members. Situational and chronic stress will affect the highly functioning family, but with each stressful situation, members learn to cope with a broader range of human problems. Chronic, sustained anxiety can activate the family projection process to a degree even in families with highly differentiated parents. However, such episodes tend to be minimally impairing. While triangulation may occur, the projection process may be spread around rather than being fixated on one family member. At the same time, even in the best families one child seems to be triangulated more than the others, and thus there is one child who tends to adjust to life less successfully.

In summation, differentiation is valued over fusion in Bowenian theory. Ideally, the family projection process fosters such differentiation—separation of emotional and intellectual functioning, with the retention of relative autonomy from the emotional issues of others, as well as an ability to operate on the basis of reasoned principles. All is relative, however, to the degree and kind of stress experienced. Normalcy is assumed and judged according to the personal characteristics one brings from the family of origin relative to the degree of stress experienced in daily living.

Finally, ideal individuals are inner-directed, establish their own goals, and assume responsibility for their own lives. These people relate to others out of strength rather than out of need. Although it is doubtful that anyone ever becomes fully differentiated, such individuals are rational, objective, and their own persons. They separate thinking from feeling and are able to remain independent of, though not necessarily out of contact with, the nuclear and extended family. To Bowen, self-differentiation was a lifelong search for intrapersonal freedom and thus for satisfying interpersonal relationships.

Therapeutic Strategies/Interventions

In the formulation of his theory, Bowen used a naturalistic research design to observe families' emotional processes. Consistent with this research paradigm, the observations were made from a neutral posture. During the course of his research, Bowen found that some families improved their emotional functioning, some stayed the same, and others grew worse. Bowen also found that families with whom a neutral research posture could be maintained did better than those families given more direct help. To Bowen this suggested that inappropriate helpfulness fosters helplessness (Bowen, 1976).

Thus, in Bowenian therapy, the basic stance of therapists is that of observers or researchers who think in terms of systems and not in terms of the emotionality of the family unit or the content of its emotional processes. This stance, of course, requires that therapists have a high degree of differentiation from their own families of origin in the sense of the ideal individuals we have described. Accordingly, the better differentiated the therapists, the more successful they will be with individuals, couples, or families. Therapists are also interested, friendly, sociable, and relaxed, which possibly models calmness and objectivity. In addition, it is the therapists' job to know when they are being hooked by the emotionality of the client system. Inasmuch as progress toward self-differentiation in clients is related to the degree of self-differentiation of therapists, the person of the therapist, rather than particular techniques, is the primary therapeutic tool. In a sense, therapy is research; what happens, happens.

It is also imperative that therapists think systems and see patterns rather than focusing on specific issues. If therapists address the content of an emotionally charged issue, the family projection process has been successful and the therapists have been triangulated. Further, therapists must keep in mind the concept that each spouse plays an equal part in the presenting problem and must not take sides. By refusing to be triangulated and by maintaining a calm, assured demeanor, therapists can help the clients differentiate and detriangulate.

Self-differentiation is the goal of therapy and, according to Bowen, it must be self-motivated and not initiated by therapists. Therapists serve as consultants, teachers, or coaches, and move clients to intellectual processing rather than falling into the trap of responding to the emotional tone. Accordingly, therapists may teach clients about systems and the intergenerational transmission process. Therapists may use genograms, questions, or any other tools that may help clients move to the intellectual level. More importantly, therapists seek to encourage thinking and to reduce intense feelings by having clients talk to (and sometimes through) the therapist. Throughout the process, therapists must maintain their emotional distance. Indeed, it is the therapists' knowledge of the family projection processes and triangulation that assists them in maintaining this distance. The theory, in its objectivity, is therefore a very useful ally that helps keep therapists on track. Therapists discuss facts more than feelings, and always maintain their calm stance. Therapists keep the focus on cognitive insight rather than on affective expressions.

Bowen's model gave rise to the *genogram,* a tool that allows the therapist and the family to examine the family in its intergenerational context. Typically, the genogram provides a three-generational map of the family. The genogram also provides a well-defined structure and method for gathering information about the family. The information relevant to the Bowen model should include, but is not limited to, the following characteristics of the family: cultural and ethnic origins, socioeconomic status, religious affiliation, physical location (proximity of family members), and frequency and type of contact between family members as well as the people or systems by whom and with whom contacts are made. Dates of marriages, deaths, and other significant events provide further information about the family system. Information about the openness or closedness of each relationship in the family system can provide data about the emotionality and rules regarding emotionality in the family system.

Guerin and Pendagast (1976, p. 452) provide the symbols illustrated in Figure 7.1, which can be used in diagramming the family system. Figure 7.2 illustrates the kind of information that may emerge and be depicted in the course of therapy. While providing only a bare outline, there is a great deal that can be learned about each of us through a careful look at our genogram. Bowen would recommend that each of you do a similar exploration of your extended family system as part of the appropriate preparation for becoming a family therapist.

The genogram provides a visual mapping that may help family members see patterns and relationships in a new light. A more objective assessment may become possible when the whole is seen in context rather than focusing only on the limited emotional experience that is each family member's narrower perception of the family.

While Bowen's theory suggests every family emotional system has its roots in its multigenerational history, the therapy proceeds via change in individuals or couples who are capable of affecting other family members. Thus, therapy proceeds from the inside out. The process of differentiation starts as a personal, individual process and progresses into the transformation of relationships in the entire family system. This follows from the belief that the emotional tone of the nuclear family reflects the emotional tone and the role each spouse played in the triangulation process in his or her family of origin. The presence of the therapist as a detached observer can stabilize the relationship between spouses, but differentiation from the family of origin is seen as crucial to continued differentiation.

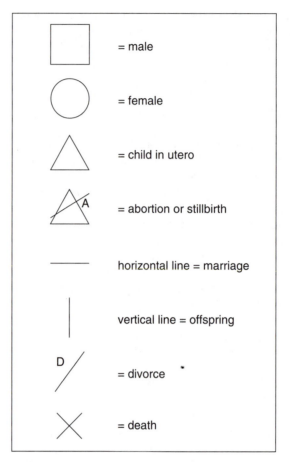

FIGURE 7-1   Genogram Symbols

Even though the focus of change is the individual or couple, the "emphasis on the extended family is one of the unique and defining features of Bowen's system" (Nichols, 1984, p. 366). Accordingly, therapy aims at reversing an hypothesized differentiation process in which fusion in the grandparent generation has resulted in problems in the nuclear family. By resolving triangles and opening up relationships in overlapping stages, differentiation is facilitated and problems are solved.

Thus, an important part of the Bowen method is to go home again. But going home is not for the purpose of seeking confrontation or reconciliation. The goal is to encourage people to know one another as they are and the family as it is rather than to establish peace and harmony (Bowen, 1976). One could speculate that knowledge of basic information about systems, the family projection process, and triangulation might provide a measure of self-differentiation. Experiencing important relationships in the context of the family of origin while newly armed with this information about systems allows clients to be aware of the attempts to triangulate

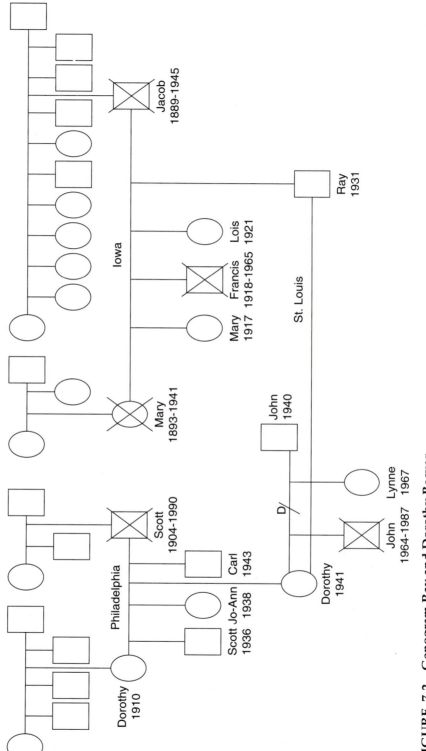

FIGURE 7-2   Genogram Ray and Dorothy Becvar

them in their usual roles and yet to have a different, intellectual awareness of the triangles and fusion processes in their original nuclear family.

This process of going home may involve renewing abandoned relationships through phone calls, visits, or letters. The therapist might suggest specific actions to pursue and may coach clients in ways to promote their own differentiation. In all cases the purpose is to gain insight. Further, such efforts at differentiation in the extended family benefit the client's nuclear family as anxiety is reduced; self-differentiation therefore proceeds beyond symptom relief. However, going home and attempting to differentiate by assuming a different role in the family is usually met not only with resistance by the family of origin but also with attempts to triangulate the clients in their usual positions.

Bowen's theory of therapy is a conceptual model and therefore does not require that every family member be seen in therapy. Working from the inside out, the parents (spouses) are seen as having the responsibility for their own self-differentiation. Consistent with this logic, Bowen also held the parents responsible for their children's problems. He thus addressed parents as responsible administrators of their own charges who can learn to deal with the symptoms of the child (Singleton, 1982). Inasmuch as the problem in the child is projected through the mechanism of triangulation, a child-focused problem becomes a parent-focused problem.

Therapists as coaches, teachers, and concerned yet neutral observers provide the tone of the therapy. Therapists come armed with their own degree of self-differentiation and objectivity provided by the theory. Through this primary vehicle, self-differentiation of the clients is begun, perhaps never to be finished, but also initiated is the projection of differentiation onto the children in their nuclear families.

Although Murray Bowen died in 1990, his theory and its applications continue to evolve through the work of his many students. Some of these include Philip Guerin, Thomas Fogarty, Monica McGoldrick, Betty Carter, Michael Kerr, Daniel Papero, Peggy Papp, and Edwin Friedman.

Systemic Consistency

Bowenian family therapy lacks systemic consistency on several counts. As you may recall from Chapter 3, at the level of cybernetics of cybernetics, the observer is part of the observed and there is an epistemology of participation. The Bowenian family therapist, in assuming the neutral posture of observer, researcher, and teacher (considered the appropriate roles for working with families) is more akin to the observer plus black box model of simple cybernetics. Thus, while the black box, or family, is seen as an entity unto itself and is understood according to process dimensions and patterns, the therapist treats the family and takes an objective stance relative to the therapy process rather than focusing on the system created by the therapist plus the client(s).

Similarly, the theory guides action in this approach. This theory is assumed to apply equally to all families and thus presupposes a right way for individuals, families, and therapists to be. Such a stance is inconsistent with the notion that good and bad, right and wrong can be judged only relative to context. At the level of cybernetics of cybernetics, making such judgments is inappropriate.

Further, linear causality characterizes the etiology and treatment of problems defined in Bowenian family therapy. There is a specific process according to which problems develop, namely, multigenerational transmission, and there is a specific remedy for dealing with these problems. According to the theory, problems will be reduced as detriangulation occurs and emotional attachments are resolved. Thus, progress is not only a possibility, but its particular dimensions are specified as a process of differentiation. Therapy is therefore a purposeful activity aimed at attaining this potential.

Finally, inasmuch as goals are defined by the therapy/therapist rather than by the client/family, the concepts of structural determinism, mutual perturbation/influence, and nonpurposeful drift are denied. In addition, although the Bowenian approach seeks to change families by changing individuals, the notion of multiple perspectives/realities is also precluded given the monistic view provided by the theory. Despite offering one of the most complete theories of family therapy, the Bowenian approach loses something in terms of systemic consistency as a function of this completeness.

Suggested Readings

Bowen, M. (1966). The use of family theory in clinical practice. *Comprehensive Psychiatry, 7*, 345–374.

Bowen, M. (1972). Being and becoming a family therapist. In A. Ferber, M. Mendelsohn, & A. Napier (Eds.), *The book of family therapy* (pp. 134–154). New York: Science House.

Bowen, M. (1974). Toward the differentiation of self in one's family of origin. In F. Andres & J. Lorio (Eds.), *Georgetown family symposium. Vol. 1.* (pp. 170–173). New York: Science House.

Bowen, M. (1975). Family therapy after 25 years. In S. Arieti (Ed.), *American handbook of psychiatry. Vol. 5.* (pp. 367–392). New York: Basic Books.

Bowen, M. (1976). Theory in the practice of psychotherapy. In P. J. Guerin (Ed.), *Family therapy: Theory and practice* (pp. 42–90). New York: Gardner Press.

Bowen, M. (1978). *Family therapy in clinical practice.* New York: Jason Aronson.

Carter, B., & McGoldrick, M. (1980). *The family life cycle.* New York: Gardner Press.

Carter, B., & McGoldrick, M. (1988). *The changing family life cycle: A framework for family therapy* (2nd ed.) Boston: Allyn & Bacon.

Ferber, A., Mendelsohn, M., & Napier, A. (Eds.). (1972). *The book of family therapy.* New York: Science House.

Guerin, P., Fay, L., Burden, S., & Kautto, J. (1987). *The evaluation and treatment of marital conflict: A four-stage approach.* New York: Basic Books.

Guerin, P. J. (Ed.). (1976). *Family therapy: Theory and practice.* New York: Gardner Press.

Guerin, P. J., & Pendagast, E. (1976). Evaluation of family system and genogram. In P. J. Guerin (Ed.), *Family therapy: Theory and practice* (pp. 450–464). New York: Gardner Press.

Hill, R. (1970). *Family development in three generations.* Cambridge, MA: Schenkman.

Kerr, M. E. (1981). Family systems theory and therapy. In A. S. Gurman & D. P. Kniskern (Eds.), *Handbook of family therapy* (pp. 226–264). New York: Brunner/Mazel.

Kerr, M. E., & Bowen, M. (1988). *Family evaluation: An approach based on Bowen theory.* New York: W. W. Norton.

Kramer, C., Bowen, M., Ferber, A., Leader, A., Boszormenyi-Nagy, I., & Whitaker, C. (1972). Being and becoming a family therapist. In A.

Ferber, M. Mendelsohn, & A. Napier (Eds.), *The book of family therapy* (pp. 134–154). New York: Science House.

McGoldrick, M., & Gerson, R. (1985). *Genograms in family assessment*. New York: Norton.

Papero, D. V. (1983). Family systems theory and therapy. In B. B. Wolman & G. Stricker (Eds.), *Handbook of family and marital therapy* (pp. 138–158). New York: Plenum Press.

Papero, D. V. (1991). The Bowen theory. In A. M. Horne & J. L. Passmore (Eds.), *Family counseling and therapy* (pp. 47–77). Itasca, IL: F. E. Peacock.

Toman, W. (1969). *Family constellation*. New York: Springer.

Toward the differentiation of self in one's own family. (1982). In M. Bowen (Ed.), *Family therapy in clinical practice* (pp. 529–547). New York: Jason Aronson.

Ivan Boszormenyi-Nagy

In Ivan Boszormenyi-Nagy's contextual family therapy we find a curious mixture of foci on interpersonal process as well as on the intrapsychic dimension. Nagy's background in the psychoanalytic tradition is evident in his theory, and yet the therapy he describes is much more active than that generally associated with psychoanalytic therapy. His approach makes us aware of the continuity of life through the traditions that get passed on from generation to generation, while dealing with both the intrapsychic and the interpersonal. In an interesting way, his theory contextualizes people and suggests that therapists need to help their clients focus not only on the decontextualized personalities of people, but to see people in context, which is a more comprehensive and fairer understanding. For Nagy, judging people out of context is not just, for people are not good or bad, saints or sinners, as our fantasies of them often suggest. People are as they are, doing the best they can in their circumstances given their heritage from their families of origin. This is not forgiveness in the usual sense, in which individuals are viewed as perverse or malicious and totally responsible for their perverseness. It is understanding. Such a focus on morality and contextualized judgments is an interesting and a useful perspective.

Basic Concepts/Theoretical Constructs

In contextual family therapy, Nagy reminds us that a new family does not start as a tabula rasa—a clean slate. Each spouse brings the heritage of past generations of families that preceded the new marriage. Indeed, according to Nagy, we cannot step out of the context of our generative rootedness. The nature of the relationships in the new family will be built on *invisible loyalties* that extend across generations. These invisible loyalties are often unconscious and are a kind of bond to the family of origin of each spouse and to the families of origin of their parents, of their grandparents, and so on. Thus, *"the struggle of countless preceding generations survives in the structure of the nuclear family"* (Boszormenyi-Nagy & Ulrich, 1981, p. 162).

Nagy postulates a basic existential human concern for *fairness* in relationships. This is referred to as *relational ethics*, which are built on a sense of equitability. Accordingly, individuals have a right to expect that their welfare will be considered and respected in a context of fairness for everyone. Thus, if in their families of origin our new spouses each experienced a high degree of equitability, they bring to their new marriage a *ledger of indebtedness and entitlements* that is balanced. They are therefore able to build their new family on the basis of a consideration of the welfare interests of each member of the family. In effect, the ledger of indebtedness notes what has been given, to what degree, and to whom. It is an interpersonal/relational account book.

There are two ethical components in the ledger. The first component is called *legacy*, which children acquire by being born of their parents and by taking on the social role (our term) that accrued to them relative to their experience in the family. For example,

> *according to the legacy of this family, the son may be entitled to approval, the daughter only to shame. Thus, the legacy may fall with gross unfairness on the two.... The children are ethically bound to accommodate their lives somehow to their legacies.* (Boszormenyi-Nagy & Ulrich, 1981, p. 163)

The legacy component is a kind of destiny, a continued enactment of the role acquired in the family of origin in one's new family. Payment of legacy obligations is possible only in the way one has been taught; for example, the child who has been beaten may beat her own children.

The second ethical component of the ledger is the record of an individual's accumulated merit by *"contribution to the welfare of the other"* (Boszormenyi-Nagy & Ulrich, 1981, p. 163). This record combines what one is due as parent or as child as well as what one merits or deserves.

Each of us brings a ledger from our family of origin; we do not live in a vacuum or start anew. Indeed, attempts to start anew indicate a ledger that reflects imbalance between indebtedness and entitlements. Consciously or unconsciously, it is existentially assumed that issues of entitlement and indebtedness exist. Balanced ledgers leave people free to build new families without excessive issues of loyalty, to consider each other's needs, to acquire merit, and to collect on their debts.

Relationships become *trustworthy* to the degree that issues of entitlement and indebtedness are faced and dealt with effectively. Mutuality of trustworthiness in relationships is a fundamental building block of family and social relationships. Thus, relational ethics have nothing to do with a set of ethical standards or moral priorities imposed from without by the therapist. They have to do with the dynamics of the family and the degree to which there is concern for and consideration of the welfare of others within the family.

A ledger of entitlement and indebtedness exists for each member of a family. One incurs a debt through merit, that is, a consideration of the welfare of others, and this debt can be repaid only to the person to whom the debt is owed. Thus, "relational ethics allow no valid substitution" (Boszormenyi-Nagy & Ulrich, 1981, p. 160). If one has acquired merit and seeks to collect on the debt, it can only be collected from the person who owes the debt. This distinction is very important in the theory, for if the spouses in a new marriage are owed debts from their families of origin, attempts to collect the debt from the new spouse are unfair. For example, if the husband attempts to repay a debt of kindness owed by the wife's parents, not only will the debt not be satisfied, but the husband may feel he has earned merit to which the wife does not feel he is entitled. The ledger of entitlement/indebtedness in their relationship thus becomes unbalanced. The husband's attempts to collect on this debt may be met with resistance—"What debt?" In such a scenario, the husband sought to satisfy a debt based on the wife's merit, but which he did not owe.

Boszormenyi-Nagy and Ulrich (1981) note that the experience of the relative balance of entitlement and indebtedness is highly subjective and that *"no family member can alone judge whether the ledger is in balance"* (p. 164). This necessitates what they call "an 'objective' balance of multilaterally-considered justice" (p. 164), which is arrived at through negotiation.

Another important part of this theory addresses the role of children in the family. Accordingly, the parent-child relationship is viewed as asymmetrical. For example, the young child naturally is more entitled than indebted. This is a necessary imbalance and describes a responsibility of the parents to gain merit without repayment during the child's early years. However, as the child approaches adulthood, an ethical balance between entitlement and indebtedness becomes more and more appropriate.

The parents, however, cannot fairly expect the child to repay the debt of early childhood. This merit is earned by the parents and they cannot justly expect repayment. Further, attempts to exploit this early merit with adolescents and young adults will be problematic. Children can be expected to maintain a balanced ledger of entitlement and indebtedness only relative to their developmental stages (our term) and capacities for accountability. In effect, as the child matures the parents can appropriately expect increasing entitlement. Moreover, it is important for the parents to expect entitlement with increasing levels of maturity.

Thus, the ledger of entitlement and indebtedness relative to children is closely tied to their ability to repay. It is problematic for the development of children for them to be encumbered with debt before their years. Such attempts can be described as drawing on an account before there is any money in that account. These attempts can take the form of asking children to be older than their years or projecting onto children a debt owed by another person either in the family of origin or in the marital relationship. The potential danger in these cases is a depletion of children's trust resources. Trustworthiness is tied to the ledger of entitlement and indebtedness and the experience that others are considering one's welfare. Thus, symptomatic behavior, which may become an enduring legacy, may result under these conditions.

For Nagy, one of the most problematic issues is a claim for loyalty by a parent at the cost of the child's loyalty to the other parent. This is referred to as *split filial loyalty*. In simple forms, mother may explain father to the children; either spouse may complain to the child about the other spouse; or children may become libidinal substitutes in the absence of a sexual relationship between the parents. A more severe form of this split filial loyalty occurs when a spouse and grandparents expect the child to join them in opposition to the other parent. The child cannot give up loyalty to either side and thus may evolve an attitude of apparently not caring. This posture is a way of balancing loyalties. It is the experience of the triangle. Further, the "I don't care" attitude may become a part of the grown child's legacy, transferred to his or her own family. Filial loyalty is the invisible loyalty. It is the universal and "central relational dynamic" (Boszormenyi-Nagy & Ulrich, 1981, p. 166).

The *revolving slate* describes the legacy, for good or ill, that "patterns shall be repeated, against unavailing struggle, from one generation to the next" (Boszormenyi-Nagy & Ulrich, 1981, p. 166). As noted previously, for a person "to do otherwise would be to step out of the context of his generative rootedness" (p. 167). With some conscious level of awareness, individuals may struggle against their legacies, but there are always unconscious binding legacies. In accordance with these legacies, individuals may feel little actual guilt in that they are in fact being loyal. Satisfaction in consciously transcending this unconscious legacy, based perhaps on existential guilt that one should be a different kind of spouse or mother or father, is compromised by guilt evolving from filial loyalty. Indeed, Nagy considers the aspect of the revolving slate to be the central issue in dysfunctional marriages and families. "The grown child of the stagnant family will be disengaged from the ongoing task of weighing what is fair in his or her relationships to spouse, children and significant others" (p. 167).

According to the theory underlying contextual family therapy, "the breakdown of trustworthiness of relationship through disengagement from multilateral caring and accountability sets the stage for symptom development" (Boszormenyi-Nagy & Ulrich, 1981, p. 171). Symptoms can take many forms and are manifested by identified patients. However, they are not necessarily restricted to categories of "mad" or "bad." Rather, a child can also be too good, too giving, too caring, or take the role of parent. Indeed, the issues of loyalty, legacy, and ledger balance affect everybody.

Theory of Health/Normalcy

The key characteristics of the well-functioning family can be inferred from the above description of the basic concepts. They include fairness, flexibility, multilateral concern, the ability to negotiate imbalances, and a sense of aliveness and thus a lack of stagnation. The anchor is parental responsibility to the process. Attempts are made to balance ledgers and to recognize situational imbalances. Relationships are trustworthy to the extent that an individual's needs are considered relative to the enhancement of personal responsibility—in other words, entitlement to take responsible action on one's own. No family member is deprived or indulged, which would detract from the ability of each to become a separate individual. The legacy thus permits autonomy. At the same time, autonomy and separateness do not contradict intimacy, for there is no genuine autonomy without relational ethics.

In addition, transitions in the family life cycle are negotiated. There is a recognition of the need for changing loyalty commitments and these needs are respected. There are open and honest efforts to balance the ledger. Indeed, "*it is the essential tenet of contextual therapy that the capacity for affection, warmth, closeness, etc., cannot be preserved if no honest effort is being made to balance the ledger"* (Boszormenyi-Nagy & Ulrich, 1981, p. 171). If parents are fair and responsible, they develop loyalty in their children, who thus receive a legacy of fairness and responsibility.

Therapeutic Strategies/Interventions

The goals of contextual therapy are to help family members take rejunctive action, or move toward relational integrity, relational commitments, and balances of fairness. Ideally, through the processes of therapy the family members will begin to gain trust from one another's trustworthy input in their honest responses to one another. The movement of the family is from an attitude of self-serving interests to one of multilateral interests. It is only through multilateral interest that the interests of the individual can be served. The goal is ethical joining.

The therapist holds everybody accountable for a multilateral perspective. Each family member has his or her own perspective. But each is also responsible for understanding the perspective of the others in the family. Each person asserts his or her own view of things. With each item of information about another, the therapist promotes an understanding of the other person's perspective if the other person is not present. If the other person is present, his or her perspective is sought.

Attention is paid to the original historical context, the relationship roots of the current family context. Clients must look at another side of each issue and each person's perspective. Honest statements are necessary, and first efforts to understand the perspective of another are seen as the beginnings of trust from trustworthy input. The therapist supports each person's self-serving efforts and those rejunctive efforts that have relational merit.

The therapeutic task belongs to family members, and everyone is held accountable for the multilateral perspective. Nagy refers to this as "'practice in accountability' for both self and others" (Boszormenyi-Nagy & Ulrich, 1981, p. 174). The evolving picture of each person includes the difficulties of his or her total life situation. Although this picture does not exonerate the person from responsibility, it helps transcend the idea that another person is a monster. The task requires specificity, challenge, interest, and curiosity to meet the goal of ethical joining. In effect, each family member needs to learn to set aside his or her own predispositions toward other members of the family and to approach each relationship with a degree of openness.

Such efforts may occur within the nuclear family and often involve going home again to reopen relational exploration. However, not all overtures within the nuclear family and with members of the family of origin will be successful. Different approaches may need to be tried. The failure of such overtures requires support from the therapist. The job of the therapist may be to help clients find reserves of strength to stand up after failure and to generate new action alternatives.

Initial efforts by the therapist may be gentle, building on curiosity and interest in an exploration of the multilateral perspectives. However, once trust has been established the therapist may be more confrontive. The therapist has faith in the basic rules of contextual therapy, and through his faith in the process a more positive attitude by the clients may be forthcoming. Clients may thus see the value in re-engagement and rejunction as opposed to the disjunction in stagnation and escalating self-interest.

There are no time limits to contextual therapy. Therapy may last a few weeks or one or two years. The family sets its own pace toward rejunctive goals. Theoretically, the ideal point of termination occurs when family members have moved toward building sufficient trustworthiness to continue rebalancing efforts on their own, but this decision is the family's. Some families terminate when symptoms stop. Others may choose to continue beyond the point of symptom cessation. The bias of the theory is toward the future families of the children. This means that ideally the family will have restored a system of balances between self-interest and the interests of others. In other words, rejunctive efforts will have proceeded to the point where the next generation of families will have different loyalties, legacy, and ledger.

In the interests of the children, the therapist prefers that the children be present in the therapy, even when the presenting problem is a marriage issue, inasmuch as parenting is viewed as an important part of any couple's marital relationship. Furthermore, the expectation that children must be a part of the therapy is made clear by the therapist. The children cannot not be affected by a marriage problem. It is highly likely their ledger will not be well balanced since issues of split loyalty are common within a context of marital conflict. The interests of the children and their unborn children are a high priority and for the therapist involve an ethical principle. As children are included and begin to experience open expression and a multidirectional perspective, they begin to trust the relationships in the family. In addition, as children see the parents being helped, the children may be relieved of the blame they may have felt about the marriage.

From the perspective of contextual therapy, the issue of individual versus family therapy is nonexistent since individual therapy is done out of the same conceptual framework as family therapy. Whether with one person or many, the therapeutic task is to "apply multidirectional partiality, a flexible sequential side-taking for everybody's entitlements and also their obligations" (Boszormenyi-Nagy & Ulrich, 1981, p. 176).

The contextual therapist therefore recognizes that all members of a family are affected by the attitudes and actions of another. Indeed, there is an ethical obligation for the therapist to be aware of these effects. The therapist is the advocate for all within the relational context, including the multigenerational extended family as well as the deceased. The therapist is not impartial. She is "multidirectionally partial," listening to each member with the same level of empathy and interest. By being partial to each, the therapist seeks to have each be accountable to the other.

The therapist does not take a prescriptive, restructuring role, nor does the therapist reframe. Reframing often attempts to put others in a good light and as such is considered to be prescriptive. Rather, the therapist seeks to elicit family members' thinking about the other persons' perspectives as well as their own. Feeling a deep hurt and blaming the other for this hurt makes the client's task of considering another person's interests and context a difficult one. Therefore, the therapist carefully balances "siding with," making it possible for people—even with deep hurts—to progress.

In contextual therapy, resistance is not resistance in the classical sense of the term. As used in this model, it is evidence of invisible loyalties, of the preservation of legacy as well as of split filial loyalty. This resistance is not interpreted or by-passed. It is seen as an ethical issue. The therapist, in his multidirectional partiality, supports the client and yet directs the client to face these issues. Anxiety is normal and expected, and movement beyond anxiety may be the first step toward devel-oping and restoring trust.

Systemic Consistency

Although contextual family therapy proposes a theory not nearly as complete or elegant as that on which Bowenian family therapy is premised, it suffers from some of the same deficits in systemic consistency. Thus, true to their psychody-namic roots, both define the etiology of pathology according to a linear model, al-though in each case symptoms are understood as being embedded in a family context. For both, the family is the focus of treatment. Bowen prefers therapy with-out children, but Nagy thinks the children must be present.

The awareness of the repetition of patterns across generations and the descrip-tion of families in terms of fairness, flexibility, filial loyalty, and parental responsi-bility are consistent with the focus on process appropriate to a systemic perspective. However, that there are certain ways families should and should not be, indeed that pathology is described at all without awareness of the role of the describer, is inconsistent with second-order cybernetics. Similarly, the notion of treating families is viable only at the level of simple cybernetics. The metaphor of the black box plus the observer is therefore an appropriate description of this mod-el on both counts.

The fundamental cybernetic characteristics of recursion and feedback are not addressed, either explicitly or implicitly, by either Bowen or Nagy. Thus, neither contextual family therapy nor Bowenian family therapy is consistent with the per-spective of cybernetics of cybernetics. Nevertheless, as first-order cybernetic theo-ries, these pragmatic approaches may successfully guide therapy when implemented out of an awareness that they may provide useful maps, but they probably do not define the territory.

Suggested Readings

Boszormenyi-Nagy, I. (1962). The concept of schizophrenia from the point of view of fami-ly treatment. *Family Process, 1,* 103–113.

Boszormenyi-Nagy, I. (1966). From family therapy to a psychology of relationships: Fictions of the individual and fictions of the family. *Com-prehensive Psychiatry, 7,* 406–423.

Boszormenyi-Nagy, I. (1976). Behavior change through family change. In A. Burton (Ed.), *What makes behavior change possible?* (pp. 227–258). New York: Brunner/Mazel.

Boszormenyi-Nagy, I. (1987). *Foundations of contex-tual therapy: Collected papers of Ivan Boszorme-nyi-Nagy.* New York: Brunner/Mazel.

Boszormenyi-Nagy, I., & Framo, J. L. (Eds.). (1965). *Intensive family therapy: Theoretical and practical aspects.* New York: Harper & Row.

Boszormenyi-Nagy, I., & Krasner, B. R. (1986). *Between give and take: A clinical guide to contextual therapy.* New York: Brunner/Mazel.

Boszormenyi-Nagy, I., & Spark, G. (1972). Loyalty implications of the transference model in psychotherapy. *Archives of General Psychiatry, 27,* 374–380.

Boszormenyi-Nagy, I., & Spark, G. (1973). *Invisible loyalties: Reciprocity in intergenerational family therapy.* New York: Harper & Row.

Boszormenyi-Nagy, I., & Ulrich, D. (1981). Contextual family therapy. In A. S. Gurman & D. P. Kniskern (Eds.), *Handbook of family therapy* (pp. 159–186). New York: Brunner/Mazel.

Object Relations Family Therapy

Object relations family therapy seeks to provide a bridge between the intrapsychic and the interpersonal theories and therapies (Slipp, 1984, 1988). While there is no overall integrated theory, this approach

> *derives from psychoanalytic principles of listening, responding to unconscious material, interpreting, developing insight, and working in the transference and countertransference toward understanding and growth. The family, however, is not related to as a set of individuals. It is viewed as a system comprising sets of relationships that function in ways unique to that family. (Scharff & Scharff, 1987, p. 3)*

Some of the important spokespersons for object relations family therapy include Samuel Slipp, David Scharff, and Jill Savege Scharff.

Object relations theory grew out of the work of Freud, who described the way in which people seek to continue receiving gratification from "lost" persons by internalizing and relating to the person's image as if it were the real person (Hamilton, 1989). An emphasis on object relations was initiated and developed within the psychoanalytic field by such theorists as Ferenczi, Klein, Fairbairn, Balint, Bion, Winnicott, Guntrip, Dicks, Kernberg, Mahler, Kohut, and Sullivan (Friedman, 1980; Hamilton, 1989; Kilpatrick & Kilpatrick, 1991). From an object relations perspective, one looks for "dynamic and personal historical reasons for problems in current relationships" (Freidman, 1980, p. 63). Thus, object relations theory is concerned with how individuals develop in relation to those around them (Hamilton, 1989).

In object relations family therapy, it is assumed that the intrapersonal and the interpersonal levels are in constant dynamic interaction. However, the resolution of current relationship problems requires an intrapsychic focus on internalized object relationships based on early interactions between parents and children. Such past influences provide the answers to questions about problems being experienced in the present (Kilpatrick & Kilpatrick, 1991). Thus, the key to understanding and working with this approach lies in familiarity with the tenets of object relations theory.

Basic Concepts/Theoretical Constructs

Splitting, as a primary developmental and psychological mechanism, is basic to modern object relations theory. Indeed, the achievement of whole object relations, as splitting resolves, is central to mature functioning in normal development (Hamilton, 1989). Thus, according to this concept, children separate their internal world into good and bad aspects in an evolving process consistent with their age or developmental stage. It originates in the infant's attempt to preserve a satisfactory relationship with the mother by separating the forbidding or dangerously exciting aspects of the relationship and forming separate internal relationships with the different part objects.

Autism describes the relative but incomplete psychological insulation with which infants are born. At about eight weeks infants move toward symbiosis, an experience in which they are one pole of a dual unity with the symbiotic mother. Separation/individuation begins at about six months. This process involves four phases, including differentiation, practicing, rapprochement, and object relations constancy. *Differentiation* occurs when children achieve the physical and intrapsychic capacities to explore properties of mother and other. *Practicing* (ten to sixteen months) is the stage in which children are exhilarated by mobility and begin to explore their world. *Rapprochement* occurs at from sixteen to twenty-four months, as children have greater awareness of their vulnerability and separateness, causing an uneasy return to the mother for refueling (Mahler, Pine, & Bergman, 1975). At this point attempts to divide the world into all-good or all-bad, nurturing or depriving are redoubled, and splitting becomes the dominant defense mechanism and an important aspect of the separation/individuation process (Hamilton, 1989; Mahler et al., 1975). *Object relations constancy* is achieved around twenty-four to thirty-six months with the child's realization of separation but relatedness to her parents and awareness that relationships are primarily good but also have some undesirable qualities (Hamilton, 1989). Ultimately, loving and destructive impulses are owned rather than projected, and the self and object are understood as separate but related, and thus whole object relatedness is achieved.

The process by means of which the relations between self and other are internalized has been described as *introjection*. It is as though interactions between parent and child were swallowed whole. Further, introjection has been seen as "the earliest, most primitive form of the internalization of object relations, starting on a relatively crude level and becoming more sophisticated as the child grows" (Kilpatrick & Kilpatrick, 1991, p. 216).

According to the concept of *projective identification*, "the individual attributes an aspect of the self to the object and reidentifies with the projected element in the other, attempting to control it" (Hamilton, 1989, p. 1554). Although it is an unconscious defense mechanism, it involves an interactional process as the other person is influenced to behave in a manner consistent with the feelings and attitudes projected onto him. *Collusion* refers to the participation by the other in this process, by acting in accordance with the projection. Transference, scapegoating, symbiosis, and family projective process are all variations on the theme of projective identification and collusion (Kilpatrick & Kilpatrick, 1991).

Winnicott introduced the concepts of the *holding environment* and the *transitional object* (Hamilton, 1989). The holding environment, which is related to the notion of good enough mothering, emphasizes the need for closeness yet separateness in order to achieve whole object relations. That is, eventually children internalize holding functions, soothe themselves, and allow for separation from their parents. An important part of this process is the development of transitional objects that are neither self nor object and yet may be treated as if they were the beloved parent and simultaneously the self. Transitional objects for children are traditionally teddy bears and blankets (Cohen & Clark, 1984); for adults they may be any object invested with energy and expected to fulfill a nurturing role.

Object relations theory focuses on the development of the psychic structure and the way in which the *ego identity* is achieved. According to Kernberg (1976), the highest level of ego identity is achieved when one's inner world of internalized objects, representing family, friends, social group, and cultural identity, provides harmonious support to the individual and depth to her current interactions. Thus, "in periods of crisis, such as loss, abandonment, separation, failure, and loneliness, the individual can temporarily fall back on his internal world: in this way, the intrapsychic and the interpersonal worlds relate to and reinforce each other" (Kernberg, 1976, p. 73).

Transference refers to elements of an individual's earlier experience and suggests that the person in a current relationship is being related to, at best, on the basis of an amended version of the actual other person involved. That is,

> *people react to and interact with not only the other actual person but also the internal other, a psychic representation of a person which in itself has the power to influence both the individual's affective states and his overt behavioral reactions. (Greenberg & Mitchell, 1983, p. 10)*

The individual therefore brings expectations to a relationship based on internal models of the way primary figures provided holding. *Countertransference* is the reciprocal interaction of the other in the face of transference, and as it is manifested, intrapsychic representations are acted out within the relationship. Each individual thus brings his own internalized object relations patterns from former relationships to the current relationship in a parallel process, the goal of which is gratification.

Theory of Health/Normalcy

The processes of introjection and identification ultimately determine the personality, the organization of mental processes, and the way individuals relate to each other. Beginning with the infant-mother relationship, psychic development can be impaired at any level, thereby having a profound effect not only on the ability to form mature relationships but also on development in the areas of perception, cognition, and sense of self. However, the impact of such impairments may not be felt until such time as the individual is required to be autonomous and self-reliant. According to object relations theorists, the key issues in development include (1) the internalization and the externalization of relationships; (2) attachment and separation; (3) introjection and projection; and (4) transmuting internalization (Hamilton, 1989). Based on a complex theory of interaction between infants and the mothering person, both parent and child, with their own unique endowments, are understood as playing a significant role in this relationship (Blanck & Blanck, 1986).

Object relations family therapists seek not only to understand the development of the individual personality within the context of the early parent-child dyad but also to "expand the family's capacity to perform the holding functions for its members and their capacities to offer holding of each other" (Scharff & Scharff, 1987, p. 62). Thus, family health equals the ability of family members to relate fully to one another. And fully relating refers to the ability to express true understanding and compassion.

Therapeutic Strategies/Interventions

New and different ways to coordinate action not only intrapsychically but also with one another are described in object relations theory in the form of (1) identifying the fragmented and/or inadequate internalized objects and insightfully "reworking" them to adequacy and wholeness; and (2) identifying, reclaiming, and insightfully "reworking" the projected objects in a similar manner (Ryle, 1985). This occurs in a therapeutic alliance that allows the manifestation of early ego functioning in order both to understand the developmental processes of the component parts and to grasp the logic of the ways in which the whole is functioning (Blanck & Blanck, 1986).

In object relations family therapy, the mutual interdependence of one with another and the reciprocal and multilevel interaction of intrapsychic and interpersonal levels are acknowledged. Thus, the therapist's role is to provide a nurturing environment in which the unconscious object relations that are interfering with current relationships may be understood and resolved. General goals for therapy include:

1. *The recognition and reworking of the defensive projective identifications that have previously been required in the family.*
2. *The treatment of the family's capacity to provide contextual holding for its members so that their attachment needs and conditions for growth can be met.*
3. *The overall reinstatement or construction of the series of centered holding relationships between each of its members to support their needs for attachment, individuation, and growth sufficient to allow each individual to "take it from there."*
4. *The return of the family to the overall developmental level appropriate to its tasks as set by its own preferences and by the needs of the family members.*
5. *The clarification of remaining individual needs in family members so that they can get them met with as much support as they need from the family. By this we specifically include individual needs for psychotherapy, as well as more general needs for other growth endeavors. (Scharff & Scharff, 1987, p. 448)*

The specific techniques for facilitating this process include working with the family's contextual transference and absorbing, understanding, and interpreting the anxieties shared by family members. The therapist may focus on individuals and/or subgroups, but there is always awareness of the impact of such interactions on the family as a whole (Scharff & Scharff, 1987). Finally, responsibility for both the determination of the specific goals as well as an assessment of the outcome of therapy are shared by the therapist and the family.

Systemic Consistency

Object relations family therapy succeeds in making significant advances toward the attainment of systemic consistency. Although this approach makes use of causal terms, particularly in the case of "problem" definition, according to Slipp (1984), an attempt to capture circularity is demonstrated in the dance of internalizing and externalizing relationships, attachment and separation, introjection and projection, and transmuting internalizations. Thus, feedback and recursion are addressed. One may also infer some aspects of the processes of mutual perturbation and an epistemology of participation in that family members share responsibility for the selection of specific therapeutic goals and decisions around termination. Similarly, there is an implicit acceptance of reality as a multiverse of individual perceptions and constructions in the recognition of each individual's developmental process and ability to relate.

On the other hand, to the extent that the therapist operates according to general goals, or a prescribed therapeutic context, within which all families' specific goals are to be achieved, the approach is inconsistent. Also inconsistent is the use of a framework according to which pathology and healthy functioning are defined and described, for this is a violation of the concepts of nonpurposeful drift and new coordinations rather than progress. Finally, there appears to be little emphasis on the notion of self-reference or awareness that the observer is part of the observed. Thus, not surprisingly given its diverse origins, we may describe object relations family therapy as a pragmatic, first-order approach that lacks systemic consistency, particularly at the level of cybernetics of cybernetics.

Suggested Readings

Scharff, D. E. (1982). *The sexual relationship: An object relations view of sex and the family.* Boston: Routledge & Kegan Paul.

Scharff, D. E., & Scharff, J. S. (1987). *Object relations family therapy.* Northvale, NJ: Jason Aronson.

Scharff, J. S. (Ed.). (1989). *Foundations of object relations family therapy.* Northvale, NJ: Jason Aronson.

Slipp, S. (1984). *Object relations: A dynamic bridge between individual and family therapy.* Northvale, NJ: Jason Aronson.

Slipp, S. (1988). *The technique and practice of object relations.* Northvale, NJ: Jason Aronson.

Chapter 8

Experiential Approaches

Experiential approaches to family therapy have their roots in the existential/humanistic orientation of individual psychology, which reached its peak of popularity in the 1960s. This was the era of encounter groups, of sensitivity training, and of an emphasis on the achievement of human potential. The focus was on here-and-now experiencing, and the goals were to get in touch with one's feelings as well as to be able to express one's emotions. Espousing a purposely positive model of humanity, this perspective reflects the desire of psychologists and family therapists to promote both individual and family growth and development.

Individuality, personal freedom, and self-fulfillment are therefore the hallmarks of experiential family therapy. Health involves the facilitation of normal change processes with an emphasis on spontaneity and creativity. Conversely, dysfunction is seen as the result of denying impulses and suppressing feelings. Thus, the primary goal of therapy is growth, especially in the areas of sensitivity and the sharing of feelings. "Symptom relief, social adjustment and work are considered important, but secondary to increased personal integrity (congruence between inner experience and outer behavior); greater freedom of choice; less dependence; and expanded experiencing" (Nichols, 1984, p. 272).

The techniques of experiential family therapy are freely drawn from the arts and include such strategies as psychodrama, sculpting, and role-playing. In fact, almost any behavior comfortable for the therapist is considered acceptable. The emphasis is on the experience in the context of therapy, and thus homework assignments are the exception rather than the rule.

Not surprisingly, experiential approaches tend to be largely atheoretical, depending mainly on the person of the therapist and his ability to respond in a rather freewheeling and spontaneous manner to the issues at hand. The therapists' strategies are therefore idiosyncratic to their personal epistemology. However, regardless of this particular orientation, there is shared agreement that the orientation is primarily toward individual family members and their personal development.

We have chosen Carl Whitaker and Walter Kempler as representatives of the experiential approach to family therapy. These two theorists/therapists provide a rich contrast to each other in terms of their fundamental epistemology, yet by this very contrast help to illustrate what is meant by an experiential approach to family therapy. Whitaker's roots are psychodynamic, while Kempler's basic world view is derived from Gestalt psychology. However, both emphasize the experiential nature of therapy and the importance of human interaction for the process of change.

Experiential approaches to family therapy have waned in popularity over the years since their introduction (Nichols, 1984). However, this shift probably reflects the difficulty in learning a model that is self-consciously not a model rather than a proven lack of effectiveness. Indeed, there is much to be learned from such approaches and, as we shall discuss shortly, they are able to provide us with a view of the therapeutic process that is probably most consistent with the perspective of cybernetics of cybernetics.

Carl Whitaker

Carl Whitaker, who died in April 1995, labeled his particular approach *experiential/ symbolic family therapy:*

> *We presume that it is experience, not education that changes families. The main function of the cerebral cortex is inhibition. Thus, most of our experience goes on outside of our consciousness. We gain best access to it symbolically. For us "symbolic" implies that some thing or some process has more than one meaning. While education can be immensely helpful, the covert process of the family is the one that contains the most power for potential changing. (Keith & Whitaker, 1982, p. 43)*

Although trained as a psychiatrist, Whitaker attributes the evolution of his therapeutic approach to the impact of World War II on personnel and placement, which resulted in major deviations from standard psychiatric training procedures (Keith & Whitaker, 1982). Originally schooled in obstetrics and gynecology, he later shifted to psychiatry as a function of a postgraduate fellowship during which he had his initial encounter with schizophrenics, with whom he was immediately enamored (Simon, 1985). His first psychiatric placement (1938–1939) was as the resident administrator in a small diagnostic hospital. The significance of this placement, as opposed to one in a larger state institution with a huge population of patients, was that its modus operandi was an outdated custodial care system, and his preparation included neither psychoanalytic nor psychodynamic psychiatry.

This experience was followed by placement in a child guidance clinic, where his practice included play therapy and his supervisor was a social worker who espoused the tradition of separate treatment of mother and child by different therapists, with no involvement of the father. Additional on-the-job training included teaching medical students to do psychotherapy during a period when he felt he knew nothing about the subject, working with delinquent teenagers, and dealing with the enormous pressures of being a psychiatrist in the understaffed Oak Ridge Hospital from 1944–1946 (Keith & Whitaker, 1982).

Both lack of experience and psychological stress led to Whitaker's use of and preference for cotherapy, which began during his tenure at Oak Ridge. He also continued to expand on the applications of play therapy and the symbolic mothering of his clients. While establishing and chairing the first department of psychiatry in the medical school at Emory University (1946–1955), Whitaker and his associates emphasized the process of therapy and began implementing an aggressive kind of play therapy in the treatment of schizophrenia. Indeed, it was at this point that Whitaker and his colleagues began to receive national recognition for their view of schizophrenic symptoms as strategies to resolve interpersonal conflicts (Nichols, 1984).

Largely as a result of his rather revolutionary view of and treatment for schizophrenia, Whitaker was dismissed from Emory in 1955. From 1955 to 1965 he worked in private practice in Atlanta, Georgia, where he continued to focus on depathologizing human experience and became increasingly interested in working with families. Thus, when in 1965 he went to the University of Wisconsin Medical School as a professor of psychiatry, he was defining himself as a family therapist (Keith & Whitaker, 1982).

Basic Concepts/Theoretical Constructs

Consistent with his emphasis on experience, Whitaker's approach to family therapy is pragmatic and deliberately nontheoretical:

> *My theory is that all theories are bad except for the beginner's game playing, until he gets the courage to give up theories and just live. Because it has been known for many generations that any addiction, any indoctrination tends to be constrictive and constipating. (Whitaker, 1976a, p. 154)*

Indeed, it is his lack of theorizing and the deliberate refusal to create a systematic model that often make his style both hard to understand and almost impossible to imitate. For Whitaker therapy is an art, and he recommends substituting for theory faith in one's own experience and the ability to allow the process of therapy to unfold in an authentic and genuinely responsive manner. In addition,

> *we must also recognize that the integrity of the family must be respected. They must write their own destiny. In the same sense that the individual has a right to suicide, the family has the right to self-destruct. The therapist may not, and does not, have the power to mold their system to his will. He's their coach; but he's not playing on the team. (Whitaker, 1976a, p. 163)*

Therapy is thus a growth process in which both therapist and client share and from which both benefit. It is an intimate, interactive, and parallel experience in which each becomes equally vulnerable and neither takes responsibility for the other. It is intuitive, it aims at increasing anxiety within a caring environment, and it proceeds via allegory, free association, and fantasy. It is experiential, intrapsychic, and paradoxical. According to Whitaker, "good therapy must include the therapist's physiological, psychosomatic, psychotic, and endocrine reactions to a deeply personal interaction system" (1976a, p. 162).

For Whitaker, the aim of therapy is both to help individuals grow and to help them be able to do so in the context of their families. Accordingly, healthy families and healthy family relationships are understood to be far more important than is either insight or understanding. The family is seen as an integrated whole, and it is through a sense of belonging to the whole that the freedom to individuate and separate from the family is derived. Thus the power of the family, as manifested in either negative or positive ways, is the key to individual growth and development. The issue of health and normalcy is therefore extremely important to Whitaker's approach to family therapy.

Theory of Health/Normalcy

For Whitaker, healthy families are self-actualizing families, or families that grow despite the pitfalls and problems they may encounter along the way. While the processes that typify such families are largely covert and nonverbal, they tend to be similar in nature. That is, everyone is included and there is an awareness of the whole, which "functions as the leader and the control system both in supporting the family's security and in inducting change" (Keith & Whitaker, 1982, p. 47). In addition, healthy families are able to understand time and space, and members are aware of their forward progress through both. While a separation of the generations is maintained, there is also role flexibility and each role is available to all members at various times. There is no rigid pattern of triangulation, and there is freedom to join and separate as appropriate. The family has its own mythology, verbal history, or set of stories—its own intrapsychic dimension. Healthy family systems are also open and available for interaction with other systems in their network. And no one member carries all of the responsibility for being the problem all of the time; thus each member can be "worked on" at different times.

Healthy families are not symptom free, but problems are handled successfully through a process of negotiation. Further, "the healthy family becomes increasingly strong as a group, therapeutic in its role to itself and its components, increasingly flexible and casual and increasingly covert" (Keith & Whitaker, 1982, p. 49). Sex, passion, and playfulness are acknowledged as important ingredients in healthy families. Indeed, according to Whitaker, "sex is more open and fun if it involves all the generations. One of the best ways is by sexual joking" (Keith & Whitaker, 1982, p. 50). It is this amalgam of patterns and processes that allows for both separation of the generations and the ability to transcend such boundaries in appropriate ways. In this manner, the healthy family facilitates individual autonomy and personal development.

The healthy family thus provides a context that is supportive of its individual members and their shared experiencing. On the other hand, dysfunctional families tend to operate in such a way that impulses are denied and feelings are suppressed. Whether enmeshed or disengaged, such a family "has excessive callouses and no craziness but is massively inhibited, or the family with 'nobody-in-it' in which the family members live back-to-back" (Keith & Whitaker, 1982, p. 52).

Dysfunctional families are self-protective and avoid risk taking. They are rigid and mechanical rather than spontaneous and free. They share a belief in the myth that confrontation and open conflict would destroy the family. Therefore, the dysfunctional family does not continue to grow. Rather, it may become stuck at a point when life-cycle requirements or external events call for change. Alienation from experience, leading to a lack of autonomy and intimacy, is the key to this stuckness, and it manifests itself both in individual intrapsychic problems and in interpersonal relationship issues. Therapy therefore aims at enabling family members to experience themselves both as a system and as individuals who are able to become unstuck. Indeed, Whitaker assumes that families come to therapy because of their inability to be close and thus to individuate. By facilitating their potential for experiencing, family members are better able to care for each other in a manner that releases their fullest potential.

Dysfunction may also arise as a result of the battle between the spouses over whose family of origin will provide the model for their family of procreation. That is, "one way to view etiology assumes there is no such thing as marriage; it is merely an arrangement whereby scapegoats are sent out by two families in an effort to recreate themselves" (Keith & Whitaker, 1982, p. 53). In this case, the aim of therapy is to enable the spouses to learn to accommodate each other's differences. However, the processes involved with achieving such goals are anything but traditional and often have been described as crazy.

Therapeutic Strategies/Interventions

For Whitaker, the basic goal of therapy is to balance and facilitate both individual autonomy and a sense of togetherness. This goal is achieved through the enhancement of creativity, or craziness, within the family so that all are freed up to grow and change. The process, as we have noted, is experiential and symbolic, or intrapsychic, and it is also paradoxical.

The apparently contradictory experiential, intrapsychic, and paradoxical elements of this brand of family therapy were reconciled and comfortably coexisted by virtue of Whitaker's unique use of himself in a way such that the latter two elements were subsumed by the former. Thus, experiential/symbolic family therapy means developing a therapist-client relationship in sequential and overlapping patterns, which includes both direct transference and countertransference as well as an existential connection in which client and therapist may "fall for" each other as in any other intimate relationship. It means becoming engaged in and, in fact, heightening the emotional and expressive feelings between client and therapist and seeking a real depth of involvement. It means allowing the therapist's own "slivers of pathology" to surface within the context of the relationship and escalating the absurdity in human behavior to create a reversal of roles, which looks paradoxical but in fact forces the family to find its own way of living and of dealing with itself: the therapist becomes crazy so the patient can become sane.

Whitaker is fond of quoting the remark by Barbara Betz that "the dynamics of psychotherapy is in the person of the therapist." The key to this dynamic vis-à-vis Whitaker is his belief that a "personal growing edge" is a central objective in every relationship and that a therapist's personal experience *as a therapist* extensively determines her work in family therapy. If experiential therapy is for her own experience, then the therapist's modeling for the client becomes real.

For Whitaker, therapy occurs in three phases—engagement, involvement, and disentanglement—during which the therapist increases, in a caring way, the anxiety with which both he and the family approach therapy. With the use of paradox he aims to escalate the pressure to produce a psychotic-like episode so that the client is impelled to reintegrate in a new and more meaningful way. During the process the therapist both belongs to and separates himself from the family, moving in and out of the intense, sane and crazy, symbiotic relationship in which intrapsychic responses are shared and roles are reversed. As the client is enabled to reconcile both sane and crazy elements within himself, to enjoy his own and the family's creativity, he achieves individuation and rebirth to the point where he is able to establish an independent peer relationship with the therapist, whose role now becomes that of consultant to the family. Thus, the paradoxical and intrapsychic elements occur within the context of experiential therapy.

Specifically, Whitaker (Keith & Whitaker, 1982) has defined seven techniques he considers important aspects of the therapy process:

1. *Redefining symptoms as efforts for growth.*
2. *Modeling fantasy alternatives to real-life stress.*
3. *Separating interpersonal stress and intrapersonal stress.*
4. *Adding practical bits of intervention.*
5. *Augmenting the despair of a family member.*
6. *Affective confrontation.*
7. *Treating children like children and not like peers.*

According to such strategies, the family is included in the problem. The family is taught how to use fantasy to expand its emotional repertoire. Family members learn to take risks. The family is offered ideas it may freely accept or reject. The absurdity of a family situation is heightened and thus underlined, and both relationship and generational boundaries are affirmed and maintained as the therapist models appropriate parenting behaviors.

Whitaker's style was both powerful and poetic, and by choosing to combine various elements, which in another context might appear contradictory and yet have relevance for him, he created a highly personal and very successful approach uniquely suited to his own being. He attempted to demonstrate his commitment to himself and to his profession by his willingness to take risks, to become involved, to share, and thus to grow. He was equally cognizant of and open about his strengths and his weaknesses and of the limitations and requirements for his type of therapy, that is, of his need for a cotherapist. He translated this personal philosophy into his own therapeutic method.

Thus, the therapy process is characterized not only by Whitaker's use of a cotherapist but also by the inclusion of extended family members. Indeed, it is a requirement that the whole family be present, and a request to see three generations is standard behavior: "I'm tempted to say over the phone before the first visit, 'Bring three generations or don't bother to start'" (Whitaker, 1976b, p. 183). This strategy enhances a sense of wholeness, dignity, and historical continuity for the family, and it is also aimed at enhancing the power of therapy:

> When the three-generation system has been assembled, whether as a preventive experience, a healing force, as consultant to the frustrated therapist, or to mediate a three-generation civil war, the long-range benefits may outweigh the immediate ones. Increased flexibility in role demands are almost automatic; frequently loyalty debts and covert collusions are altered. Involvement in the metagame of change allows new visual introjections of individuals and subgroups, thus altering each person's intrapsychic family. Discovering that one belongs to a whole, and that the bond can not be denied, often makes possible a new freedom to belong, and of course thereby a new ability to individuate. (pp. 191–192)

Finally, although Whitaker was aware that the therapist brings his own set of personal values to the therapeutic encounter, it was not his purpose to impose them on anyone else, or to tell another how he or she should be. He was aware the family is a powerful force to be reckoned with and was not afraid to implement power tactics to effect change, yet ultimately therapy is to be a joint effort in which the client is encouraged to break old patterns, to expand himself, and to create the possibility for alteration through reorganization and reintegration.

Systemic Consistency

Despite language distinctly psychodynamic in its origins and meaning, Whitaker's symbolic/experiential approach to family therapy is consistent with the systemic epistemology outlined previously. The heavy emphasis on the power and role of the system as a whole is an obvious element of this consistency. Less obvious, but nevertheless consistent, is the focus on the individual. Thus, Whitaker not only explicitly pays attention to the mutual interaction and influence (or recursiveness) of the individual relative to the system, but he also implicitly acknowledges Maturana's "multiverse" of individual personalities and the impossibility of working with a family as a unified entity sharing an identical perceptual reality.

Similarly, Whitaker's stress on experiencing rather than on educating, on spontaneity and intuition rather than on "constrictive and constipating" models is also systemically consistent. Rather than telling a family what it should do or be, Whitaker is emphatic in his belief that the therapist not "mold their system to his will." In addition, the emphasis on authenticity and personal involvement and the belief that therapists and clients are involved in a parallel growth process in which the family must "write their own destiny" compares very closely to the notions of structural determinism, structural coupling, and nonpurposeful codrifting. Thus, Whitaker did not treat families. Rather, he attempted to create, with the family, a context in which change could occur through a process of reorganization and reintegration.

Further, in his role as coach, Whitaker specifically addressed the issue of not being a member of the team, of not being able to join the family. At the same time he recognized the shared process in which all are involved. He had a model of health or normalcy in his head, but the elements of this model are all process dimensions, and growth for the family is to be defined by the family, which ultimately is viewed as its own best therapist. Whitaker explicitly did not see his role as that of a social control agent. However, by the very process of defining pathology or dysfunction, Whitaker was inconsistent with a cybernetics-of-cybernetics perspective that sees all behavior as logical or normal in context.

Throughout most of his career Whitaker wrote a great deal about his style of therapy, but mostly through the medium of case studies and examples drawn from clinical practice. In recent years, however, and specifically since his retirement from the University of Wisconsin, he paid increasing attention to explaining what he did in therapy. To the extent that he became more systematic in this description of his approach, he ran an increased risk of becoming less systemically consistent. On the other hand, given Whitaker's creative genius and years of doing otherwise, he was able to avoid this dilemma more than most other family therapists. With his death the family therapy field lost one of its most innovative and well-respected pioneers. In the words of longtime professional associate David Keith (1995, p. 7): "Carl was one of those gifted, courageous, and strong people who became a corner post of the family therapy world. Without him the world feels temporarily out of true."

Suggested Readings

Ferber, A., & Whitaker, C. A. (1972). The therapist's family, friends, and colleagues. In A. Ferber, M. Mendelsohn, & A. Napier (Eds.), *The book of family therapy* (pp. 468–479). New York: Science House.

Keith, D. V., & Whitaker, C. A. (1977). The divorce labyrinth. In P. Papp (Ed.), *Family therapy: Full length case studies* (pp. 117–131). New York: Gardner Press.

Napier, A., & Whitaker, C. (1972). A conversation about co-therapy. In A. Ferber, M. Mendelsohn, & A. Napier (Eds.), *The book of family therapy* (pp. 480–506). New York: Jason Aronson.

Napier, A. Y., & Whitaker, C. A. (1978). *The family crucible*. New York: Harper & Row.

Ryan, M. (Ed.). (1989). *Midnight musings of a family therapist*. New York: Norton.

Warkentin, J., & Whitaker, C. A. (1967). The secret agenda of the therapist doing couples therapy. In G. H. Zuk & I. Boszormenyi-Nagy (Eds.), *Family therapy and disturbed families* (pp. 239–243). Palo Alto, CA: Science & Behavior Books.

Whitaker, C. A. (1958). Psychotherapy with couples. *American Journal of Psychotherapy, 12*, 18–23.

Whitaker, C. A. (1967). The growing edge. In J. Haley & L. Hoffman (Eds.), *Techniques of family therapy* (pp. 265–360). New York: Basic Books.

Whitaker, C. A. (1972). Psychotherapy with couples. In G. D. Erickson & T. P. Hogan (Eds.), *Family therapy: An introduction to theory and technique* (pp. 164–169). Monterey, CA: Brooks/Cole.

Whitaker, C. A. (1975a). The symptomatic adolescent—An AWOL family member. In M. Sugar (Ed.), *The adolescent in group and family therapy* (pp. 205–215). New York: Brunner/Mazel.

Whitaker, C. A. (1975b). Psychotherapy of the absurd: With a special emphasis in the psychotherapy of aggression. *Family Process, 14* (5), 1–16.

Whitaker, C. (1976a). A family is a four-dimensional relationship. In P. J. Guerin (Ed.), *Family therapy: Theory and practice* (pp. 182–192). New York: Gardner Press.

Whitaker, C. (1976b). The hindrance of theory in clinical work. In P. J. Guerin (Ed.), *Family therapy: Theory and practice* (pp. 154–164). New York: Gardner Press.

Whitaker, C. A. (1978). Co-therapy of chronic schizophrenia. In M. M. Berger (Ed.), *Beyond the double bind* (pp. 155–175). New York: Brunner/Mazel.

Whitaker, C., & Bumberry, W. (1988). *Dancing with the family: A symbolic-experiential approach.* New York: Brunner/Mazel.

Whitaker, C. A., Felder, R. E., & Warkentin, J. (1965). Countertransference in the family treatment of schizophrenia. In I. Boszormenyi-Nagy & J. L. Framo (Eds.), *Intensive family therapy* (pp. 323–342). New York: Harper & Row.

Whitaker, C. A., & Malone, T. P. (1953). *The roots of psychotherapy.* New York: The Blakiston Company.

Whitaker, C. A., & Miller, M. H. (1972). A re-evaluation of "psychiatric help" when divorce impends. In C. J. Sager & H. S. Kaplan (Eds.), *Progress in group and family therapy* (pp. 521–530). New York: Brunner/Mazel.

Walter Kempler

Although less often discussed, Walter Kempler is also one of the pioneers of family therapy, and he has labeled his approach *Gestalt-experiential family therapy.* According to Kempler (1982),

> *this model focuses attention on the immediate—what people say, how they say it, what happens when it is said, how it corresponds with what they are doing, and what they are attempting to achieve. Regardless of whether discord is found within an individual or is manifest between two or more persons, treatment consists of bringing discordant elements into mutual self-disclosing confrontation. The conversational anchor point is the current conflict of the day and what can be done to resolve it in place of a more analytical or understanding (seeking why) orientation.* (p. 141)

Kempler, who began his medical career as a general practitioner, received an M.D. from the University of Texas in 1948 and later completed a residency in psychiatry at the University of California in 1959. In 1961, following several years of private practice during which he developed an interest in working with families, he established the Kempler Institute for the Development of the Family. Kempler has also written and published extensively and has produced several films of his work with families. He has been active as a freelance teacher and trainer, traveling throughout the United States and northern Europe to share his knowledge of family therapy (Kempler, 1981).

Consistent with his Gestalt heritage, Kempler's approach is derived from existential psychology/philosophy and phenomenology. Therapy is focused on expanding awareness, accepting personal responsibility, and unifying the individual, who is recognized as capable of directing and living her own life. Such acceptance of personal responsibility is necessary if the individual is to achieve maturity. Developed as part of the so-called third force in psychology, after psychodynamic and behavioral approaches, Gestalt therapy placed a heavy emphasis on a positive view of nature, or human potential. Having originated as a theory of perception that focused on the relationship between observer and observed, experiments in this area revealed that individuals view reality in terms of meaningful wholes, or Gestalts, rather than as unrelated isolates. Thus, the notions of figure and ground and the observer as participant in what is observed were key elements of this theory. Also emphasized was the here-and-now, for only the present can be changed inasmuch as the past is gone and the future is yet to come.

As translated into Gestalt-experiential family therapy, Kempler views the immediate family, or the whole of which we are all a part, as the most appropriate setting for therapeutic interaction. Like Whitaker, Kempler believes that the family holds the key to individual growth and development. In addition, the present, face-to-face, reciprocal encounter and interaction between therapist and client, in which fears, expectations, blockages, and resistant areas are explored, is the process by which change occurs.

Basic Concepts/Theoretical Constructs

For Kempler, theorizing is a means of organizing experience in order to be able to relate it to others, a frame of reference for describing behavior. However, like Whitaker he is indeed skeptical of its usefulness:

> *Theorizing, if not theory, is treacherous. Woven initially out of our fantasies, theories can become powerful, dominant, controlling shackles.... The influence of the theory/child will vary with the power the therapist/parents need to project onto the theory/child. Too often, motivated by a diminished self-worth, parents and therapist grant excessive and controlling power to children and theories. (Kempler, 1981, p. 45)*

Inasmuch as theorizing follows experience, it may be symptomatic of an *incomplete encounter*, or used as an alternative to self-disclosure. Residual discomfort and an inability to interact on a more personal level may be dealt with through the creation of cognitive explanations, which help with the accumulation of data but at the same time lead to personal stagnation. Since the experience about which a theory is created is in the past, the theory will differ tomorrow as new experience and thus a new frame of reference is acquired. On the other hand, theorizing is acceptable when used either to recognize personal arousal or for personal sharing. In addition, theories are useful if they create a new experience and thus enhance individual development (Kempler, 1970).

Consistent with this view vis-à-vis theories and theorizing, Kempler espouses an active, spontaneous, ahistoric style of therapy. At the same time he has outlined several concepts fundamental to his approach. For example, he speaks of a *psychological reality*, which is a unique combination of experience and awareness in the here-and-now. Accordingly, we perceive ourselves and the world around us by means of awareness, although this perception may or may not accurately describe our experience. Validation of the accuracy of our perceptions is provided by those whom we empower with this role—our individually chosen validators. However, our perceptions usually differ from those around us, and thus one of the basic aims of therapy is to facilitate a recognition and an awareness of individual differences in perception.

Therapy provides the opportunity for intimate personal experience—the key to growth. Rather than talking about or being educated in different awarenesses, family members are encouraged to interact more productively and thus change their perceptions. However, the first priority is the individual member and the second is the family as a whole. Therefore, "the goal of experiential psychotherapy within the family is the integration of each family member within the family" (Kempler, 1982, p. 27). And *integration* is defined as the recognition, appreciation, and expression of one's personal being.

For Kempler, the family is comprised of any two persons who are concerned about each other. Each family contains the potential to support individual development. Although human beings are motivated to cooperate with and please one another, obstructions occur. Thus, it is the role of the therapist to act as a guide toward more positive human interactions that restore more mutually beneficial interactions between family members.

According to Kempler, existence is comprised of experiences and experiences provide proof of our existence. *Encounters* are people-sequenced experiences, and good encounters are completed in such a manner that there is no residue of uneasiness. Thus, another basic aim of therapy is to provide an opportunity to experience more effective encounters on both interpersonal and intrapsychic levels (Kempler, 1967). In the effective therapeutic encounter, the focus is on the process of behavior in the here-and-now and is composed of the following four requirements:

1. *A clear knowledge of the "who I am" at any given moment. This requires a dynamic awareness of what I need from moment to moment.*
2. *A sensitive cognition or appraisal of the people I am with and the context of our encounter.*
3. *The development and utilization of my manipulating skills to extract, as effectively as I am capable, what I need from the encounter. This aspect is expressive.*
4. *The capability of finishing an encounter. (Kempler, 1981, p. 38)*

The therapist models, and thereby helps the client to share in, the experience of effective encountering. The experience of incomplete encounters is the source of psychological misperceptions; that is, incomplete encounters are characterized by an inability to express feelings aroused during the course of interpersonal interaction. They result in a sense of uneasiness, which distorts current awareness and, in turn, inhibits present encounters.

Discomfort created by incomplete encounters is often dealt with by attempts at understanding, thinking about, or talking over in a current encounter. However, such strategies move the person from the here-and-now to either the past or the future and thereby preclude his ability to experience completely. Experience of, rather than intellectual knowledge about, is considered the best teacher. Indeed, "direct, interpersonal experience is the key to the cultivation and restoration of mental health" (Kempler, 1982, p. 142), and it is the expression of what one is experiencing in the here-and-now that is indicative of responsible and responsive behavior.

Theory of Health/Normalcy

For Kempler, the healthy family provides a supportive context that allows individual members to express both their individual identity and their personal desires, to acknowledge their autonomy and accept difference on the part of others, and to function in the present moment. That is, the encounters we experience in our families have the greatest impact on our capabilities and behaviors. The individual's significant others provide the most important experience of coping, whether successful or otherwise.

In dysfunctional families, the pressures for togetherness and loyalty to the whole may interfere with personal responsibility and integrity. Individuals avoid expressing their feelings and thus preclude the possibility of attaining intimacy (Nichols, 1984). Accordingly, "symptoms are seen as signals of a distressed process: that is, a process that is not evolving suitably according to one of the points or participants in the process" (Kempler, 1982, p. 148).

Regardless of the nature of the symptom, it is always expressed as a conflict between two polarities, with one as the victim of the other and the patient inevitably describing herself in the victim role. For example, the client's presenting problem may be that she is suffering from depression, which prevents participation in desired activities. This symptomatic behavior is the client's way of saying "Ouch! I have a pain in my family" (Kempler, 1973, p. 19). Further, such "symptomatic behavior tells us that a person has a stuck process somewhere inside that obstructs his integrated flowing; that the undulating flow of some process has congealed and the two poles are deadlocked" (Kempler, 1982, p. 155).

The family is therefore dysfunctional to the extent that it has not mobilized its assets in a way that helps the symptomatic individual become unblocked. Therefore, the basic goal of therapy is to restore the ability of the family to act as a fundamental resource for its members' well-being and continued development. Achievement of this goal requires stimulating and releasing the potential of family members, "to perceive, to negotiate, and to act" (Kempler, 1982, p. 159).

Thus, the family is the client in Gestalt-experiential family therapy, while the art of processing is considered a "re-minding," or a realization for all of each individual's own life experiences (Kempler, 1981). Kempler defines the therapeutic interview as a battlefield on which both family members and therapist bring themselves forth to resolve the issues at hand. The first issue presented is usually not the problem. Rather, it is a signal of pain in the family (Kempler, 1973). For example, a request from a male client for help in dealing with his nervousness may reflect the nature of the man's relationship with his boss. It may also indicate a difficulty that his wife and children are having with him as a nervous person. Indeed, for Kempler, how well the family functions either to produce pain or to solve problems is ultimately the measure of its pathology or health.

Therapeutic Strategies/Interventions

The therapist in Gestalt-experiential family therapy acts as a catalyst who encourages individuals to confront each other in a more open and direct manner. She thus offers suggestions for alternative behaviors, provides personal observations, and gives directions or advice. If the offerings are ignored, the therapist may become frustrated and shift to the role of "passionate participant" by acknowledging the client's feelings and demanding attention. The therapist therefore both guides family interaction and relieves personal discomfort.

The personality and life experiences of the therapist are brought into the therapeutic encounter, and it is such active participation that is seen as one of the keys to effectiveness. Kempler (1968) writes that there are "no techniques, only people" (p. 99). The therapist struggles to make his perceptions known, to avoid distortions, and to facilitate a process of clarifying unique individual identities. Further, there is no objectivity in therapy and success requires an active stance. There are several characteristic behaviors that Kempler, speaking personally, feels are likely to enhance the process of therapy. A therapist *needs* to meddle in other people's lives, insists on being heard, takes risks, demands responsible behavior, tolerates differences, understands others, is contrary, is self-critical, is courageous, and acknowledges mistakes (Kempler, 1981).

Further, when the therapist is able to focus completely on the moment and to be fully present to the family, the encounter becomes therapeutic. When the therapist lets go of encounter-diminishing tactics endorsed by various psychological theories, the therapy will become more exciting and thus experiential; that is, the direction chosen by the therapist should be based on immediate perceptions and concerns and not on preconceived models of therapy. Rather than playing the role of therapist, the therapist is a total person who thereby creates an atmosphere that encourages the fullest participation and complete expression of each personality. With the exception of physical violence, any behavior or emotion is considered appropriate in therapy.

In order for the therapeutic encounter to be effective, it must have an impact on the participants. This requires either motivation on the part of the client or skill on the part of the therapist in reaching the client. The therapist must therefore display enough intensity to create a "treatable crisis," thereby making a meaningful connection with the client (Kempler, 1967). Accordingly, the therapist offers behavior rather than interpretations, while staying totally in the present. What counts is what we are and how we interact at this moment. Present experiencing of different behavior equals change for the client in his life. Historical data is relevant only as it emerges spontaneously and provides information about the client's current functioning.

Spontaneity, defined as allowing subsurface material to emerge from the therapist or the family, also characterizes the effective therapeutic encounter. Thus, affect flows freely in a safe and caring environment and the total being of the person is represented in the here-and-now. Spontaneity allows for the expression of any topic as the needs of both client and therapist become known. The therapy is kept alive through active attentiveness to these needs through either verbal or nonverbal responses: "However sparse the verbal participation may be, someone presents the complaint and everyone looks (or doesn't look), moves (or sits motionless) and responds (or fails to respond) in each moment" (Kempler, 1981, p. 159). The therapist also responds by commenting, either with a provocative statement about what is or is not happening or by sharing a personal reflection about the process.

The therapist uses his total personality and being to establish a context that supports effective encountering. Above all, she acts as a model by remaining in the present, being spontaneous, and by accepting personal responsibility for feelings, perceptions, and behaviors. The effective therapist is in tune and totally involved and uses her entire experiential repertoire to motivate or encourage responsiveness, exploration, and experimentation. To reiterate,

> no technique "works." There is no behavior that, of itself is therapeutic. All rules or actions must be filtered through the therapist-person to emerge tailored to the context. The most therapeutic intervention is the total and currently pertinent "I" statement imparted so that it will be experientially heard. (Kempler, 1981, p. 227)

Systemic Consistency

Kempler is far more systemically consistent in his description of the therapeutic process than in his delineation of the theory that guides practice. Thus, he speaks of the therapist as a catalyst who is totally involved in the process, has no objectivity, responds according to immediate perception, and makes recourse to no preconceived or definitely prescribed techniques. The observer is part of the observed, a closed system whose members interact in the here-and-now with no reference to an outside environment, an emphasis on internal structure, and an understanding of reality in terms of multiple perceptions—indeed an epistemology of participation.

On the other hand, by defining the presence of pathology as well as both its cause and the definition of its resolution (good and bad, shoulds and should nots), Kempler moves out of the realm of cybernetics of cybernetics. His extreme emphasis on the individual both in terms of location of pathology and source of health, to the almost complete exclusion of family dynamics, denies an awareness of the dimension of wholeness consistent with the cybernetic perspective. Thus, even though there is a relational focus, the notion of context is specifically addressed only as a supportive characteristic (content) and not as a dynamic in family interaction or therapy (process). Indeed, we are left with the feeling that the Gestalt-experiential approach is individual therapy in the context of the family more than it is family therapy in the purest sense of this concept.

The key to the systemic consistency of the experiential models, therefore, seems to be the degree to which they remain truly experiential or self-referentially consistent as theories that espouse no theory. While both Whitaker and Kempler built their approaches to families on a foundation of individual psychology, another measure of the degree to which systemic consistency is achieved is the relative ability of each to acknowledge the dimensions of recursion and feedback in a context of wholeness and thus make the shift to a cybernetic epistemology. Whitaker seems to have done this to a much greater extent than Kempler.

Suggested Readings

Kempler, W. (1965). Experiential family therapy. *International Journal of Group Psychotherapy, 15* (1), 57–71.

Kempler, W. (1966). The moving finger writes. *Voices, 2,* 107–111.

Kempler, W. (1967). The experiential therapeutic encounter. *Psychotherapy: Theory, Research and Practice, 4* (4), 166–172.

Kempler, W. (1968). Experiential psychotherapy with families. *Family Process, 7* (1), 88–99.

Kempler, W. (1969). The therapist's merchandise. *Voices, 5,* 57–60.

Kempler, W. (1970). A theoretical answer. Reprinted from *Psykologen.* Costa Mesa, CA: The Kempler Institute.

Kempler, W. (1974). *Principles of Gestalt family therapy.* Salt Lake City, UT: Desert Press.

Kempler, W. (1981). *Experiential psychotherapy within families.* New York: Brunner/Mazel.

Kempler, W. (1982). Gestalt family therapy. In A. M. Horne & M. M. Ohlsen (Eds.), *Family counseling and therapy* (pp. 141–174). Itasca, IL: F. E. Peacock.

Kempler, W. (1983a). *Crimes of love.* Costa Mesa, CA: The Kempler Institute.

Kempler, W. (1983b). *The myth of resistance.* Costa Mesa, CA: The Kempler Institute.

$$Chapter \quad 9$$

The Structural Approach

Salvador Minuchin is the person most frequently associated with the development of the approach known as structural family therapy:

> *The model's distinctive features are its emphasis on structural change as the main goal of therapy, which acquires preeminence over the details of individual change, and the attention paid to the therapist as an active agent in the process of restructuring the family. (Colapinto, 1982, p. 112)*

In addition to Minuchin, the other theorists/therapists who have contributed to its development are Braulio Montalvo, Bernice Rosman, Harry Aponte, Jay Haley, Marianne Walters, Charles Fishman, and Stephen Greenstein. However, since the basics of the model remain the same regardless of the therapist, we have elected to treat this approach generically and to focus only on Minuchin.

Although Minuchin and his colleagues are not regarded as originators of family therapy, the structural approach has been perhaps the most influential model in its popularization. It is a clearly articulated theory that provides a useful tool for helping people see the patterns, processes, and transactions of the family as system. As you now know, it is this kind of view that underlies the whole of the family therapy movement.

The structural approach gives the practitioner a concrete, conceptual map about what should be happening in a family if it is to be functional; it also provides maps about what is awry in the family if it is dysfunctional. The structural approach gives students and practitioners definite ideas about how the process of therapy should be carried out. However, these processes inevitably vary in practice, reflecting the personality of the therapist and the particular structure of the family (Aponte & Van Deusen, 1981).

Structural family therapy is one of the most heavily researched models, and its efficacy has been demonstrated with a variety of what are generally termed difficult families. Thus, families with a juvenile delinquent, families with an anorectic family member, families with a chemically addicted member, families of low socio-economic status, and alcoholic families (Aponte & Van Deusen, 1981) have all been successfully worked with using the structural approach. The influence of this approach may also be seen in other models of family therapy, particularly the strategic approach.

Basic Concepts/Theoretical Constructs

Minuchin's perspective suggests that the life history of a family is a series of experiments in living. Structural family therapy describes a delicate balance between stability and change, and between openness and closedness. While this model values a stable field for the family, the stability must be matched with appropriate transitions and changes in structure if it is to be a functional developmental context for its members. The image Minuchin creates for us is a series of scenarios in the life of a family:

> *All we know for sure is that each scenario is an experiment in living. Thus, by definition, it will be carried out in an unstable field, full of visible and hidden traps. The only certainty is that there will be errors and, because of them, conflict, solutions and growth. (Minuchin, 1984, p. 45)*

Structural family therapy sees the family as an integrated whole—as a system. Accordingly, it is also a subsystem in that its members belong to other agencies and organizations in the community of which it is a part and which affect its basic structure and pattern of organization. In the language of the theory there are three key concepts/constructs: *structure, subsystems,* and *boundaries.*

Structure

Structural family therapy focuses on the *patterns* of interaction within the family which give clues as to the basic *structure* and *organization* of the system. For Minuchin (1974), structure refers to the invisible set of functional demands that organizes the way the family interacts, or the consistent, repetitive, organized, and predictable modes of family behavior that allow us to consider that the family has structure in a functional sense. Thus, observations of patterns of interaction in the family provide information about how the family is organized or structured to maintain itself. A family operates through repeated transactional patterns that regulate the behavior of family members. Such patterns describe the how, the when, and to whom family members relate. The concepts of patterns and structure therefore imply a set of covert rules of which family members may not be consciously aware but which consistently characterize and define their interactions.

The structure of a family is governed by two general systems of constraints. The first constraint system is referred to as *generic,* an observation that all families everywhere have some sort of hierarchical structure according to which parents have greater authority than children. An important aspect of this generic structure is the notion of *reciprocal and complementary functions,* which can be discerned by the labels applied to family members that indicate their roles and the functions they serve. For instance, if there is an overly competent parent, the other parent could be described as incompetent. If there is a super-good kid, another child will likely be less good. Similarly, parents can be described as overinvolved-peripheral or nurturing-strict, as complements to one another. Thus, a part of the generic constraint system that can be observed relative to structure is the idea of reciprocity, or complementarity. There are things that need to be done in a family that enable it to perform its functions. Members of a family evolve roles (without a conscious awareness of their roles) to maintain the family equilibrium and to keep it functioning. These roles seem to be balanced, logical complements. Regardless of a member's description, or metaphor (tough, hard, good, healthy, etc.), one can discern another family member whose role in the family logically complements or assumes the opposite role and thus achieves a balance in the family (tender, soft, bad, sick, etc.).

A second constraint system is that which is *idiosyncratic* to the particular family. Thus, rules and patterns may evolve in a family while the reason for such characteristic processes may be lost in the history of the family. Nevertheless, the rules and patterns become a part of the family's structure. The structure of a family governs a family in that it defines the roles, rules, and patterns allowable within the family. This structure can be ascertained by watching the process of the family over time. Indeed, the key to understanding the structure of a family is found in the observation of the processes, within and between subsystems, which describe the kinds of boundaries present in the family.

Subsystems

Structural theory defines three subsystems: the *spouse subsystem,* the *parental subsystem,* and the *sibling subsystem.* The rule among these subsystems for the functional family is that of *hierarchy.* The theory insists on appropriate boundaries between the generations. Consistent with this rule, we will examine each subsystem separately.

Spouse Subsystem
The spouse subsystem is formed when two people marry and thus create a new family. The processes involved in forming the spouse subsystem are known as *accommodation,* which implies adjustment, and *negotiation* of roles between spouses. Such accommodation can best be accomplished when the spouses have attained a certain degree of independence from their families of origin. While each brings the basic rules for being a spouse and parent from the families in which they were raised, spouses who remain enmeshed with their families of origin after marriage will have difficulty accommodating and negotiating their roles relative to each other. In effect, their family of origin experiences did not provide them with sufficient

autonomy to negotiate successfully alternative roles to complement their new spouses.

Complementarity implies that each behavior has a logical complement, as described above. For example, the gender roles characteristic of traditional marriages may involve the husband working outside the home and the wife working inside the home. The early part of the marriage and the formation of the spouse subsystem necessitate evolving such complementary roles. While some of these roles may be transitory and others may be more permanent, the keys to the successful navigation of life as a family are negotiation and accommodation, especially as they concern rules and roles.

Implicit in the notion of complementarity is the idea that certain family functions must be performed in order for the family to operate effectively. The adjustment for couples may be difficult and slow, for each has certain expectations about the performance of various functions and roles. In the adjustment process each must learn to accommodate and adapt to help meet the needs of the other. This can involve small bits of behavior, such as her needing to be alone in the morning, leaving him alone in the kitchen, or how each prefers to be greeted. Larger issues, such as where to live and how to arrange the house, may also be the focus. Whatever the topics, however, the early negotiation and accommodation process in the spouse subsystem is important as a basic tool that allows the family to be functional as it adapts throughout its life. Negotiation and accommodation are enhanced to the degree that each spouse is his or her own person and is not overly tied to the family of origin or its rules, patterns, and roles.

Finally, an important requirement of the spouse subsystem is that each spouse be mutually supportive of the other in the development of his or her unique or latent talents and interests. Accordingly, neither spouse is so totally accommodating of the other as to lose his or her own individuality. There is give and take on both sides, each remains an individual, and because each accommodates the individuality, resources, and uniqueness of the other, they are respectfully bound together.

Parental Subsystem

The parental or executive subsystem is the second subsystem described by structural theory. The birth of a child instantly transforms the system, and if accommodation and negotiation have been successfully developed in the spouse subsystem, these skills will be very useful in the evolution of the parental subsystem. With children, new issues arise which demand complementarity if the functions of the family are to be performed successfully. For example, differences in parenting styles and preferences may appear and need to be negotiated. Further, with the formation of the parental subsystem, the spouse subsystem must continue to exist as a system distinct from the roles of the participants as parents. Spouses must continue to spend time together, whether it be fighting, playing, or loving. The parental subsystem exists around issues and functions about childrearing. The spouse subsystem does not involve children and children's issues.

In the parental subsystem, each spouse has the challenge of mutually supporting and accommodating the other in order to provide an appropriate balance of firmness and nurturance for the children. The parents are in charge and an important challenge is knowing how and when to be in charge about what issues. Parents need to negotiate and accommodate changes in the developmental needs of their children. For instance, one does not parent a three-year-old in the way one parents an adolescent. The former needs great care and support; the latter needs increasing independence and responsibility. Transitions in the family challenge the existing structure and require accommodation and negotiation to evolve a new structure. The children must get the message from the parental subsystem that the parents are in charge. A family is not a democracy, and the children are not equals or peers to the parents. It is from this base of authority that the children learn to deal with authority and to interact in situations in which authority is unequal.

Sibling Subsystem
By establishing the spouse and parental subsystems, structural theory also defines the sibling subsystem. The sibling subsystem allows children to be children and to experiment with peer relationships. Ideally, the parents respect the ability of the siblings to negotiate, to compete, to work out differences, and to support one another. It is a social laboratory in which children can experiment without the responsibility that accrues to the adult. Children also learn to coalesce to take on the parental subsystem in the process of negotiating necessary developmental changes.

Subsystems of the family help the family system carry out its functions relative to its structure. Individuals in a subsystem are differentially empowered and develop skills appropriate to their roles. The relationships within subsystems and between subsystems define the structure of the family. A necessary arrangement between subsystems in the functional family is described by the concept/construct of hierarchy or levels of authority. A necessary relationship between members of a subsystem is described by the concept/construct of coalition, or interaction within a level. One can speak of spouse, parental, and sibling coalitions, each of which protects its turf relative to the other. Each knows where it stands relative to the other and each has a different identity. Coalitions within subsystems and clear boundaries between subsystems enhance the security and well-being of the family.

Boundaries

In the discussions of structure and the related elements of subsystems, hierarchy, coalitions, negotiation, and accommodation, we have already exposed you to the concept/construct of boundaries. Boundaries are invisible, but they nevertheless delineate individuals and subsystems and define the amount and kind of contact allowable between members of the family. For Minuchin, the idea of boundaries implies rules, or certain preferred relationships between subsystems in the family. Each subsystem has its own identity, its own functions, and its own pattern of relationships within it. The identity, functions, and patterns of relationships within a subsystem are governed by relationships between subsystems. Thus, what happens between subsystems affects what happens within subsystems and vice versa.

We know that sounds a bit complicated, and in a way it is, and yet it isn't. The theory describes interpersonal boundaries between subsystems as falling into one of three categories: *clear, rigid,* and *diffuse.*

Clear Boundaries

The ideal arrangement between subsystems is that defined by clear boundaries. Clear boundaries are contrasted with the less-than-ideal arrangement defined by rigid or diffuse boundaries. Clear boundaries are firm and yet flexible. Where clear boundaries exist, the members of a family are supported and nurtured and yet are allowed a certain degree of autonomy. Thus, the theory suggests an ideal balance between support, nurture, and inclusion on the one hand, and freedom to experiment, individuate, and to be one's own person on the other hand.

Clear boundaries also imply access across subsystems to negotiate and accommodate situational and developmental challenges that confront the family. Thus, change in structure, rules, and roles can occur as appropriate to the process of evolving a new structure for dealing with a changing circumstance in the family or its relationship with systems outside the family. The one constant in the life of a family is that its circumstances will change. Indeed, "each scenario is an experiment in living" that necessitates negotiation, accommodation, and experimentation with a new structure over and over again until the family gets it "right," only to find its circumstances have changed once more. Although Minuchin does not specifically address the issue, we suspect that such negotiation, accommodation, and experimentation are best conducted in an atmosphere that balances concern and laughter, with an emphasis on the latter. In speaking of professionals studying the family, he notes,

> answers are born in the way we pose questions. When we look seriously at people interacting with each other, measuring their interactions and applying prevalent norms to the interpretation of our findings, our results can elicit either concern or laughter. Looking at life, as I do, as sets of unfilled promises, I think on the whole that I prefer laughter. (Minuchin, 1984, p. 45)

We do not believe we are stretching the theory too far when we suggest that Minuchin might make a similar statement about families studying themselves; that is, perhaps professionals studying families and families studying themselves take themselves a bit too seriously.

Finally, clear boundaries in a family increase the frequency of communication between subsystems, and thus negotiation and accommodation can successfully occur in order to facilitate change, thereby maintaining the stability of the family. Parents and children can belong and yet individuate. The paradox of conformity through allowing and fostering independence and autonomy is evident in our interpretation of structural theory.

Rigid Boundaries

Rigid boundaries refer to the arrangement both between subsystems and with systems outside the family. Rigid boundaries imply *disengagement* within and between systems. Family members in that instance are isolated from one another and from systems in the community of which the family is a part. Disengaged individuals and families are relatively autonomous and segregated, and when carried to the extreme, this situation may be dysfunctional. In the context of rigid boundaries, children do learn to fight their own battles and to negotiate without hovering parents protecting them from themselves. That is, parents are parents and children are children with little or no room for negotiation and accommodation, and access between subsystems is very restricted. In the extreme of disengagement, only an intense crisis or extreme stress can mobilize support. This is "Handle it yourself" or "Don't bother me, I have my own issues to deal with" carried to its outer limits. In such families, the spouses, parents, and children are so much involved with their own issues that they are slow to notice and respond when others need support. Such an arrangement may be part of the idiosyncratic structure of the family. It may not be noticed since that is the way it is supposed to be. Members in such families thus rely on systems outside the family for the support and nurturance they need and desire.

Diffuse Boundaries

The family defined by diffuse boundaries is characterized by *enmeshed* relationships. This is the polar opposite of the rigid-boundary family. In this case everybody is into everybody else's business and there is an extreme of hovering and providing support even when not needed. The parents are too accessible and the necessary distinctions between subsystems are missing. There is too much negotiation and accommodation. The cost to both the developing child and the parents is a loss of independence, autonomy, and experimentation. The spouse subsystem devotes itself almost totally to parenting functions, and as parents they spend too much time with the children and do too much for them. Consequently, children tend to rely too much on their parents and not enough on their own abilities. Such children may be afraid to experiment, afraid perhaps to succeed, perhaps to fail. They may feel disloyal to their parents if they do not want to accept what their parents offer. They probably have difficulty knowing which feelings are theirs and which belong to others. The children also tend to be uncomfortable by themselves and may have trouble building relationships with others outside the family. As these children marry and leave home, they may have trouble negotiating with and accommodating their new spouses and evolving complementary relationships with them. It is likely that they will remain very attached to their families of origin, continuing to rely on them for support and nurturance, especially if the new spouse does not provide support and nurturance to the degree experienced in the family of origin. Children in such families are too young too long. Thus, there is an absence of both the necessary developmental transitions that must occur as children mature and the necessary changes in structure to accommodate appropriate increases in responsibility and autonomy for the developing child.

In this discussion of boundaries, we hope we have made clear the theory's ideal model; that is, the clear boundary is preferred and it represents an appropriate combination of rigid and diffuse characteristics. Again, the key is balance. Also, negotiation and accommodation are balanced. One might infer that negotiation is present and valued and accommodation is valued some of the time. In the family with diffuse boundaries there is too much negotiation, accommodation, nurture, and support by all parties. In the family with rigid boundaries, we see the extreme of independence and autonomy. In the latter case, support and nurturance are minimal and typically occur only under conditions of extreme stress. Negotiation and accommodation are conspicuous by their absence. In summary, there are expected and unexpected changes in families that will require a change in structure. The family with clear boundaries is better equipped to handle and accommodate the changes—the "experiment in living" that is each new scenario for the family.

The Family over Time

Let's take a moment to elaborate on the changes that the family must make in its life as a family. As you recall from Chapter 6, various theories of family development punctuate expected transition points that require structural changes so the family may remain functional. Among these are marriage, the birth of a child, the child entering school, adolescence, and the children leaving home. These are normal and expected developmental crises or challenges that occur within our culture.

There are other challenges, or unexpected crises, that also necessitate changes in structure and realignment of roles, either temporarily or permanently. Among the changes that may confront a family are the following: winning a large amount of money, the death of a family member, deterioration of the marriage culminating in divorce, sickness of a family member, a grandparent or other relative joining the family, taking in foster children, unemployment of the major breadwinner, a parent having an affair, the arrest of a family member, or a child becoming employed.

Whether expected or unexpected, a crisis is a challenge to the previous structure of the family in the sense that in order for the family to remain functional, the structure must change. Indeed, at times of crisis the family is most vulnerable, most likely to seek therapy, and most amenable to change in therapy if the crisis is sufficiently great. Minuchin (1974) cautions, however, that we should not mistake normal developmental crises and growing pains for pathology. We will discuss this issue further in the section on therapeutic strategies and interventions.

Structural Maps of the Family

Just as Bowen provides the genogram for mapping the relationships in the extended family consistent with his theory, structural theory also provides a method for mapping the structure of the family (Minuchin, 1974). The symbols used for mapping, consistent with the theory, involve punctuating boundaries as clear, diffuse, or rigid, and transactional styles as enmeshed or disengaged. We present the symbols for the map in Figure 9.1. We follow this with examples of maps of various family structures.

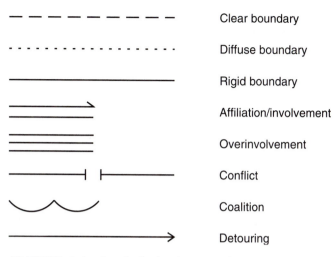

FIGURE 9-1   **Symbols for Structural Mapping (Minuchin, 1974, p. 53)**

Below is the map for the functional two-parent family, which depicts clear boundaries between the parental (executive) subsystem and the sibling subsystem.

The figure below depicts the way a map of a functional single-parent family might look:

A map of a functional stepparent family might be as illustrated below:

A functional two-parent family with an adolescent child and other children might be depicted as follows:

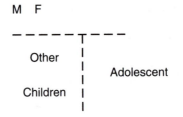

A conflictual marital relationship that has not been detoured onto a child might look like the map that follows:

A conflictual marital relationship that has been detoured onto a child is mapped as follows:

A conflictual marriage in which one parent forms a coalition with the child and thus a cross-generational breach undermining the executive subsystem might be depicted as:

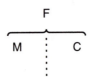

The following presents a map describing a shift in roles when father loses a job, mother takes on a job, and father takes on household duties:

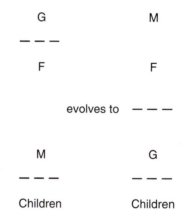

If a grandparent becomes involved in helping the family in this crisis and takes on parenting roles, the shift in roles may be mapped as follows:

One might map a dysfunctional stepparent family as follows:

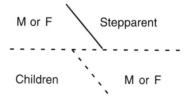

The variety of maps used to describe the functioning and nature of interpersonal relationships within the family is endless. The above maps describe just a few of the possibilities. Regardless of the situation, however, it is important to consider issues relating to developmental stage and to take note of all subsystems as well as other extrafamilial systems that may be involved with the family.

Theory of Health/Normalcy

The concept of an ideal family, regardless of its particular form, comes through loud and clear in structural theory. It is important to note, however, that Minuchin (1984) does not necessarily see the traditional family with two parents and their natural children as the only acceptable form. In fact, he suggests that holding up the traditional family as an ideal while considering other family forms—single-parent, stepparent, or blended—as anomalies and less than ideal may be counterproductive to helping these other kinds of families view themselves as functional contexts for development:

> *At this point in history, most Americans still think of the nuclear family as the norm—which automatically makes us think of other shapes as "incorrect."... We should recognize change as inevitable, even normal, and set ourselves the tasks of helping families over transitional periods.... We are still organized to defend the nuclear family. (pp. 47–48)*

For Minuchin, the ideal family builds on a spouse subsystem in which each accommodates, nurtures, and supports the uniqueness of the other. The spouses have attained a measure of autonomy from their families of origin. Ideally, in the family of origin each spouse felt supported and nurtured and yet experienced a degree of autonomy, independence, and responsibility. Similarly, spouses need to be able to maintain a delicate balance between proximity and distance. On this base the couple negotiates complementary roles that are stable but flexible and, through a process of negotiation and accommodation, evolves different structures and role complements to deal with changing circumstances. The spouse subsystem maintains itself even when children are born and the parental/executive and sibling subsystems come into existence.

As we noted, the parental, or executive, subsystem must face differences of opinion about how to raise the children and organize the family so that children get a balance of authority and nurture. However, in healthy families the autonomy of each spouse and of the spouse subsystem does not get lost in the structure shift necessitated by the birth of children. This reflects what to us is both/and rather than either/or thinking and negotiating. Thus, the children experience the security of the parental/executive subsystem. Grounded in this security and sure that they will be supported and nurtured, they are also encouraged to experiment with increasing amounts of independence and responsibility appropriate to their developmental ages.

The ideal family will face expected and unexpected crises appropriately by recognizing and facilitating necessary changes in structure. Such behavior requires a great deal of patience and wisdom. As in the beginning of the family when spouses "evolved a new culture" (Minuchin, 1984, p. 57), so with the challenge of each crisis a new culture (structure) must be evolved, in many cases a structure and transition process for which the participants have no direct experience to guide them. That is, "families are organisms in a continuous process of changing while trying to remain the same" (p. 71).

For children, their particular family structure is the only experience of family they have, and their security is grounded in this structure. Thus, for the child, what is, is normal. Consequently, a divorce is often followed by a mourning of the "structure that was lost" (Minuchin, 1984, p. 71). Certainly the structure of the family after divorce will be different. However, this differentness offers alternative possibilities for growth that the previous family structure did not. Nuclear families and divorced families are different, but not better or worse; each has the potential to be either healthy or dysfunctional.

In the ideal family the sibling subsystem feels the security and strength of both the spouse and parental subsystems. This strength provides the grounding for increasing levels of experimentation in independence and responsibility. The children know the parents will provide support and nurturance. Indeed, children's experimentation is not for real and does not carry with it the full-blown responsibility of the adult. Children can return for support and encouragement after failure and applause after success. In the case of failure, they can experience a moratorium, and, with encouragement, they can venture out to experiment anew, to fail or to succeed, or both. In addition, the sibling subsystem is the first territory where children experiment with evolving peer relationships. Similarly, as siblings negotiate with the parental/executive subsystems through clear boundaries, they learn to deal effectively with authority figures. Thus, the family is the laboratory where children learn skills to deal with systems outside the family and to apply, ultimately, to their own spouses and families.

In the ideal family of structural theory, a generation gap gradually gives way to something approximating an adult-adult relationship as the children grow to maturity. Children leave home through small incremental steps, beginning formally when they first go to school. When children ultimately leave home, they do so secure in the knowledge that the family will be O.K. without them. They have witnessed and experienced the reciprocity and accommodation in the spouse subsystem, which did not get displaced by the parental subsystem, and which maintained appropriate boundaries within and between the generations.

Therapeutic Strategies/Interventions

Few families are ideal in the sense of being problem free and handling all challenges and transitions smoothly and without growing pains. Indeed, all families experience stress from situational challenges and at transition points in their evolution. The key to the success of the family is its ability to make adaptive changes in structure relative to family circumstances and the developmental stages of its members. Behavior disorders are believed to arise when the family structures are inflexible, whether enmeshed or disengaged, and do not make appropriate structural adjustments.

Symptoms or behavior disorders in a person designated as the *identified patient* (IP) are not limited solely to the IP's relationships with others. Rather the relationships the IP has with others may reflect other relationships in the family—relationships that do not directly involve the IP. Thus, problems reflect the whole of the family, and structural theory would include all family members not only in the assessment but also in the therapy. Further, in the assessment process, other people or systems not a part of the immediate family, but which affect the nature of the structure and the relationships in the family, must be considered. This may include stressors coming from work, school, the welfare system, a recently incapacitated grandparent, or a lover in an extramarital affair. The structural therapist may even work with some of these outside agencies or people if it is deemed important for effecting successful structural change in the family. Given these outside influences, the structure of the family therefore may not be successfully changed by working only with the family.

The primary focus of structural therapy is on the structure of the family, yet structural theory strongly suggests that the therapist also be alert to problems within individuals. Minuchin, Rosman, and Baker (1978) caution therapists to avoid "denying the individual while enthroning the system" (p. 91). Elsewhere Minuchin (1974) notes: "Pathology may be inside the patient, in his social context, or in the feedback between them" (p. 9). The structural therapist must therefore be alert to identifying what might be a learning disability or a neurological problem within the individual and be able to make appropriate referrals. However, even if there is a problem within a child, for example, evolving an appropriate structure to accommodate this different child without detracting from the developmental needs of other siblings and the spouse subsystem is an important issue for the structural therapist.

Problem solving is not the goal of structural therapy. Symptomatic behavior is viewed as a function of the structure of the family; that is, it is a logical response in the family given its structure. Problem solving will naturally occur when appropriate structural adaptations have been made. Thus, problem solving is the business of the family; structural change, so that problem solving can occur, is the business of the structural therapist. Symptom removal without the appropriate change in structure would not be successful therapy from the structural perspective.

Goals of Structural Therapy

The goals for structural therapy are somewhat idiosyncratic to the family, although it is recognized that there are some general patterns and structures that recur within a given cultural context. The following general goals therefore guide the structural therapist in our society:

1. There must be an effective hierarchical structure. Parents must be in charge. Thus, there must be a generation gap based on parental/executive authority.
2. There must be a parental/executive coalition. Parents must support and accommodate each other to provide a united front to their children.

3. As the parental/executive coalition forms, the sibling subsystem becomes a system of peers.
4. If the family is disengaged, the goal is to increase the frequency of interaction and move toward clear rather than rigid boundaries. Through this shift there would be an increase in nurture and support to complement the previous independence and autonomy characteristic of families with rigid boundaries.
5. If the family is enmeshed, the general goal would be to foster differentiation of individuals and subsystems. This would reflect a respect for differences in developmental stages of the children and permission for age-appropriate experimentation with independent activity.
6. There must be a spouse subsystem established as an entity distinct from the parental subsystem.

The Process of Change

Minuchin (1974) identifies three phases in structural therapy: (1) the therapist joins the family and assumes a leadership position; (2) the therapist ascertains the family's underlying structure; and (3) the therapist transforms the family structure. The structural therapist must join the family and respect its members and its way of organizing itself. This joining and respecting is akin to what anthropologists do when studying a different culture. They attempt to understand a culture from its own perspective and not from the perspective of the anthropologist's culture. In therapy this joining is also essential, for the family must accept the therapist, and acceptance is more likely to occur if the therapist reciprocally accepts the family. Thus, the therapist gets into the family and accommodates to its usual style. Such joining is a necessary prerequisite of attempts to restructure.

The structural therapist also respects the hierarchy of the family by asking for the parents' observations first. On the other hand, if the therapist begins by first asking for the views of the children, the therapist may be rejected by the parents. As the therapist listens, she reframes and transforms the family's interpretation of events, which is usually based on an individual-pathology or outside-influences model, into a systemic or structural framework. Problems thus get redefined relative to the family structure. Reframing, among other techniques, is an important part of structural therapy. Structural therapy is action oriented and is aimed at influencing what happens in the therapy session. The therapist works with what she sees going on in the session even though the content of the discussion may be about what goes on outside the session. The therapist thus modifies even as she accepts and observes.

Structural family therapy focuses on two kinds of live, here-and-now activities: *enactments* and *spontaneous behavioral sequences*. When a therapist asks for an enactment, he seeks a demonstration of how a family deals with a specific kind of problem in order to observe the sequence. This gives the therapist clues as to the existing structure of the family. For example, mother and father may be asked to discuss an issue regarding the handling of children. In the course of the discussion, the therapist may observe a child join with one of the parents, thus suggesting a parent-child coalition, bridging of the generation gap, a weak parental/executive coalition, a diffuse boundary (enmeshment) between one parent and the child, and a rigid boundary (disengagement) between the child and the other parent. After observing the transactions in the enactment, the therapist guides the family to change the enactment. This is not done by criticizing, but by suggesting different ways of handling the interchange. Enactment thus describes the process in therapy whereby the therapist makes specific kinds of transactions occur and through which the therapist can begin to modify the structure. In our example, the therapist might suggest that the parents firmly inform the child that the issue under discussion is between them and the child may not interrupt.

Spontaneous behavioral sequences describe transactions that occur in the family as a natural part of its pattern. If the therapist successfully joins the family, the family will begin to reveal pieces of its structure through its transactions. The transaction is not specifically requested by the therapist as in the case of enactment, but offers similar opportunities to modify the transactions and thus the structure of the family.

Structural theory suggests that the therapist should observe the transactions of the family and get a sense of its pattern and structure. The therapist should avoid sweeping, a priori assumptions about family structure. However, there seem to be certain characteristic structures associated with certain kinds of presenting problems relative to the membership of the family. Therefore, hypotheses regarding existing structures can be developed before the first interview. Answers to key questions about the family can provide clues to the structure and to probable problems often accompanying a given structure. Among the questions that might be posed are:

1. How many people are in the family?
2. What kinds of people are in the family? Children? Adults?
3. What are the ages of family members?
4. What is the presenting problem?
5. What are the sexes of family members?
6. What is the religion of the family?
7. What is the family's socioeconomic status?

We will give a few examples of the kinds of clues provided by various answers to these questions.

The Single-Parent Family with One Child

When this kind of family requests therapy it is likely that the two members are enmeshed with one another. The family may reflect an adult-adult relationship in which the child is moved into an adult role before her years. A valid hypothesis is that the child spends too much time with adults and insufficient time with peers. At the same time, the child may receive too much individual attention. Indeed, parent and child may each be overly responsive to the other's needs and moods. A key issue is the mutual overdependency that such a family may build.

The Three-Generational Family

This kind of family is typically a grandmother, a mother, and a child. When such a family is experiencing problems, a key issue may be who is the child's parent? Is the mother the grandmother's "child," and thus more a peer and less a parent to her own child? There may be a different structure if the mother lives in the grandmother's house than if the grandmother lives in the mother's house. Are they competing for the role of primary parent to the child? Is there a parental coalition between grandmother and child? Who is the primary parent? The key point in this family is distinguishing and allocating appropriate roles among the three generations.

The Large Family

In the large, dysfunctional family, it is quite common that one child, often the eldest or the eldest female, will be given responsibility as the parental child. While this is not problematic in itself, it can be problematic if the child is given responsibilities he or she cannot handle or if the child is not supported by the parents. In the latter case, such a child is asked to be the parental child and yet is not sufficiently validated as having this role when another child complains. A further complication may be that the child does not have sufficient opportunities for peer relationships within the sibling subsystem or outside the family. Key points are how executive authority is delegated to the child, how it is supported, and how the child is relieved of this authority.

The Blended Family

Two single-parent families or one single-parent family and one childless spouse are joined under this arrangement. In effect, they are two families joined only at the level of the spousal relationship. When blended families become symptomatic, it is important to be aware that if there was too much enmeshment in the previous single-parent families, the issues of joining and developing a structure may be resisted by both the children and the spouses. Another key issue is the nature of the relationship with absent natural, noncustodial parents and the nature of their involvement with the family.

The patterns described by these examples are suggestive rather than definitive. The therapist must not rigidly hold to the patterns and structures suggested, but rather must be willing to rely on his observations as the most valid source of data in family assessment. This is an important part of the diagnostic process. Thus, hypotheses regarding structures are formulated and revised as the therapist observes different patterns in subsequent sessions that were not evident in the initial observations of family transactions. Again, the key is observing the family in action and not relying on the reports of family members about what is happening. Crucial issues in the therapist's mind as he observes are "who says what to whom, and in what way" (Nichols, 1984, p. 494). This observed sequence reveals family structure. For example, frequent interruptions suggest enmeshment, while a disinterested response by a parent or spouse to an emotional crisis in session suggests disengagement.

Once a pattern or structure is ascertained, the challenge becomes one of breaking the pattern. There are no specific techniques for doing this. In fact, specific techniques can interfere with the natural flow in the new "family," which includes the members plus the therapist as both member and leader. The therapist must know what he wants to say and must say it in a manner that will get the family's attention. He gets the family's attention via modulation of the analogic mode of communication; that is, voice tone, pacing, volume, repetition, and word selection are used to achieve *intensity*. Intensity in delivery is what enables family members to hear a message about what is going on and thus sets the stage for structural change.

Indeed, intensity is an important tool in structural family therapy, and *shaping competence* is another. Shaping competence refers to altering the direction of the flow and helps develop the positive, functional alternatives that the family members may already know. For example, praise for performing a difficult action (difficult relative to the existing structure) may help family members feel confident in themselves. An important part of structural therapy is the therapist's insistence that the family members are capable and can do what needs to be done. In effect, the structural therapist makes what he wants the family to do happen in the session, where the members can be encouraged to hang in there and where their success is generously praised.

Other specific activities the structural therapist might do in therapy include:

- Realign boundaries by physically altering the proximity or distance between family subsystems. This can also be accomplished by meeting separately with subsystems or individuals in order to firmly establish or acknowledge boundaries.
- Help members of disengaged families to increase the frequency of contact between them.
- Help specific dyads resolve their own issues without intrusion from other members of the family. This can be sibling to sibling, parent to parent, or parent to child. Such activities can be described as allowing each relationship to seek its own level.
- Teach aspects of structural theory to the family so the family can have its own cognitive map to understand the goals and the interventions of the therapist better.
- Change the way family members relate to one another so their perception of the other can change. Structural therapists believe that reality is only a perspective. The family members are acting on the validity of the perspective each has of the other. The therapist can also provide the family with other cognitive constructions referred to as "pragmatic fictions" (Nichols, 1984, p. 500) and thereby provide family members with a different world or family view for its experience.
- Confuse the family by using paradoxes and thus help them evolve different structures.

The fundamental processes of structural family therapy include:

1. Learning and believing in the concept of structure in families.
2. Observing transactions and patterns characterizing these processes, from which structure may be inferred.
3. Having a definite ideal structure for a family given its constituent members and circumstances.
4. Joining, accepting, and respecting the family in its efforts to organize itself to achieve its goals while assuming a leadership role.
5. Intervening in the family in respectful and yet firm ways to make happen in session what the therapist wants to have happen, consistent with the structural map deemed more likely to help the family and its members move toward the model of health described by structural theory.
6. Supporting members, challenging them to try new methods in session, and praising them generously when they are successful.

These processes may or may not occur in Minuchin's dynamic and forceful way. However, there must be an intensity sufficient to gain the attention of family members. "Tone, volume, pacing, and choice of words can be used to raise the affective intensity of statements. It helps if you know what you want to say" (Nichols, 1984, p. 494). To this we add: if you know what you want to have happen.

Systemic Consistency

Structural family therapy in general and Minuchin in particular provide a unique blend of the perspective of simple cybernetics with that of cybernetics of cybernetics. Through the way inconsistencies are balanced by consistencies, this approach offers a viable model for implementing a nonlinear framework in a linear context. The systemic theory is translated into a working model containing elements of both first- and second-order cybernetics that are so interwoven that little is lost in the translation.

For example, Minuchin articulates a theory of family and therapy that clearly defines ideal types of structures and behaviors. That is, there are absolute rights and wrongs in a theoretical context that stresses relativity. This is balanced, however, by the focus on process dimensions such as hierarchy, boundaries, rules, roles, accommodation, and negotiation as elements of health and dysfunction.

Similarly, on the one hand Minuchin feels that therapists must respect a family's organization, must join the family, must revise their hypotheses about the family as they go along, must recognize differences in members' perceptions, and must focus on changing the structure or context within which a problem is logical. On the other hand, therapists also provide a leadership role and give priorities to their own observations. Therefore, therapists must be both subjective and objective and operate according to both the black box plus the observer model and the black box model.

Mutual influence, feedback, and emphasis on internal structure are additional aspects of the consistency of this approach with cybernetics of cybernetics. Indeed, inasmuch as structure is understood as defining and determining function, Minuchin is very close to Maturana. However, deliberate interventions to break patterns and the notion of progress implicit in this process contrast sharply with Maturana's vision of structural coupling and nonpurposeful drift.

Carried to the extreme of consistency, the theoretical context of cybernetics of cybernetics precludes pathology and thus the need for therapy. In a cultural context that defines a role for both pathology and therapy, structural family therapy offers an approach that is able to exist with a great deal of ease in both contexts and to provide a bridge between the medical model and the systemic model. This is certainly a tribute to and reflection of its creator, Salvador Minuchin, psychiatrist and family therapist.

Suggested Readings

Aponte, H. (1976). Underorganization in the poor family. In P. J. Guerin, Jr. (Ed.), *Family therapy: Theory and practice* (pp. 439–448). New York: Gardner Press.

Aponte, H. (1994). *Bread and Spirit: Therapy with the new poor.* New York: W. W. Norton.

Aponte, H., & Van Deusen, J. (1981). Structural family therapy. In A. S. Gurman & D. P. Kniskern (Eds.), *Handbook of family therapy* (pp. 310–360). New York: Brunner/Mazel.

Colapinto, J. (1991). Structural family therapy. In A. Gurman & D. Kniskern (Eds.), *Handbook of family therapy* (2nd ed.) (pp. 417–443). New York: Brunner/Mazel.

Elizur, J., & Minuchin, S. (1989). *Institutionalizing madness: Families, therapy and society.* New York: Basic Books.

Minuchin, S. (1974). *Families and family therapy.* Cambridge, MA: Harvard University Press.

Minuchin, S. (1982). Reflections on boundaries. *American Journal of Orthopsychiatry, 52,* 655–663.

Minuchin, S. (1984). *Family kaleidoscope.* Cambridge, MA: Harvard University Press.

Minuchin, S., & Fishman, H. (1982). *Techniques of family therapy.* Cambridge, MA: Harvard University Press.

Minuchin, S., & Nichols, M. (1993). *Family healing: Tales of hope and renewal from family therapy.* New York: The Free Press.

Minuchin, S., Baker, L., Rosman, B., Liebman, R., Milman, L., & Todd, T. (1975). A conceptual model of psychosomatic illness in children. *Archives of General Psychiatry, 32,* 1031–1038.

Minuchin, S., Montalvo, B., Guerney, B., Rosman, B., & Schumer, F. (1967). *Families of the slums.* New York: Basic Books.

Minuchin, S., Rosman, B., & Baker, L. (1978). *Psychosomatic families: Anorexia nervosa in context.* Cambridge, MA: Harvard University Press.

Chapter *10*

Communications Approaches

The theory underlying communications approaches to family therapy is seminal to the entire field. Indeed, its basic premises are fundamental to both the structural and strategic models. "Virtually every approach now treats communication as synonymous with behavior, and concepts like the double bind and family homeostasis have been absorbed in the literature. In fact, it might be said that communications family therapy died of success" (Nichols, 1984, p. 394).

It is therefore difficult to delineate models or identify key figures who are distinctly representative of this approach today. It is no accident that those we have chosen to include in this chapter might just as easily be, and in some cases have been, discussed under other headings. We will focus first on such early members of the Palo Alto, California, group as Don Jackson, John Weakland, and Paul Watzlawick. These same people are also closely associated with and representative of the strategic approach. The second half of the chapter will be devoted to the work of Virginia Satir, who is often defined, and rightly so, as a member of the experiential school of family therapy. However, in both cases the basics of the particular models associated with these therapists emerged out of the work of Gregory Bateson and his research teams in the area of schizophrenia. Thus, in both cases, communications theory is the heart of the matter.

Essential to the focus of this theory/approach are the redundant patterns of communication and interaction within and between systems. Such patterns are seen as comprising the rules of the system and may be inferred by an outside observer. Hence, the emphasis is on the here-and-now rather than on the past, and the key question is What? rather than Why?, consistent with systems theory in general. Similarly, causality is understood as circular and recursive, and families are seen as error-activated and goal-directed systems.

More specifically, communications theorists are concerned with (1) *syntax*, or the style or manner in which information is transmitted and received; (2) *semantics*, or the clarity of communication transmission and reception; and (3) *pragmatics*, or the behavioral effects of communication, whether verbal or nonverbal (Nichols, 1984). Thus, the theme of communication and its importance, which has run throughout this book, is consistent with the impact that early research in this area has had on the development of the entire field of family therapy.

Early Researchers

Don D. Jackson

One of the earliest researchers in the area of communications theory was Don Jackson, who joined Bateson's Palo Alto research team in 1954. Jackson was hired as the psychiatric consultant to join original members Jay Haley, John Weakland, and William Fry in their study of schizophrenic communication. He was a coauthor, with Bateson, Haley, and Weakland, of the 1956 landmark article, "Toward a Theory of Schizophrenia." In 1959 he founded the Mental Research Institute (MRI) in Palo Alto, inviting Virginia Satir to join him in this enterprise.

Jackson's major contributions deal with the organization of human interaction. Thus, in addition to his role in the development of the double-bind concept, he is also responsible for the introduction of the notion of *homeostasis*. Jackson hypothesized that families develop recurring patterns of interaction that maintain the stability of the family, especially in times of stress. Therefore, families may be described as *rule-governed systems*.

According to Jackson, there are three kinds of rules by means of which a system operates. These include *covert norms, overt values*, and *metarules*, or rules about the norms and values. The process of defining rules is known as *calibration*, or the determination of behaviors considered acceptable by a family. Accordingly, a family experiencing symptoms indicates a need for recalibration and the lack of a rule for changing the rules.

Jackson's focus on relationships also led to his delineation of the symmetrical and complementary communication patterns originally described by Bateson. As you no doubt remember, *symmetrical relationships* are defined by exchanges of similar kinds of behavior, and *complementary relationships* are characterized by exchanges of opposite kinds of behavior. Jackson was also responsible for describing the concept of the marital *quid pro quo*; that is, marriage partners are said to establish this-for-that bargains by means of which they unconsciously collaborate to resolve differences and create a workable relationship.

For example, Fred does not like to go to parties or to socialize in groups of more than four or five people. Linda, his wife, is very outgoing and is comfortable in almost any kind of social situation. The expectation (covert norm) they had early in their marriage was that married couples should go out together. Thus, initially each tried to please the other, with Fred going out when he preferred not to go or

Linda staying home when her choice would have been to go out. Over the years, however, they have modified this arrangement in such a way that according to the current rules, it is acceptable for Fred to say no to certain social invitations and it is also acceptable for Linda to go out alone if she so desires. This is an example of a functional quid pro quo.

On the other hand, if Fred and Linda had not been able to modify their expectations, every social event might have been the occasion for a scene in which Fred was always late getting ready and Linda always nagged in advance and then got angry when Fred was late anyway. Although they invariably wound up going out, neither had a very good time. In this case, the this-for-that bargain is, "We will go out together but it will always be a struggle and we certainly won't enjoy ourselves." The pattern repeats, and the couple becomes more and more stuck as similar exchanges create more negative feelings. It is with such negative quid pro quos that couples may eventually come into therapy.

For Jackson, therapy was an active process, and his goals included pointing out and clarifying such family rules as those we described. He wished to upset the old homeostasis in order to facilitate the development of a new relationship balance in families. He used both insight about current patterns of interaction and paradoxical interventions such as reframing and prescribing the symptom. Further, he believed the therapist's role should be one of both model and teacher in the process of helping to create more functional patterns of communication.

John H. Weakland

John Weakland received degrees in chemistry and chemical engineering and began his career in industrial research and plant design. However, after six years of engineering practice he became interested in sociology and anthropology and turned his attention to research in the areas of Chinese culture, family, personality, and political behavior. In 1953 he moved to California to participate in Bateson's Palo Alto study of human communication. The connection here is that Bateson had been Weakland's first professor of anthropology during his graduate studies at the New School for Social Research in New York City.

As a member of the Bateson group (1954–1960), Weakland studied hypnosis and therapeutic practice with Milton Erickson. He also increased his knowledge of psychotic behavior and family therapy in collaboration with Don Jackson. In addition, he was a codirector of the schizophrenia research project (1958–1962). He also began a part-time private practice in brief family therapy (1959).

Weakland was a research associate for the Institute of Political Studies at Stanford University from 1962 to 1968. From 1965 to 1970 he was the principal investigator for MRI's Chinese Political Themes Project, and from 1965 to 1971 he analyzed Chinese feature films for the Office of Naval Research. He also conducted field studies of Chinese communities in New York and San Francisco and of the Navajo and the Pueblo Indians. Over the years he has taught for Stanford University, the California School of Professional Psychology, the Wright Institute at Berkeley, and the University of San Francisco.

Until his death in July 1995, Weakland worked as a clinical anthropologist and family therapist at MRI, where he also served as research associate and associate director of the Brief Therapy Center. In addition, he was advisory editor for the journals *Family Process* and *Family System Medicine.* During his distinguished career he published five books as well as numerous articles.

The initial focus of the Bateson group was on the observation of human communication in general. The switch to the observation of schizophrenics in particular occurred in response to the awareness that communication among members of this group illustrated the paradoxes, or inconsistencies between the report and command levels, in which the researchers were interested. An understanding of the inability of schizophrenics to distinguish between the levels of messages led to speculation about the origins of such dysfunction. Thus the double-bind theory was born, and the role of the family in the learning and maintaining of such behavior patterns was introduced into the group's theorizing (Watzlawick & Weakland, 1977).

Building on the concept of family homeostasis, the researchers began their study of communication between schizophrenics and their families. In this undertaking, the viewpoint of the group was interactional and their orientation was anthropological; families were seen as a particular culture, and the goal was to describe both normal and abnormal behavior patterns within this culture. Even though therapy with these families was not part of the original plan, an interest in helping to alleviate pain and to solve problems gradually developed among the team members. Ultimately, the outcome of this concern was the development of the concept of *brief therapy* (Watzlawick & Weakland, 1977).

According to the assumptions of the brief therapy model, only those issues defined as problems by the family should be the focus for change. Such problems are to be specified in clear behavioral terms, as are the desired outcomes of therapy. After inferring the specific interactional and communicational patterns maintaining the problem behavior, the therapist seeks to interdict this pattern through the use of paradox. Sessions are kept to a maximum of ten, and family progress is evaluated during a follow-up study several months after the termination of therapy. In 1974 Watzlawick, Weakland, and Fisch outlined the basics of this model, including the delineation of first- and second-order change, in their book *Change.* (You might want to refer back to Chapter 5 for a review of this theory.) It is difficult to isolate the particular contributions made by Weakland, but there is no doubt he was a significant force in the orientation of the study and the development of the theories described by the Palo Alto group as a whole.

Paul Watzlawick

Paul Watzlawick is a native of Vienna, Austria, and his early interests were in language, communication, and literature. He received a doctorate in philosophy and modern languages from Ca' Foscari University in Venice, Italy (1949), and then studied psychotherapy at the C. J. Jung Institute in Zurich, Switzerland. During the ten years that followed this study, Watzlawick was a training analyst in Zurich, a professor of psychotherapy at the University of El Salvador, and a research associate at the Temple University Medical Center in Philadelphia, Pennsylvania. However, frustrated with the unsatisfying results of therapy according to traditional methods, he went to MRI in 1960 to become a research associate and investigator (Bodin, 1981; Hansen & L'Abate, 1982; Kaslow, 1982).

When the Brief Therapy Center was opened at MRI in 1967, Watzlawick joined Arthur Bodin, Richard Fisch, and John Weakland in their efforts to investigate behavioral change, with a focus on interpersonal communication and its disturbances in families and other social contexts. Not only was the brief therapy approach advocated by this group successful in solving the client's presenting problems, it was found that such resolution often led to positive changes in other areas of the family. Today Watzlawick continues his association with MRI and the Brief Therapy Center in addition to teaching and consulting in the Department of Psychiatry at Stanford University.

The basic premise of Watzlawick's theory of communication is that a phenomenon cannot be understood completely without examination of the context in which it occurs and is embedded. Thus relationships, as manifested through communication, are the appropriate focus of study (Watzlawick, Beavin, & Jackson, 1967). Primarily concerned with pragmatics, or the behavioral effects of communication, the goal of therapy is problem resolution. Problems are viewed as situational, arising from difficulties in interaction. Resolving problems requires altering the client's perception of reality by changing the language employed to communicate about the problem.

According to Watzlawick (1978), the language of change is the analogic mode, which is a function of the right hemisphere of the brain. The therapist gains access to the right hemisphere through the use of homonyms, synonyms, ambiguities, and puns, which block the brain's logical left hemisphere. In addition, Watzlawick uses paradox, reframing, and requests for clients' worst fantasies. Facilitation of second-order change is achieved through making the covert overt, advertising instead of concealing, and using resistance (Watzlawick, Weakland, & Fisch, 1974). In each case, changing the rules of the system, thus altering the context, by providing information from outside the system is the road to problem resolution.

In addition, Watzlawick (1978) stresses the rule that influence is inevitable and that, therefore, therapists cannot not influence. Therapists are active and they are responsible for the moral judgments they make. Further, he believes, along with Weakland and Fisch, that schools of psychotherapy that have such patient goals as happiness, individuation, or self-actualization are working toward utopian, and therefore unattainable, outcomes:

> *With goals such as these, psychotherapy becomes an openended process, perhaps humanistic, but more likely inhumane as far as the concrete suffering of patients goes. In view of the lofty magnitude of the endeavor, it would be unreasonable to expect concrete rapid change. . . . The unattainability of a utopia is a pseudo-problem, but the suffering it entails is very real. (Watzlawick, Weakland, & Fisch, 1974, pp. 56–57)*

Problems are thus created by unrealistic expectations, and Watzlawick, Weakland, and Fisch insist that to prevent therapy from becoming its own pathology, it should confine its activity to the alleviation of suffering. Watzlawick sees all theories as perspectives on reality and believes that adherence to one's own perspective as the only reality is both faulty and dangerous.

Review Of Early Research

Since the basic assumptions underlying the communications approach of the Palo Alto theorists have been spelled out in some detail in this and other chapters, we shall merely present summaries under our usual headings of Basic Concepts/Theoretical Constructs, Theory of Health/Normalcy, and Therapeutic Strategies/Interventions. These summaries will be followed by our assessment of systemic consistency as well as a list of suggested readings.

Basic Concepts/Theoretical Constructs

The fundamental rules of communication (Watzlawick, Beavin, & Jackson, 1967) include the following:

1. One cannot not behave, and thus, by definition, one cannot not communicate. All behavior is communication at some level.
2. All communication has a report (digital) level and a command (analog) level. The command level defines the nature of a relationship.
3. All behavior/communication must be examined in context. Without contextual awareness, complete understanding is not possible.
4. All systems are characterized by rules according to which the homeostatic balance is maintained and the system is preserved.
5. Relationships may be described as either symmetrical or complementary. In the former case the context of the behavior exchange is one of equality; in the latter it is one of oppositeness, or one-up, one-down. Neither is necessarily better nor more stable.
6. Each of us punctuates our reality in different ways; that is, behavioral sequences are understood and meaning is experienced relative to the epistemology of the observer.
7. Problems are maintained within the context of recursive feedback loops of recurrent patterns of communication.

Theory of Health/Normalcy

Normal, according to the communications approach, equals functional; that is, the normal family is able to maintain its basic integrity even during periods of stress.

Changes are accommodated as needed. Communication is handled in a clear and logical manner. On the other hand, a dysfunctional family is said to be stuck. Symptomatic behavior maintains the current equilibrium and avoids change when change is needed. A problem is therefore a symptom of system dysfunction and is thus a communication about what is and is not happening in the family.

The classic example of communication in a dysfunctional family is the double bind. Accordingly, two messages, or injunctions—one verbal and one nonverbal—are simultaneously sent. Each of these messages denies or negates the other. The receiver of the message, however, is unable either to avoid or to comment upon such paradoxical messages. He ultimately "escapes" through an inability to discriminate between levels of messages, thus refusing all attempts to define the nature of the relationship.

Therapeutic Strategies/Interventions

The goal of therapy for the Palo Alto theorists is to change the recurrent pattern of communication by which a problem is maintained. There are four steps to approaching and handling a problem (Watzlawick, 1978), including:

1. Define the problem in clear and concrete terms.
2. Investigate all solutions to the problem previously attempted.
3. Define the change to be achieved in clear and concrete terms.
4. Formulate and implement a strategy for change.

As you read Chapter 11 you will recognize these steps—they characterize the strategic approach to family therapy. This approach emerged from communications theory. The major difference is that the MRI group tends to focus more on dyadic (two-person) than on triadic (three-person) interaction (Nichols, 1984). Further, in recent years the MRI group has shifted to working with only one member of the system.

The rule for therapy is that you change behavior by changing communication. Specifically, hidden messages are brought out into the open and rules governing faulty or paradoxical communication are altered. The therapeutic relationship is central to this process, and key interventions include the paradoxical injunction and the therapeutic double bind.

Systemic Consistency

The communications theorists' approach is basically intellectual and scholarly (Nichols, 1984). The therapist first theorizes about the family in general and its characteristic behavior patterns in particular. She then does therapy by operating on the family in order to change behavior. Thus, recursive feedback loops are the focus of assessment and the locus of change. This is clearly a black box approach to understanding and working with families. Indeed, it is the belief of advocates of this approach that dysfunctional, stuck families require information, hence correction, which is available only from outside the system. An avowedly pragmatic approach, it is quite systemically consistent at the level of simple cybernetics.

Consistency at the level of cybernetics of cybernetics, however, must be rejected on nearly all counts. While reality is understood as perceptually based, the observer/therapist is not included in what is observed—the family. Systems are defined as open and as having reference to an outside environment in terms of inputs and outputs. Indeed, therapist inputs are seen as essential for client change. Symptoms are described as logical to context, yet the healthy-dysfunctional polarity is delineated and an ideal model is defined. Therefore, the model may also be said to be internally inconsistent inasmuch as the practice conflicts with the theory in several instances. None of this, of course, denies the fact that this approach has proven to be extremely useful and has provided the basics for much of the field of family therapy.

Suggested Readings

Bateson, G., Jackson, D. D., Haley, J., & Weakland, J. H. (1956). Toward a theory of schizophrenia. *Behavioral Science, 1,* 251–264.

Bateson, G., Jackson, D. D., Haley, J., & Weakland, J. H. (1963). A note on the double-bind, 1962. *Family Process, 2,* 154–162.

Fisch, R., Watzlawick, P., Weakland, J., & Bodin, A. (1972). On unbecoming family therapists. In A. Ferber, M. Mendelsohn, & A. Napier (Eds.), *The book of family therapy* (pp. 597–617). New York: Science House.

Flaskas, C. (1992). A reframe by any other name: On the process of reframing in strategic, Milan and analytic therapy. *Journal of Family Therapy, 14,* 145–161.

Jackson, D. (1967). The myth of normality. *Medical Opinion and Review, 3,* 28–33

Jackson, D. D., & Weakland, J. H. (1961). Conjoint family therapy: Some considerations on theory, technique, and results. *Psychiatry, 24,* 30–45.

Ruesch, J., & Bateson, G. (1968). *Communication: The social matrix of psychiatry.* New York: W. W. Norton.

Watzlawick, P. (1963). A review of the double-bind theory. *Family Process, 2,* 132–153.

Watzlawick, P. (1965). Paradoxical predictions. *Psychiatry, 28,* 368–374.

Watzlawick, P. (1966). A structured family interview. *Family Process, 5,* (2), 256–271.

Watzlawick, P. (1974). *An anthology of human communication.* New York: W. W. Norton.

Watzlawick, P. (1976). *How real is real?* New York: Vintage Books.

Watzlawick, P. (1978). *The language of change.* New York: Basic Books.

Watzlawick, P. (1983). *The situation is hopeless but not serious.* New York: W. W. Norton.

Watzlawick, P. (1984). *The invented reality.* New York: W. W. Norton.

Watzlawick, P., Beavin, J., & Jackson, D. (1967). *Pragmatics of human communication.* New York: W. W. Norton.

Watzlawick, P., & Weakland, J. H. (Eds.). (1977). *The interactional view: Studies at the Mental Research Institute, Palo Alto, 1965–74.* New York: W. W. Norton.

Watzlawick, P., Weakland, J., & Fisch, R. (1974). *Change: Principles of problem formation and problem resolution.* New York: W. W. Norton.

Weakland, J. H. (1960). The "double-bind" hypothesis of schizophrenia and three-party interaction. In Don D. Jackson (Ed.), *The etiology of schizophrenia* (pp. 373–388). New York: Basic Books.

Weakland, J. H. (1972). We became family therapists. In A. Ferber, M. Mendelsohn, & A. Napier (Eds.), *The book of family therapy* (pp. 132–133). New York: Science House.

Weakland, J. H. (1974). "The double-bind theory" by self-reflexive hindsight. *Family Process, 13* 269–277.

Weakland, J. H. (1976). Communication theory and clinical change. In P. J. Guerin, Jr. (Ed.), *Family therapy: Theory and practice* (pp. 111–128). New York: Gardner Press.

Weakland, J. H., Fisch, R., Watzlawick, P., & Bodin, A. M. (1974). Brief therapy: Focused problem resolution. *Family Process, 13*, 141–168.

Virginia Satir

Virginia Satir, having found research a rather boring enterprise, entered the field of family therapy via education and social work, having always made it a point to get to know the families of both her students and her clients. By the time that Don Jackson invited her to join him at MRI, she had been doing family therapy for several years, had taught family dynamics in Chicago, had visited Murray Bowen in Washington, D. C., and had presented the results of her work to the Bateson group at the Veteran's Administration Hospital in Palo Alto. It was Satir who began what was probably the first training program in family therapy shortly after MRI opened (Satir, 1982).

In 1964 Satir published *Conjoint Family Therapy,* one of the first major books in the field. That same year she also became acquainted with the Esalen growth center and later became director of its residential program. At Esalen, Satir was introduced to sensory awareness, massage, group encounter, Gestalt therapy, dance therapy, body therapy, and other nontraditional therapies. As a result, she began moving toward a wholistic approach to therapy. Her model, although based in communications, is also very experiential in nature and incorporates elements drawn from many of the nontraditional therapies to which she was introduced at Esalen.

According to Simon (1989), Virginia Satir, who died in 1988, was "larger than life" (p. 37), not only literally but figuratively. An extremely sensitive person, she was able to connect with those around her in a deeply caring manner. The secret of her success was the consistency of her model with her personal being.

Basic Concepts/Theoretical Constructs

Satir (1982) termed her approach a process model "in which the therapist and the family join forces to promote wellness" (p. 12). This model is premised on the view that families are balanced, rule-governed systems that, through the basic components of communication and self-esteem, provide a context for growth and development. Underlying this model are four fundamental assumptions.

In the first place, Satir believed that the natural movement of all individuals is toward positive growth and development. A symptom therefore indicates an impasse in the growth process, which is somehow related to a balance of the requirements in the larger system, or family. Although the specifics may look different in different individuals and families, the general characteristics of this process are always the same.

Secondly, Satir assumed that all individuals possess all of the resources necessary for positive growth and development. By learning to access their physical, intellectual, emotional, sensual, interactional, contextual, nutritional, and spiritual resources, human beings can increase their potential to nourish themselves. The goal of therapy is therefore to facilitate this process.

Satir's third assumption was one of mutual influence and shared responsibility; that is, "everyone and everything is impacted by, and impacts, everyone and everything else. Therefore, there can be no blame—only multiple stimuli and multiple effects" (1982, p. 13). Accordingly, the therapist, by means of a variety of techniques, helps to bring characteristic family patterns, in which all members are involved, into conscious awareness in order to avoid the scapegoating or blaming of one member.

The fourth assumption is that therapy is a process involving interaction between both clients and therapist. While the therapist may take the lead in helping to facilitate growth, each person is in charge of himself or herself. Indeed, each family member is to become as whole as possible, and therapy is merely to provide a supportive context for such development.

Satir (1982) summarized the process of creating the above framework and its continuing evolution as follows:

> *I had developed a profound and unshakable belief that each human can grow.... My search is to learn how to touch it and show it to the persons so they can use it for themselves. That was, and still remains, the primary goal in my work. (p. 16)*

The cornerstone of Satir's model is what she called the *primary survival triad*. This triad includes the child and parents. For Satir, each child acquires identity and self-esteem relative to the constructive or destructive interactions characteristic of this triad.

A second important triad is that of *body, mind*, and *feelings*. According to Satir, body parts can become metaphors for psychological meaning, and thus physical symptoms are often an expression of emotional distress. Sculpting, or posturing, is therefore an important part of therapy, as it allows clients to experience themselves and their feelings in a safe environment and to achieve new awareness and thus new interpretations.

Perhaps the best-known examples of Satir's theorizing about communication are the stances of *placating, blaming, super-reasonable, irrelevant*, and *congruent* (Satir, 1972). According to Satir, these styles of communication are expressed by body position as well as verbal behavior. Thus the *placater* looks as well as speaks in the role of the passive, weak, self-effacing individual who always agrees with others. By contrast, the *blamer* usually disagrees no matter what, always finds fault with others, and is the picture of the self-righteous finger-pointer. The *super-reasonable* individual assumes a computerlike rigid posture devoid of feelings but is extremely logical and intellectual, at least in appearance. The *irrelevant* individual is characterized by unrelated and distracting behaviors and seems to consider neither self nor others in the process of communicating. Finally, the *congruent* individual sends level messages in which words and feelings match, and neither the self, the other, nor the context is denied. Indeed a major part of Satir's focus was on communication and the discrepancies between levels of messages:

> *The forms of discrepancy were manifest in (1) what one felt but could not say (inhibition); (2) what one felt but was unaware of (repression), and only reacted to in another (projection); (3) what one consciously felt, but since it did not fit the rules, one denied its existence (suppression); and (4) what one felt but ignored as unimportant (denial). (Satir, 1982, p. 18)*

For Satir all behavior is communication. Since communication involves the sending and receiving of information, messages must be sent and received clearly within families if individuals are to survive and flourish. The difficulty involved with maintaining clear communication is a function of the many different possible interpretations of the same message and the ways in which words may be qualified by both nonverbal processes and the context. Thus, communication is a complex business and it lies at the heart of Satir's perspective on dysfunction.

Theory of Health/Normalcy

For Satir the family is a system that operates to achieve and maintain its own balance. Symptomatic behavior is thus a homeostatic mechanism reflecting family pain, which is experienced to some degree by all family members. Further, a symptomatic child often reflects a pain in the marriage, which is manifested in incongruent communication and dysfunctional parenting.

Satir (1964) believed that problems arise in the context of marriage partners with low self-esteem, high expectations, and lack of trust in their potential to succeed. For example, two people marry in the hope of getting something, without awareness of the necessity for giving something as well. Expecting total agreement, their worst fears are realized when they discover their differentness, which is immediately labeled as badness. This leads to disagreement, which in turn is interpreted as lack of love. However, such disagreements are never brought out into the open, and communication becomes more and more covert and indirect.

Dissatisfaction in the marriage leads to increasing efforts on the part of the couple to have their needs met through the process of parenting. They may therefore use their children as a means of maintaining their self-esteem. Thus, a child may become triangulated into the marital relationship, although dysfunctional parents rarely perceive their participation in problem behavior on the part of the child. Indeed, since they lack self-esteem, they do not have any sense of their ability to be an important influencing factor. Rather, they look to the role of heredity and chemistry in the development of emotional problems.

While conceding the one-sided and linear nature of the process of symptom formation, Satir nevertheless stressed the role of the parent in the development of self-esteem in a child. She believed the parents have the power to affirm or negate the child's sense of mastery and worth as a human being. Parents do not fail intentionally, but it is this failure that is responsible for deviant behavior in children.

Accordingly, if parental messages to each other and to the child are contradictory, the child learns to communicate in a similar fashion. Further, parents who model indirect or incongruent styles of communication also send messages that undermine the child's self-esteem. This in turn contributes to the development of dysfunctional communication patterns in the child. Thus, the cycle is complete as parents with low self-esteem communicate poorly and produce children with low self-esteem, who also communicate poorly.

Illness is therefore a logical response to a dysfunctional context. It is resolved when the symptomatic individual is either removed from the context or the context is changed. On the other hand, a healthy context is one in which communication is congruent and feelings are openly expressed in an unbiased, nonjudgmental manner. Further, rules are updated as needed and discarded when appropriate. A functional family therefore provides a set of relationships in which members can ask for what they need, can have their needs met, and are supported in their movement toward individuality and self-worth. Differentness is thus accepted, and growth and development are facilitated in the processes characterizing healthy families.

Therapeutic Strategies/Interventions

Satir used the *family life fact chronology* to depict important events in the life of the family. The chronology begins with the birth of the oldest grandparents and is crucial to the technique of family reconstruction. Similar to a genogram, the therapist is able to get a sense of the context within which symptoms emerged as well as of characteristic intergenerational family patterns.

According to Satir, we all grew up in families that influenced how we think, feel, and behave today. Further, we are all striving to become whole, and thus therapy is for everyone: "My view is that we are constantly trying to make a whole out of that which was unwhole in our growing up" (Satir, 1982, p. 23). The appropriate target for treatment is thus the family, which contains the same potential to heal as it does to harm. The purpose of therapy is to change the family's style of communication in order to permit the fulfillment of its humanistic purposes. The first task of the therapist is to make contact with each family member, modeling one's own feelings of worth and equally acknowledging the value of every other person. In addition, the therapist must be spontaneous and willing to experiment in order to help clients grow. Satir advocated flexibility of time, place, and style, and set no limit on possible therapist behaviors. Indeed, the focus is on the here-and-now, and techniques such as metaphors, sculpting, games, and humor are implemented "at a moment in time to make an intervention to allow something to happen" (Satir, 1982, p. 25).

The therapist is seen as a facilitator, a resource person, an observer, a detective, and a model for effective communication. The therapist creates a setting in which clients may risk looking at themselves and their actions more clearly. He recognizes clients' fears and feelings of hopelessness and thus strives to create a context of comfort and trust, which is also characterized by a sense of purposefulness and action.

All available family members are included in the therapy, although Satir often preferred to see the marital pair first, and children under four years of age might eventually be excluded. The history taking, or family chronology, provides information for the therapist, structures the early sessions, and helps to reduce clients' level of anxiety.

Satir attempted to change faulty communication through direct intervention (Nichols, 1984). Thus, she pointed out problematic patterns, helped individuals get in touch with their feelings, and demonstrated functional interaction patterns. She also educated clients about differentness, or "the whole area of individuality, how each person is innately different from every other person" (Satir, 1967, p. 11).

Through her process model, Satir created a trusting and nurturing context in which family members could let down their defenses, risk sharing their feelings, and learn new behaviors. She believed that the most difficult family problems could be solved in therapy once access is gained to the human resources necessary and available for dealing with these problems. Thus, families can initiate change and make new choices rather than persisting in old patterns.

Once a family has learned to communicate more effectively, the system has become more open and is better able to support the fulfillment of its purpose. Clients can respond to crises and problems in a more creative and effective manner. The family has some potent and long-term resources with which to maintain itself and continue to function in a healthy manner.

Systemic Consistency

As with the communication approach discussed in the first half of this chapter, Satir's model has some problems in the area of systemic consistency. However, her emphasis on process seems to balance out these inconsistencies to some extent. On the one hand, Satir described a linear etiology of symptoms based on faulty communication and dysfunctional parenting. Similarly, she defined an ideal model of how individuals and families should be if they are to be considered healthy. On the other hand, she understood problems as logical to context and reality as perceptual and self-referential. To the extent that therapist and client are involved in a shared process during which they work together to facilitate growth and development, an epistemology of cooperation may be inferred. Thus, the therapist responds to what is going on in the here-and-now and sees the balanced nature of the system.

Although certainly systemic, Satir's model of the family ultimately is that of the black box: the therapist is external to the system, observing characteristic patterns and offering information, or inputs, without which change would be impossible. Progress is assumed as both a possibility and a goal. Thus, the requirements of cybernetics of cybernetics are not really met by this approach.

Suggested Readings

Bandler, R., Grinder, J., & Satir, V. (1976). *Changing with families.* Palo Alto, CA: Science and Behavior Books.

Satir, V. (1967). *Conjoint family therapy* (rev. ed.). Palo Alto, CA: Science and Behavior Books.

Satir, V. (1967). A family of angels. In J. Haley & L. Hoffman (Eds.), *Techniques of family therapy* (pp. 97–173). New York: Basic Books.

Satir, V. (1971). The family as a treatment unit. In J. Haley (Ed.), *Changing families* (pp. 127–132). New York: Grune & Stratton.

Satir, V. (1972). *Peoplemaking.* Palo Alto, CA: Science and Behavior Books.

Satir, V. (1978). *Your many faces.* Millbrae, CA: Celestial Arts.

Satir, V. (1982). The therapist and family therapy: Process model. In A. M. Horne & M. M. Ohlsen (Eds.), *Family counseling and therapy* (pp. 12–42). Itasca, IL: F. E. Peacock.

Satir, V. M., & Basdwin, M. (1983). *Satir step by step: A guide to creating change in families.* CA: Science and Behavior Books.

Satir, V., Stachowiak, J., & Taschman, H. (1977). *Helping families to change.* New York: Jason Aronson.

Simon, R. (1972). Sculpting the family. *Family Process, 11,* 49–51.

Simon, R. (1989). Reaching out to life: An interview with Virginia Satir. *The Family Therapy Networker, 13* (1), 36–43.

Chapter *11*

Strategic Approaches and the Milan Influence

More than any other approach, strategic family therapy brings us face to face with the received view of our culture and of traditional mental health as practiced in our culture. As you read about the various theories of family therapy, you probably noted whether or not they fit with your current belief system regarding people, change, and the process of therapy. We think this will especially be the case as you read and study about strategic family therapy. An important part of the received view of our culture is the psychodynamic/depth psychology assumptions that problems are within people, that they are deep-seated, and that we must get at the root of their causes in order to solve them. Anything less than this would be merely superficial and transitory change. From this perspective, strategic family therapy is superficial and transitory. However, like any approach, it is consistent within itself and builds on the logic of its assumptions.

The criticisms lodged by proponents of psychodynamic/depth psychology are based on the belief that their view describes reality and truth. On the basis of this assumption other theories are critiqued. Thus, we have a controversy in which one theoretical school, operating on the basis of the validity of the assumptions consistent with and underlying its perspective, critiques the theory and therapy of another theoretical school operating on equally consistent but decidedly different fundamental assumptions. However, from the perspective of theoretical relativity, each deserves to be critiqued on its own merits, within its own framework, and consistent with the assumptions of that framework.

We call your attention to this phenomenon because strategic approaches (as well as behavioral approaches, to be discussed in Chapter 12) build on assumptions that are very different from the received view of our culture, and thus we are anticipating some of your reactions (most likely resistance) to both. Paradoxically, by anticipating your possible reactions, we are also providing you with an experience in strategic therapy. That is, (1) we anticipate a highly probable response based on our assumption that you are a person socialized in Western culture and thus into the psychodynamic/depth psychology model, which is a part of the received view of the culture; and (2) in the process we place your probable resistance to strategic therapies under our control by pointing out to you the source of your resistance and saying to you it makes sense to resist. Of course, by explaining what we are doing, we have effectively negated the paradox we posed. Or have we? By explaining what we were doing, we have shared control with you. Or have we? Could it be that by presenting the paradox of anticipating your resistance and putting it under our control, and by our subsequent (presumed) honesty in explaining how we sought to control your thought, we posed a higher-order paradox through the seduction of the term *honesty?*

If, by this point in our discussion, you are thoroughly confused, we have accomplished our purpose and helped you experience a paradox, consistent with the assumptions of strategic family therapy, imposed by us as therapists on you the client. To state this a little differently, at first we were very manipulative. We then were honest. Was our apparent honesty also manipulative? Is our honesty in continuing to try to explain also manipulative? From the point of view of the strategic therapist, the answer is "Yes! It must be, it cannot not be!" The assumption about the nature of people and relationships implicit in the theory underlying strategic therapy is that manipulation is unavoidable. As such it is not unethical, which is another criticism often aimed at strategic therapists. From this perspective it is more unethical to insist that one can avoid manipulation.

The assumption that manipulation is bad is based on the belief that one can "not manipulate." By contrast, strategic therapists, building on the assumptions that one "cannot not behave" and one "cannot not communicate," describe what is generally called *manipulation* as an inevitable consequence of being in a relationship in which each member seeks to control or define its nature. Thus, manipulation is something one cannot not do. Further, while being honest about one's intention of having no hidden agendas may perhaps represent a sincere attempt to avoid manipulating the other, such honesty is still an attempt to influence such that a relationship will be defined in which the rule is: no hidden agendas. And that, of course, is also a hidden agenda! To explicitly acknowledge one's purpose or hidden agenda only reveals a higher-order hidden agenda. Indeed, there are no relationships devoid of hidden agendas, and there are no relationships devoid of manipulation.

The theory and therapy that is often set forth as the exemplar of "no hidden agendas" is that of Carl Rogers, with its warmth, empathy, genuineness, respect, and nonjudgmental orientation. It certainly feels genuine and sincere, but that of course is its manipulation from the perspective of the strategic therapist. The Rogerian therapist does not make known to the client the agenda embedded in the theory underlying therapy. For example, the Rogerian therapist does not say to the client at the outset, "I will listen to you with active interest and empathy. I will be genuine with you. I will not judge you. I will not take responsibility for your life or decisions. As I do these things with you, I believe you will 'move yourself' to self-actualize, to become a fully functioning person. I do not believe you can do this, according to the assumptions of my theory, unless I am genuine, warm, acceptant, and empathetic with you." Is the Rogerian therapist not manipulative? From the perspective of Rogerian theory she is not. From the perspective of the strategic therapist, she cannot not be, and thus the paradox.

Many people are regarded as strategic theorists and therapists. We will therefore focus first on the approach in general, saving a discussion of particular models for the latter half of the chapter. Some of the many members of the strategic club have included Milton Erickson, Jay Haley, Cloé Madanes, Lynn Hoffman, Peggy Penn, Richard Rabkin, Richard Fisch, John Weakland, Paul Watzlawick, and Arthur Bodin. Members of the group referred to as the Milan Associates, i.e., Mara Selvini Palazzoli, Luigi Boscolo, Gianfranco Cecchin, and Guiliana Prata are also included in this chapter based on the influence of strategic approaches upon the evolution of their theorizing. However, the metaphor systemic is probably more appropriate to describe in general the early work of this group and subsequent work by individual members of the group. Indeed, strategic therapy is also known by other descriptions, such as problem-solving therapy and systemic therapy.

This approach came of age with the family therapy movement, although as general concepts, the ideas of paradoxical injunction and prescribing the symptom, which often characterize strategic therapy, have been around a long time (Dunlap, 1928, 1946). In the field of family therapy, strategic therapy's entry into mainstream thought was marked by publication of the seminal book by Watzlawick, Beavin, and Jackson (1967), *Pragmatics of Human Communication.* An earlier work by Haley (1963), *Strategies of Psychotherapy,* sought to demonstrate that paradox was a common factor in all approaches to therapy and was built on the work of Milton Erickson. Haley further articulated Erickson's hypnosis techniques in *Uncommon Therapy* (1973).

The strategic approach to therapy evolved from both communications theory (which was discussed in Chapter 10) and from general systems theory. In addition, many ideas regarding intervention were drawn from Milton Erickson, and a variety of concepts and constructs were based on the work of Gregory Bateson (1972) together with Satir, Jackson, Watzlawick, Weakland, and Haley of the Mental Research Institute (MRI) in Palo Alto, California.

Basic Concepts/Theoretical Constructs

Strategic therapists build their models on common assumptions and concepts regarding the nature of people and the nature of problems. However, different strategic therapists emphasize different aspects and thus have evolved different approaches to therapy. We will begin by calling your attention to the commonalities. Later we will point out the differences in approach of different therapists.

Interestingly, while strategic therapists generally do not value providing clients with insight to help them change, a knowledge of their perspective on conceptual frameworks is basic to an understanding of the theory underlying strategic therapy. A *conceptual framework* is defined as a world view, or a set of assumptions about the world according to which similarities and differences are punctuated. A conceptual framework provides definitions of what is called problematic. Further, once a problem is defined as a problem by a conceptual framework, that framework also suggests certain ways of dealing with the problem; that is, possible solutions to a problem are limited to those that are logically consistent with the framework. Thus, if one is tired (defined as a problem), the logical solution is to sleep. Similarly, if one observes a behavior by another, perhaps throwing a temper tantrum, that is assumed to be problematic, the logical solution provided by the frame may be to stop the tantrum by coercive means. According to this theory, therefore, a so-called problem is a problem only from a frame of reference that so defines it. In addition, given the problem as defined, we are limited to a finite number of means to solve the problem, and the rule for selecting the means is that it be logical to the problem as defined. However, in a different frame of reference, what was defined as problematic from the first perspective may no longer be a problem in need of solution.

Strategic therapists are concerned with the conceptual frameworks of their clients. They are aware that the problem, as described by the metaphors and constructs of the client, gives clues about the client's conceptual framework and about solutions the client has attempted. Thus, if a parent describes a child as a "rotten kid," the therapist knows that the client behaves in a way that is logical to the metaphor "rotten kid," and might be reciprocally labeled a "tough, punishing, and restrictive parent." It is a fundamental assumption of the strategic therapist that people will behave in a way logically consistent with their conceptual frames. A further assumption is that clients are not aware the "map is not the territory" (Bateson, 1972; Chase, 1938; Korzybski, 1958), or that their conceptual frame is not the way they or others really are. Clients generally do not share the belief that their framework merely punctuates one of an infinite number of possible explanations that could be assigned to the same experience.

Clients (people) are therefore limited in two ways. In the first place, they are limited to conscious mind and to the rational solutions that arise within the boundaries of the framework of concepts and constructs through which they experience meaning. In the second place, they are limited by the fact that they do not have access to alternative frameworks. They are not aware that what they call a problem can be reframed out of existence, that it can be viewed in a framework in which it is not problematic, because they lack a conscious awareness of the alternatives offered by the metaperspective that the "map is not the territory." By contrast, when individuals with a higher-order perspective encounter problems that have remained insoluble, they might ask questions about the assumptions being made about the situations. They are therefore able to move into a different framework.

Clients who believe the map is the territory do not have the option of alternative, equally valid explanations of the same phenomenon which, paradoxically, is no longer the same phenomenon once they have a different perspective on it. That is, from this perspective, reality is based on perception. The strategic therapist believes that things are not the way they are. Rather, they are the way they are because that is the way we have perceived and conceptualized them. The therapist therefore behaves in a manner consistent with this belief in order to move people to a different perspective of the same situation. In a conversation the authors had with Milton Erickson in 1979, he explained his behavior as follows: "People come with problems they cannot solve. I give them problems they can solve." He continued: "The rational mind is a dumb, stupid mind limited by what it believes to be true and is limited to what is logical to it." He therefore used hypnosis to shut down the logical, limited framework of options and narrowness of the conscious mind. By inducing a hypnotic trance he activated what he convinced clients was the creative, expansive subconscious in which solutions existed outside the conscious awareness of the rational mind.

The perspective that the map is not the territory and that any phenomenon can be given any number of alternative, equally valid explanations also describes the essence of reframing, an important intervention in strategic therapy. However, if one believes that the map is the territory, that what I call it is really what it is, then reframing as an intervention is not a logical possibility.

Key ideas in this discussion are *frameworks* and *logic*. With logic also comes the concept of illogic. As we continue our discussion we will be making frequent reference to that which is *logical*, defined as making sense, and that which is *illogical*, defined as not making sense, and thus paradoxical. For the time being, however, we would like to do away with the logical-illogical dichotomy. To this end, Paul Dell (1986c) poses the following question in his article: "Why do we still call them 'paradoxes'?" It is a useful question, since what is viewed as illogical, or paradoxical, is only so from a frame of reference in which it does not make sense. From within its own framework, what is considered to be illogical in another frame makes perfect sense and thus ceases to be illogical. Stated differently, to see something as illogical or paradoxical is not to see its sense in context. Indeed, it is assumed that everything has meaning and makes sense from some framework.

For example, a client presents himself as having the problem of "depression," an affective condition that our society punctuates as something problematic. Consistent with the logic of the culture, he makes numerous conscious attempts to get rid of his depression. He may see his physician, whose prescription of an antidepressant confirms his belief that the depression is bad and that all possible effort should be made to get rid of it. Family and friends all try to help with their commonsense suggestions for the so-called problem referred to as depression. However, all attempted solutions fail. In fact, not only does the depression persist, it intensifies. But none of the data regarding the efficacy of these attempted solutions daunt our client or the network of therapists, some lay and some professional, in their efforts to get rid of the depression.

Enter the strategic therapist. This therapist believes that the depression makes sense; it is a behavior embedded in the social context of which the client is a part. In fact, the depression is seen as symptomatic of family disturbance. The therapist sees normalcy in context and the symptom of depression is not abnormal in a dysfunctional context. Further, the depression is seen as a communication about relationships within the system. If the symptom persists, this is information that the context is logically consistent with maintaining the behavior the client is seeking to change.

The strategic therapist also believes in a phenomenon called the *"be spontaneous" paradox*. That is, conscious attempts to control behaviors such as depression, which are not subject to conscious control by rational and logical means, only maintain the depressed behavior. They also serve to increase its intensity and to add another level of higher-order feelings (e.g., anger or guilt) about not being able to get rid of the depression as one is "supposed" to be able to do.

The strategic therapist therefore suggests not only that the client should keep his depression but also that he should intensify it. The therapist may either offer an elaborate set of reasons, or reframes, for making this suggestion or may offer no explanation at all. In either case, she has prescribed the symptom. This prescription is illogical to the framework within which depression is viewed as bad and something to be eliminated, for the client certainly does not see the symptom as a communication about, or a manifestation of, dysfunction in the family. By prescribing the symptom, however, the therapist is seeing the problem in a framework according to which (1) symptoms make sense in context and (2) the escalation of symptoms also makes sense given the failure of previous attempted solutions and the notion of the "be spontaneous" paradox. Indeed, symptoms must make sense in some framework. If they do not, it is due to the therapist's inability to get outside of the conceptual "box" she is using to decide sense and nonsense.

In strategic theory and therapy, symptoms are seen as interpersonal strategies or efforts to define the nature of relationships (Haley, 1963). They are embedded in the family's network of relationships and serve an important purpose in the family. Thus, the maintenance of a symptom is associated with complex, reciprocal feedback mechanisms within and between systems.

Accordingly, a symptom is not viewed as a discrete or isolated piece of behavior. It is an important part of the social context of the family, as are the reciprocal roles that logically complement the symptom. Symptoms are not caused (the linear view). Rather, they evolve as a necessary and logical role for the maintenance of the family. Strategic therapists are therefore not concerned about etiology. Given the concept of equifinality/equipotentiality, the focus is on pattern, and particularly that of the triad, or what may be a series of interlocking triangles, an emphasis most strategic therapists share with Bowen and Minuchin.

A typical triadic pattern is that of the peripheral father, the ineffective, overinvolved, executive mother, and the rotten kid. The rotten kid escalates his relationship with mother to the point where father becomes involved. However, father's intervention is too heavy-handed (according to mother's perspective), and mother compensates for father's toughness by being overnurturing, thus undermining her own executive function. Mother thereby continues her ineffectiveness, and father reverts to his peripheral role.

Note that we have punctuated this sequence linearly. However, from the systemic perspective, there is no cause, no beginning of the sequence, except what we punctuate for practical, theoretical, or therapeutic purposes. It is a circular pattern in which each person in the triad is simultaneously cause and effect.

This sequence also describes a form of the "game without end." Other triangles can be woven into the scenario. Father may have an affair, forming a triangle of mother, father, and paramour, in addition to the triangle of mother, father, and rotten kid. Or mother may triangulate with her mother, thus punctuating still another triangle. It is assumed by Haley (1976), Selvini Palazzoli, Boscolo, Cecchin, and Prata (1978) and Hoffman (1981) that even the relationship between couples is stabilized by a third party, either inside or outside the immediate family.

The family characterized by an escalating pattern of pathology engages in a dance between stability and change. Attempts at change are typically aimed at the person punctuated as "causing" the problem, while others stay the same. Such first-order change efforts are also consistent with the logic of the conceptual framework that describes child as rotten, father as peripheral and uncaring, and mother as overinvolved and ineffective. This is the classic "I withdraw because you nag" and "I nag because you withdraw" sequence, in which one's behavior is justified by projecting responsibility for the problem onto the other person. Thus, one logically can only attempt to change the other.

However, such attempts at change must fail, for these are attempts at unilateral change in another person with whom one has a relationship, which is, by definition, bilateral. The pathology of epistemology here is that of not seeing one's own behavior as a part of the pathological, triadic pattern in the family; not seeing the logic of the sequence of rotten kid, peripheral father, and overinvolved mother, or, as in the other example, not seeing the nagging and withdrawing as punctuating a reciprocal dance in which the problem escalates. Any attempt at change that does not recognize the logical and reciprocal roles in the pattern of the family pathology is an example of first-order change. While such attempts are sometimes successful, when failure continually results, it is time to think about second-order change.

As you may recall from Chapter 5, second-order change refers to the process whereby the pattern of the "game without end" gets broken. However, from the perspective of the linear punctuation of events and the assignment of cause to one person, second-order change strategies will make no sense. Asking father to be more peripheral, mother to be more overinvolved and ineffective, and the kid to be more rotten is illogical to the framework of the family according to which continued attempts at first-order change make sense. Thus, such requests are viewed as paradoxical, although they are illogical only to the family's frame of reference. From the perspective of the "game without end," or escalating self-defeating cycles in which each family member is reciprocally tied to all other family members, and operates on the basis of a faulty epistemology, prescriptions to continue doing more of what they have been doing make perfect sense. From the logic of the alternative framework, they are not paradoxical.

The strategic approach therefore views people and symptoms in context. Further, for most of its proponents the triad is seen as basic to the family's organization and the maintenance of its dysfunctional pattern. Theoretically, if family members had a world view in which they saw themselves as connected in reciprocal roles to one another, if they did not punctuate the behavior of others as independent of their own behavior, and if they subsequently made no attempts at change in another without reciprocal change in themselves, families would not be pathological. But would not being pathological mean the family would be normal? This is an important question and one to which only very general answers are possible.

Theory Of Health/Normalcy

It is almost a contradiction in terms to talk of health or dysfunction from the perspective of strategic family therapy. The strategic therapist sees normalcy, coherence, and fit in any family pattern regardless of its form and regardless of whether it includes a member whose behavior might be classified as dysfunctional from a perspective outside the family. All behavior is perfectly logical within the family system, and all families are viewed as functional rather than normal or abnormal.

When a family presents itself for therapy it has no awareness of its "success" in producing a schizophrenic teenager, a depressed mother, a rotten kid, or a peripheral father. However, the family is well organized to do what it does. It may reflect the cultural consensus about what comprises pathology, yet we could speculate that unilateral and logical attempts to have family members be what the culture says they are "supposed to be" may be a part of its "pathology." The family's organization reflects its normalcy.

In very general terms, strategic theorists may describe family patterns associated with the evolution of what by cultural consensus is called dysfunction or pathology. Thus, one can also surmise what would be considered normal in the sense of patterns less likely to be associated with symptomatic behavior. Systems theory insists the punctuation of health and normalcy can only be made from the point of view of cultural consensus, that is, without reference to the logic and coherence of the family. Thus, strategic family therapists cannot label families as dysfunctional or abnormal and be logically consistent with the theory underlying their work.

On the other hand, Haley (1976) does value hierarchically organized families. He also espouses a life-cycle developmental framework (Haley, 1973) similar to that discussed in Chapter 6. In addition, Selvini Palazzoli et al. (1978) note that asymptomatic families tend to have fewer covert alliances and coalitions. While there may be alliances and coalitions in healthy families, they are usually acknowledged as such. A bit of communications theory can also be seen in the belief that asymptomatic families have clear rules and a balance of stability and flexibility.

By viewing families as uniquely normal within themselves, therapy is not a logical role. In doing therapy at all, the strategic therapist violates a basic assumption of the theory underlying his work. The context of the therapy room and the metaphor of therapist imply an agreement with the assumption that there are normal and abnormal families. In spite of the theory, acceptance of the role of therapist is participation in the cultural consensus that some individuals and families are normal while others are abnormal. How strategic family therapists extricate themselves from this dilemma is the topic of the next section. (Stay tuned. Will Paula discover the duplicity of Simon? Will the strategic family therapists save their sanity and find a solution to the paradox of supposedly treating and curing normal families?)

Therapeutic Strategies/Interventions

In our last episode, as you recall, we left our strategic family therapist confronting a paradox. She is asked to change a family that according to her theory is logical and coherent within itself. The culture says, and the family agrees, that producing schizophrenics, depressives, and rotten kids is not acceptable. However, our strategic family therapist has, with the exception of Haley's hierarchical structure and developmental framework, no particular model about how a family should be. Without a specific model our therapist cannot impose a specific organization. Indeed, the therapist's value base is one of diversity and respect for different modes of organization relative to the characteristics of the members of the family.

Our therapist thus sees each family as unique, having its own rules and patterns that define its organization and identity. She watches these patterns and infers the family's conceptual framework as expressed in the labels its members assign to each other. Unable to impose values, our therapist focuses on pragmatically intervening to preclude the existing pattern and to allow a new pattern to evolve. This pattern will be unique to the family, and she hopes it will also be more useful.

Our therapist is not interested in *why* the family is the way it is from a historical perspective. Rather, *what* is going on in the family is believed to be the necessary and sufficient explanation of the family as it is. Our therapist believes that if the family is given an explanation about "what is going on," thus explaining its coherence with the goal of having insight produce change, the family will probably incorporate this new information into its current pattern of interaction rather than evolve a new pattern of organization.

Our therapist is not concerned about etiology in the classical sense of getting at the root cause. Rather, a family is believed to be the way it is because that is the way it is. More pragmatically, Watzlawick, Weakland, and Fisch (1974) suggest that family members are either (1) trying to solve a problem that is not a problem (Johnny does not smile and cheer when asked to take out the trash); (2) they are attempting solutions at the wrong level (asking Martha to be a parent to her siblings without supporting her authority); or (3) denying that a problem exists, in which case action is necessary but not taken (Cheryl is afraid to be home alone after school, which is responded to with a "she will get used to it" stance).

Our therapist does not believe that she is on the outside of the family looking in. Further, she does not have the luxury of calling a family resistant or not motivated, for these concepts and constructs are not consistent with systemic theory. If the therapy is not successful, it is because the therapist did not do her job well. Blaming the family would imply that the family must also be responsible for its own solutions to problems.

Our therapist seeks only to interrupt vicious cycles of problematic feedback loops. After identifying specific problems and clearly articulating goals, therapy is focused on altering the patterns maintaining the presenting problem. The articulated goal might be that "Johnny will be a better behaved child and will cease his temper tantrums," while the goal in the therapist's head is to break the homeostatic pattern that is the problem according to this theory. In either case, however, the family and its members are not seen as sick; rather, they are stuck.

The degree of stuckness dictates to some degree the particular form of intervention. Less stuck families, those that can use cognitive information, might be dealt with in a relatively straightforward manner; that is, the pattern the therapist sees may be described so that all the members of the family can see and make their own inferences about how to be different with each other. Some families can use this information and can make appropriate changes. However, strategic family therapists know that some families cannot be dealt with in such a straightforward manner, for they will use the therapist's analysis to confront each other. Their basic pattern will remain unchanged.

It is at this point that the use of *paradoxes,* those illogical tricks for which strategic family therapy has become famous, become appropriate. A paradox, or paradoxical injunction, is a directive used in therapy that recognizes the limitations of conscious attempts to be different, especially when the family's pattern is long standing and emotionally charged. The paradoxical injunction will appear illogical to the family, especially since the context of therapy implies change. It is, however, a logical intervention given the assumptions of the theory.

At base, a *paradoxical injunction* is a strategy that "goes with" whatever is presented, with no overt attempts to change any member of the family. It recognizes what is occurring as normal and normalizes what is occurring. For example, it makes sense to tell Susan to feel angry, disappointed, and embarrassed when she fails a test for which she studied very hard. Anger, disappointment, and embarrassment are normal. If she were not feeling these things, it would be called abnormal. Her attempts not to feel these emotions would feed and escalate her distress. Paradoxically, her acceptance of these feelings as normal responses would lessen their intensity.

Underlying the paradoxical injunction is the assumption that conscious attempts to override habitual, spontaneous behavior patterns that are embedded in a context of long-standing relationships will probably not be very effective over the long term. Further, prescribing the symptomatic behavior (asking the rotten kid to be even more rotten) requests that the behavior be engaged in consciously, thus taking away its spontaneity.

Rohrbaugh et al. (1977) also describe two other forms of paradoxical strategies. One of these is *restraining,* in which the therapist recognizes what from another framework would be called resistance and not only goes with it but even discourages the possibility of change. This strategy recognizes that the symptoms may be useful in some strange way in the person's or family's life and probably should be maintained. An additional paradoxical strategy is that of *positioning,* which describes a way of dealing with extreme resistance by exaggerating it to hopelessness. For example, when the client suggests that things look bad, the therapist adds that things are probably hopeless. Each of these strategies implies that the therapeutic relationship should not be one of persuading the client or family members to change.

Most of the work of the strategic family therapist involves giving directives. While some may be given in the session, most are assigned to be completed in the interval between therapy sessions. The directives, whether paradoxical or not, need to be designed to fit the uniqueness of the family system. We wish to reiterate, however, that although the therapist may use interventions that are called paradoxical, from the framework of systems theory they are not only not paradoxical, but they are also very respectful of the family's current pattern of interaction and organization. We realize that when you first begin to dabble in paradoxical interventions, you may do so with tongue in cheek—"I'll trick them." But when you begin to see normalcy in what by cultural consensus is called pathological, not only will paradoxical techniques make perfect sense but you also will be very sincere in your delivery and thus increase the probability of success in helping the family break its current pattern of interaction.

Paradoxical tasks can be, and often are, assigned without explanation. However, as one understands family members, their values, and their current modes of organization, one can frame the apparently illogical assignment implied by the label "paradox" in a way that it ceases to be illogical to members of the family. Such a prescription can be framed as making perfect sense, a sense that derives from an understanding of the conceptual frameworks of members of the family. Indeed, reframing becomes easier if you can set aside the normal/abnormal and functional/dysfunctional dichotomies and see normalcy in each family and its unique organization. That is, the truth or falseness of a particular way of conceptualizing a problem or a pattern lies not in any standard of external validity but rather in its usefulness to members of the family. Keeney (1983), as you may recall, refers to this as "meaningful noise."

One example of such a contextual reframe might be: "I know you want to change and to feel better about yourself. This sounds simple enough, but I want you to be aware that you have long-standing relationships with others whom you know and who know you as you have always been with them. You could change, but it might mean changing, and in some cases ending, some important relationships. This is a significant consideration. This does not mean that you should not change, however. It is merely to point out that your changing has many consequences that neither of us can anticipate. Before you attempt to be different in any way, I think you should talk to these people and together analyze the consequences for your relationship when you do change. Until then, I encourage you not to change."

Haley (1976) notes that once we begin to think systemically, we have an ethical obligation not only to our clients but also to all those who might be affected by the outcome of the therapy. The intervention we described is a restraint from change, but it is expressed as a reason that may make sense to the client and also addresses the ethical issue raised by Haley. The paradoxical directive thus ceases to be paradoxical with the new sense we have given it. To answer Dell's question, "Why do we still call them 'paradoxes'?" (1986c): we probably shouldn't, and if we do, it is because we do not see their sense.

Three Examples

As we noted at the outset, the general framework is similar for all strategic therapists. They all engage the client, focus on the symptom, define the problem clearly, and set a clear goal for therapy. All seek to actively involve each member of the family in the therapy. All accept the family where it is as well as its focus on and definition of the problem. All seek to understand the family as it understands itself rather than challenging or confronting. They offer no explanations. All give assignments for tasks to be completed outside the therapy session. Some of these directives may involve conscious attempts to change. Most assignments are likely to be paradoxical. But different therapists have devised different models for implementing this theoretical framework. To illustrate, we have chosen to focus on Jay Haley, Cloé Madanes, and then on the early work of the Milan Group.

Jay Haley

Jay Haley is acknowledged as one of the pioneers in the field of family therapy. Unlike most of the other pioneers, however, his degree is in the arts and communication rather than in psychiatry or psychoanalysis. Haley began his career in family therapy while working with Gregory Bateson in the Project for the Study of Schizophrenia. His specific focus was on communication patterns in families, as part of the group out of which the Mental Research Institute (MRI) evolved.

From MRI, Haley moved in 1967 to the position of director of family therapy research at the Philadelphia Child Guidance Clinic, where he worked with Salvador Minuchin, Braulio Montalvo, and Bernice Rosman until 1976. While at the Philadelphia Child Guidance Clinic, Haley began to train family therapists. Indeed, it is notable that both he and Minuchin sought to train therapists who had no previous experience in this field. They felt such people were better able to incorporate systemic thinking into their work since they had not previously been socialized into models of individual pathology and therapy. After leaving Philadelphia in 1976, Haley founded the Family Therapy Institute of Washington, D. C., with Cloé Madanes.

The evolution of Haley's theory is manifested in his writing. At MRI he shifted from an individual to a brief family therapy and systems perspective. Many years of association with Minuchin also left their mark, reflected in Haley's belief in the importance of a hierarchical structure in the family as well as a focus on the triad as the unit of the family that maintains stability. What is most clear in Haley's theory is his view that family therapy represents not a different treatment modality for individual problems, but rather a different perspective on the concept of change and stability.

Haley consistently identifies himself as a strategic therapist, a label he coined while writing about the work of Milton Erickson. Like other strategic therapists, Haley focuses on sequences of behavior, communication patterns, and the here-and-now. He uses directives and action plans to change behavior and creates strategies to fit the uniqueness of the family. His approach to therapy is method oriented and problem focused, with little or no attempt to instill insight. Unlike other strategic therapists, his model incorporates the importance of a hierarchical family structure.

Haley also uses the concepts of power and control in his description of family patterns, for he sees communication sequences and symptoms as attempts to control or influence. This punctuation of control as a motive in all relationships was an issue between Haley and Gregory Bateson. Bateson acknowledged the existence of the concept of control, but to him the belief that control is possible was a pathological concept both pragmatically and in terms of epistemology. Thus, Bateson addressed the issue as follows: "To want control is the pathology, not that the person gets control, because of course you never do" (Brand, 1974, p. 16). Bateson therefore wanted to get rid of the concept of control. The illusion that control is possible (which it is not, according to systems theory), keeps us trying to engage in ecologically and interpersonally destructive behavior.

Haley, on the other hand, uses the concept of control at the level of pragmatics and finds it a useful metaphor to describe patterns that seem to characterize all systems and families. According to Haley (1963), people inevitably engage in reciprocal attempts, through digital and analogic communication, to control the nature of their relationships:

> *Any two people are posed the mutual problems: (a) what messages, or what kinds of behavior are to take place in this relationship, and (b) who is to control what is to take place in the relationship and thereby control the definition of the relationship. . . . It must be emphasized that no one can avoid being involved in a struggle over the definition of his relationship with someone else. (p. 9)*

Thus, going beyond the behavior paradox that one cannot not behave, and the communication paradox that one cannot not communicate, Haley adds that one cannot not attempt to influence the definition or nature of the relationship. He notes further that "it is not pathological to attempt to gain control of a relationship, we all do this, but when one attempts to gain that control while denying it, then such a person is exhibiting symptomatic behavior" (p. 16).

Consonant with this belief, Haley points to the power of symptoms to control. Symptoms, by definition, and consistent with traditional mental and physical health practice, are behaviors that are beyond one's control. They are, however, very controlling in terms of the alternatives available to the other person who has a relationship with the symptom-bearer. Inasmuch as symptoms are behaviors or conditions one cannot help doing, they are simultaneously a denial of control. But the nonsymptomatic person in the relationship is in a relatively powerless position since it is not appropriate to try to make a person stop doing what he or she cannot help doing. Haley therefore defines certain symptoms as tactics to maintain a particular kind of arrangement in a relationship or family. By contrast, although attempts to control are inevitable, in a fair relationship it is appropriate for one to be able to comment on the other person's behavior.

The belief that the struggle for control in relationships is inevitable also leads Haley to speculate on the nature of control in families. Here we see the influence of Minuchin's structural model in that Haley believes the organization is in trouble when coalitions occur between levels of the hierarchy, for example between members of the parental and sibling subsystems. Further, while two-against-one coalitions are considered unhealthy, they are seen as particularly destructive when the necessary generation gap is breached. This is even more problematic when the coalitions are covert and are denied when commented upon.

When the stable pattern of organization within a family involves a coalition across generations, the family is stuck in a confused or ambiguous state. Symptomatic behavior in one or more family members is highly probable in this circumstance. Indeed, symptoms are clues that the hierarchical structure of the family is confused and needs restructuring, and problems are thus viewed in terms of pathological triads, or triangles.

Haley believes that the therapist must consider himself a part of the social unit that contains the problem. In fact, he views professionals as participating in the definition of the problems that families frequently come to the therapist to change. Further, any act on the part of the therapist, such as labeling, identifying, or defining a problem, joins the therapist with the family, and they thus become a single unit.

It is important at this point to take note of a few definitions. Haley (1976) defines *structure* as "repeated acts among people," *therapeutic change* as "change in the repeating acts of a self-regulating system—preferably a change into a system of greater diversity," and *pathology* as "a rigid, repetitive sequence within a narrow range" (p. 105).

In his therapy, Haley does not believe that asking *why* a problem exists is useful. The key question is *what* is being done that is maintaining a problem. He believes telling people what they are doing wrong is not only not useful but often hooks resistance in the family. Further, he believes changing behavior changes feelings and perceptions, and not vice versa.

Haley's general strategy for therapy is to intervene in such a way that the covert hierarchical structure, as reflected in the repeated sequences of behavior, cannot be maintained. This focus on a change in the structure of the family is an important difference between Haley and other strategic therapists. In addition, he seeks to change symptomatic metaphors in order to allow more adaptive ones to emerge.

The following general procedures describe the process of therapy according to Haley's model:

1. Whole families should be seen. By seeing the entire unit, the therapist is better able to control the therapy and to see pattern, infer structure, and involve all

members in the process, transforming the problem from one in the symptom-bearer to one in the family system.

2. Building on the metaphor of power, only one therapist is to work with the family. This allows her to direct the therapy more immediately and decisively and thereby to establish control.

3. A second therapist or team of therapists is to observe the family from behind a one-way mirror and serve as consultant. While joining the family is important, it has its hazards if effective control is not established. The observer(s) can help maintain control, offer insights regarding family structure, and suggest directives.

4. While there is flexibility in terms of techniques, assignments, etc., there is no flexibility about the importance of the first interview. To have a successful ending, therapy must have a successful beginning. The first session must therefore include all of the following five stages:

   a. Social engagement of the family: The therapist makes it a point to engage each member of the family, helping all to feel more relaxed. Since it is "Johnny's problem" and most family members will probably be confused about why they are there, social engagement lays the groundwork for establishing the importance of each family member, for redefining the problem as systemic, and for establishing control. The metaphor "host" is an appropriate description of therapist behavior in this stage.

   b. Definition of the problem: The therapist spends time introducing himself and his role, sharing knowledge of the family, and offering an explanation as to why he asked all family members to attend. Typically, family members are defined as resources who have valuable insights and opinions. Family members are asked to present their perspectives on the problem. All conversation is directed at the therapist, who listens carefully, validating each family member's opinion as important. Discussions between family members are avoided. After listening carefully, the therapist redefines "Johnny's problem" as a problem shared by other members of the family.

   c. Interaction stage: The focus is on having family members discuss the problem among themselves. The therapist remains in charge to the extent that he refuses to be pulled into the discussion. During this relatively open discussion between family members, patterns and structure (power, control, coalitions, etc.) are revealed to the therapist and observer(s).

   d. Definition of desired changes: The goal for the therapy is stated in terms of solving the presenting problem and is specified in behavioral terms, for example, cessation of tantrums. Thus, the focus is on solving a specific problem and not on more generic goals like insight or improving communication.

   e. Ending the interview with directives and scheduling the next appointment. Not all first sessions end in directives, but throughout the entire first session, if successful, the therapist will have orchestrated the interview with directives regarding the process. If final directives are given, they may take the form of paradoxical injunctions or direct assignments for change.

Directives are a very important part of Haley's version of strategic therapy. While generally viewed as an assignment for the family to perform outside of therapy, it is his belief that all therapist behavior in the session is a directive. For Haley, directives serve three purposes: (1) they facilitate change and make things happen; (2) they involve the therapist in the therapy by keeping him supposedly in the family during the week; and (3) they offer a stimulus, reactions to which give the therapist information about family structure, rules, boundaries, and so forth. All family members should therefore be assigned a role in homework assignments. However, this might be as simple as having someone remind other family members of the assignment(s).

Some, but not all, of the directives are paradoxical in the sense of prescribing the symptom or prescribing resistance. In either case, the therapist maintains control by anticipating family members' responses to therapy. Operant directives, such as suggestions about specific things the family members might do differently, can also be given. However, these are not likely to be effective except in relatively minor problems. Thus, while giving an operant directive, the therapist anticipates possible failure and may suggest that "this may be impossible to do." The operant suggestion plus anticipation of resistance constitutes a double bind, so that no matter what the family does (comply or not comply) the therapist is still in control. In addition, even if the family is successful in implementing change, Haley paradoxically might be skeptical about whether the changes will be long lasting and perhaps may even prescribe a relapse.

In general, paradoxical directives not to change are designed to provoke rebellion in family members. For example, the therapist might reframe and hook rebellion in family members by suggesting that if Johnny ceased his temper tantrums, other issues in the family might arise and they might want to avoid this.

Another form of directive is the *metaphoric task*. During the session the therapist might speak in a metaphor that symbolizes a problem or issue the family does not discuss. The therapist thus indirectly plants seeds for possible change. This kind of therapist behavior parallels much of the work of Milton Erickson. As either an in-session or out-of-session directive, the therapist might also have family members engage in a conversation that is not about the problem, but because of the task and the symbolism of the content of the task, may indirectly facilitate change. An example is a directive in which the parents are asked to discuss how an orchestra might be conducted successfully with two conductors, each of whom has a slightly different interpretation both of the music and of how the orchestra should perform.

If the family has an ambiguous hierarchy, change in the family structure is essential. To this end the therapist might prescribe new coalitions to promote the desired hierarchical arrangement. The therapist also might use paradoxical directives to block cross-generational coalitions and thereby realign the power structure. For example, by directing a mother to consult with her son before discussing issues with the father moves the coalition into the open and precludes its spontaneity.

Another directive used by Haley (1984) is termed *ordeal therapy*. Once again, the resemblance to some of the work of Milton Erickson is not coincidental. The magic trick here is to make it harder for the client to have the problem than it is to give it up by prescribing an ordeal that is equal to or greater than the distress of the symptom itself. It is essential to select as the so-called ordeal something that is good for the client, for example, dieting or exercise. The ordeal must also be something the client can do and cannot legitimately object to doing. Further, it must not harm the client or any other person. Thus, at the onset of the symptom, the client is directed to engage in the behavior described as good for and yet difficult for the client to do. For example, directing a client to be nice to a critical mother-in-law might be an ordeal sufficient to make the client give up her symptom. In this example, the ordeal involves achieving a social context that would be desirable. As described by Haley, there is a cultural tradition that suggests anything worth having requires sacrifice and suffering.

Basic to the notion of change from Haley's perspective is the necessity for change in style of interaction in the social unit of which the client is a member. Indeed, this is change in the system itself. While a directive may alleviate the symptom, Haley notes that change needs to be supported and maintained. A change in one aspect of the system involves other parts of the system, which also need to be modified.

Cloé Madanes

In many ways Madanes' (1980, 1981, 1984) work fits well with Haley's strategic approach to therapy. She retains the importance of the *incongruous hierarchy* in a functional family, but her model involves a greater range of creativity and playfulness. An example of the concept of play, which is also a functional paradoxical intervention as well as a means for getting family members to change behavior, is that of the *pretend technique* (Madanes, 1981). In the belief that people are more likely to experiment with different behavior if it is framed as play or pretend, clients are asked to pretend to have a symptom and other family members are asked to pretend to offer assistance. This strategy places both the symptom and the attempts to help in a different context and also implies that they are within the individual's control.

While staying within the functional approach of strategic therapy, Madanes (1990) provides a map for thinking about dynamics within families. In addition to hierarchy she believes that the issues of love and violence are the root of all problems brought to therapy. For Madanes there are four intentions of family members that are important in the development of particular kinds of problems: (1) attempts to control are associated with delinquency and behavior problems; (2) attempts to be loved are associated with psychosomatic disorders; (3) attempts to love and to protect are associated with neglect, abuse, thought disorders, and suicidal behavior; and (4) attempts to repent and forgive are associated with incest and sexual abuse.

According to Madanes' map, there are also four dimensions that appear to affect the issues involved with love and violence. The first dimension is the struggle for power and control within our lives, as well as over the lives of others. Family members may oppose each other to gain power or to influence each other. Personal gain and selfishness motivate the participating members to become exploitive in their relationships.

The second dimension focuses on the difficulties associated with the desire to be loved. Family members may be involved in a power struggle to be cared for, with the main emotion involved being that of desire. When these needs are not fulfilled, family members experience frustration. Symptomatic behaviors appear that are characterized by excessive demands for attention and affection. The main goal of therapy in such cases is to change the desire of being loved to the desire of loving others.

The third dimension of the love/violence dilemma is the desire to love and protect others. Although this desire can bring out the compassion and kindness within us, it can also lead to extreme acts of violence in the name of love. The emotion of despair is closely linked to the desire to protect those whom we love. This despair often leads to an act of violence to protect a significant other.

The fourth and most important dimension influencing this dilemma of love and violence is the ability to repent and forgive. When family members have inflicted trauma, deception, or violence upon each other, they feel shame. Attempts to place extreme guilt upon others for what they have done or have not done occur. Often finger-pointing and blame are passed around in an effort to distribute the shame within the family. The therapist must take the blame away from the victims and replace the posture of avoiding responsibility. The therapist may want to encourage family members to have compassion towards each other, hopefully leading to repentance and forgiveness.

Madanes (1990) suggests different strategies for each of these dimensions. For dimension one, domination and control, she might correct the hierarchy, negotiate and develop contractual agreements, change benefits, foster life-stage transitions through rituals, and develop ordeals which make it harder to keep a problem than to get rid of it. For dimension two, the desire to be loved, she might change a parent's involvement, prescribe the symptom, prescribe a symbolic act, and/or prescribe "the pretending of a symptom" (p. 31). For dimension three, loving and protecting, strategies may include "reuniting family members" (p. 32), "changing who is helpful to whom" (p. 34), "empowering children to be appropriately helpful" (p. 35), and/or "orienting toward the future and deeds of reparation" (p. 36). For dimension four, repenting and forgiving, she might create a positive framework, find protectors for victims, elicit compassion and/or promote unity.

For Madanes, change in therapy requires (1) leading clients to see that they can change their behaviors when they take control of their actions; (2) helping clients take control of their minds, that is, change their ways of thinking and thus change the context in which the problem lies; (3) helping clients control their anger and violence by transforming the anger into positive actions and violence into patience; (4) encouraging empathy towards all mankind, i.e, to sympathize with others and their circumstances which leads to intelligence, a sense of justice, and respect for all mankind; (5) encouraging hope and humor. Hope by the therapist engenders hope in the client, while humor allows us to learn to laugh at ourselves and helps us to conquer fears; (6) promoting compassion and tolerance toward others: "Tolerance and compassion constitute a protective environment in which young persons can grow and develop in their own particular ways" (Madanes, 1990, p. 12); (7) encouraging forgiveness of self and other and kindness toward self and others, which allows the client to survive the day-to-day challenges of living; (8) promoting harmony and balance in people's lives, "To love and be loved, to find fulfillment in work, to play and enjoy: All are part of a necessary balance" (Madanes, 1990, p. 13).

Milan Systemic/Strategic Therapy

The Milan approach to family therapy has been called systemic in the tradition of Bateson's circular epistemology (MacKinnon, 1983). However, when first formulated it also had a very strategic feel to it, at least as described by the original team of Mara Selvini Palazzoli, Luigi Boscolo, Gianfranco Cecchin, and Guiliana Prata (1978). It is on this basis that the Milan model(s) are included in this chapter. We refer to "model(s)" because in 1980 the Milan group separated into two pairs, each of which chose to follow slightly different paths. Selvini Palazzoli and Prata focused on studying the effects of a single, sustained and invariant intervention. Boscolo and Cecchin, on the other hand, concentrated on developing new training methods (Tomm, 1984a). Further, since 1982, Selvini Palazzoli and Prata have worked separately from one another. Thus, we present the initial model as well as aspects of subsequent work by members of the original team.

The original Milan team claimed to have been the first to practice family and couple therapy in Italy. Building initially on the psychoanalytic model, the group soon began to experiment with the Mental Research Institute's model (Bodin, 1981). In their transition from psychoanalysis to systemic thinking, they studied Haley (1963), Watzlawick, Beavin, and Jackson (1967), and others who represented the systems/communication perspective of MRI. Gradually, they began to develop their own theory base and techniques and sought to be consistent and coherent within their own framework. The first major publication of the Milan group was *Paradox and Counterparadox* (Selvini Palazzoli et al., 1978). This book recounts a series of trial and error learnings with dysfunctional families that focused on a search for the "pathological nodal point" (Tomm, 1984a, p. 115), which, if changed, would help the family evolve itself into a different form. It also represents an important contribution to the field of family therapy. We therefore describe the group's original team approach, which continues to be a useful model today.

The Milan group focused on overcoming the "tyranny of linguistics," which by its very nature keeps therapists and clients thinking in an intrapsychic, linear manner. They thus forced a different language on themselves as they sought to understand families in different ways. In the process they made themselves substitute the verbs *to seem* and *to show* for the verb *to be* (Selvini Palazzoli et al., 1978). They gradually moved to a perspective that saw schizophrenic families acting "as if all behaviors and attitudes of the family in schizophrenic transaction were mere moves whose sole purpose were to perpetuate the family game" (p. 27). The families were described as paradoxical in that they came to therapy to change, and yet the moves of each member of the system sought to keep change from occurring. The common message was, "We have this (problematic member who must change)...but as a family we are fine...(and intend to remain unchanged)" (Tomm, 1984a, p. 115). Slowly but surely the Milan group became aware that a major part of the family system cannot change without a complementary change in the whole.

With the understanding of the necessity for complementary changes in all family members, the group devised interventions that sought to break the impasse imposed by the family's paradoxical request for both stability and change. Such interventions took the form of a counterparadox, which effectively took charge of the paradox posed by the family: "(Although we as therapists are socially defined as change agents), we think that you should not change because it is a good thing that...." (Tomm, 1984a, p. 115). They would thus give a positive connotation to all behaviors in the homeostatic pattern and prescribe no change in the context of change (therapy), putting the family in a therapeutic double bind (Selvini Palazzoli et al., 1978).

Bateson's *Steps to an Ecology of Mind* (1972) influenced the group even further and helped them view systems as always evolving even while appearing to be stuck. They also began to punctuate what they and Bateson called epistemological errors as outdated maps of reality. They therefore began to differentiate "between the level of meaning and the level of action" and they began to see therapeutic interventions as "introducing new connections or new distinctions in thought or actions" (Tomm, 1984a, p. 115). Accordingly, information is introduced, either explicitly via reframing or implicitly through the prescription of a family ritual. In either case, the therapist acts as a catalyst and the goal is to activate a process in which the family creates new patterns of behavior and belief that are supportive of the creation of more new patterns (Tomm, 1984a).

The process which the original Milan group (Selvini Palazzoli et al., 1978) described builds on systems theory/cybernetics and information theory. They saw the world primarily as pattern and information rather than as mass and energy. Theirs was a recursive approach in that the theory and clinical practice were responsive to feedback derived from the therapy. They participated in and were a part of the families they saw.

The members of the Milan group believed mental phenomena reflect social phenomena and what is called a mental problem is really a problem in social interaction. A useful idea in practice, therapy was directed toward inferred patterns of interaction rather than toward individuals or intrapsychic problems. The model was built on a circular epistemology, and thus the observer focused on recursiveness in the interaction between parts of the family and on seeing wholistic patterns. The members of a family were understood as being caught in this recursive pattern and were viewed more with compassion than with condemnation, with significant ramifications. Espousal of a circular epistemology precludes a moral stance and requires a position of neutrality, which permits greater freedom for the family in its exploration of alternatives for change. Similarly, the systemic perspective allows for greater freedom and creativity on the part of the therapist (Tomm, 1984a).

The Milan group did not see linear thinking as incorrect, although it may be misleading because it punctuates only a part of a larger whole. The circular perspective was viewed as a more complete and coherent perspective. The members of this group were also adamant that therapists view themselves as a part of the pattern that they are observing.

As noted previously, an important part of the Milan perspective calls our attention to what Chase (1938) has described as a tyranny of words and Shands (1971) delineates as a "tyranny of linguistic conditioning" (Selvini Palazzoli et al., 1978, p. 51). We tend to take for granted the distinctions we have drawn about people on the basis of the labels we assign to them or to their behaviors. It is therefore suggested that saying a child *acts* aggressively is preferable to saying the child *is* aggressive. In addition, our language and the structure of our grammar tend to emphasize linear thinking and linear descriptive statements. Thus, we typically would say "father is depressed" rather than "father is showing depression." The former takes father out of context. The latter implies that the behavior is part of a context and cues us to consider what effect this showing of depression has on relationships in the family. While we cannot totally escape the tyranny of linguistics, we can, through conscious effort, create a semblance of circularity. Language can also be an ally in its ability to conjure up images through metaphors and stories.

Change in a family can be approached through changes in meaning or in action. However, action in the form of behavior is not directly accessible. On the other hand, meaning is accessible, and through changes in meaning, changes in action may occur. New meanings can therefore be introduced directly through reframes or indirectly by prescribing rituals, the two major categories of intervention for the Milan group.

The whole process of therapy is carefully orchestrated to be consistent with the model on which it is built. The phone call requesting an appointment is often the first contact with the client. The therapist tries to maintain neutrality from the outset in order to avoid any implication of a coalition with the caller. Accordingly, questions are carefully phrased as the therapist obtains information. For example, it is better to ask the caller, "When did you start having problems with your son?" than to ask, "When did your son start having his problems?" The difference is that in the former case, the problem is punctuated as social rather than individual.

Tomm (1984a) describes the Milan approach as "long brief therapy" (p. 122). While only ten sessions are planned, they are scheduled at one-month intervals. This monthly interval is explained to the clients as appropriate since that amount of time is needed for therapeutic change to unfold given their model of intervention.

If the therapist receives a call from a family member between sessions, he is careful to continue to maintain a neutral therapeutic stance and to avoid a coalition with the caller. If the issue raised is not an emergency, the caller is advised to bring it up in the next session. In the event of a definite emergency, as in the case of a suicide or homicide risk, the therapist ceases to be therapist and becomes a social control agent. However, this difference, as evidenced by a shift in roles in the case of an emergency, does not change the primary mode of therapy.

If therapy does not progress, the field of observation may be expanded to involve others in the therapy session. The therapist may also increase the size of her resources by including other team members and receiving additional input through supervision or consultation. Indeed, the Milan approach is a team approach and typically follows a ritual prescribed to themselves as a team. The ritual includes five components: a five- to twenty-minute presession in which the team members discuss the family; a fifty- to ninety-minute interview of the family by one therapist while the rest of the team observes; a fifteen- to forty-minute intersession in which the team members discuss the family and the session; a five- to fifteen-minute intervention in which the conclusions of the team are delivered by the therapist to the family while the other members observe; and a five- to fifteen-minute postsession in which the team holds a summary discussion (Tomm, 1984a). The metaphor for the team is that of a collective "systemic mind." The principles used by the team are described as *hypothesizing, circularity, neutrality,* and *positive connotation.*

In the presession discussion the team begins to formulate hypotheses about the family. The belief is that unless the therapist is armed with these hypotheses, she may be persuaded by the family to adopt its definition of the problem and of how to deal with it. These hypotheses can be described as metaphoric explanations about what purpose the symptom serves in the family and how the family organizes itself around the symptom. From this starting point, the therapist sets out to confirm or disconfirm her hypotheses in the therapy session as she learns about the family through information gathering and observation. An hypothesis can be set aside or revised until the team has formulated the hypothesis (explanation) that offers the best understanding of the family dynamics supporting the client's symptoms.

Possible hypotheses are restricted to those describing circularity. Thus, thinking is in terms of interaction and relationships rather than in terms of symptoms residing within a person. As the therapist gathers information, questions are geared to learning about relationships within the family. For example, the therapist might ask a child to describe the relationship between his mother and father and between his mother and another child. This information is viewed as a perspective that provides information about triangles within the family. Consistent with the idea of circularity, therapists request information about how family members respond to symptoms rather than asking for descriptions of the symptom itself. Reactions to symptoms provide more useful information about how the family is organized and reveal its ritualistic dances; that is, the meaning of a behavior lies in its context and its association with other behaviors.

The particular style of circular questioning about relationships used by the Milan group is a way of changing the meaning family members may attribute to the behavior of other family members without directly stating, "Think about your family in this way." It can be construed as an indirect form of reframing. It also may transform the tyranny of linguistics and linear punctuation necessitated by our grammar. This is a systemic reframing and the result is that family members may begin to question certain assumptions underlying their beliefs, which may influence their behavior.

Penn (1982) draws a parallel between circular questioning and Bateson's principle of double description. Quoting Keeney, she notes that

> *in order to get from one level of description to another, an act of double description is required, or views from every side of the relationship must be juxtaposed to generate a sense of relationship of the whole. Double description is, according to Bateson, the relationship. (p. 267)*

The process of circular questioning is a fundamental concept in the Milan model. According to Boscolo, Cecchin, Hoffman and Penn (1987, p. 11),

> *Questions most commonly used fall into several categories: questions about difference in perception of relationships ("Who is closer to Father, your daughter or your son?"); questions about difference of degree ("On a scale of one to ten, how bad do you think the fighting is this week?"); now/then difference ("Did she start losing weight before or after her sister went off to college?"); and hypothetical and future difference ("If she had not been born, how would your marriage be different today? If you were to divorce, which parent would the children stay with?"). Such questions comprise a series of mutually causal feedback chains creating a complex and nonlinear piece of circuitry.*

This process can be described as helping to transform the family members' perceptions of autonomous, independent individuals and linear causation to a world view of reciprocity and interdependence. This perception may contrast with a view that traits or attributes reside within individuals. It also helps family members be aware of differences in perception and the validity of these differences. The process of circular questioning joins symptom, intervention, family, and therapist in a co-evolutionary process. Circular questioning focuses on both connections and differences among people and on the nature of their relationships across time as it punctuates times when patterns in the family shifted as a natural adaptation to an event (Feinberg, 1990).

An important assumption underlying circular questioning is that "in a healthy relationship, both sides of a relationship must evolve" (Penn, 1982, p. 271). Most families presenting for therapy seek unilateral control over a relationship that is, by definition, bilateral. Any attempt at unilateral control over that which is bilateral must fail. Circular questioning seeks to punctuate the reciprocity and co-definition of any relationship and thus to promote co-evolution.

Responses to circular questions can alert the therapist to "openings," (competition, jealousy, fixed coalitions) which can lead to useful (not necessarily true) hypotheses which can be pursued in further circular questions. The process may be understood as a "nonchronological and nonlinear decision tree," (Boscolo et al., 1987, p. 11) which requires "neutrality." In this model neutrality refers to the therapist taking a nonmoral stance and promoting the feeling in family members that the therapist is aligned with no one and everyone. Thus neutrality is considered to be "multipositional" rather than "nonpositional." In addition to requiring systemic hypotheses it aligns with the idea of seeing the problem as making sense in the context of the family. Neutrality also implies not being aligned with any particular model of therapy and is nonprescriptive of the form the family should take (Cecchin, Lane, & Ray, 1993).

While maintaining neutrality, the team, through the therapist, aligns with and supports each family member. This reflects a view of the family as an organic whole rather than a composite of independent parts. No bad people and no good people are punctuated. The family is as it is and this is the only way it can be at this time.

The idea of positive connotation of the symptomatic behavior and the behavior of all other family members is at once paradoxical and confusing to family members. Symptoms are not criticized or punctuated as undesirable in any way. Symptoms, as well as the behaviors of all family members, are punctuated as important to the well-being and cohesion of the family and each of its members. Through this process the behavior of all family members is also linked. The therapists do not criticize the system and thus are not seen as outsiders threatening the system.

The prescription of rituals and the maintenance of the status quo in the context of change (therapy) is, of course, paradoxical. Further, the therapists see themselves as a part of the family system in a very real way. They do not project responsibility to the family when the therapy is not successful, nor do they accept responsibility for change. New information about the ineffectiveness of prescriptions is used to modify hypotheses and to formulate new prescriptions for the family. Thus, the therapists accept responsibility for the therapy, but not for change. A lack of success may be punctuated as evidence that the family has outwitted the team. On the other hand, it may be evidence that the family knows best what is best for it. A strong aspect of respect and yet gamesmanship is part of this approach. We suspect that if the neutrality and positive connotation derive from a respect for the family as it is, rather than as a trick to get the family to change, therapy is more likely to be successful. In effect, the therapists believe the family could not be any other way than it is at this moment. What it is and what it does are normal for this family. Prescriptions for both the continuation of the existing pattern by the symptom-bearer and the behavior of others that complements the symptom, together with a positive connotation, may be coupled with the suggestion that one day there may be change. Thus, the therapist might say, "it is probably good that you decide not to eat for a while, because it enables your parents to have meaningful conversations with each other. For the time being this is a useful way to help your family."

The prescription of a ritual is done very carefully and exactly. The prescription describes what is to be done by whom, where, when, and in what sequence. It is important to note that the ritual is not to become a permanent part of family members' lives together. Rather it is framed as an experiment. Consistent with the theory, the failure of a family to carry out the ritual prescription is not seen as the basis on which to confront the family for not complying. By contrast, failure is more likely to be punctuated as the therapist's responsibility. Finally, the ritual is designed to clarify important relationships in the family as well as to highlight intergenerational boundaries.

Among the rituals that may be prescribed are the following two examples: (1) Mother and father are to go out together without telling anyone else in the family of their whereabouts and to be mysterious about where they have been. (2) A nuclear family of four may be asked to lock the doors, take the phone off the hook, and isolate themselves for one hour each evening. Each family member can talk about the family for fifteen minutes or not talk about the family. The choice belongs to the family member, and these fifteen minutes are his or hers. No other family member is to comment during this time. A clock on the table may be a part of the ritual prescribed, and may be moved to punctuate who has the floor.

Prescribed rituals can focus on either behavior or on process or structure without specified content, as in the examples presented above. Other prescriptions may focus on content to the point where team members may prepare written statements for each family member to read to the others. Such messages may reveal contradictions, double binds, and other difficulties that family members may be experiencing in the family.

A final note on termination of the therapy seems appropriate, for it illustrates the nature and "unobtrusiveness" of the intervention. Tomm (1984b) describes it as follows:

> When a major transformation has occurred the family generally does not attribute it to therapy. They tend to associate it with non-therapy events and often do not even remember the triggering intervention. Interestingly, when no change has occurred the family tends to remember the intervention much more clearly. It is considered a therapeutic error to suggest to the family that the change should be attributed to therapy. To do so is to disqualify the family. The family members themselves must have made the changes, if, indeed, any substantive change did occur. (p. 269)

Termination may be by mutual agreement or by the therapist or the family. The team always respects and goes along with the family's decision to terminate. Consistent with the model, the family is alerted to the possibility of relapse or doubt as to whether the changes that have been effected will last. The purpose of the anticipation of a possible relapse is to suggest that minor setbacks are normal and to be expected.

As mentioned earlier, the original Milan team parted company in 1980. Since their parting, Boscolo and Cecchin have expanded and refined the ideas of the original group. Consistent with second-order cybernetics, the unit of treatment is not the family but an "ecology of ideas" (Boscolo, Cecchin, Hoffman, & Penn, 1987). They also now believe, in agreement with Maturana, that "there can be no 'instructive interaction,' only a perturbation of a system that will then react in terms of its own structure" (p. 18). They have shifted the concept of positive connotation from the implication that a symptom is needed to a connotation that the symptom is logical. Also consistent with second-order cybernetics, they believe that the "problem does not exist independently of the 'observing systems' that are reciprocally and collectively defining the problem," and thus, "the problem creates the system" (p. 14). They conceptualize their efforts as "learning to learn," and toward this end have evolved a network of teams "proliferating outward into many different contexts, and by their very nature incapable of cloning" (p. 28). Thus, the model they envision is one that never attains status as a model, but rather a model for the process of teams co-evolving with the families and teams as observing systems. Among Cecchin's more recent contributions are *Irreverence: A Strategy for Therapists' Survival* (Cecchin et al., 1992) which seeks to help therapists reject totalizing theories and "truths" of therapeutic practice and to encourage them to play with the options that may be useful to the client, and *The Cybernetics of Prejudices in the Practice of Psychotherapy* (Cecchin, Lane, & Ray, 1994). A recent work by Boscolo and Bertrando (1993), *The Times of Time*, explores variations on the theme of time and the part it plays in people's lives and in the process of therapy.

Selvini Palazzoli and Prata continued to do family systems research until 1982, when Selvini Palazzoli (Selvini, 1988; Selvini Palazzoli, 1986) formed a new group of colleagues to work with families of schizophrenics and anorectics. Processes in these families are described as a family game in which the child observes a provoking parent as winning over the passive parent, although this is an erroneous assessment on the part of the child. After siding with the losing/passive parent, the child finds that the passive/losing parent joins with the provoking parent instead of the child. The child feels betrayed and responds by escalating the disturbed behavior. Disturbed behavior is thus viewed as an attempt to show the passive/losing parent how to bring down the winning/provoking parent. The family becomes stable around the disturbed behavior, as each member resorts to "psychotic family games" in an attempt to benefit from the situation.

To break the pattern of the psychotic family games, the therapist meets with the whole family initially and with the parents alone in subsequent interviews. Beginning with the second interview, parents are given the following *invariant prescription* directives, which they are required to follow. The prescription is designed to produce a boundary between generations that is both clear and stable:

> *Keep everything about this session absolutely secret at home. Every now and then, start going out in the evenings before dinner. Nobody must be forewarned. Just leave a written note saying, "We will not be home tonight." If, when you come back, one of your (daughters) inquires where you have been, just answer calmly, "These things concern only the two of us." Moreover, each of you will keep a notebook, carefully hidden and out of the children's reach. In these notebooks each of you, separately, will register the date and describe the verbal and nonverbal behavior of each child, or other family member, which seemed to be connected with the prescription you have followed. We recommend diligence in keeping these records because it's extremely important that nothing be forgotten or omitted. Next time you will again come alone, with your notebooks, and read aloud what has happened in the meantime. (Selvini Palazzoli, 1986, pp. 341–342)*

The invariant prescription seeks to break alliances and coalitions as well as to strengthen the parental alliance and thus promote a boundary between generations.

Systemic Consistency

Strategic approaches provide some of the most cybernetically consistent models of family therapy. Accordingly, therapist and family are seen as comprising one system. The system includes the observer plus the black box, and the observer is part of the observed. In addition, reality is understood as perceptually based and self-referential. The crucial issue is What? rather than Why? and negative feedback, reciprocal influence, and recursion define systems and their characteristic patterns of interaction. Symptoms are understood as logical to context, and the normalcy, coherence, and fit of any family pattern is assumed. Thus, the logic of symptom formation is consistent with the concept of structural determinism. Similarly, the strategy of attempting to interdict old patterns so that new ones may emerge is not unlike the notion of perturbation.

On the other hand, cybernetic consistency is undermined by virtue of the fact that the theory underlies a model of therapy. That is, as soon as problems are defined and strategies are devised to solve problems, one may infer a belief in pathology and thus what would comprise wellness. As benign as such punctuations as "stuck" families may be, at the level of cybernetics of cybernetics the designations of dysfunction and health do not exist. Rather, everything functions as it functions. Haley, by contrast, considers hierarchy to be important and defines pathology as a function of rigidity. Similarly, the Milan group values clear rules and openly expressed alliances and focuses on the "pathological nodal point" in families as well as "outdated maps" of reality. However, all models of therapy will inevitably encounter this paradox, and the strategic approaches take the lead in attempting to deal with it by acknowledging its existence and reducing value judgments to a minimum.

Suggested Readings

Andolfi, M. (1979). *Family therapy: An international approach*. New York: Plenum Press.

Bateson, G., Jackson, D., Haley, J., & Weakland, J. (1956). Toward a theory of schizophrenia. *Behavioral Science, 1*, 251–264.

Boscolo, L. (1983). Final discussion. In H. Stierlin, L. Wynne, and M. Wirsching, (Eds.), *Psychosocial intervention in schizophrenia: An international view* (pp. 245–246). Berlin: Springer-Verlag.

Boscolo, L., & Bertrando, P. (1992). The reflexive loop of past, present, and future in systemic therapy and consultation. *Family Process, 31*, 119–133.

Boscolo, L., & Bertrando, P. (1993). *The times of time: A new perspective in systemic therapy and consultation*. New York: W. W. Norton.

Boscolo, L., Cecchin, G., Hoffman, L., & Penn, P. (1987). *Milan systemic family therapy*. New York: Basic Books.

Cecchin, G. (1987). Hypothesizing, circularity and neutrality revisited: An invitation to curiosity. *Family Process, 16*, 405–413.

Cecchin, G., Lane, G., & Ray, W. (1992). *Irreverence: A strategy for therapists' survival*. London: Karnac Books.

Cecchin, G., Lane, G., & Ray, W. (1993). From strategizing to nonintervention: Toward irreverence in systemic practice. *Journal of Marital and Family Therapy, 19*, 125–136.

Cecchin, G., Lane, G., & Ray, W. (1994). *The Cybernetics of Prejudices in the Practice of Psychotherapy*. London: Karnac Books.

Haley, J. (1963). *Strategies of psychotherapy.* New York: Grune and Stratton.

Haley, J. (1973). *Uncommon therapy.* New York: W. W. Norton.

Haley, J. (1976). *Problem-solving therapy.* New York: Harper-Colophon Books.

Haley, J. (1980). *Leaving home.* New York: McGraw-Hill.

Haley, J. (1984). *Ordeal therapy.* San Francisco: Jossey-Bass.

Jackson, D. (1967). The myth of normality. *Medical Opinion and Review, 3* (5), 28–33.

Keeney, B. (1982). What is an epistemology of family therapy? *Family Process, 21,* 153–168.

Kleckner, T., Frank, L., Bland, C., Amendt, J., & du-Ree Broyant, R. (1992). The myth of the unfeeling strategic therapist. *Journal of Marital and Family Therapy, 18,* 41–51.

Madanes, C. (1980). Protection, paradox and pretending. *Family Process, 19,* 73–85.

Madanes, C. (1981). *Strategic family therapy.* San Francisco: Jossey-Bass.

Madanes, C. (1984). *Behind the one-way mirror.* San Francisco: Jossey-Bass.

Madanes, C. (1990). *Sex, love and violence: Strategies for transformation.* New York: W. W. Norton.

Papp, P. (1980). The Greek chorus and other techniques of paradoxical therapy. *Family Process, 19,* 45–57.

Penn, P. (1982). Circular questioning. *Family Process, 21,* 267–280.

Penn, P. (1985). Feed-forward: Further questioning, future maps. *Family Process, 24,* 299–310.

Selvini, M. (1988). *The work of Mara Selvini Palazzoli.* Northvale, NJ: Jason Aronson.

Selvini Palazzoli, M. (1981). *Self-starvation: From the intrapsychic to the transpersonal approach to anorexia nervosa.* New York: Jason Aronson.

Selvini Palazzoli, M. (1986). Towards a general model of psychotic games. *Journal of Marital and Family Therapy, 12,* 339–349.

Selvini Palazzoli, M., Boscolo, L., Cecchin, G., & Prata, G. (1977). Family rituals: A powerful tool in family therapy. *Family Process, 16,* 445–453.

Selvini Palazzoli, M., Boscolo, L., Cecchin, G., & Prata, G. (1978). *Paradox and counterparadox.* New York: Jason Aronson.

Selvini Palazzoli, M., Boscolo, L., Cecchin, G., & Prata, G. (1980). Hypothesizing-circularity-neutrality: Three guidelines for the conductor of the session. *Family Process, 19,* 3–12.

Selvini Palazzoli, M., Cirillo, S., Selvini, M., & Sorrentino, A. (1989). *Family games: General models of psychotic processes in the family.* New York: W. W. Norton.

Selvini Palazzoli, M., & Prata, G. (1983). A new method for therapy and research in the treatment of schizophrenic families. In H. Stierlin, L. Wynne, & M. Wirsching, (Eds.), *Psychosocial intervention in schizophrenia: An international view* (pp. 237–243). Berlin: Springer-Verlag.

Selvini Palazzoli, M., & Viaro, M. (1988). The anorectic process in the family: A six stage model as a guide for individual therapy. *Family Process, 27,* 129–148.

Tomm, K. (1984). One perspective on the Milan systemic approach: Part I. Overview of development, theory and practice. *Journal of Marital and Family Therapy, 10* (2), 113–125.

Tomm, K. (1984). One perspective on the Milan systemic approach: Part II. Description of session format, interviewing style and interventions. *Journal of Marital and Family Therapy, 10* (3), 253–271.

Tomm, K. (1987). Interventive interviewing: Part I. Strategizing as a fourth guideline for the therapist. *Family Process, 26,* 3–13.

Tomm, K. (1987). Interventive interviewing: Part II. Reflexive questioning as a means to enable self-healing. *Family Process, 26,* 167–184.

Watzlawick, P., Beavin, J., & Jackson, D. (1967). *Pragmatics of human communication.* New York: W. W. Norton.

Watzlawick, P., Weakland, J., & Fisch, R. (1974). *Change: Principles of problem formation and problem resolution.* New York: W. W. Norton.

Chapter 12

Behavioral Approaches

In conceptualizing what are generally labeled as behavioral approaches to family therapy, it is useful to think in terms of both therapy and a scientific method, for the two are intricately interwoven. That is, the procedures for therapy parallel the procedures for the scientific study of behavior consistent with the logical positivist-empirical tradition of research. Research in this tradition is based on sensory experience—what can be observed, seen, heard, smelled, tasted, or touched. Behavior therapy is committed to the scientific approach in that as an applied science its procedures must be testable and falsifiable. Thus, to do behavior therapy is to do science in the positivistic tradition. The elements of the model include:

1. A testable, explicit conceptual framework.
2. A treatment derived from and consistent with the content and method of experimental psychology.
3. Therapeutic techniques that are described precisely enough to be objectively measured and replicated.
4. A rigorous experimental evaluation of treatment methods and concepts.

Of the many models consistent with this approach, that of Gerald Patterson's Oregon Social Learning Project is one of the best known. The work of Patterson's group exemplifies the marriage of behaviorism and microanalytic research. That is, while working with families to deal with child-related problems, their main focus is on process variables associated with client resistance, or the successful outcome of therapy (Chamberlain, Patterson, Reid, Kavanaugh, & Forgatch, 1984).

Behaviorism grew out of a movement in the early 1900s led by J. B. Watson, a harsh critic of subjectivity and mentalism. He sought a basis for the "objective" study of behavior. Indeed, it was John Watson who claimed overt behavior provides the only legitimate data for the science of psychology. B. F. Skinner's view was much more expansive in that he contended that the subject matter of behavioral psychology is what the person does, irrespective of the public or private nature of the events. As early as 1938, Skinner believed behavior includes phenomena such as thoughts, feelings, dreams, and memories (Thyer, 1992). In Russia, Ivan Pavlov built the basis for what is called *classical conditioning*. E. L. Thorndike's research brought attention to the rewarding and punishing consequences of behavior. The focus of research on conditioning and establishing learning principles emerged from animal research laboratories and became the basis for experimental psychology.

Many people contributed to the evolution of what is now generally referred to as behavior therapy. In 1924 Mary Cover Jones demonstrated the efficacy of the application of behavioral procedures for treating children's fears. Mowrer and Mowrer used conditioning principles to treat enuresis in 1938 (Ross, 1981). However, early attempts to use the principles derived from laboratory research did not find a sympathetic audience among psychotherapists, who had built their work on the traditional psychodynamic psychology that is a part of the received view of our culture. Indeed, there was a basic division between experimental and clinical psychologists. Behaviorism challenged the status quo, although there were attempts to bridge the gap between the two orientations. One notable example is the work of Dollard and Miller (1950), who translated psychodynamic concepts into learning theory.

Despite criticism from psychodynamic psychologists, behaviorism grew. Joseph Wolpe (1958) developed procedures based on classical conditioning principles to treat adult neurotic disorders. This treatment derived from the research on reduction of fear in laboratory animals. Wolpe's procedure became known as systematic desensitization, in which anxiety (a response of the autonomic nervous system) was reduced by inducing a simultaneous contradictory response, relaxation. Eysenck (1959) viewed behavior therapy as an applied science and gave impetus to the movement by developing the journal *Behavior Research and Therapy*. Skinner's book *Science and Human Behavior* (1953) described psychotherapy in behavioral terms. The development of the *Journal of Applied Behavior Analysis* in 1968 was also significant, and the publication of Ullman and Krasner's now-classic book *Case Studies in Behavior Modification* (1965) was a major contribution in that it gave contrasting views of medical and psychological treatment methods for the same problem.

Allegiance to the scientific method and precision in approach as well as the challenge posed to the received view of our culture were important characteristics of the model as it evolved and grew. However, behavior therapy today is no longer what it once was. While a belief in precision and the scientific method remains, it has broadened its scope to accommodate Bandura's (1969) social learning theory, which emphasizes vicarious learning (modeling), symbolic/cognitive processes, and self-regulation. There is also an increased emphasis on cognitive processes in the form of mediation variables (Mahoney, 1974; Beck, 1976; Meichenbaum, 1977). In addition, Bandura's (1982) "reciprocal determinism" brings in an aspect that is useful in describing the dynamics of relationships. Along this same line, Thibault and Kelley's (1959) theory of social exchange helps the behavioral therapist focus on family interactions.

According to the social exchange perspective, interactions are analyzed in terms of the relative amounts of supposed reward and cost to people in relationship. The assumption is that people in relationship seek to maximize rewards and minimize costs. Over time there is reciprocity so that an equilibrium is established. Thus, positive behaviors beget positive behaviors and negative behaviors beget negative behaviors. The basic approach described by Thibault and Kelley has influenced the development of behavioral marital therapies and will be discussed at greater length later in this chapter.

To a great extent, behavior therapy continues to be closely aligned with the logical positivist-empirical research tradition and the basic belief that behavior is determined more by its consequences than by its antecedents. Its approach continues to be somewhat individualistic in the sense that the person targeted as having the problem is treated by changing the consequences of the undesirable behavior and thus changing the behavior. It is linear in that it punctuates a difference between antecedent events (events preceding a behavior) and consequent events (events following a behavior).

The stimulus-response-reinforcement sequence has been modified somewhat in more recent behavioral marital therapy:

> *Since each spouse is providing consequences for the other on a continuous basis, and since each partner exerts an important controlling influence on the other's behavior, the marital relationship is best thought of as a process of circular and reciprocal sequences of behavior and consequences, where each person's behavior is at once being affected by and influences the other. (Jacobson & Margolin, 1979, p. 13)*

Even though it is strongly aligned with the scientific method, behavior therapy also acknowledges the importance of the therapeutic relationship. As Brady (1980) states:

> *There is no question that the qualitative aspects of the therapist- patient relationship can greatly influence the course of therapy for good or bad. In general, if the patient's relationship to the therapist is characterized by belief in the therapist's competence (knowledge, sophistication, and training) and if the patient regards the therapist as an honest, trustworthy, and decent human being with good social and ethical values (in his own scheme of things), the patient is more apt to invest himself in the therapy. (p. 285)*

Further, behavior therapies tend to be both deterministic and optimistic. Problem behaviors as well as functional behaviors are viewed as nonpathological problems in living. Such behaviors are learned and as such can be unlearned. Similarly, new behaviors can be learned. The approach is ahistorical in that assessment is only concerned with current determinants of behavior and analysis of the problem into its components. It is concerned with *how, when, where,* and *what* rather than *why,* characteristic of psychodynamic psychology. Treatment is built upon this assessment and targets specific components or subparts. While the basic principles of treatment are keyed to changing the consequences of behavior, treatments are designed to fit the different problems of unique individuals. In fact, what is defined as a reward or punishment for an individual is only known after the fact and by measuring whether it increased or decreased the frequency of behavior. If the frequency of behavior has increased, the consequence is defined as a reward. If there is a decrease, it is defined as a punishment.

The goals of behavior therapy are decided by the client rather than by some a priori conceptual framework about how a person or relationship should be. The *how* of the therapy is decided by the therapist. For the behavioral therapist determinism is the rule, and all forms of social engagement involve social influence. The behavioral therapist is aware of this influence process and uses it in deciding the how of therapy. Indeed, influence is an important ethical issue for behavioral therapists, and procedures have been formulated to protect human rights and dignity (Stolz, 1978; Wilson & O'Leary, 1980).

In summary, behavior therapy grew out of laboratory research. Consistent with this heritage, its ultimate goal is the understanding, prediction, and control of behavior. It is applied science that seeks to advance its science through carefully designed treatment procedures.

Basic Concepts/Theoretical Constructs

Behavioral approaches to family therapy are more a technology than a coherent theory. Therefore, in this section we provide definitions of key concepts and principles that are basic to behavior modification.

Definitions

Classical Conditioning
Classical conditioning describes the process by which an unconditioned stimulus (food), which is associated with an unconditioned response (salivation), is paired with a conditioned stimulus (bell). The simultaneous presentation of the bell and the food elicits salivation. In repeated pairings of the food and the bell, the bell will gradually elicit the salivation without the presentation of the food. This process is identified with the autonomic nervous system—what is beyond conscious control.

Operant Conditioning
Operant conditioning describes the process according to which a subject voluntarily engages in a behavior. The frequency of response is controlled by the consequences following the behavior. An *operant* is a cause. A positive consequence is called a *positive reinforcer* and describes an increase in the frequency of the behavior preceding it. If the behavior of the subject is followed by a punishment, a response that is aversive (spanking), or withdrawal of a positive (grounding), or if it is ignored, there will be a decrease in the frequency of the behavior until it ceases to appear and is said to be extinguished (extinction).

Negative Reinforcement

Negative reinforcement describes the process by which an increase in the frequency of a behavior is associated with avoiding an aversive stimulus. Leaving the house to avoid a nagging husband would be an example.

Discrimination Learning

Discrimination learning describes a response that is conditioned to occur in one context and not in another. This is an important concept when selected behaviors are desired in a particular situation. Discrimination learning is influenced by the contingencies of reinforcement and punishment in the different situations. A child is rewarded for running and jumping in the playground but not for doing so in the classroom.

Generalization

Generalization describes a process related to discrimination learning. It might be referred to as not discriminating between different situations and engaging in the same behavior in a variety of contexts other than that in which the behavior was acquired. A simulated job interview in a therapy session would transfer, or generalize, to the real-life job interview.

Social Learning Theory

Social learning theory describes the importance of clients' awareness of rules and contingencies associated with the consequences of their behavior. This concept recognizes cognitive processes and is also related to vicarious learning or modeling. That is, people can learn new behavior by observing other people or events. Thus in order to change, clients do not have to engage in a behavior themselves and may not experience any direct rewarding or punishing consequence. However, they can infer an imagined or anticipated reward. Environmental influences in terms of contingencies of reinforcement are still important. Therefore, observing other people either directly or vicariously (e.g., through videotapes) may be sufficient to result in learning or a change in behavior.

Primary and Secondary Reinforcements and Punishments

Primary and secondary reinforcements and punishments describe a difference between what is believed to be biological or natural and what is acquired through learning. A primary reinforcer might be food. A primary punishment might be a spanking. A secondary reinforcer might be a pat on the back, and a secondary punishment might be a reprimand. Secondary reinforcers and punishments are believed to be acquired through social learning.

Reinforcement Schedule

A reinforcement schedule describes the different bases for the contingencies of reinforcement of a behavior and establishes the relationship between a behavior and its consequence. A continuous positive reinforcement schedule describes the process of giving a reward each time the desired behavior occurs. An intermittent reinforcement schedule describes the giving of a positive response on an irregular schedule, sufficient to maintain the behavior, but not so widely spaced as to lead the person to believe that no reward will be forthcoming.

Shaping
Shaping describes the process in which a complex behavior is divided into sub-parts, and contingencies of reward and punishment are provided to these subparts until all the behaviors comprising the whole are elicited. Thus, if having a child sit quietly at her desk, pay attention to the teacher, raise her hand, and wait to be called on before speaking is the target behavior, one might initially reward "sitting" as a first subpart of the whole. The process is also referred to as successive approximation.

Contingency Contracting
Contingency contracting refers to a process of negotiating desirable behavior change between two parties. It defines explicit rules for interaction. The contract is developed after noncoercive, open negotiation. The contract specifies which behaviors will be performed by whom, under what circumstances, with a specific reward contingency for each party built into the contract. Typically the contract specifies that the parties agree to exchange positive, rewarding behavior with each other.

There are many other concepts we could define in this section since a variety of terms have evolved in the application of behavior modification principles to parent training, couples therapy, and sex therapy. However, these will be presented under the appropriate headings later in this chapter.

Theory of Health/Normalcy

Earlier in this chapter we noted that the client decides the *what* of the therapy and the therapist decides the *how*. However, behavior therapy has little to say about how and what a person should be or do. Indeed, the behavioral approach has been much criticized in this regard; having no implicit values, it theoretically can be used to promote any behavior. Skinner's *Walden II* (1948) was criticized on this basis, as was Orwell's *1984*. Who decides? As we have mentioned, behavioral therapists recognized the possible abuse of this technology and formulated principles to protect human rights and dignity (Stolz, 1978; Wilson & O'Leary, 1980).

While no explicit values are presented in the behavioral literature, the data in the field provide clues as to what might be termed a "good" relationship, a "good" marriage, or a "good" family. Building on Thibault and Kelley's (1959) social exchange theory, we can infer that a good relationship is one in which there is a higher proportion of rewards relative to costs. Further, the benefits to both parties in such a relationship are balanced in that the benefit or costs to one is not greater than the benefit or costs to the other. The key is balance.

Research by Wills, Weiss, and Patterson (1974) suggests that in a good relationship there is a higher frequency of pleasant behavior and a minimal amount of unpleasant behavior. In effect, this supports the idea that the relationship will be better if there is more positive reinforcement. Gottman, Markman, and Notarius (1977) suggest that good, clear communication is important. Agreement is not essential, but good listening is, as it rewards the behavior of relating to one another.

Jacobson and Margolin (1979) suggest that good relationships are not problem free, but their members have viable problem-solving skills. Further, communication is effective and the members are able to discuss issues and consider each other's perspective. Consistent with the behavioral model, the skills necessary for a good relationship are learned. Good communication and problem-solving skills can be taught. These skills form the basis for the evolving family, which must be flexible and able to adapt to its changing circumstances.

Therapeutic Strategies/Interventions

The goals of behavior therapy are defined by the client and are limited to modifying the current behavior pattern. Symptom relief is the desired outcome. No assumption is made about treating the underlying or so-called real problems consistent with the medical or disease model regarding the treatment of symptoms. The goal is to substitute desired behaviors in place of those defined as undesirable. Thus, "symptom substitution" is neither a concept nor a concern from this perspective.

Maladaptive behavior is governed by the same principles of learning and modification as is adaptive behavior. Thus, the focus is on "corrective learning experiences in which clients variously acquire new coping skills and improved communication competencies, or learn how to break maladaptive habits and overcome self-defeating emotional conflicts" (Wilson, 1984, p. 253).

As a general principle, the basic assumption underlying this approach is that "behavior will change as contingencies of reinforcement are altered" (Nichols, 1984, p. 311). A first step in the therapy is to define the problem and conduct a functional analysis of the behavior targeted for change, to assess its antecedents and consequences. Thus, the therapist/scientist engages in careful observation. The behavioral therapist would not describe what he does as art, for what he does derives from basic principles of learning theory. Accordingly, this functional analysis is conducted in order to establish a baseline of the frequency of the targeted behavior while simultaneously noting what precedes and follows it.

Behavior therapy is typically an action-oriented therapy with a focus on operant (voluntary) behavior. Assignments outside the therapy session are common and may include practicing relaxation training, self-monitoring (charting) the frequency of a given behavior, using newly learned communication or assertive training skills, and confronting anxiety-provoking situations. In the operant model, new behavior is important. A new behavior cannot be rewarded until it is engaged in. Clients can be taught to monitor and change their own contingencies of reinforcement. In effect, behavior change precedes feeling or attitude change.

An important aspect of behavior therapy is attention to the consequences of a behavior rather than to the target behavior itself. The consequences of a behavior are assumed to be rewarding to the behavior even if the consequences do not appear to be a positive reinforcement. Thus, a question to a client might be, "What do you do when Johnny does X?"

Nichols (1984) notes that "a major tenet of behavioral treatment is that behavior is better changed by accelerating positive behavior rather than by decelerating negative behavior" (p. 313). In effect, the focus on the positive behaviors often precludes the appearance of negative or coercive behaviors. Consistent with the model, behavioral therapists also reward their clients' behavior changes. While rewards may at first be continuous and primary, ultimately the therapist wishes to move toward intermittent secondary (usually social) reinforcement. In a very real sense, the therapist might be referred to as an educator rather than a therapist since she seeks to have clients gain the knowledge and the skills to monitor their own behavior.

Also, consistent with the scientific model of observation, progress in therapy is very carefully monitored and measured. The focus is on precisely defined, overt behavior. It is important to note here that resistance is another concept that is not used in behavior therapy. If what from another framework would be called resistance emerges, it is seen as a function of the scientist/therapist's failure to design the experiment carefully enough. The experiment/therapy may thus need to be redesigned by redefining and reassessing the antecedents and consequences of the behavior. Therapy is thus a behavior-change experiment (Liberman, 1972).

Three Examples

The field of behavioral family therapy continues to evolve and various models build on this framework. Cognitive behavioral approaches are focused upon attributions, that is, how members of families view and explain deviant behavior in themselves and others. In effect, proponents of this approach seek to shift the thinking of family members from projected negative traits (unmotivated, lazy) to a view that includes the behavior of other family members, thereby giving family members more of a sense of control over the lives of others in the family (Barton & Alexander, 1981; Morris, Alexander, & Waldron, 1988). Others have begun to include aspects of systems thinking in their work and to focus on relationship issues as well as behavior change (Birchler & Spinks, 1980; Spinks & Birchler, 1982). In addition to the fact that behavioral principles certainly may be applied to whole families in a more general way, three specific behavioral models include parent-skills training, behavioral marital therapy, and conjoint sex therapy. We will therefore discuss each of these models in some detail and as separate entities, although there is obvious overlap.

Parent-Skills Training

A burgeoning field, parent-skills training fits the behavioral marital and family therapist. Unlike the systems therapist, however, he accepts the parent's definition of a child as the person having the problem, and the focus of therapy is on changing the parents' response to the child and thus effecting a change in the child's behavior. Consistent with the assumptions of the model, this is a linear punctuation of the events that are antecedent and consequent to the targeted behavior.

Whether in a therapy or a workshop format, the therapist serves as a social learning educator. He is a consultant to the parents, who are expected to make direct interventions with their children according to the principles of learning theory and social learning theory. The therapist/educator/experimenter is very precise in his procedures. The following steps are typical examples of the training process:

1. Explain social learning theory principles the parents need to know.
2. Precisely define the targeted, problem behavior.
3. Analyze the antecedent and consequent behaviors around the problem behavior.
4. Carefully monitor the frequency of the targeted behavior via some form of charting, and thereby establish a baseline, or preintervention frequency count.
5. Train the parents in the specific procedures for changing the targeted behaviors. This may involve:
   a. Precisely defining the rules for and expectations of the child.
   b. Changing the conditions antecedent to the occurrence of the problem behavior.
   c. Setting up exact procedures by which to positively reward compliance, such as type of reinforcement, schedule of reinforcement to be used, and timing of the reward (immediate or delayed gratification).
   d. Setting up exact procedures for discipline, such as time out or withdrawal of privileges. In this stage parents are taught and encouraged to use natural consequences as much as possible.

Assessment is geared to finding the lawful regularities that are presumed to exist in the dyadic relationship between parent and child. Parents might be asked to describe a typical day in the family. Parents might also be asked to complete a questionnaire such as the Louisville Behavior Checklist (Miller, 1979) or the Walker Problem Behavior Identification Checklist (Walker, 1976). Consistent with the behavioral model, the linear punctuation of parent affecting child could be reversed so that, theoretically, children could be trained to affect the parents.

An important part of the assessment process is to ascertain whether parents have a realistic set of expectations regarding their children. Thus, education of the parents early in the therapy session or workshop aims at helping them to define realistic, age-appropriate expectations. These expectations might be related to self-statements (cognitive, behavioral) as well as to family traditions.

During the assessment stage, the therapist/educator/experimenter is alert to problems in other family dyads that may preclude successful parent training. However, the model does not automatically presume that there must be a marriage problem if there is a misbehaving child. Thus, the therapist proceeds with parent training (if no overt problems between other dyads are noted), and would focus on other dyads only if the parent training were not successful. The therapist might use a marital adjustment questionnaire to supplement interview and observational data if deemed appropriate.

Analysis of the antecedent and consequent events involves having the parents discriminate and pinpoint the exact behavior they seek to modify. Thus, discrimination training is essential and includes delineation of both the child's and their own behavior. In effect, the parents must discriminate between desirable and undesirable behavior and arrange the appropriate consequence (reward or punishment) when the behavior is observed.

Gordon and Davidson (1981) identify four factors that should be considered before deciding to implement parent-skills training:

1. *"First, it is important to assess the degree to which environmental control is even possible"* (p. 526). *That is, there must be sufficient control of the environment to affect the antecedents and consequences one can modify. The authors cite the example of the overloaded single parent with three "professional monsters."*

2. *"Second, interpersonal problems between the parents may preclude their working together in a collaborative set"* (p. 526). *This does not mean that satisfied spouses will automatically be successful parents. On the other hand, in some unhappy marriages the parents can set aside their differences out of their superordinate love for their children. That is, parent-skills training is enhanced to the degree that parents can work cooperatively with one another.*

3. *"Third,...intrapersonal interference factors such as depression and anxiety may severely limit parents' ability to benefit from behavioral parent training"* (p. 527). *Accordingly, systematic desensitization, cognitive restructuring, and/or altering antecedents and consequences of the behavior of the parent may be a necessary adjunct to parent training.*

4. *"Finally, the resources and motivation of the child may suggest different forms of intervention"* (p. 527). *That is, a focus on how to help the particular child develop self-control is essential.*

Continuous assessment and monitoring are important in behavioral parent training. The distinction between assessment and treatment blurs in this model, for continuously monitoring charts that indicate progress is being made is an important reward for the parents, particularly those who want the perfect kid now. The data provided by the monitoring also provide information as to whether the procedures are being correctly applied and are appropriate to the situation, or indicate a need for the therapy/experiment to be redesigned. Parents may be rewarded, perhaps paid, for compliance, in an effort both to avoid dropouts and to achieve positive outcomes from therapy (Hansen & L'Abate, 1982).

Specific parent-training procedures may include verbal and/or performance methods. The verbal methods may involve didactic instruction as well as written materials. Performance training methods may involve role playing, modeling, behavioral rehearsal, and prompting. The use of videotape may also be a part of the performance-based model. Thus, parent(s) and child are placed in a situation and are monitored, coached, cued, and encouraged. In addition, parent counseling may be indicated under some circumstances. The purpose of parent counseling is to help the parents identify and resolve those factors that are interfering with successful parent training. Parents, like children, need an optimal social learning context in order for them to be successful as parents. They therefore may need to experience some success in the other roles in their lives if the parent-skills training is to be effective.

Behavioral Marital Therapy

In the parent-skills training process we have described, the target is the child and the procedures are taught to the parents. Reciprocity in the parent-child relationship is recognized, but the treatment focus is basically linear and the pathology or problem is located in the child. While some attention is given to other relationships in the family, the punctuation of the child as the target is a focus on the individual. Behavioral marital therapy is similar and yet different, for it retains the idea of altering behavior by altering the reinforcement contingencies in the environment, while it provides a decidedly relational focus in that both spouses are viewed as participating in maintaining a pattern of rewards and punishments. Instead of a simple linear punctuation that *B*'s response to *A* has reinforcing or punishing characteristics, the behavioral marital therapist is aware that the consequent response of *B* is also an antecedent to the behavior of *A*, which in turn is a consequence of *B*'s behavior. Behavior exchanges are continuous, and the behavior of each spouse is both an antecedent and a consequence for the behavior of the other. Thus, there is a punctuation of a recursive loop in the behavior exchanged within the marital relationship.

Another difference, which we have already addressed briefly, is the social exchange theory of Thibault and Kelley (1959). This theory uses the metaphors of costs and rewards to assess the level of satisfaction in a relationship. One could hypothesize that when a couple marries, they anticipate a greater ratio of rewards to costs. When the level of costs exceeds the level of rewards for each spouse, they experience marital discord. Thus, exchange theory suggests that individuals seek to maximize rewards (satisfaction) and to minimize costs (dissatisfaction). It is assumed that each spouse has control over the satisfaction or dissatisfaction given to the other.

It is further assumed that if the reward given is perceived as a reward by the other it has a greater value. Every relationship is judged by its members on the basis of the cost/benefit ratio. This is the comparison level, but this comparison level does not occur in a vacuum. Rather, the relative cost/benefit ratio is closely tied to one's expectancies and to the alternative relationships available. These comparisons may be glorified, but they are a very real part of each spouse's evaluation of the current relationship.

Thus, two individuals enter into a relationship with certain predispositions and expectancies for costs and benefits. Each spouse will experience certain benefits at some cost. If the benefits exceed the costs and if the benefits fit expectations, then the spouses may experience a high level of satisfaction. On the other hand, the cost/benefit ratio is never static but is modified by experiences in and out of the relationship. The idea of a stable relationship is thus equated with satisfaction. However, satisfaction is very personally experienced by each spouse, subject to a wide range of diverse challenges inherent in any ongoing relationship. The same behavior in the fifth year of a marriage may not be as valued as it was during the first year. Early in the marriage there may have been a disproportionate number of rewards to costs. Over time, the costs will evolve once the newness and the novelty have worn off. Continuing accommodation over many years has its costs as well as its benefits.

Cognition and social learning theory are more in evidence in behavioral marital therapy than in parent-skills training. Consistent with the model, the focus remains on changing behavior. However, it is also recognized that modified thought (cognition) and feelings are both antecedents and consequences of changed behaviors. The sequence of treatment in this approach seems to be that of cognition, behavior, and cognition, with the therapist playing the role of educator. Clients can and do use cognitive information, which can be reinforced by their experience in doing specific behaviors, which in turn affect and reinforce the behavior and the understanding. Social learning theory in behavioral marital therapy recognizes a reciprocal determinism of people in relationship. Accordingly, human interaction is shaped by personal, behavioral, and situational forces. Assessment of these forces is essential if one is to understand the dynamics of relationships and the potential for change in these relationships.

The goals of behavioral marriage therapy include: (1) an increase in the frequency of positive (reward) behaviors and a decrease in the frequency of the negative (punishing) behaviors; (2) increased skill in communication; and (3) increased skill in problem solving. The behaviors that fit these three categories are important parts of the initial and ongoing assessment in the therapy.

These three goals punctuate a difference between content and process. The emphasis is on specific behaviors and specific content tasks, with a focus on the increase in frequency of positive behavior and a decrease in negative behavior. On the other hand, skills training in communication and in problem solving focuses on process and teaches the couple *how* to deal with problems that may arise in the future. Communication and problem-solving skills are viewed as the tools for continuing to live together successfully as a couple. Indeed, skills training has evolved as the primary focus of behavioral marital therapy (Nichols, 1984).

The initial interview in behavioral marital therapy is viewed as an important source of data about the developmental history of the relationship as well as the historical antecedents of the current problems in the marriage. While the self-report of spouses may be used, the preference is for the therapist to rely on his observation of spouse interaction. In the process of identifying and specifically defining target behaviors, the therapist helps couples state the behavior they desire rather than the behavior they find displeasing. Couples are generally quite good at describing what they don't like but much less proficient in describing the behavior they desire. The transformation from "I want her to quit nagging me" to "Be more loving" is crucial. However, even though it is positive, this goal is still too general. A goal is not deemed defined unless its description can induce a specific behavioral image of its performance; for instance, acceptable statements would be "He would tell me he loves me once a day," or "She would give me a back rub twice a week." The precision of definition is important in that the more specific the behavior, the more likely it is to be performed, and once performed, to be rewarded appropriately.

The behavioral marital therapist also has many instruments at her disposal to assess the marriage. Among those available are the Areas-of-Change Questionnaire (A-C) (Weiss, Hops, & Patterson, 1973); the Marital Status Inventory (MSI) (Weiss & Cerreto, 1975); the Locke-Wallace Marital Adjustment Test (MAT) (Locke & Wallace, 1959), and the Dyadic Adjustment Scale (DAS) (Spanier, 1976). In addition to these formal instruments, couples also may be asked to record the frequency of pleasant and unpleasant behavior experienced with each other during the week.

An assumption of the behavioral marital therapist is that it is easier to increase the frequency of pleasing behavior than it is to decrease the frequency of undesirable behavior. Indeed, one cannot not behave, and the absence of a behavior does not mean that no behavior has occurred. Rather, it must be replaced by something. The focus is thus on the behavior that replaces the displeasing behavior. The assessment concentrates on the relationship's strengths. The therapist helps the couple change their focus away from behaviors they dislike to behaviors they would like. Accordingly, a homework assignment might be to ask spouses to record those pleasing things their spouse did during the week (Azrin, Naster, & Jones, 1973). The desired shift is away from aversive means of control to positive means of control.

A specific aspect of the therapy is to help the couple reduce mind reading and to be very explicit about what each dislikes and desires. Such expressions are to be stated in precise behavioral terms and are an important component of effective communication and problem-solving skills.

In the initial stages of the therapy, particularly with highly distressed couples (those with a high level of reciprocal aversive control behavior), expressions like "I would like you to...." can be used as a basis for quid pro quo (or something-for-something) exchanges. The therapist can help the couple create a contract with explicit clauses about what each will give and what each will get in a reciprocal exchange. Thus, an awareness of the contractual, reciprocal nature of their exchanges, whether positive or negative, is facilitated.

The quid pro quo contract is one form of the contingency contract, or a contract to do contingent on what the other does. The difficulty with this contract, of course, is that the occurrence of any different behavior depends on the other spouse honoring his contract. In an extremely troubled marriage this contract can be used as a basis for the continuation of the aversive control methods: "I did my part, but you didn't."

Another form of contract is the good faith contract. In this arrangement each spouse is asked to do the contracted behaviors whether or not the other spouse lives up to his or her part of the bargain. The spouse who does the specified behavior is entitled to a prearranged reward. However, an important part of such a contingency contract is that the reward selected by the husband must not be aversive to his wife and vice versa.

The personal good faith contract is a noncontingency form of contract that builds on the developmental history of the relationship (Becvar & Becvar, 1986). For example, the couple may be asked to form visual images of those little, important, rewarding things they each did for the other in the early stages of their relationship. The therapist might suggest that these behaviors have not been used recently because the couple has been caught up in the mundane requirements of daily living. The contract evolved is not a contract in the sense we have just described. Rather it is a personal contract each spouse makes with himself or herself to increase the frequency of positive behavior and to reward success. Spouses can be cued to be alert to increases in positive behaviors in their spouses and to reward the spouse. However, the key to the contract is that the specific positive exchanges are known personally only to each spouse and thus add the dimension of surprise, which also can be rewarding to the relationship.

Typically, contingency contracts are content focused in that specific behaviors are targeted for change. Again, it is important to note that the content is that of increased pleasing behaviors rather than on decreased negative behaviors. In effect, you don't stop the negative; you put in the positive. However, putting in a positive may preclude the appearance of the negative when the pattern of aversive methods of control is replaced by a positive method of control and by a view of control as reciprocal.

Emphasis on content is important, but the therapist must focus simultaneously on the process according to which the couple negotiates and evolves specific content issues. Communication and problem solving are thus a continuing part of the therapy with or without the couple's specific awareness that this is happening.

The formal focus on communication and problem-solving skill training involves the couple's conscious awareness that they are learning specific skills to communicate and solve problems more effectively. This includes teaching couples the basic principles of effective communication and problem solving. These principles may be explained verbally or by modeling. Modeling is viewed as being very effective in that by observing and then imitating the "expert" therapist, the couple will be rewarded vicariously by emulating one who is "esteemed" (Jacobson, 1981).

Another important part of the skill training is behavioral rehearsal. This means doing the desired, new behavior in the therapy session and receiving feedback regarding performance from the therapist and the spouse. The process of giving feedback is thus modeled by the therapist, and the couple can learn vicariously by observing. The therapist also gives each spouse feedback on how he or she gives feedback. Video- and audiotaping provide powerful feedback on the skills of communicating and problem solving as well as on giving feedback.

Consistent with the basic assumptions of this model, the global behaviors are broken down into parts, and the process of therapy can be viewed as shaping, or the feedback and reinforcement of incremental gains in learning new skills. Among the specific communication skills that might be taught are the following: eye contact; using "I" statements ("I think" or "I feel"); ownership of feelings ("I was" or "I felt pleased"); paraphrasing and empathy skills ("I heard you saying...." or "You are really excited that you will get two back rubs each week"); directly articulating what is desired in behavioral terms ("I would like it if you would tell me what part of your back you prefer that I rub"); and directly stating what has been requested ("You would prefer that I focus on your shoulders when I give you a back rub"). The specific skills seen as essential may vary from therapist to therapist. However, the focus is on tasks and issues rather than on catharsis or the ventilation of negative feelings. This task orientation is important to the behavioral approach since catharsis or ventilation of feelings can make the problem worse by hooking the couple back into their usual pattern of attempts at control by aversive means. Effective communication skills are viewed as basic to effective problem solving. Skill training in problem solving focuses on specific issues and is "future-directed, and solution-focused" (Jacobson, 1981, p. 576) rather than being a format for a discussion of the past. Jacobson also punctuates an important aspect of problem-solving skills training in that "the behavioral therapist's goal is not to eliminate anger and its concomitants from marriage, but simply to help couples discriminate between arguing and problem solving" (p. 576).

Defining the problem and collaboratively developing a solution divide behavioral marital therapy into two distinct phases, and maintaining this separation is considered important (Jacobson, 1981). Jacobson's general rules for problem solving include: (1) "discuss only one problem at a time"; (2) "paraphrase" to help each spouse to listen and the other to feel understood, thus increasing the probability that each spouse will understand and consider the other's perspective; (3) avoid mind reading or assigning motives to the other; and (4) "avoid verbal abuse and other aversive exchanges" that tend to come when one reads a motive into a statement of a problem (p. 577).

More specific skills for defining a problem include the following: (1) when stating a problem, always begin with something positive ("I appreciate the many little things you have done the past few weeks"); (2) define the problems in precise behavioral terms ("I am aware that I initiate our going out more than you do, and I would like it if you would suggest that we go out and do things more frequently"); (3) express feelings ("I feel responsible when we do go out and I worry about whether you are having a good time"); (4) make sure that both spouses acknowledge the reciprocal role in maintaining the problem ("I keep initiating, which may get in the way of your initiating" or "I don't initiate, which leaves it to you" or "The more you initiate the more I don't, and the more I don't the more you do"); and (5) keep the problem definitions brief (Jacobson, 1981).

After problem definition, the remainder of the discussion is focused on solutions. Generating possible solutions is an unrestricted no-criticism-of-solution process described as brainstorming. Absurd and humorous suggestions can add a dimension of creativity to possible solutions. Since "behavior change should be based on mutuality and compromise" (Jacobson, 1981, p. 579), behavior changes on the part of both spouses are essential. In addition, a proposed solution that includes a desired behavior change that is more of a burden to one spouse than to the other is not acceptable. These rules reinforce the notion that the couple is in it together and that both share responsibility for solving problems. Whatever solution is agreed upon, it is precisely stated and put in writing—what behavior change is agreed to by each spouse, when, for how long, and under what conditions.

These general principles of behavioral marital therapy involve content and process issues, which in practice are integrated throughout the course of therapy. By way of illustration we will present an eight-stage model developed by Richard Stuart (1980), which exemplifies the basic principles we set forth and yet has its own unique twists. Stuart's model is ahistorical, action oriented, conjoint, and time limited.

The first stage in Stuart's model is a comprehensive assessment, which involves having the couple complete a lengthy marital precounseling inventory. Covered in the inventory are a variety of issues, including commitment to the marriage, general goals, satisfactions, targets for change, and details regarding daily activity.

In the second stage the couple agrees to a treatment contract. The therapy contract is important in that it contains essential aspects deemed necessary for successful therapy. These aspects include the willingness of the couple to have the therapist reveal to both all information each has provided, a statement of one or more goals, a commitment for both to come to the sessions, the minimum number of sessions (this varies from six to ten), and the therapist's remuneration. Stuart makes clear that therapy is conjoint and that he will not enter into an agreement with one spouse against the other. Further, he expects both members to initiate change and to become involved in the process of change.

In the third stage, Stuart outlines the model underlying his approach with the couple. The basic idea he imparts is that the essential focus is on having the couple increase the frequency of positive behavior. The therapist describes himself as an educator, role model, and source of reinforcement and positive feedback.

The fourth stage in Stuart's model involves instituting caring days. In preparation for caring days, each spouse makes a list of specific behaviors desired from the other. Selected behaviors (typically eight to ten) are asked for on the targeted caring day. Stuart's model does not involve the contingency contract described previously. Rather he asks for what he calls "positive risks," in which each partner is to perform caring behaviors independent of the other's actions. Each partner keeps a record of the caring behaviors given and received each day. These are viewed as a "pleasure index" and "commitment index" for that day's behavior.

The fifth stage is concerned with communication. Stuart believes in planned communication to develop the skills to send and receive honest, timely, and constructive messages. His focus is on the positive and his interventions interrupt negative exchanges (subterfuge, indirect communication, manipulation, misinterpretation) and teach positive alternatives. Stuart does not specifically teach or discuss what spouses did wrong, and thus he is an educator and a source of reinforcement.

Contracts are negotiated in the sixth stage. The focus here may be on shifting ritualized role responsibilities, developing strategies for dealing with problem areas, or on producing greater trust. The contracts take the form of something for something, or the quid pro quo agreement.

The focus of the final two stages is on effective decision making. The key skills here are formulating realistic goals and developing problem-solving skills. Stuart uses a "powergram," which helps couples see how decisions are made, by whom, when, and how in their relationship. Negotiation about decision making and responsibilities for making decisions are worked out.

The eighth and terminal stage of the therapy helps the couple focus on how to maintain the changes in their relationship. This involves summarizing what they have agreed to and the best ways to insure continuing effective communication and decision making. This agreement may involve periodic formal self-assessments to gauge progress and to make changes relative to changing circumstances. Stuart fades himself out of the therapy by scheduling sessions at wider intervals as well as by taking a less active role in the therapy.

Stuart's model is one variation of the many available in the literature on behavioral marital therapy. There are common themes in these models, however, and whatever variations exist, they are more reflective of differences in therapist style and preference than in basic principles.

Conjoint Sex Therapy

Conjoint sex therapy came of age with the publication of Masters and Johnson's *Human Sexual Inadequacy* (1970). Indeed, sexuality is an important relationship issue, and a sexual problem may be one of many presenting problems encountered by a family therapist. The question of whether the sexual problem is a symptom of other relationship issues between partners (Kaplan, 1974) or whether it is a problem in its own right remains an open issue in the field. As with any problem, however, in order to be viewed as a problem, it is necessary to have some conceptualization or expectancy of what the problem should or should not be. It is not surprising that a society with a long history of sexual taboos and inhibitions communicated through many of its institutions has set the tone for current conflicts. That is, given the recent shift in both the popular press and professional literature about the importance of accepting our sexuality and the enjoyment of sex, tension in this area is inevitable. Also, the relatively recent changes in the roles of men and women deemed appropriate in other parts of their lives inevitably sneak into the bedroom. However, such issues are beyond the scope of this book. Our focus in this chapter is on the behavioral approaches to treating sexual dysfunction.

It should not come as a surprise that many parallels to behavioral marital therapy are found in conjoint sex therapy. Thus, the behavioral sex therapist is an educator who teaches sexual physiology and techniques, changes maladaptive behavior patterns and cognitions, and uses direct methods to reduce anxiety and improve skill performance. Heiman, LoPiccolo, and LoPiccolo (1981) note that "sex education, skill training in communication and sexual technique, and attitude change procedures remain elements common to both 'behavior therapy' and 'sex therapy' " (p. 594).

Healthy Sexual Relationships

As we suggested, defining a problem is relative to the expectancy and the actual experience. Thus, it is inappropriate to discuss normalcy and abnormalcy in sexual functioning aside from the unique intimate experience of each couple. We can, however, infer the desirable from a focus on what is presented as problematic. Thus, general issues concern degree of pleasure from sexual activity, variety, degree of arousal and orgasm, and acceptance of one's own sexuality and the sexuality of the partner. The bottom line for normalcy in any unique relationship, of course, is what the couple can mutually agree upon as satisfactory.

Heiman et al. (1981) discuss general factors important in the sexual relationship. Among these are (1) "flexibility" in sex-role; (2) "openness: receptive and expressive"; (3) "active intimacy and involvement," or being "valued in the relationship and showing care and concern in ways that matter to the other person, communicating a desire to feel close, and trying to be tuned in to a partner's reactions"; (4) "trust and commitment," or a willingness to be vulnerable, spontaneous, and uninhibited; (5) "love"; (6) "erotic attraction"; and (7) "freedom, autonomy, responsibility" (pp. 597–598).

Again, the experience of a problem reveals a discrepancy between an expectancy and the actuality. These general relationship factors can influence the expectancy and become a standard against which to compare actuality, thus creating a problem. This, of course, is not exclusive to sexual problems.

Therapeutic Strategies/Interventions

The treatment of sexual dysfunction necessitates the punctuation of some means of conceptualizing the problem. Kaplan (1974) provides a useful model that is divided into three phases. The first phase is identified as sexual desire, which may involve too little or too much desire. The second phase relates to sexual excitement, which in the female may take the form of lack of sexual arousal and in the male, erectile dysfunction. The third phase is called orgasm, which may include premature ejaculation, retarded ejaculation in males, and inhibition of orgasm in females.

An important issue in understanding sexual dysfunction is the possibility of a physical basis for dysfunction, including injury, neurological disorders, or medication (legal and illegal). Therefore, the assessment process must include a consideration of this crucial dimension and may require that clients have medical checkups and take appropriate steps.

Psychological factors to be considered include aspects of history that have become a part of the current context. These may include expectations, guilt regarding sexuality, trust, religious upbringing, performance anxiety, and low self-esteem. Spouses bring their personal histories into the relationship, and a part of these histories are attitudes about self, marriage, sex, and relationships.

Relationship factors must also be considered and can reflect previous relationships as well as the dynamics of the current relationship. Heiman et al. (1981) comment in this regard that "a dysfunction can be serving purposes very useful to the structure of the relationship and the psychological needs of each individual" (p. 601). In other words, sexual dysfunction may be symptomatic of relationship problems in that the symptom serves to maintain a certain pattern of interaction between partners.

Given the various issues we have described, the assessment should be multi-dimensional. It should therefore include aspects of history, current sexual practice, beliefs, attitudes and expectations regarding sex, and the larger pattern of the couple's relationship. Physiological or medical factors also should be taken into consideration.

As with behavioral marital therapy, behavioral sex therapy involves setting specific goals. Goal setting may involve such elements as compromise or working through differences regarding expectations in the sexual relationship. The general ultimate goal is that there be greater agreement between expectations, attitudes, and experiences for the couple. The idea of reciprocity is very important in this compromise.

Also consistent with behavioral marital therapy, improved communication (directly stating preferences and understanding each other) is a major focus of conjoint sex therapy. A part of this communication involves education regarding knowledge of sexuality and means of improving sexual pleasure and expanding the range of alternative sexual behavior.

Another important part of the therapy is to be alert to overriding issues in the relationship beyond the presenting problem of sexual dysfunction and to shift to this focus or make a referral as appropriate. From the behavioral perspective it is also important to be sensitive to individual psychopathology as well as to different levels of motivation for therapy in the partners.

In this approach the therapist plays an active role. She may provide information, facilitate communication, or correct misinformation. She may use a variety of teaching methods, including films, books, and other specific means of providing clients with information regarding the physiology and anatomy of sexual response. The therapist promotes openness of communication. It is important for the therapist to be seen as knowledgeable and competent, which is one basis for the rapport necessary for openly discussing a topic or an aspect of a relationship generally associated with taboos and inhibitions. Indeed, such open discussion may be sufficient treatment of the problem, for this discussion may be part of a more general relationship enhancement which affects sexual interaction.

The techniques of behavioral sex therapy may include systematic desensitization (Wolpe, 1958) to reduce anxiety, assertive training (Lazarus, 1965) to overcome sexual and social inhibition, or learning to express individual preferences. Assertiveness training can be closely tied to communication skills training in which couples are taught to initiate sex by creating an atmosphere of intimacy. This communication may involve helping the couple say "No" in a way that is not destructive either to sexual intimacy or to other aspects of their relationship. That is, it is important that couples learn how to both initiate and refuse sex.

Sexual inhibitions can be treated and sexual communication enhanced by what is called the sensate focus, a nongenital sexual massage (Kaplan, 1974). This technique allows the couple to learn more about each other's bodies through touch and helps them to learn to communicate about which areas give them pleasure. During the sensate focus, no genital contact or sexual intercourse is allowed. This sensate focus is part of in vivo desensitization and is keyed to anxiety reduction. Indeed, anxiety reduction and overcoming inhibition, and thus changing attitudes, seems to be a key part of numerous techniques used in the treatment of sexual dysfunction.

A variety of techniques are used for specific dysfunctions. Among the dysfunctions for which viable treatments exist are premature ejaculation (the squeeze technique); erectile failure (reduction in anxiety regarding performance, paradoxical instructions that suggest the male is not expected to become aroused); and inorgasmic dysfunction (directed masturbation or becoming familiar with her genitalia and accepting her sexuality). A detailed examination of these and other techniques is beyond the scope of the present discussion. However, it is important that the family therapist become well acquainted with the many alternatives in behavioral sex therapy as well as the physiological, medical, psychological, and relationship dimensions of sexual dysfunction as a presenting problem.

Systemic Consistency

Behavioral approaches to family therapy are built on assumptions characteristic of individual psychology and the neopositivistic world view. Thus, a critique based on the assumptions of systems theory/cybernetics hardly seems appropriate. The more important question concerns whether such approaches qualify as examples of family therapy. If one accepts the proposition that family therapy is about theory and not about particular interest groups, such as parents, couples, marriages, or families, then the answer is no.

On the other hand, there are some pragmatic aspects of the behavioral approaches that are quite consistent with a cybernetic perspective. That is, problems are defined by the clients, and no ideal models of health or normalcy are posited. The emphasis is on skills and thus on process dimensions. To the extent that reciprocal determinism is understood, then circularity and mutual influence are acknowledged. Further, although antecedents and consequences of behavior are generally described in a linear fashion, this is an arbitrary punctuation and may be defined in the reverse direction.

As models of traditional science as well as of therapy, the behavioral approaches lend themselves more readily to evaluation than any of the others we have discussed. In a culture that values such a punctuation of science, this is a high recommendation. The fact is, these approaches have proven effective in a variety of situations and thus cannot be disregarded on the basis of systemic inconsistency.

Suggested Readings

Alexander, J., Barton, C., Schiaro, R., & Parsons, B. (1976). Systems behavioral intervention with families of delinquents: Therapist characteristics, family behavior and outcome. *Journal of Consulting and Clinical Psychology, 44,* 656–774.

Arrington, A., Sullaway, M., & Christensen, A. (1988). Behavioral family assessment. In I. R. Falloon (Ed.), *Handbook of behavioral family therapy* (pp. 78–106). New York: Guilford Press.

Azrin, N., Naster, J., & Jones, R. (1973). Reciprocity counseling: A rapid learning-based procedure for marital counseling. *Behavior Research and Therapy, 11,* 265–283.

Bandura, A. (1977). *Social learning theory.* Englewood Cliffs, NJ: Prentice-Hall.

Bandura, A. (1982). Self-efficacy mechanisms in human agency. *American Psychologist, 37,* 122–147.

Bandura, A., & Walters, R. (1963). *Social learning and personality development.* New York: Holt, Rinehart & Winston.

Beck, A. (1976). *Cognitive therapy and the emotional disorders.* New York: International Universities Press.

Beck, A., Rush, A., Shaw, B., & Emery, G. (1979). *Cognitive therapy of depression.* New York: Brunner/Mazel.

Berkowitz, B., & Graziano, A. (1972). Training parents as behavior therapists: A review. *Behavior Research and Therapy, 10,* 297–317.

Birchler, G., & Spinks, S. (1980). Behavioral-systems marital and family therapy: Integration and clinical application. *American Journal of Family Therapy, 8,* 6–28.

Conway, J., & Bucher, B. (1976). Transfer and maintenance of behavior change in children: A review and suggestions. In E. Mash, L. Hamerlynck, & L. Hands (Eds.), *Behavior modification and families* (pp. 119–159). New York: Brunner/Mazel.

DiGiuseppe, R. (1988). A cognitive-behavioral approach to the treatment of conduct disorder in children and adolescents. In N. Epstein, S. Schlesinger, & W. Dryden (Eds.), *Cognitive-behavioral therapy with families* (pp. 183–214). New York: Brunner/Mazel.

Eisler, R., & Hersen, M. (1973). Behavior techniques in family-oriented crisis intervention. *Archives of General Psychiatry, 28,* 111–116.

Falloon, I. (Ed.). (1988). Handbook of behavioral family therapy. New York: Guilford Press.

Foster, S., & Hoier, T. (1982). Behavioral and systems family therapies: A comparison of theoretical assumptions. *American Journal of Family Therapy, 10* (3), 13–23.

Gordon, S., & Davidson, N. (1981). Behavioral parent training. In A. S. Gurman & D. P. Kniskern (Eds.), *Handbook of family therapy* (pp. 517–555). New York: Brunner/Mazel.

Gurman, A., Knudson, R., & Kniskern, D. (1978). Behavioral marriage therapy: IV. Take two aspirin and call us in the morning. *Family Process, 17,* 165–180.

Jacobson, N. (1981). Behavioral marital therapy. In A. S. Gurman & D. P. Kniskern, (Eds.), *Handbook of family therapy* (pp. 556–591). New York: Brunner/Mazel.

Jacobson, N., & Margolin, G. (1979). *Marital therapy: Strategies based on social learning and behavioral exchange principles.* New York: Brunner/Mazel.

Kaplan, H. S. (1974). *The new sex therapy: Active treatment of sexual dysfunctions.* New York: Brunner/Mazel.

Kaplan, H. S. (1979). *Disorders of sexual desire and other new concepts and techniques in sex therapy.* New York: Brunner/Mazel.

Liberman, R. (1970). Behavioral approaches to family and couple therapy. *American Journal of Orthopsychiatry, 40,* 106–118.

LoPiccolo, J., & LoPiccolo, L. (1978). *Handbook of sex therapy.* New York: Plenum.

Margolin, G., Fernandez, V., Talovic, S., & Onorato, R. (1983). Sex role considerations and behavioral marital therapy. *Journal of Marital and Family Therapy, 9,* 131–145.

Masters, W., & Johnson, V. (1970). *Human sexual inadequacy.* Boston: Little, Brown.

Meichenbaum, D. (1977). *Cognitive behavior modification.* New York: Plenum Press.

Patterson, G. (1975). *Families: Applications of social learning to family life.* Champaign, IL: Research Press.

Skinner, B. F. (1953). *Science and human behavior.* New York: Macmillan.

Stuart, R. (1969). Operant interpersonal treatment for marital discord. *Journal of Consulting and Clinical Psychology, 33,* 675–682.

Stuart, R. B. (1976). An operant interpersonal program for couples. In D. H. Olson (Ed.), *Treating Relationships* (pp. 119–132). Lake Mills, IA: Graphic Publishing.

Stuart, R. (1980). *Helping couples change.* New York: Guilford Press.

Thibault, J., & Kelley, H. (1959). *The social psychology of groups.* New York: John Wiley.

Weiss, R. (1978). The conceptualization of marriage and family disorders from a behavioral perspective. In T. Paolino & B. McCrady (Eds.), *Marriage and marital therapy: Psychoanalytic, behavioral, and systems theory perspectives* (pp. 165–239). New York: Brunner/Mazel.

Wolpe, J. (1958). *Psychotherapy by reciprocal inhibition.* Stanford, CA: Stanford University Press.

Wolpe, J. (1969). *The practice of behavior therapy.* Elmsford, NY: Pergamon Press.

Chapter 13

Evolving Therapeutic Models

In this chapter we shift our museum tour of the various approaches to family therapy to a review of new approaches that we call evolving models. On the one hand, every therapist evolves his or her own approach to therapy while, on the other hand, in each professional field a few emerge that are perhaps sufficiently elegant, to be accorded the status of a model. Such a model may ultimately become part of the received view of the field. However, any new approach serves a useful purpose in that it challenges, stimulates the imagination, or otherwise helps people to ask different questions. Their development is important in that all fields need sources of the random, or differences that may make a difference. Otherwise the field's processes may get circular, that is, double back on themselves, defining rigid structures.

To us, most of the models of family therapy presented in this chapter fit the postmodernist, second-order cybernetics, social constructionist perspective. Included in the first part of the chapter are the approaches of Tom Andersen, Bill O'Hanlon, Steve de Shazer and Insoo Berg, Michael White and David Epston, Harry Goolishian and Harlene Anderson, and Bradford Keeney. Also included are brief overviews of two approaches which, although certainly less well known, illustrate consistency with this perspective. In the second part of the chapter we review Carol Anderson's psychoeducational model and Richard Schwartz's Internal Family systems model which we perceive as more consistent with the modernist, simple cybernetics tradition. Our classifications of these models is uniquely our own and we respectfully acknowledge the right of any of their authors (or readers) to disagree with the distinctions we make consistent with our reality.

As you recall, in our introduction to Part Two we punctuated a difference between the modernist/structuralist and the postmodernist/social constructionist traditions. Thus, in Chapters 7 through 12 we presented models in which universal codes, customs, structures, and behaviors that transcend unique contexts are assumed and searched for and all-encompassing processes are identified. To us they represent the received view of the field of marriage and family therapy. The exception is the MRI communications approach, which in our opinion is more similar to the models consistent with the postmodernist/social constructionist tradition. In therapeutic approaches consistent with the modernist/structuralist tradition, the therapist becomes the expert (e.g., coach, choreographer, director) who sets the goals as mandated by her theory and treats the real problem, which is the underlying structural flaw or faulty processes built into the system.

By contrast, we described the postmodernist/social constructionist therapist as one who is "suspicious of great subjects and all encompassing theories . . . because no social theory can make claims to validity outside a particular context and value system" (Doherty, 1991, p. 40). We also created a parallel between therapy in this mode and our perspective on second-order cybernetics. Accordingly, therapists are characterized as participant-observers who view therapy as a collaborative process between themselves and the client system. The therapist participates with the client in deconstructing the universal truth story the client brings to therapy and collaborates with the client in constructing a new story that solves/dissolves problems defined by the presenting story. The therapist might therefore be viewed as more "client centered" (Rogers rediscovered) than "theory centered"; that is, the focus is more on the client rather than on some preconception of what is *really* going on in the client system. The goal is not to impose some normative way (according to the theory of the therapist) about how the client system should be. Therapy in this tradition is more likely to resemble a conversation.

To briefly review the assumptions of second-order cybernetics:

1. It is the observer who punctuates differences and distinctions that are called *reality.*
2. The reality thus invented orients one's attitude and behaviors toward self, one's relationships, and the world.
3. There are many possible meanings (multiversa) as opposed to one "true" meaning (universum), and thus we can create many new worlds limited only by our imagination.
4. Each living system is "structurally determined," can do only what its structure (world view or ecology of ideas) allows, and thus can relate only within the limits of the modes of relating available in its repertoire.
5. Living systems are autonomous systems and, consistent with their structure, will make their own determinations about when to change, how to change, and what form change will take or cease to exist.

Consistent with these assumptions, therapists would (1) communicate respect for the system's existing structure; (2) understand that the system is doing what it does as best it can given its existing ecology of ideas, which constitutes its reality; and (3) share different versions of the same world to "structurally couple" with the existing structure of the system. Such different versions of the world may be the "difference that makes a difference" (Bateson, 1972, p. 453), if they are (1) neither too small to be noticed nor so large as to disorganize the system; (2) are communicated with respect for the system's existing structure; (3) are sufficiently nonobtrusive, that is, a perturbation rather than an intervention; (4) are sufficiently interesting, or structurally couple; and (5) are communicated in an atmosphere of safety.

The Reflecting Team: Tom Andersen

In our view, Tom Andersen and his Norwegian colleagues (Andersen, 1987, 1991, 1992, 1993) have developed a model that is clearly consistent with the postmodern, second-order cybernetics, social constructionist/narrative traditions. Andersen's journey to his present approach began in medical school and was followed by four years of work as a family physician, during which he became concerned with and curious about the social context of illness. His move into psychiatry provided no answers, but it raised many questions:

> *Could there be alternatives to the beliefs that "mentally ill patients" can be steered into health? Could there be alternatives to separating the "mentally ill" from their family, friends, jobs, and so forth? Could "patients" be called something other than "patients"? Could alternatives to standard treatment (namely, being locked behind closed doors, given medication against one's will, behavior modification, and so on) be more coherent with the context of the "patient"—family—friends— job—neighborhood? (Andersen, 1992, p. 56)*

Consideration of questions such as these led Andersen and his associates to study and attempt to apply principles derived from the work of Minuchin, Haley, and MRI, but with less success than hoped for. Thus they sought "smart" understandings of the families and their problems and "smart" instructions on how to handle them. They studied Bateson's ideas as well as those of Boscolo and Cecchin of the Milan team, and of Hoffman and Penn from the Ackerman Institute. However, attempts to apply the Milan team's ideas from the perspective of expert did not feel right and observations such as, "'This is what we see,' or 'This is what we understand,' or 'This is what I want you to do,'" gave way to "'In addition to what you saw we saw this,' or 'In addition to what you understood we understood this,' or 'In addition to what you have tried to do yourself, we wonder if you might try to do this'" (Andersen, 1992, p. 57).

With the help of Aina Skorpen, Andersen articulated an important question about the therapy process: "Why did we hide away our deliberations about the families?" (Andersen, 1992, p. 57). In 1985, this idea opened the door to the process of *the reflecting team* when it was suggested that the family and the interviewer listen to the thinking of the team which had been watching the family and the interviewer. The reflecting team sharing its thinking about the family punctuated a difference between "public language" and "private language," the latter being the language of the professionals, intellectuals, and academicians. Open-reflecting moved "professional language toward daily language," (p. 58) or language which allowed a common understanding.

This shift in process also moved the therapist into the role of participant-observer. However, the process was not yet complete and its evolution continued as the team began reflecting on the concept of difference, that is, Bateson's difference as "elementary unit of information" and his "difference that makes a difference." How much difference is too much difference (too unusual) to make a difference? Aware that the clients gave the clue, the team began observing and becoming sensitive to clients' level of participation in and discomfort with the conversation. Using the language provided by Maturana and Varela, they noted that difference is important, but a difference that cannot be integrated may mean the disintegration of the system.

Andersen also noticed that the team had fewer ideas when they talked together than when they observed silently. In addition, the team became aware that it was important that reflections initially describe an event that happened in the interview, for example, "When I heard . . ." or "When I saw . . . I thought about. . . . " Further, they believed that reflections truly must be reflections, that is, offered with uncertainty or tendered tentatively: " 'I am not sure but it seemed to me. . . . ,' or 'My thinking of that made me wonder' " (p. 60). Another important idea was that clients have the ability to say no, that is, to choose to listen to what the team is saying or not.

Building on the idea that "nothing is negative in itself; it becomes negative when the listener perceives it as negative" (p. 60), team members were encouraged not to give "negative" connotations. Thus, "I cannot understand why they did not try this or that?" becomes, "I wonder what would happen if they tried . . . ." Another important aspect of the process of reflecting is that team members are to look at one another and not to those who listen. Thus clients are freer to listen or not at their discretion.

As the conversation is turned back over to the family and the interviewer, new conversations and/or new understandings may evolve. An important assumption underlying the process is the belief that there are many ways to explain a situation rather than one right or correct way. As stated by Andersen, "Squarely spoken, we do not relate to life 'itself' but to our understanding of it" (p. 61).

To Andersen, the first two questions in the meeting are important: "How would you like to use this meeting?" avoids the idea that there is some predetermined plan of action, and "What is the history of the idea behind this meeting?" creates a context for those who are eager to talk as well as for those who are not. It is also important to help family members feel comfortable to "talk about this talk." This may involve conversation about the use of a team, where to meet, and what issues are to be talked about, with whom, in the family.

If there is no team the interviewer can have "inner and outer conversations" as family members are asked to reflect on what they heard another family member say and then ask the family member for his/her reflections on the reflections of other family members. The professional also can reflect on his thoughts and ask family members to reflect on what they heard. Andersen refers to this as the "reflecting process" (p. 63).

Andersen (1993) reports his personal difficulty with only listening and with avoiding the temptation to make up meanings about what his clients are saying. However, he believes it is very important to listen with what he calls a "co-presence" and to ask only questions that connect with what the speaker has just said. He waits until the speaker has finished "talking" and *"thinking"* (1991, p. 63, [emphasis added]). Building on the work of Heidegger, Gadamer, and Gergen, which calls our attention to metaphor and the use of language, Andersen observes that

> *Talking with oneself and/or others is a way of defining oneself. In this sense the language we use makes us who we are in the moment we use it. . . . The search for new meanings, which often comprises searching for new language, is a search for us to be the selves with which we feel most comfortable. So-called "therapeutic" talk might be regarded as a form of search; a search for new descriptions, new understandings, new meanings, new nuances of the words, and ultimately for new definitions of oneself. (Andersen, 1992, p. 65)*

Solution-Focused Therapy: William O'Hanlon

William O'Hanlon studied with Milton Erickson, and the solution-focused therapy of O'Hanlon and his collaborators, Weiner-Davis and Wilk, reflects the same pragmatism found in much of Erickson's work. Accordingly, people are understood to be caught up in the framework of meaning that defines a problem as a problem as well as the necessary more-of-the-same solutions that are consistent with the problem as defined by that particular framework. While any framework limits the number of alternatives, what is problematic is that the assumptions of the framework that define both the problem and attempted solutions are not being questioned. If assumptions of the framework are examined, problems may be redefined and new solutions may be forthcoming.

O'Hanlon's work assumes the constructionist position that reality is multiperspectival: "Solution-oriented therapists don't believe that there is any single 'correct' or 'valid' way to live one's life" (O'Hanlon & Weiner-Davis, 1989, p. 44). Thus, reality is not a given. Meaning and perception are embedded in language, and language becomes the vehicle for change as reflected in the vocabulary used; the world view is mirrored in the language.

Language is described as an interactive process through which three goals are negotiated: (1) "change the 'doing' of the situation that is perceived as problematic"; (2) "change the 'viewing' of the situation that is perceived as problematic"; (3) "evoke resources, solutions and strengths to bring to the situation that is perceived as problematic" (O'Hanlon & Weiner-Davis, 1989, p. 126). The therapist attempts to "shape" the client's complaint through therapeutic interaction: "The therapeutic problem to be worked on does not exist outside the therapist's office,... it is a product of the client's and therapist's talking together" (O'Hanlon & Wilk, 1987, p. 47).

No singular model of a normal family is espoused from this perspective: "We have come to understand that what is unacceptable behavior in one family or for one person is desirable behavior in another" (O'Hanlon & Wilk, 1987, p. 44). It is further assumed that there are no underlying purposes or ulterior motives for the problem in the family and that clients do want to change. People are believed to have the strengths and resources to solve their problems, not by attempting to solve the problem but by constructing solutions. The therapist therefore seeks to help the client feel encouraged by accomplishing small changes, for "once a small positive change is made, people feel optimistic and a bit more confident about tackling further changes" (O'Hanlon & Weiner-Davis, 1989, p. 42).

O'Hanlon's solution-oriented therapy is conversational and emphasizes the use of ordinary language:

> A "fly on the wall" who did not know we were doing psychotherapy would not necessarily suspect what we were doing: he would see and hear only an ordinary conversation. What defines the conversation as psychotherapy is simply our goal in conducting the conversation. (O'Hanlon & Wilk, 1987, p. 177)

Further, therapy moves from a problem focus to a solution focus through the steps of "joining," "describing the problem," "finding exceptions to the problem," "description of the problem," "normalizing," and "goal-setting" (O'Hanlon & Weiner-Davis, 1989, pp. 75–103). The therapist takes an active role and directs the conversation toward goal-oriented solutions.

O'Hanlon (1993, p. 14)) creates a distinction between "three domains in people's lives": experience, action, and stories. In his view it is important first of all to validate clients' experience. This validation involves "acknowledging" or communicating that their experiences are valid and valued; "giving permission" to "feel, experience, think or do things"; and "inclusion" or incorporating the experience into the conversation without impeding a move toward solutions.

The second domain is action: "Action consists of what people do that is actually or potentially under their deliberate influence" (O'Hanlon, 1993, p. 15). Through therapeutic conversation the therapist focuses the dialogue on actions that move the client "towards the stated goals" and away from actions that "lead away from stated goals" (p. 15).

O'Hanlon's third domain is stories. This domain "consists of the ideas, beliefs, frames of reference, and habits of language that the client and his/her intimates show in reference to the presenting concern in therapy" (p. 15). As with actions, O'Hanlon states that some stories are acceptable and others are not, depending on whether or not the story leads the client toward or away from stated goals.

Gale (1991, pp. 43–44), who reviewed the work of O'Hanlon and Wilk (1987) and O'Hanlon and Weiner-Davis (1989), notes ten interventions consistent with O'Hanlon's solution-oriented therapy:

1. *"Speaking the client's language" describes the therapist's attempt to join by using aspects of the client's language (words, phrases, or metaphors) as well as paralanguage (emotional tone) so that the client may feel understood.*

2. *The use of "presupposing change" questions, in which the assumption that change is forthcoming is implied. These are "when," not "if," questions.*

3. *The use of "multiple-choice questions," which have possible answers embedded in them in the direction the therapist would have the client move.*

4. *The use of "therapeutic interruption," an intervention to redirect the conversation toward the most constructive, or goal-directed, solution.*

5. *"Normalizing the problem" describes a general category of intervention that defines the problem as an everyday phenomenon rather than as a pathology.*

6. *"Summarizing with a twist" describes an intervention that summarizes a preceding conversation, but turns it in a solution-oriented direction.*

7. *"Utilization" describes a process of accepting the client's perspective rather than rejecting, disagreeing, or resisting the client's views. This involves "building a bridge from where the client is now to the eventual goal" (O'Hanlon & Wilk, 1987, p. 133).*

8. *"Providing obvious solutions" involves offering commonsense suggestions, that is, new behaviors or alternative expressions.*

9. *"Introducing doubt" describes a class of interventions that question the client's assumptions and beliefs within which the problem is embedded.*

10. *"Future focus" involves working toward specific and concrete goals, which may include anticipating obstructions to success.*

According to O'Hanlon and Wilk (1987), any such list is more illustrative than exhaustive and should not be viewed as "rigid procedures, but as guidelines for therapists" (p. 110).

Solution-Oriented Therapy: Steve de Shazer

Steve de Shazer is co-founder of and senior research associate at the Brief Family Therapy Center in Milwaukee, Wisconsin. In his orientation to brief therapy, de Shazer's work reflects the influence of his early work with MRI. In addition, de Shazer and his wife and colleague, Insoo Kim Berg, assume a social constructionist perspective and have developed a solution-focused therapy with strong allegiance to the idea that language constitutes one's experienced reality.

While there are many parallels between the solution-oriented therapies of de Shazer and O'Hanlon, there are also many differences, particularly in how they are storied. And it is in consideration of the differences we punctuate and the different ways each languages therapy that we treat them separately. However, like O'Hanlon, de Shazer's therapy is oriented to helping clients find solutions rather than to solving problems.

De Shazer (1991) articulates the philosophical and theoretical underpinnings of his model and credits his students for asking the questions, the answers to which comprise the essence of his work. He notes that students have often requested information about "causal processes" (i.e., How does it work?). De Shazer's position, which provides a clue to his philosophy and theory, which we call a metaphilosophical position, is that how it works is not something that one can know: "One can only know that it does work" (p. xvii). Attempts to know how something works involve speculation, storytelling, and fiction. Consistent with his therapy, de Shazer's response has been: "Make up your own explanation; it is as good or better than mine" (p. xviii).

In contrast both to more traditional thinking about therapy and to his early training at MRI, de Shazer (1991) makes startling assertions that deserve some speculation: " 'You do not need to know what the problem is in order to solve it,' or 'The problem or complaint is not necessarily related to the solution,' or 'The solution is not necessarily related to the problem' " (p. xiii). These assertions challenge the usual associations between problem and solution as necessarily related.

In attempting to articulate (perhaps invent) the philosophy/theory underlying his work in response to requests for clarification, de Shazer offers many of the usual definitions of family therapy, systems, and structuralist and poststructuralist thought and language. From a perspective derived from the work of Wittgenstein and Derrida, among others, he articulates what to us is a postmodernist/constructionist/second-order-cybernetics position. In an attempt to delineate the processes and the form of this therapy, it seems most useful to present some typical behaviors that de Shazer might use in the course of his "conversation" with clients. Implicit in these behaviors are his philosophical/theoretical assumptions.

The question "How do you know you are depressed?" suggests a constructionist perspective by asking for verbalization of the self-knowledge claim that the client is depressed. De Shazer might rephrase this as, "What are your criteria for assigning the metaphor depression to yourself?" The question seeks to open a door or window as "the meaning(s) of what is going on is set adrift in a sea of potential meanings" (de Shazer, 1991, p. 66). That is, the only meaning of a word that is important and possible is how the "participants in a conversation use it" (p. 69).

Client responses to a question about how they know they are depressed might include "I procrastinate"; "I lie awake at night"; "I do not spend time with my friends like I used to"; etc. Each response provides data not only about the client's definition of the word *depressed* but also for reconstructing or restorying the client's experience and developing alternative formulations of the client's goals for the therapy. Indeed, "the client's goals and solutions were more important than the problems the client depicted in the session" (de Shazer, 1991, p. 57). Thus, de Shazer draws a radical distinction between problems and solutions. Further, an important part of this opening for reconstruing or restorying is the belief that solutions to a normal difficulty are easier to find than those for a pathological problem having deep roots in infancy.

Another intervention might be, "Tell me about the times when you feel okay or good, when you do accomplish things, enjoy your friends, etc." The client's cooperation is requested in making an inversion toward solution talk. This also orients the client to see that there are exceptions to "always being depressed," which are often dismissed as trivial by the client and, unless elicited by the therapist, may remain completely unseen. The client is already doing something that works, so an important part of the therapy is to ask the client to continue to do what she is already doing some of the time. These exceptions (behaviors, perceptions, thoughts, and feelings) serve as contrasts to the complaint and have the potential to deconstruct the complaint. In de Shazer's solution-oriented therapy, the times when the client is not depressed become very important both for deconstructing the problem and for constructing a solution.

Elaborating on the concept of exception, de Shazer (1991) asserts that "random exceptions are not random" but are embedded in contexts and patterns "which if described, would allow for their being predicted and thus prescribed" (p. 88). By asking the client to "predict exceptions" the therapist is asking the client to create a "self-fulfilling prophecy." Thus, the client may be asked to predict before retiring whether the next day will be a depression-free day or perhaps to what degree it will be depression free. Exceptions can be related to client complaints, but they can also be "read as precursors to goals and solutions" (p. 90).

The concept of "creatively misunderstanding" is important in this model, both for observing team members and for the therapist. "Following the second law of thermodynamics, misunderstanding (chaos) is much more likely than understanding (order)" (de Shazer, 1991, p. 69). Thus, the more probable misunderstanding is used in creative ways to help the client "construct a reality that is more satisfactory" (p. 69). It may be the beginning of the attempt to help the client have a new way to experience himself in daily living. That is, consistent with Wittgenstein, de Shazer subscribes to the concept of *language game,* which connotes an inner state or private experience but which necessarily involves a public framework (i.e., shared meanings). Language games, including the process of therapy, have rules that constitute "whole and complete systems of human communication" and can be "understood as systems of shared meanings and shared behavior" (p. 76). In attempting to understand, one is engaging in the language game of evolving a shared meaning, which can involve an inversion from problem X to problem Y and from problem to solution. In the language game that is therapy, "binocular vision," or that which allows depth perception, evolves in the interaction between client and therapist, who necessarily have two different descriptions (binocularity), which are put together. When therapy involves a family or a therapeutic team, there is "polyocular" vision. The difference in the two descriptions must be neither too great nor too small; the descriptions must be similar and yet different.

De Shazer also describes the conversations between clients and therapists as stories or narratives. Stories have beginnings, middles, and ends, and they have plots. Therapy, like most stories, deals with human dilemmas, troubles, solutions, and attempted solutions. Stories in conversations in therapy can shift plots and be amended as exceptions and unexpected events occur. Building on a model created by Gergen and Gergen, de Shazer (1991) describes three kinds of narratives:

1. Progressive *narratives that justify the conclusion that people and situations are progressing toward their goals.*
2. Stability *narratives that justify the conclusion that life is unchanging.*
3. Digressive *narratives that justify the conclusion that life is moving away from goals. (p. 92)*

Each story type takes on the characteristics of a system in that it is "told jointly by the client and the therapist in a session that is different from the sum of its parts, which include the client's depiction of the situation and the therapist's description from a different perspective" (pp. 93–94). In therapy, progressive narratives are preferred in order to "produce transformations and discontinuities," to assess "whether desired change is occurring, to . . . allow clients to elaborate on and 'confirm' their stories, expanding and developing exception and change themes into solution themes" (pp. 92–93). Progressive narratives are contrasted with complaint-centered narratives, which are the usual form of therapeutic story construction. By asking "What is better?" rather than "How did the homework go?" (p. 130), the therapist can keep the client on a progressive narrative track.

In discussing the concept of change, de Shazer notes that it is a constant in life; that is, nothing ever repeats in exactly the same form, and "each iteration is at least subtly different" (p. 103). His goal is change that makes a difference to clients in that they will experience their lives at the end of therapy as different from what they experienced before therapy. Their experience may be one of discontinuity or second-order change. However, he cites Maruyama, Thom, and Hoffman, who suggest that "continuous causes may lead to discontinuous effects" (de Shazer, 1991, p. 96). As Maruyama (1963) notes:

Once a system is kicked in a right direction and with sufficient initial push, the deviation-amplifying mutual positive feedbacks take over the process, and the resulting development will be disproportionally large as compared with the initial kick. (p. 166)

Relative to the goals of therapy, de Shazer (1991) notes that what happens in therapy are "depictions of . . . problematic events and not the events themselves. . . . And what the client is depicting is always open to therapeutic misunderstanding . . . which involves the development of a solution-oriented language game" (p. 109). Setting goals thus becomes an important part of the process of shifting the context from complaint narratives to solution narratives. To de Shazer, "goals are depictions of what will be present" (p. 112), and workable goals are defined as:

1. *small rather than large;*
2. *salient to clients;*
3. *described in specific, concrete behavioral terms;*
4. *achievable within the practical context of clients' lives;*
5. *perceived by the clients as involving their "hard work";*

6. *described as the "start of something" and not as the "end of something";*
7. *treated as involving new behavior(s) rather than the absence or cessation of existing behavior(s). (p. 112)*

In helping clients to elicit workable goals, de Shazer may ask the "miracle question":

Suppose that one night there is a miracle and while you were sleeping the problem that brought you to therapy is solved: How would you know? What would be different?
   What will you notice different the next morning that will tell you that there has been a miracle? What will your spouse notice? (p. 113)

As de Shazer frames it, the "miracle question" is useful in the transformation necessary to sidestep structural, causal assumptions implicit in the complaint narratives that comprise the language game of most therapies. And the goal of working toward the absence of a problem is clearly different from working toward a desired future state. According to de Shazer, this process

serves to bypass the clients' historical, structural perspective and any disagreements about what the problem really is. Once the solution develops, once the clients know that the problem is solved, it no longer matters to them . . . what the problem might have been. (p. 115)

As the de Shazer model evolved, other "formula tasks" were developed which oriented clients toward a solution focus. One of these is the question about what is currently happening with the clients or in their relationships that they would like to continue. This question implies that there are some good things going on in the clients' lives and moves exploration from the dominant focus on the bad things.

Questions about "exceptions" imply that nothing is always or never and that there are times and circumstances in the past, however brief, during which the problem was not experienced. By creating a focus on exceptions, the problem may seem somewhat less oppressive and pervasive, and the door is opened to the expansion of the number and/or the duration of these exceptions.

"Scaling questions" comprise another form of questioning and "were first developed to help therapist and client talk about nonspecific topics like depression and communication" (Berg & de Shazer (1993, p. 22). A scaling question defines a problem, for example depression, in terms of a gradient and measures it in degrees. This is different than the experience of either being or not being depressed. Thus the therapist might ask, "On a scale of zero to ten, with ten representing your experience when your depression is gone and zero representing how you felt when you called for an appointment, where would you place how you feel at this time?" A client might give himself or herself a three. Further questions might be, "How did you move from a zero to a three in three days?" or "What might you do to move to a four?"

Therapy is terminated when the depictions of the client reveal that the goal(s) have been accomplished. Although not explicitly stated by de Shazer, a secondary goal may be inferred, which is that clients will have learned a new relationship between problem and solution—that there is no "real" problem, and " 'You do not need to know what the problem is in order to solve it,' or 'The problem or complaint is not necessarily related to the solution,' or 'The solution is not necessarily related to the problem' " (de Shazer, 1991, p. xiii).

Externalization and Reauthoring Lives and Relationships: Michael White and David Epston

Michael White is co-director of the Dulwich Centre in Adelaide, South Australia. David Epston is co-director of the Family Therapy Centre in Auckland, New Zealand. Their work reflects a liberation philosophy consistent with postmodernism and social constructionism as they eschew attempts to formulate universal, generic principles and in their work seek to empower clients to develop their own unique stories or narratives about themselves. Indeed, White and Epston articulate a position that asserts that the "ultimate truth stories," supported by evidence created in the tradition of logical-positivism, into which people in Western society are socialized, are a part of the problem if not *the* problem in the development and subsequent course of what is called "mental illness" and "family dysfunction." Citing Michel Foucault, they assert that what the human science disciplines do is "characterize, classify, specialize; they distribute along a scale, around a norm, hierarchize individuals in relation to one another, and if necessary disqualify and invalidate" (White & Epston, 1990, p. 74). Thus, people are objectified and their rich personal experiences and personal stories are subjugated/repressed/denied in favor of the normative classification schemes offered as the way people are supposed to experience themselves in order to be members of Western societies. In essence, people internalize and take on the identity of the "objective" category(ies) set forth and validated by human science professionals. They then describe the category or classification as within themselves or as themselves and others (e.g., "I am schizophrenic"—self/schizophrenic; "I have a behavior disorder"—self/behavior disorder; "I am paranoid," etc.). Accordingly, people begin to think about and experience themselves and the problems in their relationships and families in ways that are logically consistent with the standardized, problem-saturated story. And solutions to such internalized/normative problems are limited to options that are logically consistent with the normative stories. In Foucault's terms, to be a member of a Western society is to participate in a process of normalization and to submit to "compulsory objectification," which he describes as an insidious method of social control of which the practice of normal human science in the Western tradition is an integral part. As people internalize the normative experience offered, they may deny a large part of their "lived experience" and how this lived experience is storied.

The dilemma is that the normative story set forth by professionals in the human sciences is presented as the true story, which represents direct knowledge of the world, or the way things and people really are. And representation of a story as true precludes the search for alternative stories. However, no normative story is sufficient to include the full spectrum of lived experience:

> *Stories are full of gaps which persons must fill in order for the stories to be performed. These gaps recruit the lived experience and the imagination of persons. With every performance, persons are reauthoring their lives. The evolution of lives is akin to their process of reauthoring, the process of persons' entering stories, taking them over and making them their own. (White & Epston, 1990, p. 13)*

White and Epston's model of therapy therefore assumes a postmodern, social constructionist position and helps a client build an alternative story, which can be derived from the person's own lived experience and "which falls outside the dominant stories about the lives and relationships of persons" (p. 15). These are the stories that previously have been denied and subjugated to the normative, "true" story imposed by the society.

In response to the internalization of the problem/normative category that constitutes the client's experience of herself, therapy requires what is called externalization, which involves both the problem-saturated story and the problem. Through a process of asking such questions as "How has the problem been affecting your life?", therapists seek to separate the *problem* from the person. Externalization breaks the habitual reading and retelling of the complaint-saturated story as residing within the person. It also seeks to give people a sense of personal agency by personifying the story and giving it an existence as an entity independent of and yet influencing the lives of persons. Thus externalized, it becomes another member of the family. According to White and Epston (1990, pp. 39–40), the practice of externalization also

1. *Decreases unproductive conflict between persons, including those disputes over who is responsible for the problem;*
2. *Undermines the sense of failure that has developed for many persons in response to the continuing existence of the problem despite their attempts to resolve it;*
3. *Paves the way for persons to cooperate with each other, to unite in a struggle against the problem, and to escape its influence in their lives and relationships;*
4. *Opens up new possibilities for persons to take action to retrieve their lives and relationships from the problem and its influence;*
5. *Frees persons to take a lighter, more effective, and less stressed approach to "deadly serious" problems; and*
6. *Presents options for dialogue, rather than monologue, about the problem.*

Related questions that augment externalization include two forms of *relative influence questions*. For example, the question "How has the problem (not Johnny) influenced you and your life and your relationships?"maps the influence of the problem in the clients' lives and punctuates one direction of influence. Turning the question around punctuates another direction of influence: "What influence have you had on the life of the problem?" The goal is to help people become separated from their stories and, perhaps, to become aware of the storied, rather than the objective, nature of human experience. Relative influence questions take people "out of a fixed and static world, a world of problems that are intrinsic to persons and relationships, and into a world of experience, a world of flux" (White & Epston, 1990, p. 42).

Believing that no normative story can account for all of lived experience, the therapist might then ask questions that search for "unique outcomes," such as instances and examples in clients' lived experience that reveal "gaps" in the story, or when their performance in life denied the normative story. This could be construed as helping clients reauthor their lives. It is assumed that lived experience contains unique outcomes that are inconsistent with the complaint-saturated story. A question to solicit unique outcomes might be, "Tell me about the times when anxiety did not keep you from what you wanted to do?" It is assumed that these unique outcomes exist for all people but are often dismissed as unimportant or trivial. However, a unique outcome that reveals previously neglected "facts" must be sufficiently significant to the persons involved to contradict their problem-saturated description of life. That is, the problem-saturated map may have a long history and may have been billed as a normative "truth" by credentialed professionals. Any report of a sufficiently significant unique outcome admits new data that can serve to disconfirm or at least point to the limits of the complaint-saturated story as well as be a stimulus for people to begin to reauthor their lives. A question like "How did you manage to resist the influence of the problem on this occasion?" (White & Epston, 1990, p. 17) invites the development of a personal story. Personal agency is implied in this question, as the client's own unique experience becomes data that may serve to disconfirm the normative, complaint-saturated story he has been living.

Through the evidence of unique outcomes and the request to explain the unique outcome, groundwork is laid for alternative stories, which are available to be performed, repeated, or enlarged upon. Persons are thus invited to be "an audience for their own performance of these alternative stories," which can enhance "the survival of the stories and the sense of personal mastery" (White & Epston, 1990, p. 17). The idea of being an audience to one's own performance assumes externalization and observing oneself living within a story. Becoming an external audience to the performance of a new story that has been precipitated by the explanation of a unique outcome can augment the reauthoring by contributing new meanings, can enhance the endurance of a new story, and can affect the relationship of the audience to "the problem."

White (1991) speaks of externalization as a form of deconstruction of narrative stories which "determine real effects in terms of shaping persons' lives" (p. 28). Externalization involves "the objectification of a familiar world" so that we might become more aware of the extent to which certain "modes of life and thought" shape our existence, and that we might then be in a position to choose to live by other "modes of life and thought" (White, 1991, p. 29). Therefore, deconstruction of culture stories through externalization seeks to help people "orient themselves to aspects of their experience that contradict these cultural knowledges.... These contradictions are "unique outcomes" (White, 1991, p. 29). White also seeks to facilitate the "re-authoring" of a person's life by asking a variety of questions including *landscape of action* questions and *landscape of consciousness* questions: "Landscape of action questions encourage persons to situate unique outcomes in sequences of events that unfurl across time according to particular plots. Landscape of consciousness questions encourage persons to reflect on and to determine the meaning of those developments that occur in the landscape of action" (White, 1991, p. 30).

White believes that it is important to give *unique outcomes* both a recent history and a distant history, giving them a credibility in the face of the history of the cultural pathology story they are to displace. Thus, the identification of a unique outcome might lead to recent history questions like, "How did you get yourself ready to take this step? What preparations led up to it?" (p. 30) and to distant history questions such as, "What can you tell me about your history that would help me to understand how you managed to take this step?" (p. 31). Landscape of consciousness questions might include, "What does this history of struggle suggest about what Jane believes to be important in life, about what she stands for?" (pp. 31–32).

Other important questions are "experience of experience" questions, which "encourage persons to provide an account of what they believe or imagine to be another person's experience of them." An example might be, "How do you think my knowing this has affected my view of you as a person?" (p. 32).

As the model has been outlined above, it describes storytelling and reauthoring in the oral tradition. However, another important dimension in its application is the use of writing. In a way not possible with the oral tradition, writing allows a person to record sequences of events, or the "mapping of experience onto the temporal dimension" (White & Epston, 1990, p. 36). This promotes "the formalization, legitimation, and continuity of local popular knowledges, the independent authority of persons and the creation of a context for the emergence of new discoveries and possibilities" (p. 35).

Consistent with this position, writing letters to clients after a therapy session is an important focus of Epston's work. According to Epston (1994), a conversation may produce some useful new thoughts, but may fade when removed from the context of the conversation in which the thought was brought to life. Epston (1993) writes, "But the words in a letter don't fade and disappear the way a conversation does.... A client can hold a letter in hand, reading and rereading it days, months and years after the session" (p. 31).

In writing letters Epston is transparent about his thinking and about the therapy and does not create a distinction between what he might say outside the therapy session about the client and what he says to the client. His letters are his case notes co-created with the client as he takes "careful" notes during the session, "completely focused on the alternative story that is unfolding...and then absorbed in the retelling of it in the letter" (p. 63).

While the resolution of the problem as presented by the clients is an important goal of White and Epston's model, it is clear that they are also interested in helping their clients learn about the storied nature of human experience. Thus, clients would learn to value their own personal life experiences and stories without automatically deferring to the normative stories preferred by social science professionals. They would also learn a process whereby, if problem-saturated stories are encountered in the future in their own lives or in the lives of others, they could move up a level, externalize the problem, and reauthor their own lives or facilitate reauthoring in the lives of others.

This model is clearly intended to be countercultural and is consistent with the belief that normative science, as practiced in the human sciences, participates in creating and maintaining problems through the suggestion that knowledge of truth is being provided. As White and Epston (1990) write,

> *practices associated with the externalization of problems may be considered counter-practices to cultural practices that are objectifying of persons and of their bodies. These counter-practices open space for persons to re-author or constitute themselves, each other, and their relationships, according to alternative stories or knowledge.* (p. 75)

Therapeutic Conversations: Harlene Anderson and Harry Goolishian

The late Harry Goolishian was what we refer to as a "quiet voice" in the field of family therapy who nevertheless had a major impact on many other theorists and therapists. As early as the 1950s he developed Multiple Impact Therapy to help reduce the recidivism rate of hospitalized adolescents. His evolution as an innovative therapist continued as he collaborated with the associates of the Mental Research Institute and became a strategic therapist. His most recent shift was toward constructionism, postmodern thought, and a "language system" approach which he perceived as a move away from cybernetics. In his work with Harlene Anderson, and later Tom Andersen and Lynn Hoffman, this shift represented a move away from "the extremely interventionist and change-oriented family therapy of the past. In their model, the therapist does not lead, nor does the client lead—rather, the therapeutic conversation that is jointly created leads" (Hoffman, 1992, p. 101).

Goolishian and Anderson's (1988; Anderson, Goolishian, & Winderman, 1986) model can be called by many names, among which are "therapeutic conversation," "collaborative language systems" approach or "narrative therapy." It is unique among other models that (to us) are consistent (more or less) with second-order cybernetics, postmodernism, and social constructionism in its refusal to be formulaic in its approach. Thus, there can be no specific set of techniques. Indeed, it would probably be more appropriate to call it an attitude rather than a model.

According to this view, therapy is understood as a process of caring, empathic conversations within which to evolve new meanings with clients. The therapy of Anderson and Goolishian seeks to be "less hierarchical, more egalitarian, mutual, respectful and human, a therapy which allows a therapist to be aware of the depth, existence, and experiences of the individual" (Anderson, 1992, p. 21). Consistent with postmodernism, they do not claim expertise and they value multiple perspectives, that is, "the therapist's knowledge, experience and values are no truer than the client's—nor more final" (Hoffman-Hennessay & Davis, 1993, p. 343). Also consistent with postmodernism, they believe that if one's sense of self and others is socially constructed or constructed in conversations, it can be reconstructed in other conversations.

A collaborative conversation is not possible when the therapist assumes the role of expert and thus Goolishian and Anderson advocate a position of "not knowing" (Anderson, 1993) or what Hoffman (1993, p. 127) calls "a kind of deliberate ignorance." Further, "the therapist's pre-experiences and pre-knowledges do not lead. In this process both the therapist's and the client's expertise are engaged to dissolve the problems" (Anderson, 1993, p. 325).

An additional glimpse of the process or attitude can be envisioned through the following statement by Harry Goolishian:

> *In the therapy room I am a learner. I adopt a "puzzling" position. This flips the position of the client and the therapist. The client is now the knower, and the therapist is the not-knower. . . . It is not just the therapist trying to understand the client, collecting information and data and placing it on some kind of cognitive map in a unilateral way. Rather, it is a mutual search in which client and therapist puzzle together in search for understanding, to develop a story that has not been told before. (Winderman, 1989, p. 12)*

Goolishian (1991) also notes,

> *It is in the telling and retelling that the narrative changes. We think of the therapist as a participant narrative artist engaged in the co-construction of new meaning, new meaning and story that is coherent with the fragments of memory of the old stories. It is as if the therapist is a conversational participant, as opposed to being a narrative editor. (p. 1)*

In effect Anderson and Goolishian eliminate the concept of a family system and particularly the idea that the system creates the problem. They suggest instead that the problem (as an objectified pathology) creates the system. Thus, the system consists of a conversation or meaning system organized around the problem. As described by Hoffman (1990b), it is "the system that is formed by a conversation about a problem" (p. 12). What is defined, therefore, is a conversation or discourse that minimizes the consciousness of the therapist in pushing for, strategizing about, or designing the form of a therapeutic outcome, which is characteristic of the modernist/structuralist therapeutic posture. Anderson and Goolishian have not articulated a coherent model for the concept of therapy they envision. However, if they are to remain consistent with their beliefs, they cannot do so.

Other Second-Order Cybernetics Models

Bradford Keeney's (1990) improvisational therapy challenges the concept of therapist as a professional with a privileged kind of knowledge in favor of the concept of therapy being a performing art "where the score or script comes into play after the performance rather than before" (Tyler & Tyler, p. xi). Therapy thus becomes a conversation without a predetermined narrative. Such a conversation is not "informed" by the received-view stories that comprise the subject matter learned by most mental health professionals.

Because therapy is considered a performing art, each meeting of participants (rather than of therapist and clients) is viewed as a new scene for a conversation that is not formally guided toward some theoretically predetermined end. Keeney's model encourages the therapist as participant to "share the creative inventions of one's own imagination" (p. 5). A creative resourceful therapist will not be regarded as a "master." More specifically, Keeney suggests that therapists:

1. *Cultivate a healthy irreverence for all teachers and teachings (including this one).*
2. *Do what you want with any therapeutic model, school or orientation—utilize it, ignore it, kick it, invert it, reverse it, distort it, misunderstand it, play with it.*
3. *Be cautious when therapy doesn't feel like play, never forgetting that play is serious work.*
4. *Experience psychotherapy as theatre: When it's boring, change anything—the script, the actors, the director, the audience.*
5. *Theory is critical for evolving clinical work; with every new understanding, you become a different person—the person you previously were plus the new understanding. The new you cannot necessarily perform what worked for the previous you. This means you must learn to do something different. Doing something different leads to a new experience which in turn can be subjected to understanding. (p. 5–6).*

Keeney and Ray (1993) have developed a Resource-Focused Therapy (RFT) that fits Keeney's (1990) improvisational model. RFT uses the performance of conversation (words, behaviors, and experiences) to shift from a problematic context to a resourceful context. Therapist and clients are described as "participants," thus avoiding the tradition of the therapist as expert, narrator, or teacher and the client as student. Each session is a new context and has a beginning, middle, and end. RFT punctuates a difference between a "problem/solution context" and a resourceful context.

RFT looks at how each participant can influence the other in a resourceful way to exchange positive contributions and avoid getting stuck in a "problematic context." The therapist endeavors not to think about the constructs from a theory, which would limit creativity. Psychological labels also are avoided as they restrict movement to a resourceful context.

Douglas Flemons (1991) draws from the work of Bateson and from Taoism to develop a relational orientation to therapy. He suggests that all symptomatic relationships are disjunctive—whether between a person and himself or herself, among people, or, more broadly, between humans and the environment and the connective nature of healing relationships. Flemons would have the therapist be self-conscious about the nature of clients' questions which, if answered, would not solve the problem. When clients expect the therapist to "'change this symptom or that family member, while leaving everything and/or everyone else as is,' they are expecting a dichotomous solution to a schizmatic dilemma" (p. 118). The problem may be one of not seeing the connection in the disjunction that calls forth the problem. In other words, "To be healing, the therapist must turn people back to their questions" which "requires in the not-acting spirit of wu wei, that the question be not-answered" (p. 119). He notes,

1. *In not-answering a wrong question right away, the therapist takes care not to act with haste or unmediated purpose.*
2. *In not-answering a wrong question in a right way, the therapist responds at a more encompassing level than the query and thus avoids being organized by its dichotomous premises. (p. 122)*

Other Evolving Models

In this section we summarize Carol Anderson's Psychoeducational Model and Richard Schwartz's Internal Family Systems Model. We believe these models are more consistent with first-order cybernetics and the modernist tradition than the models presented above.

Carol Anderson

As with many new approaches, the psychoeducational model of Carol Anderson and associates (Anderson, 1988) was based on perceptions regarding inadequacies of and frustrations with existing approaches. Initial work using the psychoeducational model was focused on schizophrenics, their parents, and families. The issue of concern that gave rise to the development of the psychoeducational model was the high frequency of relapse for schizophrenics who were released to the custody of their families. Anderson and her associates observed that traditional family therapy approaches with families of schizophrenics view the etiology and maintenance of schizophrenia as rooted in family dynamics, and relapse is countered by more intensive efforts to change family dynamics. Since psychiatric treatment with schizophrenics focuses on chemotherapy, psychiatrists tend to see relapse as being caused by the patient's not complying with the medical regimen. Anderson's vision of current practices is that

> *we have blamed each other, the patients themselves, their parents, and grandparents, public authorities, and society for the cause and for the too often terrible course of these disorders. When home and money become exhausted, we frequently tear schizophrenic patients from their families, consigning them to the existential terror of human warehouses, single room occupancy hotels, and more recently to the streets and alleys of American cities. (Anderson, Reiss, & Hogarty, 1986, p. vii)*

As one might expect, such a perspective gives rise to a radical model (at least relative to the assumptions held in traditional family therapy and psychiatry) that certainly can do no worse and may do better. Indeed, a study reported by Anderson et al. (1986) suggests that the psychoeducational model is successful, using the criterion of lowering relapse rates:

> *Among treatment takers (n=90), 19% of those receiving family therapy alone experienced a psychotic relapse in the year following hospital discharge. Of those receiving the individual behavior therapy, 20% relapsed, but no patient in the treatment cell that received both family therapy and social skills training experienced a relapse. These relapse rates constitute significant effects for both treatments when contrasted to a 41% relapse rate for those receiving only chemotherapy and support. (p. 42)*

Similar results are reported by Steinglass and Horan (1988), Falloon et al. (1985), and Leff, Kuipers, Berkowitz, Eberlein-Vries, and Sturgeon (1982), all of whom utilize a psychoeducational model.

The psychoeducational model seeks to reduce the degree and frequency in families of "expressed emotion," including hostility, criticism, and emotional overinvolvement (Brown, Birley, & Wing, 1972; Brown, Monck, Carstairs, & Wing, 1962). All of these emotions seem to characterize the homes of schizophrenics with high relapse rates (Vaughn, Snyder, Jones, Freeman, & Falloon, 1984). Thus, the traditional family therapy model is turned around by focusing on the impact of the schizophrenic on the family rather than on the family's being responsible for schizophrenia and its maintenance. Instead of blaming and trying to cure, the goal is to supplement and renew families' resources, which may have been depleted by previous well-intentioned professional efforts to help, which, paradoxically, may have made things worse.

Psychoeducators accept the fact of schizophrenia and collaborate with families who are trying to do the best they can with the information they have. They seek to join, empathize with, support, and empower the families. Contrary to traditional therapy, they seek to build on the strengths of families rather than focusing on their deficits. In accepting the fact of schizophrenia, they

1. *provide the families whatever information is available about schizophrenia and how it is likely to progress;*
2. *seek to lower family members' expectations about what to expect of the schizophrenic;*
3. *present information about studies around "expressed emotion" and what this information means in terms of how the family organizes itself and deals with its internal processes;*
4. *seek to promote understanding without blame of the patient, themselves, or other professionals;*
5. *encourage families to provide an environment of low stimulation with latitude for the schizophrenic in terms of withdrawal and other behavior that may seem strange to families;*
6. *help family members see the need to set limits, including limiting behavior that interferes with the lives of other members of the household as well as assigning chores the schizophrenic is capable of performing;*
7. *reduce family members' pressure on the schizophrenic to perform normally and thus move away from the expectation of cure. (Anderson et al., 1986)*

Therapy begins with a workshop, after which a professional meets with the family on a regular basis for at least one year. While these sessions may focus on the patient and specific tasks for the patient, the atmosphere of family support described above continues. Issues brought by family members to these sessions may include the structure of the family or other personal concerns. As described, the sessions resemble structural family therapy and similar goals are sought for the family (i.e., facilitating generational boundaries, relieving children of parental roles, creating links to systems outside the family, etc.). While other issues may be dealt with that are not related to the patient, the professional does so only when requested by family members or as these relate to issues around the patient.

How does it work? While Anderson and her colleagues provide their explanation of the mechanism, as de Shazer (1991) notes, attempts to know how something works involve speculation, storytelling, and fiction. We therefore cannot help but inject our speculations about how the process evolves. Perhaps it works because it represents such a different experience for families than their previous experience with professionals. This may be a part of the "difference that makes a difference." Related to this, we are reminded of Watzlawick, Weakland, and Fisch's (1974) assertion that it is the attempted solution that is the problem. Upon noticing different behavior in their children, later diagnosed as schizophrenic, families may have initiated solutions that escalated and maintained the problem. Systems theory suggests that the way in which initial crises/differences are handled when they first appear is significant relative to what gets built into the system. Thus, the attempted solutions provided by traditional family therapy and psychiatry may also be a part of the problem.

Accepting and labeling schizophrenia as a fact that must be lived with reframes the phenomenon and may change family members' relationship with it. That is, by reifying the metaphor schizophrenia, one can destabilize it and restory it. Anderson and her colleagues tell families a story different from what they have heard previously, and they do so in a nonblaming, supportive atmosphere. While we concur with de Shazer that attempts to understand how something works are exercises in speculation and fiction, the process allows the imagination free reign and the ability to evolve more differences that make a difference.

Internal Family Systems Model

The Internal Family Systems Model (IFS) of Richard Schwartz (Nichols & Schwartz, 1991; Schwartz, 1987, 1989, 1995) seems to have aspects of the modernist/structuralist as well as the romanticist traditions. We can also see a parallel with a post-modernist/narrative approach in that the therapist elicits the stories people tell themselves about their situations. This model combines systemic family therapy with attention to the internal (psychodynamic) processes of family members. The mind is described as consisting of subminds that interact with each other in much the same manner as family members interact with each other. The internal process among subminds is similar to family process according to first-order cybernetics: "They organize into alliances, vie for control, and, at times, go to war against each other" (Nichols & Schwartz, 1991, p. 502).

Parallels between the internal processes of family members and interactions between family members are also noted. Thus, in addition to working on the dynamics between family members, the therapist also is concerned with working on and attempting to resolve the conflicts among the subminds of individual members of the family. To this end, the therapist helps a client have a dialogue between her different subminds, a procedure akin to Gestalt therapy's empty chair technique. More specifically,

> The therapist asks about the problem, and then asks each family member what they say to themselves about it. In reiterating any family member's response to this question, the therapist might ask "So a part of you says _____ about the problem, is that right?" And then, "How do you think the problem would be affected if this part of you didn't take over?;" "What's the part afraid would happen if you let you lead in this area?;" "Ask the part to let your Self lead the discussion about the problem this time and see how it goes" (Nichols & Schwartz, 1995, p. 473).

Systemic Consistency

As we have noted, the models presented in the first part of this chapter are consistent with the systems perspective at the level of second-order cybernetics, in that each sees the therapist as a participant-observer and espouses a view of therapy as a reciprocal process of creating alternative realities. However, second-order cybernetics models have been criticized by Golann (1988) as representing an insidious form of manipulation and the acquisition of power in therapy by denying the power of the conditions described above: "Power obscured eventually emerges—a therapeutic wolf clad as second-order sheep" (p. 56). According to Golann, each model has its assumptions about the processes of change and how change occurs. He also calls attention to "unconscious persuasion," which "may be said to be ethically more objectionable than excessive and explicit strategic intervention because it is potentially dishonest and because it creates an even greater power hierarchy in favor of the therapist than most other forms of practice" (p. 63). Thus, he challenges the possibility of observing systems without an observed systems stance and the possibility of co-evolving in a context that defines the therapist as expert. What he might have said and did not say explicitly is that these models, as they are presented, are equally as seductive as traditional models for therapists in training who, in their idealism, search for and believe in the possibility of respectful, non-manipulative, non-normative modes of therapeutic practice.

Thus, Golann observes the theory and practice of second-order therapies through a different lens. His observations are similar to the discussions in the 1950s about Carl Rogers's "non-directive" counseling, which to true believers in the model was noble, respectful, and truly nonobtrusive. To others, however, it also was seen as insidious manipulation, or "a therapeutic wolf clad as second-order sheep."

Indeed, there is an aspect of the concepts of co-evolving systems and observing systems, as opposed to observed systems, that is inconsistent with second-order cybernetics models. That is, one could assert that the context of therapy necessarily transforms observing systems to observed systems in spite of the best intentions of the therapist. One could therefore wonder whether or not it makes a difference if the client system is helped, but this is a pragmatic and not an aesthetic consideration. Obviously, there are those for whom it does matter and for whom it is more ethical that the therapist assume the expert role and move the client system toward so-called normative functioning rather than manipulating by the unconscious persuasion of second-order therapies.

Part of the problem may lie in the process of transforming the ontology/philosophy that is second-order cybernetics into a formal, pragmatic model for therapy. This process necessarily involves conversations about the therapeutic process, without the involvement of the client system. In other words, the creation of a model may be inconsistent with second-order cybernetics since the process necessarily transforms observing systems to observed. While this issue probably will continue, it is important to note that to punctuate a difference at one level of abstraction is to create a connection at a higher-order level of abstraction. If Golann's observations are taken as valid, perhaps the saving grace for therapists who operate at the level of second-order cybernetics lies in their stance of not imposing some normative way that client systems should be. However, it is also possible that some normative way may sneak into the client system through the process of unconscious persuasion that Golann describes.

On the other hand, is it possible to set aside the modernist, first-order cybernetics perspective of therapist as expert with privileged knowledge whose mission is "therapeutic" colonization into the world view of the therapist, which is believed to be superior to that of the "indigenous" native population (Amundson, Stewart & Valentine, 1993)? Is it possible to move beyond the concept of technique, intervention, manipulation evolving out of private conversations (Andersen, 1992) about clients? Is it possible that Rogers and "therapeutic conversationalists" are sincerely respectful of the persons (not clients or patients) who come to them for help? Can we respect uniqueness and multiversa (without abandoning concerns about abuse, poverty, injustice, and inequity)? If we can move beyond the modernist, first-order conceptions of people, human experience, and therapy to the possibilities offered by second-order cybernetics and second-order therapy, we open the doors to the concept of creating an energy field of influence through caring. We might just find that the problems we believe can only be solved by discourses about the problem may dissolve through the medium of the caring, respectful therapeutic conversations described by the second-order therapies.

Suggested Readings

Andersen, T. (1987). The reflecting team: Dialogue and meta-dialogue in clinical work. *Family Process, 26*, 415–428.

Anderson, C. M. (1988). Depression and families. In F. Walsh & C. Anderson (Eds.), *Chronic disorders and the family* (pp. 33–47). New York: Haworth Press.

Anderson, C. M., Reiss, D., & Hogarty, B. (1986). *Schizophrenia and the family.* New York: Guilford Press.

Anderson, H. (1993). On a roller coaster: A collaborative language systems approach to therapy. In S. Friedman (Ed.), *The New Language of Change* (pp. 323–344). New York: Guilford Press.

Anderson, H., Goolishian, H., & Winderman, L. (1986). Problem determined systems: Toward transformation in family therapy. *Journal of Strategic and Systemic Therapies, 5*, 14–19.

Anderson, H., & Goolishian, H. A. (1988). Human systems as linguistic systems: Preliminary and evolving ideas about the implications for clinical therapy. *Family Process, 27*, 371—393.

Berg, I. K., & de Shazer, S. (1993). *Working with the problem drinker: A solution-focused approach.* New York: W. W. Norton.

Boscolo, L., Cecchin, G., Hoffman, L., & Penn, P. (1987). *Milan systemic family therapy.* New York: Basic Books.

de Shazer, S. (1984). The death of resistance. *Family Process, 23*, 11–21.

de Shazer, S. (1985). *Keys to solution in brief family therapy.* New York: W. W. Norton.

de Shazer, S. (1986). An indirect approach to brief therapy. In S. de Shazer & R. Kral (Eds.), *Indirect approaches in therapyc.* Rockville, MD: Aspen.

de Shazer, S. (1987). Minimal elegance. *The Family Therapy Networker,* September/October, *11*(5), 59.

de Shazer, S. (1988). *Clues: Investigating solutions in brief therapy.* New York: W. W. Norton.

de Shazer, S. (1994). *Words were originally magic.* New York: W. W. Norton.

Foucault, M. (1980). *Power/knowledge: An archaelogy of medical perception.* London: Tavistock.

Friedman, S. (Ed.). (1993). *The new language of change.* New York: Guilford Press.

Gilligan, S., & Price, R. (Eds.). *Therapeutic conversations.* New York: W. W. Norton.

Golann, S. (1988). On second-order family therapy. *Family Process, 27*, 51–65.

Goolishian, H. (1991). The use of language in two different therapy approaches. In *AAMFT Annual Conference Newsletter,* p. 1.

Hoffman, L. (1985). Beyond power and control: Toward a second-order family therapy. *Family Systems Medicine, 3*, 381–396.

Hoffman, L. (1990). A constructivist position for family therapy. In B. Keeney, B. Nolan, & W. Madsen (Eds.), *The systemic therapist, Vol. I* (pp. 3–31). St. Paul, MN: Systemic Therapy Press.

Hoffman, L. (1993). *Exchanging voices.* London: Karnac.

Keeney, B. (1990). *Improvisational therapy.* St. Paul, MN: Systemic Therapy Press.

Keeney, B., & Ross, J. (1985). *Mind in therapy: Constructing systemic family therapies.* New York: Basic Books.

Keeney, B., & Silverstein, O. (1986). *The therapeutic voice of Olga Silverstein.* New York: Guilford Press.

Madanes, C. (1980). Protection, paradox and pretending. *Family Process, 19,* 457–470.

Madanes, C. (1981). *Strategic family therapy.* San Francisco: Jossey-Bass.

Madanes, C. (1984). *Behind the one-way mirror.* San Francisco: Jossey-Bass.

McNamee, S., & Gergen, K. (Eds.). (1992). *Therapy as social construction.* Newbury Park, CA: Sage.

Nichols, M., & Schwartz, R. (1991). *Family therapy: Concepts and methods.* Boston: Allyn and Bacon.

O'Hanlon, W. H. (1990). Debriefing myself: When a brief therapist does long-term work. *The Family Therapy Networker, 14,* 48–49, 68–69.

O'Hanlon, W., & Martin, M. (1992). *Solution-oriented hypnosis: An Ericksonian approach.* New York: W. W. Norton.

O'Hanlon, W. H., & Weiner-Davis, M. (1989). *In search of solutions: A new direction in psychotherapy.* New York: W. W. Norton.

Rosenblatt, P. (1993). *Metaphors of family systems.* New York: Guilford Press.

Schwartz, R. (1987). Our multiple selves. *The Family Therapy Networker, 11,* 25–31.

Schwartz, R. (1988). Know thy selves. *The Family Therapy Networker, 12,* 21–29.

White, C., & Chamberlain, S. (Eds.) (1991). *Postmodernism, deconstructionism and therapy.* Adelaide, Australia: Dulwich Centre.

White, M. (1989). *Selected papers.* Adelaide, Australia: Dulwich Center Publications.

White, M., & Epston, D. (1990). *Narrative means to therapeutic ends.* New York: W. W. Norton.

Chapter **14**

The Many Modalities of Family Therapy

In this chapter we provide an overview of some of the many other forms family therapy may take. In most of the approaches we will present, it is the client system that drives the therapy rather than the theoretical model. We will consider individual family therapy, couple therapy, group family therapy, couples group therapy, multiple family therapy, and family networking. Consistent with the format of the other chapters in Part Two, we have chosen to describe models seminal in the development either of a particular approach or of the field in general. Thus, some of the models are now either outdated or no longer widely used. However, the influence of each was felt and may still be seen in the use of specific techniques, if not in applications of the approach as a whole.

In some of our discussions we will consider a particular theorist, but in other instances this will not be appropriate. We will also devote one section to a discussion of symptom-focused treatments, for example, treatments for chemical dependency, anorexia, bulimia, and so forth. We will conclude with some general thoughts on the issue of systemic consistency in family therapy and its many modalities.

Individual Family Therapy

A frequent, and important, question asked by students who are wrestling with the concepts of systems theory and cybernetics for the first time is, What about the individual? We suspect that many of you share this concern and have wondered whether the individual gets lost in the focus on relationship, context, and pattern. A related question may be whether doing family therapy precludes doing therapy with an individual. We would guess that for both questions the crucial issue is the perceived potential of this perspective for devaluation of the individual and the concomitant denial of the uniqueness of each individual.

As you may recall from Chapter 1, it is our belief that the term *family therapy* is a misnomer. Rather, we feel a more appropriate label would be *relationship therapy* or *contextual therapy*. It is not who is in the room that determines whether the therapy is individual or family. Rather, it is the theory underlying the therapist's approach, the choice to bake a pie with a family therapy crust rather than an individual psychology crust—the selection of a model, whether it is psychodynamic, experiential, structural, communications, strategic, behavioral, or some combination of these, built on a systems theory/cybernetics perspective.

Thus, doing family therapy with an individual is certainly a viable option. However, in this case the family therapy pie is distinguished from the individual psychology pie by virtue of the therapist's consideration of the individual in context; that is, each individual is understood to be part of a larger system. Whatever symptom the individual may be evidencing, it is viewed as having emerged relative to, and as being maintained in, some context within which that symptom makes sense. The family therapist will thus consider the ecology of individuals, or the relationships and systems in which individuals have membership as well as the characteristic patterns of each.

At the same time, this focus raises the issue of the devaluation of the individual: What happens to the individual if all you care about is the relationship? The answer is, simply, balance. A concern for individuals and the pain they may be experiencing is balanced by an equal concern for the other individuals in the client's world and for the relationships they have evolved together. Obviously, one cannot have relationships without the individuals who comprise them. Indeed, it is their individual perceptual realities in interaction that define the nature of any given relationship. Similarly, as Maturana (Simon, 1985) has indicated, it is not legitimate to talk about working with a family. Rather, we must understand a family as a multiverse of unique perceptions and individual realities of that organizational entity each identifies, somewhat differently, as family. Ultimately, it is individuals with whom the family therapist works, no matter now many people are in the room. But he works differently with them than does the individual, Newtonian, medical-model psychotherapist.

For example, if Harry comes in complaining about a hand-washing compulsion, the family therapist would be concerned about such considerations as the following: How does Harry define the problem? What is the function of this behavior in Harry's marriage or on the job? How do important others respond to Harry around this issue? What would change if Harry stopped washing his hands compulsively? Accordingly, there is a very real concern for Harry the individual and for his personal reality. However, the focus is on Harry in context, and there is a simultaneous respect for Harry's relationships and for the ramifications of change within his context.

Thus, while the therapist might not choose to invite Harry's wife into therapy since Harry has not defined the problem as a marital issue, she will be sensitive to relationship dynamics. Therefore, Harry might be advised to share what went on in therapy with his wife. On the other hand, if this behavior is seen as either part of the problem or potentially destructive, Harry might be given the opposite advice, to avoid discussing the issue with anyone but the therapist until resolution has been achieved. Similarly, the therapist takes into consideration the possible impact on and response of the larger system vis-à-vis any intervention she may devise.

Despite the logic of our answer, we suspect you may continue to experience discomfort as a function of your concern for the relative importance of the individual. This is certainly to be expected and is equally understandable. In the first place, there is no question that the individual shares the limelight in family therapy. Secondly, you probably have been socialized in a context that gives primacy to the individual, hence the logic of your concern. However, we would merely remind you that each event or entity can be defined only relative to its opposite, or identity member; that is, knowledge of our individuality requires knowledge of our connectedness. We would also refer you back to our discussion of the individual from a postmodernist, social constructionist perspective in Chapter 4 and to our discussion of the internal family systems model in Chapter 13.

Couple Therapy

An important question often asked by family therapists concerns the appropriateness of designating couple therapy, or marriage therapy, as a separate phenomenon. If our focus is on systems, and thus by definition also on subsystems, why distinguish between marriage therapy and family therapy? In this case, the answer seems to relate more to the content of the issues than to the process of therapy.

For those therapists who choose to make such a distinction and to work with the couple separately, the important considerations are (1) dealing with problems specific to the marital relationship; (2) the necessity for clearly demarcating the boundary around the marital subsystem; and (3) respect for the couple's privacy. For those therapists who feel otherwise and who prefer to work with the whole family regardless of the nature of the problem, the important considerations are (1) that every issue affects all family members in some way; (2) that everyone knows, at some level, about the problems being experienced by the couple; and (3) that secrecy and mystification about the definition and location of problems is potentially destructive. However, whether one works with the couple separately or in the context of the entire family, the therapy is based on the same basic theoretical model and looks different only as a function of the people in the room and the pragmatic approach preferred by a given therapist.

For example, in a case study entitled "The Divorce Labyrinth" (Keith & Whitaker, 1977), Carl Whitaker and his cotherapist, David Keith, describe therapy revolving around "the threat of divorce in a marriage" (p. 123). Treatment included, at various times and in various combinations, the husband, the wife, the twin sons (ages five and a half at the start of therapy), the husband's girlfriend, the wife's boyfriend, and the wife's mother. Even though some therapists undoubtedly would have dealt only with the couple given this particular presenting problem, Keith and Whitaker defined the marital issue as a case of "schizophrenia in the family" (p. 127). Therapy proceeded in a manner consistent with the symbolic experiential approach described in Chapter 8.

By contrast, Murray Bowen preferred to work only with the marital dyad. No matter what the issue, problems and their solution must be dealt with at the level of the couple. Therapy thus involves the formation of a triangle that includes the therapist and the "two primary members of the family" (Nichols, 1984, p. 362), thereby allowing detriangulation and differentiation to occur within the family of the clients.

Between these two extremes, couple therapy manifests itself in dozens of ways, often combining elements of several approaches. Though somewhat dated, one of the classic books on this topic is Lederer and Jackson's *Mirages of Marriage* (1968), which provides an important example of the communications approach to understanding couples. As noted in Chapter 12, *Marital Therapy* (Jacobson & Margolin, 1979) outlines a behavioral approach based on the principles of social learning theory. The *Casebook of Marital Therapy,* edited by Gurman (1985), offers a smorgasbord of approaches currently in use.

Group Family Therapy

Group family therapy is characterized by the application of the principles of group therapy to treatment of the family and thus, in this instance, it is the underlying theory that distinguishes the therapy. The best-known proponent of this approach is John Elderkin Bell, whom we noted in our historical review is one of the less-often-acknowledged pioneers in the field of family therapy. Bell conceptualizes families as small groups, faulting psychodynamic theory for ignoring relationships and focusing exclusively on intrapsychic processes. It is his belief that action processes in families and the roles assumed by family members provide the keys to understanding and treating problems.

According to Bell, a healthy family is one that has devised complementary aims, which are being met through mutual interaction to the satisfaction of the members; in other words, the structure and functions of the family as a group are being supported. Such a family has flexibility and a variety of methods for handling conflicts, factions, and incompatible demands. The healthy family also has a method for ongoing assessment of the accommodation process and is able to adapt to change as necessary (Bell, 1975).

By contrast, dysfunctional families are unable to adapt when necessary, and roles become inflexible when rigid patterns emerge. A symptom-bearer expresses this dysfunction and ultimately becomes stuck in his role as the family operates such that the pathology is maintained: "It follows that in every instance where we have a disturbed child we have a family motivated to preserve that disturbance, seeking to perpetuate the pathology of the individual" (Bell, 1975, p. 185). Therapy therefore aims at (1) freeing up action processes; (2) allowing greater individual expression; (3) heightening awareness of the roles played by various family members; and (4) helping family members understand their interrelatedness. "The primary intent of the therapist is to change the functioning and structure of the family as a group" (Hansen & L'Abate, 1982, p. 206). The desired outcome of therapy is for family members to achieve both greater cohesiveness and individual flexibility, although specific goals are decided upon by each particular client family.

The process of therapy is based on results derived from studies of small groups and is thus understood as proceeding through a series of seven stages. These stages include initiation, testing, struggling for power, settling on a common task, struggling toward completion of the common task, achieving completion, and terminating (Bell, 1975). The nature of the group is democratic as opposed to hierarchical and the orientation is to the here-and-now rather than the past.

After an initial meeting with the parents alone, therapy includes all family members over nine years of age, plus the therapist. The focus is on the interaction between all members of this new group. The therapist acts in a predetermined role of group leader and facilitator whose behaviors consist of the following:

1. *Stating and legitimizing a leader role.*
2. *Concentrating attention on what is going on between family members.*
3. *Directing private analyses of what is happening with the family to the meaning of what are perceived of as characteristics of interactions of the total group.*
4. *Bridging gaps between family members.*
5. *Modeling the act of listening.*
6. *Distributing opportunities for family members to speak.*
7. *Confining the content in most stages to intra-family matters.*
8. *Firming up the boundaries around the family in a related way.*
9. *Adapting the pace of development of the group to that which emerges with each particular family.*
10. *Affirming the importance of each individual and of the family as a whole.*
11. *Assisting the family in exploring what will now work out of what they now know how to do.*
12. *Encouraging trials of new interactions.*
13. *Facilitating termination of the therapy (Bell, 1976, pp. 141–142).*

Through the establishment of new relationship patterns, members test out and learn new behaviors in therapy that may allow greater flexibility and a change of roles to be incorporated into the family. Unlike small groups made up of strangers, changes initiated in therapy may have immediate transfer inasmuch as family members are together both in and out of therapy.

Family group therapy is more a pragmatic approach than a theoretical model. It borrows heavily from small group theory and the techniques of group therapy, while at the same time recognizing the differences between stranger groups and family groups (Bell, 1972). Although family group therapy is certainly not successful in all cases, Bell believes family satisfaction is its usual outcome (Hansen &

L'Abate, 1982). However, this approach is not widely espoused. On the one hand, according to Nichols (1984), "Family group therapy has met the fate of many innovations; it has been a victim of its own success, and absorbed by everyone in the field" (p. 258). On the other hand, there are many aspects of group dynamics that do not fit family therapy (D. Becvar, 1982), hence its lack of popularity.

Couples Group Therapy

Couples group therapy combines the principles of systems theory and group dynamics into a format for working with couples. Ian Alger and Peggy Papp are perhaps best known for their use of this modality. However, Alger's orientation is more psychodynamic and Papp has been classified as a strategic family therapist. Accordingly, they describe their uses of couples group therapy in distinctly different ways.

For Alger (1976), careful evaluation of the appropriateness of a couple for group treatment must include such factors as the nature of the presenting problem, other life circumstances, the quality of the relationship, therapeutic expectations, and potential for involvement in the process. Three to four couples comprise the optimal size group, which may either be time limited or open ended. Ideally, the group will be led by a cotherapy team made up of one male and one female.

After two or three sessions alone, Alger may invite the couple to become part of a group. In the early stages of the couples group therapy, a structure is imposed so that each couple gets an equal amount of time in which to speak. As the group develops, however, it moves into a more dynamic and less structured format. The group evolves through stages of early anxiety to greater openness, trust, and active participation, with improved communication and system functioning the ultimate goals of the therapy process (Alger, 1976).

Alger has described the role of the therapist in couples group therapy as follows:

> *I see the therapist in the group as both a person with very human reactions to the others in the group, and also as a person whose specific role tasks are to lead the group and use his expertise to enhance the group experience so it will be as much as possible a human learning experience productive of change. (1976, p. 379)*

In addition to the usual techniques of family and group therapy, Alger also makes use of several other strategies. A member of a couple's family may temporarily join the group. The couples may be separated into subgroups in order to facilitate change. Role playing may be utilized to heighten awareness of relationship dynamics and improve communication. Choreography, video playback, and changes in meeting time and place may also be implemented as appropriate. Alger recommends couples group therapy because it is efficient, less costly for clients, provides a potentially important support system for the couples involved, enhances awareness of shared problems, and increases the therapeutic resources available.

For Peggy Papp, couples group therapy is a variation of brief therapy "that is designed to produce accelerated change through planned strategy" (1976, p. 350). Papp bases this approach on her beliefs that behavior changes as a function of action rather than insight; that change can be immediate and that the effects of such change can be long lasting; and that the rate of change is influenced by the therapist's expectations in this regard. Anticipating immediate change increases the likelihood of its occurrence.

Consistent with its strategic orientation, couples group therapy as implemented by Papp is extremely structured, focused, and directive. It is problem centered and uses choreography, prescribed tasks, and a group setting specifically to alter the form of problems so that new behavioral alternatives become possible: "The choreography redefines the problems symbolically through the use of metaphors in action; the tasks carry the redefinition pragmatically into daily living; and the group setting sustains and amplifies the redefining process" (Papp, 1976, p. 351).

Membership in a couples group is based on presentation of a problem that is clearly marital rather than child related. The group meets for twelve sessions and is comprised of four couples plus the therapist. The first session is devoted to the choreography of each relationship. Husbands and wives then meet in separate groups during subsequent sessions in which tasks are assigned and their performance is evaluated. The couples may meet together from time to time as deemed appropriate by the therapist, and the final session aims at allowing couples to summarize their experiences and speculate on future directions.

Many of Papp's assigned tasks are paradoxical in nature and are directed at revealing the absurdity in human behavior. Further, a series of interdependent tasks are usually required as the therapy process unfolds. Each task is designed to fit a specific situation. Finally, according to Papp (1976), success is a function both of the motivation of the clients and the imagination of the therapist relative to "the initial rapid improvements in each relationship" (p. 362), which universally occur in this form of couples group therapy.

We would suggest that couples group therapy might be conducted in a variety of ways. No matter what the format, both group dynamics and systemic interaction processes would be operative. However, each manifestation would be likely to vary in relation to the basic orientation of the therapist and his approach of choice.

Multiple Family Therapy

Multiple family therapy is also characterized by the interaction of systems dynamics and group processes, although in this case the group is comprised of whole families. Developed by H. Peter Laqueur in 1950, multiple family therapy (MFT) emerged in response to a situation where the number of families required that they be seen in groups rather than individually. Happily, as it turns out,

> it seems that certain mechanisms active in MFT, such as learning through analogy, indirect interpretation, and identification, make it easier for family members to improve communication and to try out new behavior in an atmosphere that is

more permissive than when only one family is the center of attention at all times. (Laqueur, 1976, p. 405)

For Laqueur, ideal families are characterized by free and open communication expressed by all members at all levels of the system. Dysfunctional families, on the other hand, are identified by seven general kinds of structures that define their particular brand of faulty communication. In the most disturbed families, each individual is a social isolate and communication occurs on only the most superficial topics. Two other kinds of disturbed families are those with a too-rigid boundary between the parental subsystem and the sibling subsystem and those with a too-rigid boundary between the males and the females. In another example of a dysfunctional family, one symbiotic pair is balanced by the isolation of all other members. In the "control tower" family, all communication is filtered through one member so that direct communication, as well as collisions, are avoided. Some disturbed families are characterized by generally good communication patterns with the exception of one member who is either weakly connected to one other member or is the scapegoat. Finally, there is the family with a too-rigid hierarchy, according to which the top dog directs the behavior of everyone else in the family.

In multiple family therapy, the group consists of four to six families who meet once a week with two cotherapists, as well as trainees in an observer role. The format is open ended and families are selected at random. For Laqueur (1976), the crucial aspect of multiple family therapy is the presence of society, or the suprasystem, in the form of other families with whom the identified patient and the family must interact. The job of the therapist requires that she have originality, flexibility, initiative, and an excellent sense of timing (Laqueur, 1970).

The goal of therapy is to change the interaction patterns that characterize the relationship between the identified patient and the family. Treatment occurs in three phases: (1) initial interest, (2) resistance, and (3) working through. Change is facilitated by a variety of group techniques, or mechanisms, including delineation of the field of interaction, breaking the intrafamilial code, competition, amplification and modulation of signals, learning through trial and error, learning by analogy, learning through identification, the use of models, creating a focus of excitation, and the use of families as cotherapists.

According to Laqueur (1976), success is defined in the following manner:

We consider a family improved if our therapeutic intervention has achieved the following: 1. Better function and creative operation of the family, even within environments that make family life more complex and difficult emotionally, economically, politically, or morally. 2. Better mutual liking and respect of family members for one another. 3. Better acceptance of shortcomings and capitalizing on each other's strengths. 4. Better ability to enjoy day-to-day living. 5. Greater capability for compassion, mutual love, understanding, support, and cooperation among family members. 6. Better insight and improved judgment. 7. Greater openness for new information. 8. Building of lasting and satisfying relationships with each other within the family, and with friends and environment. (pp. 414–415)

Like couples group therapy, multiple family therapy is certainly cost effective. In addition, it has proved beneficial with a variety of highly disturbed families. Designed to help families help themselves, Laqueur himself described this modality as "a sheltered workshop in family communication" (1976, p. 405). We might also mention that the multiple family format characterizes a variety of structured facilitation programs that may either be problem focused (Hoopes, Fisher, & Barlow, 1984) or aimed at enrichment (Sawin, 1979, 1982). It is thus not limited to either disturbed families or to a hospital setting.

Family Networking

Also known as social networking, family networking focuses on the natural, continuous relationship system of persons as individuals or in various groupings. The family or social network refers to "a relatively invisible, but at the same time a very real, structure in which an individual, nuclear family or group is imbedded" (Speck & Attneave, 1973, p. 6). This larger social context is the focus of intervention in family networking. The therapists most commonly associated with this approach to family therapy are Carolyn Attneave, Uri Rueveni, and Ross Speck.

While networks, like individuals and families, can be either functional or dysfunctional, a well-functioning network mediates stress, facilitates communication, and interprets the environment in an effective manner. Dysfunctional networks tend to be rigid and constraining and are characterized by depersonalization and alienation. Thus, individual growth is stifled and symptomatic behavior emerges (Nichols, 1984).

The networking approach attempts to deal with crisis by helping to make the larger context "visible and viable" through energizing and enhancing its inherent strengths. Ideally, the network thereby becomes a resource and support for positive growth and development. This process also attempts to redefine the context so that symptomatic behavior on the part of one member is no longer a logical response: "The network effect can scramble the cybernated pegboard, open up new feedback connections, and make everybody both an experimenter and a validator of new options. Suddenly, no one is sick" (Speck & Attneave, 1973, p. 10).

Specifically, family networking aims to:

1. *Facilitate rapid connections, familiarity, and readiness to participate, which increases the level of involvement and energy.*
2. *Develop and encourage sharing of the problems and concerns by members of the immediate family, which allows for increased involvement and exchange of a variety of viewpoints by network members.*
3. *Facilitate communication between the family and its extended network system, which emphasizes the need for network activists.*
4. *Provide direct intervention and a deeper exploration of the nature of difficulty during impasse periods, which leads to crisis resolution.*
5. *Assist in the development and formation of temporary support groups, which serve as resource consultants. (Rueveni, 1979, p. 72)*

The first step in the development of a family networking intervention is the analysis and mapping of a social context and its members. This mapping includes people within the household, emotionally significant people outside the household, casual relationships, and distant relationships, with a distinction drawn between family and nonfamily members. Within each of these categories there is a further distinction between those who make one feel uncomfortable or whom one dislikes and those about whom one feels more positively. From this map, the therapist gets a picture of the whole and can designate significant individuals to be included in the therapy process, thereby enlarging an individual's or family's potential base of support. The technique of incorporating persons from outside the family depends on the nature of the presenting problem and the particular therapist's style. In both cases, however, the therapists and family meet to discuss and negotiate the final contract specifying the participants.

Family networking is led by a team of three to six therapists and may include as many as one hundred people. The intervention occurs via a process of six ongoing and recursive phases. During the *retribalization* phase, network members and therapy team members become acquainted and define the problem. In the *polarization* phase, network members express their feelings and choose up sides around the "hot" issues. *Mobilization,* based on the repetition of old change strategies, defines the third phase. This is followed by a period of *depression* as feelings of hopelessness and resistance emerge. The *breakthrough* phase describes the expression of previously denied feelings, the experience of new behaviors, and the accomplishment of assigned tasks. The final phase is one of *exhaustion and elation,* after which the pattern repeats. Indeed, "these phases are present regardless of the frequency or duration of the social network intervention, and even tend to repeat themselves in the microcosm of the single session" (Speck & Attneave, 1973, p. 20).

The goal of crisis resolution through family networking is facilitated by a variety of techniques. Those specific to the retribalization process include milling around, screaming, whooping and clapping, circle movements, songs, speeches, and network news briefs. Polarization is encouraged through the use of exercises such as the inner and outer network circles, the empty chair, removing a family member, communicating with an absent member, and asking "Whose side do you take?" Mobilization techniques include promoting direct confrontations, simulating disengagement from home, the "death ceremony," sculpting the family network, role playing, and role reversal. For detailed descriptions of each of these techniques, the reader is referred to *Networking Families in Crisis* (Rueveni, 1979).

Problem resolution, according to the assumptions of family networking, is a function of opening previously closed or dormant networks, healing alienation, and thus changing the social context of the individual or family. As old conflicts emerge and are dealt with effectively, new sources of assistance become available. Although all of the presenting problems may not be resolved as a result of the networking intervention, it may facilitate the creation of a more supportive context. Ideally this support system will be available for assistance in future crises and thus will function in a more effective manner. There will be an ongoing awareness that help is available when needed.

In addition to its application during times of crisis, family networking has also been used as a preventive mental health technique. Individuals approaching retirement age have availed themselves of the approach in preparation for the stresses of this major life transition. It has been successfully used for the reduction of intergenerational conflict in the families of adolescents, for dealing with cross-cultural issues and tensions, and for work with the clergy (Attneave, 1976). Family networking can provide a powerful experience for participants, touching the individuals' need and desire for closeness and broadening their base of physical and emotional support. Further, the exploration of relationships beyond the boundary of the nuclear family is a logical extension of more typical family therapy approaches and seems to lend itself to a great variety of applications and styles of implementation.

Symptom-Focused Treatments

The decade of the 1980s was characterized by tremendous concern about the emergence of and treatment for specific symptoms or disorders. For example, family-based theories and approaches to chemical dependency (Black, 1981; Elkin, 1984; Wegscheider, 1981) and eating disorders (Minuchin, Rosman, & Baker, 1978) were formulated and became the basis for a flurry of activity. Workshops on these topics abounded and symptom-focused treatment centers became big business. Consistent with this trend, the 1986 Annual Conference of the American Association for Marriage and Family Therapy (AAMFT) was the scene of much discussion about whether or not to include courses on these symptom-focused treatments in the curriculum required for AAMFT accreditation.

Certainly family interventions for chemical dependency and eating disorders are appropriate to the extent that they acknowledge the relational aspect of and contextual importance relative to such symptomatic behaviors. However, if one is operating according to a systemic/cybernetic perspective, models that focus on the symptom and define the family accordingly do not qualify as family therapy approaches. Inasmuch as they are linear in nature and are consistent with more traditional medical models of pathology, they are pies baked in an individual psychology crust. As such they tend to focus on content, or the phenomenon named by the label. Thus they see the problem as "real" and the map as the territory.

To illustrate, when symptom-based models are delineated and popularized, their concepts tend to enter everyday language and are used to explain and predict feelings and behavior. It is then not unusual, for example, to hear clients or other individuals refer to themselves as ACOAs (Adult Child of Alcoholics) who experience their reality accordingly. The difference that we as systemic/cybernetic theorists want to punctuate relates to the extent we as creators of symptom-focused treatment models may have become part of the problem rather than of its solution.

From our perspective, the dilemma posed here seems to be a function of the nature of theories about human behavior. We create theories to order our reality, to explain ourselves, to make sense out of an enormous body of information. In the process, however, we tend to reify our creations. Thus, we forget that it is we who have invented the concepts, and that these order-givers do not represent truth in any absolute sense. We treat them as real and as the way it is.

Consistent with our basic orientation, we like to emphasize this point by referring to theories as myths or fairy tales. For example, we all know that Walt Disney created Mickey Mouse and Donald Duck. We can have a meaningful conversation about these characters, and in the sense that we can talk about them, we objectify them—we give them a "real" existence by having a discussion about them. At another level of consciousness, however, we are aware that they are "really" fictional characters; that is, they are Disney's creations, figments of his imagination. By contrast, when Sigmund Freud created the id, ego, and superego, for example, we tended to believe they had been discovered. In the process of having meaningful conversations about these constructs we began to see them as real.

You might assert that certainly we are not equating Mickey and the ego. But from the perspective of systems theory/cybernetics, we are. However, there is an important difference. This difference is the conscious awareness that Mickey is not really real and the lack of conscious awareness that the ego is not real except in the theory that gives it existence and meaning. Walt Disney knew he was inventing Mickey Mouse. Theorists believe they discovered the ego. We would therefore remind you that from this perspective the theory of id, ego, and superego is a potentially useful explanation, which is nevertheless a figment of its creator's imagination, and thus a myth, or story.

While all theories may be stories, they nevertheless are capable of providing us with extremely useful ways of thinking. Certainly the models underlying symptom-based treatments may offer important information about characteristic patterns of families in which chemical dependency or eating disorders exist. However, as systemic/cybernetic theorists, we feel that at best they may delineate a set of useful guidelines for understanding and working with some families. At the pragmatic, simple-cybernetics level, a problem such as chemical dependency is understood as a symptom of system dysfunction. It is embedded in an interactional context within which alcoholism, for example, represents a logical response. According to this perspective, the context is the appropriate target of intervention and change. Thus, when baked in the crust for a family therapy pie, family therapy focuses on process rather than on content. In so doing, it also recognizes that the map is a model and is not the territory.

Systemic Consistency

As you read through the brief discussions on systemic consistency at the end of each of the various approaches to family therapy, you may well have asked, So what? when inconsistencies were noted. Indeed, we have emphasized the notion that inconsistencies are inevitable in any theoretical framework, given the fact that human beings cannot transcend themselves in the process of studying themselves. However, systemic family therapy is about epistemology and about avoiding pathologies of epistemology. And in the current, postmodern era, this issue is of primary importance. Thus, we feel it essential that we as professionals not disregard our fundamental orientation and the ramifications of our theorizing for therapist behavior.

The field of family therapy has been successful in establishing its own professional identity. It has come of age and has therefore moved from a period of theory building, to a period of theory integrating, to a period of rethinking itself. Having established their credibility and having taken their place among a variety of professional groups, each of which seeks to protect its own turf, family therapists have become wary of violating the premises that defined their uniqueness in the first place and of participating in the creation of problems rather than of their solutions. As we have stated several times, from our perspective family therapy is about theory. It is built on the unifying concepts of a systemic/cybernetic perspective. However, it exists in a context dominated by an alternative paradigm and thus is vulnerable to becoming hooked into the patterns characterizing the traditional, modernist world view of our society. Hence, an emphasis on consistency is not only appropriate but essential for maintaining its effectiveness.

It is our belief that just as systems theory tells us that the key to change is a function of a change in context via a response that appears illogical from the framework of that context, the effectiveness of family therapy may lie in its being an apparently illogical response in a societal context characterized by a Newtonian, medical-model world view. To the extent that we fall into the pattern consistent with that societal world view, we simply become more of the same—a first-order response. To the extent that we remain systemically consistent, we offer the possibilities of a second-order, postmodern response. At the same time this poses a dilemma for the systemic family therapist. This dilemma is taken up in Part 3, where we consider epistemological challenges as they relate to assessment and research (Chapter 15) and so-called pathologies of epistemology (Chapter 16).

P a r t 3

Epistemological Challenges

It is time to begin the final leg of our journey together. As we anticipate the sites we are about to visit, we are also aware of those we were unable to include in our itinerary for this trip. We would therefore encourage you to do some explorations on your own in the areas of training, supervision, and the contributions of video equipment in opening up and changing the nature of both the therapy process and the process of becoming a therapist. Similarly, we believe that knowledge of the realm of family development and enrichment, both in terms of contributions to therapy and as an alternative to treatment, is essential for the competent therapist. However, the parameters of our systemic integration (as well as of time and space) require that we go in a slightly different direction at this point.

According to our map, we are approaching the territory of assessment and research. Once again, we will find a complementarity between old and new, between the familiar and the unfamiliar. Once again, you may expect to feel sometimes at home and sometimes like a stranger in an unknown land. In Chapter 15 we will consider traditional models of family classification and family therapy research. Following this discussion we will present some evolving models of qualitative research. We will then discuss approaches consistent with a systems perspective and with the findings of quantum physics, as well as the ramifications of both for assessment and research.

In Chapter 16 we will describe some of the implications of being a systemic family therapist and a teacher of systemic family therapy. We will also point out the potholes, in the form of pathologies of epistemology, that may interfere with continued travels along this road. Finally, we will offer a brief summary of the meaning of this journey for us.

Our biases are particularly apparent in these two chapters, and while we do not apologize for them, we do want to acknowledge them. We believe there are many valid ways to know, and an exclusive focus on and use of one methodology is as inappropriate and potentially harmful as is single-method, or cookbook, therapy. Further, while we may, understandably, be faulted for not having considered in greater detail the external and empirical criteria of verifiability and accountability for each of the family therapy approaches, such criticisms come out of another world view and are not consistent with the systemic/cybernetic paradigm out of which we are operating.

On the other hand, we are aware of our own inconsistency in, and might therefore justifiably be faulted for, discussing pathologies of epistemology in the context of a perspective that precludes designations of good and bad. However, given a belief in a totally conjoined universe, we become aware of certain issues that must be considered vis-à-vis the practice of therapy at the level of simple cybernetics. Thus, by *pathologies* we are referring to beliefs that, while logical in cultural context, are inconsistent at the level of cybernetics of cybernetics—one of the main considerations of our systemic integration.

Chapter 15

Assessment and Research

We now invite you to the territory of assessment and research, areas that, at first glance, may seem noncontroversial. You probably have a knowledge of assessment procedures consistent with the trait and factor classification system of individual psychology as well as a background in research in the logical positivist-empirical paradigm, for both are highly consistent with the accepted practice of science in our society. We therefore begin this chapter with a brief history of this research tradition in the social sciences. We then review the status of several family assessment/classification models as well as outcome and process research in family therapy. After that we will once again be traveling into rarefied air as we challenge you to examine many of the assumptions of the classical assessment and research paradigm from the perspective of cybernetics of cybernetics. Next, we describe the use of a systems perspective for assessment and research. Then we venture into a consideration of the paradoxes that gave rise to the new science called quantum physics. We also consider the implications for research of adopting a systemic/cybernetic perspective as well as the importance of framework-relative models. Finally, we examine the limits of what we can know and the issue of certainty and uncertainty.

History

The so-called received view of research that has evolved in our culture and has been equated with the practice of responsible, rigorous science is that of the logical positivist-empirical tradition. Indeed, the word *science* in our culture is often associated with such notions as experimentation, cause/effect relationships, control, numbers, replication, probability, hypothesis testing, dependent variables, and independent variables. This science grew out of the work of René Descartes, Isaac Newton, and Francis Bacon. Capra (1983) notes: "Since the seventeenth century physics has been the shining example of an 'exact' science, and has served as the model for all other sciences" (p. 42). Accordingly, a mechanistic world view has been employed for approximately two hundred and fifty years in the process of developing and refining the prevailing paradigm of classical physics. Consistent with this perspective, existence is premised on matter, and the metaphor used to define the material world is that of a machine. Like other machines, the so-called cosmic machine is assumed to consist of elementary parts, the discovery of which will provide knowledge of the machine's operation. Understanding thus requires a focus on reductionism, and for centuries the mechanistic and reductionistic views of classical physics have been presumed to be the correct descriptions of reality. Not surprisingly, then, the search for scientific credibility in the fields of psychology, sociology, and anthropology has led to the adoption of a similar perspective (Capra, 1983).

Key assumptions of this Newtonian research model include:

1. Valid knowledge claims can only be based on what is observed (i.e., seen, heard, smelled, tasted, or touched).
2. Control and replication are essential, particularly relative to the goal of determining cause/effect relationships.
3. Cause/effect relationships are tied to the assumption of time as absolute.
4. A reality exists independent of us as observers.
5. The experimental method seeks to eliminate subjective judgments from the practice of science.
6. Observation serves the purpose of testing theory.
7. Theory is the goal of scientific activity. The activity of science is to subject theories to disconfirming tests.
8. Reality is a constant, static, absolute phenomenon.
9. Mind transcends a reality that is independent of mind.

Until the emergence of scientific psychology, however, the study of the human mind and society (the moral sciences) had been the domain of philosophy. But the mid-nineteenth century was the heyday of Newtonian physics, and the machine metaphor, as well as research methods consistent with this world view, pushed physics to the forefront of respected science. John Stuart Mill (1806–1873) was among the investigators who sought to apply the methods and goals of the natural, physical sciences to the social sciences. Mill stated the case in this way:

> *The backward state of the moral sciences can only be remedied by applying to them the methods of physical science, duly extended and generalized.... If there are some subjects on which the results obtained have finally received the unanimous assent of all who have attended to the proof, and others on which mankind have not yet been equally successful; on which the most sagacious minds have occupied themselves from the earliest date, and have never succeeded in establishing any considerable body of truths, so as to be beyond denial or doubt; it is by generalizing the methods successfully followed in the former inquiries, and adapting them to the latter, that we may hope to remove this blot on the face of science. (Koch, 1976, p. 484)*

The labels associated with early attempts at applying the methods of classical physics to the study of the human mind, as called for by Mill, included empirical philosophy, physiological psychology, and experimental psychology. The last label reflects the focus on method. Indeed, it is primarily through the adoption of the methods of the natural sciences that the emancipation of the social sciences from philosophy was effected. One of the goals of this emancipation through the adoption of a scientific methodology was to have a basis on which to make valid knowledge claims—a certainty of knowledge and a delineation of facts rather than the rational, logical argumentation that was the methodology of philosophy.

The development of scientific psychology was in tune with the zeitgeist of the latter part of the nineteenth century. Many individuals were involved in working out how to apply scientific methods to the social sciences. Wilhelm Wundt established a psychology laboratory in Germany in 1879, generally considered psychology's birth year. Somewhat earlier, Francis Galton had suggested that "until the phenomena of any branch of knowledge have been submitted to measurement and number, it cannot assume the dignity of a science" (Misiak & Sexton, 1966, p. 57). William James noted, "I wished by treating psychology like a natural science, to help her become one" (Gadlin & Ingle, 1975, p. 1003). James McKeen Cattell asserted in 1892 that "psychology will gain greatly in clearness and accuracy by using the methods and conceptions of physics and mathematics" (Sokal, 1973, p. 279). George Fullerton wrote in 1893 that "the psychologist must accept without question the assumption upon which the natural sciences rest,—he must accept the external world, the world of matter and motion" (Sokal, 1973, p. 286).

Thus, the methodology and assumptions of the natural sciences evolved into the received view of the social sciences and have become equated with the responsible, rigorous, and accepted practice of science so highly valued in our culture today. It has become for many—laypeople as well as professionals—the only means by which to make valid knowledge claims. The social sciences adopted the world view of classical physics and its mechanistic root metaphor: "The metaphor of the world and human beings as machines expressed the conceptualizations of physical force and energy, discrete causes and effects (referred to by Braginsky and Braginsky, 1972, as billiard-ball causality), and lineal . . . thinking" (Dayringer, 1980, p. 38). In addition, the experimental method sought to preclude the investigators' subjective judgments. Indeed, objectivity was believed to be as essential for the scientific study of human beings as it was for the scientific study of nature, and it was assumed that there was a unity between the natural sciences and the social sciences.

As psychology was adopting the methodology of the natural sciences and seeking credibility as a legitimate field or discipline, a methodology different from the rational, logical argumentation of philosophy was sought, as we have said. As so often happens in the course of change, though, when we seek to move from one position, we move to its polar opposite. Thus, from a wholly subjective field without any recourse to systematic observation, psychology turned into a field that almost exclusively valued the observable. Accordingly, sensations and subjective judgments were mistrusted because they could not be observed and thus had become confused forms of knowing—Descartes's world of the mind.

While social science researchers today are not as committed to this extreme emphasis on objective, observable, controlled experimentation, they have stayed with a methodology that seeks precision. Subjectivity itself, in the form of cognition and beliefs, is now a legitimate topic for systematic, controlled observation through a variety of instruments with demonstrated validity and reliability for measuring the particular aspect of subjectivity in question. In addition, the neo-positivists do not speak of causation in the ultimate classical (billiard-ball) sense. Rather, this position has given way to one of multiple causation and probability statements about causation, as exemplified in multivariate analysis.

The idea of a value-free science has also been replaced by an effort to minimize and admit the biases and values of the researcher through controls in the research design. However, the methodology still involves hypothesis testing of a priori theories that purport to be accurate maps of the world. Further, the research design seeks to disconfirm, and only disconfirm (Popper, 1959), the theoretically predicted outcome as stated in the alternative hypothesis. While the theory being tested may be the target of the specific investigation, it is recognized that other theories are operating at the same time. These include the theory of measurement implicit in the instrument or machine used and the particular conditions of the study. On the other hand, as noted by Dawis (1984), the goal of research is a robust theory, and "a robust theory will survive many disconfirming tests. When a theory (at any order) gains near universal acceptance it can be called a fact from the Latin word, facere, meaning to make: hence, a fact is something made, a construction" (p. 468).

Thus modifications have occurred, but the basic assumptions have remained the same, or in Kuhn's (1970) terms, we have dealt with anomalies by shifts within the paradigm. Not surprisingly, many of the models that have been developed for studying the family are consistent with the traditional research paradigm. We will shift our attention now to a consideration of some of these models.

Family Assessment and Classification—General Models

Assessment and classification of families and research on families are highly interrelated, and the standard for each generally remains the logical positivist tradition we have discussed. The concept of family therapy implies an assumption that a set of categories exists by which families can be assessed to be functional and healthy or dysfunctional and unhealthy. As you read about the models of family therapy presented in Part Two, you became aware of the way many approaches provide a framework for punctuating functional and dysfunctional families. Accordingly, the successful outcome of therapy is measured by the progress of the family in the direction defined as functional by the particular model. By way of review we would like to highlight the dimensions, processes, and structures—assessment categories—that therapists using some of these approaches might observe, consistent with what the theory describes.

Assessment from the Bowenian perspective relates to the degree of differentiation of self as it is grounded in a good marriage that provides both autonomy and emotional intimacy. In healthy families, children are allowed to evolve their own personal autonomy and are capable of functioning in a variety of situations. To Bowen, stress was a normal part of living, and under conditions of chronic stress, symptoms can evolve. Therefore, the presence of symptoms is not viewed as dysfunctional.

Boszormenyi-Nagy's contextual approach values movement toward trustworthiness and consideration of the welfare of other family members. The model also stresses the importance of autonomy, relational equitability, fairness, and flexibility.

Whitaker as therapist emphasizes the importance of seeing the family as an integrated whole with a sense of itself as a system. A sense of family history and tradition exists as well as ties to extended family and systems outside the family, yet there is also loyalty to the nuclear family. Whitaker's normal family has a stability and, with a consciousness of the passage of time, can adapt and maintain a balance between dependence and autonomy.

Kempler's experiential model values a family context supportive of individuality and personal desires. The model also values autonomy and acceptance of differences by all family members, as well as a spontaneous living style. Pressures for extreme togetherness and loyalty to the family are viewed as dysfunctional.

In Minuchin's structural model, the therapist is cued by the theory to observe structure, generational boundaries, hierarchy, degrees of enmeshment and disengagement, and provision for change over time, as well as the promotion of both autonomy and interdependence. This model also suggests that assessment must consider cultural variations and the particular idiosyncrasies of the family and its circumstances.

From the communications perspective of the MRI group, the fundamental value is that the family be functional. The normal family is thus able to maintain its basic integrity even during periods of stress. Appropriate change and stability are desired. Communication is clear and direct.

Satir's model prizes feelings of self-worth as well as clear, direct, and honest communication. In addition, family rules are clear, specific, and flexible as appropriate to various circumstances.

Haley, as strategic therapist, adopts the structural perspective regarding the importance of hierarchy, clear rules, and the parental coalition. Like Minuchin, Haley also values diversity and does not talk about normalcy and abnormalcy in any absolute sense. For Haley, the key issue is whether the family is accomplishing its tasks.

For the original Milan group the family is respected as it is, as the only way it can be at this point in time. The therapist thus supports each family member. While not aligning with any particular family form or organization, this model prescribes rituals which reveal a preference for a marital coalition and a certain level of closeness from systems outside the family. The model's "value neutrality" is simultaneously an honest assessment and a therapeutic strategy.

The behavioral/social exchange models talk of healthy and unhealthy families only in a functional sense. There is no inherently good or bad behavior. The focus is on process in that desirable behavior is rewarded and undesirable behavior is not reinforced.

Family Assessment and Classification— Scientific Approaches

Classification schemata peculiar to particular theoretical models do not necessarily lend themselves to the practice of scientific research if general laws are our goal. At best their constructs may be supported and theories thus validated through the testing of hypotheses generated by each theory. However, if the desired outcomes relative to what characterizes healthy functioning are different for each theory, the relevance of comparisons between them is decidedly limited. Only when common approaches to the study of the family which transcend the different theoretical models are evolved, is generalization to the larger population possible. The objective of such approaches is the assessment and classification of family functioning on a variety of dimensions, which may include, but are not limited to, the ideals posited by the various schools of therapy. Several such models exist, most notably Kantor and Lehr's family typology (1975), Olson, Russell, and Sprenkle's circumplex model (1983), the Beavers model (1981), the McMaster model of family functioning (Epstein, Bishop, & Levin, 1978), and Constantine's tetrahedal model of family paradigms (1993).

Kantor and Lehr observed a large number of families for almost ten years in an attempt to identify different types of family structures. Their focus was on both the processes within the family and the processes used by the family to interface with the outside world. They described three family types—open, closed and random—noting that none was a pure form and that each had aspects of the other two.

Open families were described as democratic in their style of operating within the family and with agencies in the external environment. While order was evident in these families, they were also flexible, members negotiated with one another, and individual rights were respected. Loyalty to the self and to the family was expected. Open and honest exchanges with family members and with people outside the family were also in evidence.

Closed families were characterized by structures, rules, and a hierarchy of power according to which group needs were to take precedence over individual needs. In these families there was stability through tradition. Accordingly, rigid family schedules were adhered to and children were expected to inform parents about their comings and goings. In addition, outside influences, media, people, and reading material were carefully monitored.

Random families were so described because their processes appeared to be fragmented. Kantor and Lehr described these families as having the "core purpose" of exploration through intuition. That is, each person did his or her own thing, which was not necessarily connected to what other members were doing.

Few rules were in evidence. Boundaries shifted and could be crossed easily. People from the outside could come and go through the family in much the same manner as family members.

Kantor and Lehr did not describe one family type as superior to another. In the authoritarian family, rebellion is possible if the structure is too rigid. Random families can have an atmosphere bordering on chaos. Even open families may err in the direction of either authoritarianism or randomness, and thus problems may evolve.

Olson, Sprenkle, and Russell (1979; Olson, Russell, and Sprenkle, 1983) created a "circumplex" model, which involves two dimensions of family functioning, *cohesion* and *adaptability*. Cohesion is described as the degree of "emotional bonding." In the language of Minuchin (1974), families are classified as either enmeshed or disengaged. Family adaptability describes the ability of the family to balance stability (morphostasis) and change (morphogenesis). The key aspect in both dimensions is balance—between enmeshment and disengagement (cohesion) and between stability and change (adaptability).

Families can be classified in four categories on both the cohesion and adaptability dimensions, going from lowest to highest:

1. Cohesion
    a. Disengaged
    b. Separated
    c. Connected
    d. Enmeshed
2. Adaptability
    a. Rigid
    b. Structured
    c. Flexible
    d. Chaotic

The sixteen categories that emerge from the circumplex model are illustrated in Figure 15.1.

Another aspect of the circumplex model is that of family communication, what the authors call the "facilitating" dimension. That is, effective communication is seen as essential for evolving the appropriate levels of bonding and adaptability necessary for optimal family functioning.

The Beavers model (Beavers, 1981, 1982; Beavers & Voeller, 1983) seeks to integrate family systems theory with developmental theory and classifies families on two axes. The first dimension describes families relative to their *stylistic quality of family interaction*. They can therefore be either centripetal, in which case the family turns in on itself and is distrustful of the outside world, or centrifugal, in which case the family members rely on and are more trusting of relationships outside the family. On the other dimension, families are classified as *optimal, adequate, midrange, borderline,* or *severely disturbed*. Families are classified on this second axis on the basis of "structure, available information, and adaptive flexibility of the sys-

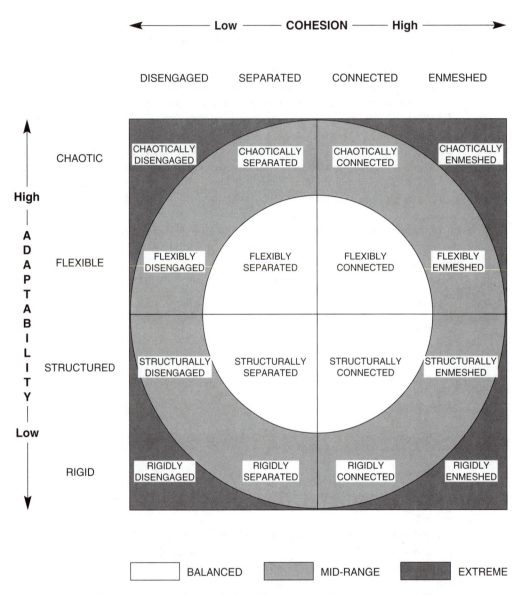

FIGURE 15-1   **The Circumplex Model (Olson, Russell, & Sprenkle, 1983, p. 71)**

tem. In systems terms, this may be called a negentropic continuum, since the more negentropic (the more flexible and adaptive), the more the family can negotiate, function and deal effectively with stressful situations" (Beavers & Voeller, 1983, p. 89). Figure 15.2 illustrates the two dimensions of the Beavers model.

The McMaster model of family functioning (MMFF) (Epstein et al., 1978; Epstein, Bishop, & Baldwin, 1982) builds on the systems model in that a family is

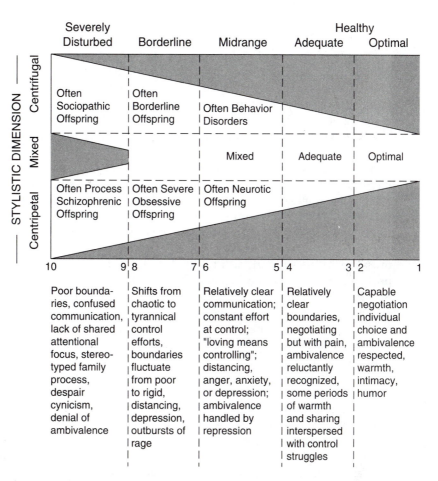

	Severely Disturbed	Borderline	Midrange	Adequate	Healthy Optimal

STYLISTIC DIMENSION — Centrifugal / Mixed / Centripetal

Centrifugal: Often Sociopathic Offspring | Often Borderline Offspring | Often Behavior Disorders

Mixed | Adequate | Optimal

Centripetal: Often Process Schizophrenic Offspring | Often Severe Obsessive Offspring | Often Neurotic Offspring

10   9 8   7 6   5 4   3 2   1

| Poor boundaries, confused communication, lack of shared attentional focus, stereotyped family process, despair cynicism, denial of ambivalence | Shifts from chaotic to tyrannical control efforts, boundaries fluctuate from poor to rigid, distancing, depression, outbursts of rage | Relatively clear communication; constant effort at control; "loving means controlling"; distancing, anger, anxiety, or depression; ambivalence handled by repression | Relatively clear boundaries, negotiating but with pain, ambivalence reluctantly recognized, some periods of warmth and sharing interspersed with control struggles | Capable negotiation individual choice and ambivalence respected, warmth, intimacy, humor |

Autonomy: A continuous or infinite dimension, related to the family system's capacity to allow and encourage members to function competently in making choices, assuming responsibility for self, and negotiating with others.

Adaptability: A continuous or infinite dimension, related to the capacity of a family to function competently in effecting change and tolerating differentiation of members.

Centripetal/Centrifugal: A curvilinear, stylistic dimension with extreme styles associated with severely disturbed families and the most competent families avoiding either extreme.

Inflexibility: The inability to change. The most chaotic families are the most inflexible owing to their lack of a shared focus of attention.

Severely disturbed: The lowest level of functioning along the adaptiveness continuum manifested by poorly defined subsystem boundaries and confusion owing to nonautonomous members having little tolerance for clear, responsible communication.

Borderline: A level of functioning between severely disturbed and midrange, manifested by persistent and ineffective efforts to rid the system of confusion by simplistic and often harsh efforts at control.

Midrange: Families that typically turn out sane but limited offspring, with relatively clear boundaries but continued expectations of controlling and being controlled.

FIGURE 15-2   The Beavers Model (Beavers & Voeller, 1983, p. 90)

viewed as an integral whole. It assumes the importance of a family's structure and organization as well as its transactional patterns. It sets forth six dimensions of family functioning, including (1) problem solving, (2) communication, (3) roles, (4) affective responsiveness, (5) affective involvement, and (6) behavior control.

Family problem solving describes a family's ability to solve problems, instrumental and affective, sufficient to maintain a functional environment for its members. *Family communication* describes the exchange of information in the instrumental and affective dimensions of family life. Communication is also classified as to whether it is direct or indirect, clear or masked. *Family roles* describe the patterns engaged in by family members to perform family functions. Accordingly, it is important that all family functions or roles be fulfilled without overburdening one or more members. Among the roles described are the provision of resources, nurturance and support, adult sexual gratification, personal development support, and maintenance and management of the family system.

Affective responsiveness refers to a family's ability to respond with the appropriate level of intensity (qualitative) and in the right amount (quantitative) relative to the situation. All feelings are valued, including "welfare emotions" (such as warmth, tenderness, love, and consolation) and "emergency emotions" (anger, fear, and sadness).

The fifth dimension, *affective involvement,* describes the degree to which family members are interested in the idiosyncratic interests of other family members. On this dimension, MMFF defines different kinds of involvement, including lack of involvement, narcissistic involvement, empathic involvement, overinvolvement, and symbiotic involvement.

The sixth dimension is *behavior control,* which describes how families "handle behavior in three areas: physically dangerous situations; situations that involve the meeting and expressing of psychobiological needs and drives; and situations involving interpersonal socializing behavior both between family members and with people outside the family" (Epstein et al., 1982, p. 128). Styles of behavior control include rigid, flexible, laissez-faire, and chaotic. In the MMFF model, "flexible" behavior control is preferred and "chaotic" is viewed as least effective.

There are many other formal models available in the professional literature. To us a formal model refers to one whose assumptions have been explicated using accepted scientific procedures for operationalizing theoretical constructs. Thus, systematic procedures for using and/or testing the model have been described. A variety of formal assessment scales that seek to assess one or more dimensions of family or couple functioning also exist. Perhaps the most comprehensive collection of available instruments is the *Handbook of Family Measurement Techniques* (Touliatos, Perlmutter, & Strauss, 1990). This volume abstracts 976 instruments, which "represent the development of measurement within the family field over the past 50-plus years" (p. 7).

All of the models presented thus far in this chapter are consistent with the practice of family assessment in the modernist/structuralist tradition. They seek and purport to describe what is really going on in the relationship or family. In the next section, we present a postmodernist/constructionist critique of formal assessment procedures, which from our perspective are inconsistent with the systemic perspective.

Family Assessment and Classification—Some Concerns

The five assessment models we have described represent attempts to define a specific set of categories in which to fit the many variations of family structures and styles one might find. Each model, in its own way, suggests we must consider variations on the general themes suggested by the model. In any such grouping, much information about the idiosyncrasies of particular families is lost. However, the assessment models tend to fit the culture in which they evolved, and one can infer common threads in them that fit the values of Western society. They are very useful for both research and therapy purposes, but regardless of this, an important concern from the perspective of ecosystemic epistemology is whether or not the categories described by the models are treated as true, accurate descriptions of the family rather than as categories we might use to understand families for therapeutic or research purposes. The metaphor of the categories often becomes the reality, for each assessment model describes a value framework, and therapists using any model to guide their interventions toward goals defined by the model necessarily impose values despite admonitions to respect cultural and situational circumstances.

A related concern is the possibility that the family will adopt the framework of the therapist regardless of its appropriateness for them. That is, assessment implicitly imposes a set of imperatives and prohibitions on the family. When therapists reify a description of a family—this family is "chaotic"—the assessment becomes an "is" rather than a label chosen from a great variety available. From the systems perspective we must be aware that our maps and our assessment metaphors or labels are not the territory. More responsibly we might say, "Let us assume for the moment that the description, 'the family is chaotic' is useful" and use it as a guide for our action as therapists. Consistent with this perspective, we would then help the family become more flexible in its control attempts. This would constitute a more appropriate balance between the rigid and chaotic categories of the MMFF model we are using. However, we would recognize that this is only one way we might help the family.

Another important issue emerges at this point, for in conventional psychotherapeutic practice, based on the scientific, medical model, assessment is viewed as something that occurs prior to treatment. Viewed systemically, however, assessment and intervention constitute an arbitrary punctuation of difference. Indeed, what the therapist treats is largely what she assessed or conceptualized to be the problem. Thus, the problems treated by the therapist who imposes a theoretical or more general assessment model on the family unit are those defined by the conceptual model used. While it is true that the family comes with its own assessment of its problem (which very probably is focused on the individual who is the symptom-bearer or identified patient), by asking the family to participate, we have already imposed the systems paradigm on the family unit. In effect, the problems treated are those invented to be treated, either by the family or by the therapist. Stated differently, we choose the problems we treat by what we choose to call them. For example, if the metaphor "depression" is assigned, then depression is what we treat. However, one could also assign Adler's term "discouraged," or Rollo May's "demoralized" to the same phenomenon. Indeed, it might be important to be aware that in some cultures the concept of depression does not exist and that its use may represent a form of "colonialism" (Gergen, 1994).

An additional dilemma we encounter from the systems perspective is that the problem assessed by either the family or the therapist is a problem only from a frame of reference that defines it as a problem, a frame of reference that reflects the values of the culture. At the level of simple cybernetics we can assess the role the problem has in the context of the family. However, at the level of cybernetics of cybernetics we can reframe or redefine and thus place the so-called problem in a different context in which it ceases to be a problem. This is an issue we will address more directly in the latter part of this chapter. For now, let us say that one cannot just observe or assess and that the phenomenon one seeks only to observe is changed by the very act of observing or assessing it. Further, the labels we use to define a person, family, or relationship are of critical importance. Clients, couples, and families tend to reify the assessment metaphors or labels we assign to them, and they begin to take on the characteristics described by these metaphors or labels.

Thus, a consideration of the models used in the assessment and classification of families is just as important for family therapists as are the results of our assessment and classification activities. The impact of our theories may be much greater than is generally assumed. Although the traditional paradigm that guides normal science in our society espouses an objective observer stance, subjectivity and influence are inevitable. In the same way, we would say that the knowledge obtained from research on family therapy is limited by the parameters employed. When viewed from the perspective of a systemic/cybernetic epistemology, a variety of similar, important issues arise and must be addressed relative to this research.

Family Therapy Research in the Logical Positivistic Tradition

In this section we present a summary of outcome and process research in family therapy. It is important to note that outcome research is based on the idea of family therapy as a treatment modality rather than as a conceptual framework. That is, family therapy outcome research seeks answers to the complex question posed by Gordon Paul (1967): "What therapy is most effective for what problems, treated by what therapists, according to what criteria, in what setting?" (p. 111).

Many authors have reviewed the research on family therapy. The most notable of these reviews are those by Gurman and Kniskern (1978, 1981), Pinsof (1981), Todd and Stanton (1983), and Gurman, Kniskern, and Pinsof (1986). The key questions dealt with in these reviews include the following:

How effective are the family therapies?

Which family therapies are the most effective?

What therapist factors, client factors, and treatment factors influence the effectiveness of family therapies?

What are the major measurement problems in family therapy outcome research?

What are the key directions for future research? (Piercy, Sprenkle, & Associates, 1986, p. 330)

In answer to the general issue raised by these questions, Gurman et al. (1986) conclude with the following observation regarding the efficacy of family therapy: "Reassuringly,... when family therapy methods have been rigorously tested, they have been found to be effective without exception" (p. 58). More specifically, and based on earlier reviews, Gurman (1983a) provides summary data on family therapy research:

1. *With family related issues, many different family therapies are more effective than individual psychotherapy.*
2. *In both behavioral and nonbehavioral marital therapies, improved couple communication seems to be the key to successful outcome.*
3. *For marital problems, conjoint couples therapy is clearly better than individual therapy.*
4. *Negative outcomes are twice as likely to occur if marital problems are treated with individual therapy rather than conjoint therapy.*
5. *Positive outcomes occur in family therapies and individual therapies in the same proportion of cases.*
6. *Deterioration can occur in family therapy. The probability of such deterioration is associated with certain styles of therapist behavior.*

The more recent review of family therapy research by Gurman et al. (1986) provides further and different insights. Among those we have selected and interpreted are the following general observations:

1. *The preferred treatment for alcohol-involved marriages is conjoint couples treatment in groups. Such treatment may be superior to individual therapy with the alcoholic spouse.*
2. *Nonbehavioral conjoint marital therapy may be more effective than individual therapy for marital problems.*
3. *Improvement can be expected in about 71 percent of childhood or adolescent behavioral problems when any one of a variety of family therapy methods are used.*
4. *No empirical evidence is offered in support of the Milan or strategic family therapies in the treatment of schizophrenia. Empirical support in the form of reduced incidence of rehospitalization is available when psychoeducational models with families of the patient are used. This is support of the latter by default given the lack of evidence available from the former.*

5. *Behavioral marital therapy may be more effective with younger couples who may be more committed and caring.*

6. *Mediation as a form of divorce therapy has been demonstrated to be effective with motivated clients with relatively uncomplicated life circumstances.*

7. *Couples participating in enrichment experiences are likely to experience brief highs in terms of positive outcome. Deterioration effects are noted with some couples, suggesting a need for better screening for the experience as well as marital therapy follow-up after the enrichment experience.*

8. *Empirical research on the efficacy of training of marital and family therapists is in short supply. However, there is indirect evidence that training can increase the number of therapeutic alternatives that the therapists in training use.*

9. *Change or outcome measures in family therapy should be chosen from multiple perspectives and should fit the therapeutic process.*

10. *Outcome studies should measure systemic variables as well as measures of change in presenting problems.*

11. *Process research is in its infancy, and while models by Pinsof (1980; Pinsof & Catherall, 1984) and Patterson's Oregon school (Chamberlain, Patterson, Reid, Kavanaugh, & Forgatch, 1984) show promise in articulating the therapeutic interventions that make a difference, the issues regarding theory specific or generic process analysis remain.*

12. *Clinicians tend not to use family therapy research. However, the research that is more likely to be used by clinicians relates to process issues regarding how to handle problems encountered in therapy.*

Gurman et al. (1986) report other interpretations based on an earlier (Gurman & Kniskern, 1978) review of research on family therapy. Among these are the following:

1. *When compared to no treatment, nonbehavioral marital and family therapies are effective in about two-thirds of cases.*

2. *Whether the identified patient is a child, adolescent, or adult is not associated with treatment outcomes.*

3. *Successful outcomes occur in relatively few (one to twenty) sessions in both behavioral and nonbehavioral marital and family therapies.*

4. *Deterioration in therapy is associated with a therapist style that involves "little structuring" and "confrontation of highly affective material" (Gurman et al., 1986, p. 572). If the therapist promotes interaction and gives support, the probability of deterioration is reduced.*

5. *Cotherapy has not been demonstrated to be superior to marital or family therapy by one therapist.*

6. *Higher level "therapist relationship skills" appear to be necessary for positive outcomes in therapy. Basic "technical skills" may prevent worsening of the problem and maintaining the pretherapy status of the family.*

Our decision to select the work of Gurman and associates was not arbitrary. There were many different reviews of family therapy research we could have selected, but Gurman and his associates' framework reflects most clearly a conscious awareness of the context and status of empirical research in the light of the systems model. Further, we find the continuity across these comprehensive reviews useful. Their interpretation of the status of research in family therapy is, of course, their interpretation and is certainly not definitive, nor is our interpretation of their reviews and our interpretation of the tensions between the empirical research models and the new ecosystemic epistemology definitive.

Other selected reviews the reader may wish to investigate include those by Wells, Dilkes, and Trivelli (1972); DeWitt (1978); Borduin, Henggeler, Hanson, and Harbin (1982), Ulrici (1983), Tolan, Cromwell, and Brasswell (1986), Hazelrigg, Cooper, and Borduin (1987), Bednar, Burlingame, and Masters (1988), and Markus, Lange, and Pettigrew (1990). Research on special populations or problem metaphors that illustrates the effectiveness and issues in family therapy modalities includes the following: (1) addictions and family therapy (Stanton, Todd, & Associates, 1982; Joanning et al., 1987; Szapocznik et al., 1986, 1988; Lewis, Piercy, Sprenkle, & Trepper, 1990; Todd & Selekman, 1991; Joanning, Quinn, Thomas, & Mullen, 1992); (2) parent management and training for conduct disorders (Patterson, 1974; Borlens, Emmelkamp, Macgillarry, & Markvoort, 1980; Fleishmann & Szykula, 1981; Kazdin, 1987, 1991); (3) behavioral marital therapy (Jacobson, 1977; Baucom, 1982; Hahlweg, Schindler, Revenstorf, & Brengelmann, 1984; Jacobson et al., 1987); (4) juvenile delinquency (Alexander & Parsons, 1973; Alexander et al., 1977; Tolan, Cromwell, & Brasswell, 1986; Barton et al., 1987; Henggeler et al., 1992); (5) psychosomatic disorders and structural family therapy (Minuchin, Baker, Rosman, Liebman, Milman, & Todd, 1975; Minuchin, Rosman, & Baker, 1978; Minuchin & Fishman, 1981; Schwartz, Barrett, & Saba, 1985; Russell et al., 1986; Dare et al., 1990); (6) psychoeducation in families with a schizophrenic member (Falloon, Boyd, McGill, Razani, Moss, & Gilderman, 1982; Leff, Kuipers, Berkowitz, Eberlein-Vries, & Sturgeon, 1982; Falloon, Boyd, & McGill, 1985; Anderson, Reiss, & Hogarty, 1986; Hogarty et al., 1986); (7) child and spouse emotional and physical abuse (Brunk, Henggeler & Whelan, 1987; Trepper & Barrett, 1989; Lipchik, 1991).

Piercy and Sprenkle's (1990) decade review of the field of marriage and family therapy identified the following trends in family therapy research:

1. A move away from *"global comparative questions to specificity questions"* (p. 1120), which would include specific presenting problems with an eye to which method is most appropriate with a particular problem or type of client.
2. A move away *"from hubris to 'mellowing,'"* as systems purists become more conciliatory to alternative explanations other than that "all human problems were a direct result of current interactional dynamics" (p. 1121).
3. A move *"from outcome to both process and outcome"* by focusing on process in relationship to outcome, "which looks at 'outcome' as a series of 'episodes' of

therapy in which some significant change occurs.... The researcher then examines what proceeds and/or follows the change in order to develop causal or at least correlational hypotheses about events that may be related" (p. 1121).

4. A trend *"from design weakness to design strength."* More studies now employ "rigorous controls, careful execution, and a variety of reliable and valid measures" and "diligent attempts to raise and eliminate the possibility of alternative explanation for their findings" and provide "excellent models of long-term follow-up and attention to attrition and relapse" (p. 1121).

5. A move *"from statistical to clinical significance"* by increasing use of meta-analysis, which refers to "statistical analysis of the standardized results of a large number of studies" in a search for the "magnitude of the effect of treatment compared to control group scores" (p. 1122).

6. A move from quantitative to both qualitative and quantitative research methodologies. Qualitative research is seen as complementing quantitative research, particularly in the " 'discovery' of relationships among variables, understanding complex events and interactions in the natural context" (p. 1122).

Piercy and Sprenkle (1990) also provide recommendations for family therapy research in the 1990s:

1. Attention needs to be focused on adequate descriptions of the treatments used in research, making sure the treatment described is the actual treatment.

2. There need to be more adequate descriptions of the nature of the client population, with attention to how external validity is limited by the population.

3. Given that therapists in studies do not necessarily believe in the treatment they are mandated to do, comparative studies should, as a part of the research, use different therapists of "equal experience, competence and allegiance" (p. 1123).

4. Attention should be given to outcome measures at the individual, couple, and family system levels as well as to the respondent and data to collection methods.

5. Standards by which to evaluate qualitative research need to be developed, drawing upon efforts in education and sociology.

6. Research needs to be accretive; that is, there is a need for developing programmatic research in which subsequent research builds on what was learned from earlier studies.

The reviews, studies, trends, and recommendations discussed and presented above reflect research in the modernist/structuralist tradition and thus the assumptions of logical positivism, which views observation as a passive process and one's observations as unbiased.

Certainly there are real tensions between the practice of so-called normal science in the tradition of the logical positivist-empirical school and the new systemic/cybernetic paradigm. The reality is that research in the tradition of Newtonian physics can be done on family therapy. However, all research is necessarily research on parts of the whole that is assumed by the systemic paradigm. It is therefore research at the level of simple cybernetics. Clearly, Gurman and his associates seek a rapprochement between the two different world views, as does Keeney (1983), who suggests that we need not give up our historical traditions. The crux of the matter seems to be that "the realization that the map is not the territory does not require that we throw away all our old maps. We must, however, keep in mind that a map is a map" (Kniskern, 1983, p. 61).

A Postmodernist, Social Constructionist Consideration of Quantitative and Qualitative Research

There are a variety of issues regarding research in marriage and family therapy which directly relate to the perspective of the theorist/therapist. An essential tension between first-order cybernetics (all the world is connected except the observers) and second-order cybernetics (all the world is connected including the "observers") describes many of these issues. Most research and assessment is implemented at the level of first-order cybernetics, consistent with the modernist and structuralist traditions of normative social science and normative mental health practice. Indeed, it seems that if marriage and family therapy is to survive as a professional field, we must play to the political and economic audience that sanctions our roles as marriage and family therapists. In other words, we must demonstrate the efficacy of systemic/cybernetic thinking to other clinicians, to our clients, and to those people who control funding for therapeutic services (Nichols & Schwartz, 1995). Failure to do so increases the "marginalization of family therapy" (Shields et al., 1994, p. 117). Accordingly, we must stay within the box of first-order cybernetics which, from the perspective of cybernetics of cybernetics and social constructionism, is a major part of the problem we are trying to solve. That is, it is as a function of social science research that metaphors assigned to classes of behavior become reified and viewed as "phenomena out there" rather than simply as constructs we have invented to make "sense" of our experience. Thus, to participate in the traditional research enterprise is to be inconsistent with our own perspective.

In academia, the site of most social science research, the rewards (promotion, tenure, salary increases) generally are meted out on the basis of obtaining funding by doing research on the questions acceptable to funding agencies using traditional quantitative research methodologies. Further, in regard to current changes in the health care system, Sprenkle (1994, p. 237) states, "I firmly believe that well-controlled process and outcome research will be necessary to legitimize MFT for third-party payers and other external audiences."

An additional dilemma is that while traditional quantitative, empirical research is recognized on many fronts as the primary way to make valid knowledge claims, traditional social science tends to focus only on socially sanctioned research questions consistent with the ideology of the society. That is, "the questions thought important to investigate are determined by the social/cultural context in which science is done, as by problems and puzzles internal to scientific inquiry" (Longino, 1990, p. 84). Dialogues on research and domestic violence (see Jacobson, 1994; 1994b; Avis, 1994; Gelles, 1994) illustrate the interrelatedness of politics and research and the idea that research questions and answers activate value and political sensitivities. Similarly, in our society the individual (personality or monad) remains the primary unit of analysis and thus "person blame explanations of social problems" (Caplan & Nelson, 1973, p. 206) are more likely to be supported and funded. Moreover, these projects also "hold the potential for reinforcing established stereotypes and thereby perpetuating the conditions of the 'problem' group" (p. 206). As an example, Caplan and Nelson (1973) note that funding is available to study the deviant behavior of delinquents, but not the deviant behavior of slumlords.

Therefore, researchers and practitioners of marriage and family therapy are caught in a double bind. On the one hand, not to comply with the rules of the system described above by justifying our claims of effectiveness with the appropriate research protocols is to preclude funding for and support of the practice of marriage and family therapy. This could spell the demise of the field or force professional practice into the model of simple cybernetics. Sprenkle (1994) rightfully points out that the results of traditional process and outcome research methodology can be useful to inform one's clinical practice. On the other hand, to comply with the rules is to be inconsistent with our theoretical perspective and to participate in creating, both for ourselves and our clients, a reality which we say we eschew.

Issues such as these open up a consideration of qualitative research, which in the literature is often juxtaposed with quantitative research. Sprenkle (1994, p. 227) notes, "I would be distressed if the field were to polarize into qualitative versus quantitative research factions." However, to us, this is not the issue or a meaningful distinction, for any distinction necessarily creates a relationship between the two concepts (Bateson, 1972; Flemons, 1991; Keeney, 1983). Rather, we prefer to see these two methodologies as logical complements, each of which may be understood as having utility relative to context.

As we see it, the primary issue is that of logical consistency within one's conceptual framework. Traditional quantitative research is consistent with the simple cybernetics, modernist tradition. Indeed, traditional, normative, medical-model mental health practice needs traditional quantitative research to be consistent with itself. However, a cybernetics of cybernetics, postmodern, social constructionist approach to research requires something different:

> *The social constructionist approach urges us to abandon the obsession with truth and representation. The phrase "social constructionist" is used to refer to analytic programs in history and sociology of science that take scientific theories and hypotheses to be the products of their political, economic, and cultural milieu. The*

*programs employ a wide range of epistemological views, but their proponents are
unanimous in rejecting the idea that science is objective or that it gives us an unbiased view of the real world. (Longino, 1990, p. 9)*

Longino also punctuates an important difference in the social constructionist
interpretation of research data regarding the efficacy of family therapy approaches:

*That a theory works, that it can be used to predict correctly the empirical conse-
quences either of naturally occurring events or of human interaction and manipulation of events in nature is often taken to be a reason for accepting it. But
accepting a theory for practical or instrumental purposes and asserting it to be
true are quite different acts. "Working" is not an epistemological notion. (p. 93)*

Thus we must be aware that in research as well as in clinical practice we can be se-
duced into believing that because something works it therefore constitutes the
truth.

To us, the spirit and underlying philosophy of qualitative research is more consistent with therapeutic practice at the level of cybernetics of cybernetics. Qualitative research has the feel of a perspective which emancipates people from the tight
boxes of normative social science and mental health practice (Lather, 1986). It attempts to understand individual human experience in great depth. Like quantitative research it also seeks commonalities across human experience just as an
anthropologist seeks to understand the world view of a different culture. However,
these commonalities do not translate into normative standards by which people
are compared with one another. It acknowledges subjectivity and that we can only
do research on our representations of the world. It accepts that "observation is theory laden," and "meanings are theory dependent," and "facts are theory laden"
(Hayward, 1984, p. 76–77). Qualitative research may or may not be theory informed in a formal way.

The spirit of qualitative research suggests that the questions of interest should
dictate the design rather than being limited to asking only those questions that fit
accepted research protocols. Designs may change midstream. Rather than seeking
to control variables that may confound the internal and external validity of a research design, all variables are viewed as part of the context and are included in
the investigation. Some forms of qualitative research move the researcher out of
the role of expert who believes his or her observations and interpretations of the
data are better than those of the subjects. Subjects of investigations may be invited
to participate and dialogue with the researcher throughout a research project. Indeed, qualitative research and therapeutic conversations may be indistinguishable
from one another.

It is also within the spirit of qualitative research to see the data and interpretations as valid only under the unique conditions of a particular project at a particular time and place. It is more likely to be discovery-oriented inquiry rather than
hypothesis-testing research (Chenail, 1994). Qualitative research may or may not

be self-consciously "praxis oriented"; that is, it may "combat dominance and push toward thoroughgoing change in the practices of . . . the social formation" (Benson, 1983, p. 338), and it may raise questions about the results of professional discourses about such things as mental illness, marriage and family dysfunction, gender and racial issues. This is its strength, which necessarily reveals its liability relative to traditional quantitative research. One can pin it down by designing standardized protocols, but doing so costs some of its spirit.

Both quantitative and qualitative research in the social sciences and mental health professions can inform clinical practice. If marriage and family therapy is to be viewed as a legitimate health care profession, we must provide information in a form that is acceptable to the institutions and agencies who fund our enterprise. While this is necessary, from the perspective of cybernetics of cybernetics and social constructionism it also provides support for the very ideas, institutions, and practices that may, as a function of the research questions that are likely to get funded for investigation, paradoxically create increasing incidence of "mental illness" and marriage and family "dysfunction." Harlene Anderson (1994, p. 148) addresses this topic as follows:

> *I favor research wholeheartedly. I agree it legitimatizes and is necessary for political positioning and economic viability. Research transforms speculation into "reality." I have no doubt that if researchers wanted to, they could establish the relationship between family variables and individual mental disorders and establish the cost-effectiveness of family therapy. Researchers, as observers, have demonstrated persuasively that they can find what they are looking for. But what do family therapists want to discover or prove, and for what purpose? What do they want to learn? Who is the audience they want to talk to and influence? What is the source of funding? Such questions influence the choice of qualitative versus quantitative research; it is not a methodological either-or.*

Indeed, the above discussion moves us further into the realm we call pathologies of epistemology, which we will examine in greater detail in the final chapter of this book. For now, we need to end this brief consideration of quantitative and qualitative research.

While generating much interest in a variety of fields, qualitative research has a rather underground feel to it in the same way that therapy from the cybernetics of cybernetics, postmodernist, social constructionist perspective also feels like an underground movement. Occasionally a qualitative research article does get accepted into major journals in the field of marriage and family therapy (Gale & Newfield, 1992; Hoshmand, 1989; Moon et al., 1990) and some reports utilizing both qualitative and quantitative research protocols have found their way into professional journals (Joanning, Newfield & Quinn, 1987; Jacobson, Schmaling, & Holtzworth-Munroe, 1987). However, research from and theorizing about qualitative approaches generally is not as readily available as quantitative research reports. Therefore, we have provided a list of suggested readings in qualitative research at the end of this chapter.

We move at this point to issues of causality, observation, and objectivity as well as to a further consideration of the ramifications of a cybernetic perspective and the meaning of research consistent with this paradigm.

A Systems View of Research

The meaning and validity of research in the tradition of logical positivism is described by the systemic perspective as inconsistent on many counts. Particular areas of concern include the following: (1) it is more appropriate to speak of a multiverse (many viewpoints) than of a universe (a single objective reality); (2) if you must speak of causes, you must refer to the multiple causes that can be discerned relative to the frame of reference used in making observations; (3) rather than focusing on subunits, the whole system, or the larger context, must be the unit of analysis; (4) the concept of independent variables influencing and affecting dependent variables describes a linear notion of causality; and (5) traditional research models offer little help in understanding the complexities of human systems.

From the systemic perspective these objections are valid, and yet the issue of alternatives to traditional research models remains since few have been forthcoming (Gurman, 1983a; Schwartz & Breunlin, 1983). Perhaps this may be explained, at least in part, by the fact that while there are many critics of the logical positivist-empirical tradition of research, alternatives to this research paradigm are often viewed as doing something other than science. In this regard we are reminded of a conversation that Richard Schwartz (Schwartz & Perotta, 1985) had with his father, an M.D. who had authored "many medical papers." After reading an article written by Schwartz as well as other articles in the journal in which the article was published, the senior Schwartz commented, "By the way, I looked through some of the rest of the articles in that issue of your journal. You know, there's a lot of bullshit in your field" (p. 29).

Indeed, from the tradition of logical positivist-empirical research, what does not measure up to this model is considered by people in the field, and certainly by others whose science is more rigorous in adhering to the logical positivist-empirical tradition, as inferior. Accordingly, the research model of classical physics has become a part of the received view and has become the preferred, if not the only, way to make valid knowledge claims.

Koch (1976) notes that "at the time of its inception, psychology was unique in the extent to which its institutionalization preceded its content and its methods preceded its problems" (p. 485). That is, previous entries into the scientific domain qualified for inclusion only after the acquisition of a recognized and respected body of knowledge. For example, it took several hundred years for physics to acquire the status of a university discipline.

One could speculate on the difference it might have made if psychology's content and problems had preceded its methods. What would a human "science" have looked like? What would its problems have been? What would we know about people and societies if we were not constrained by the methods of classical physics? We might have asked, Are people machines? Is the machine metaphor appropriate? Are the assumptions of a mind/body dualism and of nature as "out there," independent of mind (which is not matter), valid in the study of people? Of course, we can't know that the outcome would have been different, but we suspect it might have been.

Even now a strong argument can be made that people are differnent in that they are not matter and are not reactive; instead, they are active agents. Thus, Bronfenbrenner (1979) notes, "The child's evolving phenomenological world is truly a construction of reality rather than a mere representation of it" (p. 10). Kelly (1955) saw people as scientists trying to understand, predict, and control their worlds in a manner not unlike the professional social scientist. Indeed, the recognition of the perverseness of people as subjects in research (hence the reason for designing studies that involve deception or attempts to mask the true purpose of the research from the subjects) led to an effort to get them to behave more like matter. Thus, the "subject as scientist" and the "experimenter as scientist" can be viewed as engaged in a dance to "psyche" each other out. Watzlawick, Beavin, and Jackson (1967) provide an example that illustrates our belief that research on things and research on living creatures may be of a very different order:

> *If the foot of a walking man hits a pebble, energy is transferred from the foot to the stone; the latter will be displaced and will eventually come to rest again in a position which is fully determined by such factors as the amount of energy transferred, the shape and weight of the pebble, and the nature of the surface on which it rolls. If, on the other hand, the man kicks a dog instead of the pebble, the dog may jump up and bite him. In this case the relation between the kick and the bite is of a very different order. It is obvious that the dog takes the energy for his reaction from his own metabolism and not from the kick. What is transferred, therefore, is no longer energy, but rather information. (p. 29)*

People also seem to violate another of the assumptions of the logical positivist-empirical tradition. That is, they are not constant, static, and absolute phenomena. By the very process of participating in an experiment, they probably are different and may no longer be where the results of the research suggest they are. Standards for ethical conduct of research recognize this phenomenon. And methodologists seek control for this so-called nuisance factor.

In contrast to psychology, the field of systems theory and family therapy is criticized because its content has evolved through rampant theory building and claims for validity without research evidence in support of these claims (Gurman, 1983a). Indeed, Kuhn (1970) suggests that the emergence of a new paradigm, such as the systemic/cybernetic perspective might be, also implies the emergence of a methodology logically consistent with the paradigm. Gurman (1983b) and Kniskern (1983) have suggested with some justification that we have the methodology of logical positivism that can be used appropriately in research on family therapy. Certainly this is true if we are satisfied with punctuating only one arc of a relationship. In terms of the people who might consume such research—students, clinicians, teachers, and policy makers both inside and outside the field of family therapy—the positivist-empirical model has credibility as it is a part of the received view of our culture, which not coincidentally is a high-tech society. It might therefore be expedient to use the traditional model to serve the political purpose of advancing our field. To do so, however, may serve to reinforce this model and thus detract from the potential usefulness of helping the society evolve another paradigm that might become the received view.

According to Gurman (1983a), it is an "ethical imperative" that we demonstrate the efficacy of our treatment models before endowing them with more certainty than current findings warrant. Another ethical imperative might be to seek to be logically consistent within ourselves and our paradigm, and to let research methods evolve, be used, and be published even in the face of the inhospitable charges of our research as inferior. There are other methodologies available to family therapy/systemic researchers. However, they are imprecise, they are ambiguous in their results, and they do not lead to certainty—as they should not.

What seems clear, however, is that research in the logical positivist-empirical tradition will certainly continue to be preferred despite the existence of alternatives that may be more compatible with the postmodernist/constructionist tradition. For example, Lather (1986) suggests the implementation of studies that have up-front political agendas and include the subjects of investigation in the process of generating knowledge. This is Paolo Freire's "empowering," or participatory, ethnographic research. It would have subjects collaborate on the meaning to be ascribed to the observations of scientists, thereby empowering the subjects to participate in the creation of the realities through which they experience their lives. Qualitative and ethnographic research in various forms are alternatives that have stirred up considerable debate (Moon, Dillon, & Sprenkle, 1990; Atkinson, Heath, & Chenail, 1991; Cavell & Snyder, 1991; Moon, Dillon, & Sprenkle, 1991). Process research might also include conversation analysis (Gale, 1991) or discourse analysis (Chenail, 1991).

Research in the logical positivist-empirical tradition will continue to be preferred for a variety of reasons, the foremost being that it is logically consistent with the ideology of Western cultures and therefore remains the method of choice for making valid knowledge claims in most scientific disciplines. Research in this tradition has a higher probability of being published and having grant applications funded. It is the model with which consumers of our services are familiar and in which they have faith, regardless of whether or not this faith is justified.

However, there are many issues that will not be resolved in debates about the validity of qualitative versus quantitative research. That is, the idea of "objective" knowledge no longer exists when a second-order cybernetics, constructionist position is assumed. Similarly, linear causality also self-destructs and with it the concept of etiology. Further, while we may continue to equate the explanations we use in successful treatment with discoveries of the cause, perhaps the more important question is, How do we appropriately study ourselves and the systems of which we are necessarily a part? For we are necessarily our own subject matter. Clearly, one cannot transcend oneself, and "no matter what modes of perception or what sorts of world interpretation he chooses, they are still his own" (Seidler, 1979, p. 52). In effect, we do not have a human science; we have a science of our descriptions of ourselves.

We believe that through the discourse of therapy and the practice of normal science we inevitably participate in creating people's experience of themselves. That is, people experience themselves and internalize and reify the explanations offered by both therapist and scientist. This is problematic to the extent that we as designers of human experience communicate our explanations as "discovered," consistent with what is suggested by the observer-separate-from-observed paradigm. Both scientists and consumers become caught by their thoughts and begin to take their imaginations literally. We conduct science according to what we believe and, thus endowed, the belief becomes both scientific and cultural reality.

We believe that our subjects/clients should participate in inventing their own explanations and experiences of themselves and their relationships. To us this is an important ethical issue that is not addressed in any ethical code of any human science profession. Perhaps the human sciences would serve us better by providing a focus for discussion rather than the form of that science. Perhaps we can learn from the new physics in a manner akin to the way we learned from and sought to emulate Newtonian physics.

The New Physics

According to Capra (1983), physicists encountered paradoxes when they tried to understand atomic physics in terms of classical concepts. Indeed, the observations and insights from quantum physics challenge the concepts of matter as matter in the classical sense, and mind as separate from matter in the tradition of Descartes's mind/body dualism. It challenged the idea that we can, through reductionism, discover any basic building blocks.

Thus, the conceptual revolutions that have occurred in the field of physics in the twentieth century have revealed "the limitations of the mechanistic world view and lead to an organic, ecological view of the world which shows great similarities to the views of mystics of all ages and traditions" (Capra, 1983, p. 47). That is, rather than using the metaphor of a machine composed of separate entities into which it may be reduced, modern physicists now view the universe as an indivisible whole comprised of dynamic relationships that include observers as well as their minds in that which is observed. The ramifications of this position are significant, for, as Briggs and Peat (1984) note, "the whole idea of a scientific experiment rests on the assumption that the observer can be essentially separate from his experimental apparatus and that the apparatus (in Popper's term) 'tests' the theory" (pp. 32–33). In the new physics, however, the concept of "matter" is challenged inasmuch as it has characteristics of energy and does not appear to be independent of the observer. Indeed, this has been referred to as a "looking glass universe" (Briggs & Peat, 1984), in which data changes with a shift in paradigms, and paradigms generate the seeds of their own destruction. Accordingly, observer and observed influence each other, and the activity of scientific study changes what is being studied.

This position seems to reflect the essence of Einstein's statement that the theory decides what we can observe. In other words, what we can see and what is "out there" is decided by the paradigm we have in our heads. Thus, what is in our heads becomes real "out there" and takes on characteristics of the paradigm and apparatus we used in our observation. We are looking in a mirror, and what we see is our own reflection looking at us looking in a mirror.

It is of particular note that this phenomenon was delineated in the so-called hard science of physics. Certainly it was not an easy concept for physicists to accept. Indeed, there are many physicists today who do not accept quantum physics. Werner Heisenburg made the following observation about his experience of being confronted with the dilemma of paradox and self-reference, or the looking glass phenomenon:

> *I remember discussions with Bohr which went through many hours till very late at night and ended almost in despair; and when at the end of the discussion I went alone for a walk in the neighboring park I repeated to myself again and again the question: Can nature possibly be so absurd as it seemed to us in these atomic experiments? (Capra, 1983, p. 76)*

The phenomenon of the observer and the observed taking on characteristics of one another and each mirroring the other is a difficult idea to accept. However, if in the world of physics the separation between matter (the observed) and the observer is challenged, such a notion perhaps more readily fits relationships between people, for here we are more likely to acknowledge the active agency of individuals in interaction whereby each transforms the other by being in relationship. Thus, the ultimate in paradox and self-reference is that we study ourselves. Indeed, pieces of this phenomenon are found in folk wisdom: "Pick your enemies carefully for you will become like them." Minuchin (1984) also refers to the transformational power of the metaphor by which a thing is called: "Through magic incantations the named lose their own shape, and become more and more what they're called" (p. 50). From the perspective of quantum physics and, perhaps, of research with people, "things" have never had and do not have their own shape; they are what they are called.

Implications for the Social Sciences

If this phenomenon observed in the world of the new physics is accurate, and if we assume it may fit the world of psychology, the implications for the mental health profession are profound. Subjectivity, or the values and biases of the researcher, can no longer be treated simply as nuisance factors. If the theories and paradigms we use transform rather than merely describe, then we don't just study people, we influence who they are and what they might become, and vice versa. This issue raises important ethical questions for many of the activities of mental health professionals and social scientists, some of which we have just discussed in the previous section. We will discuss nonresearch issues in the next chapter and confine ourselves here to implications for social science research in terms of ethics and practice.

Both the new physics and systems theory challenge fundamental assumptions in the logical positivist-empirical science derived from classical physics. Among these challenges are the following:

1. A reality may exist independent of us, but we cannot know that reality.
2. The reality that exists for us and the reality we can observe is relative to the theory we use as a metaphor for that reality.
3. What we can observe is a function of the means (instruments, tools, and machines) we use to measure the phenomena of interest (phenomena that exist and are meaningful) and of our theories, which suggest what might be "out there."
4. Reality is a dynamic, evolving, changing entity.
5. To observe a phenomenon is to change the nature of the phenomenon observed.
6. Phenomena observed take on characteristics of the theory or model used to guide and systematize the observations.
7. The appropriate unit of analysis is not elementary parts but relationships, which should be the basis of all definitions.

Descartes's vision reflected a belief that science deals in certainty. This vision has given way to the notion that all the concepts and theories we use to describe nature are limited and that the best we can hope to achieve are "approximate descriptions of reality" (Capra, 1983, p. 48). Descartes's optimism and certainty have been replaced by uncertainty. Elementary particles are not elementary in the fundamental sense of Newtonian physics, but are meaningful only in relationship to the whole. That is, *part* is inseparable and meaningless out of the context of the *whole* in the way that the concept *dark* is meaningless without its identity member *light*.

Systems theory suggests a universe that constitutes one organism. In the purest sense of this perspective, we would not see parts or subsets of the whole. Our experience would be that of a total oneness with the universe. It would be akin to the cosmic mysticism described by Capra (1983). This is a world view in which concepts like power, control, environment, and parts would not have been invented. To systems thinkers, it is a random universe on which we impose order. The order does not lie "out there" waiting to be discovered independent of us; it is there because we believe it is there. Instead of "seeing is believing," believing is seeing. It is the theory that decides what we can observe.

From this perspective it is the cultures and ideologies into which we are socialized that define parts, cause, subsystems, differences, and a so-called ego experience of ourselves as autonomous, independent entities in a world separate from other creatures. Accordingly, cultures and ideologies give us concepts and theories to use to explain various phenomena. These theories and metaphors are couched in the language of the culture and are the basis for the organization of that culture. Indeed, we cannot not be socialized into a culture. Not surprisingly, the culture does not generally provide as a part of its socialization the message that what you experience in the culture is not what you would have experienced if you had been socialized into a different culture. Thus, the culture does not provide its members with an awareness that the world view into which they are socialized is *a* world view; the culture implies it is *the* world view.

Purists in systems theory prefer to say that we experience only the cosmic awareness of the whole. The not-so-purists concede that at the level of culture we do invent differences, isolate parts, and punctuate problems, values, and aesthetics specific to that culture. In fact, we have no choice except to live in a culture and to experience its unique way of organizing reality.

To participate in a culture and to communicate meaningfully with members of that culture there must be some consensus about the nature of experience relative to the culture's metaphors, constructs, and concepts. Similarly, to be therapists in a culture necessitates that we understand the world view of that culture (Frank, 1974). As family therapists, we often find that when we request the participation of the whole family in the treatment of an identified patient, we are proposing a radical departure from our cultural tradition. The systems theory that legitimizes our work with the entire family, or at least our thinking in terms of social system as context, challenges in a very basic way the concept of the individual as "mentally ill." On the other hand, systems theory and the culture influence each other; they cannot do otherwise. We find that family therapy theories reflect a bit of the language and concepts of the culture. At the very least this makes them more understandable. At another level, the culture sanctions our roles as family therapists and to a degree has included aspects of context in its conceptions of so-called mental illness. It is thus necessary for both systems theory and the culture to be tolerant of each other's alternative conceptions of the world. From the systems perspective there is less tolerance, however, of a lack of awareness that our cultural world view is only *a* world view.

To us, based on our own experiences and those of our students, it is essential that we be conscious of our paradigm, or *Weltanschauung* (world view). "You cannot claim to have no epistemology. Those who do so have nothing but a bad epistemology" (Bateson, 1977, p. 147). However, having an awareness of our paradigm is often uncomfortable. It is an experience of freedom, of paradoxically having no choice except to choose among alternatives arbitrarily. That is, one must live with uncertainty. There is no escape from this freedom.

We do not challenge the usefulness of the methodology consistent with the positivist-empirical research tradition. We do, however, suggest that like world views, it is but *a* way of knowing, not *the* way of knowing. It is our invention, our attempt to transcend our subjectivity by defining a specific protocol to make our subjectivity objective. Further, it is consistent with the paradigm in which it emerged. We would therefore argue for the potential of other equally useful inventions to guide our search for knowledge. We would insist that whatever methodologies we create be logically consistent with the assumptions of the paradigm we are using.

Your challenge in becoming a systemic family therapist involves learning and internalizing the alternative paradigm suggested by systems theory. A further challenge involves changing your conception of what constitutes research. Any paradigm, to be viable, must be logically consistent within itself. Many social scientists think systemically but simultaneously engage in research based on the wholly different paradigm derived from the work of Descartes, Newton, and Bacon, which is premised on a model of the universe as machine. The machine metaphor and the research methodology consistent with this metaphor are not consistent with the systems paradigm, just as they are not consistent with current models in quantum physics. Let us therefore briefly consider the kind of research methodology that would satisfy this requirement of systemic consistency.

Ramifications of a Cybernetic Perspective

At the level of cybernetics of cybernetics, we view systems theory as a metatheory. If we experience the world from this perspective, we do not discern parts or wholes and we do not experience ourselves as separate from the whole. Further, there are no problems to be solved. However, as Dell (1986b) notes, we tend to experience the world linearly, consistent with our cultural tradition. We also see cause/effect, we see parts, we discern difference, and we value—punctuating good-bad, moral-immoral, beautiful-ugly, problems-solutions.

Indeed, it is at the level of culture, the level of simple cybernetics, that we do therapy and conduct research. As social science researchers, we are members of a society that punctuates experience in specific ways. Accordingly, the paradigm of the culture provides the framework that defines problems. Thus, as a researcher or therapist, accepting for study or therapy the problem as defined by the culture typically means accepting a linearly punctuated, narrow perception of reality that is framework specific and is based on a limited view of the world. We commit what Churchman (1979) calls the "environmental fallacy":

> *It might be called the "fallacy of ignoring the environment". . . . In the broader perspective of the systems approach no problem can be solved simply on its own basis. In an even broader perspective, no problem is a problem independent of a framework of belief that defines it as a problem. Every problem has an environment, to which it is inextricably united. (p. 5)*

Assuming the validity of this perspective, systemic researchers seek to expand the boundaries of the research problem to encompass relevant aspects of the environment in which the problem exists and to expand the framework of belief to encompass more pieces of the systemic whole. By doing so they increase the probability that solutions to problems will be both meaningful and possible. Of course, this framework can be expanded to include the whole of the universe, thus transcending and defining the problem out of existence, in which case research per se ceases to be meaningful.

A parallel to systemic therapy might be seen at this point. The systemic therapist attempts to change the context of the problem as presented. He is thus consciously aware of the framework of beliefs in which the problem is conceptually valid. As such, a reframe, or an expansion of the conceptual framework, is a common therapeutic tool.

If the systemic researcher accepts the culturally defined problem and conducts research on this problem as conceptualized by funding agencies, then responsible report writing would include a description of the limitations of the research and relate it to the methodology employed. What we are suggesting is the delineation of an expanded framework. Such a framework would include relevant information about the environment in which the problem exists as well as alternative frameworks of belief that might define or solve the problem differently.

The assumption underlying such a research imperative is that conscious awareness of the problem as framework relative and environment bound is important to responsible systemic research. Research results have political consequences and influence social policy. Thus, social scientists are political activists whether they support the society's status quo or offer a different perspective of the culture or society. Inasmuch as systemic researchers have an awareness of the context in which they conduct research, and which sanctions their role as researcher, logical consistency requires that they acknowledge this awareness.

Systemic researchers, like systemic family therapists, do not impose absolutistic reality norms. They know these are not available to us as finite people without a "God's-eye view." Apparent contradictions are seen only as contradictions if they occur within the same context of reference. As systemic family therapists recognize that each family member sees and thus lives in a different family, given that each is coming from a different context of reference, so systemic researchers must view facts of their own and the research of others as relative to context, and assert valid, internally consistent propositions from within that context of reference. They responsibly limit their claims of "fact" to the context of reference used.

To reiterate, we do not challenge the received view of the logical positivist-empirical tradition as a viable way to know. Rather, our issue is methodological and ethical, and these two considerations are related. Our culture has accepted the received view and given it a certainty that perhaps it does not deserve. Goldman (1982) notes that "precision tends to be associated in people's minds with numbers and with experimental and correlational methods of research. However, there may be a spurious air of precision about those traditional methods and an equally spurious air of vagueness about the 'X' methods" (p. 88). Frederick Suppe (1977) writes that "the vast majority of working philosophers of science seem to fall on that portion of the spectrum which holds The Received View fundamentally inadequate and untenable" (p. 116). Yet, as Sarason (1981) indicates, social scientists are of, by, and for a culture, and our culture seeks certainty. The precision of which Goldman speaks fits our highly technological society and its hope that technology will provide the means to alleviate the experience of existential anxiety. However, the methodology of the logical positivist-empirical tradition creates an air of certainty it may not deserve. Indeed, Schofield (1964) suggests we may have given the impression, either inadvertently or not, that cures for the pathologies of unhappiness or the failure to be free of anxiety are known and that treatments are available. In addition, Koch (1981) accuses social scientists of "ameaningful" thinking couched in "method-fetishism" and "a-ontologism" and reminds us of Bertrand Russell's statement that "almost all the questions of most interest to speculative minds are such as science cannot answer" (p. 262). For Koch, "ameaning" refers to "a fear-driven species of cognitive constriction, a reduction of uncertainty by denial, by a form of phoney certainty achieved by the covert annihilation of the problematic, the complex and the subtle" (p. 264).

The related ethical issue concerns what Churchman (1979) describes as "disciplinary politics." Accordingly, through the process of socialization into the research tradition of a particular discipline, broad-minded students are transformed into narrow-minded professors. The idealistic search for solutions to large problems in the interest of the greatest good for the greatest number is often replaced by a focus on small problems within the accepted limits of the discipline. This focus is consistent with the mandate of the culture in which the discipline exists.

At the level of cybernetics of cybernetics, it is not possible to practice science on the *whole* we envision. Science is an activity we perform on parts of the whole that we arbitrarily distinguish as different. While parts are recursive and logical to the concept of whole, the parts we research are typically the parts, differences, and problems punctuated by the culture. This framework limits the range of relevant questions available to the researcher if she is to continue to be a part of the culture. Society would also have us provide definite answers to its questions. To do so may give credibility to our discipline in the eyes of others, but it belies the uncertainty inherent in our conceptions of reality and in the methods we use that purport to discover that reality.

A responsible reply to the cultural mandate to provide answers to the questions, to solve the problems, may be to reeducate the culture on the nature and limits of our knowledge. A part of this education might include providing the following information:

1. We don't know what is real. We don't have a God's-eye view of the world.
2. The answers we give to the questions posed are limited by the theoretical framework and the methodology employed to study the questions.
3. The solutions we provide, given theoretical and methodological limitations, are based on the study of a part, which is recursively linked to other parts comprising a whole. Because of our limited frame of reference, such solutions may solve a problem only to generate other problems at a higher order.
4. The phenomenon we studied is not the way it was before we studied it. It is different by the very act of observation.
5. Given the logic of our solution to the problem, as it was posed and as it was studied, the object of our attempted solutions will take on characteristics of the theory implicit in our model.

According to Polkinghorne (1984):

> *The activity of knowing is itself a human phenomenon. How can we turn the tools of knowledge-making on ourselves when we are the tool makers? There is no absolute point outside human phenomena from which to investigate. Moreover, the knowledge gained when we study ourselves changes the object that we are studying. (p. 427)*

Polkinghorne's statement reminds us of the question posed by Brand (1974) to Gregory Bateson: "What color is a chameleon on a mirror?" (p. 20). Bateson and Brand then speculated on the mood of the beast trying to disappear in a universe of itself. The looking glass universe of Briggs and Peat (1984), in the world of the new physics, points to a similar dilemma of trying to find ourselves in a universe of ourselves.

It is our conclusion that we can carry out our research on parts, as we probably will, for that is the reality of the political context in which our disciplinary science exists. This is pragmatic. However, the supposed precision of our instruments and research methods belies their relativity and inherent uncertainty, and is, for us, the aesthetic and moral challenge of research.

Thus, it behooves us to explore with the political, aesthetic, and moral leaders the questions they pose, considering with them the universe of possible questions that might address the problem. We might change the nature of the problem conceptually, or address the problem at a higher order of systemic/conceptual abstraction in which the problem self-destructs. If we did this, we might lose credibility at one level but gain it at another.

Again, we see parallels in this process to that of therapy. Clients come to us presenting their practical problems in living, seeking the pragmatic explanation, the solution. We can convince, persuade, assist them (if we have set the appropriate conditions in our therapy) with our confidence in what to us is *the* explanation, *the* answer, and *the* solution to their problem. This is pragmatic, but in Keeney's (1983) sense it is not "aesthetic," for it may lead to higher-order problems. We provide them with a pragmatic view based on the many theories of individual and family therapy available to us, but we do this with an air of certainty that our theories may not deserve. To us, "aesthetic" therapy would be a reciprocal, qualitative process in which the client and therapist form a partnership to explore at higher levels of abstraction the different pragmatic explanations available to us. The goal would be to evolve together with the client a higher-order solution to the problem as posed.

Indeed, what would a science of people look like if its content and problems had preceded its institutionalization and its methods? The unique characteristics of the people as objects of investigation necessitate modifications in the aims and goals of science. They may even necessitate a consideration of whether or not the received view of science is possible or desirable. We confront the paradox that the observer is the observed. Ours is a looking-glass universe, and it is through this vision that we may have discovered or created a universe that is whole.

Summary

In this chapter we have approached the issues of assessment and research from several different directions. We began with a brief history of research in the logical positivist-empirical tradition. We also described the process whereby psychology adopted this paradigm, the same foundation on which classical physics was built.

Five models for assessing and classifying families, which cut across the various approaches to family therapy, were delineated. Several issues related to the use of such models from a systemic/cybernetic perspective were addressed. These issues included the loss of information about specific families that occurs through the use of more general models; the potential that such models may be seen as describing reality or truth rather than as a map or guide; the fact that families may adopt the imperatives implicit in a model without awareness of other possible explanations; the possibility that assessment constitutes an intervention; the consideration that the model being used defines the nature of the problems observed; and the hypothesis that from another perspective a problem may not be a problem at all.

A summary of research on family therapy outcomes validated the general usefulness of this approach, and specific findings from this research were enumerated. We then noted some of the issues that emerge from a postmodernist, social constructionist perspective. In addition, many of the tensions that exist between the logical positivist-empirical paradigm and the systemic/cybernetic paradigm relative to research were considered. Thus, consistent with findings in the realm of quantum physics, it was postulated that the act of observation changes the object of that observation; that uncertainty may be inevitable; and that the universe may be a cosmic whole for which a mechanistic metaphor is no longer appropriate.

Conducting research from a systemic/cybernetic perspective requires consistency with the assumptions of this paradigm. Accordingly, family therapists and family therapy researchers are called upon to delineate the context of problems as well as that of their search for solutions. Finally, we must acknowledge our lack of certainty and specify the limits of what we can ethically claim to know.

Suggested Readings

Bogdan, R., & Taylor, S. (1975). *Introduction to qualitative research methods: A phenomenological approach to social sciences.* New York: John Wiley.

Clifford, J., & Marcus, G. (Eds.). (1986). *Writing culture: The poetics and politics of ethnography.* Berkeley, CA: University of California Press.

Crabtree, B., & Miller, W. (Eds.). (1992). *Doing qualitative research.* Newbury Park, CA: Sage.

Denzin, N., & Lincoln, Y. (Eds.). (1994). *Handbook of qualitative research.* Thousand Oaks, CA: Sage.

Gilgun, K., Daly, K., & Handeel, G. (Eds.). (1992). *Qualitative methods in the study of the family.* Newbury Park, CA: Sage.

Goetz, J., & LeCompte, M. (1984). *Ethnographic and qualitative design in education.* New York: Academic Press.

Goffman, E. (1974). *Frame analysis: An essay on the organization of experience.* Cambridge, MA: Harvard University Press.

Guba, E. (Ed.). (19). *The paradigm dialog.* Newbury Park, CA: Sage.

Hoshmand, L. K. (1990). Alternative research paradigms: A review and teaching proposal. *The Counseling Psychologist, 17*(1), 3–79.

Lincoln, Y., & Guba, E. (1985). *Naturalistic inquiry.* Beverly Hills, CA: Sage.

Mishler, E. (1986). *Research interviewing: Context and narrative.* Cambridge, MA: Harvard University Press.

Pearce, W., & Cronen, V. (1980). *Communication, action, and meaning: The creation of social realities.* New York: Praeger.

Polkinghorne, D. (1988). *Narrative knowing and the human sciences.* New York: State University of New York Press.

Strauss, A., & Corbin, J. (1990). *Basics of qualitative research: Grounded theory and procedures and techniques.* Newbury Park, CA: Sage.

Chapter *16*

Pathologies of Epistemology, Cybernetics of Cybernetics, and Family Therapy

As we have noted many times throughout the preceding chapters, people's experiences in therapy and the way they learn to think about themselves and their problems is greatly influenced by the theoretical orientation of the therapist. A parallel observation could be made that your experience of the field of family therapy will emerge in large measure as a function of the textbooks you read as complemented by the perspectives of the instructors, who in most cases participate in the selection of textbooks. As we prepared this third edition of our textbook we did so with conscious awareness that each textbook in the field of family therapy (indeed, any book related to a field) creates a unique vision of that field and cannot not be an editorial. A book can be seen as a metaphor, and every metaphor we use opens up new ways of seeing, thinking, and believing while simultaneously obscuring others. One reviewer of the first edition of this book noted, "The last two chapters of the book read very much like an editorial." In one sense, we could view the reviewer's observation as a criticism. On the other hand, we view it as a compliment for it is our intent that our editorial biases be explicit and that, in the spirit of second-order cybernetics and second-order therapy, we provide a semblance of the experience of a dialogue. A textbook is not a dialogue, but we want you to be aware that in our self-conscious editing of what we would include or not include and what we punctuated as important or not important, we were "dialoguing with you." Thus, a meta-goal for this book was to present a vision of the field of family therapy in such a way that you would have an epistemology about the field that has a conscious awareness of itself. For we believe that to provide an epistemology of the field of family therapy without a conscious awareness of itself would be to participate in the creation of what Bateson (1977) termed a bad epistemology.

Similarly, in a review of Keeney's *Aesthetics of Change* the reviewer noted, consistent with Keeney's perspective and yet clearly with tongue in cheek and with acknowledged bias, that the review informed the reader more about the reviewer than it did about the book. From the perspective of second-order cybernetics it could not be otherwise. And thus, either directly or indirectly, we have acknowledged this inevitable bias and have tried to be consistent within the framework of this bias throughout the book. Our goal was to provide a teaching/learning tool that would help students, instructors, and therapists to be able to think systematically and to translate this mode of thinking into therapeutic practice with individuals, couples, and families. The whole book, therefore, is in some sense an editorial.

We also are aware that there is probably a very large difference between our understanding of the systems perspective and what it is that you now understand. Your current understanding is only possible as it fits, or structurally couples, with what you already understood prior to opening this book. That is, as you began to read, you had an ecology of ideas that comprised your world view and anything new had to be filtered through this existing framework. Thus, when we "understand" another person, idea, or concept, we create meaning (Barnlund, 1962) according to the framework of constructs that we use to make sense of the world around us. Therefore, "it is not likely that any person can ever experience another's experience; he can only infer by the other's behavior what that person's experience is at any given moment" (Sieburg, 1985, p. 41). So, in understanding our understanding of systems theory, you must inevitably invent your own meaning, which necessarily includes your own bias. And your understanding of our book probably reveals more about you than it does about the book.

If this book had been solely about simple cybernetics, it would have been very easy to write and very easy to understand. At the level of simple cybernetics there is a "received view" body of knowledge comprised of philosophy, theory, and research, which marks the boundaries of the field of family therapy. Our challenge would then be to construct tests to measure your comprehension of the articulated content and thus the degree to which you have been appropriately socialized into the field.

By contrast, writing and learning about second-order cybernetics is much more difficult. There is no formal content "out there" that we and others have "discovered" and can thus share with you. Rather, the subject matter of second-order cybernetics is about you, about me, about you/me; about subject matters, about thinking, about how we know what we know (epistemology), and about what constitutes knowledge. It is more a philosophy and an ontology. And this difference between simple- and second-order cybernetics is where the difficulty lies. Indeed, second-order cybernetics remains almost an enigma. It challenges beliefs and practices in traditional mental health practice and research. To us it represents a paradigm shift or "scientific revolution" in the Kuhnian (1970) sense.

One shocking and controversial aspect of second-order cybernetics is its challenge to include yourself in your thinking if you are to be consistent with the assumptions of this perspective. To punctuate yourself as standing outside of and being a detached observer defines a different kind of relationship with the phenomenon you purport to observe. Another shocking and controversial aspect, which builds the bridge to constructionism, is the challenge to the idea that what we see is a mirror image of what is "out there."

From the perspective of second-order cybernetics, what registers for us as participant-observers is a function of our structure, or the framework of concepts and constructs in the ecology of ideas that is our personal epistemology. That is, we define (punctuate differences and distinctions) what we observe. Instead of the usual stance that seeing is believing, we are confronted with the idea that believing is seeing and are aware of ourselves looking in a mirror and of seeing ourselves looking in a mirror.

A third controversial aspect is the challenge posed to our thinking about ourselves as a profession. Consistent with the focus on the family as the unit of analysis, a political effort is under way to continue to define family therapy as a distinct professional identity and, perhaps, discipline. At the level of simple cybernetics this activity makes sense and is logically consistent with designating the family as the unit of analysis. However, this desired separate professional identity reflects a provincialism akin to what the early family therapists sought to overcome. Their work with families was countercultural and countertraditional relative to accepted practice in the mental health field. Our interpretation is that the efforts of these early practitioners were not undertaken in order to establish a separate professional identity but to expand the framework of concepts used by mental health practitioners and thereby to increase their effectiveness. They sought to include the social context of the so-called mentally ill as a legitimate focus of therapeutic activity in their treatment.

Perhaps the establishment of a separate professional identity is inevitable in that traditional mental health professionals have been less than open to the revolutionary concepts implied by systemic family therapy. Indeed, this response is not surprising, as Kuhn's (1970) model of the process of paradigm shifts suggests. The predictably hostile reception afforded the emerging idea of family therapy is reflected in two classic articles by Haley and by Framo. Haley's "Why a Mental Health Clinic Should Avoid Family Therapy" (1975) and Framo's "Chronicle of a Struggle to Establish a Family Unit within a Community Mental Health Center" (1976) document the resistance with which they were greeted. In each case their experience remarkably parallels Kuhn's (1970) description of resistance to an emerging new paradigm and Sarason's (1972) description of attempts to establish a new mental health clinic in an existing community context. (We think you might find it interesting to ponder the similarity between these articles and descriptions of the process of family therapy with a resistant family.)

But from the perspective of systems theory at the level of cybernetics of cybernetics, the movement toward a separate field and identity does not make sense. At this level, systems theory is not about family therapy per se. It is about individuals, families, communities, international relationships, and the cosmos. It is about epistemology, how we know what we know, the limits of what we can know, pathologies of epistemology. As a metatheory, it is a unifying framework in which no mode of experience or methodology is discriminated against. If simple cybernetics is countercultural, cybernetics of cybernetics is the paradigm shift and the revolution of which Kuhn speaks. It raises unanswerable questions. Carried to its logical conclusion, there are no problems in this world, there are no things more beautiful or moral than any other. Cybernetics of cybernetics does not punctuate parts and separateness, and when we in our rationality do so, it reminds us that our punctuations are arbitrary cuts not to be reified, and thus we are not to lose sight of our finiteness. At the level of simple cybernetics we can pose questions and find answers to the meaning of our existence. Similarly, we discover or create problems and attempt solutions. At the level of cybernetics of cybernetics we cannot.

Cybernetics of cybernetics confronts us with the limits of what we can know, with the idea that we cannot go beyond the limit set by our own minds. It presents the idea that we are one with, and not separate from, the universe (whether punctuated as things or other people), and that we fully experience freedom and responsibility as we define or create our own reality, arbitrarily choosing among alternatives. At this level we have no choice except to be free, but this freedom is painful, and while we can hypothesize that all people at certain times experience the full measure of this freedom, we also know that people are quite willing to give away this freedom at the level of simple cybernetics by deferring to the expertise of scientists, therapists, religious leaders, and assorted gurus.

The logic of cybernetics of cybernetics carries us to the level of existential meaning and purpose. In reminding us of our inevitable finiteness and freedom, and thus of a necessary uncertainty, we become aware that we create (not discover) the reality we observe. If there are problems, we have created them by inventing and trying to implement a particular political, moral, and aesthetic order. Likewise, because they are products of our imaginations and rational minds, they could also be disinvented to create a new order, although the new order would not be without problems. If we avoid what to Bateson (1979) were "pathologies of epistemology" by expanding to some degree the universe of possible relevant contexts, we perhaps can minimize what Watzlawick, Weakland, and Fisch (1974) characterize as inappropriate attempted solutions that become a part of and evolve into even worse problems. Thus, we also can minimize what Keeney (1986) suggests are higher-order problems.

In this chapter we will explore some pathologies of epistemology at the level of simple cybernetics that only become apparent when we view the world from the perspective of cybernetics of cybernetics. We will explore some of the implications for both therapy and living that can help us, if not avoid paradox, then at least be able to recognize paradoxes and problems that cannot be resolved when posed at a particular level of abstraction. However, it is important to reiterate that a problem-free world will never be available to us. The rational mind is limited and must necessarily deal with parts and logic. On the other hand, we are able to do what Bartlett (1983) calls "conceptual therapy." He suggests a pair of analogies:

1. *As human behavior at times becomes self-defeating and in need of psychotherapy, so sometimes do human concepts stand in need of therapy.*
2. *In somewhat the sense in which theories of psychotherapy express forms of therapy that are used to treat self-defeating behaviors, so is a general epistemological therapy for dysfunctional concepts possible. (p. 21)*

Albert Ellis (1962) evolved an approach (rational emotive therapy) that is conceptual therapy in the sense we use the term here, at the pragmatic or simple-cybernetics level. That is, Ellis's model, in either hard or soft form of delivery, challenges self-sabotaging beliefs by helping people examine their previously unexamined belief systems. In a similar manner, conceptual therapy at the level of cybernetics of cybernetics challenges certain previously unexamined beliefs and assumptions, which as defined by Bateson, are pathologies of epistemology at the level of culture and ideology. The implications of such a conceptual therapy for the practice of traditional science and therapy as we have come to know it are profound. We therefore consider some of these pathologies of epistemology (conceptual pathologies from the perspective of cybernetics of cybernetics) and their ramifications for therapy. This discussion will make more sense, however, if we precede it with a consideration of reality from the perspective of second-order cybernetics.

Mind and Nature/Stories

The bottom line for us is Gregory Bateson's "mind and nature," which to him were one and the same. Bateson noted that "the processes and structures found in human beings were also to be found in the rest of nature, and that the organizing relations within both were of the same stuff as stories" (Plas, 1986, p. 79). For Bateson (1972), both redwood forests and sea anemones have minds that are part of a universal mind: "There is a larger mind of which the individual mind is only a subsystem . . . in the total interconnected social system and planetary ecology" (p. 461). Further, we must think in terms of stories that are shared by all minds. Such stories establish the connections between parts, "the very root of what it is to be alive" (Bateson, 1979, p. 14). The concept of mind and nature is simple, and yet it is profound in its implications for our experience of self, of other humans, and of our relationships with other creatures and things in our world.

To speak of stories rather than reality means that truth, in the tradition of logical positivism, is no longer available to us. According to the notion of a storied reality, the form of our relationships with self, others, and creatures and things necessarily takes the form of the way we story ourselves and others. If we story the personality as residing solely within the person, we describe a relationship with a person who is independent of our participation. If we story the biblical "dominion over" rather than "stewardship" relative to nature, we create a very different relationship with the other creatures and things in the world. If we story a "survival of the fittest" concept of evolution, then we story a social Darwinism in which some cultures/creatures are superior to others. If we story either/or rather than both/ and, we establish polarities. If we create distinctions in our story, we can lose the more encompassing system that frames it, for example, predator/prey. Indeed, to "take the side of either predator or prey is to risk breaking a larger pattern of interaction," or ecosystem/species interaction, which "keeps the whole ecosystem in balance" (Keeney & Ross, 1985, p. 48).

Consistent with Bateson's perspective, second-order cybernetics is about stories, stories we tell ourselves and that we perform in the theater of life, which necessarily become our experienced reality:

> *Stories are habitations. We live in and through stories. They conjure worlds. We do not know the world other than as story world. Stories inform life. They hold us together and keep us apart. We inhabit the great stories of our culture. We live through stories. We are lived by the stories of our race and place. It is this enveloping and constituting function of stories that is especially important to sense more fully. We are, each of us, locations where the stories of our place and time become partially tellable. (Mair, 1988, p. 127)*

Howard (1991) makes the following distinctions relative to stories: "Life—Stories We Live By; Psychopathology—Stories Gone Mad; Psychotherapy—Exercises in Story Repair" (p. 194). Our stories are the houses, the families, the communities, cultures, nations, and cosmos in which we live. That is, we dwell in very different places relative to the stories according to which we operate. Howard thus sees therapy as a process of helping people to rewrite their stories and build new habitations. He asks whether he as therapist can help a fundamentalist client rewrite his story in a way that respects and allows it to remain a fundamentalist story, which ultimately is an ethical question. He notes, "I would no more engage a fundamentalist in therapy in order to move him or her out of a fundamentalist worldview than I would applaud a nonfeminist's efforts to undermine a feminist's belief system in therapy" (p. 195).

From the perspective of second-order cybernetics, the therapist engages clients to weave different stories or habitations in which to live their lives. The use of language, experimenting with different behavior, or providing different experiences for clients can be vehicles for challenging existing stories, perhaps by making clients aware at some level that the "real" world in which they have been living is but a story that has been reified. Thus, therapist and client co-evolve different coherent stories that will allow them to live meaningful lives.

Watzlawick (1984) asks, "What would the world of a person be like who managed to accept reality fully and totally as his or her own construction" (p. 326)? His answer is that tolerance would characterize the person, who would also relate to others according to this insight. A second characteristic would be ethical responsibility relative to the realities created by individual constructions. And such total responsibility would equal total freedom, for "whoever is conscious of being the architect of his or her own reality would be equally aware of the ever-present possibility of constructing it differently" (p. 327). Indeed, such people would be socialized into a paradigm that does "include a conscious awareness of itself" (Keeney, 1983, p. 13).

If people had an epistemology that had a conscious awareness of itself, they would be aware of the concept of a *weltanschauung,* world view, or ecology of ideas, which has been described as follows:

> *One does not choose to have a weltanschauung. It emerges and develops over a lifetime. It may change in certain respects but rarely in regard to its origins and bases, which remain silent and axiomatic. One's weltanschauung is more than knowledge and less than language. What one calls knowledge is largely a consequence of weltanschauung and not its cause. The knowledge one receives from others, and the way one receives and organizes such knowledge, reflects a view of man and the world. The infant and young child are unaware of this process but those responsible for rearing the child are quite aware that they are inculcating a way of viewing self and the world. But they, like the child, are unaware of how much of what they are trying to do bears the imprint of a particular weltanschauung. (Sarason, 1981, pp. 46–47)*

Pearce (1988, p. 48) also offers a narrative about the acquisition of a world view:

> *A social world view, one shared with other people, is structured from our infant minds by the impingements on us from, and the verifying responses to us by, other people. A mind finds its definition of itself not by confrontation with* things *so much as other minds. We are shaped by each other. We adjust not to the reality of a world but to the reality of other thinkers. When we have finally persuaded and/or badgered our children into "looking objectively" at their situation, taking into consideration those things other to themselves, we relax since they are being* realistic. *What we mean is that they have finally begun to mirror our commitments, verify our life investments, and strengthen and preserve the cosmic egg of our culture.*

As we pass on our weltanschauung or world view to our children, we might also have an awareness of some politically and psychologically "correct" ways of thinking that are hard programmed into us. One could think of these as ideas, stories, or values that comprise how we experience ourselves and others, our institutions, as well as other creatures and things in our world. In diagram form some of these ideas/stories/values are presented in Figure 16.1. The concepts included in the illustration of the ecology of ideas characteristic of Western Ideology do not comprise an exhaustive list. Indeed, it is doubtful that anyone can have a conscious awareness of all of the ecology of ideas/stories/values that comprise the weltanschauung of any society. Rather, we tend to become aware of aspects of our weltanschauung when it is shattered. Sarason (1981, p. 48) provides us with examples of

Representationalism

A determinate relationship between words & world

Ultrasolutions   The Work Ethic

Utopian Notions   Individual Autonomy

Responsibility/Freedom   Correct/true perceptions

"Be spontaneous" paradoxes   Unilateral Control

Survival of the fittest   Fall & Redemption Theology

Either/or thinking   Faith in Science/Technology

Separation of mind/body/society   People versus nature

Billiard ball causality   Objective, value free knowledge

Mental Health/Illness   Functional/Dysfunctional families

Certainty/Uncertainty   Normative psychology

Problems independent of values   Male dominant gender roles

Racial and ethnic superiority/inferiority   Separation of self/other

Appearance/reality   Subject /Object Dualism

Failure as moral weakness   Valuing Rationality/Devaluing emotion

Science as discovery of real reality   Observation without intrusion

The concept process   Singular/Unified Self

Searching for essences and universal truths independent of culture

FIGURE 16-1   A Map of the Ecology of Ideas Characteristic of Western Ideology

human experiences on the societal level that shatter existing world views: "Blacks being taken into slavery, Jews walking to the Nazi gas chambers, immigrants forced to go to new lands, American Indians uncomprehendingly facing white settlers, countless colleagues of Stalin's sitting numbly and dumbly in prison cells...." At a micro level, aspects of a weltanschauung might be shattered by the unexpected loss of a job, a divorce, the untimely death of a family member, or a healing that contradicts medical predictions. However, the ideas/stories/values presented in our illustration above represent (to us) some of the conceptual pathologies of which we may become aware when we think at the level of cybernetics of cybernetics or include ourselves as members of a totally connected universe.

By calling your attention to the concept of weltanschauung and the ecology of ideas/stories/values within which we live, we are trying to influence you to develop a higher-order awareness. That is, we believe that when you think and do things it is important that you have a conscious awareness of your thinking, the ideas/concepts involved in your thinking, and an awareness of the actions that logically follow from these ideas. This (to us) is the consciousness that a postmodern perspective provokes. It thus also provokes an awareness of reality as socially constructed.

This higher-order awareness is especially important in the education of social scientists and marriage and family therapists as well as other mental health professionals. We believe it is important to be sensitive to the idea that the received view of any professional group is socially constructed and is, to greater or lesser degrees, logically consistent with the socially constructed weltanschauung of the society that sanctions particular professional roles. Such sensitivity might influence therapists to question their own assumptions, stories, and values when "therapy is not progressing" rather than projecting responsibility for the lack of progress onto the client. The higher-order awareness of the relativity of "knowledge" would also temper the concept of therapist as "expert" whose word is superior and more final than that of the client. Further, such awareness would have social scientists and mental health practitioners see themselves "in the society" rather than see themselves "and the society." Indeed, such a perspective might influence and temper the "colonialism" of which Gergen (1994) speaks when describing therapists who do not respect gender, race, and ethnic differences. With our perspective on the significance of such issues as background, we proceed now to a consideration of some specific conceptual pathologies.

Conceptual Pathologies

Problems Exist "Out There"

Higher-order cybernetics suggests that there are no problems in the cosmos. It is a total, unified whole in which everything fits, is coherent, and makes sense. The problems we treat are the problems of a given frame of reference, or world view. If we did not want people to read, there would be no reading problems. If we did not have a framework that specified preferred gender roles, there would be no gender role issue or problems. If we did not value the traditional family (two biological parents and their children), we would not see divorce or single-parent families as problematic. The school dropout problem is intricately tied up with and logically connected to valuing education and enacting compulsory school attendance regulations and child labor laws. "Spare the rod and spoil the child" and "child abuse" are different problems, each sympathetic to different frameworks, and are contradictory only relative to the moral and aesthetic framework of the other.

The framework we use to experience meaning punctuates what is problematic and what is preferred. We are error-activated systems in that any framework at the level of simple cybernetics or culture necessarily punctuates good and bad, functional and dysfunctional, normal and abnormal. Cybernetics of cybernetics reminds us that problems and solutions to problems are framework relative. For example:

> *When a stick is partly immersed in water, it seems curved when one looks at it and straight when one touches it, but in reality it cannot be both curved and straight. While appearances can be opposed to each other, reality is coherent: the effect of determining reality is to dissociate those appearances that are deceptive from those that correspond to reality. (Perelman & Olbrechts-Tyteca, 1969, p. 416)*

When presented with such a phenomenon we seek to reconcile the difference, to tidy up our cognition and smooth out incompatibilities in appearance. We thus discern data that are significant and data that are misleading. For us, the stick cannot be both curved and straight. Yet, *in fact,* what we see is curved, and *in fact,* what we touch is straight. We want to see only one stick, yet both observations can be called fact. We now encounter the need for a good understanding of what a fact is.

The claim for the status of *fact* can only be made relative to a set of norms or standards agreed on within a given framework of reasoning. The typical response to the challenge posed by Perelman and Olbrechts-Tyteca is to *know* the stick is really straight. That is the *real* fact. We then develop an explanation to account for the *fact* that the stick we see is curved when immersed in water. The latter is merely an *appearance* of being curved. As we do this we are asserting a set of basic postulates of reasoning and it is from this basis that we assert our proposition. However, if we operate out of a different framework of reasoning we activate a different set of norms or standards to determine fact. Thus, we might also see the stick as really curved and explain away its appearance of being straight.

Therefore, what is an appearance from one framework may be a fact from another. The stick is, indeed, both straight and curved on the basis of sensory data consistent with the methodological mandate of the empiricist tradition. However, we yearn for the same stick, and we appeal to a higher-order explanation to get at the genuinely real stick. We seek to get rid of the apparent contradiction. A proposition and its negation cannot both be true. According to this principle, the stick is either straight *or* it is curved.

But a proposition and its negation can both be confirmed in certain theories as a function of the operation logically consistent with that theory. These are complementary facts and are only apparently contradictory when one does not consider the context of reference:

> *If it can be granted that there are numerous, distinct systems equipped to ascertain facts, formulate true propositions expressing these, and hence reach "objectively valid results," then we must also accept the fact that this view brings to our attention: that there is a plurality of sometimes divergent facts, and that the relations*

between certain of these facts will be relations of complementarity. (Bartlett, 1983, p. 129)

Thus, the assertion of contradiction, or conflict between the stick as bent and the stick as straight, can only be made from a framework of absolutist reality norms. Such apparent contradictions are not possible when we accept the doctrine of a plurality of essentially dissimilar frameworks as legitimate bases on which to make valid knowledge claims. If facts occur in dissimilar contexts of reference, it is not legitimate to judge them with the same criteria. Compatibility or incompatibility of facts can only be judged relative to whether the facts occur in the same or in different contexts of reference. In a similar way, the experience of a problem only exists relative to a given framework of reasoning.

One of the most challenging concepts to emerge from postmodern, social constructionist thinking is the idea that problems are socially constructed and are relative to the values and mores of the society. Recall Paul Dell's (1983) statement, "Clinical epistemology de-constructs pathology and leaves us to dwell in a world of our values" (p. 64). In other words, we don't treat problems; we treat values.

We also create problems by our attempted solutions to the problems depicted as needing solution. We tend to do this by "drawing attention to problems, shortcomings, or incapacities" (Gergen, 1991, p. 13). Gergen elaborates on this point:

> *To put it more broadly, the vocabulary of human deficit has undergone enormous expansion within the present century. We have countless ways of locating faults within ourselves and others.... In many respects this spiraling of deficit terminology can be attributed to "scientizing" of human behavior characteristic of the modern era. As psychiatrists and psychologists try to explain undesirable behavior, they generate a technical vocabulary of deficit. This language is slowly disseminated to the public at large, so that they too can become conscious of mental-health issues. As people acquire the vocabulary, they also come to see self and others in these terms. (pp. 13–15)*

Further, we create problems by creating unrealistic standards or what Watzlawick, Weakland, and Fisch (1974) call the "utopian syndrome" which may evolve into increased scrutiny of oneself and one's relationships. Barsky (1988) discusses this phenomenon in relation to physical health. He notes that despite improvements in general health status during the previous twenty or thirty years, the individual's sense of his or her own healthiness has declined. That is, while there has been a substantial increase in attention that individual's pay to their bodies, to the pursuit of a healthy lifestyle, and to attempts to reduce risk factors, there has been an erosion in the individual's sense of well-being. In other words, "The increased scrutiny itself amplifies discomfort and dysfunction and results in a more negative appraisal of one's health" (Barsky, 1988, p. 416). Barsky continues,

> *It is harder to feel confident about one's health when sensations and dysfunctions one had assumed to be trivial are portrayed as ominous, the herald of some hereto-*

fore unrecognized and undiagnosed disease. Feelings of ill health and disability are amplified when every ache is thought to merit medical attention, every twinge may be the prodrome of a malignant disease, when we are told that every mole and wrinkle deserves surgery. (pp. 416–417)

Barsky's observations seem relevant to similar efforts to reduce the incidence of mental, marital, and family problems, particularly through efforts at "prevention." Efforts at prevention make sense at the level of simple cybernetics, but become a part of the problem at the level of higher-order cybernetics.

The Map Is the Territory

The idea that the map is the territory suggests another pathology of epistemology. This pathology manifests itself when people do not have a conscious awareness that the framework or map relative to which they experience meaning is only one possible explanation or guide to the territory known as reality. The traditional view suggests that a thing is what it is called. Accordingly, there is a one-to-one correspondence between what is "in our heads" and what is "out there." Consistent with this belief, we tend to reify our concepts or constructs.

This lack of a higher-order consciousness in our culture, which admits to the relativity of our paradigms, fits very well with the idea that we can "discover" the real world by observation, a "real" world that exists independently of us. Indeed, this is an assumption of science in the classical Newtonian tradition. The framework of the culture thus is reified and treated as real in the sense of an absolute reality. Without the perspective that the world we experience is framework relative, we are doomed to experience problems and are limited to attempted solutions logical to the framework we are using. The lack of conscious awareness that our maps are not the territory necessarily leads to experienced contradictions when we impose our absolute reality norms on others (who do the same to us); hence conflict is inevitable.

Holding to a particular set of beliefs, or to an ideology (based on the assumption that such beliefs represent the right way, or the truth), will result in controversy when confronted by a similarly dogmatic, but contradictory, stance. The dispute between anti-abortionists and free-choicers, both of whom claim to know the territory without awareness of their respective maps, provides an example of such a conflict. Carried to its extreme, we find ourselves engaged in warfare. In either case, "paths of communication are blocked by mutually exclusionary, equally self-righteous dogmas that are accepted, usually blindly" (Bartlett, 1983, p. 26).

In daily living and in our work as therapists, the implications of committing the pathology of epistemology implied by the idea that the map is the territory has profound implications. We become single-theory people, with alternatives limited by our framework in the same way that our clients are limited by their frameworks. In the family, competing and rigidly held ideologies may resemble the kind of conflict we have just described.

In therapy we may understand the identified patient as "triangulated," "wanting attention," "scapegoated," "bridging the generation gap," "lacking structure," "devoid of nurture," and so on, consistent with the theories that offer the particular explanation. Indeed, each explanation is plausible. If we perceive that the map is not the territory, however, none of these metaphors describes the way the family really is. Rather, each description offers a possible story about the family and implies action alternatives to us as therapists. The seduction of success derived from acting on the assumption that the "generation gap has been bridged" and having the family make progress in therapy may lead us to believe that our explanation was "true"—the way the family really is. However, any one of a number of explanations, or stories, may be proved "true" through success.

The pragmatic usefulness of an explanation should not be equated with "true" in an absolute sense. Repeated success in using the same explanation may lead us to reify the explanation, which may become the explanation of choice for all families. Subsequently, in those cases where it is not a useful explanation (not successful), we may then project its lack of success on to the family, whom we may now label as not motivated or resistant, rather than on to the nature of our theory, or explanation, and subsequent action. In doing so, we have moved to a standard of absolutist reality. We want to know the real stick, the way families really are.

A reality may exist "out there," but we, as finite people, cannot know that reality. The reality that exists for us, the reality we can observe, is relative to the framework through which we filter reality. All explanation is metaphor. All explanation at the pragmatic level is simple cybernetics.

Defining Differences in Isolation

If we assume ours is a totally conjoined universe in which all events or phenomena exist in a necessary relationship to one another, then explaining a phenomenon as an independent entity constitutes a pathological definition. According to Bateson (1972), all phenomena should be defined in terms of relationship. No phenomenon has a meaning or identity in and of itself, but only in terms of its logical complement. We may punctuate a difference, but it can only be so defined relative to that from which it differs. Further, this punctuation of difference is arbitrary, given the fact that a relationship must exist in order for us to see difference. That is, although a figure may be punctuated as different, it must exist in a relationship with, and be a part of, its ground in order to be so discriminated. This is basic Gestalt psychology.

This pathology of epistemology logically follows from the assumptions of the classical Newtonian model of science in which the observer is seen as independent of the observed. Such an assumption, however, denies the necessary relationship without which the observed would have no meaning. That is, describing something "out there" of necessity puts us in a relationship to the thing by virtue of the process of describing it.

The same is true for the relationships between concepts and constructs (metaphors) used to describe the concepts. That is, a theory is a set of related concepts and constructs that exist in meaningful relationship to one another. Each concept or construct has no meaning in its own right. The relationship is one of complementarity and meaningfulness in context and only in context. In Freudian psychology, for example, id, ego, and superego are meaningful only in relationship to one another, and attempts to differentiate among them also punctuate a necessary relationship among them. This principle holds in any system that is logical and meaningful in itself. Thus, the logic of the rules of grammar define the different parts of a sentence as subject, verb, and object, which are part of the whole, defined as sentence, and are meaningful only in relationship to one another in that context.

What a thing is called makes a great deal of difference in terms of the relationship(s) implied by the particular metaphor. We do not relate to people; rather, we relate to the metaphors we assign to people, and in the process, we assign a reciprocal metaphor to ourselves and specify the nature of the relationship between us. We behave with people in a way logically consistent with the metaphor we use to describe them. Our relationships are thus characterized by logical complements to the metaphors that we as members of the relationship assign to each other. Examples of this phenomenon can be found in the names we assign to typical roles in our culture:

To define a role is to define a complementary role and thus a relationship, for their meanings are recursive. This phenomenon can also be seen in the actions that logically accrue to the assignment of a metaphor to define behaviors:

The pathology is to see difference in isolation rather than relationship between phenomena. Nothing has identity or meaning in and of itself. There is only meaning in context. Difference is not separateness—it is relationship.

Independence/Autonomy and Unilateral Control

Again, if ours is a totally conjoined universe and phenomena are meaningful only in relationship to one another, our epistemology is pathological if we attempt unilateral control over what by definition is bilateral or multilateral. Many interpersonal problems evolve from our acting on the assumption of the independence or autonomy of people who, in fact, are in relationship. People in relationship often attempt to change the behavior of others while they themselves stay the same. They thus attempt to gain unilateral control over the other in a way that maintains and escalates the pattern between them. In effect, they see the other's so-called undesirable behavior as independent of their behavior and do not recognize their part in defining and maintaining the very behavior they seek to change. Thus, people

- assertively attempt to get dependent people to be more independent;
- crab at someone for not being sufficiently loving;
- hit someone for hitting another person.

Our definitions of people necessarily define the nature of the relationship between us and thus define us as well. To be in relationship is to be, by definition, not autonomous or independent. Hence our different experiences of ourselves in different relationships. To define Jane as dependent or withdrawn without specifying the context of the definition or including ourselves as a necessary part of the definition is problematic. Indeed, our tradition of a trait-and-type psychology, in which the individual is the primary unit of analysis and is autonomous and independent, commits a pathology of epistemology from the systemic/cybernetic perspective.

You Can Do Just One Thing

The consequences of our attempts unilaterally to change one thing as an autonomous unit make us aware, sometimes painfully, of the relationships of the one thing to other things that define a whole. A striking example of this phenomenon is our experience with DDT. This chemical was designed and used for many years to eliminate unwanted insects. Insects were its target as defined by people. However, nature did not discriminate the limit defined by people. Thus, the insecticide affected plants and other animals and eventually worked its way into the human food chain. These too were targets. However, they were targets by virtue of relationship, not by virtue of being defined as the target. Similarly, in medicine we learn that certain forms of chemotherapy have side effects. But these are side effects only by limited human definition. The body does not discriminate between "desired effects" and "side effects." As far as the body is concerned, the "purposes" of chemotherapy for cancer are getting rid of hair and inducing nausea as much as destroying malignant cells. Similarly, in family therapy, if the story or the behavior of one person changes and the change is maintained, the nature of other relationships within the family cannot not be influenced. Such a change in relationship may include as one so-called side effect of the therapy its now being defined as a family of divorce. Thus, the therapist who promotes unilateral change in one family member without defining the client's behavior in relationship to other family members does therapy based on a faulty epistemology.

We define, and if our definitions do not include relationships, we risk upsetting the balance necessary for the existence of each of the parts and thus of the whole. We cannot do just one thing. Any one, supposedly insignificant thing we do in this totally conjoined universe is not independent of the whole of the universe. We may be hard pressed to see how our eating a breakfast of ham and eggs in St. Louis, Missouri, is related to what occurs in Hong Kong, but the assumption of a totally conjoined universe suggests that there is a relationship—there cannot not be a relationship.

Control Is Possible

Closely tied to the idea that we cannot do just one thing is the notion that we really can't control anything. The dispute between Haley (1963) and Bateson (1972, 1974) over the issue of control is not really a conflict. Control is an important part of Haley's theory of change. As we interpret it, control is a meaningful metaphor in our culture, and as such it may be a useful explanation of the dynamics between people in relationship who attempt to control one another unilaterally. It is a concept, or construct, in the world view of our culture.

Bateson's objection was not that the idea of control exists, but that it is a pathology of epistemology to believe that control is ever possible. Attempts to attain unilateral control over what by definition is bilateral or multilateral must fail, and failing to control creates higher-order problems, increasing attempts to control that are a consequence of trying to control unilaterally in the first place. Again, we face the interrelatedness of the universe, which seems to exist whether or not we punctuate it that way. To Bateson, control is a pathological concept that seduces us into a variety of activities that must not only fail, but also necessarily give rise to further attempts to control. This behavior is consistent with the illusion that control is possible. An example might be the transplantation of a heart, a surgical procedure which seeks to control death. We must then control the body's attempts to reject the foreign heart. The medication we administer to prevent tissue rejection has a so-called side effect of attacking the body's immune system, making bacterial infection highly probable. Therefore we medicate to control the infection, and so on. The example of DDT also fits this related concept.

Systemically, control implies changing the nature of the relationship that, from the systems perspective, always exists. Defining the family or the school as in trouble and seeking to treat either in isolation, assuming that their supposed problems exist independently of the context in which they necessarily and dependently exist, is an attempt to control a part, which can only be punctuated as a part on the basis of a pathological epistemology at the level of simple cybernetics. Similarly, attempts to control the welfare system without seeing the relationship of welfare recipients to the rest of society must fail. The illusion of control in relationships between people takes many forms, and it is reinforced by metaphors such as "managing your children," "raising a child," "overcoming resistance," and "saving the family," to mention but a few. A linear punctuation of events and the idea of cause/effect as well as the autonomy of phenomena feed the illusion. You can't do just one thing. Attempts to do one thing ignore the context, commit the environmental fallacy, and foster belief in the possibility of control.

We are reminded of an anecdote that Lewis Thomas (1979) relates. He describes a time in the history of medicine when most of the treatments were "sheer guesswork and the crudest form of empiricism" (p. 133). Thus doctors tried anything and everything to treat (control) diseases. Such treatments included "bleeding, purging, cupping, the administration of infusions of every known plant, solutions of every known metal, every conceivable diet including total fasting, most of these based on the weirdest imaginings about the cause of disease, concocted out of nothing but thin air" (p. 133).

The belief was that not treating the patient with something would inevitably be fatal for the patient. In the early nineteenth century, however, there was a gradual recognition that most of the then-available "cures" did not actually work and in many cases actually exacerbated the problem. Concurrent with this recognition was the "discovery" that "certain diseases were self-limited, got better by themselves, possessed so to speak a 'natural history' " (Thomas, 1979, p. 133).

Similarly, Bateson's (1972) classic article on and analysis of the Alcoholics Anonymous (AA) method of treatment suggests that the success of the model rests on the insistence that the alcoholic give up trying to control the alcoholism. Our interpretation of his analysis is that the idea of alcoholism as a thing that needs to be controlled and the idea that control is possible feeds the escalation of the phenomenon until it is supposedly out of control. It is the *idea* of control and the *idea* of alcoholism as a phenomenon in need of control that is the problem. Ironically, while AA is a very effective treatment, the so-called disease of alcoholism as a phenomenon that is beyond control logically hooks drinkers into proving to themselves they are in control and are winning the battle of the bottle. The questions used for self-diagnosis or diagnosis of others fuel the challenge; by not drinking in the morning or stopping after one or two drinks the person proves that she is in control. But of course, by that time the idea of control and needing to control is already in full charge. The idea of control as necessary and possible seduces and controls the person.

We wonder what the natural history of the supposed diseases of the breakdown of the family, the increasing divorce rate, and the crisis of the schools would be without attempts to control them. We wonder what a young couple would experience when they enter marriage if they were not bombarded with advice, either from well-meaning people or articles and books, and if they did not have to worry about their marriage working. We wonder how our attempts to control these "diseases" may inadvertently have contributed to the escalation of these "problems." We wonder how phenomena would be perceived if we had viewed these "problems" in the context of the broader society—filed our environmental impact statement or taken a societal history. That is, we might have seen that people are living longer; that World War II had an impact on gender roles that was irreversible; that the sixties increased our valuing of the individual; that we have increased our expectations of what is possible in a marriage; and that mobility has become the norm. Thus, we have evolved a context in which increasing divorce rates are not only predictable but logically fit. We suspect that conscious attempts to control and prevent failure may, paradoxically, increase the probability of failure. We suspect further, that if the "diseases" had been left to run their own courses, they probably would not have escalated to the present runaway degree.

We Can Just Observe

William Schofield (1964) calls our attention to a curious phenomenon of special significance to systemic family therapists. He notes that with an increase in the number of therapists, there is a corresponding increase in the number of clients, which is a strong argument for an increase in the number of therapists. You may already have guessed the next step—an increase in the number of clients, and so on. In effect, as the number of professionals increases, there is a vested interest in liberalizing the definitions of mental illness or family illness. Schofield addresses the issue as follows:

> *In essence, there is a problem of a reverse approach to diagnosis; we may define as mentally ill any person who does not have perfect mental health, and we may define perfect mental health in terms of such rigorous standards that it is a condition notable for its absence rather than its presence in a majority of the population at a given time. (p. 12)*

From the systems model, Schofield's observations are valid. We as professional therapists exist and can only define ourselves in relationship with our clients. We do not exist independently of the society. Our roles could not exist in our society without a complement, and that complement is our client. What we define as mental illness or family pathology is within our control as inventors of the categories into which we fit our clients. We cannot just observe. Observation is intervention. We do not discover—we invent.

We are faced with a phenomenon suggested by both the systems perspective and quantum physics, that not only are we a part of the society, but also that the phenomenon observed takes on characteristics of the model of the world we use to understand it. It is a pathology of epistemology to believe we can "just observe." It is also a pathology of epistemology to believe we discover "real" phenomena independent of our frameworks.

The theory decides what we see, and the phenomenon we see takes on our characteristics as observers. In our searches to understand human nature, we face the possibility that we are the inventors of our nature and that we professionals, by inventing theories that purport to be descriptions of human nature, may bring the human nature described by the theory into existence.

For example, if you are a psychoanalyst you must be concerned about the possibility that symptom substitution will occur if symptoms are removed without resolution of the underlying problem or conflict. On the other hand, if you are a behavioral therapist you may remove symptoms without fear of symptom substitution because your approach does not speak to this phenomenon. Whether this complication exists is thus a function of the theory used rather than of the human mind or human nature (Watzlawick, Weakland, & Fisch, 1974).

In Schofield's sense we can define "mental illness" or "family illness" in liberal or conservative terms. We can normalize or abnormalize people's experience. We can invent a human nature that is more benign than current conceptualizations by reinventing our categories. We can also reveal to those who consume our theories that the categories we have invented are not "real," but are merely maps. If we say our theories describe reality, we must take responsibility for participating in the development of our society's world view in that regard.

On the other hand, by communicating that the categories and the constructs and concepts described by our theories are arbitrary punctuations of difference and are invented and not discovered, we must assume a different kind of responsibility, for in so doing we would take away the certainty that people assign to our theories. We would thus replace certainty with the certainty of uncertainty.

We can let people evolve their own explanations of themselves, or we can invent theories of people that might contribute to the formation of a more just and fair society. We wonder whether our societal view of human nature, which is markedly pessimistic, would be significantly different if the cultural context out of which it evolved had been Rogerian rather than Freudian.

In therapy we may reframe a client's experience and give it a new meaning, thus defining the problem out of existence. We may move clients from a problem they cannot solve to one they can solve. We can let them evolve their own meaning, as some models of therapy suggest. However, it is doubtful that the latter is entirely possible, for therapist and client cannot not reciprocally influence one another. There are no random or meaningless events in therapy. The context of therapy, defined by seeing the therapist as expert and the client as having a problem, suggests that whatever the therapist does, the client will interpret and discern meaning because of the context. Remarks such as "Tell me about your family of origin," "How did you two meet each other?" or a selective "Uh-huh" or "I see" in the context of therapy all impose a framework and suggest that there is a purpose to the questions. By contrast, these same questions in the context of a friend's visit would mean very different things and would not be perceived as interventions.

Whether as therapist or as theorist, we cannot avoid this responsibility, and paradoxically the more we try to help clients feel responsible for themselves, the more responsibility the client may ascribe to us. Our role is that of socially sanctioned expert educated to deal with interpersonal problems. As a family therapist you may have felt this responsibility even more, for the metaphor suggested by systemic family therapy already moves the locus of the problem away from the individual and onto the social unit that is the family. If you are an Attneave, a Rueveni, or a Whitaker, you may redefine it as a problem that transcends generations within the family and even extends to other people who interface with family members. The systemic family therapy model is not immune to this value imposition. We have evolved models of normal families that are theory and culture relative. The systemic family therapy model does, however, help you to become consciously aware of the phenomenon we described. It gives you no choice except to see yourself as a part of the unit of observation, to define only in relationship, and to assume responsibility for the explanation you choose in order to explain the family to yourself and to its members.

There is a strong political tone to the categories in which we fit people. We can reinvent the categories we use. We do so in therapy as we reframe. We can do so at a more general level in terms of the theories we invent. For example, homosexuality is no longer included as a mental disorder in the *DSM IV*. Hysteria as a category was successfully lobbied against and transformed by feminists. Indeed, the selection of metaphor is crucial, and somehow we may need to label things in more benign ways. We prefer the old "melancholia" to "depression"; we also prefer Adler's "discouragement."

As therapists we reinvent the wheel for our clients each day. As therapists for our culture, we are a bit more pessimistic about our ability to be effective in this regard. We are of and in a culture, a culture that sanctions our roles to treat the problems that the culture defines for us. However, as systemic therapists we are at least called upon to consider the challenge.

The Paradox of Being a Systemic Therapist

In practice, what the distinction between the pragmatics of simple cybernetics and the higher-order cybernetics means is that therapists who have a conscious awareness of both levels face a paradox. In effect, we are faced with living a rather schizophrenic life, at least where our work is concerned; that is, at the pragmatic level we are mandated by the society that sanctions our roles to accept and solve problems as they are defined by our culture. Our general charge from the society seems to be to "help people fit," or in other words, to be more adaptive to the way we want our society to be, to fit the ideal model of a "normal" person or family for our society. Thus, we seek to help families and individuals be asymptomatic (normal) and productive (achieving and contributing) and to view themselves as autonomous, independent, responsible people. The assumption of the society is that the people who are not asymptomatic, who are not productive, or who project responsibility for problems onto others do not fit. Pragmatically, we can carry out this role without the conscious awareness of the pathologies of epistemology suggested by cybernetics of cybernetics. Indeed, the role of therapist is much easier, if less respectful, without this higher-order consciousness.

However, the perspective of cybernetics of cybernetics poses an interesting dilemma for the systemic therapist, for the logic of this model suggests that what is called maladaptive does fit. As an individual member's symptomatic behavior is a functional role in the context of the family, symptomatic family behavior is a functional role in the larger community as the family interfaces with other social systems (school, church, work, etc.). The contradiction faced by therapists is that by responding to the charge to help individuals, families, schools, or communities fit, or be more adaptive, we in essence can only do this by helping them become misfits, that is, behave in a way that is illogical to their context(s).

Further, once one internalizes the cybernetics-of-cybernetics perspective, one no longer sees the abnormal or dysfunctional. One sees normalcy in context. Whatever the behavior, it makes sense, it fits. What individuals feel is what they should be feeling given their experiences, beliefs regarding feelings, and social context. Maturana's structural determinism suggests that toasters toast—such is their organization. Schizophrenogenic families are structurally organized to have schizophrenics. Alcoholic families are families in which the complementary roles are comprised of both the alcoholic and the enabler. Each individual, family, community, or society is structurally organized to maintain itself, to do what it does. Thus, it may well be that, as suggested by Anderson and Goolishian (1986), it is the label attached to behavior (problem) that organizes the system.

Indeed, one can infer from the higher-order systems model that if societies had evolved paradigms and processes consistent with the ideals set forth by those societies, then therapy per se would not be a role in the society. A society evolves the role of therapist to deal with discrepancies between its ideals and the processes based on its paradigm, which the society activates to attain these ideals.

As we expose you to the contradiction implicit in the role of therapist when viewed from the levels of pragmatic cybernetics and higher-order cybernetics, we are aware that you may be uncomfortable and may be inclined to reject higher-order cybernetics. Certainly this is not a comfortable awareness. Pragmatically, you don't need cybernetics of cybernetics to be a family therapist. Indeed, we are aware that we may challenge your ideals and your basic motivations for becoming a family therapist, for we are suggesting that while at the pragmatic level you may be "doing good," at the higher-order-cybernetics level you may be contributing to escalating pathology in the society. All therapists do so, however inadvertently, to the extent that they sanction society's paradigm (and contradictions therein) as well as the social order as it exists. That is, at the pragmatic level, as we continue to enact our roles, we support the status quo. We feed the illusion of certainty and the status quo of existing social relationships and structures.

In society's charge to therapists to reduce the incidence of mental illness, family dysfunction, and so forth, we have not been successful. If anything, the incidence of mental illness and family dysfunction has increased. The higher-order systems model suggests that it may have increased as a function of our participating in the effort to reduce its frequency. Churchman (1979) suggests that to solve a problem, it is important to know the context of the problem. It is also important to know the ideology, model, or paradigm that defines the problem as problem. As systemic family therapists we learned to view the individual's "problems" in the context of the family. From the logic of the same model, it makes sense to view family "problems" in the context of the society. The problems defined for us as therapists are problems specific to a framework or ideology without conscious awareness of the epistemology. That is, the problems defined for us are problems that are decontextualized or restricted to a limited context, insufficient to solve the problem.

On the other hand, we can eliminate mental illness and family dysfunction. The first way is to agree with Thomas Szasz (1961), who suggests that mental illness is a myth. He defines it as irresponsible behavior. Higher-order cybernetics also suggests that we create a myth of mental illness by not seeing normalcy in context and by not seeing the pathologies of epistemology, which when translated into rules for living may lead to what is called mental illness. Either way, the behavior is normal. Indeed, the paradoxical approach to therapy normalizes or makes logical what is viewed as problematic. Given the rules of the paradigm by which people attempt to live their lives in the context of family or society, what people experience makes perfect sense. It may be painful, but it is normal in epistemological/social context. Thus, the second way to eliminate mental illness is to recognize that it is logical to context and therefore not pathology.

Watzlawick, Weakland, and Fisch (1974) pose two pragmatic questions: "'How does this undesirable situation persist?' and 'What is required to change it?'" (p. 2). In answer, we might say that we have the problems of "mental illness" and "family dysfunction" because we have invented the concepts and constructs and incorporated these into our world view. They will continue to exist so long as these concepts and constructs exist. We would not see these phenomena if we did not have such constructs as a part of our paradigm. They punctuate difference and are recursive to their identity members "mental health" and "functional families." We can get rid of mental illness by getting rid of these concepts and constructs or by redefining them. Family systems theory gets rid of these "problems" by making sense of, or seeing the fit of, symptomatic behavior in context.

There is also a third way to get rid of mental illness and family dysfunction. This way is akin to the first and is also logical to higher-order systems theory. This third way is to declare all people to be mentally ill and all families to be dysfunctional. By eliminating mental and family health we functionally get rid of mental and family illness. As we observe our society (as participants, of course) we see increasingly utopian expectations for individuals and families reflected in the popular social science literature. We see increasingly narrower ranges of normalcy, or in Schofield's (1964) terms, more liberal definitions of mental and family illness and more conservative definitions of mental and family health. What is experienced by our society as normal or abnormal and the relative range of each is suggested by the theories we professionals invent for consumption by the members of the society. This is rather like the problem of testing hypotheses in research: Do we want to risk committing alpha error or beta error? By the way we set our confidence intervals, we may reduce the probability of committing type-one error, but we increase the probability of committing type-two error, and vice versa. We believe we should increase the range of normalcy, with very, very conservative definitions of mental and family dysfunction. Of course, if we think we are "discovering the real reality" and not "inventing" it, this option is not available to us. That is, if we believe that nature exists independently of us, then we also believe that we can just observe.

Another dilemma for the systemic individual, marriage, and family therapist is posed by the question, What is your unit of analysis? What part of the totally conjoined universe do you abstract as the unit in need of therapy? We have abstracted many levels of systems, as illustrated in a map of a systems hierarchy presented in Figure 16.2 (Engel in McWhinney, 1989). In this map, the arrows between the levels of a systems hierarchy indicate that the flow extends in both directions. The map also includes our punctuation of a difference between the organismic hierarchy and the social hierarchy. However, by punctuating a difference between the social and organismic hierarchies, we also become aware of the connection between the two. This further questions the separation of mind and body, which has oriented and separated professional practices for many years. Thus, physicians tend the organismic problems and therapists tend the psychological and sociological problems. But, as the map suggests, they are not separate. Indeed, this connection may be better illustrated by Figure 16.3 (Engel in McWhinney, 1989, p. 60).

This connection also calls into question the issue of etiology: Is it mental? Is it physiological? or Is it embedded in the network of relationships? From the systems

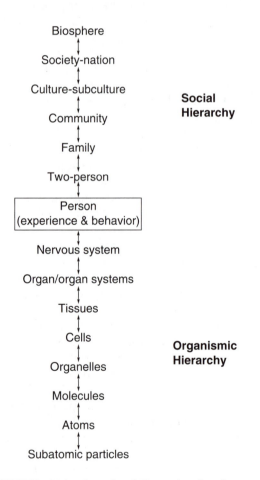

**FIGURE 16-2   Levels of Organization in a
Systems Hierarchy**

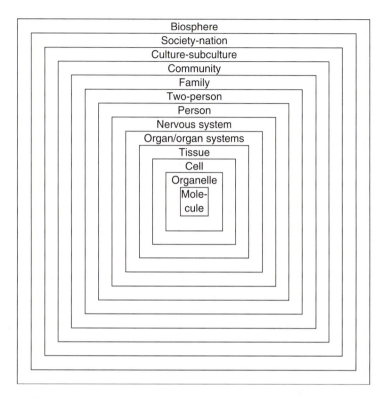

FIGURE 16-3   Continuum of Nested Natural Systems

model, the answer to all of these questions is Yes! By recognizing the research evidence relative to the connection between mind, body, and the social network, the field of family systems medicine (see Chapter 2) came into existence, and many family practice physicians currently are being trained in a manner similar to the training experienced by family therapists. Ironically, family therapists typically are not trained in seeing the connection between the organismic and the social, and few seem to have an awareness that as they help people deal with their relationships, they also have an impact at the organismic level.

But we stray from the question posed earlier, What is your unit of analysis? And yet we do not, for different professional groups, punctuate different parts of the hierarchy of abstractions described in Figures 16.2 and 16.3, and we are also aware that no level of the hierarchy can be understood by study of each part individually. For, according to Alan Watts (1972),

> *every individual is a unique manifestation of the whole, as every branch is a particular outreaching of the tree. To manifest individuality, every branch must have a sensitive connection with the tree, just as our independently moving fingers must have a sensitive connection with the body. (p. 72)*

While we may differentiate between fingers and the body, differentiation does not equal separation. And while the physical relations between human beings and the universe are different from those between the body and its parts, such connections exist.

The ideology of the society and its human science professionals, out of which emerges the normative, classifying framework described by White and Epston (1990), does not provide an awareness of the connection that the systems perspective would have us see. Thus, whatever unit of analysis is the focus of treatment, it represents an arbitrary cut and is but a part of the whole, which cannot be understood by study of that part individually. As Sluzki (1985) notes: "We treat the family because we see the family because we evoke the family with our models of inquiry" (p. 1). In fact, individuals live in complex, overlapping, changing networks of which the family is a part. It is we who impose a boundary around the family as a function of the questions we ask and the rules according to which we operate. Minuchin (1986) frames it somewhat differently:

> *What if the woman has married the kitchen, the children, the welfare system, her analyst, her church, or her bridge club? What if the man has married his workplace, the military, his psychoanalyst, the AA, or the golf club... What if the couple functions as a confused reconstituted family, each subsystem unable either to integrate or to separate? Do we family therapists tackle the "family" that members experience, or do we insist that (since the only system we know is governed by our own concept of family), they divorce their nonparadigmatic partners? (p. xii)*

But even the concept of family experienced by its members is limited by the concept of family as defined by the ideology of the society and its human science representatives.

What is our unit of analysis? From the perspective of second-order cybernetics it is the unit we create through our abstractions. The unit of analysis is limited only by the scope and vision of our imaginations as we invent and see connections that may be important for the client system. Systemic family therapy is not about who is in the room. It is about our way of thinking and the kind of reality we wish to create. This is Bateson's "mind and nature." It is mind in relationships with ourselves, others, and other creatures and things in the world. All are of the same substance. And that substance is the idea of story.

There are many reasons why you may not want to be a systemic family therapist at the level of higher-order cybernetics. To do so is to assign to yourself a share in the responsibility for participating in developing the problems experienced by our society, which you must subsequently attempt to solve. Higher-order cybernetics is not an easy level at which to think, live, and work, particularly for social scientists. From this perspective, social science is public philosophy and cannot be value free. We are of and in our society. To live in it uncritically and without conscious awareness of the contradictions in the paradigm of the society, and the social order that logically fits the paradigm, is to support the status quo.

Falzer (1986) suggests that the cybernetics of cybernetics perspective cannot be demonstrated to be a valid perspective. However, we suggest its validity is demonstrated each day in each person's life as attempts to do just one thing demonstrate the interconnected universe that Bateson (1972), Bronowski (1978), and Keeney (1983) propose. Higher-order systems theory is more than a theory about people in social systems. It is about the epistemologies that serve to guide action within social systems, for "cybernetics focuses on mental process" (Keeney, 1986, p. 270). Historical data suggest that higher-order problems do emerge when we attempt pragmatic solutions to problems without examining the underlying framework that defines the problem as a problem, thus having a limited awareness of the context in which the problem exists. A frequently cited example is that of Prohibition, which was a pragmatic solution to the drinking problem. Prohibition not only did not solve the drinking problem, but it also helped to create an increase in the number of criminals and perhaps contributed to the development of organized crime.

We are also confronted with evidence of the validity of Maturana's structural determinism in that attempts to intervene without respect for and accommodation of the individual's or family's internal organization and epistemology simply will not be meaningful. Nor can we escape the existential questions, the questions, according to Koch (1981), that are the most important to people, by losing ourselves in pragmatics. Simple cybernetics, as Watzlawick, Beavin, and Jackson (1967) suggest, is not capable of delving into existential questions. Higher-order cybernetics, on the other hand, suggests that we cannot avoid the existential and meaningful questions of living. These are the sine qua non of what it means to be a human being. Higher-order cybernetics confronts us with our finiteness, with uncertainty, and with the demand to define our own essence.

> *It is not that man must learn to live with the paradox—the human being has al-*
> ways *lived in this paradox or dilemma, from the time that he first became aware of the fact that he was the one who would die and coined a word for his own death. . . .The awareness of this, and the acting on this awareness, is the genius of man the subject. (May, 1967, p. 20)*

Teaching the Cybernetic Perspective

As we wrote this book we were continually reminded of the difficulty of describing cybernetics of cybernetics and of the inevitable struggle that new visitors to this territory would experience in reading about it. Throughout, we have punctuated differences where there were none except as we or others have chosen to see them for heuristic or practical purposes. We have confronted the frustration of our language, which limits us to use metaphor to describe metaphor and whose rules of grammar require that sentence structure be linear. That is, a book speaks to the rational mind. It seeks to explain something different and to communicate its difference in a way that is meaningful and that builds bridges to new ideas through the framework of concepts you already know. This task is more challenging when the concepts you already know and those we seek to explicate are qualitatively different.

In the same way, we are challenged by the task of teaching family therapy within a university context. In order to be consistent with our perspective, and thus create an appropriately meaningful experience for our students, we would like to design a curriculum that would look very different from the traditional format (just as this book was probably very different from the textbooks you generally encounter). Ideally, we would provide a nonevaluative setting that includes classes in such areas as biology, history, linguistics, philosophy, physics, psychology, semiotics, and theology as well as course work focused on the family and therapy. Our choice would be to work as a team with teachers from these other fields who shared an awareness that the world (and knowledge) is not described by arbitrary divisions into particular disciplines. We might therefore begin each class with something like the following statement by Casteneda (1974):

> *The first act of a teacher is to introduce the idea that the world we think we see is only a view, a description of the world. Every effort of a teacher is geared to prove this point to his apprentice. But accepting it seems to be one of the hardest things one can do; we are complacently caught in our particular view of the world, which compels us to feel and act as if we know everything about the world. A teacher, from the very first act he performs, aims at stopping that view. Sorcerers call it stopping the internal dialogue, and they are convinced that it is the single most important technique that an apprentice can learn. (p. 231)*

We would hope such an experience would create a context of confusion in which different differences might be punctuated, and a logical response might be to suspend rationality in the spirit of eastern Zen philosophy and of mysticism. Ideally, all concepts would be defined in terms of relationship, as suggested by Bateson (1972). Concepts would also be identified as concepts and not reified. Students would experience no choice except to formulate their own integrations. This would be an experience in moral philosophy as a part of the education of social scientists. Such social scientists would become increasingly aware of their epistemologies and the value and arbitrariness of their epistemologies.

We would also include in our curriculum a section on stories and storytelling, for a question we are frequently asked is, "If we would be second-order cybernetics therapists, where do we get our alternative stories?" As a partial answer to the question, it is important to realize that the therapist is not necessarily the source of the alternative story. At the level of second-order cybernetics, the preferred metaphor for the therapy process is a co-evolving, recursive system between therapist and client(s) who reciprocally perturb each other. It is out of this mutual perturbation process that a new story evolves. Indeed, if you are feeling the sole responsibility to provide an alternative story that structurally couples with the existing structure of the client, your therapy is more consistent with first-order cybernetics (i.e., you are thinking from the observed rather than the observing system perspective).

As to the source of alternative stories, if you work in a manner similar to Andersen, O'Hanlon, de Shazer, White, or Goolishian, you have an awareness that there are many client experiences that are not a part of the complaint-saturated narrative story that clients bring to therapy. Thus, by the nature of the questions you ask in your dialogue, you can call attention to those aspects of the client's life that have not been included in the presenting story. By eliciting these other events and by asking the client how he explains these events, you lay the groundwork for an alternative story derived from the client's lived experience. Another important aspect of stories relative to the client/therapist dialogue emerges from the concept that you cannot step into the same stream twice. By analogy we state: you cannot tell the same story in exactly the same way twice. Each telling of the story transforms the story. Further, the telling of the story changes relative to the audience. As therapist you can take the form of different audiences by the questions you ask and the aspects of the story upon which you focus. (As an experiment, try to tell a story of an experience in your life to at least three different persons.)

Another source of stories lies in the formal education you received to become a family therapist, social worker, psychologist, counselor, or pastoral counselor. As a part of your education you were required to learn a set of theories, or what we call stories, written in the modernist/structuralist, first-order cybernetics tradition. One might call them competing versions of "truth." Thus, a source of stories can be Freud, Jung, Adler, transactional analysis, etc., consistent with the individual psychology pie, and Minuchin, Bowen, Satir, Nagy, etc., consistent with the family therapy pie. However, while many of these theories/stories are rich in metaphor and contain many constructs that can be used in a therapeutic conversation, many of them also pathologize; that is, they provide alternative descriptions of what is wrong. Thus, we would add the proviso that you be aware of substituting another pathology-saturated story for the client's complaint-saturated story. At the same time, some constructs from these theories can be a bridge to evolving a more useful alternative story if the client's story includes aspects of the above theories. Indeed, according to the concept of structural coupling, this may well be an essential part of the therapeutic process.

Our students and supervisees often note that they are not good storytellers. One reply to this is, "You are much better than you think you are. You just do not describe what you do when you converse with another as storytelling." Another reply is that clients can evolve and validate a different story through means other than the active process of storytelling. An operant or paradoxical assignment to be performed outside of therapy can provide the client with an experience of self that may contradict the complaint-saturated story. A carefully constructed assignment that the client carries out can also facilitate the development of a story about herself as a person who can change. It has been said that a picture is worth a thousand words. A transform of this idea is that an "experience is worth at least a thousand words." Through their experience of the *how* you are with them, (i.e., treating them with respect and normalizing their experience as logically consistent with their story and context), clients can experience themselves differently, thus planting the seeds of an alternative story.

There are many sources of stories other than those mentioned above. Your imagination, which may have been disciplined by the process of formal education, can be stimulated by poetry, novels, biographies, and by visiting art galleries, attending theater performances, and attending different churches. It can be augmented by listening to people of different cultures, races, and socioeconomic levels. Your imagination can also be enriched by experiencing a quiet walk in the woods or among a crowd on a busy street. Your imagination is limited only by your imagination. While each new adventure may be difficult for you, it can help you develop a story about yourself as a person with imagination.

We suggest further that an education for social scientists that does not include helping them develop a conscious awareness of their epistemology and its arbitrariness is an incomplete education. How we teach (the process) should be logically consistent with what we are teaching (the content). Thus, the creation of a context that supports the learning of a systemic/cybernetic epistemology is essential. Additionally, it should be required that information about families and family therapy be balanced by information about individuals and individual psychology; that knowledge of a cybernetic perspective be balanced by knowledge of the positivist-empirical view of science; that teaching about contexts be balanced by a consideration of the other contexts in which students and faculty exist; and that the educational process facilitate the integration of information and the creation of a reality in a way that is most meaningful or useful for each as well as most supportive of the whole. The latter aspect naturally requires a consideration of the parameters, or contextual markers, of the setting in which the educational process occurs.

In Conclusion

As we come to the end of our journey together, we feel it is important not only to summarize its highlights but also to reflect on the experience of creating a map for your use as you visit and revisit the world of systems theory and family therapy. In the recursive process of thinking, writing, reviewing, giving and receiving feedback, thinking, and writing, we have been keenly aware of your presence as readers and thus as coparticipants in the process. We have attempted to second-guess your questions, to anticipate your struggles, and to figure out where you would perceive us as pontificating rather than presenting. Obviously, each of you will have a different assessment of the degree to which we succeeded or failed in this regard, but we hope all of you will share an awareness of what to us is inevitably an experience of mutual influence.

It is also our hope that, while we have chosen to focus on systems theory and family therapy, our emphasis on integration will overrule the tendency of some to believe that espousal of a systemic/cybernetic perspective necessitates the rejection of other world views, or that espousal of cybernetics of cybernetics requires rejection of simple cybernetics. Rather, as illustrated in Figure 16.4, it is our belief that concepts are descriptions of relationships and the punctuation of differences is possible only through distinctions of complementarity. Thus, just as the natural

FIGURE 16-4   The Both/And Perspective

sciences are defined by and distinguished from the social sciences, individual psychology and family therapy complement each other under the umbrella of the social sciences. Similarly, simple cybernetics and cybernetics of cybernetics are parts of a larger whole, which in this case we have defined as family therapy.

As we mentioned at the outset, it is our belief that *family therapy* is a misnomer and that *relationship therapy* would be a more suitable label. We also stated our perception that epistemology is what systems theory and cybernetics are about. Thus, this perspective might just as appropriately be used to view disciplines, or territories, other than family therapy.

However, we are both family therapists and we are both teachers of family therapy. It was in this field that we first encountered the systemic/cybernetic perspective and began our attempts to explain it to others. It is as a function of our experiences in this field that we began to extend our quest for knowledge into related disciplines such as physics and biology. We believe that integration should occur not only within a field but between fields. For us, the systemic/cybernetic perspective provides a bridge that makes this possible.

Postscript

The ideas of Gregory Bateson have been seminal to much of the work in the field of systemic family therapy. Many of the concepts you have been exposed to in this book have been from Bateson or from the interpretation, extrapolation, and pragmatic application by others of Bateson's thought. It therefore seems fitting that we conclude with a conversation between Bateson and Stewart Brand:

"You cannot induce a Pavlovian nervous breakdown—what do they call it, 'experimental neurosis'—in an animal out in the field."

"I didn't know that!"

More of the Bateson chortle. "You've got to have a lab."

"Why?"

"Because the smell of the lab, the feel of the harness in which the animal stands, and all that are context markers which say what sort of thing is going on in this situation; that you're supposed to be right or wrong, for example.

"What you do to induce these neuroses is, you train the animal to believe that the smell of the lab and similar things is a message which tells him he's got to discriminate between an ellipse and a circle, say. Right. He learns to discriminate. Then you make the discrimination a little more difficult, and he learns again, and you have underlined the message. Then you make the discrimination impossible.

"At this point discrimination is not the appropriate form of behavior. Guesswork is. But the animal cannot stop feeling that he ought to discriminate, and then you get the symptomatology coming on. The one whose discrimination broke down was the experimenter, who failed to discriminate between the context for discrimination and a context for gambling."

"So," says I, "it's the experimenter's neurosis that . . ."

". . . Has now become the experimental neurosis of the animal. The whole context business has a Heisenberg hook in it much worse than the atoms ever thought of." (Atomic physicist Heisenberg's famous Uncertainty Principle states that the observer constantly alters what he observes by the meddling act of observation.)

"In the field what happens?"

"None of this happens. For one thing, the stimuli don't count. Those electric shocks they use are about as powerful as what the animal would get if he pricked his leg on a bramble, pushing through.

"Suppose you've got an animal whose job in life is to turn over stones and eat the beetles under them. All right, one stone in ten is going to have a beetle under it. He cannot go into a nervous breakdown because the other nine stones don't have beetles under them. But the lab can make him do that you see."

"Do you think we're all in a lab of our own making, in which we drive each other crazy?"

"You said it, not I, brother," chuckling. "Of course." (Brand, 1974, pp. 25–27)

References

Abbot, P. (1981). *The family on trial.* University Park, PA: Pennsylvania State University Press.

Ackerman, N. W. (1937). The family as a social and emotional unit. *Bulletin of the Kansas Mental Hygiene Society, 12*(2).

Ackerman, N. W. (1958). *The psychodynamics of family life.* New York: Basic Books.

Ackerman, N. W. (1966). *Treating the troubled family.* New York: Basic Books.

Ackerman, N. W. (1967). The future of family psychotherapy. In N. Ackerman, F. Beatman, & S. Sherman (Eds.), *Expanding theory and practice in family therapy* (pp. 3–16). New York: New York Family Association of America.

Alexander, J., & Parsons, B. (1973). Short-term behavioral interventions with delinquent families: Impact on family process and recidivism. *Journal of Abnormal Psychology, 81,* 219–225.

Alexander, J., Barton, C., Schiavo, R., & Parsons, B. (1977). Systems-behavioral intervention with families of delinquents: Therapist characteristics, family behavior and outcome. *Journal of Consulting and Clinical Psychology, 44,* 656–664.

Alger, I. (1976). Multiple couple therapy. In P. J. Guerin (Ed.), *Family therapy* (pp. 364–387). New York: Gardner Press.

Allen, W. R. (1978). The search for applicable theories of black family life. *Journal of Marriage and the Family, 40*(1), 117–129.

Allport, G. W. (1964). The open system in personality theory. In H. M. Ruitenbeek (Ed.), *Varieties of personality theory* (pp. 149–166). New York: E. P. Dutton.

American Association for Marriage and Family Therapy. (1991). *AAMFT Code of Ethics.* Washington, DC: AAMFT.

American Psychiatric Association. (1994). *Diagnostic and statistical manual of mental disorders* (4th ed., rev.). Washington, DC: APA.

Amundson, J., Stewart, K., & Valentine, V. (1993). Temptations of power and certainty. *Journal of Marital & Family Therapy, 19,* 111–123.

Amundson, J. (1994). "Whither narrative? The danger of getting it right." *Journal of Marital and Family Therapy, 20*(1), 83–89.

Andersen, T. (1987). The reflecting team: Dialogue and meta-dialogue in clinical work. *Family Process, 26,* 415–428.

Andersen, T. (Ed.) (1991). *The reflecting team: Dialogues and dialogues about the dialogues.* New York: W. W. Norton.

Andersen, T. (1992). Reflections on reflecting with families. In S. McNamee & K. J. Gergen (Eds.), *Therapy as social construction* (pp. 54–68). Newbury Park, CA: Sage.

Andersen T. (1993). See and hear: And be seen and heard. In S. Friedman (Ed.), *The new language of change* (pp. 54–68). New York: Guilford Press.

Anderson, C. M. (1988). Psychoeducational model different than paradigm. *Family Therapy News, 19*(3), 10–12.

Anderson, C. M., Reiss, D., & Hogarty, B. (1986). *Schizophrenia and the family: A practitioner's guide to psychoeducation and management.* New York: Guilford Press.

Anderson, H. (1993). On a roller coaster: A collaborative language systems approach to therapy. In S. Friedman (Ed.), *The new language of change* (pp. 323–344). New York: Guilford Press.

Anderson, H. (1994). Rethinking family therapy: A delicate balance. *Journal of Marital and Family Therapy, 20*(3), 145–149.

Anderson, H., & Goolishian, H. (1986). Problem-determined systems: Towards transformation in family therapy. *Journal of Strategic and Systematic Therapies, 5,* 1–13.

Anderson, H., & Goolishian, H. A. (1988). Human systems as linguistic systems: Preliminary and evolving ideas about the implications for clinical theory. *Family Process, 27,* 371–393.

Anderson, H., & Goolishian, H. (1990). Beyond cybernetics: Comments on Atkinson and Heath's "Further thoughts on second-order family therapy." *Family Process, 229,* 157–163.

Anderson, H., Goolishian, H., & Winderman, L. (1986). Problem-determined systems: Toward transformation in family therapy. *Journal of Strategic and Systemic Therapies, 5,* 14–19.

Anderson, R. E., & Carter, I. (1990). *Human behavior in the social environment.* New York: Aldine Publishing.

Aponte, H., & Van Deusen, J. (1981). Structural family therapy. In A. S. Gurman & D. P. Kniskern (Eds.), *Handbook of family therapy* (pp. 310–360). New York: Brunner/Mazel.

Aries, P. (1963). *Centuries of childhood.* New York: Vintage Books.

Ashby, R. (1956). *An introduction to cybernetics.* London: Chapman & Hall.

Ashby, W. R. (1940). Adaptiveness and equilibrium. *Journal of Mental Science, 86,* 478–484.

Atkinson, B., & Health, A. (1990a). The limits of explanation and evaluation. *Family Process, 229,* 164–167.

Atkinson, B., & Heath, A. (1990b). Further thoughts on second-order family therapy—This time it's personal. *Family Process, 229,* 145–155.

Atkinson, B., Heath, A., & Chenail, R. (1991). Qualitative research and the legitimization of knowledge. *Journal of Marital and Family Therapy, 17,* 175–180.

Attneave, C. (1976). Social networks as the unit of intervention. In P. J. Guerin (Ed.), *Family therapy: Theory and practice* (pp. 220–232). New York: Gardner Press.

Avis, J. M. (1988). Deepening awareness: A private study guide to feminism and family therapy. In L. Braverman (Ed.), *A guide to feminist family therapy.* New York: Harrington Park Press.

Avis, J. (1994). Advocates versus researchers—A false dichotomy? A feminist, social constructionist response to Jacobson. *Family Process, 33,* 87–91.

Azrin, N., Naster, B., & Jones, R. (1973). Reciprocity counseling: A rapid learning-based procedure for marital counseling. *Behavior Research and Therapy, 11,* 365–383.

Bandler, R., Grinder, J., & Satir, V. (1976). *Changing with families.* Palo Alto, CA: Science and Behavior Books.

Bandura, A. (1969). *Principles of behavior modification.* New York: Holt, Rinehart & Winston.

Bandura, A. (1982). Self-efficacy mechanisms in human agency. *American Psychologist, 37,* 122–147.

Barker, R. G. (1968). *Ecological psychology.* Palo Alto, CA: Stanford University Press.

Barker, R. G., & Associates (1978). *Habitats, environments and human behavior.* San Francisco: Jossey-Bass.

Barker, R. G., & Wright, H. F. (1955). *Midwest and its children.* New York: Harper & Row. (Reprinted by Archon Books, Hamden, CT, 1971.)

Barnhill, L. H., & Longo, D. (1978). Fixation and regression in the family life cycle. *Family Process, 17,* 469–478.

Barnlund, D. D. (1962). Toward a meaning-centered philosophy of communication. *Journal of Communication, 11,* 198–202.

Bartlett, S. (1983). *Conceptual therapy: An introduction to framework-relative epistemology.* St. Louis, MO: Crescere.

Barton, C., & Alexander, J. (1981). Functional family therapy. In A. Gurman & D. Kniskern (Eds.), *Handbook of family therapy* (pp. 403–443). New York: Brunner/Mazel.

Barton, C., Alexander, J., Waldron, H., Turner, C., & Warburton, J. (1985). Generalizing treatment effects of functional family therapy: Three replications. *American Journal of Family Therapy, 13*(3), 16–26.

Bateson, G. (1970). An open letter to Anatol Rapoport. *ETC: A Review of General Semantics, XXVII* (3), 359–363.

Bateson, G. (1971). The cybernetics of "self": A theory of alcoholism. *Psychiatry, 34,* 1–18.

Bateson, G. (1972). *Steps to an ecology of mind.* New York: Ballantine.

Bateson, G. (1974). Double bind. In S. Brand (Ed.), *II cybernetic frontiers* (pp. 9–33). New York: Random House.

Bateson, G. (1977). The thing of it is. In M. Katz, W. Marsh, & G. Thompson (Eds.), *Explorations of planetary culture at the Lindesfarne conferences: Earth's answer* (pp. 143–154). New York: Harper & Row.

Bateson, G. (1979). *Mind and nature.* New York: E. P. Dutton.

Bateson, G., & Bateson, M. C. (1987). *Angels fear: Toward an epistemology of the sacred.* New York: Macmillan.

Bateson, G., Jackson, D. D., Haley, J., & Weakland, J. (1956). Toward a theory of schizophrenia. *Behavioral Science, 1*, 251–264.

Bateson, G., & Mead, M. (1976). For God's sake, Margaret. *The CoEvolution Quarterly,* Summer, 32–43.

Baucom, D. H. (1982) A comparison of behavioral contracting and problem-solving/communications training in behavioral marital therapy. *Behavior Therapy, 13*, 162–174.

Beavers, W. R. (1981). A systems model of family for family therapists. *Journal of Marital and Family Therapy, 7*, 229–307.

Beavers, W. R. (1982). Healthy, midrange and severely dysfunctional families. In F. Walsh (Ed.), *Normal family processes* (pp. 45–66). New York: Guilford Press.

Beavers, W. R., & Voeller, M. N. (1983). Family models: Comparing and contrasting the Olson circumplex with the Beavers systems model. *Family Process, 22*, 85–98.

Beck, A. (1976). *Cognitive therapy and the emotional disorders.* New York: International Universities Press.

Becvar, D. S. (1982). The family is not a group—Or is it? *The Journal for Specialists in Group Work, 7*(2), 88–95.

Becvar, D. S. (1983). *The relationship between the family and society in the context of American ideology: A systems theoretical perspective.* Unpublished doctoral dissertation, St. Louis University, St. Louis, MO.

Becvar, D. S. (1985). Creating rituals for a new age: Dealing positively with divorce, remarriage, and other developmental challenges. In R. Williams, H. Lingren, G. Rowe, S. Van Zandt, P. Lee, & N. Stinnett (Eds.), *Family Strengths, 6* (pp. 57–65). Lincoln, NE: University of Nebraska—Lincoln Press.

Becvar, D. S. (1986). Strengths of a single-parent family. *Growing Times, 4*(1), 1–11.

Becvar, D., & Becvar, R. (1986). Building relationships. *Marriage Encounter, 15*, 26–28.

Becvar, R., & Becvar, D. (1994). The ecosystemic story: A story about stories. *Journal of Mental Health Counseling, 16*(1), 22–32.

Becvar, R. J. (1974). *Skills for effective communication.* New York: John Wiley.

Becvar, R. J., & Becvar, D. S. (1982). *Systems theory and family therapy: A primer.* Washington, DC: University Press of America.

Becvar, D., & Becvar, R. (1993). Family therapy: A systemic integration. Boston: Allyn and Bacon.

Becvar, D., & Becvar, R. (1994). *Hot chocolate for a cold winter night.* Denver: Love Publishing.

Becvar, R. J., Becvar, D. S., & Bender, A. (1982). Let us first do no harm. *Journal of Marital and Family Therapy, 8*(4), 385–391.

Becvar, R. J., Becvar, D. S., Newell, J. P., & Andresen, S. A. (1991). An open letter to family practice residents. Unpublished manuscript.

Bednar, R. L., Burlingame, G. M., & Masters, K. S. (1988). Systems of family treatment: Substance or semantics. In M. R. Rosenzweig & L. W. Porter (Eds.), *Annual Review of Psychology* (pp. 401–434). Palo Alto, CA: Annual Reviews.

Beer, S. (1974). Cybernetics. In H. von Foerster (Ed.), *Cybernetics of cybernetics* (pp. 2–3). Urbana, IL: Biological Computer Laboratory, University of Illinois.

Bell, J. E. (1961). *Family group therapy.* Public Health Monograph No. 64. Washington, DC: U. S. Government Printing Office.

Bell, J. E. (1972). A theoretical position for family group therapy. In G. E. Erickson & T. P. Hogan (Eds.), *Family therapy: An introduction to theory and technique* (pp. 138–149). Monterey, CA: Brooks/Cole.

Bell, J. E. (1975). *Family therapy.* New York: Jason Aronson.

Bell, J. E. (1976). A theoretical framework for family group therapy. In P. J. Guerin (Ed.), *Family therapy: Theory and practice* (pp. 129–143). New York: Gardner Press.

Bellah, R., Madsen, R., Sullivan, W., Swides, A., & Tipton, S. (1985). *Habits of the heart.* New York: Harper & Row.

Benson, J. (1983). A dialectical method for the study of organizations. In G. Morgan (Ed.),

Beyond method: Strategies for social research (pp. 331–346). Beverly Hills, CA: Sage.

Berg, I. K., & de Shazer, S. (1993). Making numbers talk: A solution-focused approach. In S. Friedman (Ed.), *The new language of change* (pp. 5–24). New York: Guilford Press.

Bertalanffy, L. von (1968). *General system theory.* New York: George Braziller.

Billingsley, A. (1968). *Black families in white America.* Englewood Cliffs, NJ: Prentice-Hall.

Bircher, G. R., & Spinks, S. H. (1980). Behavioral-systems marital therapy: Integration and clinical application. *American Journal of Family Therapy, 8,* 6–29.

Black, C. (1981). *It will never happen to me.* Denver, CO: M. A. C.

Blanck, R., & Blanck, G. (1986). *Beyond ego psychology: Developmental object relations theory.* New York: Columbia University Press.

Bodin, A. (1981). The interactional view: Family therapy approaches of the Mental Research Institute. In A. S. Gurman & D. P. Kniskern (Eds.), *Handbook of family therapy* (pp. 267–309). New York: Brunner/Mazel.

Borduin, C. M., Henggeler, S. W., Hanson, C., & Harbin, F. (1982). Treating the family of the adolescent: A review of the empirical literature. In S. W. Henggeler (Ed.), *Delinquency and adolescent psychopathology: A family ecological systems approach* (pp. 205–222). Boston: John Wright.

Borlens, W., Emmelkamp, P., Macgillarry, D., & Markvoort, M. (1980). A clinical evaluation of marital treatment: Reciprocity counseling versus system-theoretic counseling. *Behavioral Analysis and Modification, 4,* 85–96.

Boscolo, L., & Bertrando, P. (1983). *The times of time: A new perspective in systemic therapy and consultation.* New York: W. W. Norton.

Boscolo, L., Cecchin, G., Hoffman, L., & Penn, P. (1987). *Milan systemic family therapy.* New York: Basic Books.

Boszormenyi-Nagy, I. (1966). From family therapy to a psychology of relationships: Fictions of the individual and fictions of the family. *Comprehensive Psychiatry, 7,* 406–423.

Boszormenyi-Nagy, I. (1987). *Foundations of contextual therapy.* New York: Brunner/Mazel.

Boszormenyi-Nagy, I., & Framo, J. (Eds.). (1965). *Intensive family therapy: Theoretical and practical aspects.* New York: Harper & Row.

Boszormenyi-Nagy, I., & Spark, G. (1973). *Invisibility loyalties: Reciprocity in intergenerational family therapy.* New York: Harper & Row.

Boszormenyi-Nagy, I., & Ulrich, D. (1981). Contextual family therapy. In A. S. Gurman & D. P. Kniskern (Eds.), *Handbook of family _therapy* (pp. 159–186). New York: Brunner/Mazel_.

Boulding, K. E. (1968). General systems theory—The skeleton of science. In W. Buckley (Ed.), *Modern systems research for the behavioral scientist* (pp. 3–10). Chicago: Aldine Publishing Company.

Bowen, M. (1976). Theory in the practice of psychotherapy. In P. J. Guerin (Ed.), *Family therapy: Theory and practice* (pp. 42–90). New York: Gardner Press.

Bowen, M. (1978). *Family therapy in clinical practice.* New York: Jason Aronson.

Brady, J. (1980). Some views on effective principles of psychotherapy. *Cognitive therapy and research, 4,* 271–306.

Braginsky, B., & Braginsky, D. (1972). *Mainstream psychology: A critique.* New York: Holt, Rinehart & Winston.

Brand, S. (1974). *II cybernetic frontiers.* New York: Random House.

Briggs, J. P., & Peat, F. D. (1984). *Looking glass universe.* New York: Simon & Schuster.

Broderick, C. B., & Schrader, S. S. (1981). The history of professional marriage and family therapy. In A. S. Gurman & D. P. Kniskern (Eds.), *Handbook of family therapy* (pp. 5–38). New York: Brunner/Mazel.

Bronfenbrenner, U. (1979). *The ecology of human development.* Cambridge, MA: Harvard University Press.

Bronowski, J. (1978). *The origins of knowledge and imagination.* New Haven, CT: Yale University Press.

Brown, G. W., Birley, J. L., & Wing, J. K. (1972). The influence of family life on the course of schizophrenic disorders: A replication. *British Journal of Psychology, 121,* 241–258.

Brown, G. W., Monck, E. M., Carstairs, G. M., & Wing, J. K. (1962). Influence of family life on the course of schizophrenic illness. *British Journal of Preventive and Social Medicine, 16,* 15–68.

Brunk, M., Henggeler, S., & Whelan, J. (1987). Comparison of multisystemic therapy and parent training in the brief tre: tment of child abuse and neglect. *Journal of Consulting and Clinical Psychology, 55,* 171–178.

Caplan, N., & Nelson, S. (1973). On being useful: The nature and consequences of psychological research on social problems. *American Psychologist, 28,* 199–211.

Capra, F. (1983). *The turning point.* New York: Bantam Books.

Carter, E. A., & McGoldrick, M. (Eds.) (1980). *The family life cycle: A framework for family therapy.* New York: Gardner Press.

Carter, E. A., & McGoldrick, M. (Eds.) (1988). *The changing family life cycle.* New York: Gardner Press.

Casteneda, C. (1974). *Tales of power.* New York: Simon & Schuster.

Cavell, T., & Snyder, D. (1991). Iconoclasm versus innovation: Building a science of family therapy—Comments on Moon, Dillon and Sprenkle. *Journal of Marital and Family Therapy, 17,* 181–185.

Cecchin, G., Lane, G., & Ray, W. (1992). *Irreverence: A strategy for therapists' survival.* London: Karnac Books.

Cecchin, G., Lane G., & Ray, W. (1994). *The cybernetics of prejudices in the practice of psychotherapy.* London: Karnac Books.

Chamberlain, P., Patterson, G., Reid, J., Kavanaugh, K., & Forgatch, M. (1984). Observation of client resistance. *Behavior Therapy, 15,* 144–155.

Chase, S. (1938). *The tyranny of words.* New York: Harcourt, Brace.

Chenail, R. (1990). Introduction. *The Qualitative Report, 1*(1), 1–2.

Chenail, R. (1991). *Parents' talk concerning their child's heart murmur: A discourse analysis.* Norwood, NJ: Ablex.

Chenail, R. (1994). Qualitative research and clinical work: "Privat-ization" and "Public-ation." *The Qualitative Report, 2*(1), 1–12

Christensen, O. C., & Schramski, T. G. (Eds.). (1983). *Adlerian family counseling.* Minneapolis, MN: Educational Media Corporation.

Churchman, C. (1979). *The systems approach and its enemies.* New York: Basic Books.

Cochran, M., & Brassard, J. (1979). Child development and personal social networks. *Child Development, 50,* 601–616.

Cohen, K. N., & Clark, J. A. (1984). Transitional object attachments in early childhood and personality characteristics in later life. *Journal of Personality and Social Psychology, 46*(1), 106–111.

Cohen, W., & Milberg, L. (1992). The behavioral pediatrics consultation: Teaching residents to think systemically in managing behavioral pediatrics problems. *Family Systems Medicine, 10*(2), 169–179.

Colapinto, J. (1982). Structural family therapy. In A. M. Horne & M. M. Ohlsen (Eds.), *Family counseling and therapy* (pp. 112–140). Itasca, IL: F. E. Peacock.

Constantine, L. (1993). The structure of family paradigms: An analytical model of family variation. *Journal of Marital and Family Therapy, 19*(1), 39–70.

Coontz, S. (1992). *The way we never were.* New York: Basic Books.

Corsini, R. (1984). *Current psychotherapies.* Itasca, IL: F. E. Peacock.

Dare, C., Eisler, I., Russell, G., & Szmukler, G. (1990). The clinical and theoretical impact of a controlled trial of family therapy in anorexia nervosa. *Journal of Marital and Family Therapy, 16,* 39–57.

Dawis, R. (1984). Of old philosophies and new kids on the block. *Journal of Counseling Psychology, 31,* 467–469.

Dayringer, S. (1980). *Experimentation in behavioral science research: Status and prospectus.* Unpublished doctoral dissertation, St. Louis University, St. Louis, MO.

Dell, P. F. (1980). Researching the family theories of schizophrenia: An experience in epistemological confusion. *Family Process, 19*(4), 321–335.

Dell, P. F. (1982). Beyond homeostasis: Toward a concept of coherence. *Family Process, 21,* 21–41.

Dell, P. F. (1983). From pathology to ethics. *Family Therapy Networker, 1*(6), 29–64.

Dell, P. F. (1986a). Can the family therapy field be rigorous? *Journal of Marital and Family Therapy, 12*(1), 37–38.

Dell, P. F. (1986b). In defense of "lineal causality." *Family Process, 25,* 513–522.

Dell, P. F. (1986c). Why do we still call them "paradoxes"? *Family Process, 25,* 223–235.

Dempsey, J. J. (1981). *The family and public policy: The issue of the 1980's.* Baltimore, MD: Paul H. Brookes.

de Shazer, S. (1985). *Keys to solutions in brief therapy.* New York: W. W. Norton.

de Shazer, S. (1988). *Clues: Investigating solutions in brief therapy.* New York: W. W. Norton.

de Shazer, S. (1991). *Putting difference to work.* New York: W. W. Norton.

Dewey, J., & Bentley, A. (1949). *Knowing and the known.* Boston: Beacon Press.

DeWitt, K. N. (1978). The effectiveness of family therapy: A review of outcome research. *Archives of General Psychiatry, 35,* 549–561.

Dinkmeyer, D., Jr., & Dinkmeyer, D., Sr. (1991). Adlerian family therapy. In A. Horne & J. Passmore (Eds.), *Family counseling and therapy* (pp. 383–401). Itasca, IL: F. E. Peacock.

Dinkmeyer, D. D., & McKay, G. D. (1973). *Raising a responsible child.* New York: Simon & Schuster.

Dinkmeyer, D. D., & McKay, G. D. (1976). *Systematic training for effective parenting (STEP).* Circle Pines, MN: American Guidance Service.

Doherty, W. J. (1991). Family therapy goes postmodern. *The Family Therapy Networker, 15*(5), 36–42.

Doherty, W. J., & Baird, M. A. (1983). *Family therapy and family medicine.* New York: Guilford Press.

Dollard, J., & Miller, N. (1950). *Personality and psychotherapy.* New York: McGraw-Hill.

Dunlap, K. (1928). A revision of the fundamental law of habit formation. *Science, 67,* 360–362.

Dunlap, K. (1946). *Personal adjustment.* New York: McGraw-Hill.

Duvall, E. (1962). *Family development.* Philadelphia: Lippincott.

Efran, J., & Lukens, M. D. (1985). The world according to Humberto Maturana. *The Family Therapy Networker, 9*(3), 23–28, 72–75.

Efran, J. A., Lukens, R. J., & Lukens, M. D. (1988). Constructivism: What's in it for you? *The Family Therapy Networker, 12*(5), 27–35.

Elkin, M. (1984). *Families under the influence.* New York: W. W. Norton.

Ellis, A. (1962). *Reason and emotion in psychotherapy.* New York: Lyle Stuart and Citadel Books.

Engel, G. (1977). The need for a new medical model: A challenge for biomedicine. *Science, 196,* 129–136.

Engel, G. (1992). How much longer must medicine's science be bound by a seventeenth century world view? *Family Systems Medicine, 10*(3), 333–346.

Epstein, N. B., Bishop, D. S., & Baldwin, L. M. (1982). McMaster model of family functioning: A view of the normal family. In F. Walsh (Ed.), *Normal family processes* (pp. 115–141). New York: Guilford Press.

Epstein, N. B., Bishop, D. S., & Levin, S. (1978). The McMaster model of family functioning. *Journal of Marital and Family Counseling, 4,* 19–31.

Epston, D. (1994). Extending the conversation. *The Family Therapy Networker, 18*(6), 30–37, 62–63.

Erickson, E. H. (1963). *Childhood and society.* New York: W. W. Norton.

Eysenck, H. (1959). Learning theory and behavior therapy. *British Journal of Medical Science, 105,* 61–75.

Falloon, I. R., Boyd, J. L., & McGill, C. W. (1985). *Family care of schizophrenia.* New York: Guilford Press.

Falloon, I. R., Boyd, J. L., McGill, C. W., Razani, J., Moss, H. B., & Gilderman, A. M. (1982). Family management in the prevention of exacerbations of schizophrenia. *New England Journal of Medicine, 306,* 1437–1440.

Falloon, I. R., Boyd, J. L., McGill, C. W., Williamson, M., Razani, J., Moss, H. B., Gilderman, A. M., & Simpson, G. M. (1985). Family management in the prevention of morbidity of schizophrenia: Clinical outcome of a two-year longitudinal study. *Archives of General Psychiatry, 42,* 887–896.

Falzer, P. (1986). The cybernetic metaphor: A critical examination of ecosystemic epistemology as a foundation of family therapy. *Family Process, 25,* 353–364.

Family therapy and family medicine: A new partnership. (1990). *Family Therapy News,* July/August, p. 9.

Feinberg, P. H. (1990). Circular questions: Establishing the relational context. *Family Systems Medicine, 8*(3), 273–277.

Fisch, R., Weakland, J., & Segal, L. (1982). *The tactics of change.* San Francisco: Jossey-Bass.

Fleishmann, M., & Szykula, S. (1981). A replication of Patterson's A community setting replication of a social learning treatment for aggressive children. *Behavior Therapy, 12,* 115–122.

Flemons, D. (1991). *Completing distinctions.* Boston: Shambala.

Foerster, H. von (1981). *Observing systems.* Seaside, CA: Intersystems Publications.

Foley, V. D. (1974). *An introduction to family therapy.* New York: Grune & Stratton.

Foucault, M. (1978). *The history of sexuality: An introduction.* Middlesex: Peregrine Books.

Foucault, M. (1979). *Discipline and punish: The birth of the prison.* New York: Pantheon.

Fox, D. (1990). Health policy and the politics of research in the United States. *Journal of Health, Politics, Policy and Law, 15*(3), 481–499.

Framo, J. J. (1976). Chronicle of a struggle to establish a family unit within a community mental health center. In P. J. Guerin (Ed.), *Family Therapy: Theory and practice* (pp. 23–39). New York: Gardner Press.

Frank, J. (1974). *Persuasion and healing.* New York: Shocken.

Frankel, C. (1963). The family in context. In F. Delliquadri (Ed.), *Helping the family in urban society* (pp. 3–22). New York: Columbia University Press.

Friedman, L. J. (1980). Integrating psychoanalytic object-relations understanding with family systems intervention in couples therapy. In J. K. Pearce & L. J. Friedman (Eds.), *Family therapy: Combining psychodynamic and family systems approaches* (pp. 63–79). New York: Grune & Stratton.

Fromm-Reichman, F. (1948). Notes on the development of schizophrenics by psychoanalytic psychiatry. *Psychiatry, 11,* 263–273.

Gadlin, H., & Ingle, G. (1975). Through a one-way mirror: The limits of experimental self-reflection. *American Psychologist, 30,* 1003–1009.

Gale, J. E. (1991). *Conversation analysis of therapeutic discourse: The pursuit of a therapeutic agenda.* Norwood, NJ: Ablex.

Gale, J. (1993). A field guide to qualitative inquiry and its clinical relevance. *Contemporary Family Therapy, 15*(1), 73–91.

Gale, J., & Newfield, N. (1992). A conversation analysis of a solution-focused marital therapy session. *Journal of Marital and Family Therapy, 18,* 153–165.

Garfield, R. (1982). Mourning and its resolution for spouses in marital separation. In J. C. Hansen & L. Messinger (Eds.), *Therapy with remarriage families* (pp. 1–16). Rockville, MD: Aspen Systems Corporation.

Gelles, R. (1994). Research and advocacy: Can one wear two hats? *Family Process, 33,* 94–95.

Gergen, K. (1982). *Toward transformation in social knowledge.* New York: Springer.

Gergen, K. J. (1985). Social constructivist movement in psychology. *American Psychologist, 40,* 266–275.

Gergen, K. (1991). *The saturated self.* New York: Basic Books.

Gergen, K. (1994). Exploring the postmodern: Perils or potentials? *American Psychologists, 49*(5), 412–416.

Germain, C. B. (1991). *Human behavior in the social environment.* New York: Columbia University Press.

Gilligan, C. (1982). *In a different voice.* Cambridge, MA: Harvard University Press.

Golann, S. (1988a). On second-order family therapy. *Family Process, 27,* 51–65.

Golann, S. (1988b). Who replies first? A reply to Hoffman. *Family Process, 27,* 68–71.

Goldenberg, I., & Goldenberg, H. (1985). *Family therapy: An overview* (2nd ed.). Monterey, CA: Brooks/Cole.

Goldman, L. (1982). Defining non-traditional research. *The Counseling Psychologist, 10*(4), 87–90.

Goldner, V. (1985a). Warning: Family therapy may be hazardous to your health. *The Family Therapy Networker, 9*(6), 19–23.

Goldner, V. (1985b). Feminism and family therapy. *Family Process, 24,* 31–47.

Goldner, V. (1988). Generation and gender: normative and covert hierarchies. *Family Process, 27*(1), 17–31.

Goldner, V. (1993). Power and hierarchy: Let's talk about it! *Family Process, 32,* 157–162.

Goolishian, H. (1991). The use of language in two different therapy approaches. In AAMFT Annual Conference Newsletter, p. 1.

Gordon, S., & Davidson, N. (1981). Behavioral parent training. In A. S. Gurman & D. P. Kniskern (Eds.), *Handbook of family therapy* (pp. 517–555). New York: Brunner/Mazel.

Gottman, J., Markman, H., & Notarius, C. (1977). The topography of marital conflict: A sequential analysis of verbal and nonverbal behavior. *Journal of Marriage and the Family, 39,* 461–477.

Greenberg, J. R., & Mitchell, S. (1983). *Object relations and psychoanalytic theory.* Cambridge, MA: Harvard University Press.

Guba, E. (Ed.) (1990). *The paradigm dialogue.* Newbury Park, CA: Sage.

Guerin, P. J. (1976). Family therapy: The first twenty-five years. In P. J. Guerin (Ed.), *Family ther-*

apy: Theory and practice (pp. 2–22). New York: Gardner Press.

Guerin, P. J., & Pendagast, E. (1976). Evaluation of family system and genogram. In P. J. Guerin, (Ed.), *Family therapy: Theory and practice* (pp. 450–464). New York: Gardner Press.

Gurman, A. S. (1983a). Family therapy research and the "new epistemology." *Journal of Marital and Family Therapy, 9*(3), 227–234.

Gurman, A. S. (1983b). The old hatters and the new weavers. *The Family Therapy Networker, 7*(4), 36–37.

Gurman, A. S. (Ed.). (1985). *Casebook of marital therapy.* New York: Guilford Press.

Gurman, A. S., & Kniskern, D. P. (1978). Research on marital and family therapy: Progress, perspective and prospect. In S. Garfield & A. Bergin (Eds.), *Handbook of psychotherapy and behavior change: An empirical analysis* (2nd ed.) (pp. 817–902). New York: John Wiley.

Gurman, A. S., & Kniskern, D. P. (1981). *Handbook of family therapy.* New York: Brunner/Mazel.

Gurman, A. S., Kniskern, D. P., & Pinsof, W. M. (1986). Research on the process and outcome of marital and family therapy. In S. Garfield & A. Bergin (Eds.), *Handbook of psychotherapy and behavior change* (3rd ed.) (pp. 525–623). New York: John Wiley.

Fruggeri, L. (1992). Therapeutic process as the social construction of change. In S. McNamee & K. Gergen (Eds.), *Therapy as Social Construction* (pp. 40–53). Newbury Park, CA: Sage.

Hahlweg, K., Schindler, L., Revenstorf, D., & Brengelmann, J. C. (1984). The Munich family therapy study. In K. Hahlweg & N. Jacobson (Eds.), *Marital interaction: Analysis and modification.* New York: Guilford Press.

Haley, J. (1963). *Strategies of psychotherapy.* New York: Grune & Stratton.

Haley, J. (1973). *Uncommon therapy.* New York: W. W. Norton.

Haley, J. (1975). Why a mental health clinic should avoid family therapy. *Journal of Marriage and Family Counseling, 1,* 1–13.

Haley, J. (1976). *Problem-solving therapy.* New York: Harper Colophon.

Haley, J. (1984). *Ordeal therapy.* San Francisco: Jossey-Bass.

Hall, C. S., & Lindzey, G. (1978). *Theories of personality* (3rd ed.). New York: John Wiley.

Hamilton, N. G. (1989). A critical review of object relations theory. *American Journal of Psychiatry, 146*(12), 1552–1560.

Hamner, T. J., & Turner, P. H. (1985). *Parenting in contemporary society.* Englewood Cliffs, NJ: Prentice-Hall.

Hansen, J., & L'Abate, L. (1982). *Approaches to family therapy.* New York: Macmillan.

Hare-Mustin, R. T. (1978). A feminist approach to family therapy. *Family Process, 17,* 181–194.

Hare-Mustin, R. (1994). Discourses in the mirrored room: A postmodern analysis of therapy. *Family Process, 33,* 19–35.

Hareven, T. K. (1971). The history of the family as an interdisciplinary field. In T. K. Rabb & R. I. Rotberg (Eds.), *The family in history: Interdisciplinary essays* (pp. 211–226). New York: Harper & Row.

Harper, J., Scoresby, A., & Boyce, W. (1977). The logical levels of complementary, symmetrical and parallel interaction classes in family dyads. *Family Process, 16,* 199–210.

Hayward, J. W. (1984). *Perceiving ordinary magic.* Boston: New Science Library.

Hazelrigg, M. D., Cooper, H. M., & Borduin, C. M. (1987). Evaluating the effectiveness of family therapies: An integrative review and analysis. *Psychological Bulletin, 101,* 428–442.

Heiman, J., LoPiccolo, L., & LoPiccolo, J. (1981). The treatment of sexual dysfunction. In A. S. Gurman & D. P. Kniskern (Eds.), *Handbook of family therapy* (pp. 592–627). New York: Brunner/Mazel.

Heims, S. P. (1975). Encounter of behavioral sciences with new machine-organism analogies in the 1940's. *Journal of the History of the Behavioral Sciences, 11,* 368–373.

Heims, S. P. (1977). Gregory Bateson and the mathematicians: From interdisciplinary interaction to societal functions. *Journal of the History of the Behavioral Sciences, 13,* 141–159.

Held, B. S. (1990). What's in a name? Some confusions and concerns about constructivism. *Journal of Marital and Family Therapy, 16,* 179–186.

Held, B. S., & Pols, E. (1987). Dell on Maturana: A real foundation for family therapy. *Psychotherapy, 24*(3), 455–461.

Henao, S. (1985). A systems approach to family medicine. In S. Henao & N. P. Grose (Eds.),

Principles of family systems in family medicine (pp. 24–40). New York: Brunner/Mazel.

Henggeler, S., Borduin, C., & Mann, B. (1992). Advances in family therapy: Empirical foundations. In T. Ollendick & R. Prinz (Eds.), *Advances in clinical child psychology*, vol. 15. New York: Plenum.

Herzog, E., & Sudia, C. E. (1972). Families without fathers. *Childhood Education, 49,* 311–319.

Hill, R., & Rodgers, R. H. (1964). The developmental approach. In H. Christensen (Ed.), *Handbook of marriage and family therapy* (pp. 171–209). Chicago: Rand McNally.

Hill, R. B. (1980). *Black families in the 1980's.* Unpublished paper.

Hoffman, L. (1981). *The foundations of family therapy.* New York: Basic Books.

Hoffman, L. (1985). Beyond power and control. *Family Systems Medicine, 4,* 381–396.

Hoffman, L. (1988a). Reply to Stuart Golann. *Family Process, 27,* 65–68.

Hoffman, L. (1988b). A constructivist position for family therapy. *The Irish Journal of Psychology, 9*(1), 110–129.

Hoffman, L. (1990a). Constructing realities: An art of lenses. *Family Process, 29,* 1–12.

Hoffman, L. (1990b). A constructivist position for family therapy. In B. Keeney, B. Nolan, & W. Madsen (Eds.), *The systemic therapist* (Vol. 1) (pp. 3–31). St. Paul, MN: Systemic Therapy Press.

Hoffman, L. (1992). A reflexive stance for family therapy. In S. McNamee & K. Gergen (Eds.), *Therapy as social construction* (pp. 7–24). Newbury Park, CA: Sage.

Hoffman, L. (1993). Exchanging voices: A collaborative approach to family therapy. London: Karnac.

Hoffman-Hennessay, L., & Davis, J. (1993). Tekka with feathers: Talking about talking (about suicide). In S. Friedman (Ed.), *The new language of change* (pp. 345–373). New York: Guilford Press.

Hogarty, G., Anderson, C., Reiss, D., Kornblith, S., Greenwald, D., Javna, C., Madonia, M., & the EPICS Schizophrenia Research Group. (1986). Family psychoeducation, social skills training, and maintenance chemotherapy in the aftercare treatment of schizophrenia: I. One year effects of a controlled study on relapse and expressed emotion. *Archives of General Psychiatry, 43,* 633–642.

Hoopes, M. H. (1974). *Who's who in family therapy.* Provo, UT: Brigham Young University.

Hoopes, M. H., Fisher, B. L., & Barlow, S. H. (1984). *Structured family facilitation programs.* Rockville, MD: Aspen Systems Corporation.

Horne, A. M. (1982). Counseling families—Social learning family therapy. In A. M. Horne & M. M. Ohlsen (Eds.), *Family counseling and therapy* (pp. 360–388). Itasca, IL: F. E. Peacock.

Hoshmand, L. (1989). Alternate research paradigms: A review and teaching proposal. *The Counseling Psychologist, 17,* 1–79.

Howard, G. S. (1991). Culture tales. *American Psychologist, 46,* 187–197.

Howe, R. H., & Foerster, H. von (1975). Introductory comments to Francisco Varela's calculus for self-reference. *International Journal of General Systems, 2,* 1–3.

Jacobsen, D. S. (1979). Stepfamilies: Myths and realities. *Social Work, 24*(3), 203–207.

Jacobson, N. (1981). Behavioral marital therapy. In A. S. Gurman & D. P. Kniskern (Eds.), *Handbook of family therapy* (pp. 556–591). New York: Brunner/Mazel.

Jacobson, N., & Margolin, G. (1979). *Marital therapy: Strategies based on social learning and behavior exchange principles.* New York: Brunner/Mazel.

Jacobson, N. S. (1977). Problem-solving and contingency contracting in the treatment of marital discord. *Journal of Consulting and Clinical Psychology, 45,* 92–100.

Jacobson, N., Schmaling, K., & Holtzworth-Munroe, A. (1987). Component analysis of behavior marital therapy: Two-year follow-up and prediction of relapse. *Journal of Marital and Family Therapy, 13,* 187–195.

Jacobson, N. (1994). Rewards and dangers in researching domestic violence. *Family Process, 33,* 81–85.

Jacobson, N. (1994a). Contextualism is dead: Long live contextualism. *Family Process, 33,* 97–100.

Joanning, H., Newfield, N., & Quinn, W. (1987). Multiple perspectives for research using family therapy to treat adolescent drug abuse. *Journal of Strategic and Systemic Therapies, 6,* 18–24.

Joanning, H., Quinn, W., Thomas, F., & Mullen, R. (1992). Treating adolescent drug abuse: A comparison of family systems therapy, group therapy, and family drug education. *Journal of Marital and Family Therapy, 18,* 345–356.

Jung, C. G. (1928). Problems of modern psychotherapy. In H. Read, M. Fordham, & G. Adler (Eds.), *The collected works of Carl G. Jung* (Vol. 8) (pp. 53–75). Princeton, NJ: Princeton University Press.

Kantor, D., & Lehr, W. (1975). *Inside the family.* San Francisco: Jossey-Bass.

Kaplan, H. S. (1974). *The new sex therapy: Active treatment of sexual dysfunctions.* New York: Brunner/Mazel.

Kaslow, F. (1982). Profile of the healthy family. *The Relationship, 8*(1), 9–25.

Kazdin, A. E. (1984). The treatment of conduct disorders. In J. Williams & R. Spitzer (Eds.), *Psychotherapy research: Where are we and where should we go?* New York: Guilford Press.

Kazdin, A. (1987). Treatment of antisocial behavior in children: Current status and future directions. *Psychological Bulletin, 102,* 187–203.

Keeney, B. (1990). *Improvisational therapy.* St. Paul, MN: Systemic Therapy Press.

Keeney, B., & Ross, J. (1985). *Mind in therapy: Constructing systemic family therapies.* New York: Basic Books.

Keeney, B., & Silverstein, O. (1986). *The therapeutic voice of Olga Silverstein.* New York: Guilford Press.

Keeney, B. P. (1983). *Aesthetics of change.* New York: Guilford Press.

Keeney, B. P. (1986). Cybernetic foundations of family therapy. In I. Piercy, D. Sprenkle, & Associates (Eds.), *Family therapy sourcebook* (pp. 262–287). New York: Guilford Press.

Keeney, B. P., & Sprenkle, D. (1982). Ecosystemic epistemology: Critical implications for the aesthetics and pragmatics of family therapy. *Family Process, 21,* 1–19.

Keith, D. (1995). Remembering Carl Whitaker. *AFTA Newsletter, 60,* 7–8.

Keith, D. V., & Whitaker, C. A. (1977). The divorce labyrinth. In P. Papp (Ed.),. *Family therapy: Full length case studies* (pp. 117–131). New York: Gardner Press.

Keith, D. V., & Whitaker, C. A. (1982). Experiential/symbolic family therapy. In A. M. Horne & M. M. Ohlsen (Eds.), *Family counseling and therapy* (pp. 43–74). Itasca, IL: F. E. Peacock.

Kelly, G. (1955). *The psychology of personal constructs* (Vol. I). New York: W. W. Norton.

Kempler, W. (1967). The experiential therapeutic encounter. *Psychotherapy: Theory research and practice, 4*(4), 166–172.

Kempler, W. (1968). Experiential psychotherapy with families. *Family Process, 7*(1), 88–99.

Kempler, W. (1970). A theoretical answer. *Psykologen.* Costa Mesa, CA: Kempler Institute.

Kempler, W. (1972). Experiential psychotherapy with families. In G. D. Erickson & T. P. Hogan (Eds.), *Family therapy: An introduction to theory and technique* (pp. 336–346). Monterey, CA: Brooks/Cole.

Kempler, W. (1973). *Principles of Gestalt family therapy.* Costa Mesa, CA: Kempler Institute.

Kempler, W. (1981). *Experiential psychotherapy with families.* New York: Brunner/Mazel.

Kempler, W. (1982). Gestalt family therapy. In A. M. Horne & M. M. Ohlsen (Eds.), *Family counseling and therapy* (pp. 141–174). Itasca, IL: F. E. Peacock.

Kern, R. M., Hawes, E. C., & Christensen, O. C. (Eds.). (1989). *Couples therapy: An Adlerian perspective.* Minneapolis, MN: Educational Media Corporation.

Kernberg, O. F. (1976). *Object relations theory and clinical psychoanalysis.* New York: Jason Aronson.

Kilpatrick, A. C., & Kilpatrick, E. G. (1991). Object relations family therapy. In A. M. Horne & J. L. Passmore (Eds.), *Family counseling and therapy* (2nd ed.) (pp. 207–235). Itasca, IL: F. E. Peacock.

Kleinman, J., Rosenberg, E., & Whiteside, M. (1979). Common developmental tasks in forming reconstituted families. *Journal of Marital and Family Therapy, 5*(2), 79–86.

Kniskern, D. P. (1983). The new wave is all wet. *The Family Therapy Networker, 7*(4), 60–62.

Koch, S. (1976). Language communities, search cells and the psychological studies. In W. J. Arnold (Ed.), *Nebraska symposium on motivation, 1975* (Vol. 23). Lincoln, NE: University of Nebraska Press.

Koch, S. (1981). The nature and limits of psychological knowledge. *American Psychologist, 36*(3), 257–269.

Kohlberg, L. (1981). *The philosophy of moral development.* San Francisco: Harper & Row.

Korzybski, A. (1958). *Science and sanity: An introduction to non-Aristotelian system and general semantics* (4th ed.). Lake Shore, CT: Institute of General Semantics.

Kuhn, T. (1970). *The structure of scientific revolutions*. Chicago: University of Chicago Press.

Ladner, J. A. (1973). Tomorrow's tomorrow: The Black woman. In J. A. Ladner (Ed.), *The death of white sociology* (pp. 414–428). New York: Vintage Books.

LaFarge, P. (1982). The joy of family rituals. *Parents, 57*(12), 63–64.

Laqueur, H. P. (1970). Multiple family therapy and general systems therapy. In N. W. Ackerman (Ed.), *Family therapy in transition* (pp. 99–124). Boston: Little, Brown.

Laqueur, H. P. (1976). Multiple family therapy. In P. J. Guerin (Ed.), *Family therapy: Theory and practice* (pp. 405–441). New York: Gardner Press.

Lather, P. (1986). Research as praxis. *Harvard Educational Review, 56,* 257–277.

Lax, W. (1992). Postmodern thinking in clinical practice. In S. McNamee & K. Gergen (Eds.), *Therapy as Social Construction* (pp. 69–85). Newbury Park, CA: Sage.

Lazarus, A. (1965). The treatment of a sexually inadequate male. In L. Ullman & L. Krasner (Eds.), *Case studies in behavior modification* (pp. 208–217). New York: Holt, Rinehart & Winston.

Lederer, W. J., & Jackson, D. D. (1968). *Mirages of marriage*. New York: W. W. Norton.

Leff, J. P., Kuipers, L., Berkowitz, R., Eberlein-Vries, R., & Sturgeon, D. (1982). A controlled trial of social intervention in the families of schizophrenic patients. *British Journal of Psychology, 141,* 121–134.

Leff, P., & Walizer, E. (1992). The uncommon wisdom of parents at the moment of diagnosis. *Family Systems Medicine, 10*(2), 147–168.

Lewis, D. K. (1975). The Black family: Socialization and sex roles. *Phylon, XXXVI* (3), 221–237.

Lewis, J. M., Beavers, W. R., Gossett, J. T., & Phillips, V. A. (1976). *No single thread*. New York: Brunner/Mazel.

Lewis, R., Piercy, F., Sprenkle, D., & Trepper, T. (1990). Family-based interventions for helping drug-abusing adolescents. *Journal of Adolescent Research, 13,* 35–44.

Liberman, R. (1972). Behavioral approaches to family and couple therapy. In C. J. Sager & H. S. Kaplan (Eds.), *Progress in group and family therapy* (pp. 329–345). New York: Brunner/Mazel.

Lidz, R. W., & Lidz, T. (1949). The family environment of schizophrenic patients. *Journal of Psychiatry, 106,* 332–345.

Lipchik, E. (1991). Spouse abuse: Challenging the party line. *Family Therapy Networker,* May/Jun, 59–63.

Locke, H., & Wallace, K. (1959). Short-term marital adjustment and prediction tests: Their reliability and validity. *Journal of Marriage and Family Living, 21,* 251–255.

Longino, H. (1990). *Science as social knowledge*. Princeton, NJ: Princeton University Press.

Lowe, R. N. (1982). Adlerian/Dreikursian family counseling. In A. M. Horne & M. M. Ohlsen (Eds.), *Family counseling and therapy* (pp. 329–359). Itasca, IL: F. E. Peacock.

Lowe, R. (1991). Postmodern themes and therapeutic practices: Notes towards the definition of 'Family Therapy: Part 2.' *Dulwich Center Newsletter, 3,* 41–42.

Lowenthal, M. F., & Chiriboga, D. (1973). Social stress and adaptation: Toward a life course perspective. In C. Eisdorfer & M. P. Lawton (Eds.), *The psychology of adult development* (pp. 281–318). Washington, DC: American Psychological Association.

MacKinnon, L. (1983). Contrasting strategic and Milan therapies. *Family Process, 22,* 425–440.

Madanes, C. (1980). Protection, paradox and pretending. *Family Process, 19,* 457–470.

Madanes, C. (1981). *Strategic family therapy*. San Francisco: Jossey-Bass.

Madanes, C. (1984). *Behind the one-way mirror*. San Francisco: Jossey-Bass.

Madanes, C. (1990). *Sex, love, and violence: Strategies for transformation*. New York: W. W. Norton.

Mahler, M. S., Pine, F., & Bergman, A. (1975). *The psychological birth of the human infant*. New York: Basic Books.

Mahoney, M. (1974). *Cognition and behavior modification*. Cambridge, MA: Ballinger.

Mair, M. (1988). Psychology as storytelling. *International Journal of Personal Construct Psychology, 1,* 125–138.

Markus, E., Lang, A., & Pettigrew, T. (1990). Effectiveness of family therapy. *British Journal of Family Therapy, 12,* 205–221.

Marotz-Baden, R., Adams, G. R., Bueche, N., Munro, B., & Munro, G. (1979). Family form or family process? Reconsidering the deficit family model approach. *Family Process, 28*(1), 5–14.

Martin, E. P., & Martin, J. M. (1978). *The Black extended family*. Chicago: University of Chicago Press.

Maruyama, M. (1963). The second cybernetics: Deviation-amplifying mutual causal processes. *American Scientist, 5,* 164–179.

Masters, W., & Johnson, V. (1970). *Human sexual inadequacy.* Boston: Little, Brown.

Mathis, A. (1978). Contrasting approaches to the study of black families. *Journal of Marriage and the Family, 40*(4), 667–676.

Maturana, H. (1974). Cognitive strategies. In H. von Foerster (Ed.), *Cybernetics of cybernetics* (pp. 457–469). Urbana, IL: University of Illinois.

Maturana, H. (1978). Biology of language: The epistemology of reality. In G. A. Miller & E. Lennerberg (Eds.), *Psychology and biology of language and thought: Essays in honor of Eric Lennerberg* (pp. 27–63). New York: Academic Press.

Maturana, H., & Varela, F. (1980). *Autopoiesis and cognition.* Dordrecht, Holland: D. Reidel.

Maturana, H. R., & Varela, F. J. (1987). *The tree of knowledge.* Boston: New Science Library.

May, R. (1967). *Psychology and the human dilemma.* Princeton, NJ: D. Van Nostrand Company.

McAdoo, H. P. (1980). Black mothers and the extended family support network. In L. Rodgers-Rose (Ed.), *The black woman* (pp. 125–144). Beverly Hills, CA: Sage Publications.

McDaniel, S., Hepworth J., & Doherty, W. (1992). *Medical family therapy: A biopsychosocial approach to families with health problems.* New York: Basic Books.

McGoldrick, M. (1982). Ethnicity and family therapy: An overview. In M. McGoldrick, J. K. Pearce, & J. Giordano (Eds.), *Ethnicity and family therapy* (pp. 3–30). New York: Guilford Press.

McWhinney, I. R. (1989). *A textbook of family medicine.* New York: Oxford University Press.

Meichenbaum, D. (1977). *Cognitive behavior therapy.* New York: Plenum Press.

Midelfort, C. (1957). *The family in psychotherapy.* New York: McGraw-Hill.

Miller, L. (1979). *Louisville behavior checklist.* Los Angeles: Western Psychological Services.

Miller, W. (1992). Why family medicine? The sound of bells. *Family Systems Medicine, 10*(3), 347–357.

Minuchin, S. (1974). *Families and family therapy.* Cambridge, MA: Harvard University Press.

Minuchin, S. (1984). *Family kaleidoscope.* Cambridge, MA: Harvard University Press.

Minuchin, S. (1986). Foreword. In L. Wynne, S. McDaniel, & T. Weber (Eds.), *Systems consultation: A new perspective for family therapy.* New York: Guilford Press.

Minuchin, S., Baker, L., Rosman, B., Liebman, R., Milman, L., & Todd, T. (1975). A conceptual model of psychosomatic illness in children. *Archives of General Psychiatry, 32,* 1031–1038.

Minuchin, S., & Fishman, H. C. (1981). *Family therapy techniques.* Cambridge, MA: Harvard University Press.

Minuchin, S., Montalvo, B., Guerney, B., Rosman, B., & Schumer, F. (1967). *Families of the slums.* New York: Basic Books.

Minuchin, S., Rosman, B. L., & Baker, L. (1978). *Psychosomatic families: Anorexia nervosa in context.* Cambridge, MA: Harvard University Press.

Misiak, H., & Sexton, V. (1966). *History of psychology: An overview.* New York: Grune & Stratton.

Moon, S., Dillon, D., & Sprenkle, D. (1991). On balance and synergy: Family therapy and qualitative research revisited. *Journal of Marital and Family Therapy, 17,* 187–192.

Moon, S. M., Dillon, D. R., & Sprenkle, D. H. (1990). Family therapy and qualitative research. *Journal of Marital and Family Therapy, 16,* 357–373.

Morgan, E. S. (1956). *The Puritan family.* Boston: Trustees of the Public Library.

Morris, S., Alexander, J., & Waldron, H. (1988). Functional family therapy. In I. R. Falloon, (Ed.), *Handbook of behavioral family therapy* (pp. 107–127). New York: Guilford Press.

Moynihan, D. P. (1965). *The Negro family: The case for national action.* Washington, DC: Office of Policy Planning and Research, U.S. Department of Labor.

Napier, A. Y., & Whitaker, C. A. (1978). *The family crucible.* New York: Harper & Row.

Neugarten, B. L. (1976). Adaptation and the life cycle. *Counseling Psychologist, 6*(1), 16–20.

Newmark, M., & Beels, C. (1994). The misuse and use of science in family therapy. *Family Process, 33,* 3–17.

Nicholl, W. G. (1989). Adlerian marital therapy: History, theory and process. In R. M. Kern, E. C. Hawes, & O. C. Christensen (Eds.), *Couples therapy: An Adlerian perspective* (pp. 1–28). Minneapolis, MN: Educational Media Corporation.

Nichols, M. P. (1984). *Family therapy—Concepts and methods.* New York: Gardner Press.

Nichols, M. (1985). Checking our biases. *The Family Therapy Networker, 9*(6), 75–77.

Nichols, M. (1987). *The self in the system: Expanding the limits of family therapy.* New York: Brunner/Mazel.

Nichols, M. P., & Schwartz, R. C. (1991). *Family therapy: Concepts and methods.* Boston: Allyn & Bacon.

Nichols, M., & Schwartz, R. (1995). *Family therapy: Concepts and methods.* Boston: Allyn and Bacon.

Nobles, W. W. (1978). Toward an empirical and theoretical framework for defining Black families. *Journal of Marriage and the Family, 40*(4), 679–688.

O'Hanlon, W. H. (1990). Debriefing myself: When a brief therapist does long-term work. *The Family Therapy Networker, 14,* 48–49, 68–69.

O'Hanlon, W. H. (1993). Possibility therapy: From Iatrogenic injury to Iatrogenic healing. In S. Gilligan & R. Price, (Eds.) *Therapeutic Conversations* (pp. 3–17). New York: W. W. Norton.

O'Hanlon, W. H., and Weiner-Davis, M. (1989). *In search of solutions: A new direction in psychotherapy.* New York: W. W. Norton.

O'Hanlon, W. H., & Wilk, J. (1987). *Shifting contexts: The generation of effective psychotherapy.* New York: Guilford Press.

Olson, D. H., Russell, C., & Sprenkle, D. H. (1983). Circumplex model of marital and family systems: VI. Theoretical update. *Family Process, 22,* 69–83.

Olson, D. H., Sprenkle, D. H., & Russell, C. (1979). Circumplex model of marital and family systems: I. Cohesion and adaptability dimensions, family types and clinical implications. *Family Process, 18,* 3–28.

Olson, D., Bell, R., & Portner, J. (1985). *FACES III manual.* Department of Family Social Science, University of Minnesota, St. Paul, Minn.

Orwell, G. (1949). *1984.* New York: Harcourt, Brace, Jovanovich.

Otto, H. (1979). Developing human family potential. In N. Stinnett, B. Chesser, & J. Defrain (Eds.), *Building family strengths* (pp. 39–50). Lincoln, NE: University of Nebraska Press.

Papp, P. (1976). Brief therapy with couples groups. In P. J. Guerin (Ed.), *Family therapy: Theory and practice* (pp. 350–363). New York: Gardner Press.

Papp, P. (1977). *Family therapy: Full length case studies.* New York: Gardner Press.

Pask, G. (1969). The meaning of cybernetics in the behavioural sciences (The cybernetics of behaviour and cognition: Extending the meaning of "goal"). In J. Rose (Ed.), *Progress of cybernetics* (Vol. 1) (pp. 15–43). New York: Gordon & Breach.

Patterson, G. R. (1974). Interventions for boys with conduct problems: Multiple settings, treatment, and criteria. *Journal of Consulting and Clinical Psychology, 42,* 471–481.

Patterson, G. R., Chamberlain, P., & Reid, J. B. (1982). A comparative evaluation of a parent-training program. *Behavior Therapy, 13,* 638–650.

Paul, G. (1967). Outcome research in psychotherapy. *Journal of Consulting Psychology, 31,* 109–188.

Pearce, J. (1988). *The crack in the cosmic egg.* New York: Julian Press.

Pedersen, F. A. (1976). Does research on children reared in father-absent families yield information on father influences? *The Family Coordinator, 25*(4), 459–463.

Penn, P. (1982). Circular questioning. *Family Process, 21*(3), 267–279.

Perelman, C., & Olbrechts-Tyteca, L. (1969). *The new rhetoric: A treatise on argumentation* (J. Wilkinson & P. Weaver, Trans.). South Bend, IN: University of Notre Dame Press.

Piaget, J. (1955). *The language and thought of the child.* New York: World Publishing.

Piercy, F. P., & Sprenkle, D. H. (1990). Marriage and family therapy: A decade review. *Journal of Marriage and the Family, 52,* 1116–1126.

Piercy, F. P., Sprenkle, D. H., & Associates. (1986). *Family therapy sourcebook.* New York: Guilford Press.

Pinsof, W. M. (1980). *The family therapist coding system (FTCS) coding manual.* Chicago: Center for Family Studies, Family Institute of Chicago, Institute of Psychiatry, Northwestern Memorial Hospital.

Pinsof, W. M. (1981). Family therapy process research. In A. S. Gurman & D. P. Kniskern (Eds.), *Handbook of family therapy* (pp. 669–674). New York: Brunner/Mazel.

Pinsof, W. M., & Catherall, D. R. (1984). *The integrative psychotherapy alliance: Family, couple, and individual therapy scales.* Unpublished paper. Center for Family Studies, The Family Institute of Chicago, Institute of Psychiatry, Northwestern Memorial Hospital, Chicago, IL.

Plas, J. M. (1986). *Systems psychology in the schools.* New York: Pergamon Press.

Polkinghorne, L. (1984). Further extensions of methodological diversity for counseling psychology. *Journal of Counseling Psychology, 31*(4), 416–429.

Popper, K. (1959). *The logic of scientific discovery.* New York: Basic Books.

Powers, W. T. (1973). Feedback: Beyond behaviorism. *Science, 179,* 351–356.

Rappaport, R. A. (1974). Sanctity and adaptation. *The CoEvolution Quarterly,* Summer, 54–68.

Ray, W., & Keeney, B. (1993). *Resource focused therapy.* London: Karnac Books.

Reeves, R. (1982). *American journey.* New York: Simon & Schuster.

Remembering Virginia. (1989). *The Family Therapy Networker, 13*(1), 27–35.

Riskin, J. (1982). Research on non-labeled families: A longitudinal study. In F. Walsh (Ed.), *Normal family processes* (pp. 67–93). New York: Guilford Press.

Rohrbaugh, M., Tennen, H., Press, S., White, L., Raskin, P., & Pickering, M. (1977). *Paradoxical strategies in psychotherapy.* Symposium presented at the American Psychological Association Convention, San Francisco, CA.

Rorty, R. (1979). *Philosophy and the mirror of nature.* Princeton, NJ: Princeton University Press.

Rosenblueth, A., Wiener, N., & Bigelow, J. (1943). Behavior, purpose, and teleology. *Philosophy of Science, 10,* 18–24.

Ross, A. (1981). *Child behavior therapy.* New York: John Wiley.

Rubin, Z. & Mitchell, C. (1976). Couples research as couples counseling. *American Psychologist, 30,* 17–225.

Ruesch, J., & Bateson, G. (1951). *Communication: The social matrix of psychiatry.* New York: W. W. Norton.

Rueveni, U. (1979). *Networking families in crisis.* New York: Human Sciences Press.

Ruitenbeek, H. M. (1964). *Varieties of personality theory.* New York: E. P. Dutton.

Russell, G., Szmukler, G., Dare, C., & Eisler, I. (1987). An evaluation of family therapy in anorexia nervosa and bulimia nervosa. *Archives of General Psychiatry, 44,* 1047–1056.

Rychlak, J. F. (1981). *Introduction to personality and psychotherapy* (2nd ed.). Boston: Houghton Mifflin.

Ryle, A. (1985). Cognitive theory, object relations and the self. *British Journal of Medical Psychology, 58,* 1–7.

Sarason, S. (1972). *The creation of settings and the future societies.* San Francisco: Jossey-Bass.

Sarason, S. (1981). *Psychology misdirected.* New York: Free Press.

Satir, V. (1964). *Conjoint family therapy.* Palo Alto, CA: Science and Behavior Books.

Satir, V. (1967). *Conjoint family therapy* (rev. ed.). Palo Alto, CA: Science and Behavior Books.

Satir, V. (1972). *Peoplemaking.* Palo Alto, CA: Science and Behavior Books.

Satir, V. (1982). The therapist and family therapy: Process model. In A. M. Horne & M. M. Ohlsen (Eds.), *Family counseling and therapy* (pp. 12–42). Itasca, IL: F. E. Peacock.

Satir, V., Stachowiak, J., & Taschman, H. (1975). *Helping families to change.* New York: Jason Aronson.

Sawin, M. M. (1979). *Family enrichment with family clusters.* Valley Forge, PA: Judson Press.

Sawin, M. M. (1982). *Hope for families.* New York: Sadlier.

Scharff, D. E., & Scharff, J. S. (1987). *Object relations in family therapy.* Northvale, NJ: Jason Aronson.

Schofield, W. (1964). *Psychotherapy: The purchase of friendship.* Englewood Cliffs, NJ: Prentice-Hall.

Schultz, S. J. (1984). *Family systems therapy: An integration.* New York: Jason Aronson.

Schwartz, R. (1987). Our multiple selves. *The Family Therapy Networker, 11,* 25–31.

Schwartz, R. (1988). Know thy selves. *The Family Therapy Networker, 12,* 21–29.

Schwartz, R. (1994). *Internal family systems therapy.* New York: Guilford Press.

Schwartz, R., Barrett, M., & Saba, G. (1985). Family therapy for bulimia. In D. Garner & P. Garfinkel (Eds.), *Handbook for the psychotherapy of anorexia nervosa and bulimia* (pp. 280–310). New York: Guilford Press.

Schwartz, R., & Breunlin, D. (1983). Why clinicians should bother with research. *The Family Therapy Networker, 7,* 22–27.

Schwartz, R., & Perotta, P. (1985). Let us sell no intervention before its time. *The Family Therapy Networker, 9*(4), 18–25.

Seaburn, D., Gawinski, B., Harp, J., McDaniel, S., Waxman, D., & Shields, C. Family systems therapy in a primary care medical setting: The Rochester experience. *Journal of Marital and Family Therapy, 19*(2), 177–190.

Seidler, M. (1979). Problems of systems epistemology. *International Philosophical Quarterly, 19,* 29–60.

Selvini, M. (1988). The work of Mara Selvini Palazzoli. Northvale, NJ: Jason Aronson.

Selvini Palazzoli, M. (1986). Towards a general model of psychotic games. *Journal of Marital and Family Therapy, 12*, 339–349.

Selvini Palazzoli, M., Boscolo, L., Cecchin, G., & Prata, G. (1978). *Paradox and counterparadox.* New York: Jason Aronson.

Shands, H. C. (1971). *The war with words.* Paris: Mouton.

Shields, C., Wynne, L., McDaniel, S., & Gawinski, B. (1994). The marginalization of family therapy: A historical and continuing problem. *Journal of Marital and Family Therapy, 20*(1), 117–138.

Sieburg, E. (1985). *Family communication: An integrated systems approach.* New York: Gardner Press.

Simon, G. (1992). Having a second-order mind while doing first-order therapy. *Journal of Marital and Family Therapy, 18*, 377–387.

Simon, G. (1993). Hierarchy again: On accepting limitations. *Family Process, 33*, 101–103.

Simon, R. (1982). Behind the one-way mirror. *The Family Therapy Networker, 6* (1), 18–59.

Simon, R. (1985). Structure is destiny: An interview with Humberto Maturana. *The Family Therapy Networker, 9* (3), 32–43.

Simon, R. (1989). Reaching out to life. *The Family Therapy Networker, 13* (1), 37–43.

Simon, T. B., Stierlin, H., & Wynne, L. C. (1985). *The language of family therapy: A systemic vocabulary and sourcebook.* New York: Family Process Press.

Singleton, G. (1982). Bowen family systems theory. In A. M. Horne & M. M. Ohlsen (Eds.), *Family counseling and therapy* (pp. 75–111). Itasca, IL: F. E. Peacock.

Skinner, B. F. (1948). *Walden II.* New York: Macmillan.

Skinner, B. F. (1953). *Science and human behavior.* New York: Macmillan.

Slipp, S. (1984). *Object relations: A dynamic bridge between individual and family therapy.* Northvale, NJ: Jason Aronson.

Slipp, S. (1988). *The technique and practice of object relations family therapy.* Northvale, NJ: Jason Aronson.

Sluzki, C. (1985). Families, networks, and other strange shapes. AFTA *Newsletter, 19*, 1–2.

Smelser, N. J., & Halpern, S. (1978). The historical triangulation of family, economy and education. In J. Demos & S. Boocock (Eds.), *Turning points* (pp. 288–315). Chicago: University of Chicago Press.

Smith, M. B. (1994). Selfhood at risk: Postmodern perils and the perils of postmodernism. *American Psychologist, 49*(5), 405–411.

Sokal, M. (1973). APA's first publication: Proceedings of the American Psychological Association, 1892–1893. *American Psychologist, 28*, 277–292.

Spanier, G. (1976). Measuring dyadic adjustment: New scales for assessing the quality of marriage and similar dyads. *Journal of Marriage and the Family, 38*, 15–28.

Speck, R. V., & Attneave, C. L. (1973). *Family networks.* New York: Pantheon.

Spinks, S. H., & Birchler, G. R. (1982). Behavioral systems marital therapy: Dealing with resistance. *Family Process, 21*, 169–186.

Sprenkle, D. (1994). Editorial: The role of qualitative research and a few suggestions for aspiring authors. *Journal of Marital and Family Therapy, 20*(3) 227–229.

Stanton, M. D., Todd, T., & Associates. (1982). *The family therapy of drug abuse and addiction.* New York: Guilford Press.

Staples, R., & Mirandé, A. (1980). Racial and cultural variations among American families: A decennial review of the literature on minority families. *Journal of Marriage and the Family, 42*(4), 403–414.

Stein, H. (1992). "The eye of the outsider": Behavioral science, family medicine, and other human systems. *Family Systems Medicine, 10*(3), 2293–304.

Steinglass, P. (1991). An editorial: Finding a place for the individual in family therapy. *Family Process, 30*(3), 267–269.

Steinglass, P., & Horan, M. (1988). Families and chronic medical illness. In F. Walsh & D. Reiss (Eds.), *Chronic disorders and the family.* New York: Haworth Press.

Stolz, S. (1978). *Ethical issues in behavior modification.* San Francisco: Jossey-Bass.

Stuart, R. (1980). *Helping couples change.* New York: Guilford Press.

Suppe, F. (1977). *The structure of scientific theories* (2nd ed.). Urbana, IL: University of Illinois Press.

Szapocznik, J., Kurtines, W., Foote, F., Perez-Vidal, A., & Hervis, O. (1986). Conjoint versus one-person family therapy: Further evidence for the effectiveness of conducting family therapy through one-person with drug abusing adolescents. *Journal of Consulting and Clinical Psychology, 54*, 385–387.

Szapocznik, J., Perez-Vidal, A., Brickman, A., Foote, F., Santisteban, D., Hervis, O., & Kurtines, W. (1988). Engaging adolescent drug abusers and their families in treatment: A strategic/structural systems approach. *Journal of Consulting and Clinical Psychology, 56*, 5522–557.

Szasz, T. (1961). *The myth of mental illness.* New York: Hoeber-Harper.

Tessman, L. H. (1978). *Children of parting parents.* New York: Jason Aronson.

Thibault, J., & Kelley, H. (1959). *The social psychology of groups.* New York: John Wiley.

Thomas, L. (1979). *The medusa and the snail.* New York: Bantam Books.

Thomas, W. I., & Thomas, D. S. (1928). *The child in America.* New York: Knopf.

Thyer, B. (1992). Personal communication.

Tilley, K. (1990). Family medicine-family therapy joint task force established. *Family Therapy News,* July/August, p. 1.

Todd, T., & Selekman, M. (Eds.) (1991). *Family therapy approaches with adolescent substance abusers.* Boston: Allyn & Bacon.

Todd, T., & Stanton, M. (1983). Research on marital therapy and family therapy: Answers, issues and recommendations for the future. In B. Wolman & G. Stracker (Eds.), *Handbook of family and marital therapy* (pp. 91–115). New York: Plenum Press.

Tolan, P. H., Cromwell, R. E., & Brasswell, M. (1986). Family therapy with delinquents: A critical review of the literature. *Family Process, 25*, 619–649.

Toman, W. (1976). *Family constellation: Its effects on personality and social behavior* (3rd ed.). New York: Springer.

Tomm, K. (1984a). One perspective on the Milan systemic approach: Part II. Overview of development, theory and practice. *Journal of Marital and Family Therapy, 10*(2), 113–125.

Tomm, K. (1984b). One perspective on the Milan systemic approach: Part II. Description of session format, interviewing style and interventions. *Journal of Marital and Family Therapy, 10*(3), 253–271.

Touliatos, J., Perlmutter, B., & Strauss, M. (Eds.). (1990). *Handbook of family measurement techniques.* Newbury Park, CA: Sage Publications.

Trepper, T., & Barrett, M. (1989). *Systemic treatment of incest: A therapeutic handbook.* New York: Brunner/Mazel.

Truxall, A. G., & Merrill, F. E. (1947). *The family in American culture.* New York: Prentice-Hall.

Tyler, S., & Tyler, M. (1990). Foreword. In B. Keeney, *Improvisational Therapy* (pp. ix–xi). St. Paul, MN: Systemic Therapy Press.

Ullman, L., & Krasner, L. (1965). *Case studies in behavior modification.* New York: Holt, Rinehart & Winston.

Ulrici, D. (1983). The effects of behavior and family interventions on juvenile recidivism. *Family Therapy, 10*, 25–36.

Varela, F. J. (1979). *Principles of biological autonomy.* New York: Elsevier North Holland.

Varela, F. J. (1981). Introduction. In H. von Foerster, *Observing systems* (pp. xi—xvi). Seaside, CA: Intersystems Publications.

Varela, F. J., & Johnson, D. (1976). On observing natural systems. *The CoEvolution Quarterly,* Summer, 26–31.

Vaughn, C. E., Snyder, K. S., Jones, S., Freeman, W. B., & Falloon, I. R. (1984). Family factors in schizophrenic relapse: Replication in California of British research on expressed emotion. *Archives of General Psychiatry, 41*, 1169–1177.

Visher, E. F., & Visher, J. S. (1982). Stepfamilies in the 1980's. In J. C. Hansen & L. Messinger (Eds.), *Therapy with remarriage families* (pp. 105–119). Rockville, MD: Aspen Systems Corporation.

Walker, H. (1976). *Walker problem behavior identification checklist.* Los Angeles: Western Psychological Services.

Walsh, F. (1982). *Normal family processes.* New York: Guilford Press.

Walters, M., Carter, B., Papp, P., & Silverstein, O. (1988). *The invisible web: Gender patterns in family relationships.* New York: Guilford Press.

Watts, A. (1972). *The book.* New York: Vintage Books.

Watzlawick, P. (1976). *How real is real?* New York: Vintage Books.

Watzlawick, P. (1978). *The language of change.* New York: Basic Books.

Watzlawick, P. (Ed.). (1984). *The invented reality.* New York: W. W. Norton.

Watzlawick, P., Beavin, J., & Jackson, D. (1967). *Pragmatics of human communication.* New York: W. W. Norton.

Watzlawick, P., & Weakland, J. H. (Eds.). (1977). *The interactional view: Studies at the Mental Research Institute, Palo Alto, 1965–74.* New York: W. W. Norton.

Watzlawick, P., Weakland, J. H., & Fisch, R. (1974). *Change: Principles of problem formation and problem resolution.* New York: W. W. Norton.

Wegscheider, S. (1981). *Another chance.* Palo Alto, CA: Science and Behavior Books.

Weiss, R., & Cerreto, M. (1975). *Marital status inventory.* Unpublished manuscript. University of Oregon.

Weiss, R., Hops, H., & Patterson, G. (1973). A framework for conceptualizing marital conflict, technology for altering it, some data for evaluating it. In L. Hamerlynck, L. Handy, & E. Mash (Eds.), *Behavior change: Methodology, concepts and practice* (pp. 309–342). Champaign, IL: Research Press.

Wells, R. A., Dilkes, T. C., & Trivelli, N. (1972). The results of family therapy: A critical review. *Family Process, 11,* 189–207.

Wheeler, E. (1985). The fear of feminism in family therapy. *The Family Therapy Networker, 9*(6), 53–55.

Whitaker, C. A. (1975). Psychotherapy of the absurd: With a special emphasis in the psychotherapy of aggression. *Family Process, 14*(1), 1–16.

Whitaker, C. A. (1976a). A family is a four-dimensional relationship. In P. J. Guerin (Ed.), *Family therapy: Theory and practice* (pp. 182–192). New York: Gardner Press.

Whitaker, C. A. (1976b). The hindrance of theory in clinical work. In P. J. Guerin (Ed.), *Family therapy: Theory and practice* (pp. 154–164). New York: Gardner Press.

White, M. (1991). Deconstruction and therapy. *Dulwich Center Newsletter, 3,* 21–40.

White, M., & Epston, D. (1990). *Narrative means to therapeutic ends.* New York: W. W. Norton.

Whitehead, A. N., & Russell, B. (1910). *Principia mathematica.* Cambridge, England: Cambridge University Press.

Wiener, N. (1948). Cybernetics. *Scientific American, 179*(5), 14–18.

Wills, T., Weiss, R., & Patterson, G. (1974). A behavioral analysis of the determinants of marital satisfaction. *Journal of Consulting and Clinical Psychology, 42,* 802–811.

Wilson, G. (1984). Behavior therapy. In R. Corsini (Ed.), *Current psychotherapies* (pp. 230–278). Itasca, IL: F. E. Peacock.

Wilson, G., & O'Leary, K. (1980). *Principles of behavior therapy.* Englewood Cliffs, NJ: Prentice-Hall.

Winderman, L. (1989). Generation of human meaning key to Galveston paradigm: An interview with Harlene Anderson & Harold Goolishian. *Family Therapy News, 20*(6), 11–12.

Wittgenstein, L. (1963). *Philosophical investigations.* New York: MacMillan.

Wolin, S. J., & Bennett, L. A. (1984). Family rituals. *Family Process, 12*(3), 401–420.

Wolpe, J. (1958). *Psychotherapy by reciprocal inhibition.* Stanford, CA: Stanford University Press.

Wylie, M. S. (1991). Family therapy's neglected prophet. *The Family Therapy Networker, 15*(2), 24–37.

Wynne, L. C., Ryckoff, I. M., Day, J., & Hirsch, S. I. (1958). Pseudo-mutuality in the family relations of schizophrenics. *Psychiatry, 21,* 205–220.

Wynne, L., Shields, C., & Sirkin, M. (1992). Illness, family theory, and family therapy: I. Conceptual issues. *Family Process, 31,* 3–18.

Zukav, G. (1980). *The dancing wu li masters.* New York: Bantam Books.

Name Index

Subject Index